Internet Horror,
Science Fiction and
Fantasy Television Series,
1998–2013

Internet Horror, Science Fiction and Fantasy Television Series, 1998–2013

VINCENT TERRACE

McFarland & Company, Inc., Publishers
Jefferson, North Carolina

Library of Congress Cataloguing-in-Publication Data

Terrace, Vincent, 1948–
Internet horror, science fiction and fantasy television series, 1998–2013 /
Vincent Terrace.
p.   cm.
Includes bibliographical references and index.

ISBN 978-0-7864-7993-1 (softcover : acid free paper) ∞
ISBN 978-1-4766-1645-2 (ebook)

1. Internet television—Encyclopedias.   2. Science fiction television programs—
Plots, themes, etc.—Encyclopedias.   3. Horror television programs—
Plots, themes, etc.—Encyclopedias.   4. Fantasy television programs—
Plots, themes, etc.—Encyclopedias.   5. Internet entertainment—
Encyclopedias.   I. Title.
PN1992.924.T47 2014   384.550285'4678—dc23   2014012455

British Library cataloguing data are available

On the cover: Laptop computer (Mike Powell/Comstock Images);
screen image from *The Cipher Effect* showing Dee Marshall and
Beau Ballinger (Phillip Hudson/Rhinomotion Productions)

Printed in the United States of America

McFarland & Company, Inc., Publishers
Box 611, Jefferson, North Carolina 28640
www.mcfarlandpub.com

TABLE OF CONTENTS

PREFACE

Internet television series are produced typically without either the backing of a sponsor or distribution through a broadcast or cable network. They are considered "no budget" or "low budget" productions and have also been tagged as Web Television Series, Internet Television Series, Webisodes, and Online Programming. Most of these series follow formats that have been established by the major television networks and many encompass the serial-like storytelling of the 1930s and 1940s theatrical movie serials. As such, these Internet television series range from exceptional (broadcast worthy) to horrendous, with production values and/or acting often falling somewhere between professional to amateurish.

In 1995 before the creation of such Internet sites as YouTube, a lone program called *The Spot* became the first worldwide, American-produced Internet series. Since then thousands of such online series, covering every known genre (including animation, comedy, drama, Horror, science fiction, and reality) and from countries around the world have found their way onto the Internet. Some establish their own websites while others find a home at an overall sharing site (e.g., youtube.com, blip.tv, and dailymotion.com). Internet users interested in this relatively new format/venue of television generally find these shows by chance or through word of mouth. Until now there has been no single guide in print or on the Internet that one can

use (like *TV Guide*) to find all the Internet television programs that fit a specific genre.

The series contained within this book cover not only those produced in the U.S., but also those created in England and Canada and the very few from Hong Kong, Spain, Latin America, and Norway that have worldwide distribution. Most of the series listed in this volume can still be viewed although some are no longer active shows and, for the most part, have been withdrawn from active viewing (actual episodes are not viewable, but teasers or trailers often still remain).

The purpose of this book, the first of its kind, is to explore specific Internet-produced series genres and present the shows that encompass these categories with detailed listings. Each of the 405 alphabetically arranged series in this volume contains: 1) a website where the series was viewable at the time of publication; 2) year(s) of production; 3) a detailed storyline; 4) cast and credits (producer, writer, and director), along with comments on the show; and 4) a descriptive episode guide. Episode running times have been provided where available. Forty-eight photographs accompany the text and an index completes the book.

For this particular book, the horror, science fiction, and fantasy genres are covered from their beginnings in 1998 through the end of 2013. It does not include broadcast and cable television programs that are streamed over the Internet (as these are not series produced exclusively for the Internet). Simple as it may sound, this book was not simple to do. For example, there was no single source (including Google, Bing, and Yahoo) that tracked all the shows that fit within a specific genre. As such, finding and researching potential entries was a major hurdle. Once this difficulty was met, gathering specific program information proved to be an even greater concern. Often story synopses and listings of episodes produced for a series were available, but they were often very short and not very informative. In many instances there were no episode descriptions and, sometimes, synopses did not match what the actual series was really about. In addition, I found a considerable amount of conflicting data regarding the number of episodes, especially with those shows that appear on several sharing websites. (For example, episode listings, titles, and running times were not always identical; casts differed in name spellings, and synopsis information also varied.) For reasons that are perhaps known only to the producers of some shows, casts and/or credit information was not listed. Problems of this sort that could not be overcome have been listed appropriately. Viewing the American and foreign-produced series that could be found became the only viable solution to the researching problem. In fact, it was the only way a book such as this could be done effectively; avoiding the viewing aspect would have resulted in a poorly constructed, not very informative volume.

Resolving conflicting information, especially with name spellings (as many are unusual) were taken from the screen (where possible) as opposed to various Internet sources (such as reviews and third-party sharing websites). Unfortunately, some episode information vanished and had been removed from the Internet both before and during the research aspect of this book. (Thus it was not possible to present episode descriptions for several shows.) In cases where partial episode information remained but varied from site to site, the information was edited to present an episode listing as accurate as possible. As of December 31, 2013, all websites listed herein were open (except where noted) and all programs were able to be viewed. Many of these series (including ones that are no longer viewable) have been released on DVD in edited versions (made to look like a feature film as opposed to a serial). In some instances these series are being adapted to regular broadcast television. Conversely, some series are Internet spinoffs from a broadcast or cable television series (here including the *Star Trek*, *Battlestar Galactica* and *Doctor Who* listings), and some are spoofs of feature films (like *Pink Five,* a take-off on *Star Wars*).

As noted, compiling this volume presented a number of intriguing challenges. However, it also brought to light an exciting new world of television programming that, for the most part, has been overlooked by the general public. It can surprise you just how good Internet television series can be (better, in some cases, than what is actually on broadcast and/or cable television). It is also the case that some of the shows are awful (except to diehard lovers of schlock). Delving into the genres presented in this book, one will discover a detective who is also a zombie (*Hamilton Carver, Zombie P.I.*), beautiful female superheroes (*Batgirl*, *Supergirl*, and *Vexika*), demons, angels, Shadow Men (beings that can bend time and space), vampires, time travelers, ghosts, ghouls, and things that go bump in the night. There are werewolves, medieval (and modern-day) demon fighters, haunted houses, wizards, strange cities, life in outer space and on other planets and struggle in post-apocalyptic worlds.

If you have never seen an Internet series or you have based your judgment on a knee-jerk reaction to the new format itself or just word-of-mouth, then watching what has been produced in the horror, science fiction, and fantasy genres may stir your interest to view some or more of the series based on the information presented in this book. It could change your perspective and make you wonder: why isn't this Internet series on television?

This is the first volume in a series of books that will also cover Internet-produced series in the fields of comedy, drama (including crime drama, mystery and suspense), and animation.

The author would like to thank James Robert Parish for his assistance on this project.

THE SHOWS

1 **The Abandon.** theabandon.com. 2013 (Science Fiction).

Five college friends (see cast) embark on a camping trip only to discover on the first night that, after an alien invasion, they are apparently the only surviving humans—and also the target of aliens, who to keep their invasion secret, must kill them. The program, which stresses loyalty, survival and manhood, charts their experiences on the run.

Cast: Billy Eugene Jones (Jeff), Sterling K. Brown (Kendall), Jordan Mahome (Craig), Morocco Omari (Dennis), Jamie Lincoln Smith (Aaron). **Credits:** *Producer:* Kamilah Forbes, Walter Greene IV, Constana Mortell, Karin Gist. *Writer-Director:* Keith Josef Adkins. **Comment:** The writer and director, Keith Josef Adkins worked on the television series *Girlfriends* and created *Abandon* as a means to "see black and brown people work in the sci-fi genre." The statement is kind of deceiving because blacks and browns have worked (and starred) in Internet horror and science fiction series (examples being *Body Jumpers* and *Osiris*). Disregarding the statement, the program is intriguing (no matter what race were the principals) and the possibilities far reaching (Adkins states that future episodes will use flashbacks to introduce family members, friends and the hours leading up to the invasion. He also mentions that the men will find another survivor—a woman played by Asha Jones). Adkins used a fund raiser to produce the show—and for the $8,000 it cost to make the pilot, the money was well spent.

Episodes:
1. The Pilot. Establishes the story line as described above.

2 *Abigail.* red-raccoon.com 2012–2013 (Horror).

In the not-too-distant future, artificial intelligence has been developed by Adam Robotics and brought to a point where it is impossible to tell created humans from real humans. Such is the case with a beautiful android named Abigail. Abigail, contained in a low security facility off the grid, is a seemingly nor-

Abigail **poster art featuring Meghan Moonan (copyright Meagan O'Neal of Meagan O. Photography and Ben Salley [digital artist]).**

mal woman. She is married and hopes to begin a family. Her skin is soft; she can bleed if she is cut and can cry real tears. What Abigail doesn't realize is that she is not human. She is actually a test subject of an experiment called Project Saul. Abraham, the CEO of Adam Robotics, secretly created Abigail (the reason why is not revealed) and to protect her has programmed his lapdog Seth to watch over the facility. But is Abigail really safe and a secret? For reasons that are known only to him, Luke, an employee of Adam Robotics, assembles a team (Fox and

Gabrielle) to abduct Abigail. The abduction is successful but complications set in when Abigail learns she is an android and her life was not real, and Gabrielle, appearing as a normal woman, sees a copy of herself and discovers she too is an android, a creation of a flawed experiment called Project Lion (over time, Gabrielle's system will break down and she will need repairing). Is Abigail Gabrielle's salvation (as discovering her system makeup could begin the production of flawless androids) or is Abigail something more relevant (or sinister), something apparently known only to Luke? Although the program ends unresolved (as of March 2014) a second season of episodes will reveal why Luke abducted Abigail, focus on their growing relationship and possibly solve the overall mystery surrounding Project Saul.

Cast: Meghan Moonan (Abigail), Darla Warnock (Gabrielle), Olubajo Sonubi (Luke), Scotty Gannon (Seth), Gavin Llambes (Fox), Michael Stille (Saul), Brandon Wentz (The Tenant). **Credits:** *Producer-Director:* Nathaniel Collum. *Writer:* Nathaniel Collum, Martin Smith. **Comment:** Intriguing concept with excellent production values and acting. Although, at present, the program ends unresolved, it is well worth watching as it brings television-created androids (such as *My Living Doll* and *Small Wonder*) out of infancy and into adulthood to show that such creations may not always be for the greater good. Each episode runs as an arc and needs to be watched in order to appreciate the story.

Episodes:

1. Wake Up O'Sleeper (5 min., 21 sec.). Abigail's life begins to change forever when she is kidnapped and taken to a secret location within the Adam Robotics facility.

2. Stand By Me (5 min., 6 sec.). Luke seeks a way to disengage Abigail's tracking unit to protect her from her pursuers.

3. Flash (6 min., 4 sec.). Abigail learns she is not human and her life including her apartment, are an illusion (she has actually been in a lab).

4. Not Human (7 min., 14 sec.). Abigail becomes unstable as she tries to comprehend what Luke has just revealed to her.

5. Temperature Rising (10 min., 27 sec.). Luke learns that Abigail is really "The Tenant," a computer that thrives within her and controls her thoughts and actions.

6. Catalyst (9 min., 54 sec.). In an attempt to escape from the facility, Luke makes a deal with The Tenant—to help him escape in exchange for information about Project Saul.

7. Blood and Electricity (12 min., 17 sec.). Luke, guided by "The Tenant" installs a virus inside Abigail to activate her defense system. The episode concludes with Abigail and Luke escaping from the lab, but leaving Gabrielle behind—and Luke expressing his feelings that their escape was too easy.

3 *Absolution: The Series.* scifinal.com. 2008 (Fantasy).

In Las Vegas (the program setting) the Devil exists more in reality than anywhere else. People who require something can trade their souls for that desire. In return, the Devil acquires his or her soul for all eternity. Such "sellers" can seek absolution and redeem themselves by finding a new soul ("soul searchers") and trading it. One such searcher is Shelley, a young woman who becomes a pawn between good and evil as she seeks a new soul to acquire salvation. The Devil has chosen Shelley as one of his slaves, to do his bidding (acquire him souls for Hell), while a savior (who appears as an Elvis impersonator) battles for the same souls but for redemption. Shelley's experiences as she seeks her own absolution are depicted.

Cast: Andrea Swain (Shelley), Yuri Lowenthal, Jesse Bernstein, Jamie McMahon, Paul Brindley, Hartley Sawyer, Greg Crafts, Eric Shelley, Matt Lepage. **Credits:** *Producer-Writer-Director:* John Gardiner. **Comment:** Easily expandable program to continue focusing on Shelley as she seeks her own salvation, but helps others achieve theirs first. The acting is very good and the story fast-moving. Production values and direction are also good.

Episodes:

1. Episode 1 (4 min., 42 sec.). Introduces the soul searchers, in particular a young woman (Shelley) as she begins her quest.

2. Episode 2 (5 min., 30 sec.). While searching, Shelley comes to the aid of a man being attacked by two thugs.

3. Episode 3 (3 min., 13 sec.). A Savior, a Las Vegas Elvis impersonator, is introduced.

4. Episode (2 min., 54 sec,). As Shelley continues her search she finds herself becoming more involved in the world of the supernatural.

5. Episode 5 (3 min., 32 sec.). Shelley, believing she found her new soul learns that she cannot have it as someone much needier requires it.

6. Episode 6 (4 min., 12 sec.). Ignoring what she has been told by the Savior, Shelley seeks the soul for herself.

7. Episode 7 (3 min., 41 sec.). Shelley's continual defiance could mean damnation for a soul meant for salvation.

8. Episode 8 (3 min., 45 sec.). Shelley learns that she is more than a soul searcher, but one who must keep the balance between good and evil—souls meant to be saved and souls meant for damnation.

9. Episode 9 (5 min., 27 sec.). Shelley, instructed to deliver a soul to the Devil (who appears in shadows and greenish in color) encounters difficulty when she is confronted by Alex—the man who requires that soul for salvation.

10. Episode 10 (5 min., 58 sec.). Alex confronts Shelley and steals the soul (which appears to be contained in a small box).

11. Episode 11 (6 min., 31 sec.). Shelley catches the thief—but finds she can do nothing as he is protected by the Messenger.

12. Episode 12 (7 min., 4 sec.). With Alex receiving salvation, Shelley moves on seeking another soul, but not knowing when such will occur.

4 *Ace.* webserieschannel.com. 2012 (Science Fiction).

Christopher Roy is 17 years old and a student in the ACE Educational System, Section E. Like his past school experience, he considers school boring and just coasts through the year. A new student, Eden, changes his perspective when he becomes infatuated with her. It becomes such an attraction that he is thrust into events beyond his control. Also experiencing the mysterious (if not supernatural) Eden are Christopher's friends, Brooklyn, a school journalist seeking that story of the year, Gunner, the rebel and Edward, an obnoxious young man. The program relates what happens as Eden becomes a part of their lives. **Cast:** Alina McLeod (Eden), Andrew Fosseneuve (Christopher Roy), Jason Kucey (Edward), Max Pedley (Gunner), Dakota Hebert (Brooklyn). **Credits:** *Producer-Writer-Director:* Tyler Smeding. **Comment:** Intriguing program that does tell the viewer "The outcome is unclear; however, one thing is certain: high school will never be the same again." At present, the viewer will be drawn into the mystery surrounding the beautiful Eden but may be disappointed that there is no conclusion. Good acting and production values prevail and it is worth watching.

Episodes:

1. Welcome to E-Section (11 min., 25 sec.). The appearance of Eden has an effect on the lives of the students, especially Christopher, whose experiences with her have him questioning what the truth is and what it is not.

5 *The Adventures of Chadwick Periwinkle.* chadwickperiwinkle.com. 2011 (Science Fiction).

In a future era (sometime in the year AD 4010) a young man named Chadwick Periwinkle is an intergalactic couch potato. He just wants to be left alone, sleep and watch television. But the futuristic world frowns on people like Chadwick. It is a time when space travel is common, jobs are no longer just earthbound, clones are common and insurance companies, in order to protect their holdings, incorporate heavily armed public relations warships to deal with their enemies. Unfortunately for Chadwick and others like him, they are considered an abomination to the Universe and it has been ordered that such trash must be eliminated. Before he can be terminated, Chadwick flees and episodes follow his various adventures as he seeks to avoid the Universe hit men out to get him.

Chadwick was once a happy-go-lucky young man who had a nice smile and was friendly to everyone. He is now a futuristic hoodlum—eager to steal from anyone and use his ill-gotten gains on hookers, booze and drugs. His reputation has grown from nice guy to incompetent drug smuggler (although he legitimately works as a part-time insurance agent) to guilty-by-association mass murderer. As people say, he's a pain in the butt but Chadwick doesn't see himself as a good guy or bad guy; he's an "indifferent guy."

Hal-E is the artificial female intelligence attached to Chadwick's ship, The *Deus Ex-Machina*. She is constantly abused by Chadwick, suffers from paranoia and plagued by the numerous viruses that have infiltrated her system and trying to take over her thought processes. Although she is not human, she has feelings for Chadwick (although she also says she will make Chadwick's life a living hell for his indifference towards her).

The Dream Girl is the gorgeous imaginary woman that haunts Chadwick's dreams. But is she just a dream vision or is she a mysterious foreshadower (in Chadwick's dreams, she appears to have a message to relay).

Baron Von Nazty-Kins is a cyborg bounty hunter that has been programmed in the image of a World War II Nazi. He calls himself "A Nazi-Cyborg-Bounty-Hunter-Serial Killer from Space." He pilots the ship *The Donkey Punch* and is dead set on capturing Chadwick.

Chevey Periwinkle is Chadwick's older brother, a renowned womanizer and adventurer whose ship, *The Feral* is his portable bachelor pad. His job appears to be copyrighting catch phrases then turning them into hits. His current "hit" is "You've been Periwinkled."

Cast: Stimson Snead (Chadwick Periwinkle), Shayla Keating (Hal-E), Wonder Russell (Dream Girl), Charissa Adams (Li'l Red), Bjorn Whitney (Chevey Periwinkle), Gene Thorkildsen (Baron Von Nazty-Kins), Marty Krouse (Jack Manly), Lizzie Officer (Madame Bubala), Ian Lindsay (Johnson J. Jackson), Parker Mathews (Hacifert), Bryan Bender (Big Dog). **Credits:** *Producer:* David Purdy. *Writer-Director:* Stimson Snead. **Comment:** Comically played space adventure that, despite its absurd premise is amusing with good acting and production values. The Dream Girl is especially appealing and Hal-E's issues add to the fun.

Episodes:

1. Chadwick Periwinkle, the Inaction Hero (9 min., 11 sec.). After discovering how really insignificant he is in the Universe, Chadwick decides to get high and true to his nature, fails to do anything to save a group of people from certain death.

2. Chadwick Periwinkle and the A.I. from Hell (7 min., 10 sec.). Hal-E, Chadwick's female-formed

computer, rebels against his ineffectual ways and threatens to leave him if he doesn't turn his life around.

3. Licensed to Slack (7 min., 17 sec.). After he is fired from his job for doing nothing to save the lives of 500 people, Chadwick learns that the crazed captain of the *Helvitica*, the warship commissioned by the Universe, has been sent to terminate him.

4. I've Had Worse Days (6 min., 52 sec.). The blood-thirsty Nazi-like cyborg bounty hunter from the stars, Baron Von Nazty Kins, learns of Chadwick's whereabouts.

5. Chadwick's Ugly Little Mind (8 min., 33 sec.). A look into Chadwick's mind—wherein lurk such "horrors" as an inflated super ego, a lust monster and filth beyond imagining.

6. If Your Problems Don't Include Nazi Cyborgs (8 min., 5 sec.). Chadwick comes face-to-face with the crazed Baron Von Nazty Kins.

7. The Cursed Planet of Cursed Doom (6 min., 37 sec.). Escaping the Baron, Chadwick crash lands on an alien planet where he becomes tormented by Boob Monsters, little people, mirages, hallucinations and images that resemble "Star Wars" characters. For Chadwick—just another day (but he does manage to get a decent meal when he encounters a green Muppet-like alien that cooks up well).

8. Chaddy O'Periwinkle an' Da Little People (7 min., 40 sec.). In a forest Chadwick succumbs to a sickness and dreams of being the prize in a battle being fought by two pint-sized tribal warriors.

9. Oh Ricky! (6 min., 56 sec.). Still marooned on the planet from episode 7, Chadwick faces another enemy—Hal Von Na-zi—the crazed computer of the crazed Baron Von Natzy Kins.

6 *The Adventures of Shakespeare and Watson: Detectives of Mystery.* shakespeareandwatson.com. 2013 (Fantasy).

Although it is the 1890s master detective Sherlock Holmes possesses a time traveling walking cane that allows him and his biographer, Dr. John Watson to travel throughout time to solve crimes. During a case called "The Riddle of a Thousand Faces" (wherein a killer leaves Shakespearian quotes on his victims' bodies) Holmes and Watson travel back in time to the era of William Shakespeare seeking clues. Suspicion points to Professor Moriarty, Holmes' arch enemy (how Moriarty was able to travel back in time is not explained). A plan by Moriarty to stop Holmes from capturing him backfires and breaks the time cane. A temporal storm is formed that transports Holmes and Moriarty to an unknown time and Watson and Shakespeare to present day Williamsburg in Brooklyn, New York. With no immediate way of returning to either of their past times, Shakespeare and Watson decide to make the best of the situation and open a detective agency (Shakespeare and Watson—Detectives of Mystery). The modern world also becomes fascinating for both men: Shakespeare is attracted to designer drugs and Dr. Watson becomes in awe with Brooklyn's seemingly endless supply of handsome men. With their individual addictions brought into the open the program charts their efforts to not only control them but solve crimes and find a way to return home.

Cast: David Blatt (William Shakespeare), Chris Miskiewicz (Dr. John Watson), Nick Abadzis (Sherlock Holmes), Paul Mosche (Prof. Moriarty), Ozzie Martinez (Cracky). **Credits:** *Producer-Writer:* Chris Miskiewicz. *Director:* Christopher Piazza. **Comment:** Watson dresses as he did in his era and Shakespeare as in his era—but nobody seems to notice (or care). Light humor is mixed with fantasy as two men, totally out of their element, attempt to adjust to a life thrust upon them by fate. The production values are good and the actors chosen for the leads well represent their historical counterparts.

Episodes:

1. Russian Sundae. Watson comes to Shakespeare's aid when he is pursued by thugs for stealing a bag of cocaine.

2. Ground Control to Arizona. Explores Dr. Watson's efforts to find a way to build a new time cane (suggesting that it was Watson who built the original cane for Holmes).

3. Sweets. As Shakespeare's addiction to drugs grows stronger Watson finds that he cannot rely on his partner for help on a current case and must solve it alone.

4. Who Will Save Us? Moriarty, transported to the future (the year 2555) manages to travel back in time to 2013 and to Brooklyn to capture Watson and Shakespeare.

5. Cracky's Pet. Moriaty's efforts fail and he is taken prisoner by Shakespeare and Watson who place him for safe-keeping with Shakespeare's drug-addicted friend, Cracky.

6. The Riddle of a Thousand Faces. Watson finds, during a case investigation wherein the killer leaves Shakespearian quotes on his victims' bodies, that it is somehow related to the case he and Holmes were attempting to solve over 100 years ago.

7 *The Adventures of Superseven.* super7 evenspy.com. 2011–2013 (Fantasy).

T.H.E.M. is an organization of goodness and kindness dedicated to battling evil wherever it exists. T.H.E.Y is an organization of nastiness dedicated to controlling the world. And wherever evil exists there is one man who has dedicated his life to destroying it—Superseven, a masked, man of mystery who dons a crimson costume and becomes whatever the situation calls for to right wrongs—from adventurer and scientist to lover and man about the world. Danger, he claims is his code name, and the gorgeous Sandra West is his partner, a girl who risks her life to not

The Adventures of Superseven. Jeremy Kokich as Superseven and Olivia Dunkley as Sandra West (copyright 60 Second Film School Productions).

only save Superseven, but her own to battle evil (from aliens and robots to assassins and madmen bent on conquering the world).

Cast: Jerry Kokich (Superseven), Olivia Dunkley (Sandra West), Anne Leighton (Sparky), Michelle Jubilee Gonzalez (Thunderpussy), Glenn Takakjian (The Fez), Rosanna Rizzuto (Angela Rome), Joe Foley (Boris), Vanessa Suarez (Madame Wasaby), Kelly Dolson (Paula Bishop), Inga Van Ardenn (Natasha), Milena Gardasevic (Sasha Banacek), Michelle Martonick (Lexi Savage), Kurt Carley (Big), Maria Leicy (Ilsa), Crystal Coney (Dr. Drexler), Krysle Martin (Emma Steel), Emerald Robinson (Jessica Logan). **Credits:** *Producer:* Olivia Dunkley, Jerry Kokich, Andrew Palmer, Scott Rhodes, Terry Shane. *Director:* Scott Rhodes, Jerry Kokich. *Writer:* Scott Rhodes, Andrew Palmer. Jerry Kokich, Olivia Dunkley. **Comment:** Well produced, directed and acted spoof of everything from superheroes to super spies. Sandra West, representing the great granddaughter of James T. West (television's *The Wild Wild West*) and the granddaughter of television's *Honey West,* is alluring as the heroine. Jerry Kokich is perfectly cast as a straight-faced superhero and Anne Leighton as Superseven's mechanic is sexy even in overalls and grease smears. One of the better comical fantasies that could easily make it as a regular broadcast or cable presentation.

Episodes:

1. Operation: Triple Cross. Introduces Superseven and Sandra as they seek information from a rogue agent about a sinister T.H.E.Y. plot.

2. Operation: Breakdown. A deadly assassin (Mamba) threatens the lives of Superseven and Sandra.

3. Operation: Four Play, Part 1. A look at the possibility of a romance between Superseven and Sandra.

4. Operation Four Play, Part 2. Sandra and Superseven battle a husband and wife team of assassins.

5. The Superseven Interview. A look at the man who is "the world's greatest masked superspy."

6. The Sandra West Interview. A look at the woman who is "a sultry and lethal secret agent."

7. Operation: Red Shark. Sparky, Superseven's mechanic, upgrades the Red Shark, Superseven's crime-fighting car.

8. Operation: Prime Time. Superseven and Sandra probe a former T.H.E.Y. agent turned Hollywood producer.

9. Operation: Trapezoid Conundrum. Sandra uncovers a plot to assassinate Superseven on live television.

10. Operation: Get Sandra West. Sandra, working alone while Superseven is on assignment in Japan, finds her life in peril when she investigates a tip on stolen information.

11. Operation: A Coffin for Sandra West. As Superseven plots to destroy an enemy missile base, Sandra is captured by T.H.E.Y. agents.

12. Operation: Death Trap Burbank. With Sandra missing, Superseven begins a search to find her.

13. Operation: Diabolical. Superseven's search continues while Sandra, being held captive by T.H.E.Y. faces interrogation from Thunderpussy, Big O and Dr. Diabolical.

14. Operation: Blueprint for Danger. Still seeking Sandra, Superseven arranges a meeting with "The Fez," a triple agent, hoping he may be able to help.

15. Operation: Spy Trap. Information leads Superseven to The Cave of Death to rescue Sandra.

16. Operation: 8 Spies Too Many. Superseven finds Sandra but encounters more than he expected as T.H.E.Y. agents have set a deadly trap for him.

17. Superseven: The Captive. In a take off on the television series *The Prisoner*, Superseven awakens after rescuing Sandra to find himself in a surreal village called The Hamlet.

18. Operation: 3 ... 2 ... 1 ... Die! Superseven and Sandra become targets as agents for T.H.E.M. are becoming victims of an unknown assassin.

19. Operation: Body Count. Sparky continues to upgrade Superseven's arsenal as Superseven and Sandra seek the assassin.

20. Operation: Permission to Kill. The mysterious assassin devises a plan to outsmart T.H.E.M., especially Superseven.

21. Operation: Permission to Kill. The assassin gains control of Sandra's mind, forcing her to kill T.H.E.M. agents in his image.

22. Operation Kiss Kiss, Kill Kill, Part Uno. As Sandra's killing spree continues, Superseven matches wits with a beautiful double agent that has been assigned to kill him.

23. Operation Kiss Kiss, Kill Kill, Part Duo. Superseven arranges a dinner date with the beautiful agent hoping to uncover the identity of the mysterious assassin controlling Sandra.

24. Operation: Kill or Die Trying. Superseven escapes the agent's attempts to kill him but fails to uncover the information he needs to stop Sandra's killing spree.

25. Operation: Shaken, Not Stirred. The mysterious assassin forces Sandra to steal the components for a death ray machine for T.H.E.Y.

26. Operation: Have Silencer, Will Travel. Superseven again seeks help from "The Fez" to learn the mysterious assassin's identity while Sandra confronts the evil Thunderpussy.

27. Operation: From T.H.E.Y. with Love. Sandra is programmed to assassinate Superseven, who is safe for the moment (on vacation in space).

28. Operation: Grand Slam. As the death ray is completed, Superseven learns that Sandra has retreated to the Island of Doom.

29. Operation: Heads I Win, Tails You Die! Sandra finds her life is also in danger as she has been targeted for elimination by the League of Assassins.

30. Operation: High Tension. Superseven finally rescues Sandra—but they are soon targeted by an old nemesis and his sultry accomplice.

31. Operation: A Funny Thing Happened on the Way to Save Sandra West. An angered Thunderpussy, having failed to eliminate Sandra (from episode 26) assigns two assassins to do the job.

32. Operation: Video Musicale. An episode featuring the cast in a song and music romp.

33. Superseven A Go Go. Continuing from the prior episode with a 1960s-style music video.

34. Operation: Next Episode. Although Superseven rescued Sandra, the mind-control chip that had been implanted in her brain causes concern for Superseven who is now thinking about liquidating her.

35. Operation: One Shot ... One Kill. Thunderpussy attempts to lure Sandra into a trap and finally eliminate her.

36. Operation: Doom Service. Superseven and Sandra enter a hotel, hoping for information, but are unknowingly walking into a trap.

37. Operation: Destructo. Bizarre side-effects continue to plague Sandra from the chip implanted in her brain.

38. Operation: Hard Kill in Fresno. Sandra and Superseven are unknowingly being stalked by a deadly assassin.

39. Operation: Red Herring. The concluding episode that finds Superseven attempting to help Sandra deal with a chip implant side-effect: a strange journey in which she encounters people from her past.

8 *After Judgment.* afterjudgment.com. 2009–2010 (Fantasy).

The world has come to an end although there are survivors. For these people death does not exist and the sun never sets. It is believed there is one last remaining, fabled entrance into paradise. Through the guidance of an ex-priest (Father Steven), a group of mismatched survivors begin their last journey, a journey of revelations as they seek the mysterious entrance into another realm. Their guiding light appears to be a mysterious child, who has appeared to them and whom Father Steven believes is the key they have been searching for.

Steven's faith was put to the test when the end neared and his parishioners sought redemption. Unable to handle the situation and coupled with the fact that he had prior knowledge of impending doom, Steven left the church and turned to alcohol. But that has changed. The world ended 100 years ago and Steven has a new calling—Humanity's savior.

The Stranger was a high ranking member of the federal government who had knowledge of the world ending. He kept quiet for over 100 years, choosing instead to become an observer to watch and listen to everything. He is now a part of Steven's group and, as the keeper of great knowledge, his observations are essential to completing their journey.

Michelle is a beautiful young woman who calls herself "a default prostitute." Though she detests what she does, if she tries something else she will always revert to selling her body for money. She has a talent for manipulating men and does not let sentiment get in the way of what she does. She is not a religious person but feels compelled to follow Steven, to find what she had been seeking but could never find.

Susan is a clairvoyant and can sense things before they happen. Susan, a writer, grew up in New York but moved to California after her third book was turned into a motion picture. Although she did not regret the move she felt that she did not fit in with the Hollywood lifestyle. Her ability gave her the sensation that something important was about to happen with Steven and felt compelled to be with him as he began his journey.

Lawrence is the eldest child of eight siblings and their caretaker since the death of their parents. Like The Stranger, Lawrence had a unique knowledge of the signs of the apocalypse and sought the help of Father Steve after only him and his brother, Xavier, survived. It was Xavier, who discovered a rare piece of scripture that revealed the truth about the world ending. Although he told Lawrence, they both decided to keep it a secret, fearing panic would result if they shared their knowledge.

Bill Reynolds is a misguided soul who earned a living as a painter and artist. When the world ended, Bill lost his son and retreated into a world of self-pity. It was when he met Father Steven, who had knowledge of a lost boy that Bill believed it could be his son and joined him.

Dusty was a character actor who has spent the last 100 years alone, mostly recounting plays and films in his mind. Father Steven has given him a new hope and Dusty has become one of his followers. **Cast:** Joel Bryant (Steven), Taryn O'Neill (Michelle), Stephanie Thorpe (Elizabeth), Monika Jolly (Susan), Tim Halling (The Stranger), Jim McMahon (The Cop), Kristen Huff (Mrs. Reynolds), Michael Thyer (Bill Reynolds), Gregor Manns (Lawrence), Michael McMillan (Xavier). **Credits:** *Producer:* Mike Davies, Jr., Taryn O'Neill, Stephanie Thorpe. *Writer-Director:* Mike Davies, Jr. **Comment:** A potentially good idea that is very amateurish with a weak and somewhat muddled plot (at times it just doesn't make sense). The acting is not good and the story is filled with inconsistencies (for example, since it is the apparent end of the world, where does electricity and food come from?). It's hard to say what the producers were thinking when they made this show. It doesn't appear it was to impress people; perhaps it was to make a sublime web series with a distinct point of view. If that was the case, they succeeded on one level, but distanced themselves from the general viewing audience.

Episodes: (5 minutes each)

1. Apathy Is the Enemy. Establishes the storyline as Steven and Michelle begin their search for the mysterious child.

2. Death Is All Relative. As Steven and Michelle search, they encounter two Trainers, members of a deadly group also seeking the child.

3. Time Has No Meaning. Steven begins to contemplate his life in a world without salvation if he cannot find the child before the Trainers.

4. My Life for One Star. As the Trainers continue their search Steven witnesses their attacking an innocent woman for no apparent reason.

5. Justice After Judgment. After witnessing the attack, but doing nothing to help, Steven returns home—only to be confronted by a woman whose threatening actions force him to shoot her.

6. No More Time. A Los Angeles pizza shop becomes a haven from this point on and introduces another survivor Steven befriends, The Cop.

7. Sunset and the Afterglow. A moment of intimacy occurs between Michelle and Steven during their discussion of the plight of the world.

8. Trainers. The dressed-in-black Trainers continue their search, this time attacking a young woman then pursuing Michelle and Steven.

9. I Bleed for You. Escaping from the Trainers, Steven and Michelle enlist the aid of The Cop as they again begin a search for the child.

10. Since the Day. Michelle and Steven encounter a couple (Mr. and Mrs. Reynolds) and learn that they are the parents of the child that is being sought.

11. Stranger Than Real Life. Now, joined by the Reynolds, the group continues their search, this time encountering The Stranger, a man with knowledge of prophecies that relate to the child.

12. We Stay Together. As the search becomes tiresome and seemingly fruitless, Steven recalls the night the world changed.

13. Sins of Our Father. As Steven dreams about the night he lost his family, he is awakened by two other survivors, Xavier and Lawrence, who have stumbled onto their camp looking for food.

14. Time Waits for No One. Now joined by Xavier and Lawrence, the group heads back to the pizza shop to rethink their situation.

15. Heaven Is So Far Away. At the pizza shop the group discusses what has happened since the child was seen and what course of action they need to take.

16. A Time for Change. An earthquake aftershock rocks the pizza shop and the survivors themselves when they realize the end may only be the beginning.

9 *Afterworld.* youtube.com. 2007–2008 (Science Fiction).

Russell Shoemaker, an advertising executive married to Janelle and the father of Kizzy, lives in Seattle Washington. With a hope of advancing his position, Russell travels to New York City to present a campaign idea to the company's main office. Tired and looking forward to what the next morning will bring, Russell retires early. The following morning, however, is nothing like Russell imagined: an unknown force has disabled all technology and it appears that most of humanity has vanished in what survivors have termed "The Fall." As Russell begins a dangerous trek back to Seattle to be with his family, stories, narrated by Russell, relate his adventures as he interacts with survivors and seeks answers to what really happened.

Cast: *Narrator:* Roark Critchlow. Credits: *Producer:* Brent W. Friedman, Stan Rogow. *Director:* Stan Rogow. *Writer:* Brent W. Friedman. **Comment:** The computer animated series consists of 13 twenty-three-minute episodes that have been edited and streamed as 130 three-minute episodes. The original episodes have also been retooled by Sony Pictures Television for broadcast television and made available to local stations as a half-hour television series.

Episodes: There are 130 episodes that are divided by the cities Russell encounters as he journeys across the country. The city story is listed followed by the episodes contained in that city.

1. The New York Story (10 episodes). *1.* The Big Day. *2.* Detritus. *3.* Purgatory. *4.* Delondre. *5.* Central Park. *6.* Hibakusha. *7.* Homeland Insecurity. *8.* Darwin's Ghost. *9.* Man of the House. *10.* 3000 Miles.

2. The Philadelphia, PA, Story (5 episodes). *11.* Call Me Eli. *12.* Terror Within. *13.* House of the Speaker. *14.* Detour. *15.* Revelations.

3. The New Eden, PA, Story (5 episodes): *16.* New Eden. *17.* Divine Intervention. *18.* Polaroid. *19.* Devil Among Us. *20.* Battle Lines.

4. The Aurora, OH, Story (5 episodes). *21.* Aurora. *22.* In Short Supply. *23.* Messenger. *24.* Mr. Shoemaker Goes to Ohio. *25.* The First Horseman.

5. The Peebles, OH, Story (5 episodes). *26.* 47 minutes. *27.* Subterranean. *28.* Looking Glass. *29.* A Quiet Place. *30.* An Offering to Uktena.

6. The Southern Ohio Story (5 episodes). *31.* The New World Historians. *32.* Fail Safe. *33.* Conflicting Reports. *34.* The River. *35.* Conspiracies Come True.

7. The Nashville, TN, Story (5 episodes). *36.* Rose Mansion. *37.* Nashville. *38.* Spontaneous Combustion. *39.* Temptations. *40.* The Second Horseman.

8. The Memphis, TN, Story (5 episodes). *41.* Graceland. *42.* The Virus. *43.* Control Group. *44.* Do No Harm. *45.* A Good Life.

9. The Ozarks Story (5 episodes). *46.* Truth or Consequence. *47.* Off the Grid. *48.* The Hunter. *49.* Wanted. *50.* R.I.P.

10. The Salina, OK, Story (5 episodes). *51.* Oklahoma. *52.* Electricity. *53.* Parthia. *55.* Gone, Baby, Gone.

11. The Wichita, KS, Story (5 episodes). *56.* The Cobalt Clock. *57.* Team Alpha. *58.* Faith in Science. *59.* Eve of Destruction. *60.* Holiday Spirit.

12. The Amarillo, TX, Story (5 episodes). *61.* Morning Star. *62.* Warning Signs. *63.* Complications. *64.* What Child Is This? *65.* The Brother.

13. The Santa Fe, NM, Story (5 episodes). *66.* Manhunt. *67.* The Settlement. *68.* Sanctuary. *69.* Fight or Flight. *70.* Change of Heart.

14. The Sedona, AZ, Story (5 episodes). *71.* Welcome to the Jungle. *72.* Something Is in the Air. *73.* Burden of Guilt. *74.* Prey. *75.* Déjà vu.

15. The Ghana Story (5 episodes). *76.* Helpless. *77.* Gone to Ghana. *78.* Solitary. *79.* Almost Home. *80.* The Remedy.

16. The Flagstaff, AZ, Story (5 episodes). *81.* The Walker. *82.* Bad Reputation. *83.* Ultimatum. *84.* Hidden Agenda. *85.* The Ever-Changing Truth.

17. The Needles, CA, Story (5 episodes). *86.* The Cartel. *87.* A Window of Opportunity. *88.* The Berserker. *89.* Like Clockwork. *90.* Fair Trade.

18. The Las Vegas, NV, Story (5 episodes). *91.* The Suicide Squad. *92.* Debt to Society. *93.* Showtime. *94.* Double Bill. *95.* Convergence.

19. The Red Rock, NV, Story (5 episodes). *96.* The Third Horseman. *97.* Change of Plans. *98.* End of the Road. *99.* The Grim Reaper. *100.* Monumental.

20. The Mount Charleston, NV, Story (5 episodes). *101.* Road to Redemption. *102.* NORAD. *103.* Prisoners of Fate. *104.* Pushing Buttons. *105.* Simple Pleasures.

21. The Lake City, NV, Story (5 episodes). *106.* Lake City. *107.* What Lies Beneath. *108.* The Devil Inside. *109.* Bottom Line. *110.* Pathological.

22. The Sierra Forest Story (5 episodes). *111.* The Fourth Horseman. *112.* Bitter Pill. *113.* The Story of the Gun. *114.* A Little Help from My Friends. *115.* Treasure Island.

23. The San Francisco, CA, Story (5 episodes). *116.* The Shipment. *117.* First Edition. *118.* On the Record. *119.* The Sting, Part 1. *120.* The Sting, Part 2.

24. The San Rafael, CA, Story (5 episodes). *121.* A New Chapter. *122.* Project Continuum. *123.* Truth in the Clouds. *124.* Matter of Time. *125.* Unholy Alliance.

25. The Seattle, WA, Story (5 episodes). *126.* North By Northwest. *127.* The Emerald City. *128.* Shoemaker & Associates. *129.* 809 W. Blaine Street. *130.* When the Levee Breaks.

10 *Aidan 5.* aidan5.com. 2009 (Science Fiction).

In a futuristic time, human cloning has become traditional and clones live among the population. James Aidan, a police detective, is one such man who has been cloned. However, when his clones are being systematically killed, he and his partner, Morgan Riley, begin an investigation. The program follows their efforts to uncover the killer and the reason why.

Cast: Bryan Michael Block (James Aidan), Maya Sayre (Morgan Riley), Bryan Coleman (Faceless Man), John Michael Stubbins (Frank), Jon Osbeck (Charles Mabon), Megan Moore (Janice), Amber Mikesell (Amelia), Nick Baldasare (Senator Kendrick), John Newkirk (Roger), Emily Bach (Lauren), Jessica Cameron (Rachel Taylor). **Credits:**

Producer: Ben Bays, John Jackson, Shawn Likely. *Director:* Ben Bays, John Jackson. *Writer:* Ben Bays, John Jackson, Tim Baldwin, Vidas Barzdukas, Noell Wolfgram, Joe Wink. **Comment:** Presented like a comic book with sketched art and made with an all volunteer cast and crew. What has been accomplished here (using volunteers) should make broadcasters take note: quality can be produced for minimal cost (equipment and sets). Although the idea is not original (the 1979 syndicated series *Jane* used the same concept) it is well done and filming in black and white also adds to the show's mystique.

Episodes:

1. The Rooftop (6 min., 42 sec.). The mystery begins as Aidan and Riley investigate a series of killings.

2. Infinity (9 min., 34 sec.). As he investigates, Aidan deducts that he is the sought target, not his clones.

3. Chasing Shadows (6 min., 57 sec.). Aidan and Riley are attacked by an unknown assailant.

4. The Enemy of My Enemy (8 min., 46 sec.). Aidan deducts that the cloning corporation, Infinity, is somehow connected to what is happening.

5. In Sheep's Clothing (7 min., 20 sec.). Aidan and Riley serve Infinity Cloning Corporation with a warrant to search their files.

6. Off the Tracks (6 min., 50 sec.). Before they can search Infinity's files, the cloning database is stolen.

7. The Life of Riley (9 min., 18 sec.). A flashback to the day Aidan was cloned.

8. Down the Rabbit Hole, Part 1 (8 min., 56 sec.). Aidan seeks information regarding his family's sudden disappearance.

9. Down the Rabbit Hole, Part 2 (5 min., 47 sec.). Aidan confronts his informant for more information and learns that unauthorized clones are being made, presumably by one such scientist, the Man with No Face.

10. A Date at the Docks (10 min., 28 sec.). Aidan and Riley seek more information about the information they just obtained.

11. Inquisition (14 min., 3 sec.). Aidan is captured and interrogated by one of his clones— Matthew.

12. Inferno (9 min., 51 sec.). After being interrogated (to see how much he knows), Matthew releases Aidan (who then joins with Riley). As they continue their probe, they discover there are illegal cloning centers throughout the city.

13. Revelations (9 min.). After infiltrating an illegal cloning station, Aidan learns that Infinity had released 500,000 clones before discovering a deficiency defect wherein only the fifth clone of a person retained the memory of the original clone (Matthew appears to be Aidan's fifth clone). While Aidan learns more about Infinity, Riley sees that she is unknowingly being cloned—but why and for what purpose? She is only able to destroy a handful of her clones (by shooting them) before the screen turns to black and the series ends.

11 *Alien Planet.* facebook. com/AlienPlanetWebSeries. 2012 (Science Fiction).

Futuristic tale of an astronaut, stranded on an alien planet when his craft crashes, who finds himself

Aidan 5. **Bryan Michael Block and Maya Sayre in their roles as James and Morgan (copyright Aidan 5 Productions, LLC).**

not only seeking a way to return home, but survive when he encounters the Alien Master, a being who rules over a population that are determined to see that their unwanted visitor never leaves their planet alive. **Cast:** Tim McLean (Alien Master), Jack Hinton (Astronaut). **Credits:** *Producer:* Tim McLean, Jack Hinton. *Director:* Tim McLean. *Writer:* Tim McLean, Jack Hinton. **Comment:** You have to see it to believe it. An adult (Tim) and a young boy (Jack) are the "stars" and do they not only need acting lessons, but writing and directing skills as well. The child's bedroom is the center of the action where he battles the Alien Master and attempts to repair his cardboard box space ship. Who ever holds the camera doesn't know the meaning of the word steady (as the scenes are annoyingly shaky). The over-abundant close-ups of the child are also a bit too much to take. It has to be assumed the program was made as a joke and nothing more.

Episodes:
1. The Awakening (2 min., 16 sec.). The astronaut's plight begins as he awakens after crash landing and encounters an alien.
2. Escape Pod (3 min., 5 sec.). The astronaut attempts to repair his escape pod.
3. The Wheel (3 min., 46 sec.). The Alien Master devises a plan to rid his planet of the astronaut.

12 *Alpha Planet*. renrobot.com/alpha planet. 2010 (Science Fiction).

After a futuristic holocaust in the year 2056, surviving members of earth's population are rescued and placed aboard the refuge ship *A.R.C.* As time passes (200 years) and the food supplies dwindle, four explorers are returned to Earth to not only find food, but search for signs of new life. **Cast:** Michael Sweeney (Adam Landrey), Jen Tobin (Karin Dawson), Don Jeanes (Luke Brodie), J.D. Mendonca (Ian Scott), Arron Marie Fenton (Kira), Jay Preston (James Dagney), Megan Franich (News Anchor), Steven Gaston (Grease), Brad Hills (Edge). **Credits:** *Producer:* Mike Darling, Arron Marie Fenton. *Director:* Mike Darling. *Writer:* Mike Darling, Arron Marie Fenton. **Comment:** Acceptable as a standard science fiction yarn although some of the dialogue contradicts itself (like the explorers saying there are no signs of life when they are surrounded by plant and tree growth then later discovering there are plants and trees). The acting is good, but the director's use of the shaky camera method is not needed, especially on wide angel shots where everything is bobbing up and down and from side to side.

Episodes:
1. News Prelude (2 min., 43 sec.). The crew (Adam, Karin, Luke and Ian) of the *A.R.C.*'s explorer ship, *Columbus II*, lands on Earth.
2. Prodigal Sons (6 min., 43 sec.). The explorers begin their probe of the devastated planet.

3. Diversilobum (4 min., 47 sec.). Shortly after Karin discovers that revitalized plant life can do more harm than good, a sudden dust storm engulfs the crew.
4. When on Earth (4 min., 29 sec.). With few supplies left, the crew continues their trek along the scarred landscape.
5. Wild Rovers (3 min., 33 sec.). Luke discovers remnants of a society that no longer exists.
6. Snake in the Grass (3 min., 28 sec.). The crew begins to gather up relics but something sinister is watching.
7. Scars (5 min., 48 sec.). Karin discovers signs of animal life—a snake that bites her; the sun sets as the crew seeks a place to spend the night.
8. Left Behind (5 min., 55 sec.). As Karin recovers from her snake bite, she has a dream of a strange figure warning her of danger. Was it real or just a side effect of the snake venom? Whatever, she urges her crew to move on.
9. Love Child (4 min., 4 sec.). Ian discovers the first sign of human life on the planet—a girl named Kira and he must now find out where she came from.
10. The Favored (3 min., 54 sec.). It is revealed that a man named Dagney has been tracking the crew since they landed; Kira is caught stealing food and flees before she is caught.
11. Dagney (5 min., 21 sec.). The team is split into two when Luke and Adam pursue Kira; Ian and Karin are left with Dagney.
12. One Government, One Earth (6 min., 12 sec.). The program ends with Dagney explaining how he came to be here and Luke, Adam, Karin and Ian wondering, now that signs of human life have been found, what their mission will be.

13 *Always Night*. blackamericatv.com. 2013 (Science Fiction).

Valerie and Roger Lennix appear to be couple that has it all—a lovely home, good friends, health and wealth. They have been married for five years and on the occasion of their latest wedding anniversary, their lives are about to change forever. As the viewer sees the couple for the first time there is an immediate sensation that all is not right with them. Roger is indulging in self-involved reflection while Valerie appears to be struggling with something. It appears they have grown apart and just how far comes to light when Valerie approaches Roger and tells him how perplexed she is that humans, being as fragile as they are, have managed to survive for such an extended period of time. As a bewildered Roger listens, Valerie confesses that she is not completely human—and not of this earth. She warns Roger that she is not alone, that others are here and the planet will face an enemy like it has never known before. Valerie then vanishes in a burst of light and Roger must now become a savior—but who to tell and will anyone believe him?

Cast: Delila Vallot (Valerie Banks), Harry Lennix (Roger Banks). **Credits:** *Producer:* Delila Vallot, Harry Lennix, Summer Luna. *Director:* Carl Weathers. *Writer:* Art Washington, Zachary Waterfire. **Comment:** Thus far only the pilot episode has been released and leaves the doorway open for an intriguing concept. The production values are good as is actor Carl Weathers' directing.

Episodes:

1. The Pilot. Establishes the series story line as described above.

14 *American Heart.* americanheart.com. 2008–2009 (Horror).

It has been thirty-four days since a zombie outbreak occurred in a small Southern town and a small group of survivors has taken refuge inside a hospital called American Heart. They are led by a somewhat ineffectual sheriff (Joe) and are also stranded with a reality television series crew that happened to be filming at the hospital at the time of the outbreak. The group "occupies their time by playing games with hospital equipment, teasing zombies and having sex with each other." As the survivors wait rescue, the television crew films the story as it happens with people, aware of the camera, speaking directly to it and relating short messages about the day's events. To bring attention to themselves, the group posts You Tube videos hoping that someone will see they need help and send the National Guard. Lucy Simms is the television star (the host of a reality dating show), Neil is a washed-up actor; Rachel is Joe's younger sister; Eric is Rachel's boyfriend.

Cast: Crystal Arnette (Lucy Simms), Jim Babel (Sheriff Joe Keller), Wayne Crawford (Neil Stahl), Rebecca Wolf (Rachel Keller), Ben Yannette (Eric Milius), Jesse Threatt (Jeremiah), Ali Bill (Alberta Roberta), Joe Flanders (Eugene), Jared Threatt (Cameraman), Lindsay Senior (Sweet Tits Zombie). **Credits:** *Producer:* Jessica Baker, Simon Woo. *Writer-Director:* Graham Bowlin, Andrew Mitchell. **Comment:** Comedy bits accent the program (like bowling with severed heads) and there are a number of "boob shots" of the females (one in particular of "Sweet Tits Zombie"). The mix of horror and comedy works and the program is well worth checking out.

Episodes:

1. The Hospital. Establishes the storyline thirty-four days after a zombie outbreak.

2. If the Guard Says It's True. Signs point to the fact that one of the survivors (Eric) may have become infected.

3. The World Wide Dead. Joe seeks a way to activate the Internet so the group can post their videos for help.

4. I Only Played a Hero on TV. With the Internet opened, but with their only laptop out of power, one member must venture outside the hospital to Jerry's van to retrieve a charger.

5. The Alamo. With zombies infesting the hospital, the group makes one last ditch effort to escape and find a new safety zone.

American Heart **series poster art (copyright Jessica Baker).**

15 Amongst Angels, Demons and Those In Between. webserieschannel.com. 2010 (Science Fiction).

As a woman, dressed in black, walks through the streets of Manhattan, we learn that every day guardians protect those who are in danger. These protectors risk their lives to save innocent people from lurking danger. "You have never heard of us," the woman in black says, "But now it is time to share our stories in the hope to spread some light on the darkness that plagues us all with insanity." As our Lady in Black exclaimed, stories of such encounters are explored as both good and evil battle for the souls of humans.

Cast: Kristina Varshavskaya (Alexa), Kristine J. Martinez (Angela), Delia Flores (Wolf), Kayla Perez (Grace), J. Rivera (Sasha), Stephanie Rodriquez (Jessica), James Guzman (Adam), Michael Ferrari (Chris), Albert De Jesus, Jr. (Sin), Clinton J. Marrast (Sy), Yu Lew (Luigi). **Credits:** *Producer-Director:* Delia Flores, Kristina Varshavskaya. *Writer:* Delia Flores. **Comment:** The good vs. evil aspect has been done countless times before in movies and on television. Here, it appears that a sense of harsh reality was sought as the episodes are filmed on the streets of New York (although the camera movement is annoyingly jerky). The performers are mostly believable in portraying real people with problems, but foul language abounds and is even used in front of children. No parental warning appears.

Episodes:

1. Amongst Angels and Demons (7 min., 18 sec.). Explores two women: Grace, who trains with angels and Alexa who has fallen prey to the dark side.

2. Just (7 min., 54 sec.). A 12-year-old boy, with help from angels, guides adults along the right path in life.

3. Adam the Little Demon (6 min., 27 sec.). Sasha, a soldier in the Devil's Army, seeks the soul of a truly wicked young boy named Adam.

4. Beginnings (5 min., 53 sec.). A young woman is torn between good and evil when she attempts to meet a mysterious stranger.

16 Amy Kidd, Zombie Speech Pathologist. youtube.com. 2013 (Horror).

Amy Kidd was a speech therapist whose practice has suffered greatly since a zombie apocalypse destroyed most humans and left her without patients. Amy, however, is resilient and revises her practice to help zombies. Since zombies are unable to speak, Amy feels she can help them and opens a zombie charm school. Stories were to follow Amy as she attempts to help zombies adjust to society.

Cast: Audrey Noone (Amy Kidd), Brooke Solomon (Look Out Girl), Curtis Reid (Joey), Chris Estes (Arnold Milquetoast), Talli Clemons (Look Out Man). **Credits:** *Producer-Writer-Director:* Audrey Noone. **Comment:** Played strictly for laughs, but presenting zombies in a new light, the potential series looks good from the pilot presentation but could suffer from monotony as to how far can the concept be stretched.

Episodes: Only a pilot (8 min., 6 sec.) has been produced that establishes how Amy chose to begin her new profession.

17 Angel of Death. crackle.com. 2009 (Fantasy).

Eve is a young woman with an unusual occupation: hired killer (called "The Angel of Death"). During one assignment a murder-for-hire goes wrong and Eve becomes the victim: struck in the head by her target with a knife. Eve, however, does not die; she is saved by a drug-addicted doctor (Rankin) who removes the knife from her skull but the wound leaves her with haunting visions of the people whose lives she has taken. She is now driven to seek revenge by eliminating those who ordered her to take the lives of others.

Cast: Zoe Bell (Eve), Doug Jones (Dr. Rankin), Lucy Lawless (Vera), Ted Raimi (Jed Norton), Vail Bloom (Regina Downes) Brian Poth, (Graham Prescott), Monica Staggs (The Madame), Jake Abel (Cameron Downs), Justin Huen (Franklin). **Credits:** *Producer:* Mark Battaglia, Paul Etheridge, John Norris. *Director:* Paul Etheridge. *Writer:* Ed Brubaker. **Comment:** Well paced thriller that, despite the foul language that is unnecessarily used, is well acted and produced.

Episodes:

1. Edge (7 min., 23 sec.). Establishes the storyline as Eve becomes impaired with a knife in her head.

2. Conscious (8 min., 56 sec.). Eve miraculously survives her ordeal when Dr. Rankin successfully removes the knife.

3. Workday (9 min., 43 sec.). Visions begin to impair Eve's abilities when she begins her quest to destroy those (the Downes family) that put a hit out on her.

4. Made Man (8 min.). As the visions continue to haunt Eve, she seeks a way to stop them from occurring.

5. Clean Up (7 min., 52 sec.). During a confrontation with someone who can possibly lead her to the people she is seeking, Eve has a seizure that totally disables her.

6. The Family (8 min., 39 sec.). Overcoming the seizure, Eve finds help from her neighbor, Vera. Meanwhile Eve's assassins attempt to get a handle on where she may be hiding.

7. Old Man (6 min., 57 sec.). Eve continues in her quest, but moves more cautiously than ever as she is now not sure who she can trust.

8. Innocents (6 min., 39 sec.). Regina, a member of the family seeking to kill Eve, instructs her brother,

Cameron to stop Graham, Eve's friend, from teaming with her.

9. The Hunt (6 min., 52 sec.). Eve becomes enraged when, to get to Eve, they kill Vera and Graham. Eve, now more determined than ever, seeks to bring down the entire Downes family.

10. Absolution (11 min., 20 sec.). Concludes the saga as Eve may just achieve her revenge—or lose her life in a final confrontation.

18 *Animus Cross.* youtube.com. 2009 (Horror).

The Civil War has ended and people are just struggling to overcome the tragedies and devastation the war has inflicted on the South. Two years later, in the Inland Northwest woods in the Idaho territory, the small settlement of Animus Cross has been established. However, with its establishment, also came an unknown evil that lurks in the darkness—and evil that appears to be unstoppable as it preys on the settlers. The story follows the efforts of three men to fight another war and destroy the beast that is destroying their lives.

Cast: Jerry L. Buxbaum (Alban Sarcous), Katherine Bukowski (Sarah Wilson), Judith Wilson (Trish Egan), Jeff Hime (Ethan Carver), Ira Kortum (Nathan Thomas), Harold Phillips (Henry Foray), Mercedes Rose (Margery), David Steen (Pastor Carver). **Credits:** *Producer-Writer-Director:* Amanda Steen. **Comment:** A rarity in web series as it can be considered both a horror series and an historical series for its setting. It is a straight, well done story with no nudity, foul language, jokes or scantily clad girls. The landscapes are well chosen; the production values comparable to any television series; the acting very good and the sets and costumes very impressive (and authentic). Well worth watching.

Episodes:

1. Hell Runs This Way, Part 1. The terror begins as a group of settlers are attacked in the dark woods by something unknown.

2. Hell Runs This Way, Part 2. Recovering from the attack, the settlers continue their trek to Animus Cross.

3. Hell Runs This Way, Part 3. Although the settlers are considered outsiders, they receive help from the local sheriff (Sarcous) as they continue their journey home.

4. Hell Runs This Way, Part 4. The trek becomes more treacherous when the settlers become stranded in the middle of Carver Pond.

5. Hell Runs This Way, Part 5. As night falls the settlers take precautions as the darkness descends on their campsite. Tension and fear also settle in as each wonders if they will ever live to see Animus Cross again.

19 *The Apocalypse Diaries.* theapocalypse diaries.com. 2011 (Science Fiction).

Experimentation on the world's largest supercollider appears to have minimal effects at first. However, as tests continue, it has repercussions over the entire planet as explosions begin to initially only affect Los Angeles but then slowly spread across the globe. The program follows one woman, Jen Cross, and her experiences facing such a crisis and of a resistance group struggling to prove that it was a government-created incident that was to blame.

Cast: Laurel Marlantes (Jen Cross), Graham Hamilton (Evan Dillon), Kris Haddad (Nurse). **Credits:** *Producer:* Clea Frost, Nicole Sacker, James Tuverson. *Writer-Director:* Clea Frost. **Comment:** Fast moving story with good special effects and acting. Though each episode is very short, it presents what happens from one week after the accident to the day before and how the government attempts to suppress disasters that are of their own doing.

Episodes:

1. Los Angeles, Day 5 (2 min., 51 sec.). Introduces a young couple, Jen and Evan, as they experience the after shocks of the explosions.

2. Los Angeles, Day 7 (1 min., 26 sec.). Jen fears for Evan's safety when he ventures outside the safety of their apartment.

3. Los Angeles, Day 9 (1 min., 43 sec.). Los Angeles begins to experience environmental contamination as a result of the continuing explosions and people become infected with what is called "The Orange Plague" (as it turns skin orange).

4. Los Angeles, Day 11 (51 sec.). Jen comes to the aid of a neighbor when she hears cries for help.

5. Los Angeles, Day 12 (46 sec.). Jen's efforts to help fail as the situation around her grows increasingly worse.

6. Los Angeles, Day 12 (1 min., 33 sec.). Struggling to overcome her inhibitions that she could not help save a life, Jen begins to wonder if the situation that is occurring is extraterrestrial or man made.

7. Los Angeles, Day 13 (1 min., 15 sec.). As the explosions continue, Jen feels she must venture outside to survive.

8. Los Angeles, Day 14 (58 sec.). Jen discovers that her suspicions may be true as a resistance group begins transmitting evidence from within the Los Angeles blast zone of what they uncovered.

9. Los Angeles, Day 1 (59 sec.). Presents a look at what happened during the first explosions that rocked Los Angeles.

10. Sydney, Day 1 (56 sec.). The resistance group realizes that the destruction goes beyond the United States when they receive footage of similar occurrences happening in Australia.

11. Los Angeles Before the Blast (1 min., 37 sec.). Shows home videos of Jen and Evan before the blast.

12. Puerto Vallarta, Day 1 (1 min., 21 sec.). Footage of the disaster spreading to Mexico and Switzerland.

13. Los Angeles (1 min., 9 sec.). Fearing the

resistance, the government seeks a way to end their transmissions of events.

14. D.C., Day 1 (1 min., 17 sec.). Washington, D.C. begins to experience its first effects of the explosions.

15. Episode 15 (2 min., 29 sec.). A government scientist risks his life to reveal that it was an experiment that caused the explosions. This and the following episode focus totally on the scientist who appears in a blur to hide his identity.

16. Episode 16 (2 min., 16 sec.). The scientist reveals a government cover up in the aftermath of the supercollider accident.

17. Los Angeles, Day 30 (1 min., 18 sec.). The Los Angeles situation grows increasingly worse with no apparent hope of stopping the devastation.

18. Episode 18 (1 min., 49 sec.). Footage from inside the blast zone is released to the media with the devastation it has caused in Los Angeles.

20 *Arcana.* vimeo.com. 2012 (Fantasy).

Is the world in which we live real or just imaginary? Stairs (as he is called) is a young man who begins a journey of self discovery to answer that question. He has a degree in anthropology but works as a clerk in a video store. He feels his life is going nowhere until he touches a Tarot card (that for some unexplained reason is lying on a coffee table) and is drawn into the world of The Gambit (an ancient magic ritual) and must solve riddles presented to him by the mystical prophet Major Arcana of the Tarot deck. Each riddle sends Stairs deeper into The Gambit and in contact with a mysterious being called the Phoenix. As he continues his journey, Stairs slowly begins to understand the nature of his reality—something that is not as it seemed (especially when he sees events from the past unfold before his eyes [seen in a brief flashback]). The story follows Stairs as he tries to encompass a spiritual enlightenment that could also drive him insane. **Cast:** Joe Homes (Stairs), Meredith Adelaide (Eliza), McKenzie Coffee (Phoebe), Austin Hillbrecht (Brenden), Dennis Fitzpatrick (Xerxes). **Credits:** *Producer:* Barry Morgan, Kristin Blyler, Vinicius Kfuri. *Writer-Director:* Barry Morgan. **Comment:** Although two episodes are listed, they are actually a pilot film that has been edited into two parts. The story is intriguing but hampered by poor sound quality and photography. It is also limited by what can occur if additional episodes are produced. The fantasy aspect can be stretched only so much before it begins to border on ridiculous. **Episodes:**

1. The Runner, Part 1 (6 min., 36 sec.). Stairs begins his mysterious journey.

2. The Runner, Part 2 (5 min., 44 sec.). Having solved the riddles of Major Arcana, Stairs now questions whether his reality is true or an illusion.

21 *Ark.* hulu.com. 2009 (Science Fiction).

After falling asleep on her living room sofa, a young third grade school teacher (Connie) in the year 2008 awakens to find herself aboard a space craft (*Ark*) many millions of miles away from earth. A young astronaut (Carl) from the year 1959 has also experienced the same fate. But how and why? As they explore the ship they encounter a woman (whom they call "Crazy Lady") who speaks a language which neither understands. It is obvious she needs their help but the language barrier prevents them from comprehending. Stories explore what happens as the trio investigates their new surroundings and seeks a way to find out what happened to them and why. **Cast:** Renee O'Connor (Connie), Adam Cardon (Carl), Marjo-Rikka Makela (Crazy Lady). **Credits:** *Producer-Director:* Trey Stokes. *Writer:* Robbie Thompson. **Comment:** Impressive science fiction series featuring Renee O'Connor (from the television series *Xenia: Warrior Princess*). The special effects and sets are good and the stories well thought out. Unfortunately, the series concludes in a cliff hanger without any resolutions (an apparent second season was hoped for, but it never materialized). The idea is quite good although it does show the slightest similarity to the 1973 television series *The Starlost* (but only in the aspect wherein a trio of passengers is stranded aboard a space craft drifting in space). Other than that, it goes far beyond that series to present its own intriguing premise. **Episodes:**

1. Episode 1 (4 min., 23 sec.). Connie awakens aboard the ship with no recollection as to how she came to be there.

2. Episode 2 (3 min., 59 sec.). As Connie begins to explore the ship she discovers she is not alone and discovers Carl.

3. Episode 3 (4 min., 45 sec.). Connie and Carl discover that the world they each knew is gone and that they are in the unknown regions of deep space.

4. Episode 4 (7 min., 16 sec.). Connie and Carl continue to unravel the mystery.

5. Episode 5 (3 min., 22 sec.). A clue emerges as to what may have happened.

6. Episode 6 (3 min.). Connie ventures deeper into the ship for answers.

7. Episode 7 (4 min., 55 sec.). Carl attempts to save Connie, who is trapped in a lower deck after an explosion.

8. Episode 8 (6 min., 1 sec.). Connie, injured during the explosion, finds "The Crazy Lady" next to her and apparently killed in the explosion.

9. Episode 9 (9 min., 53 sec.). Connie finds some unexpected evidence (her son's headless action figure) from her decade and a mysterious male voice asking for help.

22 *The Art of Zombie Killing.* scifinal.com. 2010 (Horror).

Narrated animated tales of a zombie hunter, operating from a junkyard in a post-apocalyptic world, as he pursues and disposes of his targets. **Cast:** Michael Kelly (Narrator). **Credits:** *Producer-Animator:* Thomas Bosworth, Wayne Tully. **Comment:** Unusual animated project that uses more still drawings than actual movement. The zombie hunter is vicious and the program somewhat violent but it is an interesting concept that is enjoyable.

Episodes:

1. Fat Zombie (57 sec.). The zombie hunter seeks to eliminate an overweight zombie.

2. Vulcan (54 sec.). A zombie leader is sought by the zombie hunter.

3. Bored (1 min., 12 sec.). The zombie hunter shows how he can use garbage as weapons against the enemy.

4. Horde (1 min., 14 sec.). The zombie hunter disposes of a horde of approaching zombies.

5. Rescue (1 min., 21 sec.). The zombie hunter risks his life to rescue a group of people facing certain death from zombies.

23 *Astro-Cons.* youtube.com. 2012 (Science Fiction).

The Department of Space is a federally-funded agency that spends tax dollars "to build a brighter tomorrow." The trouble is, it is staffed by morons and when that tomorrow will be is anybody's guess—but at least they have the money to do what they need. The story relates one problem the agency faces: an impending catastrophe from space is threatening the planet—but the agency has no idea what to do about it. **Cast:** Will Hessler (Brian), Jeff Ronan (Jake/Director Spivak), Mario Bueno (Dr. Milson), Amanda Van Norstrand (Jess), Taylor Marsh (Cobie). **Credits:** *Producer:* Ben Friedberg. *Writer-Director:* Leo Caine. **Comment:** A lively animated project that is more comedy than science fiction. The animation is acceptable although it does not measure up to today's sophisticated computer animation. After a minute or so of watching the first episode, the animation becomes appealing and the series is easily watched.

Episodes:

1. Wolverines (3 min., 20 sec.). Dr. Milson makes a startling discovery—but he can't reveal it until he figures out exactly what his agency does.

2. Michael Bay! Boom (4 min., 8 sec.). Before deciding to have lunch, the team struggles to figure out the department's responsibilities.

3. Little Orphan Garrett (3 min., 47 sec.). Dr. Milson reveals that a great cosmic catastrophe is going to destroy the earth.

4. Monkey Rockets (3 min., 56 sec.). Brian believes that since space exploration began with monkeys, launching a space ship with a monkey could divert the catastrophe when the aliens come in contact with such a creature.

5. Almost the Greatest Episode Ever (4 min., 51 sec.). Brian puts his knowledge of propulsion into effect (which surprises everyone as he only displayed knowledge of quotes from obscure 1980s movies).

6. Is This Thing On? (2 min., 15 sec.). When the members of the Department of Space realize that they are not a government agency unless they hold a press conference, they decide to hold one to inform the world about what is going to happen.

7. Day with the Damned, Part 1. (5 min., 29 sec.). When Brian associates the impending doom with movies he has seen about the future he theorizes that children should be their top priority.

8. Day with the Damned, Part 2. (6 min., 47 sec.). Ethan, the nephew of team member Cobie, is brought to the center to learn what his government does for him (well, at least in theory).

9. That's Debatable (4 min., 3 sec.). With election time approaching, a Presidential debate causes a rift among the center members.

10. Alejandro (4 min., 20 sec.). A congressman's negative remarks about the Department of Space angers team members who want revenge (and hopefully set the record straight—that they do have a purpose, they think).

11. Barry Bostwick! (4 min., 52 sec.). Actor Barry Bostwick's name is used in a concluding episode that finds agency director Spivack emaciating himself in the world of government corruption (perhaps the only way to survive that impending doom).

24 *Asylum.* hulu.com. 2010 (Horror).

Six years ago a renowned psychiatrist, Dr. Patrick Aubert, transferred his stately mansion into an asylum for the criminally insane. He hired a staff and advertised for volunteers to receive treatment—"perhaps for a bit; perhaps forever. I'm Dr. Aubert and this is my asylum." The asylum is anything but normal as it appears to have an eerie link to the supernatural. Patients are susceptible to something more than appears normal and stories follow one physician (Dr. Suli Urban) as she treats patients who seem to progress deeper in their psychosis rather than get better. **Cast:** Sophie King (Dr. Suli Urban), Dingani Beza (Dr. Patrick Aubert), Christopher DeMaci (Marvin Ulrich), Danielle Vinas (Jessica Cartwright), Carey Fox (Joseph Vasiliev), Jen Kuhn (Camille Ulrich), Samantha Kelly (Jenny Wilkins), Jason Paul Field (Bill Stockton), Sharon Gardner (Belinda Stockton). **Credits:** *Producer:* Louis Blitzman, David Odio, Ryan Romero, Dan Williams. *Director:* Scott Brown. *Writer:* Dan Williams. **Comment:** Intriguing little yarn that, although the idea of a haunted hospital has been done numerous times before, effectively presents its own version of the idea.

Episodes:

1. Marvin Ulrich, Part 1. During the diagnosis of

a patient (Marvin Ulrich), the staff receives an unexpected visit from Patrick Aubert, now the Deputy Director of the Department of Mental Health.

2. Marvin Ulrich, Part 2. As Aubert observes, Marvin's condition worsens with doctors unable to find an effective medication.

3. Jessica Cartwright, Part 1. A patient (Jessica Cartwright), diagnosed with strange delusions, seems to be following in the path of Marvin and getting progressively worse.

4. Jessica Cartwright, Part 2. Patrick fears something is affecting patients and begins a probe into the asylum's past.

5. Eugene Wilson, Part 1. An elderly man, with delusions of being only 15 years old, baffles doctors who are unable to find a proper means of treatment. Meanwhile, Patrick digs deeper into the asylum's past.

6. Eugene Wilson, Part 2. Patrick confronts Suli regarding the hospital's administration and what he has learned.

25 *Auror's Tale.* aurorstale.com. 2012 (Fantasy).

In what appears to be the present, Dark Magic rules the underworld. In New York City, the program's setting, the Department of Magical Law Enforcement of the Ministry of Magic has been established to solve crimes related to the Dark Arts and detain witches and wizards. A new breed of criminal has also arisen, the depraved wizard gang, the Hellhounds. One man, Lokai Hawthorne, the department's latest recruit (police officers are called Auror), is also magical and the gang's biggest threat. The program charts Hawthorne's efforts to stop the rampage of the Hellhounds.

Lokai Hawthorne is a Junior Auror (the son of a father who brought down criminal organizations but mysteriously disappeared). Lokai attended the Salem Academy of Magic (although head of the dueling club, he was also quite mischief). Just before his graduation, his father disappeared and Chief Munro (of the New York City Auror Office) approached Lokai to take up where his father left off. As Lokai began his training, his mother returned to Vietnam to grieve her husband's loss in her own way. Determined to do what his father did, Lokai became a Junior Officer (Auror) and is also determined to find out what happened to his father (believing the Hellhounds were responsible).

Christopher Munro, the Chief of the Auror Office, is a decorated and seasoned cop. He is a graduate of the Salem Academy of Magic (1991) and first worked as a secretary in the Department of Magical Law Enforcement before becoming a wizard. He married Amelia Flores in 1994 and one year later they became the parents of a boy (Anthony). He next became an Auror Officer and worked with Special Forces until 2004 when he was promoted to Senior Officer and partnered with Deputy Margaret Kellion. Five years later he and Amelia divorced (they share joint custody of Anthony) at the same time Christopher had been afflicted with a failing memory loss (although it does not stop him from doing his best as leader of the Auror's).

Margaret Kellion is second-in-command at the Department of Magical Law Enforcement. She graduated from the Salem Academy of Magic in 1993 and, due to her remarkable academic achievements, was immediately made an Auror-in-Training. She became an officer in 1995 and worked as a Junior Auror in the White House Relations Unit before becoming a Senior Auror in 1997. The business of politics also tarnished Margaret's record as rumors spread that she had minor involvement with the Hellhounds from 1999 to 2003. A year later she left the White House and, despite her shadowy past, was accepted for the job of Deputy for New York's Department of Magical Law Enforcement. Margaret, who has no tolerance for nonsense in her department, uses defensive magic and is a formidable duelist.

Cast: Leo Kei Angelos (Lokai Hawthorne), Leanna Renee Hieber (Margaret Kellion), Pascal Yen-Hieber (Christopher Munro), Morgan McGrath (Victoria Barron), Christopher Lopez (Felix Quintero), Tabetha Ray (Sarya Steelwing), Isaac Haldeman (Sebastian Twist), Philip Willingham (Jasper Trickett). **Credits:** *Producer:* Leo Kei Angelos, Christopher Lopez, Choncy Shu. *Director:* Leo Kei Angelos. *Writer:* Cassandra Johnstone. **Comment:** Potentially good idea with plenty of action and good special effects but with less than 90 seconds of programming made available, it is not possible to make a judgment call.

Episodes: Only a teaser that runs 1 minute and 27 seconds has been released.

26 *The Ballad of Mary and Ernie.* maryandernie.com. 2010 (Fantasy).

It is the 1890s and in a typical Old West town of the era stands a big man—Marshall Ernie, the town's only source of law and order and a Marshal who stands fifty feet tall. Ernie believes he was born in the town but others believe he was born in outer space and came to the town as a baby. As he grew Ernie considered the town his home and the townspeople his people—people he has sworn to protect. Also sharing Marshall's height problem is Mary Venezuela, a mysterious girl who is unaware of where she came from and who has just recently arrived in town (she is the town's saloon owner). Blad Bart is the town villain, a once prosperous wine salesman with 12 children. But during the famine of 1888 his life changed forever when making an honest living became impossible and people ate whatever they could to survive. Soon Blad's family mysterious disappeared (hinting that he survived on them) and came to realize that being an outlaw was his only choice. The Kid (his first name is The) is Ernie's best friend, an orphan. His parents were killed in a "train robbery/earthquake/typhoon/cheese cake factory explosion" and he has since attached himself to Ernie. The Kid is in love with Mary and excels at "cross-dressing, running faster than cattle and tennis—which won't be invented for another 30 years." Nan Iceberg is the normal-sized woman who is engaged to Ernie (while Mary is Ernie's size, she is not too fond of him and hates the town). Stories relate events in the lives of an Old West town that is anything but typical as Marshal Marshall Ernie deals with the prospect of upholding the law.

Cast: James Lane (Marshall Ernie), Vanessa Celzo (Mary Venezuela) *Voice Cast:* Darcy Halsey (Nan/Vinnie), Catherine Reitman (The Kid), Jesse Corti (Blad Bart). **Credits:** *Producer-Writer-Director:* Robert Stadd. **Comment:** Clever take on the *Gulliver's Travels* segment set in Lilliput. Ernie represents Gulliver while the townspeople the Lilliputians. Ernie and Mary are the only live-action characters while others are toy dolls (coupled with miniature sets) to give the illusion that Ernie and Mary are 50 feet tall. Simple as it seems, it works. Ernie does have a horse (that he carries with him rather than riding) and, even though The Kid and Nan are toys, their voices and movement give them an impression as being real. Overall the idea is good; the acting and production values also good and there are definitely numerous possibilities to explore with such a premise should the producers decide to continue the series.

Episodes:

1. I Got a Kidney Bigger Than Yours (5 min., 11 sec.). The Kid warns Ernie that Blad Bart is coming to town gunning for him.

2. A Fun Day Was Just Outside of Town (5 min., 25 sec.). Ernie learns from The Kid that killer sheep are on the prowl and he must do something about it.

3. Back in Town (5 min., 57 sec.). Mary and Ernie discuss town matters, including their origins (and hope of discovering who they are).

4. And Just Outside of Town (6 min., 42 sec.). As rustlers plague ranchers, the Kid (dressed as a girl) and Ernie (disguised as a 50-foot sheep) go undercover to capture them.

5. Jealous (5 min., 57 sec.). Nan becomes jealous, having been engaged to Ernie for eight years, when she sees him and Mary heading out for a picnic.

6. The Flashback Show (6 min., 1 sec.). As Ernie continues his bid to uphold the law, a flashback sequence reveals that Ernie was left with a childless couple as a rather large infant with a rather small flying saucer seen departing through the cabin's window. Ernie had always maintained that his height is due to the fact that his mother said "I was big for my age."

27 Barry the Demon Hunter. barrythedemonhunter.com. 2005 (Horror).

In the year AD 1118, a group of monks formed a society (the Templar Knights) to battle the supernatural forces that threaten innocent people. Over time they grew to be rich and powerful but spread fear among people that they may be something more than they appear. Two hundred years later those fears became manifested when people believed they were devil worshipers and began a revolt against them. Those that survived the revolt continued their battle in secrecy over the centuries. It is the present day when the series begins and the monks have merged into the new First Knights Templar. One such knight, Barry has just completed ten years of training. He is a priest by day and a demon hunter by night. Episodes follow his night time activities as he seeks and destroys supernatural creatures.

Cast: Oliver McNeil (Barry), Lydia Holtom (Brooke), Richard Alan (Vicar). **Credits:** *Producer-Writer-Director:* Oliver McNeil. **Comment:** One of the earliest of the Internet horror series that was filmed by Oliver McNeil "to fill the void left between the television series *Buffy the Vampire Slayer* and *Angel.*" Considering it was filmed on a tight budget over two nights, it is a remarkable achievement and has only played on the Internet (even before the inception of YouTube). There is very little information regarding the program as it has succumbed to the fate of early television programs: it was then but not now. Four episodes appear on YouTube but only two on its official website (where "This Video No Longer Exists" will pop up). It is also difficult to determine how many episodes there actually are as only five could be found (press material states that episodes are approximately ten minutes long; but the YouTube episodes run longer).

Episodes:

1. Snatched (14 min., 21 sec.). The episode establishes Barry's dark world as he kidnaps a young woman to protect her from a demon.

2. Punch (14 min., 21 sec.). Simon, the vicar, becomes trapped in a deadly fight between the forces of good and evil.

3. Echoes (15 min., 11 sec.). Gives insight into how the Templar Knights came into being.

4. Stripped (13 min., 51 sec.). Barry seeks a demon who has taken cover in a strip club.

5. Revelations (15 min., 1 sec.). Barry begins a search to find the demon responsible for killing Templar Knights and stealing their Templar emblems in an attempt to end the Templar reign.

28 The Basement. recklesstortuga.com. 2009 (Horror).

Hoping to find a quiet place to study for exams, six college students (see cast) decide to use the school's basement as their sanctuary. While cleaning, they come across an old Ouija board that one of the students, Rosie (whose mother is a witch) feels they should not touch. The others, curious to play it, ignore Rosie's warnings. As the students use it, they conjure up an evil spirit that possesses Freddy and turns him into a zombie. The spirit traps the students in the basement and the story follows their efforts to escape by outsmarting a zombie that has set its goal to kill each one of them.

Cast: Lynsey Bartilson (Blaire), Kim Fifield (Rosie), Lindsey Reckis (Claire), Jared Bell (Freddy), Eric Pumphrey (Michael), Tommy Savas (Jason). **Credits:** *Producer:* Eric Pumphrey, Lindsey Reckis, Jason Schnell, Rachel Miner. *Director:* Jason Schnell. *Writer:* Lindsey Reckis **Comment:** Silly but enjoyable horror-comedy yarn that is well acted and produced. From the attention-getting opening theme song to the last seconds of the last episode, the program is well worth watching. There is brief nudity (blurred) and bleeped foul language suggesting that it may have originally run with those scenes in tact. It is also available on YouTube and thus may have been censored for that reason.

Episodes:

1. More Than Meets the Eye (5 min., 11 sec.). Six college students, setting up a study room in the school's basement, find an old Ouija board.

2. Do or Die (2 min., 51 sec.). Despite the objections of Rosie, whose mother is a witch, the group decides to play it.

3. Finger-in-Butt (2 min., 15 sec.). The Ouija board brings forth an evil spirit that immediately possesses Freddy.

4. It's Alive (1 min., 59 sec.). The Ouija board is destroyed—as the spirit that possesses Freddy turns him into a zombie.

5. Time to Die (3 min., 30 sec.). Freddy claims that one of the group must die. Blaire becomes the victim, only she pretends to die after drinking soda with pop rocks candy.

6. I Wish I Were a Super Hero (2 min., 57 sec.). Rosie believes that by casting a spell, she can extract the spirit from Freddy.

7. I'm Hot and You're Not (1 min., 57 sec.). Rosie begins the chant that she hopes will save them all.

8. Just Banish Him (3 min., 26 sec.). The spell sort of works—it banishes the spirit from Freddy, allows the upstairs door to be opened and allows the students to escape—but is Freddy really cured? Ends unresolved.

29 *Batgirl: Spoiled*. youtube.com. 2012 (Fantasy).

Adaptation of the *Batgirl* legend, here based on the Stephanie Brown version of the comic book. Although Batgirl's history, as the daughter of the Police Commissioner of Gotham City, is the best known version (wherein Batgirl, alias Barbara Gordon, fought alongside Batman and Robin), here Batgirl

(now alias Stephanie Brown), battles evil alone, after a close call lead to her and Batman breaking ties. Stephanie, a student at Gotham University, had turned vigilante crime fighter until she met Barbara Gordon, alias Oracle, who convinced her to give up her lone crusade and join her in the battle against evil. In order to work as a team and constantly keep in contact with each other, Barbara secured a position as an assistant professor at Gotham University. Stephanie patrols the streets at night, seeking to keep Gotham City safe, but also suffers from inner demons as she re-examines her place in the world. Stephanie attends college (Barbara was a librarian), tries to have a social life and seeks help in battling evil from the various superheroes that inhabit the city. The program depicts Stephanie's dual life and the problems she now encounters trying to keep both worlds separate.

Cast: Marisha Ray (Stephanie Brown/Batgirl), Jessica Kent (Oracle), Tara Strand (Harley Quinn), Robin Sol (Catwoman), Tim Powers (Penguin), Jennifer Newman (Black Canary), Eric Cash (Tentacles), Bryan Morton (Batman), Matthew Mercer (Batman's voice).**Credits:** *Producer:* Sax Carr, Marisha Ray. *Director:* Damian Beurer. *Writer:* Sax Carr, Marisha Ray, Sam Weller, April Wahlim, Zack S. West. **Comment:** Unfortunately only two episodes were produced as the program showed great potential as being something to look forward to seeing. Marisha Ray is perfect as Batgirl and her befriending and battling other characters familiar to the Batman/Batgirl legend would have only enhanced the program. The acting and production values, writing and directing are very good (comparable to any broadcast or cable television series). The one major drawback is that there is no character background information given; Batgirl is just there; even a short narration explaining the premise would have helped as not everyone is familiar with Stephanie's history.

Episodes:

1. Blindside (12 min., 52 sec.). Stephanie investigates a plot by the evil Penguin that appears to be linked to gun smuggling.

2. Little Lost (Bat) Girl (11 min., 48 sec.). Batgirl's lone pursuit of the gun-smuggling gang results in her capture and almost certain death—until she is saved by her guardian angels—Siren and Batman. Although it appears that Batman and Batgirl have broken ties, Batman apparently still cares for her.

30 *Batgirl: Year One*. ovguide.com. 2009 (Fantasy).

An animated adaptation of the Barbara Gordon DC Comics character as she just decides to become the crime fighter Batgirl. Barbara, a recent college graduate, has returned to Gotham City and has a sincere desire to battle crime—but not like her detective (later police commissioner) father James Gordon. Although Gotham City is protected by Batman and

Robin, Barbara feels there is a need for another mysterious figure for justice and dons her Batgirl costume for the first time to stop an evil criminal (Killer Moth). Although Batgirl is initially dismissed by the Dynamic Duo, Barbara proves herself and Batgirl becomes a mysterious symbol for justice in Gotham City. Stories follow Barbara as Batgirl, as she battles crime, but also seeks to adjust to a dual life.

Voice Cast: Kate Higgins (Barbara Gordon/Batgirl), Erin Fitzgerald (Vicky Vale/Black Canary), Lex Lang, Keith Silverstein, Neil Ross. **Credits:** *Producer:* Richard Scott Russo. *Director:* Stephen Fedasz IV. **Comment:** Fast-moving story that is animated in a panel-by-panel style wherein the characters are basically stationary with moving graphics and sound effects. Takes a minute or so to adapt to, but enjoyable once you do.

Episodes:

1. Masquerade, Parts 1, 2 and 3. Introduces Barbara as she dons her Batgirl costume for the first time to capture the notorious criminal Killer Moth.

2. Future Tense, Parts 1 and 2. The elusive Killer Moth crashes a masquerade ball where he takes people hostage before encountering Batman and Robin.

3. After Glow, Parts 1, 2 and 3. Batgirl arrives at the ball but Killer Moth manages to escape and organizes fellow criminals in an effort to stop the Caped Crusaders. Meanwhile, Detective James Gordon assigns Batman the task of capturing Killer Moth.

4. Cave Dweller, Parts 1, 2 and 3. Seeing that Batgirl is now a part of Gotham City, Batman and Robin bring her (blindfolded) to their secret Batcave where she is shown how they fight crime.

5. Moth to a Flame. Batgirl, Batman and Robin, now working as a team, set their goal to capture Killer Moth.

6. Bird of Prey, Parts 1 and 2. The Black Canary teams with Batgirl to protect her father when it is learned Killer Moth is seeking him.

7. Hearts of Fire, Parts 1 and 2. Batgirl and Black Canary face off against Killer Moth at a bar hangout for criminals.

8. Seasoned Crime Fighter. Barbara proves herself as Batgirl when she intervenes in a hostage situation but also arouses the suspicions of her father who feels his daughter is hiding something.

9. Gotham Police Station Ablaze. Batgirl proves her ability when she works with (and not against) Batman to bring Killer Moth to justice.

31 *Batman Adventures: Mad Love Motion Comics.* tv.com. 2008 (Fantasy).

An unusual program that, based on a one issue only comic book of the same title (by Paul Dini and Bruce Timm) that delves into the life of Gotham City criminal Harley Quinn. Before turning evil Harley was a respected psychologist (Dr. Harleen Qunizel) but her encounter with the manipulative Joker at the Arkham Asylum for the criminally insane changed Harley's life (when she fell for the Joker's lies about his troubled childhood then fell in love with him). To be with her new love, Harley turned to a life of crime as the Joker's accomplice. The Joker, however, has a fixation about killing Batman in a spectacular manner and declines Harley's advances, knowing Batman is more important. To win back the Joker Harley sets out on a path to Kill Batman herself—something that infuriates the Joker. The episodes follow both Harley and the Joker as they each seek to kill Batman but for different reasons.

Voice Cast: Cindy Airey (Harley Quinn), Billy Davis (Batman/Joker), Paul St. Peter (Alfred/Commissioner Gordon). **Credits:** *Producer:* Dan Smith. *Director:* Stephen Fedasz IV. **Comment:** Short animated project that uses comic book–like panels with moving backgrounds and sound effects. Enjoyable, fast-moving story.

Episodes:

1. Dental Hi-Jinx/Crazy in Love. A dental checkup places Commissioner Gordon's life in danger when the Joker appears as the dentist.

2. Psycho Therapy/In Like Quinn/The Grand Decep. A look at how Harley became a criminal and obsessed with the Joker.

3. A Fish Tale/Breaking Up Is Hard to Do. Harley captures Batman and plans to kill him by feeding him to a swarm of piranhas.

32 *Batman: Black and White.* tv.com. 2008–2009 (Fantasy).

Original stories coupled with adaptations that showcase adventures encountered by the Caped Crusader, Batman, throughout the years.

Voice Cast: Michael Dobson (Batman), Janyse Jaud (Angelica), John Fitzgerald (Commissioner Gordon), Adam Fulton, Joseph May, Keifer Dobson. **Credits:** *Producer:* Ian Kirby, Ralph Sanchez. *Director:* Ian Kirby, Adam Fulton. *Writer:* Bob Kane, Doug Alexander, John Arcudi, Ed Brubaker, Kelly Puckett. **Comment:** Each animated episode is presented like a snippet as opposed to a full story. The animation is presented like a comic book—with characters basically still with moving backgrounds and sound effects.

Episodes:

1. I'll Be Watching. A janitor recalls a chance meeting with Batman who later saved his life.

2. Here Be Monsters. A criminal slips Batman a drug that produces hallucinations wherein he sees people as monsters.

3. Broken Nose. A rarity—Batman suffers a broken nose while battling a criminal.

4. Two of a Kind. A profile of Harvey Dent (a.k.a. Two Face) when he attempts to deceive his wife's twin sister.

5. Case Study. The origin's of the mater criminal The Joker are recalled.

6. Black and White Bandit. Batman's pursuit of the master thief Roscoe Chiara.

7. Punchline. The villainess Harley Quinn attempts to outsmart Batman during a robbery.

8. Good Evening Midnight. A surprise party, arranged by Alfred (Bruce Wayne's butler), awaits an unsuspecting Bruce Wayne.

9. Hide and Seek. Batman teams with Commissioner Gordon to track down a criminal who has taken refuge in the city's subway tunnels.

10. Night After Night. Crime fighting takes a toll on Batman when he begins having recurring nightmares.

11. Perpetual Mourning. Batman becomes obsessed with solving the murder of a young woman.

12. Catwoman. A World War II episode wherein Batman attempts to stop Catwoman from stealing diamonds from a Nazi spy.

13. Legend. A look at how Batman becomes a legend in a futuristic Gotham City.

14. Heroes. A look at World War II Gotham City.

15. In Dreams. Batman attempts to help a woman who is experiencing nightmares involving the Caped Crusader.

16. Sunrise. An elderly woman helps an injured Batman recover from his wounds.

17. Hands. A disturbing incident for Batman when he discovers the remains of a child in a subway tunnel.

18. A Game of Bat and Rat. A game of cat and mouse where, to trap a killer, Batman allows the culprit to think he may have been killed.

19. Monster in the Closet. Batman battles a deranged scientist capable of creating deadly mutants.

20. The Call. An elusive criminal almost costs Batman his life when he misjudges his adversary's actions.

33 Battle Lords. fantasywebseries.net. 2011 (Fantasy).

A young man (Chris) plagued by dreams of a magical, medieval land (possibly from playing video games), finds his dreams are not just dreams, but a means of escaping the reality of modern-day life to experience life one can only imagine. His friends, Karl and Liza, at first disbelieving him, are drawn into his dream world and stories, which rotate between reality and fantasy, follow Chris as he becomes a champion in "real life" (fighting the forces of darkness) as opposed to it just happening in video games.

Chris, known as Kenshin in the dream world, is a construction foreman and unsure as to which side he should ally himself. He is strong and uses a variety of weapons. Karl, known as Bram in the dream world is a former martial arts instructor who is now a satellite dish installer. As Bram he fights with a two-handed sword he calls Envy. Liza, the manager of a cell phone store, is known as Tiradora in the dream world (although not a gamer, she was pulled into the game through her husband, Nick). Tiradora, attired in Renaissance-style clothing fights with a shield and scimitar. Nick, Liza's husband, is a college student (studying to become a history professor) who is known as Araduin in the dream world. He is attired in leather armor, possesses a mysterious emblem and fights with his "great sword." Sarah, known as Menelwyn in the dream world, is studying to become a school teacher, Like Liza, who is not a gamer, Sarah is pulled into the dream world through her boyfriend Chris. She too wears Renaissance-like clothes and wields a sword. Akuragano is a dream world figure whose soul is possessed by a mysterious mask that, when worn, renders him evil. Six Fingers, the leader of the Barbarians, fights alongside Akuragano and other dark forces and only cares about defeating the enemy.

Cast: Chris Royce (Chris/Kenshin), Karl Lutes (Karl/Bram), Liza Lepczyk (Liza/Tiradora), Nicky J. Allison (Nick/Araduin), Sarah Kearney (Sarah/Menelwyn), Craig Millar (Akuragano), Jason Pontzer (Six Fingers), Nicole Morris (Nicole/Scarlet), Jacob Hassar (Brog the Barbarian). **Credits:** *Producer:* Liza Lepczyk, Nicky J. Allison. *Director:* Nicky J. Allison, Danie Jones. *Writer:* Nicky J. Allison. **Comment:** Nicely presented medieval dream sequences with good sets and costume design. The acting is a bit overplayed in the modern-day sequences (not quite convincing) but compensated for when Chris enters his dream world.

Episodes:

1. Episode 1. Establishes the storyline as Nick, suffering from dreams of a magical land, tries to convince a disbelieving Karl and Liza that they are real.

2. Episode 2. Karl and Liza try to accept what Nick reveals as actually happening and is not just a dream.

3. Episode 3. Liza and Karl are drawn into Nick's dream world.

4. Episode 4. As the Dark Army closes in on Nick and Liza, Bram and Araduin seek the help of Tiradora.

5. Episode 5. Chris struggles with his inability to choose sides; Tiradora is captured by the Dark Forces.

6. Episode 6. The concluding episode finds Tiradora escaping the clutches of Vors and Brog while Nick battles his inner demons.

34 Battlestar Galactica: Blood and Chrome. youtube.com. 2012 (Science Fiction).

The first of four web spin offs from the Syfy Channel series *Battlestar Galactica* that is actually a prequel to the series that depicts the early years of William Adama, the future captain of the Battlestar ship *Galactica*, as a young graduate from the Colonial Fleet Academy (during the tenth year of the first

Cylon War) and his first experiences as crew member of the *Wild Weasel*, a Raptor transport ship.

Cast: Luke Pasqualino (William Adama), Ben Cotton (Coker Fasjovik), Karen LeBlanc (Lt. Jenna), Adrian Homes (Decklan Elias), Lili Bordan (Dr. Beka Kelly), Zak Santiago (Armin Diaz), Tricia Helfer (Cylon Voice), Jill Teed (Cmdr. Ozar), John Pyper-Ferguson (Xander Toth). **Credits:** *Producer:* Michael Taylor. *Director:* Wayne Rose, Felix Enrique Alcala. *Writer:* Michael Taylor. **Comment:** Well done program whose episodes were re-edited and made into a two-hour television movie for Syfy that aired on Feb. 10, 2013. The program has all the production qualities of the Syfy series on which it is based.

Episodes: (Each runs 12 min.)

1. Day 4,561. Introduces William Adama as he graduates from Starfleet Academy and receives his first assignment aboard the Raptor transport ship *Wild Weasel*.

2. The Hangar. During an assignment to transport a software engineer (Dr. Beka Kelly), Adama and his co-pilot, Coker, tread dangerous waters as they near the bordering Cylon air space.

3. Operation Raptor Talon. As Adama and Coker near Cylon space, they are spotted by a Cylon war ship and pursued. After escaping the Cylon pursuit, Adama's ship reaches its destination but finds a fleet of abandoned ships, presumably destroyed in a Cylon battle.

4. Free Fall. As they investigate, Adama and Coker find the commander of one of the destroyed ships but are unable to help as Dr. Kelly holds the key to defeating the Cylon robots and must be transported to embedded Colonial operatives on the planet Djerba, a resort planet within Cylon territory.

5. The Lab. Again spotted by Cylon war ships, the *Wild Weasel* disembarks and continues its mission.

6. Survivors. After being attacked, Adama, Coker and Dr. Kelly land on Djerba. As they trek through the harsh wind and snow they find a cave and Xander Toth, the lone survivor of a Cylon attack. With Toth's help, Adama and party are led to what appears to be an abandoned compound.

7. Escape. Safely at the compound Adama learns from Toth that it was previously used to store spare Cylon parts; Dr. Kelly emphasizes that the Human-Cylon war must end and she needs to get to her destination.

8. Episode 8. Dr. Kelly discovers, after exploring the compound that Cylon robots are made of both mechanical and human parts and can feel pain.

9. Episode 9. Dr. Kelly reveals that her mission is to upload a virus into the Cylon's communications system and disrupt their programming. However, when Coker sees that Dr. Kelly is transmitting information about the destroyed ships to the Cylons, he is shot by Dr. Kelly who revels herself as a traitor (her plan was to end the war by having humans and

Cylons negotiate). Adama destroys Dr. Kelly's communicator and takes a wounded Coker to their disabled ship, leaving Dr. Kelly behind.

10. Episode 10. As Adama and Coker wait for a rescue ship, Dr. Kelly meets her fate when a Cylon approaches her and kills her.

35 *Battlestar Galactica: Razor Flashbacks.* syfy.com. 2007 (Science Fiction).

Deleted scenes from the SyfyTV Movie *Battlestar Galactica: Razor* that were used to preview the movie before its airing. Although technically not a web series (as it does not use original material created specifically for the Internet) it is considered one due to the fact that the seven episodes aired as a separate entity. The story itself begins during the final stages of the First Cylon War (before the twelve planets were destroyed and sent the *Galactica* on a mission to find its 13th colony, the Earth) wherein a younger Adama is seen as a fighter pilot of a Razor ship as he sets out to find a Cylon secret weapon concealed on a mysterious planet of ice.

Cast: Nico Cortez (William Adama; young), Edward James Olmos (William Adama; older), Allison Warnyca (Jaycie McGavin), Matthew Bennett (Aaron Doral), Jacob Blair (Banzai), Campbell Lane (Hybird). **Credits:** *Producer:* Ronald D. Moore, David Eick. *Director:* Wayne Rose, Felix Enriquez Alcala. *Writer:* Michael Taylor. **Comment:** Like other entries in the *Battlestar Galactica* web franchise, a well done, well worth watching program even if one is not a fan of the Syfy network series.

Episodes:

1. Day 4,571. Introduces William Adama as a fighter pilot aboard *Galactica*.

2. The Hangar. Chronicles the beginnings of a mission against the Cylons called Operation Raptor Talon.

3. Operation Raptor Talon. As Adama's squadron battle Cylon raiders, he is drawn into the ice planet's atmosphere.

4. Free Fall. Explores Adama's experience in the ice planet's atmosphere when he encounters a Cylon Centurian.

5. The Lab. While exploring the ice planet, Adama discovers the remains of a Cylon laboratory where it appears experiments were conducted on humans.

6. Survivors. As he continues to search, Adama finds several human subjects in a room while, at the same time, a Cylon war ship is approaching their location.

7. Escape. Adama and the rescued humans attempt to avoid the Cylon war ship while, unknown to Adama, a truce has been signed between the humans and the Cylons.

36 *Battlestar Galactica: The Face of the Enemy.* syfy.com. 2008–2009 (Science Fiction).

A filler series that was broadcast between the mid-season break of season four of the series *Battlestar Galactica*. It tells the story of the tensions that mount aboard a Razor ship, piloted by Felix Gaeta, when both human and Cylon passengers must work together to find a killer who is amongst them.

Cast: Alessandro Juliana (Felix Gaeta), Grace Park (Number 8), Michael Hogan (Saul Tigh), Jessica Harmon ("Easy" Esrin), William C. Vaughn (Finn). **Credits:** *Producer:* Ronald D. Moore, David Eick. **Comment:** Short, suspenseful extension based on *Battlestar Galactica* that has all the qualities of the parent series, although all the action takes place in a confined space.

Episodes:

1. Episode 1. Felix Gaeta, a Raptor ship pilot, begins his mission to transport both human and Cylon passengers.

2. Episode 2. A ship malfunction strands the ship (Raptor 718) in space—with the air supply rapidly being depleted.

3. Episode 3. One of the crew (Hard 8) is killed (electrocuted) attempting to reconnect a wire that controls the oxygen supply. It is discovered that the wire's insulation had been stripped off.

4. Episode 4. An investigation discloses that someone also removed the protective coating from the pliers that were used in an attempt to reconnect the non-insulated wire.

5. Episode 5. The crew, unable to bring the body of Hard 8 back to *Galactica* have no other choice but to jettison her into space, leaving Sweet 8 mourning her loss.

6. Episode 6. The condition on Raptor 718 continues to worsen with the air supply now down to nine hours and 25 minutes.

7. Episode 7. Sweet Eight believes that she can solve their problem by reprogramming the ship to get them back to their home base before their oxygen supply is depleted.

8. Episode 8. As additional deaths occurs on Raptor 718, Gaeta discovers that Sweet 8 is the culprit as she found it necessary to eliminate the others to enable her and Gaeta to survive due to the dwindling oxygen supply.

9. Episode 9. As Sweet 8 recounts the reasons why she did what she did, Gaeta unexpectedly grabs a scalpel and kills Sweet 8 (stabbing her in the neck).

10. Episode 10. Now alone on the disabled ship, Gaeta is about to kill himself when a rescue ship, dispatched from *Galactica* intercepts Raptor 718 and takes Gaeta aboard. Back on *Galactica* Gaeta learns that what happened on 718 will not be investigated as doing so will threaten an already uneasy alliance the humans have with the Cylon robots.

37 *Battlestar Galactica: The Resistance.* syfy.com. 2006 (Science Fiction).

The events that occur on New Caprica beginning with the 65th day of occupation by the invading Cylon Empire. The web episodes, meant to bridge the gap between the last episode of season two of *Battlestar Galactica* and the start of its third season specifically follows Colonel Saul Tigh as he becomes leader of the resistance group that is battling the evil Cylon robots.

Cast: Michael Hogan (Saul Tigh), Nicki Clyne (Cally Tyrol), Aaron Douglas (Galen Tyrol), Dominic Zamprogna (Jammer Lyman), Emily Holmes (Nora Clellan), Alisen Down (Jean Barolay), Matthew Bennett (Number 5). **Comment:** Episodes run two-to-five minutes each and were written as one 26-minute episode that has been edited to form a web series. The stories are not complete in themselves and only make sense when watched all together. The production values compare to the Syfy series *Battlestar Galactica* on which it is based.

Episodes:

1. Episode 1. Tyrol and Tigh begin their resistance movement on New Caprica after the Cylon occupation. Jammer, Duck, and his wife Nora discuss the Cylon-run and human-staffed New Caprica Police.

2. Episode 2. The resistance group seeks a secretive place to hide their weapons from the New Caprica Police Department.

3. Episode 3. With their weapons stored in a temple, Nora, who is hoping for a child, learns that Duck was approached to join the resistance but refused.

4. Episode 4. The Cylons, believing that the resistance has hidden weapons in the temple, attack it and kill Nora.

5. Episode 5. Nora's killing not only angers a distraught Duck, but appears to be a catalyst in bringing support for the resistance.

6. Episode 6. Although Nora and nine other people lost their lives in the Cylon attack on the temple, the resistance group has grown with hundreds of new recruits.

7. Episode 7. Jammer is captured by the Cylons and interrogated by Number 5 about the temple incident.

8. Episode 8. Number 5 attempts to persuade Jammer to become an informant on the resistance movement, claiming his information will save the lives of humans.

9. Episode 9. Jammer is released by the Cylons and returns—under suspicion that he may have sold out.

10. Episode 10. Duck joins the New Capria Police in an attempt to gather information on the resistance. Meanwhile, as resistance fighters Tihland and Barolay plan to destroy a grain silo, Jammer appears to be a spy as he possesses a key card that allows him access to Cylon headquarters.

38 *Beast Spirit Hakujin.* youtube.com. 2013 (Fantasy).

A young architect (Dalton) dissatisfied with his life begins to wonder if the world would be better off without him. One day he believes he can end his suffering and goes to a mysterious grove in the nearby woods. While contemplating what to do he finds a strange-looking artifact (a small silver canister) under a rock. While examining it, he releases a mystical Beast Spirit (sort of like a genie in a bottle) that remembers only that he is to help the one who frees him. The Beast Spirit has been imprisoned in the container but appears somewhat like a nerd, complete with glasses. Dalton becomes fearful of the spirit and, in his attempt to return him to the bottle, injures him when a ray emanates from the canister. With help from a friend (Svetlana), the Beast Spirit is nursed back to health, but Dalton's problems have only just begun: he encounters a Beast Hunter and learns that the spirit he released was a prisoner and sentenced to remain locked up forever. Stories follow Dalton as a new meaning comes to his life, but also sends him on a dangerous quest when he learns that what he has set free can also destroy him.

Cast: Kayle Smith (Dalton Rigsby), Ben del Mundo (Beast Spirit), Julia Nikitina (Svetlana), Ashley Napier (Lisa Miller), Courtney Joseph (Beast Hunter). **Credits:** *Producer-Writer-Director:* Ben del Mundo **Comment:** Although it can be said that aspects of the feature film *It's a Wonderful Life* were encompassed (not to mention genies in bottles), the program is smartly done and well produced. You actually want to find out what happens to Dalton as he ponders what to do himself.

Episodes:
1. The Mysterious Grove Near the Woods (2 min., 57 sec.). Dalton's decision to enter the woods is about to change his life forever.
2. Beast Spirit and Hakujin (5 min., 17 sec.). Dalton finds an artifact and releases a Beast Spirit that had been contained in a Light Prison but has no memory of his past.
3. Arrival (7 min., 41 sec.). When Dalton injures the Beast Spirit he enlists the help of his friend Svetlana to nurse him back to health.
4. The Beast Hunter Appears (6 min., 47 sec.). As the Beast Spirit recovers, Dalton discovers that a Beast Hunter is seeking to destroy the spirit he has released.
5. Siege in the Sacred Forest (8 min., 7 sec.). Dalton confronts the Beast Hunter but is unwilling to reveal where his Beast Spirit is concealed.
6. Christmas Spirit (10 min., 57 sec.). Dalton learns from his friend Lisa that her brother, now deceased, once claimed he encountered a Beast Spirit. Dalton continues to ponder his decision: protect the Beast Spirit or surrender it to the Beast Hunter.
7. Arbogast, the Beast Spirit of Earthen Woods (6 min., 40 sec.). The Earthen Woods Beast Spirit appears to Dalton to warn him that releasing an imprisoned spirit could cost him his life unless it is destroyed.

8. Lisa No En Casa (4 min., 59 sec.). Lisa confronts Dalton to tell him that her brother's life was claimed by a Beast Spirit.
9. Kaede, Beast Spirit Consular (7 min., 10 sec.). The freed Beast Spirit is summoned to the Beast Spirit World for a meeting with Kaede, the Beast Spirit Consular (who also looks like a nerd), on what he is to do now that he has been released.
10. World's Apart (6 min., 24 sec.). Dalton finds that his recent experiences have also changed the course of his life as he seeks out a date; the Beast Spirit leans from Kaede that he has been summoned to become a Beast Hunter.

39 *Becoming Human.* bbc.co.uk. 2011 (Science Fiction).

A web extension program based on the British television series *Being Human* about a vampire (Adam), a beautiful werewolf (Christa) and a ghost (Matt) who befriends them. In the web series Adam (a vampire) has entered school in an attempt to learn how to become human. He quickly discovers that fellow student Christa Stammers is concealing a secret (that she is a werewolf). Christa, however, has a stalker—Matt Bolton, a boy that only she and Adam can see as he is a ghost (forced to remain on earth as he has unfinished business). Matt was murdered but he cannot remember by whom. Adam and Christa have resolved to help him investigate so he can move on and stories follow that investigation.

Cast: Craig Roberts (Adam Jacobs), Leila Mimmack (Christa Stammers), Josh Brown (Matt Bolton), Simon Ludders (Mr. Swan). **Credits:** *Producer:* Toby Whithouse. *Writer:* Brian Dooley, Jamie Mathieson, John Jackson. **Comment:** Fast moving program with good acting, directing and writing.

Episodes:
1. Episode 1 (12 min., 25 sec.). Adam hopes to become more human-like by returning to school and observing fellow students.
2. Episode 2 (5 min., 8 sec.). Adam befriends Christa but they also find they have another friend—a ghost (Matt) that only they can see.
3. Episode 3 (5 min., 45 sec.). After learning why Matt is earthbound, Adam and Christa agree to help him find his body.
4. Episode 4 (6 min., 46 sec.). As the group begins their investigation they find more questions than answers.
5. Episode 5 (6 min., 25 sec.). An inspection of the surveillance tapes on the night of the murder reveals that those particular tapes are missing.
6. Episode 6 (6 min., 43 sec.). Armed with a map of the surveillance camera locations, Adam and Christa try to figure out where the killer took the body.
7. Episode 7 (7 min., 6 sec.). With Matt still unable to remember who killed him, Adam and Christa believe the body may be hidden in the basement of the school building.

8. Episode 8 (6 min., 31 sec.). The body is found but can Adam and Christa discover who did it and why so Matt can move on?

40 *Bennight Brothers.* bennightbrothers. com. 2012 (Fantasy).

The last will and testament of John Bennight to his sons, Brice, Carter and Warner, states, in part that for more than a century the Bennight family has searched for the thirteen magical keys that open a gate containing the greatest treasure in the universe. The keys, however, are mystical and possessed by living spirits who chose to conceal their presence from the world. John and his wife spent many years searching for the keys with John continuing the search alone after the birth of their first son, Carter. John had managed to uncover 12 of the keys with the elusive thirteenth key being the key to solving the mystery. "I have left you the trunk in the attic. Within its dusty cover lay all the answers you will ever need to find the last key. But most importantly, the trunk contains the means to control your abilities.... My sons you must find the last key and decipher the map that will lead to the treasure."

With a strange map of Rhode Island of 1890, as their guide, the brothers begin their quest to find the elusive thirteenth key and the wealth the keys will unlock. The map, created by a family member in 1890, is beyond comprehension. It exhibits properties unknown to science at the time. These include it apparently being made from an aerial view at a time before the Wright Brothers and when hot air balloons were incapable of reaching such heights; and how, before the invention of the X-ray machine, were the mysterious symbols found beneath the surface of the ink on the map able to be seen—and how were they put there?

Carter is the oldest and most aggressive of the brothers; Brice, the middle child, is the mediator between his siblings. Although at times he appears to be bossy and aggressive, he fears failure. Warner, timid and shy, is reserved and afraid of change. **Cast:** Joseph Marketos (Carter Bennight), Curtis Reid (Brice Bennight), David Marcos (Warner Bennight), Robert L. Lopez (John Bennight), Adam Hohler (Rey Kaylan). **Credits:** *Producer:* Robert L. Lopez. *Director:* Chris Machado, Robert L. Lopez. *Writer:* Robert L. Lopez. **Comment:** Good story idea and well presented although there are some discrepancies. Storyline information indicates that the father found 12 of the 13 keys and only the last key needs to be uncovered. The episodes indicate that the brothers must find all 13 keys and need to follow the mysterious symbols on the map as each symbol is a key's location (it is not really made clear, but it could mean that the father had hidden each key as a safety precaution and only the owner of the map can uncover them). **Episodes:**

1. The Triggers. The three brothers begin their dangerous quest for a mystical key that has remained hidden for untold ages.
2. Spark. The map leads the brothers to the Northern Forests of Rhode Island where they must put their bickering aside and work together to decipher the clues.

41 *Bewildering Life.* bewilderinglife.com. 2009 (Fantasy).

In a mystical land called Tir Na nOg, live three most unusual friends: Sam (half elephant), Diarmuid (half leprechaun) and Oisin (half donkey). In such a land, the three are considered "Wasters" as they do nothing but waste their time by not doing anything constructive. They believe otherwise as their days are spent battling the unreal—and those unreal encounters form the basis of stories. **Voice Cast:** Enda O'Connor, John Rogers, Rory O'Kelly. **Credits:** *Producer-Writer-Director:* Enda O'Connor. **Comment:** From the theme song to dialogue in the program itself, foul language is the norm. The animation is acceptable but by no means comparable to today's computer generated images. The stories are, as they are meant to be, ridiculous but the decision to use foul language, especially in a cartoon that would attract children was not a wise choice.

Episodes:
1. Don't Mess with the Rabbits. A simple walk in the countryside means danger for Diarmuid as he encounters a group of angry, raping rabbits.
2. Bewildering Life, Episode 2. A simple trip to town finds the trio annoying then being chased by an unemployed banker in a wheelchair.
3. Bewildering Life, Episode 3. Diarmuid and Oisin battle a demented self-service machine.
4. Bewildering Life, Episode 4. Sam becomes fearful of the TV License Bureau enforcers when he realizes he hasn't paid the bill (which is punishable by death).

42 *Bigfoot Roommate.* webserieschannel. com. 2013 (Fantasy).

While strolling through the woods, a young man (Joe) crosses the path of the legendary man-beast, Bigfoot. Finding that the Bigfoot is friendly but saddened because progress has left him no place to stay, Joe hits on the idea of letting him share his apartment. The mishaps that occur as Joe and Bigfoot become the most unlikely of roommates are depicted. **Cast:** Joe De Witt (Joe), Cody Ruch (Bigfoot), Joe Martino (Voice of Bigfoot). **Credits:** *Producer-Writer-Director:* Joe De Witt. **Comment:** A *Harry and the Henderson's* movie and television parody that is well done and it is ashamed that each episode plays out in so short a period of time (actually even less time as the animated, singing theme song takes up that time too). Joe is likable as the Felix Unger–like roommate with Bigfoot as his sloppy Oscar Madison counterpart (from *The Odd Couple*). Production qualities are excellent and the voice syncing for Bigfoot is perfect. There is no doubt longer episodes would play just as well.

Episodes:

1. Rent (1 min., 11 sec). With the rent due, Bigfoot finds that he doesn't have enough money for his share.

2. Razor (51 sec.). Joe tries to figure out why Bigfoot used his razor.

3. Toilet Paper (48 sec.). It's Bigfoot's turn to do the shopping—but doesn't.

4. Clothes (58 sec.). Joe wonders why Bigfoot, who doesn't wear clothes, has clothes strewn all over the apartment.

43 *Bitchcraft.* britishwebseries.com. 2013 (Fantasy).

After losing her job and breaking up with her boyfriend, a young woman (Gemma) returns to her former family home to begin a new life. Here she not only discovers that her mother (Jeeda) and brother (Nick) have become involved with witchcraft and dark magic but she too possesses the inherited powers of a witch (from her mother's side of the family). Gemma has the ability to choose the powers of light or dark witchcraft and the program charts her efforts to become a good witch—and bring her mother and brother to the light side of magic. **Cast:** Jahannah James (Gemma Black), Fay Ripley (Jeeda Black), Sam Swann (Nick Black), Noel Sullivan (Reece), Javone Prince, Max Wrottesley, Matt Gammie, Jamie Lennox, Darcy Thomas, Nick Dutton, Marc Small. **Credits:** *Producer:* Jamie Lennox, Riyad Barmania. *Director:* Luke Hyams. *Writer:* Isabella Hyams, Michele Craig, Luke Hyams. **Comment:** With the exception of the title, the subject has been done countless times before, especially on television (both comically, like here and dramatically). The program is produced in England and a bit hard to understand at times due to the British accents. Jahannah Jones is delightful as Gemma as she struggles to overcome all the embarrassing situations witchcraft causes her (like her striptease and body switch). Production values are good and the acting well executed.

Episodes:

1. Real Witch Exposed (3 min., 42 sec.). Shortly after Gemma returns home, she discovers that all is not right with her mother.

2. Witch Striptease Job Interview (3 min., 53 sec.). Gemma realizes that her mother is a witch when her mother evokes a spell to make her perform a comical striptease during a job interview.

3. Boy and Girl Body Swap (3 min., 42 sec.). A spell cast by Nick causes him and Gemma to switch bodies; it's a delight for Nick, but Gemma fears what Nick will do with her body.

4. Dick in a Box (3 min., 27 sec.). Gemma's powers are beginning to develop and she becomes fearful of what she can do.

5. Worst Speed Date Ever (3 min., 27 sec.). Hoping to find romance, Gemma decides to try speed dating—but encounters anything but what she is seeking.

6. The Howling Man (3 min., 16 sec.). Gemma tries to help a man cursed to howling when the moon is full.

7. Neighborhood Witchcraft Exposed (4 min., 1 sec.). Gemma confronts her mother and brother in a showdown over their witchcraft.

44 *Bite Me.* youtube.com. 2010–2012 (Science Fiction).

Jeff, Greg and Mike are three video game nerds who, after a zombie apocalypse, find that they are the saviors of the world and must use their gaming skills to outwit and destroy the increasing zombie killers. To make matters worse only they have the skills and even worse the U.S. Army must take orders from them as only they know what has to be done. **Cast:** Yousef Abu-Taleb (Jeff Meyer), Justin Giddings (Greg Williams), Ryan Welsh (Mike Rowe), Dani Lennon (Shawna), Risdon Roberts (Lauren), Morgan Benoit (Derrick), Ricco Ross (Gen. Joseph McRuby), Tom Lommel (Col. Smithson), Phil LaMarr (Rod Putman). **Credits:** *Producer:* Cindi Rice, Andy Shapiro, Allen DeBevoise. *Director:* Jarrett Lee Conaway. *Writer:* Bob Quinn, Andy Shapiro. **Comment:** Comical zombie "saga" of video game nerds finding more mishap than anything else as they seek to save the world. The cinematography is above average and the acting and writing a bit above par for a low budget Internet series (people familiar with playing zombie-based video games will find the most enjoyment from the program).

Episodes:

1. Outbreak (9 min., 23 sec.). A zombie apocalypse has occurred, but three gamers have yet to become aware of the fact.

2. Dead Guy Rising (8 min., 45 sec.). Roommates Jeff and Greg seek a new roommate when Mike moves out (to live with his girlfriend Lauren). Their choice: "a strange-looking dude" (Brian) from Craigslist.

3. Craigslist Guy (7 min., 8 sec.). The "dude" turns out to be a zombie—and now Jeff and Greg must find a way to dispose of him when he goes on a rampage.

4. Night Vision (10 min., 31 sec.). As Jeff and Greg attempt to deal with Brian, Mike tries to convince Lauren that, because of their zombie knowledge, Jeff and Greg are the only ones who know what to do.

5. Night Makes a Stain (9 min., 58 sec.). As the zombie outbreak increases, Mike realizes that he must act fast and with his vast knowledge of zombies, leads the battle against the undead.

6. The Beginning (14 min., 4 sec.). Escaping from their home after it becomes overrun with zombies, Jeff and Greg team with Mike to begin their job of saving the world.

7. Shotgun (11 min., 7 sec.). The gamers, now on the run, encounter difficulty attempting to buy food when a diner owner mistakes them for zombies.

8. Point of Entry (11 min., 58 sec.). As they find a new safe house, the gamers set traps to protect themselves from the ever increasing zombie population.

9. Viral (14 min., 51 sec.). The gamers turn to the Internet to post videos about their experiences when they find they can no longer play Xbox day and night.

10. Open for Business (11 min., 45 sec.). As the gamers reputation grows as heroic zombie hunters, they begin a business charging for their services while the military feels they too need to access their help.

11. Resistance (13 min., 23 sec.). The gamers team with Gen. McRuby and his troops to stop the zombies by organizing a resistance and prepare for battle.

12. The Source (13 min., 34 sec.). Gen. McRuby feels the gamers growing business is hindering his plans and seeks a way to shut them down.

13. Caught (14 min., 41 sec.). The gamers are outsmarted by a zombie patrol and captured and now face interrogation.

14. Breakout (11 min., 2 sec.). In an effort to escape, Greg is bitten by a zombie and Jeff and Mike fear the worse unless they can find a way to cure him.

15. The War (15 min., 51 sec.). As Greg survives his bite, the gamers feel they must take a stand and battle the enemy. It's now or never.

45 *The Black Dawn.* theblackdawn.com. 2009 (Science Fiction).

A bio weapon has been created and its devastation unleashed on Los Angeles. The intent of the weapon is to destroy life but keep everything else in tact. It appears to work although thirteen college students have miraculously survived. A black cloud now hangs over the city and all sunlight has been blocked. Stories follow the survivors as they seek to find out what happened and why.

Cast: Jordan Warren (Adam), Eamon Glennon (Lee), Misty Madden (Julie), Tristan Scott (Noah), Kevin Harland (Wally), Christy Giannestras (Kristen), Kerri Hellmuth (Elyse), Todd Tetreault (Mack), Joel Sappington (Dwayne), Missy Walker (Grace), Amanda Turner (Elizabeth), Bobo Chang (Alex), Skip Pipo (Dr. Wilkins). **Credits:** *Producer-Director:* William Hellmuth, Joshua Sikora. *Writer:* William Hellmuth, Brian Walton, Abraham Sherman, Kevin Christensen, Joshua Sikora. **Comment:** If one can accept the fact that scientific principals have been drastically altered, a somewhat intriguing "end of the

world" story is attempted. Unfortunately, the misuse of science hinders the story and distracts from the intent (for example, the sun has been blocked from Los Angeles yet the ground temperature remains constantly warm; in reality it would become increasingly cold; the bio weapon, called a virus by the survivors, is actually a toxin). The introduction of a zombie menace adds to the overall effect. The acting and production values are good, but the writing hinders the overall effect the producer was trying to achieve.

Episodes:

1. Nightfall. Establishes the storyline as a mysterious black cloud engulfs Los Angeles, leaving only thirteen survivors.

2. Ghost in the Dark. Ten days have passed and the survivors are desperately seeking a way to acquire help from the outside world.

3. Deadly Consequences. Tension among the survivors forces them to split into two separate groups.

4. Enemies Among Us. Information about the incidents leading up to the "black plague" is revealed through Dr. Wilkins and Lila Reed.

5. Blindsided. Further information about the "black plague" is revealed as Dr. Wilkins is seen (in a flashback) coming to terms with a colleague's betrayal.

6. The Longest Night. Zombies have now begun to rise and the survivors seek weapons to protect themselves.

7. Dawn. The survivors manage to find a place of refuge—but it may not be for long as zombies are all around them.

46 *Blackout.* fearfilm.com. 2010–2011 (Horror).

One night, during an electrical storm, a young woman (Sara), kills her husband, claiming that it was in self-defense. Was it? Later, after a police interrogation and being cleared of a murder charge, Sara begins to experience strange dreams and visions of her husband returning from the grave to seek revenge for his murder. The program follows Sara as she struggles to cope with a situation that was created by her own doing (explained in the episode listing).

Cast: Katharine Leis (Sarah), Jon Fish (Derrick), Nick Colemo (Husband), Rick Michaels (Det. Bill Thomas), Bob Glazier (Det. Frank Peters), Eryn Simpson (Missy). **Credits:** *Producer-Writer-Director:* Robert J. Massetti. **Comment:** Although the story begins in a police interrogation room, and knowing the story borrows elements of Edgar Alan Poe's "Tell-Tale Heart," does not really distract from a suspenseful, well written program that evolves. The acting and direction are also very good.

Episodes:

1. Part 1 (3 min., 21 sec.). On the night of July 29 a young woman (Sara) is being questioned by police detectives regarding the death of her husband.

She claims she cannot remember what happened (she blacked out) and is released due to insufficient evidence.

2. Part 2 (6 min., 36 sec.). As Sara returns home she is stopped by a man (Derrick) she does not know. He offers to help her and hands her his phone number.

3. Part 3 (5 min., 38 sec.). That night, Sara begins to experience strange visions as she tries to sleep.

4. Part 4 (5 min., 36 sec.). Fearing that something mysterious is happening, Sara calls Derrick asking for his help.

5. Part 5 (5 min., 48 sec.). Derrick allows Sara to stay with him—but the situation becomes worse when Sara believes her husband's ghost has come back seeking revenge.

6. Part 6 (5 min., 47 sec.). The ghost takes over Derrick's body and the viewer sees Sara's husband as mean and controlling.

7. Part 7 (5 min., 25 sec.). Sara reflects on what happened on the night of her husband's murder (she is seen stabbing him to death but it is not made clear why).

8. Part 8 (6 min.). Derrick, now free of the ghost, tells Sara who he is (a man who loaned her husband money to get him out of debt). Sara, who killed her husband to steal the money, believes Derrick is the only one who can expose her and kills him. Thinking she is free, she is engulfed by her husband's ghost and knocked unconscious. The police, whom Derrick previously called, arrive to see Sara standing over the body. The program concludes how it started—with Sara being questioned by the same detectives and claiming she blacked out and can't remember what happened.

47 *Bleed.* bleed.com. 2010 (Horror).

Brian and Perry are friends who believe that their lives are heading nowhere, especially Brian, who, at the age of 29, has a menial, low-paying job as a cashier at Blockbuster Video. Brian and his friend, Perry, have been influenced by horror movies, especially those dealing with vampires, and have misguided illusions about how much better their lives will become if they too were vampires. Enter Evil Lynne, a girl (also a vampire) who attaches herself to Brian and grants his wish, turning him into a creature of the undead. Brian eventually convinces Perry to "join the ranks" and life doesn't really change for Brian and Perry—they were losers as humans and are losers as vampires. **Cast:** Eric Morales (Brian), Alan Seales (Perry), Whitney Griffin (Evil Lynne), Mallory Culbert (Stacy), Jessica Fleming (Morgan), Sara Hoots (Succubus), Hillary Trelease (Mistress Carmela), Tanner Barklow (Gay Paseur). **Credits:** *Producer:* Matt Lawson. *Director:* Amy Taylor, Ben Snyder. *Writer:* Ben Snyder. **Comment:** Light humor based project with good acting and a good story line that, unfortunately

uses the shaky camera method of filming that many people find simply annoying.

Episodes:

1. Pilot (5 min., 36 sec.). Establishes the premise as Evil Lynne grants Brian's wish.

2. Best Friends Forever (4 min., 55 sec.). Evil Lynne stalks Perry, hoping to make him one of the undead.

3. Poseurs and Catblood (7 min., 4 sec.). Now, as full-fledged vampires, Brian and Perry seek their first meal.

4. Stacy (8 min., 41 sec.). Old feelings are ignited when Perry runs into his ex-flame, Stacy, who is unaware of his change. Complications ensue when he also meets Mistress Carmela, the beautiful vampire temptress.

5. Bad Education (9 min., 30 sec.). Not amused by Brian's inability to fully adapt to his new life, Evil Lynne takes it upon herself to teach him the rules of evil.

6. Kill Brian (7 min., 43 sec.). Brian tries to convince his ex-girlfriend, Morgan, to join him in his undead world.

48 *Blood and Bone China.* bloodandbone china.com 2011 (Horror).

It is the year 1897 and Anna Fitzgerald is a journalist for a newspaper called the *Sentinel*. However, because of the era (where women did not hold such jobs) she is forced to write under a male pseudonym. Anna was born in Caverswall, a community in Stoke-On-Trent, in 1875. She has always been fascinated by reading and writing and has made it her goal to become a journalist. Her story about the capture of a notorious jewel thief earned her a job as the paper's first female writer. Anna, however, is not pleased by the fact that she must hide her true identity and is looking for the one story that will open the door for female journalists to be recognized as equals to their male counterparts.

As the story begins Richard Howell, a local doctor, has begun an investigation into a series of mysterious disappearances. When Richard finds that the police have uncovered no such evidence and disbelieve him about his findings, he feels he needs help and contacts a journalist at the *Sentinel* (believing publicity will bring attention to his claims). On the night he is to meet the journalist (Anna) Richard becomes a victim himself when he is attacked by a vampire (Lady Victoria) and disappears. When Newlyn, Richard's younger brother, a doctor in the town of Buxton, learns of his disappearance, he travels to Stoke-On-Trent and eventually meets Anna and the two begin an investigation to discover what is behind the strange happenings in Stoke-On-Trent. (It is later revealed that Leonora, the teenage daughter of Linus Hemlock, a wealthy ceramic factory owner, was responsible, turning Lady Victoria, her father's mistress, into a vampire. One summer day in 1895

Blood and Bone China. **Lara de-Leuw as the vampire Lady Victoria (copyright Chris Stone 2011).**

Leonora wandered into Bluebell Woods and disappeared. Two weeks later she returned to her home [Hemlock Manor] as a vampire. Linus could not kill Leonora and allowed her to feed on those who would not be missed [prostitutes, the sick and the homeless]. Leonora brought her victims to her home and Linus disposed of their bodies by burning off the flesh in his kin, then grinding up the bones as china clay. When he discovered that the bones made the most elegant china, he began controlling Leonora to bring more victims his way.)

Cast: Anthony Miles (Newlyn Howell), Rachel Shenton (Anna Fitzgerald), Ryan Callaghan (The Servant), John James Woodward (Alexander Pyre), Ellie Astley (Leonora), Lara de-Leuw (Lady Victoria), David Lemberg (Linus Hemlock), Simon Hooson (Richard Howell), Jeffrey Kidner (Rev. Thomas Lilley), Brian Gorman (Insp. Cooper), Michelle Chalmers (Vampire Prostitute), Peter Greenall, Allan Law, Nyesha Jane Farag, Nina Gilgooly, Daniella Eckhardt (Vampires). **Credits:** *Producer:* Paul Bailey, Chris Stone, Stephanie Cooper. *Director:* Chris Stone. *Writer:* Stephanie Cooper, Chris Stone. **Comment:** Well produced, suspenseful series with good acting, authentic sets and costumes and a real feel for the Victorian era that it depicts. There are no recaps so it is necessary to watch each arc episode to enjoy the series. It is also not made clear exactly what will happen to Anna and Leonora in the concluding episode.

Episodes:

1. Oblivion and Paradise (10 min., 14 sec.). A series of mysterious disappearances begin to occur in Stoke-On-Trent. When his brother, Richard, becomes one of the victims, Newlyn, a veterinarian, decides to investigate.

2. The Enigmatic Mister Pyre (8 min., 14 sec.). The mysterious Alexander Pyre, the man who informs Newlyn of Richard's disappearance, accompanies Newlyn to Stoke-On-Trent.

3. Anna of the Six Towns (4 min., 50 sec.). Journalist Anna Fitzgerald joins Newlyn as he begins a search for Richard.

4. The Devil in the Potteries (10 min., 28. sec.). Introduces Leonora, the beautiful vampire who feeds on humans and whose father (Linus) creates china from the bones of her victims.

5. There's No Such Thing as Vampires (4 min., 50 sec.). Anna discovers vampires actually exist when she encounters Leonora—who is determined to make her one of her victims.

6. The Sword of Silver (8 min., 30 sec.). Pyre is revealed to be a vampire hunter when he uses a silver sword to destroy a vampire.

7. The Gates of Wrath (11 min., 58 sec.). Anna, Newlyn and Pyre become curious about the unusual, translucent china cups they find in a murder victims' home.

8. Leonora (11 min., 30 sec.). At Hemlock China,

Anna, Pyre and Newlyn meet Linus—and discover that Leonora is responsible for the carnage that has befallen the town.

9. Goodbye Happiness (6 min., 46 sec.). Linus instructs Leonora and his vampire slaves to hold captive his unwelcome visitors.

10. Through the Eyes of a Child (15 min., 35 sec.). Anna, being held captive at the china factory, encounters Richard and learns that he is a vampire.

11. The Silver Lining (9 min., 15. sec.). No longer cowering in fear, the villagers take up arms and are now determined to rid their town of vampires.

12. Of Gods and Monsters (15 min., 26 sec.). A battle rages between vampires and villagers. Pyre and Newlyn are killed; Anna is turned into a vampire and Leonora, in a surprise twist, uses her power to stop the battle. Who actually won is not shown. An epilog then appears. The setting is the early 1940s. The place: Transylvania. Richard had escaped the carnage and, while still a vampire, has established himself as a Nazi leader conducting experiments to turn soldiers into vampires. Overlooking the camp are Anna and Leonora, both good vampires who see Richard's plan as a threat to the rest of the world. Suddenly, silver arrows are seen killing the soldiers—an attack ordered by Anna to destroy evil. The scene turns to black as the credits roll.

49 Blood Light. bloodlight.com. 2010 (Horror).

Billed as "This is NOT a show about Vampires, it's a show about people who happen to be Vampires." Ethan and his girlfriend Alex, become members of the undead world when they are bitten by a vampire. Alex and Ethan, however, are not the black-caped, blood-sucking vampires familiar to legend and feature films, but young people now struggling to cope with a situation where being a vampire is not all that it is cracked up to be (as they are not cool or sexually alluring). The comical science fiction mix follows two vampires as they navigate a world in which they not only feel out of place, but have no apparent way to remedy the situation. Sharing their life is Connor, a human who pretends to be a vampire in the hopes of attracting beautiful women.

Cast: Andrew Kimler (Ethan), Nicole Hodges, Karen Bray (Alex), Justin Perez (Phillip), Cooper D'Ambrose (Cooper), Josh Breslow (Logan), Julia Falamas (Dee). Credits: Producer-Writer-Director: Chris Russell. Comment: There is a needless abundance of foul language and, while there is no nudity, there are scenes of scantily clad women. The attempt to mix comedy with vampire mythology works at times, but the comedy often falls flat. Interesting for the subject it tackles with average acting and production values.

Episodes: Twenty-three episodes were produced but only five are online (the others have been withdrawn). Descriptions are not presented as there is no continuity.

50 Bloodstone Diaries. bloodstonediaries.com. 2010 (Science Fiction).

Bettie and Sam Lawrence are a married couple that have fallen on hard times. They are now living in a homeless camp and survive on what little Bettie, a tough woman who lets nothing stand in her way, can make by stealing what she can from the nearby town. One day Sam's friend, Anthony Pace, a man of faith, mentions a mysterious relic known as the Bloodstone, which is said to have been created by Jesus Christ from his own blood. The Bloodstone is magical and whoever possesses it also gains great power. Intrigued, Sam begins an online search of the relic but unknowingly triggers an alert that brings him to the attention of the government. Before agents, called The Men in Black, can stop him, Sam steals the red jewel and Sam, Anthony and Bettie soon find themselves on the run when the agents arrive at the camp. The agents are ruthless and possessing the jewel costs Sam and Anthony their lives. Bettie, now with the jewel manages to escape—but into a world she didn't see coming—as a protector of the Bloodstone. It appears that since the creation of the Bloodstone, it had been protected from those who would use its power for their own gain by a Protector. It had been sought by dictators, kings and thieves. Now, as the latest in that long line of Protectors, Bettie finds herself not only on the run from the mysterious Men in Black but must learn how to control the relic's power (said to be able to bring about the end of the world) and struggle with two decisions: use the power of the jewel to avenge Sam's death or forfeit her life (until another Protector is found) to save the world.

Cast: Katy Allen (Bettie Lawrence), Ian Moore (Sam Lawrence), C. Tucker Steinmetz (Anthony Pace), Eric Wilson, Russell Hoffman, Patrick Beam (Men in Black). Credits: Producer: Susan Alturi, Eyren Mills, Eric Wilson. Director: Gerry Bruno. Writer: David Koon. Comment: Although only two episodes have been produced, the second actually leading into the first, it is well done with limited but excellent special effects. Situations are tense with good acting, writing and directing.

Episodes:
1. Sleeper. While the second episode should be watched first to gain a better sense of the story, here Bettie is on the run and uses the power of the Bloodstone (which she wears as a charm around her neck) to extradite herself from people seeking the stone (the jewel gives Bettie the power to levitate and thus manipulate items to defeat her enemies).

2. The Thief of All Things. A prequel episode that establishes how Bettie came to be in possession of the Bloodstone.

51 *Bloody Cuts*. bloodycuts.com. 2012 (Horror).

Anthology-styled program (like *Tales from the Crypt*) that presents short tales of people's encounters with the unknown terrors that lurk in the dark. **Credits:** *Producer:* Ben Franklin. *Director:* Ben Franklin, Neill Gorton, Jake Cuddihy, Ben Tillett. *Writer:* Joel Morgan, Ben Franklin. **Comment:** Truly creepy and shock surprise ending tales of terror that are expertly produced and acted. Even though each episode is considerably short, they pack a wallop and keep you interested from start to finish.

Episodes:

1. Lock Up (3 min.). Surprisingly chilling tale, told in a very short time, about how a man's (Josh Burdett) fears get the better of him when he finds himself locked in an empty office building at night.

2. Stitches (5 min.). Creepy tale about a babysitter (Bethen Hanks) whose principal concern becomes not for the children, but for her own safety when she soon realizes that the unnatural is also a part of the house. With Paul Ewan, Jason Loborik and Ryan Gipp.

3. Prey (8 min., 1 sec.). A sexual predator becomes the prey of a seemingly normal girl—who shows her true side—a vicious demon when he tries to seduce her. Starring Fergal Philips, Jessica Blake and David Blood.

4. Mother Died (7 min., 18 sec.). Following her mother's death from a zombie infection, a young woman plots a way to kill the horde of zombies that are roaming her neighborhood. Starring Sarah Winter and Carol Storey.

5. Suckablood. (7 min.). Narrated "fairy tale"–like story of a young girl who is terrorized by her mother into believing that if she sucks her thump an ancient, terrifying creature will come for her. Narrated by Ben Tillett and starring Holly Jacobson, Robin Berry and Sam Metcalf.

6. Don't Move (13 min., 56 sec.). Six friends, gathering for their monthly night of games, accidentally unleash a demon that now threatens to kill them all. Starring Rachel Bright, Jake Hendricks, Kate Braithwaite, Bet Cooper.

7. Dead Man's Lake (9 min., 17 sec.). Five teenagers on a camping trip trespass on land forbidden to enter only to encounter an unknown being bent on killing them. Starring James Powell, Carolina Haines, Sarah James Honeywell, Lewis Osborne, Jon Campling. Contains graphic scenes of horror and is preceded by a parental warning.

8. Death Scenes (7 min., 8 sec.). A police detective, believing that he has captured a suspected serial killer, finds that what he has apprehended is more than what he expected (a demon). Starring Robin Berry, Ayden Callaghan, Charlie Bond, Carol Storey, Charlotte Barrett.

***Bloody Cuts*. Behind-the-scenes photograph from the episode "Don't Move" (copyright www.BloodyCuts.co.uk).**

52   *The Bloody Mary Show.*
bloodymaryshow.com. 2012
(Horror).

There is a legend called Bloody
Mary wherein if you face a mirror
and say the name Bloody Mary three
times, her ghost will appear to tell
your future. Here, however, in a
comic twist, Bloody Mary and her
friends, Abdabs, Samantha, Malevolent and Viscera, are ghouls, who
haunt the living when summoned to
help—not harm them, and in their
off time, share their experiences at a
pub called Hemingways.

Bloody Mary is a sweet girl who
wants only to help people who are
facing a difficult choice to make.
The program is based on the American urban version of the legend, not
the British version, wherein Bloody
Mary is a demon and only out to kill
those who summon her—whether
intentionally or not.

Chris is a musician with a drinking problem and self-destructive
streak whose life changed when he
summoned Bloody Mary and fell for
her.

Viscera is described as "the old
hag you will meet during an episode
of sleep paralysis." She is Bloody
Mary's best friend and, unlike Mary,
she has mood swings and thinks
nothing of telling people what she
thinks of them.

Abdabs, Viscera's brother, is a
Grim Reaper who, despite his hor-
rifying appearance, is "a cherry and happy fellow who
accepts his role with joy."

Malevolent is a banshee who had a very sheltered
upbringing and today is a bit naïve and a bit ditzy.
Like all banshees, she tends "to float around and not
doing much for most of her existence."

Samantha is a pretty blonde who is not only a rich
bitch but a top succubus who is also self-confident
and aloof.

Amicus is an incubus (the male version of a succubus—a creature that, through a kiss, draws the life
spirit out of a person.)

Herzog is the mysterious owner (a Wraith) of the
Hemingways Bar and appears to know the secrets
people possess.

Bloofer and Bathory are Samantha's equally beautiful succubus friends who idolize her. Bloofer is
named after the original *Dracula* novel while
Bathory takes her name from a rather infamous Hun-
garian Countess.

Rutherford and Cadinot are friends who are con-

The Bloody Mary Show **cast, left to right: Elizabeth Webster, Hollie
Taylor, Thomas Coombes and Craig Daniel Adams (copyright Darren
Chadwick, Bloody Mary Show Productions).**

sidered the Other Realms "Eurotrash" as they do as
they want when they want.

Carabosse is Malevolent's mother, who was named
after the wicked fairy godmother in *Sleeping Beauty*.
She is pure evil and a threat to anyone who crosses
her.

The Wraith lives on the edge of the world and patrols the world seeking those succumbing to an addiction or pain to feed off their energy.

Cast: Hollie Taylor (Bloody Mary), Elizabeth
Webster (Viscera), Craig Daniel Adams (Chris),
Thomas Coombes (Abdabs), Erica Emm (Saman-
tha), Jenny Fitzpatrick, Tanya Duff (Malevolent),
Richie Hart (Amicus), David McGillivray (Herzog),
Shinead Byrne (Bloofer), Cristina Lazaro (Bathory),
Robert Feldman (Rutherford), Antonio Piras
(Cadinot), Judith Rosenbauer (Carabosse), Tim
Frost (The Wraith). **Credits:** *Producer:* Darren
Chadwick-Hussein, Timur Charles. *Director:* Victo-
ria Howell. *Writer:* Darren Chadwick-Hussein.
Comment: British produced series that captures the

flavor of the urban legend as opposed to the actual legend. The cast is creepy enough to convey that ghoulish look and the acting, writing and directing are very good. Well worth watching for something different.

Episodes:

1. Halloween: The Bloody Mary Show Episode 1 (9 min., 5 sec.). With Halloween approaching, Bloody Mary seeks to find some romance, preferably with a mortal young man named Chris.

2. Halloween: The Bloody Mary Show Episode 2 (6 min., 28 sec.). As Bloody Mary has her dream come true and attempts to keep a midnight rendezvous with Chris, Malevolent gets dumped and Samantha introduces one and all to her succubus friends (Bloofer and Bathory) at Hemingways.

3. Halloween: The Bloody Mary Show Episode 3 (6 min., 5 sec.). Bloody Mary's delight is shattered when Viscera catches her and Chris in bed; Malevolent discloses that she is pregnant.

4. Halloween: The Bloody Mary Show Episode 4 (5 min., 15 sec.). As Bloody Mary and Chris have their first argument over Viscera's discovery (that a ghoul and mortal are dating), Malevolent's wicked mother, Carabosse, arrives at Hemingways to stir up trouble. Meanwhile, no one seems to care about Malevolent's announcement.

5. Halloween: The Bloody Mary Show Episode 5 (9 min., 21 sec.). Samantha becomes enraged when she discovers that Abdabs, her boyfriend, has a secret relationship with Amicus.

6. Halloween: The Bloody Mary Show Episode 6 (10 min., 39 sec.). Bloody Mary's heart is broken when she finds Samantha has seduced Chris.

7. Halloween: The Bloody Mary Show Episode 7 (10 min., 39 sec.). Bloody Mary attempts to save Chris from an attack by an evil being called the Wraith.

Poster art from *Body Jumpers* and *Body Jumpers—Origins* (copyright Alex Fernandez).

53 Body Jumpers. facebook.com/Body Jumpers. 2012–2014 (Science Fiction).

On the Planet Euclid 6, which is millions of light years from Earth, an organization called IDA (The Interplanetary Department of Agents) has been established to protect other planets from whatever may threaten their safety. One such threat, the evil Primus, a being from a race called Body Jumpers (beings who are able to assume the form of any living thing and become it) invades Euclid 6 and steals its advanced technology—technology he plans to use to conquer other worlds, including the Earth. Although Euclid 6 has been left in a state of turmoil, stopping Primus is a prime directive of the IDA. Detecting that Body Jumpers have already established themselves on Earth, Shia'ra, an IDA agent from the City of Aura, is dispatched to Earth to terminate the Body Jumpers.

Shia'ra establishes herself in the Bedford-Stuyvesant section of Brooklyn, New York, where she appears as an ordinary African-American woman known as Amy Brooks. As her mission becomes increasingly difficult, Nexus, of the IDA, assigns her a partner—Agent Azreal. Their quest, however, becomes more dangerous as Primus has dispatched assassins to terminate them: Kora, a deadly and brutal woman with the ability to discharge flames from her arms and create devastating fire storms; Seraphim, an expert fighter and swordswoman with a deadly touch (power that can kill). It is suggested that Seraphim may not be a Body Jumper, but something even more treacherous. And Furia, a deadly space Ninja with only one desire—to kill ("If you have seen her, you're already dead"). Stories follow Shia'ra, possessed of the power to project rays from her hands, protect herself with energy shields and soar through the air, begins the ultimate test of her career—stop Primus and his Body Jumpers from becoming rulers of the universe.

In January of 2014 Producer Alex Fernandez released a prequel series called *Body Jumpers—Origins* that provides the back story to the creation of Euclid 6 and how Shia'ra, seen as a teenager (born in the year 5473), would become the woman of the original series. The legend begins as Shia'ra explains (over scenes of the formation of her world) that, "At first there was only darkness, but from that chaos came my world, Planet Euclid 6." Comic book–like panels then appear to show a young Shia'ra with her parents and how, at age 10 her world would change when the evil Lord Primus stole advanced Euclid technology and used it to conquer other worlds. Five years later, Shia'ra's father felt it was time for her to assume her role as a warrior and become a member of the IDA (Interplanetary Department of Agents) where she would learn the skills needed in later life to battle Lord Primus (who, at this time, has begun using the stolen technology to conquer Earth). The pilot details Shia'ra's first experiences as a warrior-in-training and her early encounter with the evil Mistress Raven.

Note: There is also an audio/video episode called "Body Jumpers Audio Message from Darius" that should be watched first as it is an excellent introduction to the series and its characters. The episode runs 4 minutes and 41 seconds and finds IDA Agent Darius (voice of Harold B. Gibson) attempting to warn Earth about Primus and his Body Jumpers army.

Cast (Body Jumpers): Patricia Lisanne (Shiarra), Irina Kaplin, Joanna-Sien Kiewicz (Furia), Gretchin Noel (Seraphim), Linda Delmonico Prussen (Kora), Mark D. Law (Agent Azreal), Harold B. Gibson (Agent Danus), A. Marie Walter (Nexus), Bow-legged Lou (Lord Primus). **Credits (Body Jumpers):** *Producer-Writer-Director:* Alex Fernandez. **Comment:** The original series is well produced with good special effects and acting and a story that holds your interest from the very beginning. The series has also been released on DVD and Blu-Ray. **Cast (Body Jumpers—Origins):** Zoe Leid (Teenage Shia'ra), Michelle Annette George (Mistress Raven). **Credits (Body Jumpers—Origins):** *Producer-Writer-Director:* Alex Fernandez. **Comment:** Compelling story with amazing special effects. Zoe Leid is the perfect counterpart of her future self and, just based on the pilot, it appears to be a series worthy of the Syfy channel's attention—and what can be accomplished by one person on a limited budget.

Episodes (Body Jumpers):

1. Commencement (6 min., 30 sec.). The pilot film that establishes the program's premise.

2. Search and Destroy (5 min., 49 sec.). Shia'ra, now based in Brooklyn, begins her search to find an assassin (Furia).

3. Destruction (6 min., 1 sec.). Shia'ra learns that Furia has teamed with a renegade (Kora) from her planet and must stop them.

4. Primus (4 min., 53 sec.). Primus, the evil inter-galactic criminal who masterminded the theft of Euclid technology, becomes Shia'ra's mortal enemy as he has now established himself in Brooklyn.

5. Enter Seraphim, Part 1 (6 min., 10 sec.). Feeling that Shia'ra requires help, Nexus (her superior on Euclid) assigns an agent (Azreal) to assist her. Meanwhile an unknown threat (Seraphim) is about to complicate Shia'ra's mission.

6. Enter Seraphim, Part 2 (8 min.). Shia'ra, contacted by Nexus, learns that a powerful enemy (Seraphim) has been dispatched to kill her.

7. Heroes and Villains (7 min., 59 sec.). As Shia'ra laments over the fact that she has been on Earth for six months and accomplished little, Azreal finds the tables turned on him when he confronts Furia (to take her back to Euclid to pay for her crimes) and is captured.

8. The Return of Furia (7 min., 32 sec.). Azreal finds that he is the bait in a trap to lure Shia'ra to Furia.

9. A Christmas Story (11 min., 1 sec.). A clever take on the Charles Dickens story *A Christmas Carol* wherein Primus receives a visit from three ghost who attempt to make him see the evil of his ways.

Episodes (Body Jumpers—Origins):

1. Genesis 8 min., 14 sec.). The pilot episode that establishes the premise (as explained above).

54 *The Book of Jer3miah.* jer3miah.com.

2009 (Fantasy).

Outside the Manti Library in Utah, a college freshman (Jeremiah Whitney) meets a woman who presents him with the sacred Mesoamerican Box and that it is his sacred obligation to protect it. He soon regrets his decision to accept the box when he learns that he has become the target of a conspiracy that requires his faith and courage to survive. The program, created by a group of faculty and students at Brigham Young University, follows Jeremiah as he seeks the truth about the box and why he has become a liability (the last episode reveals that his birth father is one of the Three Nephites, the immortals who serve Christ until his second coming on earth).

Cast: Jared Shores (Jeremiah Whitney), Jeffrey Blake (Porter Coolbrith), Camee Anderson Faulk (Megan Halling), Becca Ingram (Claire Warren), Blayne Quarnstrom (Ammon), Jourdan Lance (Lilah), Christopher Davis (Simon Ackerman). **Credits:** *Producer:* Jeff Parkin, Jared Cardon. *Director:* Jeff Parkin, Jared Cardon. *Writer:* David Jon Banks, Jared Cardon, Scott Clarke, John Forbyn, Taylor Rose, Lyvia A. Martinez, Matt Pieper. **Comment:** Although the program has religious overtones, it is a well-plotted and acted thriller that moves right along; well worth watching.

Episodes:

1. A Gift, a Record. Jeremiah's life changes when he receives a message stating simply "Manti Library."

The Book of Jer3miah series poster art (copyright Tinder Transmedia).

2. A Sacred Trust. Intrigued by the strange appearance of the message, Jeremiah follows its instructions and enters the library where a woman hands him the mysterious Mesoamerican box and his mission—to protect the box.

3. Detour. Unknown to Jeremiah, he is being followed by persons unknown—people who later cause the death of his parents in a car crash.

4. Porter's Call. In his dorm room, Jeremiah receives comfort from his friends Simon, Brian and Porter, but it is Porter who becomes more than a friend, but a protector when a disembodied voice instructs him to protect Jeremiah—"for he is my only son."

5. Departure. Although unsure as to how he must protect Jeremiah and from what, Porter abides by what the voice told him.

6. Coming Home. More intrigue enters Jeremiah's life when he returns home to Seneca Falls, New York, for his parents' funeral and becomes the target of two men who are apparently trying to kill him.

7. Back to School. After escaping from the men, Jeremiah returns to school where he finds that his room has been trashed.

8. Abide with Me. Seeing what has happened, Porter comes to realize that Jeremiah is in danger when he explains about the box and the attempts on his life.

9. Lineage. Jeremiah, who was adopted, refuses to listen to Porter about finding who his real parents were as it could explain what is happening to him. However, when Jeremiah attends an Old Testament class at school and learns about spiritual lineage, he decides to trace his roots.

10. Constance. Porter and his girlfriend, Lilah, make an appointment with Constance, Lilah's grandmother, the head of the Family History Center hoping she may be able to uncover records of Jeremiah's birth. Constance reveals that such records are sealed and suggests that Jeremiah take a DNA test. As Constance approaches her car to get the test kit, she is approached by a man who gives her a note for Jeremiah.

11. Mile Marker 3. Constance hands Jeremiah the note, which instructs him to go to the Mile Marker 3 in Manti, Utah. Here Jeremiah meets a man named Ammon. Together they travel to a sacred cave where Jeremiah learns that only those who were divinely chosen can enter. He also learns that his real parents were of divine ascension.

12. The Box. With the hope of discovering who he really is and what the box means, Jeremiah questions Ammon about his destiny. Ammon, however, cannot answer his questions until he can prove he is worthy.

13. Call on Him Often. Angry and frustrated at what is happening, Jeremiah returns to his dorm room to contemplate what Ammon told him.

14. Promises. To get his mind off what is happening Jeremiah begins helping his friend Claire set up decorations for an upcoming party when Claire asks him to teach a lesson in their Family Home Evening class. Although Jeremiah had plans to attend a music concert, he agrees.

15. Secret Combinations. Porter becomes concerned over Jeremiah's continuing depression while Claire and Jeremiah are apparently becoming closer, especially since they will be teaching a class together.

16. The Date. Megan, the school newspaper reporter and Jeremiah's friend, convinces Jeremiah to skip the teaching assignment and join her at the concert he gave up to teach. At the concert, Jeremiah realizes he made the wrong decision and should be with Claire. However, before he is able to leave, he is kidnapped by an assassin—all of which is witnessed by Megan.

17. The Break. Jeremiah, tied to a chair, is being questioned by persons unknown who want the box. Megan is revealed to be helping Brenna, a school faculty member, who appears to be part of the organization seeking the box.

18. Interrogation. As Jeremiah is being interrogated, he learns that his interrogator is the man who killed his parents. Jeremiah's continual refusal to turn over the box takes a turn for the worse when Claire is produced and becomes the bargaining chip—her life for the box. When Jeremiah refuses to break his oath to protect the box and Claire is about to be shot, they both miraculously disappear, leaving the assassin all alone.

19. Friends and Family. Lilah reveals the results of the DNA test: Jeremiah's mother's bloodline traces back to Guatemala while his father's bloodline could not be traced.

20. Birthright. Jeremiah and Claire appear at the cave in Manti after vanishing from the assassin. Ammon tells Jeremiah that he has passed his test of faith as he was willing to forfeit his life to protect the box. The program ends with Ammon solving his father's mystery: he was one of the Three Nephites—the immortals who will serve Christ until his second coming.

55 *The Booth at the End*. fxtv.com and hulu.com. 2010–2012 (Fantasy).

There is one booth in a diner that is always occupied by the same man. He appears normal but he possesses the ability to grant wishes—for a price. People who come to the diner seeking The Man (as he is called) tell him what they want. In return, they must complete a task as determined by The Man then return to the diner and describe every detail of their experience. Anthology-like episodes follow people who, to achieve their desires, perform tasks that would normally be inconceivable to them. The Man, however, does not force anyone to do something. It is totally up to each of his "clients" to do what they believe is right.

Cast: Xander Berkeley (The Man), Matt Nolan (James), Kate Maberly (Jenny), Matt Boren (Willem), Norma Michaels (Mrs. Tyler), Jennifer Del Rosario (Melody), Jack Conley (Allen), Sarah Clarke (Sister Carmel), Timothy Omundson (Simon), Jenni Blong (Doris), Jake Richardson (Richard), Anthony Brandon Wong (Gerald), Brendan Chadd Thomas (Bobby), Keegan Boos (Conner), Michelle Allsopp, Noel Fisher (Dillon), Romina Peniche (Maria), Danny Nucci (Henry), Dayton Callie (Jack), Abby Miller (Theresa). **Credits:** *Producer:* Stephen A. Cohen, Noel Bright, Lou Fusaro. *Director:* Jessica Landaw. *Writer:* Christopher Kubasik. **Comment:** Exactly who or what The Man is (God? The Devil?) is never revealed. All the action is set in that Booth at the End and it is basically a conversation between The Man and his client as the client reveals what happened during the performance of his or her task. It is well written to keep the viewer totally interested despite the single scene setting (although it will take some adjustment time to accept the style of filming). Episodes, short as they are (about four minutes) pack a wallop as to how much can be accomplished within that time frame. Xander Berkeley (The Man) is an old pro, having worked on numerous television series, and handles the role perfectly. Intriguing to see what people may attempt to do (they are not forced) and what is their sense of right and wrong. Although the idea has been done before on television on shows like *The Millionaire* and *Nightmare Café* it is still worth watching to see what people desire—and what lengths they will go through to achieve it. The episodes have been edited and have been seen on the FX cable network as a series of nine episodes: Start, See What Happens, What One Begins, One Must Finish, How You Do It Is All Up to You, I Have My Reasons, Our Deal Here Is Done, A New Reality, It's Not Supposed to Be Easy, The Rules of the Game and Nothing More, Nothing Less.

Episodes: Characters from each episode appear in various aspects of each story, thus making for a complex situation. Rather than explain and repeat information for each episode, information regarding each character's desire is presented.

1. James. To save his son, who is suffering from leukemia, James approaches The Man. His task: kill a young girl of his own choosing. But once selected (Elizabeth) he cannot choose another child.

2. Jenny. To become more attractive, The Man assigns a young woman (Jenny) her task: steal $101,043 from either one bank or a series of banks. Desperately wanting her wish granted, Jenny begins preparations by buying a gun.

3. Willem. Infatuated with a girl who posed as a centerfold in a girlie magazine, Willem approaches The Man with a desire to have her. His task: protect a young girl (Elizabeth) from a man (James) who is plotting to kill her.

4. Mrs. Tyler. Seeing that it is the only way to cure her husband's Alzheimer's disease, a woman is charged with a strange task by The Man: build a bomb to kill people at a location of her choosing.

5. Melody. A 17-year-old girl, concerned about the welfare of her father since his business had faltered approaches The Man with a simple request: to make her father happy again. Her task: persuade a shut-in to leave the prison of his home. Complications set in when Melody discovers that he is a serial killer—and she may be his next target (see also numbers 11 and 15 below).

6. Allen. A detective with a desire to be reunited with his son is assigned the task of concealing a fellow police officer's corrupt actions (stealing from murder victims). Allen's situation is complicated when he learns that his son, Richard, has teamed with Jenny (from number 2 above) to rob a bank.

7. Sister Carmel. A test of faith situation wherein a nun in her mid-thirties begins to lose faith in God and asks The Man to restore her belief. Her task: become pregnant.

8. Simon. An artist with a desire to make his paintings more beautiful is assigned the task of becoming a father. By fate (?) he meets Sister Carmel (from number 7 above) and not only paints her portrait but begins a relationship with her.

9. Doris. A slight departure from the premise wherein Doris, the diner waitress, has been observing The Man and the people he meets and approaches him to learn more about him—and the mysterious book he carries with him. See also number 21.

10. Richard. Richard, the man who teams with Jenny (number 2 above) and the son of Allen (number 6 above) wants only to be left alone. The Man has assigned him the task of helping Jenny rob banks in order to be free of his father.

11. Gerald. Melody's father (from number 5 above) seeks The Man's help in bringing back Melody (who was killed by the shut-in). Unfortunately the program (the season finale) ends without a task or resolution.

12. Bobby. Although the Man is somewhat reluctant to help children, he offers one (Bobby) a task: find a missing person and his desire to help his friend (Conner) will be granted. The second season premiere has The Man located in a different diner in a different city.

13. Conner. Conner joins Bobby in his quest to find a missing woman (Cheryl) and bring her home in order for his wish to be granted: stop Conner's father from drinking and disrupting his family.

14. Cheryl. Cheryl, the woman found by Bobby and Conner, approaches The Man with her own desire: cure her daughter of an undisclosed debilitating disease. Her rather harsh task: find a woman without friends or family and torture her. When Cheryl is unable to do what she has been asked, The Man offers her an alternative task: abandon her family for three weeks without notice.

15. Melody. Melody, the 17-year-old girl from

number 5 above, returns as a spirit to The Man (as she was killed by the shut-in) demanding to know if she is really dead or that another woman died in her place. To find out her task is to make something worth living for.

16. Dillon. A young man, distraught over his fathers' death in Afghanistan, wishes to live forever without changing. The Man assigns him the task of inflicting bodily harm on three people of his own choosing—but can he destroy the lives of others for his own greed?

17. Maria. A young Latina wanting only to bring happiness to her mother after the death of her father and the confinement to an institution of her drug-addicted sister, finds a most unusual task from The Man: make five people cry—a task that is more difficult than it seems.

18. Henry. Realizing that he married the wrong woman, a man (Henry) approaches The Man to ask that he be happily married to his past love. His task, which conflicts with his atheist beliefs: become a servant to a higher power.

19. Jack. The eldest of The Man's clients is assigned a most vicious task: kill twenty-two people in public with witnesses able to testify that he is the culprit. In return, The Man will grant protection to his grandchildren.

20. Theresa. A plain looking woman approaches The Man with a desire to be loved. Her task: approach men and make sexual advances towards them. It is something she must force herself to do—and receives help from a stranger (possibly The Man) who appears at her home one night to tell her she need not degrade herself. She is worth more.

21. Doris. Doris (from number 9 above) returns and approaches The Man, telling him that they may both be of the same origins and possess the same powers. Having tested people but never been tested himself The Man gives Doris the mysterious book (that records what happens) and asks her for a task so that he may understand people and why they do what they do. His task: choosing one person and helping him. The series concludes with Doris wanting to make a deal also: that he (The Man) love her.

56 *Border Guardians of Ackernon.* blip.tv. 2012 (Fantasy).

Ackernon is a medieval-like village that is protected from evil (especially the Pert) by its Border Guardians, graduates of the University, which trains young men and women to operate in the shadows against their enemies. While episodes one through six are basically an introduction to the University and how it trains operatives, the remaining six episodes relate the adventures of one such group of Border Guardians as they set out to protect Ackernon from the evil Pert.

Cast: Paige Natsues (Galiene), Danielle Golden (Roanue), Paul Pavelski (Vardin), Angela Aro (Pet-

rina), Troy Fidis (Gayorg), Cole Escovido (Marloff), Shanna Martin (Kara), Katie Simmons (Vanessa), Lydia Xiong (Charity), Truly Vang (Charley), Raymond Castelan (Max). **Credits:** *Producer:* Ray Olson. *Writer-Director:* Paul Best. **Comment:** Fantasy spiced with light comedy combined with lavish costumes and sets makes for a worthwhile program.

Episodes:

1. Family (5 min., 57 sec.). Introduces viewers to several of the former students at the University, especially Galiene, the program's heroine.

2. I Have Nothing to Hide (3 min., 35 sec.). Vardin, Galiene's informant (a smuggler), complicates her life when he comes to the University.

3. Vardin, Why Are You Here? (4 min., 58 sec.). At the Musky Ox tavern, Galiene questions Vardin why he has suddenly re-entered her life.

4. Without Magic, There Is No Ackernon (5 min., 23 sec.). It is learned at the University that magic is dangerous and that each student must encompass it, not let it control her (as magic is not for the faint of heart or one who lets her mind wander).

5. I Am Not a Spy (7 min., 11 sec.). Galiene and Vardin become close, but find their lives about to change when Marloff, a gentleman of questionable means, approaches them.

6. Guys, Where's the Camp? (6 min., 32 sec.). Five counselors, lost in the Sierras after a storm, seek their way back to their camp.

7. I Saw Nothing but Rumors (8 min., 48 sec.). Galiene and her team of former students gather in the woods for a strategy meeting.

8. Maybe It Was a Tornado (4 min., 11 sec.). As the camp counselors continue their search, they come across three men, armed with swords, battling a female warrior (Roanue).

9. Holy Crap, What Just Happened? (6 min., 48 sec.). Roanue, wounded during the fight, is mysteriously healed by one of the camp counselors (Charity). Charity and the others soon begin to wonder where they are, why they are here and if they will ever find their way home.

10. Who Wants Num Nums? (6 min., 50 sec.). A bit in a daze following her cure, all Roanue can utter is "Take me to Arges." The campers, not exactly sure what Arges is, carry Roanue on a stretcher as they seek the park road.

11. Do You Happen to Have a Phone? (8 min., 9 sec.). On the road, the campers find Arges—an odd hermit living alone in the woods, who seems to know a bit about each of the campers—and who tells them that their future is not too bright.

12. Be Quiet and Run Faster (11 min., 10 sec.). Roanue, now completely recovered, seeks a place of safety (the Glen of the Third Crossing) when she discovers that they have been spotted by a Pert patrol.

57 *Bounty: Inner Orbs.* youtube.com. 2012 (Science Fiction).

In the year 2112, earthlings have evolved into a race of super beings as their senses have all been heightened. It is also a time when The Red Syndicate rules but is opposed by H.O.P.E., an underground group that are fighting the syndicate and hoping to change the laws it established and expects citizens to obey. Chief and Lakland are bounty hunters who have become immersed in the battle between the two and the program relates their efforts to maintain the balance.

Cast: Andrew Valdez (Chief), Brittney Cardella (Lady Red), Jon Graham (Lakland), Katherine Pulker (Jaden), Lance Lash (Foxtrot), Jeff Jenkins (Rehdik), Jean-Francois Donaldson (Doc), Sydni Takacs (Celsius), Kevin Morales (Fade), Chelsea Magnano (Temple), Joel Strickland (Torque), Mark J. Richman (Tesula/Inquisitor), Corey Brown (Brink), Amanda Defrances (Façade). **Credits:** *Producer:* Andrew Valdez, Jeff Jenkins. *Director:* Jon Graham. *Writer:* Andrew Valdez. **Comment:** The special effects are good but the acting is questionable (comes off as very unprofessional). Production values change from episode to episode—from acceptable to what were they thinking.

Episodes:
1. Episode 1 (7 min., 6 sec.). Establishes the series storyline.
2. Episode 2 (9 min., 42 sec.). Lakland and Chief infiltrate the headquarters of H.O.P.E.
3. Episode 3 (13 min., 46 sec.). Joined by a new ally (Jaden), Chief and Lakland attempt a rescue of innocent people at a Red Syndicate warehouse.
4. Episode 4 (10 min., 14 sec.). A mission goes sour when Chief and Lakland find themselves involved in jungle warfare.
5. Episode 5 (10 min., 2 sec.). An enemy infiltrates the ranks of H.O.P.E.
6. Episode 6 (11 min., 16 sec.). Part 1 of a two part finale finds the war between the two factions increasing with only Chief and Lakland able to stop it (or at least curtail it).
7. Episode 7 (5 min., 33 sec.). Concludes the story but leaves it open-ended for additional episodes as H.O.P.E. continues to battle The Red Syndicate.

58 *Brain Eatin' Zombie Babies.* youtube. com. 2010 (Horror).

A mother's efforts to raise three children: a normal teenage son and two zombie babies—a boy (the older, called Baby) and the infant one-year-old Daisy. There is no background information on how a normal woman acquired her zombie babies (which are hand puppets).

Cast: Alyson Court (Mother). **Comment:** While baby is ravishingly disgusting, the program does come with a warning: "This Video Not Suitable for Small Children." Alyson Court as the mother is perfectly cast as she sees her zombie babies as just normal kids. The short sequences play very well and see-

ing what Baby does is just fun to watch. It is also the first time baby zombies where placed front and center—even if they are hand puppets.

Episodes: Thirty episodes were produced but only the following are still online (they are presented with descriptions as each is complete in itself).
1. Swing Time (1 min., 20 sec.). Baby is enjoying his swing ride in the local park when he is pushed a bit too high by Mom and flies off. Not to fear, he lands on a park patron to enjoy some brains.
2. Snack Time (1 min., 15 sec.). Baby sees his older brother as a snack and chases him for some brain food.
3. Subway (1 min., 54 sec.). Mom and Baby take a subway ride—where Baby spies a passenger and some brains to eat.
4. The Salesman (1 min., 16 sec.). A door-to-door salesman picks the wrong house when he chooses the one in which Baby lives.
5. The Big Burp (1 min., 4 sec.). Mom has to contend with Baby after he burps a disgusting liquid all over her.
6. Happy Birthday (50 sec.). Daisy celebrates her first birthday and gets her wish—a brain to eat.

59 *Bravest Warriors.* cartoonhangover. com. 2012–2013 (Science Fiction).

Futuristic cartoon (set in the year 3085) that follows four teenagers (Chris, Beth, Danny and Wallow) as they use their powers to protect the defenseless beings of all worlds. Chris is the leader of the Bravest Warriors and uses a weapon animal called Little Bee (which can form a sword with a honeycombed hilt and a swarm of bees). Beth is Chris's girlfriend and has a cat, which can transform into a cat-o-nine tails as her animal weapon. Wallow is the smartest member of the team whose glove contains a computer named Pixel. His animal weapon is a falcon that transforms into an axe. Danny formed the Bravest Warriors and his animal weapon is a dog that can transform into a sword or gattling gun. Plum is Beth's friend, a Merewif (a girl who can morph her legs into a mermaid's tail when in the water). She is the unofficial fifth member of the team. Emotion Lord is the old man with warping abilities who is linked to Chris's emotions. Catbug is the child-like creature that is part cat and part ladybug.

Voice Cast: *Pilot:* Charlie Schlatter (Chris Kirkman) Tara Strong (Beth Tezuka), Dan Finnerty (Wallow), Rob Paulsen (Danny Vasquez); *Series:* Alex Walsh (Chris Kirkman), Liliana Mumy (Beth Tezuka), Ian Jones-Quartey, Maria Bamford (Pixel), John Omohundo (Danny Vasquez), Tara Strong (Plum), Breehn Burns (Emotion Lord), Michael Leon Wooley (Impossibear), Sam Lavagnino (Catbug). **Credits:** *Producer:* Breehn Burns, Will McRobb, Chris Viscardi, Fred Seibert. *Director:* Randy Myers, Pendleton Ward, Breehn Burns. *Writer:* Pendleton Ward, Breehn Burns. **Comment:**

Comical animated science fiction fantasy that would play even better on the Cartoon Network. The animation is good and the stories as silly as animated spoofs are meant to be.

Episodes:

1. Time Slime. The warriors attempt to help a professor reverse an experiment that has the Moon of Glendale in continual spin of an overlapping time loop.

2. Emotion Lord. After a mission on the planet Zgraxxis, Danny is stricken with a mysterious fever that is apparently being controlled by a being called the Emotion Lord.

3. Butter Lettuce. Beth becomes outraged when she discovers that Danny programmed her image in a video game—and made her much sexier than she really is.

4. Memory Donk. A bus is out of control and heading for the Mars Convention Center. The warriors have been affected by a memory loss and can't figure out how to stop a pending disaster.

5. The Bunless. The warriors must figure a way to get two beings to fall back in love to save the people of Bunless 9 from enduring 99 years of war and darkness.

6. Lavarinth. The return of the Emotion Lord reveals that he is from the future—and team member Chris is his younger self.

7. Gas Powered Stick. The Emotion Lord presents the team with a stick that never runs out of gas.

8. Dan Before Time. To take revenge on the Low Gravity Pack, who made his childhood miserable, Danny creates a time machine to send him back in time.

9. Cereal Monster. Acquiring a bowl of Moon Frosted Double Dolphin Smax cereal for Beth causes problems for Chris when the Cereal Monster refuses to make it and Chris's latent Emotion Lord powers surface to ensure that she gets her cereal.

10. Ultra Wankershim. A mishap in the Holo-John (the hologram room) unleashes a Wankershim that grows to an enormous size and has the warriors baffled as how to stop it.

11. Catbug. The warriors are faced with problems when Catbug figures out a way to travel from their zone to the See-Through Zone but returns with a strange virus that mutates into a door and traps them with no apparent way out.

12. Sugarbellies. The warriors must figure out how to get a planet back on track after it goes out of alignment causing its Sugarbellie residents to no longer speak clearly.

13. Moo-Phobia. The warriors seek a way to help Chris overcome his fear of cows so they can begin a mission.

14. Drama Bug. Catbug's obsession with toys has the team worried when he believes the toys are real.

15. Browser Fail. Danny begins an investigation to discover who shaved off his eyebrows while he was asleep.

16. Impossibomb. Wallow's present from Impossibear causes problems for the team when they discover it contains a bomb.

17. Terrabeth Bytes. Beth and Wallow sumo wrestle to determine the better of the two.

18. Aeon Worm. Beth's journey to the See-Through Zone reveals that her father, known as Ralph Waldo Pickle Chips (voice of Billy Mumy) serves the evil Aeon Worm.

19. RoboChris. Danny's efforts to create a robotic version of Chris backfires creating anything but what was desired.

20. The Lost Episode. The original pilot that finds the warriors seeking to save the Brian Dogs from the Tickle Monster.

60 Brillig. brilligseries.weebly.com. 2013 (Fantasy).

Update of the Lewis Carroll story *Alice in Wonderland*. After her adventures in Wonderland came to an end, Alice returned to a normal life and eventually married—but she had always dreamed of returning to Wonderland. Many years later, after the death of her husband, Arthur Grey, Alice returns to England to find that her family estate has fallen on hard times due to her brother's (Robert) mishandling finances. Alice discovers that the only way she can save her estate is to marry Lord Dudley, the man who will save Robert from debtor's prison by paying off the debt. Before the marriage takes place, Alice's dream becomes a reality when the Mad Hatter appears to her in her world. While Alice is both amazed and delighted to be reunited with her friend from Wonderland, the Mad Hatter has come to her on very special mission: save her from a soul collector. The story follows Alice and the Mad Hatter as they embark on a mysterious journey to expose and defeat the demon seeking Alice's soul. **Cast:** Linda Goetz (Alice), James Fitzpatrick (Mad Hatter), Marley Malloy (Jane), Chuck Schwager (Lord Dudley), Stephen Cooper (Azrael). **Credits:** *Producer-Writer:* Linda Goetz. *Director:* Adam Schroeder. **Comment:** Brillig is an English term that refers to tea time or broiling food for dinner. It is also defined as one chapter ending while waiting for another to begin. And those moments between endings and beginnings can lead one to other worlds. Encompassing that second definition, the series attempts to relate aspects in Alice's adult life, here for the first time, as she battles to save her soul. The program has its moments but is somewhat talkative and, being produced in England, a bit hard to understand at times. The acting and production values are good although some scenes are very dark and difficult to see. The program also suffers from terrible closed captioning—misspelled words and captioning dialogue that does not match the words spoken by the actors.

Episodes:

1. If You Believe in Me, I'll Believe in You (10 min., 18 sec.). Alice faces the unwanted prospect of marrying Lord Dudley.

2. Episode 2 (8 min., 40 sec.). The Mad Hatter appears to Alice.

3. Episode 3 (10 min., 10 sec.). Alice and the Mad Hatter begin their quest to uncover the Soul Collector.

4. Episode 4 (13 min., 57 sec.). Alice learns that the Mad Hatter is her guardian (and has always been) and has been sent to her world to protect her.

5. Episode 5 (12 min., 10 sec.). Alice and the Mad Hatter encounter strange Wonderland-like characters as they continue their quest.

6. Episode 6 (11 min., 18 sec.). Alice and the Mad Hatter uncover—and now face the wrath of the Soul Collector—Lord Dudley.

61 *Bring Me Alice's Head.* youtube.com. 2013 (Fantasy).

After her experiences in Wonderland, Alice had returned to the real world but had always dreamed of one day finding the White Rabbit that enticed her when she was a child. Alice is now grown and has isolated herself from the world, hoping to one day find happiness in Wonderland. Her only pleasure appears to be spending time with her pet white rabbits. Her wishing becomes reality when the White Rabbit appears to her and she asks him to take her back to Wonderland. Before she can get a response, the White Rabbit disappears; however, a stranger overheard Alice and the White Rabbit talking about the magical world of Wonderland. In Wonderland, the White Rabbit relates what happened (a stranger now knows about Wonderland) to the Queen of Hearts who becomes infuriated with Alice for revealing that such a place exists. In retaliation, she orders that Alice be silenced forever (had additional episodes been produced, they would have followed Alice's new adventures as she attempts to escape the Wonderland assassins hired to kill her). **Cast:** Raffaella Anzalone (Alice), Andrea Beretta (White

Rabbit), Vincenzo De Falco (Queen of Hearts), Simone Baldassari (Cheshire Cat), Martina Rusolo (Lori). **Credits:** *Producer-Writer-Director:* Marco Latour. **Comment:** A confusing update of the Lewis Carroll story *Alice in Wonderland.* The program is produced in Italy and captioned in English, but one must activate the closed captioning icon for the subtitles. The acting is acceptable but the production is very dark and hard to see what is happening. Having to use the subtitles is also a bit distracting as it draws your attention away from the visual aspects of a scene. The program ends with no conclusion but leads the doorway open for additional episodes.
Episodes:
1. Bring Me Alice's Head (16 min., 4 sec.). Establishes the story with the Queen of Hearts demanding that Alice be silenced for revealing facts about Wonderland.

62 *The Broken Continent.* thebrokencontinent.com. 2013 (Science Fiction).

***Broken Continent* cast, left to right: Kelly Slagle, Danny Gavigan and Bette Cassat (photograph by Roy Cox, copyright Broken Continent, LLC).**

In a time long ago the center of the world's knowledge and culture was beheld in Ars Exilior, the capital city of a kingdom known as Elyrion. Its rulers possessed a mastery over magic that could be found no where else on earth. One such ruler, Demarien, was said to have a power that could bring the dead back to life. For one hundred years the citizens prospered under their belief in the True God, Relios until Demarien, now called Demarien the Unchallenged presented himself as a god and angered Relios. In retaliation for such blasphemy, Relios broke the continent of Elyrion into five entities: The Blade, the Crown, the Eye, the Fist and the Heart. The new entities were then plunged into an age of darkness called The Fracture and both Relios and Demarien vanished, never to be seen again. As the centuries passed, foreign invaders occupied and pillaged what was known as The Broken Continent. Three thousand years later in the entity known as the Heart (in the ruins of Ars Exilior) Eadwyn Redway now rules. His father, Ardwyn the Great, defeated the evil king of Selgren (of the Blade) and helped unify the rule over the Heart and the Blade. Eadwyn, however, is ambitious and now seeks to conquer the remaining three nations and acquire absolute power. However, with peace finally restored, not all citizens are loyal to Eadwyn and a resistance is building. Leading the resistance are the Daughters of Tairol, who have defended the sacred Ironleaf Forest in the name of the god Tairol (the forest provides a sanctuary for the widows and orphans whose spouses and/or parents were killed in Eadwyn's campaign of terror). With an uprising brewing and with the guiding hand of the Daughters of Tairol, the program presents the Daughters efforts to stop Eadwyn, who has been dubbed Eadwyn the Wicked.

Cast: Danny Gavigan (Eadwyn), Ariana Almajan (Malkyn), Bette Cassatt (Brenn), Ricardo Frederick Evans (Diarmait), Dorea Schmidt (Cedany), Kelley Slagle (Ayleth), Joseph Carlson (Roylon), Rebecca A. Herron (Orla), Kelly Gray (Jolenta), Nick De-Pinto (Tybolt), Blythe Coons (Lorica), Jean Hudson Miller (Usmay), Joy Jones (Nerida). **Credits:** *Producer:* Francis Abbey, Kelley Slagle, Bjorn Munson. *Writer:* Francis Abbey. **Comment:** As complex as the story sounds, the program does take a bit of adjustment to understand what is happening. The costumes, sets, acting and production values are all good and all work well to present a compelling fantasy adventure.

Episodes:

1. Episode 1 (3 min., 57 sec.). The Daughters of Tairol plot to stop Eadwyn in his plan to conquer the five Shards of Elyrion.

2. Episode 2 (9 min., 22 sec.). As a war rages in the Heart, a band of survivors makes its way to the Ironleaf Forest to assist the Daughters.

3. Episode 3 (7 min., 20 sec.). Eadwyn enlists the aid of deadly swordsmen to ensure his winning the battle by destroying the Daughters.

63 *Broken Saints.* newgrounds.com. 2001–2003 (Fantasy).

Animated tale of four modern-day people (Kaminura, Oran, Raimi and Shandala), strangers to each other and from the quiet corners of the world, who each receive similar visions of impending doom and each of whom begins an uncertain journey to search for answers. As they are drawn together and journey they begin a quest to seek the truth about the world, themselves and each other (while also battling their inner demons) only to discover the power of love.

Shandala Nisinu, 18 years old, is an altruist and living on the uncharted Fiji island of Lomalagi (Heaven). Her element is water and she was found as an infant floating on the ocean's waves and adopted by the island chief, Tui Misinu.

Raimi Matthews is 24 years of age and was born in Canada (his element is fire). He is a Catholic (though non-practicing) and now lives in Coast City in the U.S. where he works as a software security developer for a telecommunications company and the Bicom pharmaceutical company.

Oran Bajir is 29 years old (element air) and is a devout Muslim from Iraq and was involved in an armed resistance against Western domination before he began his journey.

Kamimura, age unknown, is from Japan and has the element earth. He is an elderly Shinto mystic and former Buddhist who was disavowed from his order for aiding in the theft of relics.

Principal DVD Voice Cast: Janyse Jaud (Shandala), Kirby Morrow (Raimi), Colin Foo (Kamimura), Michael Dobson (Oran). **Credits:** *Producer:* Jonathan Bogner, Brooke Burgess. *Creator:* Brooke Burgess, Andrew West, Ian Kirby. *Artist:* Andrew West. **Comment:** The program is made up of 24 chapters, ranging from 10 minutes to over an hour each (runs 10 hours and 30 minutes which is quite long for a web series). It is presented as a hybrid program, combing elements of still comics (characters remain static with dialogue presented in speech balloons) and limited animation (with music and sound effects heightening the story as it progresses). In 2006 the program was released on DVD and used upgraded animation (for the first nine chapters) and added voice talents to make the story easier to follow. While there are religious overtones, the story can be seen as both excellent and preachy (and, at times a bit hard to follow). The art work and writing are excellent and the characters well developed (although it does take 5 chapters just to introduce the characters). The episodes themselves can range from boring to exciting but, as previously mentioned, sometimes difficult to follow and their meanings could be interpreted two different ways. Because of the complexity of the situation, where chapters have been frequently subdivided into multiple acts, summaries are complex, sometimes confusing and thus not presented here.

Episodes: Due to release of the program on DVD all episodes, including descriptions, have been taken off line.

64 *Brood.* webserieschannel.com. 2012 (Fantasy).

It is a time when prominent vampire families, called Broods, have lost their control on the human population and a civil war has broken out amongst the vampire clans. The female vampire, being the most cunning of the species, killed off their male counterparts and began seeking human prey—but humans proved to be a strong adversary and drove the vampires underground. Some of the Broods are planning to strike back while others have gone into hibernation, waiting to be freed and join a new arising. One family, the Hoppers have vowed to keep the blood from spilling over—but they aren't always successful. With particular focus on Cassandra, a beautiful female vampire, stories follow the battle for struggle and power within the various vampire families as they conspire to fulfill their goal and take over the world.

Cast: *Original Pilot:* Nicole Brokaw (Cassandra), Tina Emani (Tara), Keri Wayne (Amanda Keys), Armando Alarcon (Det. Thomas Kyle), T. Falagan (Shane Harper), Gilbert Songalia (Andi), Joseph Bossey (Terry), James Ryan (Cannon), Deborah Fabiano (Poolside girl); *Series:* April Bay (Cassandra), Savannah Moore (Hopper), Marissa E. Macias (Deana Kaine), Michael Adler (Jordan Woodbine), James Shelledy (Det. Keys), T. Falagan (Narrator), Ricardo A. Romero, Candice Dalsing, Micha Hamilton. **Credits:** *Original Pilot: Producer:* T. Falagan, Deborah Fabiano-Falagan, J.J. Wauge, John Wesley. *Writer-Director:* T. Falagan; *Series: Producer:* Deborah Fabiano-Falagan, T. Falagan. *Writer-Director:* Ted Falagan. **Comment:** Although there is no conclusion, the program is well produced with good acting and directing and being filmed in black and white adds a more sinister feel. The story is captivating and the final episode leaves the doorway open for additional episodes.

Episodes:

1. Brood: Episode 1 (6 min., 33 sec.). Cassandra, a beautiful, but heartless vampire, is awakened from her centuries-long sleep to a modern world that is now controlled by a rival vampire family.

2. Brood: Episode 2 (13 min., 10 sec.). Becoming aware of a new presence, a tough police detective (Hannibal Keys) begins an investigation into a series of unusual deaths (victims drained of blood). Unknown to Cassandra, she is also being sought by the vampire hunter (Hopper).

3. Brood: Episode 3 (4 min., 41 sec.). Deana Kaine, a Pure Blood Vampire, a member of the family that once ruled humans, begins her plan to change all that and retain her place as ruler.

4. Brood: Episode 4 (4 min., 56 sec.). Deana brings to life Jordan Woodbine, the heir to the Woodbine fortune.

5. Brood: Episode 5 (4 min., 13 sec.). Deana and Jordan team to begin their take over (the concluding episode).

6. Brood: The Original Test Pilot (24 min., 18 sec.). Although not a part of the series, it is a look at how the series was originally planned: Police detectives (Amanda Keys, Thomas Kyle), seeking a serial killer, stumble onto a nest of vampires and must now battle a new evil. The original concept is just as good but somewhat sexier (as the female vampires [Cassandra and Tara] wear no bras and their unbuttoned blouses reveal almost everything).

65 *Brothers Barbarian.* fantasywebseries.net. 2011–2013 (Fantasy).

Art, a 17-year-old know-it-all, and Russ, his 16-year-old brother, live in a barbaric age and find their lives changing for the worse when an evil witch casts an aging spell on them. Now, as middle-aged "men," the brothers begin a quest to find the witch and have the spell reversed.

Art, who wears a horned helmet, and Russ, a red bandana, look out for each other as they travel through strange lands and meet unusual characters. Although neither Art nor Russ is educated, they are "street smart" and do not let a lack of education stand in their way of getting what they want. The Old Wizard is Art and Russ's advisor and mentor but his spells often misfire and make things worse than they already are. Marnack, an Orc (can't be killed no matter how many times people try) is a hard worker who is plagued by a nagging wife and annoying kids. The Party (The Fighter, The Dark Elf, The Yellow Mage and The Cleric) are a group of adventures who travel through the Midlands apparently looking for fun by "kicking ass." Stinki and Lord Brian rule the Orcs and are seeking to take over the Midlands. Nicky and Nacky, also known as The Bone Sisters, roam the Midlands pretending to be damsels in distress as a poly to rob "suckers" of their gold. The Red Wizard is an employee of the gods who uses his powerful magic to carry out their wishes.

Cast: Tim Gooch (Art), Ken Whitman (Russ), Larry Elmore (Old Wizard), Josh Logsdon (Marnack), Robert Hatfield (The Fighter), Herschel Zahnd (The Dark Elf), Travis Huber (The Cleric), Christopher Folan (Yellow Mage), Philip Allgeier (Lord Brian), Tyler Neal (Stinki), Margaret Weis (Evil Witch), Alexandra Whitman (Grandma), James Wallace Walton (Nasty), Nycole Huber (Nicky), Rebecca Wright (Nacky), William C. Eriksen (The Red Wizard), Bryan T. Huber (Cleric), Tana Stalcup (Taana). **Credits:** *Producer:* William C. Eriksen, Chuck Wagner. *Director:* Tim Gooch. *Writer:* Kim Whitman. **Comment:** Well done period piece with good sets and costumes. While there is not a lot of action, the story does move along and the plot is easy to follow.

Episodes:

1. Something Wicked. Just when everything seems to be going their way, the Evil Witch casts her aging spell on Art and Russ.

2. Double Trouble. The now middle-aged "boys" encounter The Old Wizard, who becomes their advisor as they journey.

3. Baby, Don't Hurt Me. Although only teens, Art and Russ become attracted to the older Nicky and Nacky and hatch a disastrous plan to become "their beaus."

4. To the Death. Trouble looms when the trio encounter Stinki and Lord Brian.

5. Everything Changes. Art and Russ find hope of reversing the spell when they meet Taana and The Red Wizard.

66 *Bumps in the Night.* youtube.com. 2009 (Horror).

Ghost Hunters (Syfy channel) parody (a fake reality program) that follows three bumbling paranormal enthusiasts (Emmett, Greg and John) who, by day are pool cleaners (for Senor Agua Pool Cleaners) but by night are ghost busters who run a company called NOGHOST.

Cast: Emmett Furey (Emmett), Greg Benevent (Greg), John Reha (John). **Credits:** *Producer:* Emmett Furey, John Reha, Greg Benevent. *Director:* Stuart Davis, Rudy Jahchan, Taryn O'Neill, Samuel Proof, Alethea Root, Greg Benevent, Emmett Furey, John Reha. *Writer:* Greg Benevent, Emmett Furey, John Reha, Ian Abrams. **Comment:** A comical paranormal spoof and nothing more with competent acting and adequate production values.

Episodes:

1. Ghost in the Pool, Part 1. A routine job to clean a pool becomes more of a mystery when strange things begin happening.

2. Ghost in the Pool, Part 2. The team captures a questionable image on film.

3. Ghost in the Pool, Part 3. Analyzing the film, the team believes they have captured the image of a ghost and must now act.

4. Ghost in the Pool, Part 4. With strange occurrences still happening, the team is now prepared to dispose of their angry spirit through a séance.

5. The Haunted Apartment? The team moves into a new apartment where Greg appears to be possessed by the former, deceased occupant—a crazed fitness expert.

6. Evil Parking Garage of Evil? The team investigates an evil that lurks in a parking garage.

7. Anti-Love Seat? John and Greg purchase a new couch—only to find that it is haunted and a threat to their lives.

8. Evil Whisperers. The team comes to the rescue

of a young housewife who is being terrorized by a demonic voice.

9. An Exorcise in Futility? The team tries to help a man who believes his girlfriend is possessed by the Devil.

10. Why Can't They All Be Psychic Girls? Assisted by Betsy (Shanrah Wakefield), a television psychic, the team investigates strange happenings at the infamous McGutty Murder House.

11. The Pink Scare. The team investigates an artist who claims that his studio is haunted.

12. Too Much Chicken and Waffles Presents the Inaugural All Valley Ghost Hunting Tournament. The team encounters a team of ghost hunters even crazier then they are.

67 *Buried Alive.* fearnet.com. 2007 (Horror).

Five young adults (Becca, Rick, Wylie, Sage and Curtis), for reasons unknown, have been abducted and each placed in a box-like coffin. While there appears to be no immediate escape they can talk to each other through openings between the caskets. It is learned through conversations that the five know each other, having attended the same high school. Unknown to them, miniature video cameras are concealed within the coffins and they are being observed by their mysterious abductor. The victims soon discover that each of their coffins contains a clue to their abductor's identity and that it is most likely someone they each know. Escaping is not that easy as each coffin appears to be booby trapped and a wrong move could kill them. The program intensifies when a friend (Melanie) and her brother (Travis) realize they are missing and set out to find out what has happened to them. Episodes relate the victim's anguish as they try to figure out who abducted them and why.

Cast: Greyson Chadwick (Becca), Nikki McKenzie (Sage), Natalie Wachen (Wylie), Jeff Blum (Travis), Augusto Aguilar (Tommy), Brit Morgan (Melanie), Bram Hoover (Rick), J.R. May (Curtis), John Charles Meyer (Hayden). **Credits:** *Producer:* Paul Etheredge, Donna Fewell, John Norris. *Director:* Paul Etheredge. *Writer:* Padraig Reynolds. **Comment:** More of a psychological thriller than a true horror series, it is presented as a first person perspective (the footage from the concealed video cameras) with video from Melanie and Travis's camcorders as they document what is happening during their search. The program itself is very amateurish (especially with the annoying jerky footage seen from Travis's camcorder). The girls are very attractive and the program does hold one's interest despite the fact that it lacks real directing and was produced on a tight budget.

Episodes: Only 5 of 12 produced episodes remain online: The Pilot, Needle in the Mouth, Lesbian Affair, Drowning in Dirt and Covered in Blood.

68 *The Cabonauts.* cabonauts.com. 2009 (Science Fiction).

It is the year 2183 and the vastness of space has been conquered. Travel from planet to planet has been achieved and to transport people from one place to another, rocket-powered taxi cabs have also become a part of the system. There are countless outposts and colonies in space and simply by calling Cabonauts, your destination is assured. Two such cab drivers are Cyril, a cynical, veteran driver, and Harry, his young, naïve partner (who is training to get his hack license). While acquiring passengers and bringing them to their destination begins each episode, the story quickly becomes a musical with an original song and music video to depict the trip.

Cast: Hayden Black (Cyril), Norm Thoeming (Harry), Monica Young (Lolita), Nichelle Nichols (CJ). **Credits:** *Producer-Writer-Director:* Hayden Black. **Comment:** A unique idea, combining elements of the television series *Glee* and *The Hitchhikers Guide to the Galaxy* that is a surprisingly good change from what could have simply been a futuristic version of the television series *Taxi*. Based on what has thus far been released, the program does show promise although producing a musical comedy requires far more than the low (or no) budget series (including talent that can sing, dance and act). The addition of former *Star Trek* regular Nichelle Nichols (Lt. Uhura) only adds to the show's future promise (although, being that the pilot was made in 2009, that future does not look too promising).

Episodes:
1. The Pilot. Introduces the series premise.

69 *Camera Obscura.* webserieschannel.com. 2010 (Horror).

After her grandfather (Sam), a crime scene photographer for the Los Angeles Police Department passes away, a young woman (Clara) inherits a seemingly innocent camera, the camera he used as part of his work. Clara soon discovers that her grandfather was more than just a photographer, but a demon hunter whose camera was quite special: it captures the images of unearthly creatures that cannot be seen in their true form by the human eye. Now, with an unwanted legacy, Clara finds herself stepping into the shoes of her grandfather and continuing where he left off: destroy the demons who pose a threat to humans. The episodes have been re-edited into a feature film of the same name.

Cast: Regan Dale Neis (Clara Parsons), Timm Sharp (Det. Chad Ellwood), Charlotte Bjornbak (Off. Rachel Hallan), Don Jeffcoat (Jason), Michelle L. Gardner (Mother), Jack Klugman (Sam), David Woldson (Mr. Hurt), Edin Gali (Dean), Azure Parsons (Magoria), Diona Hungerford (Dr. Abhazred). **Credits:** *Producer:* Max Goldenson, Drew Daywalt, Robert Kandle. *Writer-Director:* Drew Daywalt. **Comment:** Although not an original concept (similar ideas go back to *The Twilight Zone*) it is suspenseful, well executed and worth watching despite commercials (that cannot be deleted or sped through). The series is notable as it was Jack Klugman's (Oscar Madison on television's *The Odd Couple*) last acting performance.

Episodes:
1. The Book (7 min., 13 sec.). Clara discovers her grandfather's diary and learns that he was a demon hunter.
2. The Camera (3 min., 50 sec.). As she continues to search, Clara uncovers a very unusual camera.
3. The Tape (3 min., 17 sec.). Clara's questions regarding her grandfather's secret life are answered through a video tape that she finds.
4. The Hollow Mask (6 min., 50 sec.). As Clara plays the video tape left by her grandfather, she learns that demons are a part of society and that the camera he created can see and capture the unearthly creatures in a photograph.
5. The Cop (2 min., 44 sec.). Feeling she is unable to battle evil alone, Clara seeks help from Chad, the police officer who knew her grandfather.
6. The Search (4 min., 21 sec.). Clara begins her investigation into a series of killings in which the victims were all doctors.
7. Splinter (6 min., 18 sec.). Clara sets a trap to capture the demon responsible for the killings.
8. Solitude (2 min., 34 sec.). Clara reveals the fact of the camera to Chad.
9. Hero (3 min., 52 sec.). Clara feels that what she is doing is part of her legacy and does not want to be praised as a hero.
10. Tonight (2 min., 39 min.). The demon Clara has been seeking (Magoria) surfaces.
11. Magoria (6 min., 16 sec.). Clara's fears are realized when she encounters Magoria (but escapes unharmed).
12. Ally (5 min., 41 sec.). Jason, the son of a murdered police officer, sides with Clara in her quest (knowing what she is attempting to do and can't do it alone).
13. Trophies (5 min., 43 sec.). Clara begins to assemble a record of her grandfather's encounters with demons.
14. Missing (6 min., 21 sec.). Clara seeks Chad, who disappeared while investigating a case.
15. Mr. Hurt (6 min., 33 sec.). After finding Chad, Clara faces a demon called Mr. Hurt.
16. The Bag (5 min., 14 sec.). Believing she is safe after escaping from Mr. Hurt, Clara finds her life threatened by a demon that uses a body bag to kill humans.
17. Love (3 min., 54 sec.). Clara finds herself becoming attracted to Jason.
18. Source (3 min., 47 sec.). When her camera becomes inoperative, Clara and Jason try to figure out its power source.
19. The Bad Place (4 min., 33 sec.). Clara, drawn

to a mysterious dark corridor, begins to wander through it—and finds her grandfather—alive.

20. Farewell (6 min., 25 sec.). Clara's joy is quickly dissipated when her grandfather's image becomes that of a demon—the demon that killed her grandfather and that know seeks to kill her.

70 *Cannibal Run.* tv.com. 2009 (Horror).

In an attempt to get out of a ratings slump, the sports network USPN devises a unique if not weird series called *Cannibal Run* wherein twenty-five of America's greatest zombie athletes will descend on Santa Monica, California and compete in a cross-country car race. With a crew as ineffectual as the network they operate, USPN sets out to cover the race with the program relating all the problems associated with bringing a group of brain eaters together and releasing them on the public. **Cast:** P.J. Ochlan (Sean Andrews), Dave Shalansky (Leaping Lenny), Courtney Rackley (Christine). **Credits:** *Producer:* John Katzman, Daniel Schechter. *Director:* Erin Cantelo. **Comment:** Horror comedy spoof of the Burt Reynolds feature film *The Cannonball Run* that plays just as crazy as the movie on which it is based.

Episodes: All have been taken off line. *1.* Welcome to Cannibal Run. *2.* Lemonade Stand. *3.* Heads Will Roll. *4.* 73 Dead. *5.* Paul's P*ssed. *6.* Ratings Gold. *7.* Smoking. *8.* Newsman Bloopers. *9.* Check Out My Hair. *10.* Lisa's Frustrated. *11.* Bathroom Attack.

71 *Captain Blasto.* captainblasto.com. 2008 (Fantasy).

Colin Carter is a high school student who feels life is a drag. He is bored, tired of the same old routine and feels the future is not all that bright. To bring some excitement into his life, Colin decides to become a super hero. Basing his character on his favorite comic book, *Captain Blasto*, Colin begins by designing a costume then, to become that hero, hires a group of people to play the villains in staged criminal acts that Colin will resolve as the mysterious Captain Blasto. The program itself limits itself to what happens when the crimes Colin devises become all too real and he must literally put an end to what has become a crime wave. **Cast:** Christopher Preksta (Colin Carter), Daryl Karameikos (Aaron Kleiber), Evan Archer (Curt Wootton), Mark Tierno (Michael Lee), Sam Nicotero (Sam Seigel), Chris Hammel (Tom Moore), Melissa Urbaniak (Abbey Green), Michael Dirocco (Eddie Bendis). **Credits:** *Producer:* Aaron Kleiber, Christopher Preksta, Ashley Urbaniak. *Director:* Christopher Preksta. *Writer:* Aaron Kleiber, Christopher Preksta, Ben Shull. **Comment:** Clever mix of black and white and color images. While not an original idea, it is well presented (although it drags in places) with good acting and comedy spread throughout the production.

Episodes:
1. Episode 1 (5 min., 39 sec.). Colin decides to bring excitement into his life by creating a super hero based on his favorite comic book.
2. Episode 2 (6 min., 59 sec.). Colin begins his quest by hiring friends to become his villains.
3. Episode 3 (5 min., 58 sec.). Colin secures a job on the local newspaper in an attempt to report the crimes he creates.
4. Episode 4 (9 min., 15 sec.). Colin instructs his crew to rob a local hardware store.
5. Episode 5 (7 min., 32 sec.). Colin's plan appears to be working as stories about Captain Blasto appear in the newspaper.
6. Episode 6 (7 min., 4 sec.). Colin feels a super villain is needed and hires a friend to play the comic book's nemesis Professor Fandango.
7. Episode 7 (6 min., 44 sec.). Colin plans his biggest caper yet—robbing patrons at a movie theater.
8. Episode 8 (6 min., 47 sec.). Colin discovers the supposed fake movie theatre theft was not and he is in possession of stolen money.
9. Episode 9 (5 min., 44 sec.). As Colin looks back at what has been happening he realizes that the robberies he staged were carried out as real.
10. Episode 10 (7 min.). Having planned the fake robbery of a church, Colin sets out to stop his gang before they actually rob it.
11. Episode 11 (9 min., 58 sec.). Believing he actually has super powers, Colin, as Captain Blasto, decides to capture his gang and bring them to justice.

72 *Captain Canuck.* youtube.com. 2013 (Animated Fantasy).

Equilibrium is a Canadian-based organization of superheroes that was organized by Michael Evans, the older brother of Tom Evans, alias Captain Canuck. Michael, a scientist, possesses degrees in physics and biology and Tom is not an ordinary superhero. Michael enhanced Tom's body with nanotechnology that not only gave him the abilities of wisdom and strength, but speed and an Eidetic Memory (he can learn simply by watching). He has a strong sense of right and wrong and believes that ignorance and prejudice are the greatest enemies of mankind. Now, as Captain Canuck, Tom battles injustice in a slightly altered world where Canada is a technological superpower.

Redcoat is a top Equilibrium agent and Captain Canuck's constant assistant. She grew up in Brixton in the South of London and is only known by her code name of Redcoat. She learned the lessons of life growing up on the mean streets and at the age of 18 she chose to join a British Army initiative for social undesirables (as she was classified) rather than spending time in jail. The experience changed her life and she distinguished herself in hand-to-hand combat as well as exhibiting extraordinary abilities as a pilot. She was selected to join the SAS Mobility Troop where she became one of their top pilots (one of Lord West's "Redcoats," the shadow arm of the SAS that perform deep-cover espionage missions). When Equilibrium was formed and Lord West became its head, Redcoat also became a member of the organization.

Mister Gold is a billionaire industrialist bent on conquering the world. He was educated at the finest schools and is a master manipulator and funds a weapons manufacturing empire. While he outwardly appears as a gentleman (thanks to his public relations department) he is really brutal and ferocious and takes great pleasure in eliminating anyone who stands in his way. He is secretly financing war and instability around the world and is Tom's number one nemesis.

The Blue Fox is an elusive and deadly killer on which very little is known. She is skilled in the martial arts and is a master assassin. She is also a master of disguise and never lets her targets see she is coming or ever let anyone know she was there. Her services go to the highest bidder but she is always her own master, shifting alliances as she pleases.

Voice Cast: Kris Holden Reid (Captain Canuck), Tatiana Maslany (Redcoat), Laura Vandervoort (Blue Fox), Paul Amos (Mister Gold). **Credits:** *Producer:* Fadi Hakim, Jonas Diamond. *Director:* Sam Chou. *Writer:* Paul Gardner, Dean Heniy. **Comment:** Spectacular animation coupled with a fast-moving story that, unfortunately, ends in an unresolved cliffhanger.

Episodes:

1. Happy Canada Day (4 min., 46 sec.). Captain Canuck and his assistant, Redcoat suspect that the evil Mister Gold will somehow attempt to ruin the Canada Day celebration in his attempts to become ruler of the world.

2. Outfoxed (5 min., 12 sec.). The Captain's suspicions were right as he has detected a bomb that is set to destroy the Parliament Hill, the seat of the Canadian government.

3. Turned Tables (5 min., 13 sec.). As the Captain attempts to diffuse the bomb, he is captured by Mister Gold.

73 *The Carrier.* blip.tv. 2012 (Science Fiction).

At an unspecified time in the near future, personal freedom and the right to make decisions have been taken away from the general public. A secret organization, known as The Network, holds the key to returning society to a time before government control—"the package." The package, however, is never in one place long enough to be found or tracked. A single carrier is in possession of the package and al-

ways in transit, thus protecting it from government officials who want to retrieve it and bring down The Network. Stories follow the Carrier as he seeks to protect the package from those who would do anything to get it, including killing him. For the program, a man named Arthur is the Carrier and his attempts to protect it from the evil government official (Mr. Creed) are depicted (the package is actually a white attaché case that contains vital information regarding the government's handling of a viral outbreak "some 30 or 40 years ago" wherein it had developed a cure but withheld it, causing death to millions of people around the world. No known vile of the cure now exists but it is hinted that "the package" contains the formula, which, if the outbreak should resurface, the government would have the only means of preventing its spread—by manipulating who and what they want; should The Network retain control, all of mankind would be saved).

Cast: Patrick Elliott, Jeff Briggs, Jody Vines, Colleen Guest, Owen Daly, Leah Long, James Kirk Sparks. **Credits:** Producer: Matt Haas, John Ray. Director: Roger Franks. Writer: Roger Franks, Patrick Elliott. **Comment:** Intriguing story but the acting is just not natural with no emotion or ability to convince the viewer as to what is happening (especially in episode 7 when Arthur's father explains the secret of the package, you just want him to say it—don't drag it out). The writing is thus affected because its delivery is often strained. Production values are fine.

Episodes:

1. Pilot. Establishes the storyline as Arthur becomes the new Carrier, taking over a job held by a man named Vic.

2. Episode 2. Creed becomes aware that the package has changed hands.

3. Episode 3. Creed begins plotting to kill Arthur and acquire the package.

4. Episode 4. Arthur becomes suspicions that his actions are being monitored.

5. Episode 5. Creed's plan begins to take effect when he hires an assassin (Sam) to acquire the package.

6. Episode 6. Knowing that he is now being followed, Arthur takes refuge at his father's home and learns that he was the original Carrier.

7. Episode 7. The secret behind the package is revealed.

8. Episode 8. Arthur realizes that the only way to protect the package is for him to kill Creed.

9. Episode 9. Arthur must make a determined decision when he comes face-to-face with Creed.

74 *Casualty.* youtube.com. 2013 (Science Fiction).

In the year 2531 terrorists unleash a deadly virus that begins to affect people in all nations of the world. Affected people are now outcasts, but those who have not been contaminated have a chance to escape what is happening by returning to the past. It is also a time when time travel has been accomplished but the process is a one way trip—once sent back in time, the traveler can never return to his or her present. Dr. Sarah Genesee is one such person who has chosen to return to the past. She has selected the early 21st century and she has been implanted with a medical device that will erase all memories of her life in the future once she reaches her destination. She is also forbidden to bring anything from her time to the past to ensure that her future experiences will not change the past and thus affect the future. The program follows Sarah as she begins a new life in Seattle, Washington, a place she soon discovers is a haven for a secret society of time travelers; and her experiences in her country's past but with memories slowly returning of her life in the future—and what could happen if both worlds should merge.

Cast: Carolynne Wilcox (Dr. Sarah Genesee), Glynis Mitchell (Holly Wells), Trin Miller (Lisa), Ben Andrews (James Wells), Joseph R. Porter (Tony), Gregory Marks (Santa), Ralph Fontaine (Jude), Pearl Klein (Emma), Alexander Roan Andrews (Elijah). **Credits:** *Producer:* Glynis Mitchell, Ralph Fontaine. *Writer:* Glynis Mitchell, Michael Montoure. **Comment:** Based on the pilot episode, the program is intriguing, well acted (although Sarah is the only character profiled), written and directed. Other performers are seen in the trailer but special effects, which are prominent in the pilot (and well done) appear to be encompassed less in future episodes.

Episodes:
1. Dr. Genesee: Year 2531. Establishes the story with Sarah being informed of the consequences of her returning to the past.

Note: There is also a trailer that highlights scenes from additional episodes, but those episodes have not been released.

75 *Cataclysmo and the Battle for Earth.* youtube.com. 2008 (Science Fiction).

A spin off from *Cataclysmo and the Time Boys* (see entry) that reunites time travelers Johnny and Bucky and their present-day earth companion, Samantha, as they attempt to save earth from an army of ravaging gorillas and the effects of Dr. Crankshaft's Cataclysmo diabolical experiments to rule the universe.

Cast: Brian Walton (Johnny Zanzibar), Erin Evans (Samantha), Chris Hartwell (Bucky Stallion), Nate Bell (H.G. Welles), Kal Bennett (Queen of Atlantis), Jai Khalsa (Ameila Earhart), Jesse Grotholson (Dr. Crankshaft). **Credits:** *Producer:* Joshua Sikora, Nathan Jeffers, Chris Hartwell. *Director:* Anthony Parisi. *Writer:* Kevin Christensen, Anthony Parisi, Joshua Sikora. **Comment:** All episodes have been withdrawn thus accessing the program is not possible.

76 *Cataclysmo and the Time Boys.* you tube.com. 2007–2008 (Science Fiction).

A war has broken out in a futuristic time period. It is theorized that the war can be stopped from happening if it never occurred. To accomplish the task, a time machine is built and two young men (Johnny and Bucky) are chosen to return to the earth of 2007 and prevent a mad scientist (Dr. Crankshaft) from setting in motion the events that will lead to war in the future. Johnny and Bucky are sent back in time and, in 2007, they immediately befriend a girl of the time, Samantha, who agrees to help them after she is convinced they are who they say—people from the future (when Bucky proves it by demonstrating his ray gun). The program follows the trio as they try to stop a disaster before it happens. See also *Cataclysmo and the Battle for Earth*, the spin off series.

Cast: Brian Walton (Johnny Zanzibar), Erin Sullivan (Samantha), Chris Hartwell (Bucky Stallion), Jesse Groth Olson (Dr. Crankshaft), Kenlyn Kanouse (Mildred Crankshaft). **Credits:** *Producer:* Joshua Sikora. *Director:* Kevin Christensen. *Writer:* Kevin Christensen, Anthony Parisi, Joshua Sikora. **Comment:** Only the first five of 24 produced episodes remain online (and only at the official website). These episodes present some insight into Johnny and Bucky's life in the future (where Johnny is a soldier and Bucky a chef) and how they travel back in time (via a glowing force field overseen by H.G. Welles) to stop Dr. Crankshaft, meet Samantha and deal with gorilla warriors from their time who have used the force field to wreck havoc on earth. Although not view-able, the remaining episodes relate the trio's efforts to defeat the diabolical Dr. Crankshaft. The special effects are minimal, the gorillas are obvious as actors in costume, and similar ideas have been done before, but the program is, with its mix of comedy and science fiction, well done and amusing to watch (at least in what is available).

Episodes: *1.* Under Crimson Sky. *2.* They Died with Their Pants On. *3.* In the Land of the Blind. *4.* Men Like Gods. *5.* The House at the End of the World. *6.* Strangers in a Strange Land. *7.* The Day the Internet Stood Still. *8.* Meanwhile, in the Underwater Lab... *9.* Across the Stars. *10.* Gorillas in the Midst. *11.* Monkey Bar Skirmish. *12.* A Close Call. *13.* Trapped Under the Tide. *14.* The Underwater Demise. *15.* Forget Me Not. *16.* Sands of Chaos. *17.* The Origin of the Species. *18.* The Food of the Gods and How It Came to Earth. *19.* The Shape of Things to Come. *20.* Blockade Runners. *21.* The Last Stand. *22.* Heart of Darkness. *23.* The Good, the Mad and the Ugly. *24.* There's No Place Like Home.

77 *Chronicles of Humanity.* chronicles ofhumanity.com. 2011 (Science Fiction).

In the year 2340, a devastating accident destroys a mining colony on the planet Titan. One person,

Katherine McDonald, a television journalist (for SBC News) covering an uprising occurring within the colony becomes convinced that it was no accident (due to faulty equipment) and that the government was behind it.

Katherine has established herself as a well-respected and trusted journalist. Her assignment to cover the Titan uprising was her first job on another planet. Admiral Yasuko is the commander of the Earth Navy (which defends Earth from alien invaders). She commands the flagship *Praetorian*. The Agent, a spy and assassin, has been hired by Yasuko and it is believed she incorporates his services for the better good (he is a known spy but all his files are highly classified and no information has been released). Captain Heyman is skipper of the ENF (Earth Navy Force) *Hellstrom*, a patrol ship that assists civilians in trouble. Commander Fuller is a firm believer that aliens exist although in such a future time, no evidence has been found to support it (sort of contradicts Admiral Yasuko's job). Fulmer joined the Navy to explore space and hopefully encounter an extraterrestrial (she is also a member of the Unity of Species, an organization that searches for signs of alien life). Her current assignment is Executive Officer aboard the *Hellstrom*. Adam Halesberth is the pilot of the *Nightingale*, a small transport ship that carries cargo between Earth and the colonies. Ravyn Halesberth is Adam's wife and co-pilot. Amanda Wood is Katherine's friend and an anchor on the SBC television newscasts.

Voice Cast: Elizabeth Cameron (Katherine McDonald), Kim Genly (Admiral Yasuko), Damien Valentine (The Agent), Richard Grove (Captain Rex Heyman), Ingrid Moon (Elaine Fulmer), Charlie Allen-Wall (Adam Halesberth), Felicia Day (Amanda Wood), Gabrielle Pugliese (Ravyn Halesberth). **Credits:** *Producer-Director:* Damien Valentine. *Writer:* Kim Genly, Damien Valentine. **Comment:** Poorly computer animated project. The characters are stiff, the movement jerky and the program just difficult to watch for its entire run. The story is good but its animated presentation is rather lifeless.

Episodes:

1. Titan (7 min., 16 sec.). Faulty equipment causes a mining disaster on Titan, a moon of Saturn.

2. Aftermath (11 min., 53 sec.). A rescue ship is dispatched to help the survivors of Titan.

3. Counteraction (8 min., 20 sec.). Ravyn and Adam, two of the rescue team, arrive on Titan to begin rescue operations.

4. Crossroads (7 min., 15 sec.). Katherine, a reporter assigned to cover the story, begins her investigation of the accident.

5. Contagion (12 min., 20 sec.). Following her experiences on Titan, which has left her devastated by what she saw, Katherine and the crew of the ship *Nightingale* embark for the distant desert planet of Lubyanka, the home of a newly established prison colony.

6. The Red Planet (9 min., 24 sec.). The *Nightingale* continues its journey as it approaches Mars where a conference about possible alien life is being discussed.

7. Breakdown (8 min., 7 sec.). When sensitive government documents are stolen from Navy Headquarters on Earth and transmitted to Katherine, she comes under suspicion as being a traitor.

8. Insurgency (15 min., 18 sec.). Katherine's continual probe of the Titan incident brings her closer to uncovering the truth but her investigation also incites a rebellion against the government.

9. Breakout (6 min., 13 sec.). Believing that her actions caused the rebellion, Katherine finds herself being imprisoned as the rebellion continues to spread.

10. Forward (7 min., 28 sec.). Katherine, aided by Ethan escape from prison and return to Earth. Learning what has happened, Admiral Yasuko and The Agent, begin a hunt for them.

11. Fugitives (11 min., 39 sec.). Katherine and Ethan, now considered fugitives, continue with their mission by breaking into the government's office.

12. Politics (9 min., 59 sec.). Katherine manages to broadcast what has happened—with the government countering the rebel broadcast with assurance that it has the best interest of its colonies at heart.

13. Rebellion (15 min., 49 sec.). The government broadcast fails to convince everyone and additional rebellions are breaking out with people of Earth colonies now willing to fight for their freedom from the government's rule.

14. Tactics (9 min., 34 sec.). As the situation worsens, Captain Yasuko implements martial law on Earth and begins preparations to secure other colonies with military force.

15. Death (8 min., 42 sec.). The uprising continues with rebels preparing their campaign against the government.

16. End (11 min., 22 sec.). The confrontation between the rebels and the government could determine the future of the Earth and its colonies.

78 *Chronicles of Syntax.* chroniclesofsyntax.co.uk. 2013 (Fantasy).

Unknown to virtually all of the population there are special people that have been assimilated into society. These individuals possess traces of information that are locked deep within their DNA and hold the key to preventing a forecast apocalypse. Sian Lovat and Steven Bramwell are two such people. They are part of a larger group of such individuals and only when all members are found and assembled as a group will their memories become unlocked and their abilities combined to prevent a future disaster. In the meantime, Sian (later called Syntax) and Steven, agents for The Fallen Angels Network, a secret facility of the British government, perform missions that will enable them to meet others like them and hopefully convince them to join their cause. Episodes relate Sian and Steven's experiences as they seek their ultimate goal: regain their memories and discover who or what they really are.

Cast: Laura O'Donoughue (Sian Lovat), Liam Dryden (Kairan Fisher), Victoria Hopkins (The Lady), Daniel Tyler-Smith (Steven Bramwell), Lucy Meredith (Kelly Gilforth), Anna Wilde (Trystanne), Tara Muir (Heather Falkirk), Dita Tantang (Shia), Richard Buxton (James Black), Sarah Pitard (Liza), Rachel Lucy (Daynah Donoughue), Chris Holbrook (Chell), Ronin Traynor (Hemlock). **Credits:** *Producer:* Susan E. Clarke, April Kelley, Ian Wilson. *Director:* Jack Ayers. *Writer:* Susan E. Clarke. **Comment:** Although the episodes are rather long for a web series, they are fast moving, well produced and acted and enjoyable to watch.

Episodes:
1. The One That Ran Away (36 min., 32 sec.). Sian and Steven are assigned to find a new team member (Kia).
2. A Fighting Choice (29 min., 43 sec.). For her next assignment Sian seeks a woman named Trystanne.
3. Head Strong, Heart Strong (37 min., 3 sec.). A former police officer (Heather Falkirk) uncovers the existence of the Fallen Angels Network.
4. Taking Candy (23 min., 46 sec.). As Trystanne begins to work independently of the team (feeling she can accomplish things on her own), it is learned that something sinister is threatening them.
5. Carnage (25 min., 3 sec.). An assignment involves Sian in a dangerous situation when she infiltrates the criminal underworld.
6. Sugar and Ice (29 min., 26 sec.). Timid team member Kai risks his life to help Sian escape from the underworld.

79 Chronicles of the Dead. chroniclesoft hedead.com. 2012 (Horror).

While at a party a young man (Winston) becomes attracted to a young woman, who unknown to him, has been infected with a zombie virus. As they become romantic, the girl bites Winston and infects him with the virus. As his life begins to change, and with the help of his best friend, Omar, Winston seeks a cure for his affliction before he becomes a creature of the undead that feeds on human brains.

Cast: Brad Watson (Winston Porter), Erin Feaster (Elizabeth Studor), Sione (Omar Harris), Elizabeth Smith (Sarah Daniels), Stuart Arthur (Roman Daniels), Catherine Gilman (Vanessa Sands), Devin Flannagan (Danny Kato), Brandon Olsen (Andrew Delaney). **Credits:** *Producer:* Monica Louise Bryant, John Marshall, Danny Guerrero. *Director:* John Marshall. *Writer:* Mary Louise Bryant, John Marshall. **Comment:** A take off on the zombie feature films of the 1930s and 40s (like *White Zombie* and *I Walked with a Zombie*) that is played more for laughs than anything else. The camera work, directing, writing and acting are amateurish and there is no real interest to see what happens after the first episode or what becomes of Winston as he tries to adjust to becoming a zombie.

Episodes:
1. Pilot (11 min., 48 sec.). Winston's life begins to change when he becomes infected with a zombie virus.
2. Denial (6 min., 42 sec.). Winston, feeling the urge to feed on humans, seeks a way to resist the temptation.
3. Anger (7 min., 19 sec.). Now, fully aware as to what has befallen him, Winston and Omar begin a quest to find a cure.
4. Bargaining (6 min., 17 sec.). Omar tries to help Winston overcome his increasing desire for human nourishment.
5. Regret (5 min., 22 sec.). Winston and Omar seek help from a man who appears to know what has befallen Winston.
6. Acceptance (6 min., 44 sec.). Winston tries to come to terms with what he has become.
7. Hope (7 min., 38 sec.). Winston realizes there is no hope for a cure and he must accept what he has become.

80 The Cipher Effect. thecithereffect.com. 2013 (Science Fiction).

It is the year 2013 and limited time travel has been perfected. It is also a time when the Earth is being devastated by mysterious wormholes (which, in turn are causing an apocalypse). To hopefully stop what is happening in the present, a scientist is sent back in time one year to find a physicist at the Fairwater Physics Lab and hopefully prevent the wormholes from occurring in the future. A side effect of time travel is the Cipher Effect—he is forgotten by people he has met in the past—even though he may again meet them in the future. The story, limited to only a pilot film, charts the beginning of his journey.

Cast: Dee Marshall (Beth), Beau Ballinger (Scientist). **Credits:** *Producer:* Phillip Hudson, Glen Settle. *Director:* Phillip Hudson. *Writer:* Glen Settle. **Comment:** Good special effects and a promising storyline but thus far only a short pilot film has been released. Beau Ballinger as the scientist plays the role well, somewhat confused as to what is happening to him, yet eager to adjust to his new time while Dee Marshall as Beth plays the wide-eyed girl who, at first can't believe what she is witnessing, but aligns herself to him for the greater good.

Episodes:
1. Pilot Film (7 min., 40 sec.). Establishes the fact that something is wrong when a girl (Beth) witnesses the scientist's appearance (in a glowing ball of light) and agrees to help him in his quest.

The Cipher Effect. **Dee Marshall and Beau Ballinger (copyright Phillip Hudson, Rhinomotion Productions).**

81 *Co-Op of the Damned.* coopofthedamn ed.com. 2012 (Horror).

A seemingly normal Manhattan apartment building provides the setting for anthology-like stories about the supernatural residents of the building, or as they have been called, roommates from Hell.

Cast: Varied by episode, see episode listing. **Credits:** *Producer:* Holy Bailey, Brian Steele, Ned Ehibar. **Comment:** Short, right-to-the-point horror stories that are well calculated to present comical takes on traditional horror stories. Desiree Cooper, in the "Puppet from Hell" segment is especially endearing as the little girl unknowingly being sized up for a killing by her puppet but who constantly foils his attempts by snuggling him.

Episodes:

1. Party Killer (2 min., 33 sec.). A masked killer (reminiscent of Jason from *Halloween*) crashes a party—but, being his first "job" can't figure out who to kill first. Starring Marcus Jones, Andrea Bosch, Kennelin Stadwick.

2. The Naked Dead (2 min., 11 sec.). A man begins to question his sanity when only he and no one else can see a beautiful naked girl when night falls (the girl is discreetly covered by objects around his apartment). Starring Kendra Montagne, Jim Fastante.

3. Puppet from Hell (2 min., 36 sec.). The spirit of a serial killer, called "The Kiddie Killer" has been cursed to spend eternity as a puppet. He is now in the possession of a young girl who calls him "Mr. Snuggleface." Mr. Snuggleface is anything but happy and plots to kill the little (annoying to him) girl who now owns him. Starring: Desiree Cooper.

4. Rosemary's Other Baby (2 min., 49 sec.). A young couple, new to the building are asked to become surrogate parents to the Devil—but later rejected when research reveals that the wife has lead too good a life. Starring: B.J. Gallagher, Rebekka Johnson, Robert Valderraman.

5. Sexorcist (3 min., 21 sec.). A man attempts to curtail his wife's sexual activities by performing a "sexorcism" (tying her to her bed and preventing her from doing anything). Starring: Avi Rothman, Enzo Milieti, Steve Benaquist.

6. Hell's Kitchen (3 min., 50 sec.). The Devil, requiring new digs, rents Apartment 29 to carry out his Hell sentencing—beginning with a man who is sentenced to wash dishes for eternity. Starring: Will Greenberg, Holly Hyman, Rosie Tisch.

7. Braaaaiinss (2 min., 34 sec.). A young woman has fallen in love with two men and must choose one: her human boyfriend or her zombie lover (the title is an exaggerated take on "Brains" as zombies thrive on them). Starring: Jamie Renee Smith, Chris Marquette, Paul Teller.

8. Vacancy (2 min., 8 sec.). A new apartment becomes available but the rental agent finds herself faced with a tough job finding a tenant willing to live among supernatural beings. Starring: Lizzy Cooperman, Melissa Cueva.

82 *Continuum.* youtube.com. 2012–2013 (Science Fiction).

A young woman (Raegan) awakens to find herself aboard a space ship with no memory of who she is or how she came to be aboard the craft. As she explores the craft, which is adrift in deep space, she is disturbed by the disembodied voice of a young girl that speaks to her. When she discovers the voice is emanating from the ship's computer, Raegan requests that the computer (which she names Tara) change its voice to that of a woman. From Tara, Raegan learns that she has been in sleep mode for one year, six months longer than her programmed mission (due to a system malfunction). The craft, Raegan discovers was on a mission, but the system malfunction has apparently deleted the aspects of the mission and Raegan's purpose. As Raegan becomes increasingly uneasy with Tara (who constantly monitors everything she does) she slowly begins to have flashes of her prior life, including moments with her fiancé, Tipton—whom Raegan later discovers is also aboard the ship—and whom Tara believes is a threat to Raegan's mission. As Raegan struggles to recall who she is and the purpose of her mission, she comes to realize that she built Tara but can she now trust her? Stories follow Raegan as she seeks to uncover the memories of her past, why she is adrift in space and whether Tipton is a friend or someone out to kill her.

Cast: Melanie Merkosky (Raegan), Brad Hawkins (Tipton), Taryn O'Neill (Computer Voice). **Credits:** *Producer-Writer-Director:* Blake Calhoun. **Comment:** Fast-moving, well acted story with good writing and directing. The sets are authentic looking and the computer and special effects well done.

Episodes:

1. Supernova Caine. Establishes the story line as Raegan awakens aboard a ship adrift in deep space.

2. The Eagle Has Landed. Raegan soon discovers that the ship is controlled by a computer with a child-like voice.

3. Step Back to the Future. After finding that the computer is unable to help her, Raegan begins an exploration of the ship.

4. Event Horizontal. Raegan's search uncovers another passenger and begins to question him.

5. Han Solist. Raegan's questioning of the man she found reveals that he is Tipton, her fiancé.

6. Two Close Encounters. As Raegan and Tipton form a team, he begins to remember incidents from their past, but the computer has warned Raegan that Tipton cannot be trusted.

7. Lost in My Space. As Tipton recalls moments from his and Reagan's past, Raegan comes to believe that for some reason, the computer is seeking to drive them apart with its concerns.

8. The Ex-Terminator. Tipton discovers the computer is a virus and the purpose of his (and Raegan's) mission—to kill the computer, which escaped before it could be destroyed.

9. A Space Oddity. Tipton believes that their only option is to destroy the computer and reprogram the ship to return to Earth.

10. The Terminator's Salvation. Having programmed the computer Raegan realizes that if they destroy the computer to kill the virus then they will also destroy themselves as Tara controls the ship.

11. Solo System. As Tara deducts that Tipton and Raegan are plotting against her, she continues to warn Raegan that Titpon is the enemy.

12. Houston, We've Got Another… A flashback is used to recall incidents in the lives of Raegan and Tipton before their mission.

13. The Empress Strikes Back. Believing that Tipton really is who he claims to be, Raegan attempts to convince him that she loves him also.

14. Minority Reporting. Raegan realizes the computer is the virus and that she helped to create it.

15. Artificial Intelligence. Raegan and Tipton devise a plan to destroy the computer but encounter a setback when the computer reveals that she loves Raegan and will protect her at all costs.

16. The Wrath of a Con. To confuse the computer so that their plan can work, Raegan attempts to distract it (by threatening to kill herself) while Tipton works to disable it.

17. Phone Home. After removing a panel from the computer's control center, Tipton finds the name D.A.N.L—the name of Reagan's daughter, Danielle, after whom Raegan named the computer.

18. The Final Frontier. Raegan gains control over the ship and reprograms Tara to return to Earth—but Tara has other plans—to reverse time so that Raegan again wakes up aboard the ship with no idea of who she is or how she got there.

83 *Continuum: The Series.* syfy.com. 2012 (Science Fiction).

In the year 2077 world governments are controlled by powerful corporations that have also stripped people of their privacy and basic rights. In one such city, Vancouver, Canada, a group of terrorists, intent on restoring their country to the way it was, begin a series of attacks that, unfortunately, kill thousands of people as well as destroying multiple buildings in their attempt to eradicate the powerful 20 members of the Corporate Board. Seven of the terrorists however, are caught and sentenced to death. But, before they can be executed, they escape. Kiera Cameron, an officer with the futuristic police department, CPS Protector, is assigned to apprehend the escaped terrorists. Her investigation leads her to her target but, as the terrorists are about to use a time machine to escape six years into the past, Kiera intervenes, and all are sent back 65 years into the past to 2012. With time travel not yet developed in 2012, Kiera finds herself trapped—but with a mission to capture the terrorists before they can alter events that could affect the future. Having to conceal her real identity, Kiera pretends to be a detective from the Portland, Oregon Police Department and forms an uneasy alliance with Carlos Fonnegra, a detective with the Vancouver P.D. Before she is able to settle in, the terrorists attack police headquarters in an effort to kill Kiera, the only person who stands in their way. Accepting Kiera for who she claims to be, the police chief (Dillon) partners her with Carlos to bring down the terrorists (Liber8). Stories relate their efforts—aided more by Kiera when she befriends Alec Sadler, a teenage tech genius who will become the future technological genius responsible for the development of time travel, when one of his inventions allows him to communicate with Kiera and see through her eyes or replay events she has witnessed.

Kiera Cameron is a detective with the Vancouver City Protective Services (CPS). She is married to Greg and the mother of a seven-year-old son (Sam). But that is in her future and her separation from them causes her great pain and she is determined to find a way back to them—and she knows the only way that can happen is to preserve her future by stopping Liber8. When her cover as a police detective is blown, she poses as a member of a government anti-terrorist group called Section 6.

Carlos Fonnegra is a dedicated detective who helps Kiera—hoping to reunite her with her family although he is unaware that she is from the future. He is the son of immigrant parents (his father was killed by drug lords, forcing his mother to flee to America). He grew up in poverty and knows what suffering is all about. He married at a young age and the marriage ended soon after making Carlos aware of what it means to make a commitment.

Sonya Valentine is a former research scientist for the corporate military turned opportunist. She is attractive and cunning and her interest in genetics led her to create a stronger human that could survive the next great disaster. She created the future super soldier program and, against her will, was forced to use humans (such as Travis Verta) as test subjects to the point of their deaths. To survive the ordeal, she numbed herself as to what she was doing. This all changed when she traveled back in time, met Travis (before he was a test subject) and became drawn to him. But she is also trapped in the present and is being drawn closer to Liber8.

Travis Verta is one of Sonya's creations, a man who has been enhanced through futuristic science to be a lethal killing machine. He was a conventional soldier that was chosen to become a test subject and now feels his freedom has been taken away as he must follow orders without question and destroy the enemy without remorse.

Alec Sadler is a 17-year-old whiz kid and the future hope of mankind (although he is not aware of that until after he meets Kiera). His father was a genius who became wealthy through the technology he created. When his father passed and Alec found his diagrams and devices, Alec picked up where his father left off. Knowing what the future holds has also made Alec uneasy as he now wonders if he chose his own path or has destiny already set it for him.

Matthew Kellogg is a master manipulator, trained as a psychologist, who created a hedonistic paradise until he was caught and sent to prison. Even with the restrictions of prison, Matthew managed to secure an early release by digging up dirt on the warden. It was at this time that he met Kagame and joined in the revolution as a means to create a world that would serve his own unethical means.

Lucas Ingram is, in the future, a scientist working for Alec's firm Sadler's Sad Tech. But in the present he is one of the Liber8 (in the future Lucas developed a weapon that could bend time for the military. However, when he realized that his inventions were being used for evil, he balked and was falsely accused of being a traitor. Fearing for his life, Lucas joined the rebels when he was given a sense of belonging).

Inspector Dillon is a no-nonsense, old school cop. As a beat cop he earned the nickname "No Compromise Dillon" when he arrested his uncle for running a numbers racket. To Dillon the law is the law and affiliations do not matter. He detests being kept in the dark or having authority thrust upon him.

Continuum. Melanie Merkosky as Raegan (copyright Loud Pictures).

Cast: Rachel Nichols (Kiera Cameron), Victor Webster (Carlos Fonnegra), Erik Knudsen (Alec Sadler), Stephen Lobo (Matthew Kellogg), Jennifer Spence (Betty Robertson), Lexa Doig (Sonya Valentine), Omari Newton (Lucas Ingram), Roger

R. Cross (Travis Verta), Luvia Petersen (Jasmine Garza), Richard Harmon (Julian Randol), Brian Markinson (Insp. Dillon), Janet Kidder (Ann Sadler Randol), Tony Amendola (Edouard Kagame), John Reardon (Greg Cameron). **Credits:** *Producer:* Pat Williams, Simon Barry, Jeff King, Matthew O'Connor, Lisa Richardson. *Director:* Pat Williams, David Frazee, Mike Rohl, William Waring, Jon Cassar, Paul Shapiro, Amanda Tapping, Rachel Talalay. *Writer:* Simon Barry, Jonathan Walker, Jeremy Smith, Floyd Kane, Andrea Stevens, Sam Egan, Jeff King, Shelley Eriksen. **Comment:** Although a bit talkative at times, the well-done story does move along making for a suspenseful outing. The acting and production values are also very good.

Episodes:

1. A Stitch in Time. Depicts the terrorists (from the Liberate group) escaping into the past. With Kiera also swept back in time, she contacts Alec Sadler, the genius who will control events in her future, for help.

2. Fast Times. When Kiera's Portland detective cover is blown, Alec creates a profile depicting her as a government agent in deep undercover so that no one can figure out who she is. Kiera also learns that the terrorists are seeking a way back to their time— something she needs to follow closely if she is to return to her husband and son.

3. Wasting Time. A series of strange deaths (victims with cylindrical holes in the back of their necks) leads Kiera and Carols to discover that a special gene that would be used in a futuristic super soldier, have been removed.

4. Matter of Time. Kiera and Carlos investigate the murder of a professor who was experimenting with a high energy device—something she believes could be used by the terrorist as his notes were also stolen.

5. A Test of Time. In a devious plan to rid himself of Kiera, head terrorist Edouard Kagame, plots to kill Kiera's grandmother (Lily Cole) so that Kiera will never be born.

6. Time's Up. The terrorists have begun inciting violent protests and Kiera believes that the powerful corporation, Exotrol, may be assisting them.

7. The Politics of Time. Kiera and Carlos begin an investigation into the death of a woman Carlos knew and whom Kiera suspects was somehow involved with the terrorists.

8. Playtime. Two strange suicides (where the killers committed suicide after eliminating their victims) leads Kiera to a gaming company developing an immense holographic program—and into a trap when Edouard tests the game on her and disrupts her internal abilities, putting her in his control. Alec begins a desperate attempt to "reboot" her.

9. Family Time. A large purchase of farm fertilizer arouses Kiera's suspicions as it could be used by the terrorists to build a bomb when mixed with chemicals.

10. End Times. Kiera meets a man (Jason) who claims he is from the year 2077 and was in the control room when she and the terrorists were sent back in time. Only he was sent back to 1992 and has waited 20 years for his meeting with Kiera—to warn her that on this day the terrorists will set off a bomb that will change the future forever.

11. Second Chances. As the terrorist attacks continue, Kiera and Carlos are too late to stop one in which the Mayor is killed.

12. Split Second. Kiera begins to suspect there is a mole in the police department as the terrorists are always one step ahead of her.

13. Second Thoughts. Kiera suspects that members of a biker gang (the Coalition Kings) are responsible for the mayor's killing and that a woman (Sonya) is seeking to unite biker gangs to join with the terrorists (called the Liber8).

14. Second Skin. When Alec's sensor picks up the fact that another time traveler has arrived in 2012, Kiera sets out to find her (turns out to be her friend Elena, who is later killed by the terrorists).

15. Second Opinion. With concern that there is a mole within the department, Dillon is replaced by Insp. Nora Harris, who is determined to uncover the informant.

16. Second Truths. Carlos's suspicions are aroused about Kiera when they investigate a murder case involving a serial killer and Kiera, who had studied the case in 2077, states that there were 38 victims and the killer was never caught.

17. Second Degree. Kiera becomes bitter when she visits the grave of a friend (Elena) only to discover her body has been removed (she suspects it to be someone who knew she was from the future).

18. Second Listen. Kiera, teaming with an agent from the CSIS (Gardiner) learns that two additional bodies have been stolen from a morgue; their efforts to locate them or who was behind the snatchings prove fruitless.

19. Seconds. In an unexpected turn of events, Dillon is re-instated as the chief and he is now authorized to stop Liber8. It is believed that Julian Randall, a suspected terrorist, is the key to uncovering the person behind Liber8.

20. Second Wave. Alec unknowingly becomes a threat to Kiera when his girlfriend (Emily) gives him a new phone that transmits everything he does to the head of Liber8.

21. Second Guess. A sudden cyber attack that not only affects the Internet but traffic signals and ATM's as well, has Kiera concerned over what Lyber8's plans are as these events may have already affected her future.

22. Second Last. Kiera is more fearful for her life when Agent Gardner is killed. Alec, close to developing time travel, warns Kiera that history has already been changed and what she once had in the future may no longer exist.

23. Second Time. The cliff-hanging conclusion

wherein Kiera and Carlos uncover the plot for stealing the corpses while Alec, bitter over Emily's death vows to bring her killer to justice, thus complicating the Lyber8 investigation.

84 *Count Gore De Vol's Creature Feature.*
countgore.com. 1998 (Horror).

The earliest Internet horror series wherein the "classic" horror films of the 1930s through the 1980s are streamed and hosted by the vampire Count Gore De Vol. In addition to the Count's comical hosting, the program also features celebrity interviews. The program is based on the local Washington, D.C., television series *Creature Feature* that ran from 1973 to 1987 and was hosted by Dick Dyszel as M.T. Graves.

Cast: Dick Dyszel (Count Gore De Vol). **Credits:** Not available. **Comment:** Like the pioneering television horror host, John Zacherley in the 1950s and 60s and the sexy Cassandra Peterson as Elvira of the 1980s, Count De Gore is an enjoyable presentation that takes forgettable horror films and attempts to breathe a new life into them.

Episodes: 434 episodes were shown, most of which are no longer online. They comprised a mix of independently produced films and re-edited versions of horror motion pictures. Among the feature films presented were *Doctor of Doom, Terror from Beneath the Earth, I Was a Teenage Werewolf, How to Make a Monster, The Giant Gila Monster, Frankenstein vs. the Creature from Blood Cave, House on Haunted Hill, Revolt of the Zombies.* Independent film titles include *Tibs, The Tunnel, Year of the Ox, Mesmerize, Death Scene, Beyond, Happy Meal Horror* and *Stranded.*

85 *Craig and the Werewolf.* tv.com. 2009 (Horror).

Craig and Brett and are roommates with everything apparently normal as the two get along with each other. One day, Craig returns unexpectedly and sees that Brett is a werewolf and eating a victim in their apartment. Brett admits to the fact and Craig sort of accepts it as he doesn't want to move and lose his security deposit. Complications ensue when Brett is bitten, becomes a werewolf and both must now try to live two lives—ordinary people and werewolves when the moon is full.

Cast: Craig Frank (Craig), Brett Register (Brett), Haley Mancini (Haley), Katy Stoll (Katy), Angie Cole (Angie), Daniel Norman (Daniel). **Credits:** *Producer-Writer-Director:* Brett Register. **Comment:** Comical parody of the werewolf legend with a focus on how a werewolf adjusts to everyday life (and eats people). The acting and production values are good but the werewolf eating people aspect is so badly presented (and so obviously overplayed) that it distracts from the overall intention of the program.

Episodes:
1. I, Roommate. Craig returns to the apartment early to see Brett devouring his latest victim.
2. While Grown Men Sleep. Brett admits to Craig that he is a werewolf—and Craig accepts the fact as long as he keeps his distance.
3. I'm Going Through Changes. Living with a werewolf isn't as easy as Craig thought when Brett bites him.
4. What Beautiful Eyes You Have. Craig's efforts to romance his girlfriend (Haley) backfire when he tries to tell her what he really is and she mistakes him for being gay.
5. Requiem for a Werewolf. Craig assures Haley that he is not gay—but a werewolf. She, in turn surprises him—she is a vampire.
Note: The following second season episodes have been taken off-line: *6. Worst Werewolf Ever. 7. This Sucks. 8. The Intervention. 9. When Trojan Horses Collide. 10. Let's Face the Music and Slay.*

86 *The Crawling Dead.* crawlingdead.com. 2013 (Horror).

A young couple, Rachel and Eric York, expecting their first child, have purchased their first home and have just moved in when the program begins. Unknown to them, their Realtor, Burt Fleming (who also claims to be a doctor and monster hunter) has used the basement for a back alley abortion clinic—but as a clinic for the birth (and his killing) of zombie babies. The program follows the events that occur as Rachel and Eric slowly come to realize that all is not right with their new dream home.

Cast: Lindsey Davis (Rachel York), Elvis McComas (Eric York), Brian Gunnoe (Burt Fleming), Missy Dawn (Susan Wilcott), Whitlee Flinn (Veronica), Bianca Barnett (Marjorie), Lindsey Rae Gunnoe (Janice), Stephen Hensley (Mr. Wilcott), Angela Pritchett (Meg Cobb), Nick McGrew (Felix Wilcott). **Credits:** *Producer:* Miles Reed, Jackson Simpkins, Missy Dawn, Brandon Thomas Black. *Writer-Director:* Eamon Hardiman. **Comment:** The first episode is a grabber as you do not know what to expect until the last few seconds of the story. The zombie makeup on the young woman in episode 1 is exceptionally well done—but from that point on, and beginning with the second episode, it becomes a slow-moving story of who cares what happens next. The accompanying tag to buy the DVD version "with all the nudity and gore" sort of explains why the web series suffers as all the "good stuff" has been edited out. If interested, the program is well acted and produced.

Episodes:
1. Episode 1 (5 min., 57 sec.). Sets up the story before Rachel and Eric's appearance with a gorgeous young woman giving birth to a zombie baby—and it being destroyed by Burt in his basement abortion clinic.

2. Episode 2 (6 min., 24 sec.). Rachel and Eric move into what they believe is their dream home.

3. Episode 3 (8 min., 48 sec.). As the couple settle in, a pregnant Rachel becomes uneasy as she feels all is not right with their home.

4. Episode 4 (6 min., 38 sec.). In an unusual situation, the episode has been pulled from all sharing websites with no explanation given (not even a description).

5. Episode 5 (5 min., 45 sec.). The concluding episode that finds Rachel suspecting something is terribly wrong (and not realizing that Burt may be her biggest fear). Is she carrying a zombie baby? Ends without a conclusion.

87 The Crazies Motion Comic. otakusandgeeks.com. 2010 (Horror).

Ogden Marsh is a small, rural Iowa town that is literally destroyed by a tainted water supply (occurring when a military plane, containing an alien, crashes into the town's bog). Most of the town's inhabitants have become infected (physical and mental degradation) and are now a dangerous threat to those who have remained immune. The program follows a group of unaffected people as they struggle to live within the government-contained town (to prevent the spread of the disease and until a cure can be found).

Voice Cast: James Arnold Taylor (Nathan), Daniel Spink (Jesse), Heath Freeman (Red), Kyle Newman (Pvt. Babcock), Dean Paris (Infected). **Credits:** *Producer:* Jeff Krelitz, Andy Collen. *Director:* Kyle Newman. *Writer:* Marc Andreyker. **Comment:** Inspired by the George Romero feature film, the program uses animated comic panels with moving backgrounds, music and special effects. The voice talent, drawings and writing are very good and the series, despite its short length, is worth watching.

Episodes:

1. Hopman Bog. A military plane, with an alien hitchhiker, crashes into the Ogden Marsh bog, spreading a deadly madness virus.

2. Ogden Marsh. The government quarantines the town as Ground Zero in an effort to contain "The Crazies" and prevent the spread of the disease.

3. Dwyer Creek. Explores how the madness affects seemingly normal people.

4. Black Pond. As the disease spreads, survivors have taken to securing themselves from The Crazies who are on the prowl.

88 The Crew. youtube.com. 2007–2009 (Science Fiction).

It is the distant future and space is now being explored. The U.S. has a number of vessels that can travel great distances into the atmosphere and to other planets and one such ship is the *Azureas*. Unfortunately, the *Azureas* is not equipped with the most intelligent or effectual crew in the fleet (sort of its misfits). Stories relate the missions undertaken by the *Azureas*, missions that are accomplished more by accident than anything else.

Cast: Philip Bache (Tom Wilkerson), Ariel Lazarus (Andrea Lee), Craig Frank (Patrick Fargent), Amy Kline (Jennifer Parker), Michael Hart (Stewart Kobbler), Michelle Exarhos (Sarah Clauson), Cathy Baron (Dr. Talia), Brett Register (Tim Waterson), Angie Coe (Amber), Taryn O'Neill (Corrine), Daniel Norman (Evil Patrick), Robin Thorsen (Agule), Jessica Rose (Map), Payman Benz (Laurent). **Credits:** *Producer-Writer-Director:* Brett Register. **Comment:** Fun space spoof with good acting and production values. The program moves right along and scenes are not dragged out although special effects, while limited, are good for an Internet series.

Episodes:

1. Pilot. Shortly after beginning a mission, an error sensor indicates that an engine coil is malfunctioning, causing the crew to scramble and fix the problem.

2. Last Romantics. Having solved one problem, the crew encounters another as a virus unleashes romantic feelings.

3. Ghost Ship. As their mission continues, the *Azureas* encounters a seemingly uninhabited craft (a ghost ship).

4. Poop Deck. As Kobbler gets stuck cleaning up the engine room, the crew beings an investigation of the ghost ship.

5. An Explanation of Sorts. The crew returns to a cleaned engine room as they complete their mission.

6. Departed. The *Azureas* is assigned to track a mysterious signal that is emanating from deep space.

7. No Escape. The crew indulges in R&R (rest and relaxation) when their ship undergoes a system update.

8. Barfly. Shipmates Amber and Jennifer decide that a night out is called for after months in space aboard the *Azureas*.

9. Verdict. After a night of R&R, the crew returns to the drudge of their jobs.

10. Call the Doctor. As the crew receives a medical checkup, a problem develops in the ship's engine room.

11. Break Ups and Make Ups. The captain's (Tom) affections for Dr. Talia become more apparent, making the girl who loves him, Andrea, jealous.

12. Clones 1. The crew is assigned to investigate a mysterious rock that is floating in space.

13. Clones II. The investigation reveals that the rock was a cloning station and that clones are now attempting to take over the ship.

14. Cloned III. The crew attempts to figure out who is real and who are the clones.

15. The Signal. The crew continues on a course to track down the source of the signal (from episode 6).

16. Survival. The signal leads to the discovery of a black hole—which engulfs the ship then propels it to the other side of the galaxy.

17. Pirates. The other side of the galaxy proves to be unfriendly when the *Azureas* is overtaken by space pirates.

18. A Pirate's Life. The crew investigates the pirate ship and finds a girl with a treasure map on her back.

19. Misguided. Thinking of noting but gold, the crew abandons their mission to return home to seek the treasure indicated on the map.

20. Baby on Board. Jennifer and Tim discuss their future plans while Andrea seeks a way to win Tom's heart.

21. Rendezvous. The season finale finds the crew of the *Azureas* beginning a new mission (that would lead into additional episodes).

89 *Crime Scene X.* koldcast.tv. 2010 (Science Fiction).

Jonathon Moon is a late night radio talk show host (of "Full Moon") known as "The Prince of the Paranormal." Tony Rustic is a veteran L.A.P.D. homicide detective who knows that certain crimes go beyond the ordinary and sometimes into the world of the supernatural. He has teamed with Jonathon and together they use their combined skills to solve bizarre crimes. In the story presented, Jonathon and Tony seek an extraterrestrial serial killer.

Cast: Frank Piciullo (Jonathon Moon), Jeff Prewitt (Tony Rustic), Zarah Mahler (Sarah, Moon's assistant), Marc Mahoney (Killer). **Credits:** *Producer:* Robert LeRoy, Richard Hays. *Writer-Director:* Robert LeRoy. **Comment:** While not a copy, the television series *Something Is Out There* used a similar format. For whatever reason, most of the episodes are no longer view-able and based on what can be seen (although incomplete storyline wise) it appeared to be an interesting series. The acting is good as are the production values and the atmospheric presence given to the Jonathon Moon character.

Episodes: Forty episodes were produced but only the first 12 remain on the official website while sharing sites have only episodes 4 through 12.

90 *CTRL.* webserieschannel.com. 2008 (Fantasy).

Stuart Grundy is an ordinary guy working at an ordinary, boring office job. When his boss spills a liquid (Nestea) on his computer keyboard, Stuart discovers that by using the CTRL key with other keys, he can accomplish amazing things (like using CTRL+B to confront his immature boss; CTRL+Z to return to his past; CTRL+Y to return to the present). The first stand alone web series to be produced by a major broadcast network, NBC (its digital studios division). Based on the short film *CTRL Z* by

Robert Kirbyson (winner at the Sundance Film Festival in 2008).

Cast: Tony Hale (Stuart Grundy), Emy Coligado (Elizabeth), Steve Howey (Ben Piller), Zaden Alexander (Jeremy), Richard Karn (Arthur Piller). **Credits:** *Producer:* Thomas Bannister, Tony Hale, Robert Kirbyson, Barney Oldfield. *Director:* Robert Kirbyson. *Writer:* Robert Kirbyson, Bob Massey. **Comment:** Nicely played, comical fantasy program that is well produced and acted. A change of pace from the normal programs of the genre.

Episodes: (5 minutes each)

1. CTRL. Establishes the premise as Stuart's keyboard becomes infected by a spilt cup of Nestea.

2. CTRL B. By pressing CTRL plus B (for Bold) Stuart receives the ability to confront his boss but only to wind up being fired.

3. CTRL Z (Undo). Stuart breaks into his old office to find that his sticky keyboard has been replaced by a new one.

4. F1 (Help). Elizabeth, Stuart's friend, becomes concerned over his obsession with the keyboard.

5. CTRL C, CTRL V (Copy and Paste). Stuart finds the original keyboard but accidentally makes three copies of himself.

6. CTRL Home. While Stuart tries to figure out how to delete his duplicates, the Home key sends Elizabeth to her parents home in the Philippines.

7. CTRL X. Ben, Stuart's friend becomes aware of the magical keyboard and seeks to acquire it for himself.

8. CTRL Zzzzzzzz. When Stuart replaces the missing Z key with one from another keyboard, it jams in the repeat motion and sends him back to his first day on the job.

9. CTRL Y. Stuart uses the CTRL plus Y (redo) keys to return to the present.

10. CTRL, ALT, DEL. Stuart uses the keys to restart his life.

91 *Cupic: Diary of an Investigator.* blip.tv. 2012 (Science Fiction).

CUPIC (Central Unidentified Phenomenon Investigation Committee) is an organization, funded and composed primarily of members of the scientific community that investigates supposed legitimate cases of unexplained happenings in an effort to reach a scientific conclusion. The program follows team members as they explain what they do (in the presented episodes).

Cast: April Espinoza (Johanna Leoni), Katarina Matusek (Janet Raphael), Dwight Schendel (Murray Douglas), Deidre Bo (Dr. Ruth Max), Mike Sliwa (Gavin Leoni), Curt Belfy (Dr. Arnold Nevin). **Credits:** *Producer-Writer-Director:* Rod Washington. **Comment:** Very talkative program that will easily lose viewers unless they are interested in hearing endless chatter about aliens and UFOs. Although the episodes are short, it takes ten such episodes to lead up to what is probably planned for the future—actual case investigations.

Episodes:

1. Introduction (5 min., 12 sec.). Johanna Leoni, the lead investigator, and other members of CUPIC are introduced.

2. Intro to UFOs (3 min., 46 sec.). Johanna and investigator Murray Douglas explore the world of UFOs (Unidentified Flying Objects).

3. Close Encounters (5 min., 1 sec.). Johanna and Murray begin an examination of a classified CE-1 UFO sighting.

4. Squawker Sightings (5 min., 26 sec.). The team investigate reports of a Squawker (half man, half bird-like creature) being seen by locals in Oregon.

5. Mysterious Aircraft (6 min., 42 sec.). The team tries to make a connection between experimental aircraft (like the X-planes of the 1960s) and UFO sightings.

6. Pilots and the Unknown (5 min., 38 sec.). Team investigator Dr. Gavin Leoni delves into reports of pilots and their encounters with UFOs.

7. Contact (3 min., 57 sec.). The team examines supposed first contacts between humans and aliens.

8. Abductions (5 min., 30 sec.). Investigator Dr. Ruth Marx explores stories of alien abductions.

9. McAllister Affair (5 min., 50 sec.). A case of first contact (the McAllister Affair) is probed.

10. End of Introductions (3 min., 14 sec.). The team prepares for their first actual investigation of a UFO incident.

92 *A Cure for Dead.* acurefordead.com. 2011 (Horror).

It is the future and the entire world is in danger of extinction: a plague has been unleashed that kills people and resurrects them as zombies. A group of scientists, working in secret, develop a serum that can stop the spread of the disease. Their efforts however, seem in vain when a test subject, believed to have been cured, breaks loose, destroys the lab and all but one scientist—Arlin. With all hope seemingly lost, Arlin finds that his work was not in vain—one vile of the cure still exists. Now, unable to continue his work alone, he embarks on a lone journey to a lab in a heavily fortified city over the Nevada border called the District of Nevada. As Arlin journeys, he meets three survivalists (Emma, Cassie and Tread) who have overcome the zombie apocalypse by fighting the enemy as a team. When they realize that Arlin may have the only real means by which to battle the enemy, they join him in his quest. The story follows their treacherous journey as they not only seek the lab, but protect the last surviving vile of "The Cure" so it can be replicated and save mankind.

Cast: Erik Sundquist (Arlin), Ilea Matthews (Cassie), Rae Wright (Emma), Matthew Donaldson (Tread). **Credits:** *Producer:* Matthew Harmon, Wes

Young. *Director:* Wes Young. **Comment:** Difficult to judge on the only two episodes produced. The story does show potential and could have progressed into a thrilling race against time for the survivalists to outwit the zombies and reach their destination.

Episodes:

1. The Doc (6 min., 36 sec.). Establishes the premise as a bio-engineer (Arlin) begins a quest to replicate a serum that can end a deadly zombie disease.

2. It's What's for Dinner (7 min., 45 sec.). Three survivalists join Arlin as he journeys to a well-equipped lab in the District of Nevada.

93 *Cursed.* blip.tv. 2010 (Fantasy).

The Book of Revelations reveals that at one time angels engaged in a rebellion and for the angels that were defeated there was no turning back into the goodness of God. A young woman named Crystal Jones is such a fallen angel and she has vowed to redeem herself and get back into God's graces. But to do so she must kill. Crystal is a single mother (of Harris) and the daughter of Vincent. She works as a hired killer and stories follow Crystal as she seeks redemption in a most unusual way. As she says, "I'm Crystal ... mother, lover, daughter, fallen angel ... and this is my story."

Cast: Yuri Brown (Crystal Jones), James Black (John-Gerard Washington), John Wesley (Vincent Jones), Alex Skinner (Harris Jones), Roy Werner (Thomas Wise). **Credits:** *Producer-Writer:* Yuri Jones. *Director:* Jeff Kanew. **Comment:** The short first episode is very well done with good acting, writing and directing and leaves you wanting for more. The program establishes that Crystal has a connection to the FBI to get information on targets but lacks information as to how Crystal came to know that she needs to become a killer for redemption.

Episodes:

1. Cursed, Episode 1 (7 min., 46 sec.). Introduces Crystal as a fallen angel and hired killer.

94 *Cyphers.* minglemediatv.com. 2010 (Science Fiction).

In New Mexico two corporations are experimenting with mutating plants and animals in an attempt to control the world's water and food supply. If they succeed the course of civilization will be changed forever. The experiment, called The Pandora Project, is a failure and all records of its experiments are destroyed after a mutated seed (from a tomato plant that had been injected with a fish gene [a flounder] to enable it to grow in the cold) is discovered to cause harmful side effects in humans. The seeds, however, have been released into the atmosphere when winds spread them from seeding mature experimental plants. A reporter (Helen Sawyer) who covered the story from the beginning becomes suspicious of a cover up when all evidence of The Pandora Project

Cyphers. **Debrianna Mansini and Frederick Lopez (photograph by David Forlano, copyright A Scary Pants Production, 2010).**

is suddenly disavowed. Stories follow Helen's experiences and those of a group of people who are drawn together by inexplicable phenomena and must now work together to decipher and expose the unethical conspiracy that now reaches beyond their community.

Cast: Debrianna Mansini (Helen Sawyer), Frederick Lopez (Jaxsen Raumer), Carmela Rappazzo, Danielle Reddick (Quinn), Drago Sumonja (Neelam Beckett), Tom Romero, Lori Tirgrath, Jody Hegarty, Jonathan Dixon, Ellen Blake, Vivian Nesbitt, J.D. Garfield, Drew VahnBrun. **Credits:** *Producer:* Debrianna Mansini, Lori Romero, Carmela Rappazzo, David Forlano, Tom Romero. *Writer:* Lori Romero, Debrianna Mansini, V.A. Director: V.A. *Creator:* Debrianna Mansini. *Note:* The director has chosen to remain anonymous and has used V.A. (Vox Anonymous) as the credit. **Comment:** Smooth flowing program that holds your interest from the very first episode. The acting is superior and the production values very good. The exploration of what could result from such mutations could be an on-going concept for the series if Helen is kept from exposing what she has found and stumbles across more hideous abominations.

Episodes:

1. Coincidentia Oppositorium (7 min., 3 sec.). The mystery begins as Helen discovers that The Pandora Project never existed. The episode also explains the meaning of coincidence of opposites and suggests that in the 17th century Sir Francis stumbled upon the same theory of controlling the food and water system.

2. Will-O-Wisp (6 min., 58 sec.). The mystery

deepens and, as Helen discovers, plants were developed and an unexplained drought could be the results of The Pandora Project.

3. A Seed Hidden (6 min., 39 sec.). Helen begins to suffer from the effects of the experiment with throat irritation. A glimpse of the plant experiment is presented.

4. Snow After Fire (5 min., 33 sec.). It is revealed through Helen's investigation that the desert winds spread the mutated seeds and that experiments were conducted on humans.

5. Imaginary Keyholes (6 min., 15 sec.). A young woman (Quinn) begins to have strange experiences—as she was the test subject.

6. The Second Gate (6 min., 34 sec.). The mysterious glowing red flower is seen as Quinn inexplicably acquires the ability to replicate the formula for the mutated seeds.

7. The Egg of the Phoenix (8 min., 34 sec.). Quinn becomes increasingly ill with a strange green rash appearing on her back.

8. When Fishes Fly and Forests Walk (5 min., 53 sec.). The mystery deepens as plants begin emerging from the walls of Quinn's apartment.

9. Where Old Stones Lie Sunning (5 min., 19 sec.). A strange episode that focuses totally on two blue-flower plants as they discuss issues (presumably indicating that the mutated plants will have the ability to communicate with each other).

10. Ten White Ashes (7 min., 15 sec.). It is explained how tomato seeds were mutated with a flounder gene to enable farmers to grow plants in the dead of winter (as flounders are immune to the cold). The program concludes with Helen uncovering the

evidence she needs—but will she be stopped from revealing it?

95 Daemonium. the7thmatrix.com. 2013 (Science Fiction).

In an alternate universe where magic and technology rule and humans co-exist with demons, a rebellion is growing wherein the two factions seek to become the governing power. One human, Razor, has become a leader and stands for the new government image—but first he and his followers must defeat all that stands in their way. The program relates the war between Razor and an enemy that destroys anything that gets in their way. **Cast:** Caro Angus, Erika Boveri, Dany Casco, Paty Ace Vedo. **Credits:** *Producer:* Simon Ratzel, Dany Casco. *Director:* Pablo Pares. **Comment:** Stunningly photographed (visually striking) foreign produced (in Argentina) series that was helmed by Pablo Pare, one of the most respected filmmakers in Latin America. Even though the program is in Spanish and one needs to use the English close captioning, the visual aspects make up for that shortcoming. **Episodes:**

1. Bautismo (Baptism; 13 min.). Focuses on a young school girl who enters a warehouse and is confronted by demons—but is she an innocent or about to be inducted into the demon society?

2. La Hora Cero (The Zero Hour; 23 min.). Having nothing to do with the prior episode and more of an introduction to the series wherein a band of mercenaries seek a wizard to force him to open a portal to the Netherworld so that they may bargain with a demon.

96 Damon Dark. youtube.com. 2006–2011 (Science Fiction).

A continuation of the Australian television series of the same title (1999) after its broadcast cancellation and revision as a web series. Damon Dark, a member of Australia's Department 6 (a secretive organization that protects the Earth from alien invaders) and assisted first by Candy Ryan then Veruca Stone, is a man with a single-mined goal: investigating and uncovering evidence that aliens are a threat to the planet. For Damon it began as a child when he witnessed a UFO sighting, became intrigued by what it could be and set his goal to uncover evidence that life does exist on other planets. In the television version, aliens (in their true form) were not seen as they operated through the human hosts they possessed. The web series expanded on the alien concept when Damon became a member of Transdimensional Control, an organization of friendly aliens that protect the Earth (aliens had become aware of Damon's abilities. When the alien force, Cygnus Collective, became a threat, Transdimensional recruited him to help stop a pending galaxy war). Stories, set mostly on Earth, follow Damon as he incorporates a time portal to investigate reports of alien occurrences. See also *The Young Damon Dark Adventures* and *Vincent Kosmos*, the spin off web series.

Cast: Adrian Sherlock (Damon Dark), Susan Leigh Anderson (Candy Ryan), Niobe Dean (Veruca Stone), Chris Heaven (Vincent Kosmos), Robert Trott (Gary Sutton), Trea Cotton (Dr. Lansing) **Credits:** *Producer:* Adrian Sherlock. **Comment:** Although it does not encompass the high qualities associated with television series, the program holds its own as well done and acted—and what can be done on a very tight budget. The stories are interesting and the series well worth watching. **Episodes:**

1. The Possessed a.k.a. The Bomb. Three arc story (also encompasses the episodes "The Human Host" and "Time as a Weapon") wherein Damon confronts a former Department 6 agent, Gary Sutton, abducted by aliens and returned to Earth with a deadly doomsday bomb.

2. The Time Entity. Explores how Damon, after being dismissed from Department 6 for shooting the serial killer who murdered his girlfriend, becomes an agent for Transdimensional Control.

3. Night of Terror. Damon investigates a situation wherein a father, camping with his two sons, vanishes after a meteorite crashes into their campsite area.

4. The Dark Planet News Broadcast. Damon pilots a space shuttle to investigate a rogue planet that is causing disruptions on Earth.

5. The Ghost. Strange episode wherein Damon finds himself in a haunted house and encounters a ghost with information about what actually happened in the U.S. in Roswell, New Mexico (and what may contained in Area 51).

6. The Souls of Cygnus. Damon faces ghostly survivors of the dead planet Cygnus that are seeking to possess humans and assimilate them into a Collective (similar to the *Star Trek* enemy, the Borg, who assimilate minds as one collective).

7. End Game. Damon faces a terminator called The Destroyer when he investigates an alien complex and is believed to be a traitor. A story arc adventure that incorporates the episodes "Destination Moon," "Earth Base One," "Trial of a Traitor" and "The Destroyer."

8. Terror 9/11. Damon and his former adversary from episode 1, Gary, find themselves transported by the Collective to the World Trade Center thirty minutes before the terrorist attacks.

9. Death Trap. Damon attempts to divert the course of a space shuttle that has been programmed to crash into the sun.

10. The Undertaker. Introduces the character of Vincent Kosmos in an arc story wherein Damon battles an enemy called The Undertaker. Includes the episodes "Dark Revelation," "The Undertaker," "The Time Thief" (the pilot for *Vincent Kosmos*), "The Demon's Embrace" and "Encounter in Space."

11. The Socrad Attack. A four-part story wherein Damon and Vincent battle a robotic enemy called Socrad.

12. Darkness Falls. Damon attempts to escape the spirit of Mary Raven, a deceased doll maker whose evil spirit has possessed one of her creations.

13. Shadow Walker. Damon battles his evil side—his doppelganger.

14. Misspent Youth. Introduces Jack Knoll as a teenage Damon Dark and Josh Tuckwell as a young Vincent Kosmos in a story where they team to battle an alien (the pilot for *The Young Damon Dark Adventures*).

15. The Shapeless. Establishes a simpler format with Damon resigning from Transdimensional Control to becoming a traveler in time and space. Here he seeks to stop an alien that assumes a person's image then sends him back in time to replace him.

16. Space Prison. Vincent Kosmos appears in an episode where he risks his life to save Damon from an alien.

17. The Cosmic Magician. Damon encounters a time traveler who is seeking to alter earth's past by changing the outcome of historic events.

18. The Parallel Man. In a parallel world to earth (where Nazi Germany won World War II) Damon's duplicate seeks to open a time portal that will enable him to encounter the Damon of our world.

19. Escape from the Mirror World. Dr. Lansing, a scientist involved with the time traveling experiment, Tempus Project, opens a time rift that pulls Damon's parallel self out of his Nazi-dominated world into our world.

20. Fear in the Night. Damon battles an enemy capable of assuming human form with orders to kill.

21. Revenge of the Magician. Dr. Lansing appears to be Damon's only hope of survival when the Cosmic Magician casts a psychic attack on Damon.

22. Earth Under Siege. Damon and Dr. Lansing become allies in an attempt to stop the robotic Socrad, now a part of the Collective, from attacking Earth.

23. From Out of the Shadows. Damon encounters Hecate (Gillian Martin), an evil witch when he investigates the sudden disappearance of students at a local college.

24. The Return of Hecate. Damon attempts to stop Hecate as she continues to abduct humans for a sinister plan to conquer the earth.

25. UFO Hunter? Damon tries to clear himself of a murder charge when a news broadcast accuses him of being a delusional killer (Damon had killed an alien possessed human but the media saw it as something else—cold blooded murder).

26. The Face of the Enemy. Damon's last adventure wherein he battles the Chameleon, a shape-changing alien.

97 *Dark Pool.* the7thmatrix.com. 2011 (Science Fiction).

Jim Krall is a consultant a Tesserack, a financial management corporation. He is married to Tracy and the father of a six-year-old daughter (Sarah). One day the unthinkable happens—his daughter is kidnapped in front of his eyes—but no one, including his wife, seems to care. When Jim finds it appears that his daughter never even existed, he begins a lone quest to not only find her, but find out what has happened. Stories follow Jim as he encounters alternate realities, multiple dimensions and time travel to discover what has happened (it appears that he and his daughter are the keys in a struggle between powerful forces called Shadow Cabinets—who can travel through time and change events to accomplish their goals).

Cast: Jason Kuykendall (Jim Krall), Sierra Hersek (Tracy Krall), Chloe Hersek (Sarah Krall), Gary Pannullo (Jack), Patrick Murphy (Roger), Kelley Ogden (Susan). **Credits:** *Producer:* Rick Gott, Karen Pollard, Mike Malmberg, Lynn Malmberg. *Director:* Rick Gott, Rich Malmberg. **Comment:** Although a similar idea has been presented on the television series *Nowhere Man* in 1995, *Dark Pool* rises above that and presents a much more intriguing concept. The program captures the viewer's attention from the start and is well produced and acted to keep interest until the conclusion.

Episodes:

1. Pilot (5 min., 12 sec.). Introduces Jim, his family and their life in the suburbs.

2. Gotcha (4 min., 44 sec.). Jim's job promotion appears to be the catalyst that will change the course of his life.

3. Big Day (7 min., 41 sec.). Jim and Tracy celebrate Sarah's birthday with Jim's life about to change forever.

4. Worry Wart (6 min., 8 sec.). During Sarah's party, she is kidnapped in front of everyone—but no one no seems to have seen it happen.

5. Who's Sarah (6 min., 31 sec.). Jim ponders Sarah's disappearance but is mystified why no one knows who she is.

6. Okay (9 min., 5 sec.). Jim believes something is wrong especially when he sees constant reminders of Sarah.

7. The Captain (9 min., 57 sec.). A stranger (The Captain) approaches Jim and claims he knows what has happened.

8. In and Out of Time (7 min., 16 sec.). The Stranger, who possesses supernatural powers, explains that he (Jim) and Sarah are pawns in a power struggle.

9. Spinning Out (8 min., 26 sec.). Jim learns that his company is connected to what has happened.

10. Pull the Trigger (9 min., 31 sec.). Jim's worlds collide when he sees that alternate universes exist and that what may be in one world may not be in the other.

98 Dark Things. webserieschannel.com. 2013 (Fantasy).

Strange tales of people that encounter things that go bump in the night.

Cast: Matt McVay (Nick), Andrew Staton (Gerald). **Credits:** *Producer:* Naathan Phan, Steven Sewell, Paul Kosmala. *Director:* Paul Kosmala. **Comment:** It is difficult to tell from the only produced episode whether it would continue from where this first story left off (and leave it up to the viewer to determine the outcome—which has been done on series like *Alfred Hitchcock Presents*) or begin a new terror tale with each episode. The initial presentation has it creepy moments although it is all talk and no action. The annoying shaky camera should not have been used as the scene is set at a diner table and there is no need to bounce the scene from side-to-side and up-and-down (unless the intent was to make the viewer sea sick; would have played a lot better with a stationary scene). The idea to have the Gerald character munching on potato chips is okay—but the loud chewing sounds are truly annoying).

Episodes:

1. Truth (4 min., 58 sec.). Two men (Gerald and Nick) seated at a diner table, begin a conversation about dark things and the fears humans have about the unseen demons and spirits that are by our sides. As Gerald leaves (magically—as Nick does not see him leave) Nick becomes frightened and wonders what just happened. Will he encounter those dark things? There is no conclusion.

99 The Darkness Descending. thedarkness descending.com. 2009 (Science Fiction).

Chelsea Henderson is a graduate student and filmmaker who chose to devote her thesis on a documentary about the homeless in New York City. While doing investigative work, Chelsea discovers a vast network of abandoned subway tunnels and passage ways deep beneath the streets of Manhattan. As Chelsea begins filming the stories of people who live in the dangerous subterranean world, she comes to realize that something else lurks in the darkness—a mysterious figure (Angel) living deep below and who has declared a war on the outside world. Angel has been born of rumors that became the myths that evolve into legends. It is said that he lives off the flesh of rats and has supernatural powers. It is also said, as Chelsea discovers, he can see in the dark and is the leader of The Chosen, a mysterious and dangerous cult. Stories follow Chelsea as she becomes involved in a dangerous quest to stop a war (by The Chosen) that could not only destroy the world underground, but the above world as well.

Cast: Kinga Philipps (Chelsea), Danny Trejo (Angel), Wylie Small (Harmony), Frank Kruger (Jake Armstrong), Wylie Small (Harmony Rhodes), Daryl Crittenden (Chosen), William Romeo (Dante), Michael Rene Walton (Skeeter). **Credits:** *Producer:* Frank Kruger, Wylie Small, James Duval, Darren Darnborough. *Director:* Marc Clebanoff. *Writer:* Frank Krueger. **Comment:** What starts off as a seemingly uninteresting story about a girl and her school project quickly moves into a tense portrait of a girl involved in a mysterious quest to save the lives of innocent people. While visions of the CBS series *Beauty and the Beast* will immediately come to mind as that too was set in the abandoned subway tunnels beneath Manhattan, *Darkness* is much more compelling and mysterious and is aided by good acting and production values.

Episodes:

1. Redemption. Introduces Jake Armstrong, a former NYPD police officer who, after the tragic loss of his family, becomes homeless—and living in the subway tunnels he once patrolled.

2. Lost. Chelsea begins her documentary and meets with Skeeter, a man with unique wisdom and experiences.

3. Darkness. The mystery deepens as Chelsea becomes aware of an unseen, lurking presence.

4. Harmony. Chelsea meets with Harmony, a homeless muralist (and graffiti artist) as she describes her life in the tunnels.

5. The Chosen. Chelsea discovers that in the shadows deep beneath the city, a group of angry and lost souls (The Chosen) are following the teachings (revenge) of the mysterious Angel.

100 Date a Human.com. youtube.com. 2010 (Science Fiction).

The future has changed drastically. It is now a time wherein humans and aliens (from outer space) can live peacefully and marry each other. Unfortunately, the alien population has grown to outnumber the human population and human women are now expected to have as many children as possible to increase the human aspect. Allie is a young human woman who, after getting her heart broken by a human male "for the last time" ("as all they want are babies; can't they think of anything else?") she takes the advice of Ruthie, her cat-like roommate, and begins a quest to find an interspecies romance. Episodes follow Allie and her experiences with what she meets on DateAHuman.com.

Cast: Anne Griffin (Allie), Brooke Lyons (Ruthie), Cathy Shambley (Allie's mother). **Credits:** *Producer:* Amber J. Lawson, Joy Gohring, Lauren Schnipper. *Director:* Joy Gohring. *Writer:* Joy Gohring, Paul Malewitz, William Weissbaum. **Comment:** Interesting reversal on dating and matchmaking programs with good acting and amusing stories.

Episodes:

1. Pilot. Establishes the story as Allie, fed up with human relationships, decides to date aliens instead.

2. Space Dumped. Allie finds trouble at home when her mother objects to her dating aliens.

3. Alien Filth. Allie's dating experiences take a

turn for the worse when she is matched with a sex trophy-winning alien.

4. Lava Lips. Aliens have copied a human practice—using a photo other than their own as Allie meets an Alien who looks nothing like his profile picture.

5. Total Rip-off. Still concerned over Allie's dating habits, her mother attempts to set her up with a human date.

6. The Love Bug. Dating Blues. Allie finally believes she has met the alien of her dreams, but cannot get passed the kissing stage with him.

101 *A Day in the Life of Death*. webseries channel.com. 2009 (Fantasy).

Fed up with his job as the Grim Reaper, Bob (as he is also known), quits and decides to experience life as a normal human being. His experiences are shared with on-line viewers.

Cast: Julian Byrne (Death), Andrew Kines (God). **Credits:** For unknown reasons, credits do not appear on screen or on the program's website. **Comment:** A comical fantasy that has potential as Bob attempts to figure out the human side of life.

Episodes:

1. Pilot. Bob approaches his boss (God) and pleads his case.

2. The Grim Reaper Makes a Vlog. Bob, granted his wish, begins his quest by trying to figure out how You Tube works.

3. Cereal Confession. Bob relates his feelings about how sugary sweet breakfast cereals have become.

4. Deadly Procrastination. Bob relates the fact that he has many things to do—but doesn't feel like doing them.

5. What's in the Grim Reaper Bag? Bob reveals the things he carries in his mysterious black bag—from his wallet to an alarm clock that he uses since his deadly hour glass broke.

6. Grim Reaper Fails. A short sequence wherein Bob takes a tumble down a staircase.

7. The Grim Reaper Caught on Tape. Uncovered footage that the Grim Reaper really exists.

8. What Happens When You Read the Light. A bright light fills the screen, indicating something sinister is about to happen when the screen suddenly goes black—and Bob is seen replacing the light bulb in his lamp.

102 *Day Zero*. dayzerotv.com. 2011 (Science Fiction).

In the year 2109, science and technology had advanced to a point where it had exceeded ethical bounds. An attempt was made to reverse its course by the United Nations Bioethics Committee but global dictators violated the treaty and secretly began stockpiling weapons. American was soon attacked (thus beginning World War IV) and, in retaliation, nuclear weapons were used to annihilate the enemy.

Day Zero cast, left to right: Crystal Udy, Bill Gillaner, Colin McDermott and Flo Donelli (copyright 2014 Fofanugget Productions, all rights reserved. Used with permission. No portion of this information and its accompanying photograph may be reproduced by any means without permission in writing from the copyright owner).

The attacks devastated the Western Hemisphere and destroyed virtually the entire population. But from the devastation arose Hybrids, radiation-affected humans that became ravenous beasts and who now outnumber the unaffected. The program not only focuses on one group of unaffected humans, living in Utah, as they battle the Hybrids for survival, but on the struggles faced by other survivors, the internal threats such people encounter and how the radiated areas of the world have changed the landscape of the planet.

Cast: Richard Scott Dean (Blake Edwards), Emilyne Guglietti (Kat Finch), Ken Applegate (Russell Braddock), Deven Skye (Rachael Shore), Cal Nguyen (Jim Lecter), Leo Lynton (Cameron Clark), Juliet Touchet (Rosie Parker), Ethan Aguilar (Landon Parker), Kabrina Miller (Erica Jordan), Jonathan C. Young (Micah Sloane), Bill Gillane (Ben Lott), Colin McDermott (Tiras Abel), Flo Donelli (Diana Cantaray), Crystal Udy (Sarah Edwards), Morgan Mabey (Namaah Cain), Scott Smith (Andrew Mallory). *Cast Note:* Deven Skye originally worked under the name Deven Baldwin for season one of the series. **Credits:** *Producer:* Cal Nguyen, Desiree Haymond. *Director:* Cal Nguyen, Denver James Harward. *Writer:* Cal Nguyen, Kelsi Swensen, T.J. Nguyen. **Comment:** Well done and worth watching, with good acting, production values and a story that holds your interest from the very beginning. *Day Zero* is also one of the very few Internet series to become a broadcast television series with its episodes being run on the digital channel Tuff TV.

Episodes:

1. Lethal (22 min., 30 sec.). Blake Edwards, one of the unaffected, has turned to drugs to escape what is actually happening but soon realizes drugs are not the solution for survival.

2. Requital (17 min., 42 sec.). As Blake tries to overcome his addiction, survivors Rachael and Cameron's efforts to devise a defense plan is not as secure as they believe.

3. Suspicion (24 min., 53 sec.). A group of human survivors from another camp finds a lukewarm welcome from the Utah group.

4. Betrayal (21 min., 55 sec.). As the new members settle in, loyalties are tested among the survivors.

5. Memoriam (19 min., 42 sec.). Camp members Kat and Russell reflect on how they met shortly after Day Zero.

6. Dementia (31 min., 5 sec.). Camp member Jim Lecter's delusions begin to have an effect on other members of the compound.

7. Phoenix (13 min., 27 sec.). Russell struggles with a decision that could affect the rest of his life (the possibility of he and Kat becoming parents).

8. Metamorphosis (15 min., 35 sec.). Following the attack, plans are made to leave and find another place of refuge where the survivors have not established a base.

9. Dawn (11 min., 8 sec.). One of the camp members, Cameron, begins to show signs of a changing behavior, one attributed to the Hybrids.

10. Dusk (22 min., 44 sec.). While still contemplating a move, the humans soon realize a decision is needed quickly as Hybrids have increased their numbers and thus decreased their hope for survival if they should attack.

Note: A second season is planned and as of February 2014, the following episodes have been produced but not released: "Requiem," "Redemption," "Revelations," "Sacrificial Lamb," "Resurrection" and "Return to Sender."

103 *Daybreak.* daybreak2012.com. 2012 (Science Fiction).

Ben Wilkens is the son of a theoretical physicist who developed a new metal but was killed by persons unknown seeking the formula. To cover up the physicist's death, it was reported as due to heart problems—something he did not have. Ben accepted the explanation until a reporter aroused his curiosity that his father was working on something that could change the world. Ben disbelieves him until he digs into his father's effects and finds a mysterious sphere—a creation of Ben's father that will soon change the course of his life. Shortly after, Ben is kidnapped by members of a group that were friends of his father and who now want to protect him from a corrupt group (the Torrents) seeking the sphere and its formula. The program charts Ben's experiences as he attempts to protect the sphere and uncover the truth regarding his father's death.

Cast: Ryan Eggold (Ben Wilkens), Sarah Roemer (Sarah), Michael O'Keefe (Aaron), Ryan McPartlin (Eric), Frank John Hughes (William), Shannon Lucio (Katherine), Eugene Byrd (Charles). **Credits:** *Producer:* Tim Kring, Jules Daly, Tracie Norfleet, Esther Lee, Tom Dunlap. *Director:* David Carter. *Writer:* Raven Metzner. **Comment:** The program begins badly (with a car chase) and is an immediate turn off as the viewer has no idea as to what is happening. Even after watching the entire first episode, it is difficult to comprehend the story line (the website's synopsis does not help). However, a good story is presented if one has the patience to venture into the second episode (and possibly re-watch the first episode). The acting and production values are television series quality and the program is backed by AT&T (it has noticeable product placement throughout the episodes that showcase their then current products). There is no doubt money and efforts were put into the project but why it was decided to present the program without an easy-to-follow storyline and begin in the middle of something is the mystery.

Episodes:

1. Chapter 1 (9 min., 8 sec.). Digging into his father's personal effects, Ben uncovers a mysterious object that could change the course of the world.

2. Chapter 2 (14 min., 38 sec.). Ben learns that he is being sought by a corrupt group of people who want the object (a large clear sphere) and its formula.

3. Chapter 3 (14 min., 25 sec.). Ben, wanting to learn what actually happened to his father, reluctantly joins a group of scientists seeking to protect the sphere and its secrets.

4. Chapter 4 (10 min., 49 sec.). The Torrents, the people seeking the sphere, manage to trap Ben and take the sphere.

5. Chapter 5 (9 min., 34 sec.). Ben, determined to retrieve the sphere, begins his quest to not only retrieve it, but find out who killed his father.

104 Dead End City. youtube.com. 2008 (Science Fiction).

Spoof of the hard boiled private detectives of 1940s movie fame and of early television. Sam Fu's is a nightclub that is not only the prime hangout of a private detective named Murphy, but of the notorious underworld figures that control the city. Murphy is a ladies' man and a gambler and a guy who appears to become involved in situations that he really wants no part of. The program would chart his efforts to deal with the cases he just stumbles upon and sets out to solve. Brandy is the bar owner; Sally a waitress and Tzu Ki, the club dancer. **Cast:** Gary Graham (Murphy), Misty Madden (Sally), Dani Landon (Brandy), Mandy May (Zena), Trinh Tran (Tzu Ki), Matthew Nicolau (Scarza, the Zombie), Tennessee Webb (The Prophet), Faread Sayed (Sam Fu). **Credits:** *Producer-Writer-Director:* Jeff Varga. **Comment:** Immediately captures your attention with its surreal-like settings and the use of mostly black and white filming (the opening scenes of the bar are in color as is the dance performed by Tzu Ki—where only she appears in color against black and white backdrops). Gary Graham's narration as Murphy is reminiscent of Tom Selleck's character on the television series *Magnum, P.I.* The acting and production values are comparable to most television and cable series.

Episodes:

1. The Pilot (14 min., 53 sec.). When a patron, dressed as a Nazi, is killed in the bar, Murphy reluctantly becomes involved when the victim returns as a zombie and threatens to wreck havoc seeking the person who shot him.

105 Dead End Days. deadenddays.com. 2003–2004 (Horror).

In a time when humans and zombies co-exist, advertising companies realize there is a new market to target—the undead. Creative minds create a soda called Brain Cola as well as other brain-themed products. Ad campaigns are created and companies are rushing to capitalize on an untapped market. But beneath the surface, multinational corporations are seeking to ignite a zombie-human war to further create zombies and increase their earnings—regardless of the cost. A war had changed the world and created the zombie population. Peace was accomplished and now both factions survive together. In this new world five people are trying to adjust: Eric, a video store clerk who traffics in selling bootlegged copies of classic horror films; Ashley, a life insurance agent who spends her days coping with undead policy holders; Bridget and Sam, freelance zombie hunters; and Bruce, a zombie rights activist. The program follows the events that spark their lives. **Cast:** Erin Whitehead (Ashley), Shane Arbuthnott (Eric), Brooke Kemp (Bridget), Robert Fox (Duncan). **Credits:** *Producer:* Brad Fox. *Director:* Matthew Hoos. *Writer:* Jason Patrick Rothary. **Comment:** Comedic zombie yarn that probes a new way to target an undead market. The program is well produced and acted and, while not a laugh-out loud comedy, does have a few chuckles.

Episodes: Forty-eight episodes were produced but have been taken off-line due to a DVD release of the program.

106 The Dead Hour. thedeadhour.com. 2010–2012 (Horror).

The Dead Hour is a weekly radio program hosted by DJ Raven. Raven, however, is not your ordinary radio host. She is a young woman who has experienced the terrors of "things that go bump in the night" and relates tales of the unknown to her listeners. Anthology-like stories combine elements of horror and fantasy as ordinary people encounter a world of fear that could cost them their lives. **Cast:** Melissa Holder (DJ Raven), Mark Booker, Nic Roewert, Michelle Schrage, Jazmyne Van Houten, Chelsie Hartness, William Wassem, Melanie Gillis. **Credits:** *Producer:* Wendy Iske, Michael Lang, Shawn Watson. *Director:* Daniel B. Iske. *Writer:* Scott Coleman. **Comment:** With the exception of "Cannibal Girls," which is a bit talkative, stories are well calculated, a bit chilling and a bit creepy. The acting, directing and production values are good and the series tag line, "What scares you" lives up to its meaning.

Episodes:

1. Fright Fest (17 min., 24 sec.). When creatures from a horror film begin to emerge from the screen, a timid young man (Finch) battles the monsters to save his girlfriend (Frankie).

2. Fame (16 min., 31 sec.). A young woman (Cara) hoping to become an actress but stuck in a dead-end job, meets a producer who offers her ultimate fame if she will star "in the film of all films" (a snuff film) and sacrifice her life (by hanging) on screen. Contains brief female nudity.

3. Backseat (17 min., 55 sec.). A serial killer of teenage girls (Jason) finds more than he bargained for when he begins dating Heather—a girl who knows his secret and plots to do away with him.

4. Inside Man (22 min., 12 sec.). A man (Tony) who suffers from agoraphobia (afraid of the outside world) finds he must live with or overcome his fear when a monstrous force invades the security of his home.

5. Gross Anatomy (15 min., 31 sec.). Medical school students find their lives threatened when cadavers come to life to experiment on them.

6. Alcoholic Vampire (18 min., 50 sec.). A vampire (Vic) seeking to end his addiction to alcohol, finds that the more he tries, the deadlier his addiction becomes.

7. Cougar (14 min., 26 sec.). Miss Juniper could be considered a cougar, an older woman seeking a man. As she moves into a new home, she becomes noticed, especially by the local high school boys— who learn just what type of woman she is when they each get to know her (and her real cougar-like self).

8. The Hole (17 min., 14 sec.). Finding that he has noting to do after retiring, a man (Arthur) becomes obsessed with digging a hole in his backyard. As the hole becomes increasingly large and his wife attempts to get him to turn his attention to something else, a scuffle ensues. The wife is knocked unconscious and falls into the hole. Arthur now knows why the dug the hole—to bury his nagging wife.

9. Cannibal Girls (17 min., 23 sec.). Two young women, the survivors of a near apocalyptic disaster and stranded in the barren fields of middle America, find the only way they can stay alive is to feed on humans when the food supply is eliminated.

10. Donor (17 min., 20 sec.). A man, recently fired from his job, but unable to tell his wife and children, finds a way to provide for them—selling his spare body parts to a doctor with a specialized client list.

107 Dead Man's Blood. webserieschannel. com. 2013 (Horror).

Unreleased series about a young man (Ryan Redding) who, after returning to his home town (Haddonfield) for his father's funeral, becomes involved in a quest to solve a series of mysterious killings (committed by an unknown assailant dressed in black with a skull mask) that have been occurring since his father's death. **Cast:** Johnny Viel (Ryan Redding), Emily Callahan (Izzie Crane), Jon-Michael Miller (Robbie Harding), Miranda Kahn (Bonnie Green), Courtney Case (Monica Coleman), Virginia Hill (Piper Redding), Greg Adair (Harry Redding), Taylor Larbarbera (Billie Forbes), Luke Bartholomew (Alexander Hunt), Karen Mowery (Kelly Donovan), Jason Spina (Ash Tanner), Misha Braun (Freddie Scott). **Credits:** *Producer:* Kenneth Price, James Tucci. *Writer:* Kenneth Price, James Tucci, Tariq Simmons. **Comment:** Based on the teasers, the program appears to be quite gory (over use of "blood" in the killing

scenes) and a take off on the *Halloween* series of feature films.

Episodes: Only two Teaser Trailers are available (Teaser 1 runs 90 seconds; Teaser 2, 72 seconds) that highlight what can be expected in the near future.

108 The Dead Must Die. matthewsnyman. com. 2009 (Horror).

Light comedy blends with horror as two video game nerds, each named Steve (Steve and Steve 2) attempt to deal with reality when, after a Zombie Apocalypse, they must face a whole new world of circumstances, especially when Steve 2 becomes a zombie and Steve must protect him from the human survivors who, to survive, must kill the dead. **Cast:** Stephen Russell (Steve), Jonny Helm (Steve 2), Liza Callinicos (Mysterious Ninja Chick), Donna White (Mother), Steven Snyman, Andy Cooper (Zombies). **Credits:** *Producer-Writer-Director:* Matthew Snyman. **Comment:** Steve and Steve 2 have dreamed of such an event and now they know that "The Dead Must Die." The comedy stems from their being totally unprepared for what happens (even though they had "A Case of Zombie Invasion Evacuation Kit") while the so-called horror is really not as Steve tries to save Steve 2.

Episodes:

1. A Tale of 2 Steves (7 min., 24 sec.). The "big day" arrives—although Steve and Steve 2 are unaware of it.

2. Bring the Rain (4 min., 54 sec.). A news bulletin while watching television informs Steve that he must find Steve 2 and tell him about the zombie outbreak.

3. The Worst Zombie (5 min., 51 sec.). Unfortunately, Steve is too late to save Steve 2, who has become a zombie (and a bad one at that).

4. Pillow Talk (5 min., 51 sec.). As Steve struggles to protect Zombie Steve from humans, he meets a mysterious girl ("a ninja chick") who could be his and Steve 2's salvation.

5. These Hills Also... (3 min., 51 sec.). Steve ponders his fate: should he trust the mysterious ninja girl or try to save Steve 2 on his own.

6. A Bad Case of the... (4 min., 32 sec.). The ninja girl, called The Mysterious Stranger, becomes an ally when she helps Steve find food; unfortunately, the situation gets the best of Steve and he descends into madness.

7. Every Zombie Has... (7 min., 28 sec.). Steve and Steve 2 hope to find light at the end of the tunnel as the series ends; if not, they will have to remain as the newest members of an undead society.

109 Dead Road. deadroad.net. 2008–2013 (Horror).

The Earth, infected by a virus that kills millions, leaves only pockets of survivors across the planet. As the infected (zombies) return as the undead, they become a threat to every human left alive. With supplies and safety also becoming a problem faced by survivors, groups have been formed in order to work together and increase their chances for survival. The program follows one such group (Bert, Rich, Paige and Chris) as they struggle for survival in a world where it appears that only zombies will dominate the planet.

Cast: Rich Ruperto (Rich), Humberto Rivera (Bert), Julie Robbins (Paige), Edwin Rivera (Chris), Rodrigo Bustamante (Guts), Corrado DeRobertis (Captain Hawkins), Linda Rollino (Meghan), Mario Torres (Mario). **Credits:** *Producer-Writer-Director:* Corrado Gadaleta. **Comment:** Zombie-infested program that presents a good storyline with good acting, writing and directing. The original run was rather dragged out with many months of waiting for succeeding episodes.

Episodes:

1. Episode 1. Introduces Bert and Rich who have secured themselves in a seemingly unaffected area of New Jersey.

2. Episode 2. Although they appear to be safe, Bert and Rich decide to head for a safe settlement down South.

3. Episode 3. As Bert and Rich take to the road (by car) they cross two other survivors (Paige and Chris).

4. Episode 4. The group begins to get to know each other as they near their destination.

5. Episode 5. Arriving at the compound, the group is met by Captain Hawkins and welcomed to what appears to be a safe, well-stocked settlement.

6. Episode 6. As Bert, Paige and Chris adapt to their new surroundings, Rich becomes uneasy that something is just not right, especially with the excessive security.

7. Episode 7. Several months have passed since their arrival and, although secure in a zombie infested area, Chris feels he and the others should escape and move on.

8. Episode 8. The concluding, unresolved episode wherein Chris, Paige, Rich and Bert ready their car to leave the compound for a safer haven.

---

110 *Dead Wait.* youtube.com. 2010 (Science Fiction).

It is the present day and fears of an apocalypse are growing. Most people just ignore it but one young man, Adam, has become a bit of a recluse, fearing such a prophecy is about to come true. He has prepared himself for "the event" and now just waits until it happens. The program, complete in the episodes presented, follows Adam when the apocalypse occurs and he sets out to save himself.

Cast: Dan Hillaker (Adam Aldrid), David Crawford (Jared), Vanessa Severo (Zoe), Kate O'Neill (Cassie). **Credits:** *Producer:* Justin Gardner, Justin Parlette. *Writer-Director:* Justin Parlette. **Comment:** Horror mixes with comedy to present an entertaining program with capable acting and good production values.

Episodes:

1. Black Friday (3 min., 48 sec.). It has happened and Adam is all prepared—or at least he thinks he is.

2. What Do We Pay You For? (2 min., 6 sec.). Adam, armed with his weapon of choice (a baseball bat with protruding nails at the top) wanders out of his apartment to warn the doorman to keep zombies out of the building.

3. Hobosplosion (4 min., 37 sec.). Adam's friend Jared believes Adam is overly cautious as nothing will happen.

4. Sharp Things (3 min., 11 sec.). Adam still fearing the worst warns Jared that all is not right outside the building.

5. Survivor Man (4 min., 40 sec.). Adam ventures outside the building; has a phone call from his mother; chats with a girl (Zoe) then returns to his apartment.

6. The End of the Beginning Is the End (4 min., 57 sec.). The zombie population is rising but Jared is bitten before he can return to the safety of Adam's apartment.

7. Zombies (2 min., 22 sec.). Adam now fears for is life when Jared becomes one of the undead.

8. Empty Rooms (4 min., 20 sec.). Adam and his baseball bat escape from the apartment but he is followed by Jared.

9. 5:28 (2 min., 14 sec.). Outside of what appears to be his abandoned building, Adam desperately seeks Zoe.

10. Going Down (2 min.). Adam begins battling a horde of zombies and realizes his apartment building is no longer safe.

11. Cassie (1 min., 54 sec.). Adam seeks refuge in the parking garage and believes he is safe—until zombies begin approaching him.

---

111 *Death's Door.* youtube.com. 2011 (Science Fiction).

Marcus is a very unusual man. He inexplicably dies (usually from collapsing) then mysteriously returns to life. Each new life has a different meaning to Marcus and doctors have no medical explanation as to what his condition is or any prognosis on how to cure it or even stop the occurrences from happening. He can come back to life without medical assistance (like CPR) and each new life is a mystery for Marcus as he ponders why it is happening and could there be others like him? As the condition persists Marcus becomes fearful, confused and isolated and begins a quest to find out why so he can enjoy a solitary new life.

Cast: Jeff Berg (Marcus), Jessica Vera (Jessica), Geoffrey Pomeroy (Steve), Stephen Medvidick

(Chris), Alexandra Rosario (Diane), Ann Marie Yoo (Beth), Tom Patella (Bob), Elizabeth Bove (Jan), Jose Alvarez (Max), Miriam BoCricks (Erin O'Kane). **Credits:** *Producer:* Stephanie Dawson. *Writer-Director:* Ben Schaeffer. **Comment:** An interesting subject that could go well beyond the four released episodes to present intrigue as Marcus seeks to solve the mysteries of his own death. Good acting and production values make it a short, but worthwhile series to watch.

Episodes:

1. Marcus Dies (4 min., 57 sec.). At his engagement party (set to marry Jessica), Marcus collapses and is considered a lost cause when efforts to save him are apparently failing.

2. Marcus Comes Back (4 min., 46 sec.). After all chances to save Marcus fail, he miraculously returns to life—but no one has any explanation as to why.

3. A Day in the Park (4 min., 10 sec.). Marcus tries to explain to Jessica what has been happening to him.

4. Marcus Knows (5 min., 42 sec.). When Marcus suffers another attack, he realizes that he must find the answers he needs to live a normal life.

112 *Déjà vu.* dejavuserieweb.com. 2013 (Science Fiction).

Sebastian is a young man with the strange ability of déjà vu: he can see tragedies before they happen and is thus given the opportunity to change them. Stories, presented in Spanish with English subtitles, follow Sebastian as sets out to change the future—but in doing so he must also be careful as changing future events could alter events of the present and put his and other's lives in danger. **Cast:** Juan Trujillo (Sebastian), Clara Mejia (Isabela), Alejando Aguilar (Lucas), Andres Bejar (Victor). **Credits:** *Producer:* Edwin Herrera Ruiz. *Writer-Director:* Juan Francisco Perez Villalba. **Comment:** While not totally an original idea (seeing the future had been done in movies like *It Happened Tomorrow* and on television in series like *Early Edition*) the Spanish production is well done and takes the consequences aspect one step above most others of its kind. While dubbing can become costly, using subtitles is a bit distracting but the essence of the project is still kept in tact.

Episodes:

1. The Gift (7 min., 7 sec.). Sebastian discovers that he possesses an unusual power.

2. At Risk (4 min., 59 sec.). Sebastian's first vision is that of a businessman in danger.

3. The Decision (5 min., 25 sec.). As Sebastian envisions the future, he sees that Isabela, the woman he loves, is in danger from a man with a similar power—Victor.

4. Trapped (5 min., 40 sec.). Sebastian envisions danger at a local bank.

5. A Curse (6 min., 3 sec.). To prevent what he

envisioned from happening, Sebastian risks his life to stop it.

6. Persecuted (7 min., 22 sec.). Sebastian begins to wonder why he can see the future and if there are others like him.

7. Deceive (9 min., 7 sec.). Sebastian's doubts are sequestered when he meets Lucas—who possesses the same abilities.

8. Heroes (6 min., 26 sec.). Having had the power much longer than Sebastian, Lucas explains that he should see his powers in a different way (as a gift not a curse).

9. The Truth (6 min., 1 sec.). It is learned that Victor possesses a mental ability that he is using to not only avenge the murder of his wife, but anyone "he feels is scum," including Sebastian.

10. The Revelation (6 min., 3 sec.). Lucas and Sebastian learn the truth about their abilities—a condition that was handed down from generation to generation in their respective families.

11. The Sacrifice (6 min., 17 sec.). Isabela is used as a lure to trap Victor.

12. The End (9 min., 55 sec.). A final showdown as Sebastian and Isabela confront Victor.

113 *Delta.* webserieschannel.com. 2012 (Horror).

In the town of Delta, Colorado, a serial killer's (Paul Schmidt) terror spree is ended when he is captured by the brother (Christopher Pine) of one of his victims. Paul is tried and convicted to four life sentences in the Delta Colorado Correctional Facility. Delta has returned to normal, but Paul cannot rest and plots a daring escape. Now, with only vengeance on his mind, Paul seeks to destroy the family whose testimony caused his incarceration. The unreleased series follows Christopher as he once again seeks to stop Paul before he strikes again. **Cast:** Matt Thorpe, Jeanne Carr, Robert Keasler, Peyton McDavitt, Sharon Powers, Nicole Keyes, Keith Meinke. **Credits:** *Producer-Writer-Director:* Kohl V. Bladen. **Comment:** The series was scheduled to premiere in the fall of 2012 and based on the trailer, it is difficult to provide an opinion other than it does look promising as a deranged killer seeks revenge on those he believes betrayed him. It is also questionable why the program has been tagged as horror (other than the killing that presumably would occur) based on what has been released.

Episodes: Only a 43-second trailer has been made available that briefly highlights the series storyline.

114 *Delura.* youtube.com. 2010 (Science Fiction).

Aiden, a mine ship operator for TIMCO Tor (Tanadrine Interplanetary Mining Company, Tor Division) in the Delura Galaxy, wakes up after an accident in space to find himself in a strange hospital-like ward but mostly devoid of his memories of who he is or where he came from. His entire lifetime appears to have been erased from his memory. Because he cannot return to his past, Aiden begins a new life with animated stories following his experiences with strange creatures, not knowing who he was or what he will become.

Voice Cast: Taben Royce (Aiden), Edwyn Tiong (Lucius), Frank Hunter (Charlie), Edward Biscoe (Rudo), Karen Kahler (Senate), Debbie Grattan (Rayvazevexine), Ryan Royce (Silgrarian Doctor/Karnagie). **Credits:** *Producer-Director:* Taben Roye. *Writer:* Taben Roye, Ryan Roye. **Comment:** Computer animated project with really out-of-this world characters. The story is compelling enough to find out what really happened but it concludes with a cliffhanger and leaves the doorway open for more episodes.

Episodes:

1. Episode 1 (3 min., 58 sec.). Aiden's plight begins after an accident aboard his mine ship lands him in the hospital.

2. Episode 2 (6 min., 26 sec.). Aiden awakens with no memory of who he is.

3. Episode 3 (7 min., 46 sec.). Details about the mine disaster that caused Aiden's predicament are revealed in a global broadcast message.

4. Episode 4 (2 min., 29 sec.). Realizing that without his memory he cannot go back to what he was, Aiden begins to explore his strange new universe.

5. Episode 5 (2 min., 11 sec.). Was the mining accident an accident or a plan to destroy Tanadrine by an unknown enemy. As Aiden continues his exploration, he stumbles upon information that could provide the truth.

115 *A Demon's Destiny: The Lone Warrior.* youtube.com. 2010 (Science Fiction).

In a time and dimension other than our own, a demon army has risen and the peace that had been preserved by the demon King Surbius in the First Universe has been shattered. Sarcon, an evil demon has taken the thrown from Surbius and has begun a conquest of other planets within the universe, including Earth. While hope for some planets appears to be lost as invading demon armies destroy all the opposition, one hope does remain for Earth—Kennedy, a lone warrior (half demon, half human) who has been sent to Earth by his people, the Yergan, to somehow stop an impending demon invasion. Kennedy, however, is not alone; he teams with earthlings Donna and Michael and together they set out on a quest to save the Earth by journeying to the Demon Universe and halt the attack before it occurs.

Billed as "A live action anime" (Japanese animation) that has been "influenced" by the syndicated animated television series *Dragonball Z.* When *Dragonball Z* was made into a feature film (*Dragonball Evolution*) but performed poorly in theaters,

studios are now reluctant to tackle such projects again. Web producer Devin Rice claims such a live-action film can be made (and be successful). *A Demon's Destiny* was made "to show them how it's done (and with no budget)."

Cast: Devin Rice (Kennedy), Jacqueline Monique Corcos (Donna), Nick Pasqual (Michael), Jessica Brandick (Kara), Peter DiVito (Zygon), Tony Evangelista (Carbon), Frederick Harris (Sangreen), Alex Lake (Ugon). **Credits:** *Producer:* Devin Rice, Joe Torres. *Writer-Director:* Devin Rice. **Comment:** For a no budget project (as producer Devin Rice states) a quality, intriguing and entertaining series evolved. The acting is good, the special effects, though minimal, are well executed and overall he accomplished his goal—a live action version of an anime television series can be accomplished. If the individual episodes were edited to form a feature film, it could make a good candidate for the Cartoon Network.

Episodes:

1. Arrival (6 min., 10 sec.). After an exhausting battle in the Demon Universe, Kennedy arrives on Earth to begin his mission.

2. Awakening (8 min., 16 sec.). Kennedy, called "The Lone Warrior," takes refuge in a home owned by Donna and Michael.

3. Confrontation (5 min., 43 sec.). As they return home, Donna and Michael encounter Kennedy.

4. Discover (4 min., 36 sec.). Donna and Michael learn who Kennedy is and why he has been sent to Earth. Unknowingly, Kennedy's enemy, Zygon, has followed him.

5. Love and Redemption (6 min., 51 sec.). Kennedy confronts Zygon only to learn that he has mentally enslaved Kara, the woman Kennedy loves most.

6. Contention (4 min., 14 sec.). As Kennedy begins a battle to rescue Kara from Zygon, Donna and Michael come to his aide.

7. Problems (3 min., 54 sec.). Having rescued Kara, Donna and Michael learn that Kennedy is possessed by demons (his demon side).

8. Next Steps (3 min., 6 sec.). Kara, Michael and Donna seek a way to help Kennedy control his demon side.

9. Control (5 min., 9 sec.). Kara reveals that Zygon still has control over her while Donna and Michael continue in their struggle to help Kennedy.

10. Collateral Damage (5 min., 4 sec.). Kennedy releases and kills one of his demons but is having a difficult time retaining his human side. Kara is taken captive by Zygon.

11. The Demon Universe (5 min., 51 sec.). With Donna and Michael by his side, Kennedy journeys to the Demon Universe to save Kara.

12. Sadistic (5 min., 28 sec.). Kennedy attempts to save Kara from Carbon, a demon who is torturing her.

13. Breakout (4 min., 36 sec.). Kennedy evokes his demon powers in an effort to save Kara.

14. Losing Control (4 min., 40 sec.). As Kennedy and Carbon fight, Kennedy's demon side begins to take control of his human side.

15. Feelings (7 min., 2 sec.). As the battle ends, Kennedy's demon side appears to be controlling him.

16. Lost (5 min., 57 sec.). Kennedy struggles to gain his human side before his demon side harms Donna and Michael.

17. The Gatekeepers (6 min., 34 sec.). With Kennedy now able to control his rage, he, Donna and Michael continue their journey to Sector 15 and encounter Sangreen and Ugon, demons who guard the portal to the Demon Universe.

18. Heroes (5 min., 57 sec.). Their experiences in the Demon Universe have an adverse effect on Michael and Donna as they become possessed by the demons Cameron and Juliette.

19. The Final Battle! (10 min., 26 sec.). With the demons extracted from Michael and Donna, Kennedy confronts Sangreen in a final standoff.

116 *The Device.* webserieschannel.com. 2011 (Science Fiction).

During her understudy work as physics major, a young woman (Claire) and her fiancé, Julian, began experimenting with the theories of time travel. When Julian was killed in a car accident, Claire retreated into a world of self pity. Two years later, she returned to finish the work she and Julian began. Ten years later Claire develops a prototype device that enables a person to travel back in time. Claire experimented on herself and attempted to go back in time to before Julian was killed. But she made a mistake ("Don't ask me what," she says) and other people have become aware of her creation—people who apparently want to use it for their own unethical means. As Claire struggles to protect "The Device" (as it is called) and escape the pursuing "Mysterious Man," she crosses the path of Ryan on the street and gives him the device (wrapped in paper) and tells him not to open it. A dazed Ryan takes the device back to his apartment where he and his roommate, Serhat, open the package. They soon become involved in Claire's plight when she finds them, explains what has happened and they must now not only save Claire, but "The Device" (which they will apparently use to travel through time).

Cast: Serhat Arslan (Serhat), Ryan Matthew Stewart (Ryan), Carmen Elena Pinto (Claire), Djilali Rez-Kallah (Mysterious Man). **Credits:** *Producer-Writer-Director:* Serhat Arslan. **Comment:** The story has possibilities but with only the one episode released, it is difficult to predict how it would progress. "The Device" is a rather sad-looking box (with a television signal splitter as the most prominent feature) that doesn't appear to have the capability of doing anything, not alone send people back in time. The best part of the program is Claire, who convincingly explains how she came to create the time machine. The production values are okay and acting by the other three cast members is typical of most Internet series (adequate).

Episodes:

1. Episode 1 (10 min., 32 sec.). A pilot film that establishes the program's storyline but ends without any conclusion.

117 *Devil's Trade.* fearnet.com. 2007–2008 (Horror).

In New Jersey during the 1890s, one tree, called the Devil's Tree became infamous as cursed due to the many people who were hanged from it. Over the years the legend grew and crosses, made from twigs and branches from the tree, have been sold as souvenirs. It is 2007 when three teenagers (Anna, Jim and Darren) find the website devilstrade.com and purchase one of the souvenir crosses. Their thoughts of it bringing them good luck are quickly displaced when they find nothing but bad luck. But is it the cross that is causing the bad luck? In an attempt to find out, the teens discover, via videos posted by similar buyers, that the cross is bad luck and the only way to end its curse is to get rid of it by selling it to someone else. With that as their only means of salvation, the teens set out on a quest to find the rightful owner and end the curse.

Cast: Ginny Weirick (Anna), Edward Canossa (Jim), Michael Gene Conti (Darren), Marina Resa (Gabby). **Credits:** *Producer:* Jim Burns, Jay Chapman. *Director:* Toby Wilkins. *Writer:* J.R. Young, Ben Ketai. **Comment:** Well done take on a cursed object although the idea has been done countless times before.

Episodes:

1. The Purchase. Three teens (Anna, Darren and Jim) discover the ominous website and purchase what they believe is a good luck wooden cross.

2. Premonition. Soon after receiving the cross, a string of bad luck befalls the teens.

3. Hanging. Using the Internet to research the cross, Darren finds that it is cursed and the only way to survive is to get rid of it.

4. Anna's Plan. Anna devises a plan to give the cross back to its original owner to break the spell of bad luck.

5. The Burning Tree. Darren appears to be the one most affected by the power of the cross and is drawn to a burning tree.

6. Sell It. Although never really boyfriend and girlfriend, the cross brings Anna and Jim closer—until their romantic interlude is disrupted by their encounter with a walking dead man—a former lynching victim.

7. An Awful Truth. Unable to sell the cross or find its original owner, the teens learn that until such time, they will be cursed forever.

118 Devine Intervention. devineinterven tionshow.com. 2012 (Fantasy).

Eleanor Devine is a young woman who feels she has a dead-end job (technical analyst) and a dull and boring life. One night Eleanor sees two men engaged in a fight and, although she is not the type of person to involve herself with others, intervenes. Her intervention causes the death of one man and allows the other to escape. Immediately, Eleanor is confronted by a man (Dro) who seems to appear from out of nowhere. Dro explains to Eleanor that she has nothing to fear. He is an Angelic Handler and the man who was killed was a Champion of Heaven, an agent specially chosen to protect the world from evil and ensure that The Plan (God's blueprint to ensure good) remains in tact. Eleanor learns that the killer was a demon and because of her actions she has been selected to become a Champion of Heaven to replace the prior agent. Although reluctant, Eleanor eventually accepts her calling as a Champion of Heaven, Northeast Sector. Demons are not happy as her existence means The Plan is still functioning and that the only way to disrupt The Plan is to eliminate Eleanor. Eleanor is not the most proficient of demon fighters and stories follow her efforts to live two lives—technical analyst by day and demon slayer by night.

Cast: Marley Malloy (Eleanor Devine), Jonathan Thomson (Dro), Trish Gruspe (Anne), Michael Underhill (Brian), Karl Schmith (Bob), Emily Correa (Gertie). **Credits:** *Producer-Director-Writer:* Adam Carl, Erin Schroeder. **Comment:** Well done comical fantasy with good acting and production values. Although the program ends with a cliff-hanger situation, it does leave the door open for Eleanor to continue her demon battles.

Episodes:

1. Not Invited (8 min., 19 sec.). Establishes the storyline as Eleanor becomes a demon fighter.

2. Not Supposed to Be You (12 min., 30 sec.). Eleanor attempts to adjust to the fact that while she still maintains her boring day job, she must now work nights to save The Plan.

3. Not Too Old (10 min., 22 sec.). Eleanor becomes concerned about a lack of weapons as she battles a demon called DJ.

4. Not Good Enough (10 min., 54 sec.). Seeing that her night job is becoming as dull as her day job, Eleanor attempts to change that by plunging head first into her battle against demons.

5. Not a Superhero (11 min., 14 sec.). Eleanor's ineptness becomes evident when she fails in an attempt to defeat the demon Dagris.

6. Not a Demon (12 min., 8 sec.). Eleanor must pose as a high school student to track down a demon.

7. Not Supernatural (17 min., 28 sec.). Eleanor uncovers evidence of an impending apocalypse—with the city doing nothing to prevent it.

8. Not Too Late (11 min., 32 sec.). Eleanor de-cides that she must accept her dual life and vows to do the best she can to save The Plan despite the efforts of demons to kill her and destroy The Plan.

9. Epilogue (57 sec.). Hints that Eleanor will continue her battle against demons.

119 The Diary of Tortov Roddle. youtube. com. 2009 (Fantasy).

The travels of a man (Tortov Roddle) and his companion (a large pig, presumably descended from the Dali elephants) and their encounters with strange animals and fantasy-like cities. Each story is told through grainy water color drawings and contains no dialogue (although there are cutaway dialogue inserts like those found in an old silent movie).

Cast: Tortov Roddle (Himself). **Credits:** *Director-Animator-Creator:* Kunio Katou. **Comment:** There are no real plots to speak of, as each episode merely presents Tortov in a situation with no explanation as to how he got there. The program does not encompass a narrator as stories are told strictly through visual art and the dialogue inserts, translated from the original Japanese cartoon, are not well done (poor English). Once accustomed to the still-like presentation and accepting the fact that Tortov magically appears in places, the program becomes an interesting alternative to the standard animated productions that are typical of movie and television programs.

Episodes:

1. The City of Light (16 min., 7 sec.). Charts Tortov's arrival in the Northern Plains.

2. Midnight Café (2 min., 15 sec.). Tortov takes a break from his travels at an all-night café.

3. The Little Town's Movie Gathering (2 min., 25 sec.). Tortov attends the screening of a movie.

4. Moonlight Travelers (2 min., 38 sec.). As Tortov tries to sleep a group of midnight travelers keeps him awake.

5. Melancholy Rain (2 min., 49 sec.). Tortov's travels are delayed slightly by a rain shower.

6. The Flower and the Lady (4 min., 26 sec.). Tortov has a brief encounter with a woman in a field of flowers.

120 Dirigible Days. day304.com. 2012 (Science Fiction).

Pinkerton Cornell and his associate Salazar are two of the most dangerous criminals in the universe. Having been tried and convicted by the Cult of Cthulhu, they are placed aboard the dirigible S.S. *Beatrix* to be transported to prison. Santiago Dunbar captains the ship; Josie is the mute pilot; and Hooper is the engineer. Stories follow the crew's efforts to get their prisoners to their destination despite the numerous obstacles they encounter.

Captain Dunbar was born in the Vilalba Sky Mines and raised on the sky island of Manitowak.

The costumed cast from *Dirigible Days* (photograph by Gary Lobstein, copyright Day 304 Productions).

He previously served as a Sky Inspector in the International Constabulary and served on several different ships during the Evacuation of Kilimanjaro (a pirate battle wherein he lost his left arm; this forced him to retire at the age of 29). Shortly after he bought the *Beatrix* and joined with Josie Devereaux in a in a cargo hauling business. Profits from the business allowed him to purchase a prosthetic left gun arm—something that comes in handy in an age of ruthless pirates.

Josie, the pilot of the *Beatrix*, was injured in a mysterious accident that left her mute, and now communicates in shorthand on a small blackboard. Despite her handicap, she is one lady who can look out for herself.

Cast: James Bragado (Santiago Dunbar), Julie Wilhelm (Josie Devereaux), Gary Lobstein (Salazar Strega), Jeff Gruhala (Hooper Jefferson), Adam Goforth (Pinkerton Cornell), Jason Orsega (Lincoln Keitel), Anthony Daniels (Narrator). **Credits:** *Producer:* David B. Farley, Joel M. Meier, Michael G. Drzyzga, Abbie Davis, Anthony Daniels. *Director:* Gary Lobstein. *Writer:* James Bragado. **Comment:** Billed as a "steampunk inspired series" that features

music from such bands as Vernian Process, Professor Elemental and Victor Sierra. The sets and costumes are nice and the dirigible effects are convincing. Anthony Daniels (C3PO from *Star Wars*) narrates.

Episodes:

1. Adventure Is Inescapable (10 min., 27 sec.). When the *Beatrix* breaks down and is stranded until repairs can be made, Captain Dunbar learns that Woe Claw, an enemy of Pinkerton, and his mercenaries are looking for his prisoner (to retrieve cargo that was stolen from him by Pinkerton).

2. Strange Cargo (10 min., 27 sec.). With repairs made, the *Beatrix* begins its journey.

3. Grasping at the Shadow (12 min., 35 sec.). Discovering that Pinkerton is aboard the *Beatrix*, Woe Claw and his accomplice, Keitel, set a course to intercept the ship.

4. Hierophant Unbound (10 min., 2 sec.). Escaping from the brig, Salazar takes Josie captive, manages to sabotage the engine room, take control of the ship and steer it toward the sunken city of R'Leyh.

5. What Has Sunk May Rise (9 min., 39 sec.). As the crew battles to regain control of the ship, Woe Claw's airship, the *Vandal* catches up with the *Beatrix*.

Commodore Keitel and his mercenaries make plans to board the *Beatrix* and settle an old score.

121 *Divine the Series*. divinetheseries.com. 2012 (Fantasy)

An immortal being known as Cesar Divine can change the course of the lives of people who face a crisis of faith. Such people can either choose salvation or damnation as man's free will allows him to make such decisions. Divine has committed an unknown sin and to gain penance, he must protect humanity from the evil supernatural beings that inhabit the dark corners of the city and the souls of its people. He has acquired the assistance of four people each of whom has their dark secrets: Deacon Jim, a seemingly devout and compassionate man of the cloth; Father Andrew, a young priest facing a crisis of faith; Jin, a woman of mystery who is Divine's companion; and Father Christopher, a priest struggling to cope with his inner demons.

Cast: Misha Collins (Father Christopher), Chasty Ballesteros (Jin), Allen Sawkins (Deacon Jim), Dan Payne (Cesar Divine), John Emmet (Tracy Scorn), Lisa Marie Caruk (Lon), Haig Sutherland (The Prophet), Ben Hollingsworth (Father Andrew). **Credits:** *Producer:* Misha Collins, Jason Fischer, Ivan Hayden. *Director:* Ivan Hayden. *Writer:* Misha Collins, John Fischer, Ivan Hayden, Kirk Jaques. **Comment:** Well plotted program that tests free will and how people can (or will not) change their lives if something extraordinary happens to them in a moment of crisis. The acting and production values are also good.

Episodes:

1. Divine. On his reassignment to an inner city mission, Father Christopher first meets Divine.

2. Choices. Father Christopher attempts to help a man whose soul is being sought by the Devil.

3. Feed Him for Life. Divine intervenes in the life of a young priest (Father Andrew) who has fallen from grace.

4. Simple Men. Although he has been offered the way to return to his faith, Father Andrew must decide for himself if that is the path he needs to take.

5. Bestiality. A young woman with a checkered background finds a possible new meaning to life when Divine saves her from a demon. But will she see it as a miracle?

6. Lips of Men. Divine's intervention in the lives of Fathers Christopher and Andrew lead them to experience a crisis of faith.

122 *Doctor Who: Besieged*. besieged.co.uk. 2013 (Science Fiction).

Based on the long-running British television series *Doctor Who* (about a time traveler from the planet Gallifrey who, with his time machine, the TARDIS [Time and Relative Dimensions in Space] helps good defeat evil throughout the universe, especially on the planet Earth). Doctor Who, as the traveler is called, boards the British military research vessel, the *HMS Archer* to battle an unknown and extremely dangerous alien force.

Cast: Ray Hendrick (The Doctor), Jennifer Byrne (Lydia), Natalie Clark (Ade), Stephen Clyde (Cooper), Frankie MacEachen (Lt. Ryder), Hamish Wilson (Dr. Hiller). **Credits:** *Producer-Writer:* Ray Hendrick. *Director:* Lauren Lamarr. **Comment:** Although the episodes are series length (as would be seen on television) and rather long for a web series (breaking them down into more chapters would have been wiser) they capture the feel of the *Doctor Who* series and will not disappoint any *Doctor Who* fan.

Episodes:

1. Episode 1 (43 min., 8 sec.). The Doctor is summoned to assist the crew of a military vessel.

2. Episode 2 (54 min., 28 sec.). The Doctor's battle against a deadly alien force begins.

123 *Doctor Who: Pond Life*. bbc.co.uk. Year: 2010 (Science Fiction).

A mini *Doctor Who* adventure wherein the Doctor's efforts to repair the malfunctioning Helmic Regulator on his TARDIS (time traveling machine) has him appearing everywhere in time and space—and accidentally leaving an alien in the home of his earth friends, Amy Pond and her boyfriend Rory.

Cast: Matt Smith (The Doctor), Karen Gillan (Amy), Arthur Darvill (Rory). **Credits:** *Producer:* Steven Moffat, Caro Skinner. **Comment:** A comical episode in the *Doctor Who* saga that is just as enjoyable as if it were a regular episode of the series.

Episodes:

1. Pond Life, Part 1 (54 sec.). The Doctor is seen in various times as his TARDIS becomes affected by the Helmic Regulator.

2. Pond Life, Part 2 (1 min., 13 sec.). The Doctor appears in the home of Amy and Rory but is unaware that an alien has followed him.

3. Pond Life, Part 3 (54 sec.). Amy and Rory discover the alien the Doctor left behind.

4. Pond Life, Part 4 (1 min., 26 sec.). The alien, who is friendly, takes on the chores of butler to what he believes are his new employers.

5. Pond Life, Part 5 (1 min., 33 sec.). The Doctor, realizing that his alien passenger is missing, sets a course to retrieve him.

124 *Doctor Who—The Power of the Daleks*. youtube.com. 2013 (Science Fiction).

On the television series *Doctor Who*, which tells of a time-traveling alien from the planet Gallifrey, the Doctor's most feared enemy were the Daleks, highly sophisticated robots that sought only to kill. On a remote island in the South Atlantic, a mysterious capsule is discovered by and held in bay at the

Vulcan Corporation. When the Doctor learns of its find, he immediately sets a course for the island and arrives as the capsule is being opened. Three dormant Daleks are found and appear to be friendly—a ruse to take control of the island. The program charts the Doctor's battle against his old adversaries.

Cast: Nick Scovell (The Doctor), Suzy Needle (Janley), James George (Hensell), Phil Cottrill (Lesterson), Nick Bridges (Dalek Voices), Barnaby Edwards (Prime Minister), Lisa Bowerman (Admiral Cunningham), Vincent Adams (Colonel Harvey), Paul Denney (Bragan), Sarah Strange (Resno). **Credits:** *Producer:* Rob Thrush. *Writer-Director:* Nick Scovell. **Comment:** Like the television series, the web episodes are produced in the same manner and just as compelling. Not just for *Doctor Who* fans but anyone who likes a good science fiction adventure.

Episodes:

1. Part 1 (17 min., 1 sec.). The Doctor arrives on the island as the capsule is about to be opened.

2. Part 2 (17 min., 26 sec.). The released Daleks attempt to win the trust of the humans while rebuilding their strength to take over the base.

3. Part 3 (17 min., 2 sec.). As the Daleks gain strength and start to multiply, the familiar "Ex-ter-min-ate, Ex-ter-min-ate" phrase is uttered by their leader and the attack on humans begins. The Doctor, however, is surprised to learn the Daleks no longer fear him and must devise a new way to destroy them.

125 *Dominion.* youtube.com. 2010 (Horror).

A detective's (Jeremiah Grey) search for a missing woman leads to more than he anticipated when his investigation involves him in the world of the supernatural. Jeremiah, like Thomas Magnum on *Magnum, P.I.* believes in rules and has one for each occasion. As he says, "If you want to make it in this business there are a few simple rules. I take them seriously.... Trust me on this, I'm a professional." Jeremiah begins each episode with a rule and its explanation and there is a very brief action scene that follows that highlights that rule.

Cast: Sean Field (Jeremiah Grey), Maia Nicholson (Jennifer Marco), Claudia McLain (Franz), Steve Carter (Simon), Jaime Lee (Emma), Pedro Colon (Karl), Theik Smith (Slugger), Patrick Foster (Arys), Steve Kasan (Steve), Molly Montgomery (Crystal), Dulcie Felix (Kira). **Credits:** *Producer:* Rodney Smith, German Jimenez, Aubry Padmore, Sean Field. *Director:* Rodney Smith. *Writer:* Andrew Stoute, Rodney Smith. **Comment:** Difficult to assess series based on the very brief excerpts presented. Only action sequences are shown and, based on that, it proves to be an interesting concept as Jeremiah faces the unnatural.

Episodes:

1. Stranger Danger (1 min., 31 sec.). Rule 178: The Contact.

2. Easy Jobs (1 min., 31 sec.). Rule 14: The Investigation.

3. Trust (1 min., 34 sec.). Rule 57: Expect the Unexpected.

4. The Righteous (1 min., 33 sec.). Rule 66: Trapped.

5. Shimmer Man (1 min., 20 sec.). Rule 42: Sometimes It's Best to Keep Your Damned Mouth Shut.

6. The Old Guard (1 min., 36 sec.). Rule 123: I Can Do This Job.

7. No Escape (1 min., 38 sec.). Rule 101: Not to Be Deterred from a Mission.

8. Turning Points (1 min., 23 sec.). Rule 101, Part 2: Don't Trust Your Blackmailer.

9. The Coming Storm (1 min., 37 sec.). Rule 91: Apologies Don't Always Work.

10. Blood in Water (1 min., 31 sec.). Rule 84: Knowing When to Give Up.

11. Fiends in Low Places (1 min., 20 sec.). Rule 21: Stick to a Plan.

12. Only Human (2 min., 34 sec.). Rule 1: To Stay Alive, Lie.

126 *Doraleous and Associates.* fantasyweb series.net. 2010 (Animated Fantasy).

Nudonia is a magical territory in a land of many kingdoms. To protect the various territories, especially the vulnerable Nudonia, a band of warriors called Doraleous and Associates has been established. Stories follow the band of noble warriors (Doraleous, Drak, Broof, Neebs, Mirdon and Sir Walken) as they battle evil, especially Titanus and his Nanadoo Army.

Voice Cast: Jon Etheridge (Mirdon), Bryan Mahoney (Drak), Nate Panning (Doraleous), Tony Schnur (Sir Walken), Brent Triplett (Neebs). **Credits:** *Director:* Brent Triplett. *Writer:* Jon Etheridge, Bryan Mahoney, Nate Panning, Tony Schnur, Brent Triplett. **Comment:** An amusing, sometimes funny take off on the medieval age saga of warriors defending their kingdom. The animation is good, the jokes not overly crude (worse is seen on Fox's *The Family Guy*) as the creators considered children might be watching. Episodes are short enough so as not to become a burden to watch in multiple groups.

Episodes:

1. Open for Business (7 min., 49 sec.). Doraleous establishes his small band of heroes and sets out to protect Nudonia—and pick up extra compensation from citizens who might require their help.

2. The War Room (5 min., 5 sec.). Associates member Mirdon attempts to master a spell that involves cats.

3. The Toll Bridge (4 min.). The Associates attempt to cross an impassable bridge to get to the Wetalds.

4. The Wetalds (5 min., 44 sec.). After figuring out how to cross the bridge, the Associates meet King

Calas and the mighty Titanus in the Village of the Wetalds.

5. Worst vs. Worst (3 min., 55 sec.). The Associates watch as the worst soldier from the Wetalds battles an ineffectual warrior in Titanus's Nanadoo Army.

6. Mightopolis (4 min., 38 sec.). The Associates travel to the kingdom of Mightopolis where they are immediately imprisoned.

7. The Dungeon (5 min., 51 sec.). Using the power of all their thoughts, the Associates seek a way to escape from their dungeon prison.

8. Unexpected Gift (4 min., 39 sec.). The Associates escape and return to their castle.

9. No Horse for Walken (5 min., 13 sec.). A Trojan Horse spoof wherein Doraleous is puzzled about what to do with a large wooden horse he receives as a gift.

10. Party Cancelled (5 min., 31 sec.). Doraleous seeks advice from his guide, the mysterious Lady in the Lake.

11. Digger Town (6 min., 51 sec.). A call for help sends the Associates to the Meh Kingdom, which is in danger of attack.

12. Hero Punctuation (5 min., 37 sec.). In Meh, the Associates receive a cold reception from Lord Yahtzee, who doesn't appear to want their help.

13. The Pyramites (7 min., 12 sec.). In an effort to defeat the invading Bungards, the Associates team with the opposing Pyramites.

14. Dongo Tavern (7 min., 3 sec.). With the Bungards defeated, the Associates decide to return to Mightopolis.

15. Girl in Mightopolis (6 min., 22 sec.). In Mightopolis, Doraleous searches for a girl named Aleena.

16. The Gladiator (7 min., 43 sec.). A mistake by Doraleous places him in a Gladiator tournament where he must face the ferocious Graboonie.

17. Arzon Prison (5 min., 13 sec.). Having survived the battle, Doraleous and the Associates find refuge outside of Mightopolis, where Sir Walken recalls his time at Arzon Prison.

18. No Horse for Walken (8 min., 1 sec.). Figuring they have seen enough trouble in Mightopolis, the Associates decide to head back home.

19. Goodbye Drak (7 min., 6 sec.). As they journey, the Associates learn that trouble is brewing in The North.

20. The Canyons and Ramparts (8 min., 7 sec.). Broof sees his mighty hero, Testiclees as the Associates attempt to establish peace between the Cayous and the Ramparts in The North.

21. Old World Gate (7 min.). With no time to rest, the Associates investigate a supposed attack on The Gate to the Old World.

22. Brothers of the Old World (7 min., 25 sec.). The Associates find that in the kingdom of Dongo, the Brothers of the Old World are causing problems and must find a way to stop them.

23. Battle in Dongo (5 min., 29 sec.). The Associates confront (and put an end to) the Brothers of the Old World.

24. The Theater (11 min., 40 sec.). With peace restored, the Associates depart from Dongo.

25. Untitled (8 min., 42 sec.). Although weary, the Associates decide to push on and return home.

26. Geigh Kingdom (8 min., 9 sec.). Doraleous must make a decision as what to do when he stumbles upon Geigh, a kingdom he didn't know existed and is now in the midst of turmoil.

27. Needbs vs. Titanus (4 min., 9 sec.). The Associates get more than what they bargained for when Titanus appears in Geigh.

28. Queer Village (6 min., 26 sec.). Doraleous and the Associates attempt to protect the Queers (of Queer Village) from Titanus.

29. Last Straw (7 min., 2 sec.). The Associates face inner conflict when Neebs, Doraleous and Broof have an argument.

30. Battle of Hyleria (6 min.). The Associates battle wooden soldiers in the kingdom of Hyleria.

31. Testiclees (7 min., 40 sec.). The Associates team with Testiclees.

32. Wizard Duel (7 min., 21 sec.). Mirdon faces a confrontation with an old wizard friend who has turned to dark magic.

33. Giopi Invasion (8 min., 28 sec.). With time running out, the Associates head for Geigh Kingdom to warn them of a Giopi Invasion.

34. The Black Cloaks (8 min., 19 sec.). A new evil—The Black Cloaks, has become a threat to the safety of the kingdom and its territories.

35. Ampherny (6 min., 49 sec.). When a strange noise (a man screaming) is heard coming from the forest, the Associates stop to figure out which one of them should investigate.

36. Broom Salesman (6 min., 58 sec.). With their conquest ended, Doraleous seeks guidance as what to do next as Broof returns to his job as a broom salesman.

127 Draculette. watchdraculette.com. 2012 (Horror).

It is the present day and a group of misfit vampires have been shunned by the normal vampire clans. The misfits (Draculette, Morbidelia and Victoria) have banned together and though they have shortcomings (like Draculette having a fear of blood), have established their own little covet. The program follows the girl vampires as they attempt to deal with and overcome their problems to one day return to the Colony from which they have been expelled.

Cast: Jennifer Lauer (Draculette), Amanda Troop (Morbidelia), Ivana Shein (Victoria), Alec Tomkiw (Thurston). **Credits:** *Producer:* Jennifer Lauer, Chris Lauer. *Writer:* Jennifer Lauer. *Director:* Chris Lauer. **Comment:** Outcast vampires are something new to the Internet. While the presentation and acting are good, only a pilot episode has been produced.

Draculette **poster art featuring Jennifer Lauer (copyright 2012 Kings of Kontent).**

Episodes:

1. Moonbathing (4 min., 1 sec.). The pilot episode that establishes the storyline as Draculette, "The Vampire with a Eating Disorder," seeks professional help to overcome her fear of blood (if she fails she will lose her fangs and will not be able to survive).

128 *Dragon Age: Redemption.* youtube. com. 2011 (Fantasy).

In an unstated medieval age all magic is controlled by a demonic dimension called the Fade. People who encompass such powers become susceptible to demonic possession and face opposition from the Templars, the holy warriors of a religious state called the Chantry. The Chantry, however, is in conflict with the Qunari, a religious sect whose inhuman followers convert humans, dwarves and elves into "Qun" who must adhere to their strict following (disobedience to the "Qun" is a sin and punishable by death). Over time war has broken out with Chantry and Qunari factions seeking ultimate power. A disgraced Elven assassin, Tallis, is the focal point of the program. She has been spared death by the Qunari and, to redeem herself, she must stop a rogue mage (Saarebas) bent on creating a global crisis. Episodes chart her journey as she is joined by Cairn, a Chantry Templar, Josmael, a young Elven wizard, and Nyree, a vicious mercenary.

Cast: Felicia Day (Tallis), Masam Holden (Josmael), Marcia Battise (Nyree), Adam Rayner (Cairn), Doug Jones (Saarebas), Marissa Cuevas (Fina), Alex Huynh (Ludd), Anna Campbell (Inn Keeper), Tara Macken (Lune), Michael Munoz (Rukk). **Credits:** *Producer:* William Mesa, Emily Wallin. *Director:* Peter Winther. *Writer:* Felicia Day. **Comment:** Adaptation of the "Dragon Age" video game that assumes the viewer knows what the game is all about because without prior knowledge, it can become a bit of a chore to watch and figure out what is going on. While this could be considered a drawback, the series does have a lot going for it: great costumes, sets and locations. Felicia Day, cleavage and all, is especially appealing as Tallis, as well as the other members of the cast who handle their roles quite well. The dialogue is a little bit flat but the photography is comparable to anything television has produced. The special effects are very good but the fight sequences are not well choreographed and look unrealistic.

Episodes:

1. Tallis (9 min., 1 sec.). Tallis begins her assignment by forming a group of companions—people who are not always loyal to one another or each other's beliefs.

2. Cairn (10 min., 4 sec.). Cairn, a Chantry Templar, begins to question the mission when his goals rival those of Tallis.

3. Josmael (10 min., 44 sec.). As Tallis journeys, she meets Josmael, a Dalish Mage (a healer), who joins her quest.

4. Nyree (11 min., 24 sec.). Tallis hires Nyree, a Reaver Mercenary who has been betrayed by Saarebas and now seeks revenge.

5. Mercenaries (9 min., 9 sec.). Loyalties clash as Tallis and her party argue over the merit of their mission.

6. Saarebas (13 min., 44 sec.). Tallis and the party come face-to-face with Saarebas, who is conducting a blood magic ritual to open a rift into the Fade.

129 *Drawn by Pain.* blip. tv. 2007–2009 (Horror).

Emily Waters is a young girl who occupies her time by sketching beings of all shapes and sizes. She has also been living in fear as her father has been abusive to both her and her mother. One day, when her father kills her mother and next seeks Emily, the illustrations she had been sketching come to life to protect her. In a fit of rage, Emily transfers into an animated alter ego of herself and kills her father, thus avenging her mother's death. The situation caused trauma and Emily grew into adulthood as a sheltered and bitter woman. Over time, Emily's illustrations (her demons) have gained control her life and have, in essence, turned her into a monster. What she once feared she has now become. In public Emily appears normal, but inwardly she is vengeful; she is able to control what happens simply by tearing up the sketch she made. But her demons have become stronger and now possess her to a point where anyone who crosses her will face the anger of her demon side. She has now become a predator, forged by demonic beings of her own creation. Stories follow Emily as she struggles to control her mind in the real world and stop the killing before she loses all touch of reality.

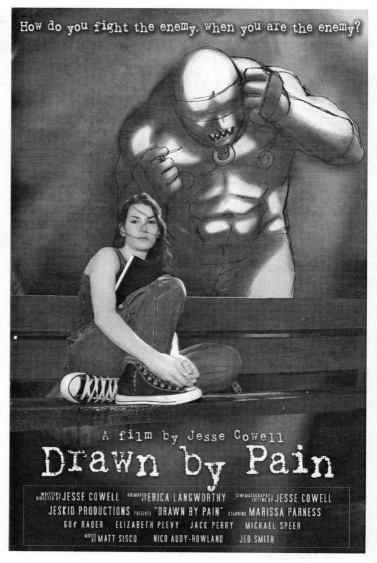

How do you fight the enemy, when you are the enemy?

A film by Jesse Cowell

Drawn by Pain

WRITTEN & DIRECTED BY JESSE COWELL ANIMATION ERICA LANGWORTHY CINEMATOGRAPHY & EDITING BY JESSE COWELL JESKID PRODUCTIONS PRESENTS "DRAWN BY PAIN" STARRING MARISSA PARNESS GUY RADER ELIZABETH PLEVY JACK PERRY MICHAEL SPEER MUSIC BY MATT SISCO NICO AUDY-ROWLAND JED SMITH

Drawn by Pain, the live-action/animaged Webby-Award winning series by writer/director Jesse Cowell, chronicles the life of a young woman searching for salvation as her animated madness fights for her sanity in the real world. Poster art featuring Marissa Parness (copyright 2008 JesKid Productions).

Cast: Marissa Parness (Adult Emily), Elizabeth Plevy (Young Emily), Guy Rader (Douglas), Michael Speer (Emily's father), Sharon Hawk (Emily's mother). **Credits:** *Producer-Writer-Director:* Jesse Cowell. *Animation:* Erica Langworthy. **Comment:** Good acting, story and production values. Live action is combined with animation and viewer interest is held from Emily's early childhood to her struggles as an adult.

Episodes:

1. Part 1. Establishes the series storyline as described above (also shows that Emily was picked on by classmates at school).

2. Part 2. Finds Emily as a grown woman, bitter and disillusioned with signs that her anger is building into something evil.

3. Part 3. As Emily dwells deeper into her psychosis, it is revealed that in her world she is not entirely alone as her inner demons are beginning to manifest themselves.

4. Part 4. Having a difficult time controlling her demons, Emily lashes out at anyone who crosses her—with deadly results.

5. Part 5. Emily struggles to control her demons and finds that by tearing up an illustration she can destroy them—at first.

6. Part 6. Emily believes she has everything under control and is struggling to convince herself that she is not insane.

7. Part 7. Emily's efforts to control what she has created is becoming more difficult and destroying the illustrations is now not a solution.

8. Part 8. Emily's past and present collide, making her more vicious than ever as her vengeful demons have grown stronger.

9. Part 9. Knowing that she must control the evil she has created, Emily struggles to regain her own being.

10. Part 10. Emily's inability to fully control her demons sends her on a rampage to kill anything that gets in her way.

11. Part 11. The situation becomes increasingly tense as Emily's every essence is being controlled by evil.

12. Part 12. The series finale wherein Emily's fate is determined as she seeks a way to end what she started.

130 *Drifter: Broken Road.* drifterseries.com. 2011 (Science Fiction).

It has been five years since a second civil war ravaged America. One woman, known only as Drifter, has survived, as have other humans, but there is no government, no laws and the only way to survive is to become a scavenger. Drifter, called a "Non-Believer" because she will not resort to the barbaric ways of others, wants to live free and live her life the best she can—but can she can live long enough to do that? In one way Drifter is a scavenger, taking what she can from the land, and has her life again turned upside down when she is forced to kill three vicious scavengers when they attempt to rape her. Stories relate one incident in her life when she befriends a brother and sister (Ed and Emily) who run a trading post and must risk her life to protect them when a scavenger (Gunpowder) seeks to kill her for killing three members of his tribe.

Drifter was an FBI agent and skilled in hand-to-hand combat as well as in the use of firearms. At the beginning of the Second Civil War she fought on the side of the U.S. government. When she discovered the government was actually deceiving people, she joined the Loudon Rangers, a Virginia militia group; she began her lone journey following the war.

Vanessa Leinani | Dale Gehris | Hannah Duncan

WRITTEN DIRECTED & PRODUCED BY JASON BRASIER
EXECUTIVE PRODUCERS CHRISTOPHER JOHNSON BRITTNEY GREER

www.drifterseries.com

Drifter: Broken Road. **Vanessa Leinani and Ryan Smith in their roles as Drifter and Ed (copyright 2012 American Wasteland Entertainment, LLC).**

Ed and his younger sister Emily are the only surviving members of their family (their parents were killed shortly after the war began during a hunting expedition). To survive, they began their trading post where passerby's can purchase or trade for supplies.

Prior to the Second Civil War, Emily was a popular high school girl and head of the cheerleading team. The war changed her life and she had to face the harsh realities of fighting for survival, joining her brother, Ed, by operating a trading post.

Prior to the war Gunpowder, known by a different (but not revealed) name was a construction worker. Like many others, the war changed him. He now leads a band of men who regulate the back roads and paths through the Midwest. His legend has grown and he is known and feared.

Prior to the war Cottonmouth was a rebel in the world of arena football. His real name is not revealed but he was given his current nickname for his short temper and habit of snapping back at others.

Drain was the host of a cable television show about hunting before the war ended all transmissions. Drain, an expert on weapons, is now Gunpowder's right hand man (they crossed paths during a gunfight and became friends when they were the only two left standing).

Cast: Vanessa Leinani (Drifter), Ryan Smith (Ed), Hannah Duncan (Emily), Nick Herra (Gunpowder), Todd Hansard (Cottonmouth), Ryan Shields (Drain), Jerry-Mac Johnston (Henry Longabaugh), Dale Geris (Agent Sands), Blake Flageolle (Ruckus). **Credits:** *Producer:* Brittney Greer, Jason Brasier. *Writer-Director:* Jason Brasier. **Comment:** Nicely enacted tale of a lone woman just trying to survive in an era that has turned to lawlessness and savagery. Production values, costumes and sets are also good. The idea is compelling enough and offers endless story possibilities for conversion into a network television series.

Episodes:

1. Chapter 1 (8 min., 9 sec.). Drifter is introduced in a world five years after the Second Civil War. She appears defenseless (walking with a cane) until she is attacked by three scavengers and is forced to kill them to save her own life.

2. Chapter 2 (7 min., 26 sec.). As she wanders, Drifter befriends Ed and Emily, a brother and sister who run a trading post.

3. Chapter 3 (7 min., 46 sec.). Unknown to Drifter, she is being sought by Gunpowder, the leader of the scavenger group whose members were killed by Drifter.

4. Chapter 4 (7 min., 50 sec.). Gunpowder and his henchmen (Cottonmouth and Drain) uncover clues as to the killer they are seeking.

5. Episode 5 (4 min., 30 sec.). Drifter, about to leave the trading post, has a change of plans when Gunpowder confronts her.

6. Chapter 6 (10 min., 46 sec.). Drifter risks her life in a confrontation with Gunpowder to save the lives of Ed and Emily.

131 Drone. webserieschannel.com. 2012 (Science Fiction).

Unmanned drones are currently being used by the military as the nature of warfare has changed in the 21st century. In the year 2023 drones have taken the form of humanoids and are being deployed to the front lines. One such drone is 237. He, like others of his kind, is the new breed of soldier—faster, stronger and better than their human counterparts. They are autonomous by design and are programmed to operate by a code of war. 237 is an exception as he develops a sense of morality and cannot kill as programmed after he is damaged. The program follows what happens when programmers attempt to return 237 to what it once was and hopefully prevent other drones from deviating from their programming. Nissen is the corrupt military commander seeking to use 237 as a means for other than what it was intended.

Cast: Lance Reddick (Nissen), Eli Presser (Drone 237), Sara Arrington (Programmer), Stacy-Love Belizaire (Nissen's daughter), Jeremy Bassett (Lab technician), William Mapother (Supervisor). **Credits:** *Producer:* Justin Lin. Andrew Nagel. *Director:* Robert Glickert. *Writer:* Robert Glickert, Daniel Casey. **Comment:** Intriguing concept as what could happen if drones develop the ability to think for themselves. The acting and production values are good although it is a bit violent and contains unnecessary foul language.

Episodes:

1. Episode 1 (6 min., 28 sec.). Introduces the program's concept.

2. Episode 2 (5 min., 57 sec.). Problems begin to develop for programmers when Drone 237 begins to deviate from its programming.

3. Episode 3 (8 min., 33 sec.). Drone 237 is taken out of service and tested.

4. Episode 4 (11 min., 2 sec.). Drone 237 goes on a rampage with the military seeking to stop him and programmers hoping to restore its android memory.

132 The Edge of Normal. wonderly.com. 2013 (Fantasy).

Gretchen, Evey, Natalie, Riley, Kimmi and Kris are teenage girls who each possess an extraordinary, dangerous and mysterious power. Their differences have united them and they have become a unique family. Stories relate their efforts to not only control their developing powers but encompass them for the greater good (battling evil).

Gretchen Summers, age 18, has a photographic memory and can biologically control electronic equipment (called an "Electronic Symbiant"). She is the daughter of Francine and Frank Summers and currently lives with her mother (her father, mentally unstable, abandoned the family nine years ago). Gretchen encompasses her powers to monitor government, police and civilian activity. She has anonymously captured criminals and the police have labeled her as "The Mysterious Vigilante." Gretchen can easily elude detection and cover her tracks but her excessive drive makes her reckless and endangers her life.

Evey Simms, age 15, has the ability to use her voice to involuntarily control the actions of those who hear her (called "Auditory Inducer"). Studies have indicated that Evey's powers interact with the cortical language areas of the brain thus allowing her to control others. She is the daughter of Sandra Simms who has since abandoned the family. Evey is also able to direct her commands to selected individuals or groups as she sees fit (she has used her abilities to escape from her guardians and her powers can develop into something very dangerous).

Natalie Reed, age 17, is a "Visual and Aural Telepath" (able to not only read minds but hear the thoughts of others and, through eye contact, see and feel their memories). She currently lives with her maternal grandmother (her parents and brother reside in another state). Natalie's powers could increase as she grows older but at present, she must take medication to help her control them (as sometimes they can become over-powering).

Riley Marks, age 18, is a "Passive Shape Shifter" (she can change her physical appearance based on what she observes). Riley appears to those who see her as an idealized projection of what each perceives her to be (almost always sexual in nature which, in turn, causes unwanted propositions and harassment). Although she possesses a great ability, she does not incorporate it for personal gain. She has currently attached herself to Natalie, who can see Riley as the person she actually is.

Kimmi Freeman, age 12, is the youngest member of the group. She is a "Sensory Precognitive" (can project her consciousness forward in time allowing her to perceive future events). She lives with her mother (Bonnie) and older sister (Kris). Her father's whereabouts is unknown. Her powers are progressing at an alarming rate and she can currently see several minutes to several days in the future. It is theorized that in a few years she will be able to see forward several decades, possibly even centuries. If encompassed, her abilities could be used to harness unimaginable technology before their actual creation.

Kris Freeman, age 17, is Kimmi's older sister. She is a "Radiant Transducer" (she can generate energy pulses and render people unconscious). She lives with her mother (Bonnie) and sister Kimmi. Kris is secretly Gretchen's vigilante associate and uses her powers to render criminals unconscious. Her abilities, however, do come with a price: if she becomes angered or emotionally charged, her powers can become involuntarily triggered and pose a danger to those around her at the time. As she grows older it is likely she will have the ability to increase her force and range and even induce permanent repercussions (such as paralysis or death).

Cast: Anna Rubley (Gretchen), Devin Brooke (Natalie), Nik Isbelle (Kris), Sarah Colbert (Evey), Allie Shea (Kimmi), Katie Orr (Riley Marks), Mike Peebler (Frank), Stephanie Manglaras (Francine), Sara Arrington (Sandra), Hayley Bensmiller (Young Evey; flashback), Dana Lee Ryan (Evey, age 8), Theron Harrison (Billy), Jeff Hersh (Oscar), Antonio Alverez (Off. Hicks). **Credits:** *Producer:* Tiffany L. Gray, Samantha Covington. *Writer-Director:* Amanda Overton. **Comment:** Any fantasy (or horror) program encompassing pretty teenage girls with extraordinary powers is an attention grabber and often becomes a hit on television (such as *Buffy the Vampire Slayer* and *Sabrina, the Teenage Witch*). The Internet has such a program here as the six teenage leads are likable, can act and are placed in a well-produced series that holds attention from the very beginning.

Episodes:

1. Natalie (6 min., 5 sec.). Introduces Natalie as she meets Evey, alone and destitute, for the first time. They soon become friends and Evey soon meets Gretchen, who has unpleasant news for Natalie.

2. Gretchen (5 min., 41 sec.). Gretchen and Kris have teamed to bring criminals to justice, but Gretchen's world becomes troublesome when she announces that her father (Frank) has returned.

3. Kimmi (4 min., 4 sec.). As Frank becomes a threat to Gretchen, Kimmi becomes a life saver when she uses her ability to see Gretchen's future.

4. Riley (4 min., 55 sec.). Kimmi's future visions reveal that there is another girl with powers, Riley, whom they must find in order to save Gretchen from Frank (who is planning to kill Gretchen).

5. Kris (7 min., 57 sec.). Feeling she can be of the most help, Kris attempts to stop Frank, alone but her actions place her and Gretchen in extreme danger.

6. Evey (10 min., 56 sec.). Feeling she owes a debt to her new found friends, Evey risks her life to save Gretchen and Kris from the mentally unstable Frank.

Note: The additional bonus episodes are also available:

1. Natalie's Vlog. Contains the following episodes: "I'm Not Alone," "Gretchen's Power," "Gretchen's Dad," "Kimmi's Power," "Fear Is Good," "Gretchen's Dangerous" and "Evey's Gone."

2. Kris's IPhone Videos. Contains the following episodes: "Kris Meets Gretchen," "First Success," "Who's Next?," "Something's Wrong" "We Need to Quit."

3. Director's Diary. Behind-the-scenes footage.

4. Meet the Cast. Cast members are profiled.

133 *8:13.* 813series.com 2012–2013 (Horror).

A pandemic has occurred (at 8:13 p.m.) and people are becoming infected with a deadly virus. As the virus kills all its victims, it also resurrects them as zombies, causing military officials and scientists alike an even greater problem—how to stop the spread of the virus and deal with the growing zombie threat. One city, Los Angeles, is the center of attention as martial law is instituted with stories relating how most people survived the virus—and their efforts to survive long enough until a cure is found. The title is taken from Romans 8:13: "For if yee live off the flesh yee shall die. But of yee through the spirit mortify the deeds of the body, yee shall live."

8:13 cast, from left to right: Beau Ryan as Johnny Dixon, Chris Dorman as Toby, Craig Frank as Kennedy and Traycee King as Erika (copyright Kitty Quilt Pictures).

Cast: Beau Ryan (Johnny Dixon), Chris Dorman (Toby), Traycee King (Erika), Marisha Ray (Sonia), Craig Frank (Jack Kennedy), Richard Lara (Greg Frost), Dangerfield Moore (David Leon), Emily Button (Agent Cooper), Rebecca Denise (Laurana Lynn), Maria Olsen (Shelly Harris), Sara Fletcher (Hannah), Paula Rhodes (Mary). **Credits:** *Producer:* Traycee King. *Director:* Rachael King, Mando Franco. *Writer:* Traycee King, Mando King, Rachael King. **Comment:** Producer Traycee King has attempted something different when it comes to a web series. Instead of presenting a straight forward story, she chose to intrigue viewers by starting at the end and progressing to the beginning. The gimmick works because the opening scene has you wondering what is (has) happened. The zombie effects are above average (some scenes are a bit bloody when the creatures are killed) and Erika's sacrificial sequence in episode 21 is a bit unsettling (tied down and forced to drink blood). Other than that, the acting and production values are very good and the program is well worth watching.

Episodes:

0. Unknown Video (2 min.). A newscast reports incidents of vandalism against a pharmaceutical company called Rundberg. As the report continues it is believed, by the graffiti scrolled "M" on the walls that a radical group called M.A.R.S. (Movement Against Rundberg) is responsible, but there is no proof.

1. The Interrogation (2 min., 4 sec.). Opens the actual program with a young man (Johnny) being interrogated by a group of men for what he may know about the vandalism incident.

2. The Hacker (4 min., 24 sec.). It is revealed that M.A.R.S. was responsible as they believe Rundberg had something to do with the disaster that occurred at 8:13 p.m.

3. Dinner for One (5 min., 23 sec.). Introduces Sonia and Johnny as Sonia becomes upset with Johnny as he leaves her alone to join Toby to report (via their Internet blog) what is happening in their city.

4. Destruction (3 min., 30 sec.). It is 7:50 p.m. and a police sting operation to bust a drug dealer is about to go down.

5. Sting (2 min., 27 sec.). The sting operation goes bad when one the agent's is killed.

6. 8:14 p.m. (1 min., 43 sec.). It is one minute after the fatal occurrence and the first evidence of a zombie uprising occurs when the deceased female agent returns to life.

7. Trespassing (4 min., 20 sec.). More evidence of zombies appears as the dead are now walking the streets.

8. Barb (1 min., 12 sec.). Johnny and Toby begin a search to find their partner, Barb, who has disappeared.

9. Shoot for the Head (5 min., 33 sec.). FBI agents Frost and Leon are forced to kill their former associate as she threatens them.

10. Home Sweet Home (4 min., 8 sec.). Follows three women (Erika, Sonia and Laurana Lynn), previously seen riding in a car, as they reach their destination—their home and danger when their fourth roommate, June (now a zombie) attacks them.

11. Kennedy (3 min., 29 sec.). Agent Kennedy and his team find themselves surrounded by zombies following the sting operation.

12. Cornered (3 min., 41 sec.). As Johnny and Toby continue their search for Barb, she finds them—turned and now seeking to kill them.

13. The Getaway (6 min., 35 sec.). Kennedy and his team manage to escape the approaching zombies but encounter more trouble when they run into a

seemingly normal couple (who stay in the shadows—to conceal their zombie transference).

14. Dead End (3 min., 2 sec.). Erika and Sonia, unable to save Laurana Lynn from June's rampage, manage to escape.

15. 1 Little, 2 Little, 5 Little Indians (3 min., 36 sec.). Fate unites Erika and Sonia with Johnny and Toby while Agents Kennedy, Frost, Cooper and Leon escape the "nice" couple.

16. United They Fall (3 min., 36 sec.). Fate again comes to the rescue when the agents encounter Erika, Sonia, Johnny and Toby and, to protect each other, become a team.

17. All That's Left (3 min., 3 sec.). A car accident separates Sonia from the group.

18. Casualties of War (2 min., 7 sec.). A search for Sonia places Erika in danger when Sonia, turned, approaches her.

19. Sanctuary (5 min., 44 sec.). As Erica is saved when Sonia is shot, the team now seeks a safe haven.

20. The Lion's Den (2 min., 44 sec.). Believing they have found a safe house, the team is tricked into entering by the leader of a mysterious cult.

21. United They Fall (3 min., 38 sec.). A hastily made plan by Kennedy to escape backfires when Erika is killed in a sacrifice and Toby is injured.

22. Last Words (2 min., 19 sec.). Toby, knowing he is going to become a zombie, pleads with Johnny to kill him.

23. Enter M.A.R.S. (2 min., 21 sec.). As Johnny contemplates his actions he becomes surrounded by zombies but is saved when he is kidnapped by the radical group M.A.R.S.

24. Noah's Ark (3 min., 40 sec.). At M.A.R.S. headquarters, Johnny recounts the incidents of the last 12 hours and is asked by Noah, the group leader, to join them and prove Rundberg is responsible for what happened.

134 Electric City. uk.screen.yahoo.com. 2012 (Science Fiction).

It is a time after an apocalypse ended the world as it was once known. One region, called Electric City, represents peace and security around the crumbling remnants of what was once society. But the bad has also resurrected—from back alley dealings, crimes and corruption. Electric City, like other such places around the globe has resorted to producing natural electric power as fossil and nuclear fuel has been depleted. Everyone in such communities must contribute to society's welfare ("All in Service to All") and undesirables (such as criminals) are put to work as "muscle power" in the utilities that produce power. Each facility is connected by power cables, but all non-essential uses for power have been termed illegal and a punishable crime if caught wasting electricity. When the world ended, a group of war survivors established Electric City and now strictly maintain the use of power as a weapon of control over the city and

its citizens. One resistance group, the Tap Coders, has risen from the depths and is determined to circumvent the current social and power restrictions. Stories follow the battle that begins to brew as the Tap Coders fight to restore society to a time as it existed before the apocalypse.

Principal Characters: Cleveland Carr was a former leader of the Allied Municipal Patrol (AMP) who, after being stripped of his life and identity (formally known as Lorenzo Seventeen) now works as a grid operative and assassin for Ruth Orwell, one of the founders of Electric City (which has the nickname "The Knitting Society"). She operates along with founders Mrs. Stoddart and Mrs. Zelaski. Hope Chatsworth is the city's radio newscaster (for station Wire 6) and Cleveland's girlfriend. Frank Deetleman is secretly a Tap Coder and works as Hope's technician. Roger Moore is a spy for AMP. Gladys Elba is a member of the Electric City Youth Auxiliary. Garrison "Knobs" Butler is the crook who sells illegal radios to citizens. Commander Welles is the AMP commander. Sah is the owner of the restaurant that fronts for the Tap Coders.

Voice Cast: Tom Hanks (Cleveland Carr), Holland Taylor (Ruth Orwell), Jeanne Tripplehorn (Hope Chatsworth), Joey Kern (Frank Deetleman), Edith Fields (Mrs. Zelaski), Lindsey Stoddart (Mrs. Emerson), Tara Sands (Roger Moore), Kristin Klabunde (Gladys Elba), Jason Antoon (Garrison Butler), Georg Stanford Brown (Commander Welles), Eric Bauza (Sah) **Credits:** *Director:* Joel Trussell. *Writer:* Tom Hanks, Josh Feldman, Bo Stevenson. **Comment:** Video material accompanying the episodes has been taken off line (the message, "This Video No Longer Exists," will appear) although one trailer has survived on YouTube.com. Based on what can be viewed, the animated program is well done and the voice characterizations fit the characters well. Tom Hanks created the program and voices the principal character, Cleveland, with television actress Holland Taylor also lending support.

Episodes: *1.* Truth or Consequences. *2.* The Voice of the City. *3.* Survivors. *4.* Young Daughter of God. *5.* We're Social Animals. *6.* All in Service to All. *7.* What Aren't We Capable Of. *8.* The Time Has Come. *9.* The Saddest of Reasons. *10.* Never the Two Shall Meet. *11.* Necessary to Hide. *12.* Lost Souls. *13.* Lorenzo Seventeen. *14.* Trail of Dead Bodies. *15.* Strategic Casualties. *16.* No One Is Untraceable. *17.* People Like a Good Show. *18.* The Outside. *19.* Such Beauty from a Box. *20.* Illumination Night.

135 The Ennead. youtube.com. 2009 (Science Fiction).

For untold centuries, a battle has been waged between good and evil. At the heart of the conflict are The Eternals, nine supernatural beings (known as the Ennead) who have shaped the destiny of the world since the beginning of time. When the

Eternals suddenly vanished both sides engaged in a quest to find them and acquire their power. It has also been prophesied that a mysterious comet would enter the Earth's atmosphere and signal a return of the Ennead. It is the present and a comet has come as predicted. Five people, apparently unknown to each other, awaken in a forest, unsure of who they are or what they may be. The program charts their experiences as their memories slowly begin to return—with each starting to believe they have known each other (five of the nine Eternals is hinted and they may be the only hope to save the planet from a second Dark Age).

Cast: Melissa Kelly (Flick), Chanel Taylor (Princess), Casey Manderson (Cats), Renee St. Cyr (Teeth), Steve Thackray (The Captain), Candace Chase (Nova), Kristine Cofsky (Polly), Clive Bethel (Lucian), Tyler McMaster (U-Turn). **Credits:** *Producer-Writer-Director:* Terry Miles. **Comment:** Long but well done program that holds the viewer's interest from start to finish. Production values, including the acting, writing and directing, are exceptional and worthy of an edited, broadcast television version. To lesson viewing time, episodes 5, 15 and 16 could be skipped as they have no impact on the story; in fact, now that production has been completed, they actually distract from the story.

Episodes:

1. Episode 1 (5 min., 51 sec.). Five people, unaware of whom or what they are, awaken in a wintry-like forest.

2. Episode 2 (5 min., 17 sec.). As they begin to wander through the forest, each ponders what could have happened and why they are where they are.

3. Episode 3 (6 min., 48 sec.). As night approaches, the group decides it would be best to make camp and begin fresh in the morning.

4. Episode 4 (5 min., 19 sec.). Hints as to what happened are revealed as several people are seen in what appears to be an observatory and seeking to find five missing people.

5. Episode 5 (2 min., 4 sec.). A message from the producer that acts as a prelude to upcoming episodes 6 and 7.

6. Episode 6 (7 min., 2 sec.). A sixth member joins the group and spreads some light as to who they are and a mission they must complete: stop an assassination or something bad will happen.

7. Episode 7 (6 min., 2 sec.). It is revealed an accident occurred that caused a loss of memory; the group must find the target of the assassination within three days (on Sept. 9, 2009).

8. Episode 8 (5 min., 56 sec.). As their memories begin to return, the name Xavier is recalled, but who he is or what connection he has to them is not known.

9. Episode 9 (8 min.). Two strangers, identifying themselves as agents from Nova, appear but find it difficult gaining the group's trust when they say they have been sent to help them.

10. Episode 10 (5 min., 37 sec.). Fearing they are in danger, an unknown ability manifests itself and the group is able to tele-transport themselves to safety.

11. Episode 11 (5 mi., 40 sec.). It appears that since the comet, each member of the group's psychology has changed: their aging process has slowed, their cells are re-directing themselves and they are able to have slight visions of the future.

12. Episode 12 (6 min., 24 sec.). A clue to what the mission entails is revealed when the drawing of a symbol that translates as "L'Est Asi" is found.

13. Episode 13 (6 min., 42 sec.). The clue, it is learned, is one third of a puzzle that was created many centuries ago by beings known as Cylons to protect a great profit from evil. The puzzle (a map), called The True Cross, was divided into three parts with each Cylon receiving one part. Once done, the Cylons simply vanished. The map, however, does not lead to a where or what—but a who.

14. Episode 14 (7 min., 49 sec.). Further research reveals to the group that the symbols date back to the Babylonian age and a copy of the entire map exists at the local library.

15. Episode 15 (10 min., 56 sec.). A break in the series that gives a behind-the-scenes look at the program's production.

16. Episode 16 (6 min., 48 sec.). A recap of what has happened so far.

17. Episode 17 (7 min., 56 sec.). By the strangest coincidence, a business card stating "Historia Nova" is found.

18. Episode 18 (8 min., 22 sec.). The card just adds to the mystery—and time is running out to discover and save the target.

19. Episode 19 (8 min., 22 sec.). The group, now in possession of all three parts of the map (from the library) attempt to figure out what the symbols mean.

20. Episode 20 (7 min., 58 sec.). The symbols appear to indicate that there are strategically placed evil beings that will strike (the target). The target is a symbol of a rebirth and if it is destroyed, evil will rule and there will be another Dark Age.

21. Episode 21 (9 min., sec.). The previously found card becomes the means of finding the target—Michael Constantine—when it leads the group to the ninth floor of a skyscraper on the ninth day of the ninth month (the previously stated date of 09-09-09).

22. Episode 22 (12 min., 34 sec.). It is realized that each member of the group is an Ennead and have been reborn to save Michael, the Great Profit, from those who seek to destroy that rebirth. If the Enneads fail, darkness will prevail upon the earth.

136 *Epilogue.* epiloguetheseries.com. 2012 (Science Fiction).

It is the present (2012) and mankind faces its most

devastating fate: In May a world-wide plague has emerged that is resistant to all modern-day cures. By July many people have succumbed to the disease. With only one hope of stopping its spread, scientists believe that a legendary 14th century French village, Pujols-Le-Harve, may hold the key as it is known for having survived the original Bubonic Plague. Dr. Samay of the Sequell Laboratory heads a team that appears to be mankind's only hope of survival. Two team members, Roz and Arch, become the guinea pigs and are sent back in time (via an injected serum) to discover the past's knowledge to save the modern world.

Rosalind "Roz" Griggs is an ex-marine and Iraq War vet who, to hopefully escape the memories of the death and destruction she faced, joined Dr. Samay at Sequell Labs to assist Dr. Samay in his time traveling experiments. Brandon Rucker, an expert on France, is an historian and scholar whose knowledge of the past could save the present-day world. Dr. Sid Samay is the founder of Sequell Labs and inventor of a miracle drug called Xanity as well as biological time travel. Archimedes "Arch" Donovan is a medical technician for Sequell Labs who built the protective EM field that surrounds the lab and helped Dr. Samay develop the time travel serum.

Cast: Sam Long (Roz Griggs), Jordan Fox (Brandon Rucker), Jon Herbert (Sid Samay), Nathan Shelton (Arch Donovan). **Credits:** *Producer:* Diana Botsford, Deborah Larson, Kenneth Mackey, Jes Mutchell, Kenneth Mackey, Celestina Jaime. *Director:* Adam Wagner, Erika Brame. *Writer:* Diana Botsford. **Comment:** Time travel is nothing new to feature films or television and even the concept presented above has been done before (in the 1978 television movie *Time Travelers* wherein a team seeks past knowledge to save present-day earth). *Epilogue* is well produced and acted and an enjoyable tale— no matter how many time traveling movies or television shows you have seen. The program's major fault is the over-abundant use of the shaky camera style of filming; scenes are just too unsteady and bouncy.

Episodes:

1. The Past Is Prologue (16 min., 7 sec.). Before returning to the 14th century, Dr. Samay's team must return to 1962 and retrieve an artifact (a knife) that will enable their journey to past centuries.

2. Bad Trip (14 min., 38 sec.). Roz and Brandon are sent to France in 1348 but Roz's strange behavior (acting as if she were in 2012) has villagers believing she is a witch.

3. Viability (14 min., 39 sec.). Before she is able to be caught and burned at the stake as a witch, Roz and Arch inject themselves with the time-traveling serum and return to the lab in 2012.

4. Imperfections (15 min.). With time running out and the 2012 plague spreading Dr. Samay theorizes that by going into the future he can change the past so that the plague never happened.

5. Broken (11 min., 11 sec.). Against the wishes of all concerned, especially Professor Rucker (who believes you cannot change a singular event in the past; everything will change) Dr. Samay journeys into the future.

6. Ripples (13 min., 53 sec.). Roz and Prof. Rucker follow Dr. Samay into the future, hoping to stop him from completing his task. Roz and Rucker fail and the past is changed—it is 2012 and Roz is seen as the owner of an antique store when a stranger (Arch) enters. Did Dr. Samay actually prevent the plague from happening? Or is an altered world about to face the plague under a different set of circumstances?

137 eScape. youtube.com. 2012 (Fantasy).

Camp Quest is a seemingly typical summer camp owned and operated by James Fantaro, owner of the video game company Fantaro Games. Suddenly, without warning, the campers find they are alone when the adult counselors mysteriously disappear. The children soon realize they are trapped in one of the video games created by Fantaro and must use their gaming skills to escape. Stories follow their efforts, given powers by the programmer, as they battle monsters and attempt to overcome various video game quests to win their freedom.

Cast: Noah Berliner (Jack), Patrick Reilly (Steven), Emma Guilfoyle (Myrna), Jake Prescott (Joshy), Sarah Sharifpour (Lexa), Livi Prescott (Olivia), Belle Babcock (Belle), Jessica Babcock (Caitlyn), Alex Wesley (Chris), Spencer Worley (Spencer). **Credits:** *Producer-Writer-Director:* Mike Feurstein. **Comment:** While not an original idea (the Australian television series *Pirate Islands* used the same trapped-in-a-video game format), it is an interesting variation and one of the very few live action web series specifically tailored to children.

Episodes:

1. Jooker (11 min.). Establishes the storyline as a group of children are suddenly stranded in their camp without counselors.

2. Aggro (9 min.). The children realize they are trapped in a video game and divide themselves into clans (like on the television series *Survivor*).

3. Zling (9 min., 30 sec.). With supplies like food dwindling, the campers seek a way to replenish their resources.

4. Romo (10 min., 30 sec.). Tensions arise within the clans as they realize that the father of one of their own is responsible for their plight.

5. Kite (9 min., 30 sec.). As the campers seek a way to escape, they discover an old train station— the possible way out of the game.

6. Rollerback (18 min., 30 sec.). As the campers decide to once again band together, a mysterious man dressed in white (head of a rival video game company) could spell the end for Fantaro Games and leave the children trapped in the game forever. Season 1 finale.

7. Episode 7 (11 min.). The season 2 premiere that picks up the story with Jason Fantaro attempting to wrestle the camp game away from The Man in White.

8. Guild. Although Jason has the game, the campers must still overcome game pitfalls to win their freedom.

9. Bot. The campers discover that Lucas, whom they thought was one of them is actually a robot.

10. Drop. The campers begin to learn more about each other and how they need to think as one to figure out an escape plan.

11. Mirror. The campers discover that another group of children are also trapped in the game but dealing with totally different game situations.

12. Retcon. The campers' skills are put to the test when they face a monster, but fail in their quest to do so when one of them is injured.

13. Rez. The campers seek a way to help their friend, but no one seems to have the power to heal.

14. Torrent. The second season concludes with the campers increasingly unable to defeat the game's monsters.

138 *Evolve*. webserieschannel.com. 2013 (Science Fiction).

Donia Reyes is a 15 year-old girl that has lived a somewhat sheltered life and has been brought up with strict traditions by her parents (Eric and Sylvia) for something she is currently unaware of but will face when she turns 18. Fate intervenes and when Donia turns 16 she realizes she is different and becomes a concern to her parents as she has developed earlier than predicted. Eric and Sylvia are members of a secret society called the Clon, people with special abilities that control the balance between the Clon (the good) and the Oden (the evil), a separate group of ex-Clon's who do not believe in the rules of absolute secrecy and could pose a threat to the world should they use their abilities for personal gain. The program charts Donia's experiences as she must now learn to accept what she is and become a fighter in a struggle between the two factions as the Clon believe the Oden are up to something evil and that something needs to be stopped before it destroys both sects. **Cast:** Jasiah Lovell (Donia Reyes), Rachel Drayke (Troi Lawson), Tisa Key (Sylvia Reyes), Eric Holter (Craig Reyes), Kajuana Shuford (Cami Knowles), Justin Hurtt-Dunkley (Ian Oscar). **Credits:** *Producer-Writer-Director:* Kia Barbee. **Comment:** Totally unconvincing acting by Jasiah Lovell as Donia. Donia couldn't care less about her abilities (like mentally moving objects) and is more concerned (totally concerned) about not being able to have her Sweet 16 party (which she complains about through most of the pilot). The pace is very slow and Donia's whining from the start is enough to turn anyone off. The parents are also not as convincing in relaying the message that they are part of the good and must defeat the evil. The idea is very good but the presentation poorly issued. *Evolve* is one of the few African American themed science fiction Internet series and a search for a better (and more likable) lead actress coupled with a faster pace would have made a world of difference.

Episodes:

1. Abilities (6 min., 37 sec.). Establishes the storyline as Donia discovers she has special abilities.

2. Birthday (8 min., 9 sec.). Donia must adjust to the fact that learning how to control her abilities is more important than a Sweet 16 birthday party.

3. Forced (7 min., 17 sec.). Eric and Sylvia feel that a different approach is needed in dealing with Donia.

4. Arrival (7 min., 54 sec.). A new girl (Troi Lawson) in town appears to be a threat to Donia.

5. Recognition (8 min.). Donia and Troi, a foreign exchange student, meet for the first time and each feels something is not right with the other. Ends unresolved.

139 *Exile*. exile.tvheaven.com. 2012 (Science Fiction).

It is days following an apocalyptic event when a group of survivors are seen in an abandoned movie theater. They all appear to be okay but their food supply is dwindling. With no other choice but to venture outside, five members (Charles, Jenni, Jake, Miss and Jesse) volunteer. It appears to be just in time as the other theater survivors are overcome by an unknown virus that turns them mad then kills them. The program follows the five remaining survivors as they attempt to find safety amid the devastation and now crazed humans who attack anything that moves. **Cast:** Peter Gaughran (Charles), Eden Suarez (Jenni), Joseph Golden (Jake), Akiko Day (Missy), James DiFlorio (Jesse). **Credits:** *Producer-Director:* Jesse Kalavoda, Marvin Day. *Writer:* Andrew Stirling. **Comment:** Poorly constructed storyline with no real explanation as to what happened to change the world. The characters are dull and interest is lost shortly after the first episode begins.

Episodes:

1. Shelter from the Storm (30 min., 1 sec.). Introduces the theater survivors and the predicament they face as their supplies begin to dwindle.

2. The Family You Choose, Part 1 (14 min., 27 sec.). A five-member group leaves the safety of the theater to search for supplies and hook up with another group of survivors.

3. The Family You Choose, Part 2 (22 min., 45 sec.). The hook up is only short lived when each must fight for his or her life when they are attacked by the zombie-like creatures that result from the apocalypse.

140 Fallout: Nuka Break. vtfilms.com. 2011 (Science Fiction).

A nuclear war has ravaged the planet. The radiation fallout has left the landscape harsh and uninhabitable and those that managed to survive must become scavengers. Three such people are Twig, Scarlett and Ben, people who are not heroes, only survivors and on a quest to find happiness—the perfect Nuka Break. As they journey, their quest becomes more difficult when wanted posters are discovered that has offered a reward (of "200 Caps") for Scarlett, a former "sexy ex-slave" who escaped from her master (Leon), an evil being who now wants her back—at any cost. As Scarlett, Twig and Ben journey they must now avoid Leon's mercenaries who will stop at nothing, including killing anyone who gets in their way as they attempt to retrieve their prey—Scarlett (after being purchased by Leon, Scarlett was spotted by Twig and Ben as she was being transported to her new master. When the opportunity arose, Twig and Ben raided her campsite and freed her; she then chose to remain with them). Ben is a disfigured survivor of what is called "The Fallout" (his face has been affected by radiation). **Cast:** Zack Finfrock (Twig), Tybee Diskin (Scarlett), Aaron D. Giles (Ben), Steven Dengler (Raz), Cameron Diskin (Ranger), David Castro (Leon), Anna Rose Heyman (Penelope), Chris Avellone (Chris), Bonnie Bower (Bonnie), Howard McNair (Daniels), Michele Specht (Red). **Credits:** *Producer:* Steven Dengler, Melanie Wagor, Anthony Clementi. *Director:* Julian Higgins, Zack Finfrock. *Writer:* Brian Clevinger. **Comment:** Immediately the viewer gets the sensation of a world devastated by an unthinkable war by the well-chosen backgrounds as Scarlett, Twig and Ben journey across it. The story moves right along and the writing and directing are right on. The acting is excellent and Scarlett, being "the sexy ex-slave" is sexy in her black attire. Although the program is not resolved, it will become obvious that the trio will survive but what will they do (seek to end their problems by killing Leon or move on to encounter new adventures as they search for Nuka Break)? Well worth watching.

Episodes:

1. Episode 1 (9 min., 3 sec.). As they journey, Twig, Scarlett and Ben have a confrontation with bounty hunters.

2. Episode 2 (7 min., 29 sec.). The journey to find Nuka Break becomes treacherous when the trio discovers a wanted poster on Scarlett.

3. Episode 3 (12 min., 5 sec.). Although they are now being cautious, Leon's mercenaries (called the Legion) manage to close in on the trio.

4. Episode 4 (7 min., 48 sec.). The Legion's efforts to dispose of Twig and Ben and capture Scarlett fail with the trio escaping after a bloody conflict.

5. Episode 5 (7 min., 46 sec.). Leon, learning of his mercenaries' miserable failure to apprehend his runaway slave, formalizes as new plan while Twig, Scarlett and Ben continue their trek across the Wasteland.

6. Episode 6 (12 min., 35 sec.). In what appears to be a foolish plan, Leon launches a torpedo-like missile, equipped with a nuclear warhead—with its target being Scarlett and her two comrades. Ends without resolution.

141 Fear Clinic. fearnet.com. 2009 (Horror).

Dr. Andover is a renowned psychiatrist whose cure for phobias has gone beyond medical practices and cost him his license. But that has not stopped him. His invention, the Fear Chamber, is a devise wherein a patient is made to face his fears as the doctor believes that the only way to overcome a fear is to confront it. Each episode focuses on a phobia and what happens to each patient when they enter and endure the "Fear Chamber." **Cast:** Robert Englund (Dr. Andover), Lisa Wilcox (Nurse Owens), Danielle Harris (Susan), Kane Hodder (Villatoro), Angel Oquendo (Garcia), Kate Nauta (Jackie), Tory Kittles (Jonte), Lucas Till (Brett), John F. Beach (Ajax). **Credits:** *Producer:* Mark Benton Johnson. *Director:* Robert Green Hall. **Comment:** While well done, it is not an original idea. Such a concept was presented on "The Fear Merchants" episode of the television series *The Avengers* (although not to cure, but to kill). Robert Englund in the title role has that mysterious Freddy Kruger aura about him (from his character in the *Friday the 13th* film series) and adds that needed touch to make for an entertaining experience.

Episodes (each runs 6 min.):

1. Hydrophobia. The fear of heights is explored in a way more terrifying than the condition.

2. Scotophobia. Unpleasant episode about a patient who suffers from a fear of fecal matter.

3. Entomophobia. The fear of bugs is one of the phobias Dr. Andover has yet to solve. In the case of his patient, Jackie, he has chosen to keep her captive until he can find a cure.

4. Misophobia. A patient, suffering from a fear of sound discovers just how loud noise can be.

5. Claustrophobia. Can imprisoning his patient in a small room cure his fear of small places?

142 Flare. rides.tv. 2013 (Science Fiction).

It appears like any other day. The sun is shining, people are working and children are playing. Suddenly, without warning, there is total darkness. The sun, the moon and the stars have all vanished. Panic sets in and society begins to fall apart. One year after what is called "The Darkness," an enormous, extremely bright flare appears in the sky and lights up the world. Has light returned to the earth? People believe so until the flare disappears into the atmosphere sixty seconds later. However, every twenty-four hours, and at the exact same time, the flare reappears to take the world out of darkness. Is it a sign the world will be once again become bright or is it the end?

Cast: Mark Moses (Dale), Jamie McShane (Burke), Ashleigh Craig (Anna), Noah Hunt (Sid). **Credits:** *Producer:* Jim Stewartson, Sean Stewart, Zach Shiff-Abrams. *Director:* Dan Brown. *Writer:* Olumide Odebebunmi, Tolu Awosiko. **Comment:** Appears exciting based on the brief trailer. Production values also look promising.

Episodes: Only a 76-second trailer has been released that is titled "Flare: The Hunt." It shows two people, Dale and his son Sid, using the Darkness for their own unethical means and of a man, Burke, seeking them for robbing him.

143 *Forests of Mystery.* forestsofmystery. com. 2009 (Science Fiction).

Video case file reports by Dewey Lansing and Jeff Collins, undergraduate forest research students (at Pacific Cascade University), as they seek answers to strange happenings in the Cascade Forest Research Center located in the deep woods of the Oregon Coast Range.

Cast: Benjamin Farmer (Dewey Lansing), Matt Ediger (Jeff Collins). **Credits:** *Producer:* Robert C. Bruce, Cary Flock. *Writer-Director:* Robert C. Bruce. **Comment:** Well paced story that, despite having no resolution, is well worth watching. Some of the case file scenes are a bit distracting (to give the effect of camera movement) but the writing, acting and direction are good.

Episodes:

1. File Case 1. Establishes the storyline as Dewey and Jeff begin their probe of the forest.

2. File Case 2. Jeff and Dewey try to determine the origin of unusual fungi and get the sensation that all is not right.

3. File Case 3. At a local bookstore, Dewey and Jeff discover from the owner that spirits exist in the deep woods.

4. File Case 4. Jeff and Dewey seek a reclusive paranormal expert that could help in their investigation.

5. File Case 5. As Jeff and Dewey continue their investigation, something sinister appears to be observing them.

6. File Case 6. Jeff and Dewey's probe indicates that an incident occurred some years ago in the deep woods that involved some loggers.

7. File Case 7. At the logger's museum, Jeff and Dewey uncover evidence of something unnatural occurring in the woods.

8. File Case 8. The search is bringing Jeff and Dewey closer to uncovering the truth—but it could cost them their lives.

9. File Case 9. Jeff and Dewey uncover evidence

that a town, called Aquadea, once existed in the woods but mysteriously vanished.

10. File Case 10. Jeff and Dewey venture back into the woods with a map showing the location where Aquadea once stood.

11. File Case 11. As they investigate, Jeff and Dewey become lost in the site of Aquadea—now a sunken valley.

12. File Case 12. The concluding episode finds Jeff and Dewey seeking a way out of the sunken valley while being pursued by something unknown.

144 *Forge Apollo.* forgeapollo.com. 2013 (Science Fiction).

Anthology-like program of brief tales involving an ordinary person's encounter with strange phenomena.

Cast: Angie Michael, Eric Larsen. **Credits:** *Writer-Director:* Gabe Michael. **Comment:** While each episode is left for the viewer to decide its outcome, the special effects, especially in the first episode, are excellent. The acting and other production values are also up to par.

Episodes:

1. The Historian (3 min., 13 sec.). While playing outdoors with her doll, a young girl witnesses the crash landing of an alien spacecraft. Curious she investigates to discover a silver-like ball emerging from the wreck and of a recorded image telling her that prophecies are about to come true. Ends without a conclusion.

2. The Outliners (3 min., 35 sec.). A young photographer finds a strange camera on the grounds of a park. When he asks his girlfriend to pose for a picture, he sees through the camera's lens that she is surrounded by ghostly-like images. Guardian Angels?

3. Hikers Get the Finger (2 min.). It actually involves two skiers, one of whom finds a glove in the snow—a glove from which an enormous hand emerges to give them "the finger."

4. SS6: Shape Shifters (3 min., 23 sec.). Unearthly Shape Shifters take human form to foil the plot of illegal arms dealers.

5. L.A. Underwater (2 min., 40 sec.). While posing for pictures, a young model and her photographer witness what could be the end of the world—a huge planet-like object overshadowing the earth.

6. Velocity Technium (1 min.). Explores the wonders of computer-generated shapes.

7. Exploration Technium (1 min.). A further exploration from where the prior episode left off.

145 *4Villains.* webserieschannel.com. 2012 (Science Fiction).

In a world where heroes are adored and villains are considered the low life's of society, four villains (Shadowsnake, Psynapse, Evil Hidden, Dr. Don't) want to change all that and get some respect. To accomplish their goal, they establish 4 Villains, a guild where the downtrodden, unworthy and unwanted villains of the world can become as one and create their own presence in the world's villainous community. The program follows "our heroes" as they establish their organization and seek to make names for themselves. Although the setting is Viktem City, common citizens know it as Victoria City; heroes maintain that it is called Victory City; villains know it as Viktem [Victim] City. While heroes and villains continue to argue over a proper name, the common citizens see them both as more of a danger to their safety than the vigilantes who are also commonplace. There is no government regulation and because of that both factions are accepted.

Cast: Jeff Saamanen (Shadowsnake), Laura Lapadat (Psynapse), Devin Douglas (Dr. Don't), Justin Guthrie (Evil Hidden). **Credits:** *Producer-Writer:* Lucas Erskine. *Director:* Jeff Saamanen. **Comment:** While only a lengthy pilot has been released, it is an intriguing, comical twist on organizations that hold only superheroes in esteem (like The Justice League of America). The production values and acting are good and there is potential for some intriguing stories if the villains are allowed to perhaps, once achieve some villainy and recognition as opposed to always remaining downtrodden.

Episodes:

1. Crucifired (24 min., 32 sec.). Establishes how 4 Villains came to be. When Dr. Don't, an employee of the government sanctioned organization of villainy called the Crucible is fired for not meeting their standards, he feels his life is going to become a drudge until he meets Shadowsnake, a time traveling Ninja from the sixteenth century who has just been rejected for membership in the Crucible. The two share a drink and hit on a plan to form their own unsanctioned society of villains—the 4 Villains (with Psynapse and Evil Hidden as its other principal members).

146 *14 Grimm Street.* webserieschannel. com. 2013 (Horror).

The home at 14 Grimm Street in London, England, may not sound like the most inviting of addresses, but it was for many years a respectable residence. That is until two squabbling friends, Sid and Julian, decided to become housemates. The address seems appropriate as Sid and Julian share a secret— they are both serial killers. The program charts their experiences as they try to live a normal, peaceful life despite what they do in their spare time—seeking victims to satisfy their hunger for killing. Produced in England.

Sid is a renegade punk artist by day and "a happy slasher" by night. He is sort of a maverick—makes his own rules but never follows them. Julian is longsuffering legal clerk by day and "surgery obsessed vengeance killer by night." He is outwardly passive and used to being pushed around and walked over; it is only at night that his hatred comes forth to manifest itself in killing the varmints of society.

Cast: Tom Kilby (Sid), Jordan Moore (Julian), Eleanor Stephenson (Nancy), Mark Townley (Klaus). **Credits:** *Producer-Writer:* Chris Armstrong, Neil Evans. **Comment:** Enjoyable horror spoof as two friends encompass what they are and how to deal with it.

Episodes:

1. Episode 1 (4 min., 46 sec.). Julian becomes annoyed when Sid decides to use his best kitchen knife for a killing.

2. Episode 2 (5 min., 43 sec.). The boys become attracted to Nancy, their next-door neighbor—but the attraction could be fatal (for Nancy).

3. Episode 3 (5 min., 5 sec.). While trying to impress Nancy, Sid embarrasses Julian at the same time an unexpected guest arrives (Klaus).

4. Episode 4 (6 min., 48 sec.). Nancy has left unharmed; Julian becomes suspicious of Klaus, whom he believes is not the quirky foreigner he pretends to be.

5. Episode 5 (4 min., 36 sec.). Julian's suspicions turn out to be true when he discovers Klaus is a killer but are he and Sid safe? The cliff hanging final episode.

147 *Freelancers.* watchfreelancers.com. 2013 (Science Fiction).

The setting is an ancient time where there are no heroes, no moral messages and no sagas—"just flawed characters with extraordinary skills just trying to make a living." The program opens with the beautiful thief (she has to make a living) Caitlin Marcks stealing a valuable artifact from a powerful sorcerer and two bounty hunting mercenaries Nick the Bold and Ivan Strang seeking her for the reward. The duo soon becomes a trio when Nick and Ivan have to risk their lives to protect her from rival bounty hunters until they can collect their reward. The three eventually become a team and stories follow their trail as they do whatever it takes to earn the money to pay the bills.

Caitlin Marcks is beautiful but stubborn and gifted as a thief (she is also an expert swordswoman but over confidence could get her killed). Ivan Strang is wizard (who likes to go barefoot) and talented as a mind bender who thrives on hallucinogens. Nick the Bold is a warrior of incredible strength and bravery who has been immune to pain since being struck in the head by one of Ivan's misfired arrows. Kristian the Shadowbender is an ambitious, cold-hearted (but beautiful) sorceress who yearns to control the denizens of Hell. Ava the Marchioness is a girl who went from rags to riches through military prowess and is a brilliant commander, tactician and dragon slayer. Quill is an assassin who strikes from the shadows. She is also a seer of ghosts and a drug user who gets high to forget her past killings. Marcus the Marked Priest wields Joseph's hammer as a serial killer for God. Saoirse is the bold, wicked and ruthless businesswoman who inherited her great wealth after her husband turned into a werewolf. Paul the Saint is a psychopath who believes he is a saint. Bradley the Soft is a happy-go-lucky killer-for-hire. The Viscountess Anastasia is the scorned debutante seeking revenge against those who scorned her. Kilimanjaro is the alchemist whose loyalties lie with the shadowy characters that can help him achieve his goal of climbing the social ladder.

Cast: Caitlin Geier (Caitlin Marcks), Ivan Borntrager (Ivan Strang), Nicholas Givanio (Nick the Bold), Holiday Kinard (Kristian the Shadowbender), Ava Brunini (Ava the Marchioness), Mayra Rodriquez (Quill), Jared Moore (Kael the Killer), Marcus Natividad (Marcus the Marked Priest), Jeff Doda (Verlinden), Jody Mortara (Saoirse), Paul L. Benton (Paul the Saint), Bradley Greenwell (Bradley the Soft), Debradawn Shockey (The Viscountess Anastasia), CJ Johnson (Kilimanjaro the Alchemist). **Credits:** *Producer:* Ignatius Fischer, Brian Dillon. *Writer-Director:* Ignatius Fischer. **Comment:** Comically played tale of an ancient time that never existed. The girls are gorgeous and the guys, well, typical of what you would expect—not the brightest of beings. The costumes are expertly designed, the locales well chosen and the acting and production values very good (the cinematography is especially appealing). The plot could be tightened a bit by editing to increase its flow. The program ends unresolved but additional episodes are planned.

Episodes:
1. The Key (5 min., 4 sec.). Introduces the main characters with Nick and Ivan battling rival bounty hunters for Caitlin's reward.
2. Thief (9 min., 6 sec). Nick appears to be falling for Caitlin (but not she for him) while Ivan finds he still has feelings for his ex-girlfriend, Kristian the Shadowbender.
3. Verlinder (8 min., 15 sec.). Ivan "attacks" Kristian with kisses; rival bounty hunter Kael the Killer catches up with Caitlin looking for the artifact she stole and, believing she has hidden it in her bosom, proceeds to check when Nick stops him.

148 *Frequency.* frequencywebseries.com. 2012 (Fantasy).

The first Internet lesbian fantasy series (with the tag line, "Most importantly, the girl gets the girl"). Deanna, a telepathic, and Claire, a clairvoyant, are future lovers—Deanna lives in the 1980s and Claire in 2012. One night Claire has a dream about a girl she doesn't know—Deanna, a dream so vivid that she cannot get her out of her mind. The following day, while walking on the street, Claire, has a brief encounter with what she believes is real—the girl in her dream—but she appears like a ghostly image than

vanishes. In the present, Claire is not a lesbian and is dating a police detective (Travis). There is also a third girl that will enter their lives—Jackie, who has the power to heal. Deanna, knowing that she and Claire are destined to be lovers but sensing that Claire is in danger, uses her power of time travel to be with Claire in the present. Unknown to them, Travis is a threat to both and the danger Deanna felt in the past. The story follows Deanna as she struggles to protect Claire to ensure that their paths will intersect as destined in the correct time and space.

Cast: Meredith Sause (Claire DuMurier), Lisa Gagnon (Deanna Shelley), Kat Froehlich (Jackie), Jenn Evans (Susan), Anthony Hughes (Travis). **Credits:** *Producer:* Monique Velasquez. *Writer-Director:* Piper Kessler. **Comment:** The program gives the viewer just what he (or she) is looking for—several erotic kissing scenes—coupled with a good story and acting. The plot is quite intriguing and played so that you never can predict what is going to happen next. The kissing sequences (there is no nudity) are quite convincing and the series would be the ideal candidate for the gay cable channels Here! or Logo. While not in any of the genres covered here, Frequency has four additional lesbian web series: *Easy Abby, Girl/Girl Scene, Lesbian Cops* and *Sunny Reign.* Since the story was left unresolved, it does leave the viewer with an interest to see more—not only to find out who or what Travis is, but what happens to Deanna, Claire and Jackie.

Episodes:
1. Episode 1. Introduces the main characters as Claire and Deanna meet physically for the first time.
2. Episode 2. Although she is not a lesbian, Claire becomes strangely attracted to Deanna and the two share their first sexual encounter.
3. Episode 3. As Claire and Deanna begin a relationship, a murder will soon change the course of their lives.
4. Episode 4. Envisioning the murder, Deanna rushes to the scene, where she encounters the mystical Jackie, who is trying to save the victim.
5. Episode 5. Knowing that Jackie is innocent, but sensing the police will think otherwise, Deanna shelters Jackie from the approaching authorities.
6. Episode 6. With Jackie safe in Claire's home (where Deanna also lives), Deanna meets another girl (Susan) who also envisioned the murder and also learns that someone she knows is a threat.
7. Episode 7. As Deanna's love for Claire grows stronger, Deanna senses that not all is right with Travis and he may be the threat.
8. Episode 8. In the 1980s Deanna meets a child—Claire in the park and realizes she will be her future lover. She also visualizes Travis killing a man and returns to 2012.
9. Episode 9. It is learned that Deanna and Claire have teamed to help injured people with Jackie providing the needed healing (and Deanna erasing the incident form their minds). Deanna reveals that

Travis "is out there mucking up the world" (killing) and needs to be stopped.

10. Episode 10. Deanna has a vision of Claire being attacked by Travis, but arrives too late to save her. Jackie, however, is able to bring her back to life at the same time Travis receives a message (from unknown sources) that he failed in his assignment. As Travis returns to complete his task, Deanna kills him (or at least she believes so when he vanishes after being shot). Now, with their presence known by something seeking to kill them, Deanna, Claire and Jackie begin a run for their lives. The series ends.

149 *Fringe—"Past+Present+Future."* side reel.com. 20011 (Science Fiction).

An Internet companion to the Fox series *Fringe* that introduces viewer's to the strange world of Fringe (where the past, present and future can coexist). Stories are narrated by series star John Noble.
Cast: John Noble (Walter Bishop), Anna Torv (Olivia Dunham), Joshua Jackson (Peter Bishop).
Comment: The series has been taken off line following the cancellation of its parent series and episodes are no longer available for viewing. Credits for the web series are not given although the television version is produced by J.J. Abrams. It was a worthy companion to the series and, with Fox behind it, well produced.
Episodes:
1. Past+Present+Future (4 min., 20 sec.). An introduction to the series concept.
2. A Tragic Past (4 min., 30 sec.). Introduces Walter Bishop, a cutting-edge scientist and his genius son Peter.
3. A Tale of Two Walters (3 min., 50 sec.). Walter's alternate self (from another universe) is revealed.
4. Fringe Takes Flight (3 min., 50 sec.). Explores how Olivia Dunham, a former Marine Corps Investigator, becomes part of the Fringe world.
5. Echoes of the Past (4 min., 25 sec.). Walter's work with fringe science (all that is beyond belief) has been responsible for many of the cases investigated by Fringe Division.
6. The Other Side (4 min., 35 sec.). Walter uncovers a Fringe Division in an alternate universe.
7. Over There (5 min.). Walter and Olivia cross over to the alternate Fringe world.
8. A Double Agent (3 min., 55 sec.). A strange and dangerous twist of events occurs as the alternate Olivia appears here while our Olivia is trapped in her alternate's world.
9. The Journey Home (2 min., 25 sec.). The two Olivia's desperately seek a way to return to their rightful worlds.
10. Facing Destiny (3 min., 55 sec.). Peter risks his life to return things to normal, but the unexpected happens when he vanishes into time.
11. The Future Is Now (2 min., 25 sec.). Peter's fate is revealed as he finds himself 15 years into the future.
12. A Different Choice (4 min., 45 sec.). Knowing through Peter what the future will bring has Walter attempting to change what will happen.

150 *Frontier: Prelude to Darkness.* blip.tv. 2011 (Science Fiction).

It is the year 2296 and skirmishes between two empires, the Terran Imperial Union and the Dakota Republic has escalated into a war with each faction seeking to control the known sectors of the Milky Way. John Caine, a retired Air Force Major, is recalled to active duty and placed in charge of the Union Army's Saber Squadron with a mission to find a civilian transport vessel (U.S.S. *Asimov*) that mysteriously disappeared after leaving the Van Gaal system. The program charts his experiences as he and his crew venture into the dangerous and unknown realms of outer space seeking the ship but also becoming involved in the conflict between the two warring factions. Rick Devers is a private assigned to John's command and a new recruit in the Union Army. Sarah Keller, an Ensign, is the communications officer.
Voice Cast: Lewis Roscoe (John Caine), Malcolm Klassen (Rick Devers), Ashley Holland (Sarah Keller), Kevin McCulley (Lt. James Sears), Stephen Richards (Arnold Wexler), Lewis Roscoe (Capt. Ellis Webster), Steve Schnier (Joahnnes Krauer), Sarah Orr (Michelle Goren), Rachael Rigda (Velina Guitterez), Tim Clough (Daniel Gaff), Dan Scott (Cleeves), Wesley Ferguson (Cmdr. Gatlander).
Credits: *Producer-Writer-Director:* Lewis Roscoe.
Comment: Well done animated project that holds viewer interest with an exciting story (would have been too costly to produce as a live-action series) and pacing that does not become boring.
Episodes:
1. Chapter 1. Establishes the storyline as the conflict between the two factions escalates into a full scale war.
2. Chapter 2. John Caine is recruited when the *Asimov* disappears while on a scientific mission in the war zone.
3. Chapter 3. Caine and his crew begin preparations to enter the war zone to search for the missing ship.
4. Chapter 4. Captain Wexler, the man in charge of the Black Operations Service Squad, prepares his team to attack the Dakota Republic.
5. Chapter 5. Caine and his wing commander, Webster, take charge of their ship, the U.S.S. *Patton* while its sister ship, the U.S.S. *Hornblower* leaves Earth for a rendezvous with the invasion forces in the Sol Sector.
6. Chapter 6. The *Patton* and *Hornblower* arrive in the orbit of Fiersis to meet with Commodore Greene, head of the Reinager Invasion Group, and

commander of the U.S.S. *Canberra* (it was in the vicinity of the enemy planet of Toyr'diablo in the Reinager System that the *Asimov* disappeared).

7. Chapter 7. The invasion begins as the *Patton* launches its fighter wing ships. Meanwhile the *Canberra* detects approaching Dakota ships and Caine's ship is dispatched to intercept.

8. Chapter 8. With the invasion underway, Devers and his platoon, aboard a UC-78 Raven, head toward the planet's surface. Meanwhile a wormhole opens and something unknown is ejected. Commodore Greene orders Lt. Sears (from the ship U.S.S. *Hammer*) to investigate.

9. Chapter 9. The previously dispatched Raven crash lands on the planet with the crew stranded in a forest; the *Hammer* takes aboard the strange object ejected from the wormhole.

10. Chapter 10. A rescue squad is sent to help the stranded Raven crew; the mysterious object retrieved from space becomes a threat to the crew when an alien presence is discovered.

11. Chapter 11. The rescue party meets up with the Raven crew; however, something unknown begins picking off them off one by one and to make matters worse, a Dakota squadron is patrolling the area.

151 *Frontier Guard.* blip.tv. 2010 (Science Fiction).

In October of 1957 while on a camping trip in Truckee, California, a father (James) and his 14-year-old son (Connor) are asleep when a strange sound awakens them. Connor investigates, encounters an alien and is swept away in its spaceship to another planet. Five hundred years later Connor is found in suspended animation on a ship called *The Ark*. But why was he abducted and by whom? Questions that require answering, but until that can happen, Connor is made a part of Earth's new world by training to become a cadet at the Frontier Guard Academy (future police force) and assigned to the training vessel starship *Polaris*. Stories, which hint that Connor is the key to being the savior of the world, relate his efforts to adjust to a new life while trying to overcome the past and what happened to him. **Cast:** Corey Jones (Connor Blake), Julia Morizawa (Zyta Campbell), Andrew Gilbert (Kasper Gribb), Ryder Bach (Jack Tawn), Michelle Laurent (Trem Warrick), Nick Cook (Devore). **Credits:** *Producer:* Rob Caves, Jennifer Cole. *Director:* David O'Neill, Sharon Savene. *Writer:* Rob Caves, Brian S. Matthews. **Comment:** Only three of twelve produced episodes remain online. They establish the story line with a flashback to that fatal camping trip in 1957 to Connor's first days as a cadet at Frontier Guard Academy. What results, however, is a disappointing *Buck Rogers in the 25th Century* copy that begins with excellent special effects than spirals quickly downward. The story idea, although being

abducted by aliens is nothing new, holds interest until the victim (Connor) is found and he is inducted into a new life. The plot then becomes a bit muddled—why was Connor abducted and by whom and for what purpose is not clearly stated (at least not in the available episodes). The casting is not right on here; the performers chosen to play the roles, especially Connor, just do not seem to fit the image the producer tries to create (especially when it appears some are looking at the camera to read their lines off a teleprompter). Special effects are essential to a science fiction series, but such effects can also be its downfall. Here there is an excessive use of CGI and computer generated backgrounds that are relatively static (as the actors are playing against green screen technology). A good intention that does not play well. **Episodes:** *1.* Sputnik. *2.* Copernicus. *3.* Connor Blake. *4.* Polaris. *5.* Spin Shock. *6.* Rippers. *7.* Revelation. *8.* Lab Rat. *9.* The Aqarii. *10.* Gallant. *11.* The Ark. *12.* Paulson.

152 *The Further Adventures of Cupid and Eros.* cupidanderos.com. 2010–2011 (Fantasy).

Cupid and Eros, believed to be the same ancient God of Love, are actually two such gods. They are both regulated from Mt. Olympus to making love happen between mortals but each in a different way. Cupid, considered "the original nice guy," is sweet, charming and "a mortal's best friend." Eros is just the opposite, a sex-crazed goddess who believes she is irresistible to any god, mortal or anything in between. Cupid is thus the ultimate romantic while Eros, as beautiful as she is, is thus the ultimate personification of sexuality. While their main goal is to perform matches and stem the tide of divorce and infidelity, they are also confused about what they create. Stories follow their efforts to really understand what they do and what happens when their matches are not "made in heaven." **Cast:** Jo Bozarth (Eros), Josh Heine (Cupid), Aliza Pearl (Isis), Kiera Anderson (Jo), Bradford Anderson (Achilles), Sheila Thiele (Lacey), Jeffrey Cannata (Apollo), Kaathleen Curran (Psyche), Dexx Hillman-Sneed (Thoth), Taryn O'Neill (Athena), Courtney Richards (Shango), Nikki Storm (Earth Goddess). **Credits:** *Producer:* Avi Glijanksy, Andy Wells. *Writer-Director:* Avi Glijansky. **Comment:** Amusing series with good acting and production values. Taking ancient gods and placing them in modern times is nothing new, but the way it is presented here is different and well thought out. If it was meant to show that gods are people too—and have the same problems as mortals, then it was achieved.

Episodes:

1. I'm Fine. Introduces Cupid and Eros as modern day match makers—not the Greek gods they once were. Cupid, depressed since his love, Psyche,

abandoned him, now longs for someone, even an obscure Egyptian goddess, to accompany him to a social gathering. To help Cupid, Eros decides to take him to a bar—and find a mortal woman to woo.

2. Two Gods Walk Into a Bar... As Eros and Cupid enter a bar, Eros finds him a woman—then goes off in search of a mortal man for herself.

3. Hopeless Romantics. As Cupid attempts to seduce the woman Eros has chosen, Eros learns that the woman is destined for someone else and she must make that match. But Cupid, unable to see anyone but the girl, feels he is in love and struggles with a decision to terminate his job or find happiness with a mortal.

4. Good Idea/Bad Idea. Unable to abandon his immortality, Cupid leaves the girl of his dreams and returns to his misery over losing Psyche.

5. Hello, My Pantheon Is. Eros hatches a plan to get Cupid and Psyche back together at the upcoming Inter-Pantheon Mixer. Unfortunately all does not go well when Cupid fails in an attempt to impress the goddess Isis. As Cupid encounters his share of problems, Eros faces her own dilemmas when she meets Aveta (the fertility goddess and her friendly enemy) and Apollo, who is seeking a lady friend.

6. Dueling and Diapers. With Psyche about to arrive, Apollo drunk and now challenging Cupid to do battle for stealing Psyche from him, Aveta hitting on gods and Cupid becoming even more depressed, Eros seeks a way to orchestrate a happy outcome for all concerned.

7. Will You Be My... Explores how Valentine's Day began and how Cupid feels about it. In the three-part episode, Cupid laments that he hates the holiday and how commercial it has become; Eros, on the other hand, sees it as a day off when she can become a part of earth life and have some unsupervised fun. However, when Cupid decides he has had enough with Valentine's Day, Eros must somehow convince him otherwise or his decision will mark the end Valentine's Day and Eros and Cupid's matchmaking career.

153 *Fury of Solace.* furyofsolace.com. 2009 (Fantasy).

In the modern-day world a young man named Emmett is the self-proclaimed hero the Fury of Solace, a red-masked vigilante that uses whatever means available to him to deal with those he perceives as being evil. Emmett, however, is no angel himself. Ten years ago he received a prophecy from a mysterious man named Augur about a young girl (Laurel) who would grow up to become a superhero and save people from a catastrophic event. However, for that to happen, her parents must be killed. Emmett takes Augur's word as gospel and kills Laurel's parents. Feeling untold remorse for the act he just committed but believing it was the wrong thing for the right reasons, Emmett theorizes that if taking the lives of an

innocent couple could benefit the world, what would happen if he destroyed those who truly deserve it? Donning a red mask and calling himself the Fury of Solace, Emmett turns his attention to eliminating the corrupt politicians and corporate presidents (especially of the Mason International Corporation) whose greed holds the world in a stranglehold. Meanwhile, Laurel, who had witnessed the killing of her parents in a Los Angeles alleyway, had vowed to avenge their deaths by devoting her life to helping those in need. Now grown, and calling herself The Orphan, she has begun her crusade. While it is not shown how they meet, Laurel and Emmett are a couple—with Laurel unaware that her boyfriend is the man who killed her parents and secretly the Fury of Solace.

Max Mason is the head of Mason International, a pharmaceutical company fraught with charges of corruption, bribery and flagrant violations of domestic and international law. Uroboros, a computer hacker who wears a crude black mask (to remain anonymous) runs a conspiracy blog called "The Flashlight" wherein he has vowed to expose Mason and bring him to justice. Damien Durand is Mason's head of security; Starla Carter is host of the television program *Crisis* wherein she tries to expose crime and believes that those vigilantes (like the Fury of Solace) that patrol the city should be held accountable for what they do if they can't work within the system. Harlan Stone is the Los Angeles Police Commissioner who believes superheroes are important and is seeking to incorporate them into the L.A.P.D. Temperance Jones, a psychologist and author of the book *The Superhero Complex* provides counseling to Los Angeles-based superheroes. Augur is the mysterious man who claims to be able to see the future. His predictions are known to be accurate and he is embraced by both the superhero and villain community. But he is also selective in what he reveals about the future.

Cast: Emmett Furey (Emmett/Fury of Solace), Laurel Rankin (Laurel Warren), Todd Livingston (Max Mason), Sara Jo Elice (Sara), Matt Hartman (Cameraman), Maxwell Glick (Uroboros), Robert Ryan Kline (Marcus Arnold), Carly Jones (Temperance Jones), Christopher Duzan (Harlan Stone), Stephanie Thorpe (Starla Carter). **Credits:** *Producer-Director:* Matt Hartman, Emmett Furey. *Writer:* Emmett Furey. **Comment:** Although the series ends unresolved, it has a good story with similar acting and production values.

Episodes:

1. The Storming of Mason Tower. Emmett, as the Fury of Solace, declares his battle against Max Mason via an online video posting.

2. Bad Press. Emmett's attempt to kidnap Max fails when Laurel, believing Max is innocent of the charges brought against him, rescues him.

3. Heroes for Hire. With his initial attempt a failure, Emmett attempts to prove that Mason is up to

no good when his company acquires a booth at Comic-Con International and begins hiring superheroes as bodyguards.

4. Just Because You're Paranoid. Emmett is not alone in his suspicions as the mysterious blogger, the Flashlight, has also posted information that Mason International has a connection with the Los Angeles underworld.

5. Between the Lines. Emmett and Laurel have chosen to move in together, making Emmett's abilities to conceal his alias from Laurel more difficult.

6. Crisis Management. A *Crisis* television report wherein Temperance Jones probes the recent bombing of Mason Tower.

7. Eye-Witness News. Mason International hosts a charity event for the victims of the Mason Tower bombing—but is the money for something more devious? Apparently not as Temperance discloses.

8. Out of the Blue. Laurel begins her own vlog to address issues that are now affecting the people of Los Angeles.

9. Opposition Research. Uroboros, hacking into Mason International's mainframe, uncovers evidence of the company's illegal activities.

10. Between Jobs. Emmett, a former ex-Marine and now full-time superhero, finds that to make ends meet, he needs a job—and acquires one as a corporate security officer.

11. Mole Hunt. Uroboros, as the Flashlight, posts hacked Mason International surveillance footage that shows dissention in the ranks (between Mason's head of security and the rest of the security team).

12. Making People Better. The Fury of Solace forms an alliance with the Flashlight to battle Mason International together as opposed to each attempting it on their own to bring Mason down.

13. No Stone Unturned. Relates the Police Commissioner's on-going battle to get the department to approve of superheroes becoming a part of the system.

14. Under Protest. The Flashlight and his supporters stage a protest against Mason International, hoping to gather attention from the press.

15. Be the Change. While reviewing the hacked footage he acquires from Mason International, Uroboros uncovers evidence of genetic experimentation on human subjects.

16. The Fugitive. Unable to comprehend what he has seen, Uroboros kills the doctor (Marcus Alrand) involved in the experiments and is now a fugitive and sought by the police.

17. Uroboros Unmasked. Uroboros, still on the run from the police, has turned deadly vigilante, creating crude pipe bombs and destroying anything and anyone associated with Mason International.

18. The Charity Case. Laurel reveals on her vlog that she uncovered evidence of a long-lost witness to her parents' murders and enlists the help of the L.A.P.D. to track him down.

19. How Do You Kill a Snake? A site created by Uroboros called "The Lighthouse" reveals that acquired evidence links Mason International with the King criminal empire.

154 *The Future Machine.* thefuturemachine.tv. 2010 (Science Fiction).

Matt and Tom are two less-than intelligent roommates. The day after a night of drinking Matt and Tom have an argument over who owns a bear costume that hangs in their apartment. With no normal way to settle the argument, they decide to transform a German-built microwave oven into a time machine and travel into the past to discover who bought the bear suit and thus determine its rightful owner. The program charts their harebrained attempts to build a time machine—and what happens when they actually succeed in doing so.

Cast: Matthew Okine (Matt), Andrew Ryan (Tom), Cariba Heine (Katie Hill). **Credits:** *Producer-Writer:* David Barker, Matthew Okine, Tom Sheldrick. *Director:* David Barker. **Comment:** While comedy overpowers the scientific aspects of the program, it does attempt to display an illusion of what could happen if time traveling were developed, although the approach here is a bit far-fetched.

Episodes:

1. That's My Bear Suit. Matt and Tom's initial attempts at building a time machine transports a future Tom to the present.

2. The Rules of Time Travel. Tom of the present learns from Tom of the future that the time machine will ultimately kill him while Matt dreams of all the money he will make.

3. How to Get Rid of a Body. Matt and present Tom try to figure out a way to dispose of future Tom when the time machine kills him.

4. Phantom Limb. Matt tries to convince Tom to continue perfecting the time machine despite the fact that it will kill him in the future.

5. Building a Time Machine. Tom's continual work results in an actual time machine—but now they must decide who will test it.

6. Boys Become Men. Matt becomes the test subject and, upon activating the machine, disappears from the apartment.

7. Return Trip. Matt returns after a week of time traveling to a depressed Tom who realizes that if he uses the machine, it will cost him his life.

8. Our Friends Are Animals. Hoping to save Tom, Matt sends him back in time then must change the past to save Tom in the present.

155 *Gabriel Cushing Versus the Zombie Vampires.* gabrielchushing.com. 2012–2013 (Horror).

Gabriel Cushing is a world renowned supernatural investigator whose specialty is the study of demons. Gabriel often finds that cases of the unnatural are often too real and not easily dismissed as being pranks by authorities. Little Eaton is a British town that outwardly appears as just a typical, charming country-like town. It hides, however, a deep, terrifying secret: it is the breeding ground for demons that have never before existed: zombies who are also vampires.

When Gabriel and his assistant, Ben, learn of a series of mysterious and unexplained deaths that have occurred in and around Little Eaton, they begin a probe into the situation. Gabriel's suspicions prove all too real and he must now face and find a way to destroy a new evil: zombies who not only prey on the flesh of humans, but their blood as well.

Cast: David Curtis (Gabriel Cushing), Samantha "Sam" Herbert (Melanie Lancely), Connor McKenzy (Ben Romanov), Nicj Orchard (Ancient Vampire), Marley Hamilton (Lucinda), Andy Chaplin (Hoodie). **Credits:** *Producer-Writer-Director:* Mark Adams. **Comment:** Well-acted, fast-moving British produced serial that is suspenseful at times and, although episodes are meant to be watched as an arc (one leading to another), the story can easily be followed when select episodes are sampled on websites like YouTube.com.

Episodes:

1. The Arrival (9 min., 56 sec.). Establishes the concept as Gabriel begins his investigation of strange deaths in Little Eaton.

2. Into the Woods (9 min., 35 sec.). Gabriel's investigation of the Old Wisp Woods uncovers evidence that the killings are caused by what he calls zombie vampires.

3. Night Terrors (9 min., 18 sec.). A villager (Melanie) comes forward to help Gabriel and Ben learn the truth about what is happening in Little Eaton.

4. Myths and Legends (10 min., 53 sec.). Gabriel encounters Lucinda, an emissary of the Ancient, a centuries-old vampire who has resurrected zombies to destroy the human race.

5. First Blood (11 min., 34 sec.). Uncovering positive evidence that Old Wisp Woods is the hiding place of the Ancient, Gabriel, Ben and Melanie seek to find him—unaware that the Ancient has set a trap to destroy them.

6. Hunted (9 min., 20 sec.). Gabriel and Ben begin a desperate quest to find Melanie—who has become separated from them and is being sought by the Ancient.

7. Satan's Grove (6 min., 47 sec.). After finding Melanie, Gabriel and Ben come face-to-face with the Ancient and learn of the threat that the undead will rule the earth.

8. The Last Stand (16 min., 8 sec.). With Melanie, safe and by their side, Gabriel and Ben seek a way to kill the Ancient and end his reign (as his death will also destroy the zombie vampires).

156 Gasland: 2012 Aftermath. youtube. com. 2010 (Science Fiction).

The Earth, once fertile and rich, is now a vast wasteland following a crack in the earth's core that released a gas with deadly results: those overcome by it were transformed into cannibalistic creatures called "Gassers" while others, who retain their essence, are the hunted and must fight for survival. Two young women, Eve and Nikki have survived unharmed but now they must find a place of refuge before they become the victims of the deranged humans that roam the region. The program follows their journey as they document (via a video camera) what happens along the way.

Cast: America Young, April Wade, Trent Duncan, Kathy Borloski, Emily Grace Morrison, Christian Calloway. **Credits:** *Producer-Writer-Director:* Trent Duncan. **Comment:** Intriguing tale of survival that holds interest from beginning to end. The acting is good and the outdoor locations, with homes still in tact, fit the project perfectly.

Episodes:

1. Welcome to Gasland (3 min., 31 sec.). Introduces Nikki and Eve as they begin their journey across a desolate landscape.

2. The History (2 min., 31 sec.). The girls encounter a survivor (Walker) who tells them about a place of safety called the Damn.

3. Nikki's Past (3 min., 2 sec.). Nikki recalls her life before the world changed.

4. The Journey (2 min., 50 sec.). An approaching sandstorm threatens the trio as they head toward the Damn.

5. Trust (2 min., 53 sec.). Walker's actions have Nikki and Eve wondering if Walker has been honest about the Damn or if he is leading them into something sinister.

6. The Damn (2 min., 25 sec.). With the Damn now in sight, Nikki and Eve see that it is guarded by someone who appears to be anything but friendly. A confrontation ensues and the program ends without resolution.

157 The Gauntlet. silverrainentertainment. com. 2013 (Fantasy).

Everleigh High is a boarding school with a mysterious, supernatural past. It is here that four teenage students (Chloe, Stella, Madison and Nina) are beginning to encompass their powers of black magic. Suspicion for unexplained happenings has never been a concern to the school until a new student, Alice McIntyre, enrolls. Her father, constantly traveling around the world on business, felt it would be best for Alice so as to not continually uproot her and disrupt her education. Alice appears to be adjusting normally until she is assigned a roommate, Chloe Adams, the school's Queen Bee. Chloe's cold attitude toward Alice and her secretive behavior has Alice feeling that something is not right with the school.

Cast members from the series *The Gauntlet* (Copyright Silver Rain Entertainment).

Alice soon becomes aware that Chloe is concealing something when she spies her sneaking out of their dorm room one night for an unknown destination. The following day Alice befriends Bailey Sheer, the dorm president and learns that many unexplained happenings have occurred at the school and that she too suspects that Chloe is hiding something. The program relates Alice's attempts to uncover Chloe's secret—and the secret of what lies behind the hallowed halls of Everleigh High School.

Cast: Giselle Van Der Wiel (Alice McIntyre), Cristina Ventresca (Chloe Adams), Tara Jay (Bailey Sheer), Ash Vlahos (Madison Cartwright), Jessica Vumbaca (Stella Cabrelli), Alex Cubis (Ryan Sanders), Adrian Lee (Luke Alston). **Credits:** *Producer:* Rachel Lu. *Director:* Kimberly Melville. *Writer:* Kimberly Melville, Rachel Lu. **Comment:** The program opens with a teenage girl (Nina) running for her life through a wooded area. She is being pursued by something unknown. Suddenly there is a scream and the screen turns to black. It reopens with Alice arriving at the school. The viewer's attention is immediately caught and curiosity sets in— you want to find out what happened. The female leads are very attractive and handle their roles quite well. The production values are comparable to any television series and the program, as eerie as it is, is well worth watching.

Episodes:

1. Episode 1 (6 min., 40 sec.). Alice's first day at school finds her encountering a cold reception from her roommate (Chloe).

2. Episode 2 (5 min., 46 sec.). Alice befriends a girl (Bailey) who tells her about the school's eerie history while one of the students, Nina has disappeared and another student, Madison, has become a suspect. It is suggested that Nina, who uncovered something, has been killed to keep the school's centuries-old supernatural past (a demonic power) secret.

3. Episode 3 (5 min., 6 sec.). It is revealed in a flashback that Chloe, Madison, Stella and Nina are involved in black magic and that Madison, the group leader, felt that Nina was a threat to them, and used her magic to kill her.

4. Episode 4 (5 min., 54 sec.). Following through with her suspicions about Chloe, Alice searches their room and finds a video camera cassette.

5. Episode 5 (7 min., 36 sec.). That night Alice follows Chloe as she sneaks out of their room to a secret room where she, Madison and Stella are seen encompassing their supernatural powers.

6. Episode 6 (5 min., 39 sec.). Alice plays the tape and sees that Chloe, Madison and Stella were responsible for Nina's death (they felt Nina was a threat and could expose them).

7. Episode 7 (7 min., 2 sec.). Hoping to expose Nina's killers, Alice brings the tape to the school principal (Hamilton) but finds disbelief as he refuses to do anything about it (as it would expose the school's secret of a connection to the supernatural).

8. Episode 8 (5 min., 38 sec.). Stella approaches Chloe and tells her that she fears Madison, whom she feels is becoming too powerful.

9. Episode 9 (6 min., 22 sec.). Madison is revealed as the one Chloe and Stella should fear as she has learned to use her powers on her own. (It had previously been shown that the girls' powers could only be invoked if two or more members of the group were involved.)

10. Episode 10 (6 min., 36 sec.). The concluding episode wherein the mysteries surrounding the school deepen with Alice now more determined than ever to expose Chloe and her connection with the supernatural.

158 *Gemini Division.* youtube.com. 2008 (Science Fiction).

Anna Diaz is a streetwise undercover detective with the NYPD. She is engaged to Nick Korda and drawn into a dangerous mystery when Nick is killed and Anna discovers he was involved with Gemini Division, a secret and sinister organization involved with covert military operations and simulated humanoid life forms (called Simulants). The story follows Anna as she infiltrates Gemini Division, performs their assignments and seeks to not only discover why Nick was eliminated, but the reason and technology behind the Simulants (also called Sims). The program is presented as a video conversation between Anna and the viewer with flashbacks used to explain aspects of the story she is relating.

Cast: Rosario Dawson (Det. Anna Diaz), Justin Hartley (Nick Korda), Elizabeth Bogush (Dr. Elizabeth Gavillan), Allison Scagliotti (M+M), Kevin Alejandro (Amasso), Tony Curran (Walken), Daz Crawford (The Cleaner), Matt Bushell (Det. Pete Vacarella). **Credits:** *Producer:* Stan Rogow, Brent Friedman. *Director:* Stan Rogow, Neal Israel. *Writer:* Andy Black, Lawrence Frank, Jacqui Zambrano, Brent Friedman. **Comment:** With the exception of a brief trailer on YouTube, all 50 episodes have been withdrawn from the Internet (at the official site "This Video No Longer Exists" will appear). Based on the trailer, the program is well produced and intriguing as it presents a mystery that grows deeper with each succeeding episode.

Episodes:
1. Eyes Wide Open. 2. Tug of War, Love Costs. 3. Note to Self 1: Lost. 4. In Deep. 5. Note to Self 2: The Rabbit Hole. 6. Clean Sweep. 7. Murder Will Out. 8. This Ain't Queen. 9. Ask the Dusk. 10. This Is What We Know. 11. Slamming Doors. 12. Dead End. 13. Insertion Point. 14. Deep Cover. 15. Fail Safe. 16. Kill Jill. 17. To Catch a Sim. 18. O.F.C. 19. Closed Circle. 20. Salvation. 21. Conejo Blanco. 22. Sub Rosa. 23. Eye for an Eye. 24. Manwich to Go. 25. The Tightening Noose. 26. Toy Soldiers. 27. Le Mujer Dormida. 28. Smart Cow. 29. Training Day. 30. Laszlo. 31. The Taking of G-D Mountain By Surprise. 32. Bound. 33. Rendition. 34. Operation Heirloom. 35. Termination Date. 36. This Is What You Don't Know. 37. Underground. 38. File No. 38. 39. Anna's Got a Gun. 40. Savior. 41. Amasso. 42. Thanatos. 43. Ringu. 44. Hell Without the Fire. 45. Finding Laszlo. 46. The Lighthouse. 47. In the Region of Ice. 48. Linnaea. 49. Kill Switch. 50. Icebreaker.

159 *Generic Girl.* gogenericgirl.com. 2012 (Fantasy).

Gillian Romero is a very pretty girl who idolizes comic book super heroes. Her friend, Pete Kirby, also a comic book geek, envisions himself as the super hero Captain Freelance (a man who acquires super powers after being struck by lightning). Each lives in a dream world until a package, meant for the evil and diabolical Dr. Mascalzone, is delivered to Gillian by mistake. As Gillian opens the package she discovers it to contain a rather beat-up looking box that is able to speak and proclaims itself to be god. Meanwhile, when the doctor learns what has happened to his package, he instructs his gorgeous, but dense daughter, Hildy, to get him that box (as he needs it in his harebrained plans for a death ray). Hildy finds Gillian but when she is unable to get the box, she kidnaps Pete as a bargaining chip for the box. Adapting the heroics of her comic book heroes (but considering herself a Generic Girl hero) Gillian begins her quest to save the world—and Pete from Hildy's mad father, his dim-witted henchmen and Hildy (whose ability to seduce any man appears to be her only ability).

Cast: Alexandra Olson (Gillian Romero), Matthew Bohrer (Pete Kirby), Sarah Ho (Brunhilda "Hildy" Mascalzone), Robert Amico (Deus Ex Machina), Matthew Farhat (Sgt. Catarsis), Richard Hawkins (Dr. Mascalzone), Christy Keller (Angelika Doom), Kristin McCoy (Miss Mayhem), Jordan Preston (Major Thunder), Jade Nicole (Lexis), Darcell Hoover (Mercedes), Nataly Pena (Candy), Sarah Roberts (Persia), Rochelle Roepke (Charity) **Credits:** *Producer-Writer-Director:* Steven Itano Wasserman, Aaron Hartley, Victor Solis. **Comment:** Gillian is adorable; Hildy is sexy; Pete is a nerd and Dr. Mascalzone is stark raving mad. All the ingredients needed for a comical science fiction story about good defeating evil (well, it has to be assumed so as the series ends without a resolution). The acting and production values are good and it plays better than some of the so-called comedies that are on network television.

Episodes:
1. Exposition (5 min., 48 sec.). Introduces Gillian and Pete, the mysterious box that Gillian possesses and of the evil Dr. Mascalzone's efforts to acquire it.

2. Requiem for a Henchman (5 min., 31 sec.). Dr. Mascalzone becomes even madder than he is when he discovers the box has been delivered to Gillian.

3. A Barrage of Bosom Burning Fire (7 min., 46 sec.). The sexy Hildy is dispatched by her father to get the box back.

Generic Girl **promotional art featuring (top left) Sarah Ho and Matthew Bohrer, (top right) Alexandra Olson, and (bottom right) Sarah Ho and Richard Hawkins (copyright Hachitan Entertainment, Inc.).**

4. Gillian's Love Box (9 min., 37 sec.). As Gillian and Pete examine the box, they begin to wonder how it can talk and what it wants.

5. Peter Envy (7 min., 36 sec.). Hildy finds Gillian and Pete and, realizing that she will not be able to get the box simply by stealing it, she begins to seduce Pete.

6. Scent of a Henchman (7 min., 32 sec.). With Pete under her spell, Hildy takes him to the doctor's lair.

7. Teabags for Two (8 min., 49 sec.). When Gillian discovers that Pete is missing, she begins distributing fliers around town then decides to visit the police department's Abduction Department (where she finds more confusion then help).

8. The Last Meow (8 min., 14 sec.). The doctor feels Gillian is also a threat and dispenses his henchmen to get her.

9. One More Into the Breeches (7 min., 14 sec.). Taken to the doctor's lab, Gillian finds her and Pete's

life threatened—although help may come in a most unexpected form.

10. Generic Girl Climaxes (10 min., 54 sec.). Hildy has fallen for Pete and defies her father. In an ensuing struggle, Hildy's gun discharges and Pete is shot. Gillian rushes to his side but it appears she is too late. But is Pete really dead? Is the box really God (and can save him)? Will there be a conclusion?

160 *Georgia.* webserieschannel.com. 2012 (Fantasy).

A psychiatrist (Georgia) attempts to help people with various phobias and fears by encompassing her own brand of therapy (which borders on the unusual)—but also finding that after she deals with patients, she is the one who needs help. **Cast:** Mary Elizabeth Ellis (Georgia), Harold Perrineau (Michael), Nancy Carell (Davinie), Mark Povinelli (Victor), Debra Azar (Sunshine). **Credits:** *Producer:* Diane Lavin, Robbie Tolin. *Writer-Director:* Martin Kaufman. **Comment:** More comedy than fantasy; perhaps the strange clients Georgia helps have given it the fantasy tag. The acting is good, as are the production values and stories. **Episodes:**

1. Hello, I Am Davinie (8 min., 24 sec.). Georgia tries to deal with a client who hates touching (sort of like Adrian Monk on the series *Monk*) and deal with a delicate situation with her fiancé (Michael)—should they marry.

2. Hello, I Am Victor (8 min., 45 sec.). A client (little person) with a big sense of humor seeks help. Georgia and Michael continue their discussion about marriage.

3. Hello, I Am Sunshine (10 min., 17 sec.). After seeing a client with a big heart but who feels nobody loves her, Georgia feels she needs some help herself (especially after spending the afternoon with two girlfriends who discussed the benefits of having large breasts—something Georgia does not possess).

161 *Ghost Class.* youtube.com. 2011 (Horror).

Tales of spirits, trapped in a purgatory-like world, who must find a way to redeem themselves in order to move on—all with the guiding help of the mysterious Simon D. **Cast:** Daniel Gordon (Simon D). **Credits:** *Producer:* Katj Bojic MacIntosh, Gemma Purkiser, Matylda Gauzo, Theo Smart. *Director:* Ester Hogan, Matt Hutchings, Rushana Adnan. **Comment:** Although the subject matter has been done countless times before, it is still an interesting concept and as long as there are circumstances there are stories to tell. **Episodes:**

1. Bruised (8 min., 57 sec.). To move on a bully must return to earth to protect one of his victims—the man he attacked but who killed him. Starring Theo Smart, Jordan Okaid.

2. A Case of Identity (12 min., 14 sec.). A university professor is returned to earth to learn the identity of the student who viciously killed him. Starring Derek Elwood, Sam Kermer, Emma Jixson.

3. Rose (9 min., 1 sec.). Agonizing over the fact that she was unable to say goodbye to her family before her death, a woman is returned to earth to fulfill that desire. Starring Dympara Peaston, Becca Bond.

4. Noir (6 min., 42 sec.). In order to move on a man is sent back to earth to repent his actions over the woman who killed him—but whom he dearly loved. Starring Michael Ajih, Alexandra Veyers, Helene Fletcher, Emily Wilsher.

5. Unrequited (6 min., 50 sec.). A young woman, killed in an accident before she can tell the man she secretly loves how she feels, is sent back to earth to get that chance. Starring Shane Frater, Nic Lamont.

6. The Last Note (8 min., 44 sec.). Simon D tries to persuade a self-absorbed rock star who refuses to listen that, to redeem himself, he must make amends with the mother he neglected. Starring Tyrine Relph, Mary Sheen.

7. Epitaph (12 min., 5 sec.). In the final episode, Simon D attempts to help a young girl come to terms with what she did after she commits suicide. Starring Gina Abolins, Julia Seifert.

162 *Ghost Ghirls.* screen.yahoo.com. 2013 (Horror).

Heidi and Angelica are the Ghost Ghirls—not spirits but two very pretty ghost hunters. Heidi and Angelica believe they have the ability to detect spiritual activity and that ability can make them money. They have established a business called The Ghost Ghirls (with a rather primitive web site they designed) and stories follow their efforts to help people threatened by ghosts. Heidi is a bit off-the-wall while Angelica is more down-to-earth. They have disagreements as to how a case should be handled and often feel each has the better solution when in reality neither one does; it is when they put their heads together and work as one that they achieve their goal. **Cast:** Amanda Lund (Heidi), Maria Blasucci (Angelica). **Credits:** *Producer:* Maria Blasucci, Amanda Lund, Jack Black, Sheila Stepanek. *Director:* Jeremy Konner. *Writer:* Amanda Lund, Maria Blasucci, Jeremy Konner, Ryan Corrigan. **Comment:** Charming mix of comedy and horror with excellent acting and production values. Although the subject of ghost hunters has been done countless times before—from the very good to the very bad *The Ghost Ghirls* falls within the very good category. Heidi and Angelica are perfectly matched and the stories are well written and directed. Would be a perfect candidate for network television; too bad the producers didn't take that route. **Episodes:**

1. Home Is Where the Haunt Is (8 min., 6 sec.). Complications arise when Heidi and Angelica, called into investigate reports of a haunted house encounter a spirit with designs on Heidi.

2. Hooker with a Heart of Ghoul (12 min., 34 sec.). Heidi and Angelica pose as prostitutes to help the police capture an elusive killer who preys on women at a local brothel.

3. Field of Screams (9 min., 29 sec.). A group of kids hire Heidi and Angelica to rid their baseball field of "Bloody Bat," a ghost that supposedly decapitates children and drinks their blood.

4. Will You Scarry Me? (10 min., 56 sec.). Heidi and Angelica attempt to help their friend Megan (Larisa Oleynik) who believes her late husband's spirit is preventing her from moving on with her love life.

5. Ghost Writer (11 min.). When Heidi finds an old typewriter, she becomes possessed by a spirit that compels her to write his racist manifesto.

6. I Believe in Mira-Ghouls (10 min., 46 sec.). Heidi and Angelica attempt to exorcise the ghost of a hip club owner that is now haunting (by partying as if it were the 1970s) a drab accounting office.

7. Comedy of Terrors (10 min., 24 sec.). Heidi's dyslexia sends her and Angelica to the wrong house—where they encounter their rivals, the Ghost Bros. (Jason Ritter, Jason Schwartzman)—crooks who pose as ghost hunters to rob homes.

8. School Spirit (11 min., 40 sec.). Heidi and Angelica relive their school days when they are hired by a middle school boy who is being bullied by a ghost.

9. The Golden Ghouls (11 min., 28 sec.). Heidi and Angelica enter a retirement home to help a resident who believes she is being haunted by her deceased husband's best friend.

10. Something Borrowed, Something Boo (10 min., 25 sec.). The Ghost Ghirls are hired to exorcise the ghost of a bridesmaid who died before her wedding ceremony and who is now haunting weddings at a spa retreat.

11. Spirits of '76, Part 1 (11 min., 30 sec.). Heidi and Angelica are called in to exorcise the spirits of a 1970s country rock band that are now haunting a recording studio.

12. Spirits of '76, Part 2 (12 min., 42 sec.). When Heidi and Angelica discover that the ghost band always argued and were never able to finish their last song, they arrange for a recording session that will allow them to record the song and move on.

163 *Ghost Mine.* syfy.com. 2013 (Horror).

Sumter is a relic of a time long ago. It is a former boom town located in the peaks of the Elkhorn Mountain Range in rural Oregon. There is also the Crescent Mine, an 80-year-old abandoned mine that was once rich with gold. It is also rumored to be haunted by the spirits of the miners who lost their lives there searching for riches. Larry Overman is the mine's current owner and he believes there may still be gold inside the mine. The reality-like series follows Larry and his team of veteran miners (and two greenhorns) as they set out to explore the mine and retrieve its possible wealth. Patrick and Kristen are the paranormal investigators who accompany them. Jerod, Keith and "Fast" Eddie are the miners; Jay and Jamol, the greenhorns.

Cast: Larry Overman, Patrick Doyle, Kristen Lumen, Stacie Sisk-Overman, Jay Verburg. **Credits:** *Producer:* Jay Bluemke, Dave Caplan, Ben Samek. *Director:* Jay Bluemke, Phil Davis. **Comment:** Considering there are abandoned gold mines and adding the possibility that gold may still exist makes for an interesting concept. But throw in the possibility of them being haunted is even more intriguing and *Ghost Mine* presents a well produced excursion into an area of supernatural possibilities that have not been explored before.

Episodes:

1. Pilot. Larry and his team arrive at the mine to begin preparations to explore it.

2. The Lost Chamber. As the crew breaks through the barrier covering the entrance, they discover a ballroom.

3. Phantom Intruder. Paranormal activity is encountered as the team begins blasting.

4. Wandering Spirits. Patrick and Kristen begin their investigation of the mine's unseen presence.

5. Ghosts of the Geiser Grand. Patrick and Kristen's search uncovers evidence that leads them to investigate the Geiser Grand Hotel in nearby Baker City.

6. Mystery Train. The search for clues next leads the investigators to explore the historic Sumter Train.

7. Massacre at Hells Canyon. A mysterious fire breaks out in the mine.

8. Supercharging the Supernatural. The team attempts to use electricity to force the spirits out of the mine.

9. Town Wide Terror. As the paranormal activity appears to have ceased, the miners return to work.

10. Passageway Into the Unknown. Apprehension grips the crew as they dig deeper into the mine.

11. Shadows in the Drift. The team discovers a previously unknown mine shaft.

12. The Final Barrier. As the miners approach what could be the mother lode, Patrick and Kristin attempt to put all the pieces of the puzzle together. Season one ends.

13. Ghost Mine: Back to the Mountain. The miners and investigators gather around a campfire to recall events of the prior season.

14. Return to Darkness. The crew returns to work but all is not easy as strange occurrences are again beginning to affect their efforts to find gold.

164 Ghost Whisperer: The Other Side.
youtube.com. 2007–2008.(Horror).

An extension of the CBS series *Ghost Whisperer* that explores the spirit world from the perspective of the earthbound spirit as opposed as through the eyes of Melinda Gordon (Jennifer Love Hewitt), a young woman who has the ability to see and speak to ghosts. The first story focuses on a spirit (Zach) and his attempts to "live" among the living while at the same time search for answers surrounding his death. Sarah is Zach's spirit world teacher; Shadow Spirit is the spirit from the Dark Side. A second story tells of Meg Tyler, her husband James and their young daughter, Daisy. As the Tyler's move into a new home they soon discover that an unknown presence is hindering their happiness. When that presence, a ghost, makes a disturbing bond with Daisy in an attempt to make the family leave, Meg and James team to find a way to destroy the ghost before it overtakes Daisy. The third story follows an engaged couple's (Olivia and Marc) efforts to rid themselves of a ghost when it attaches itself to Olivia.
Cast: *First Story:* Mark Hapka (Zach), Robin Hines (Sarah), Graham McTavish (Dark Spirit), Matthew Alan (Danny), Lanre Idewu (Shadow Spirit Leader), Peter Douglas (Luke), Lucas Alifano (B.J.); *Second Story:* Kasey Wilson (Meg Tyler), Mark Lutz (James Tyler), Hailey Sole (Daisy Tyler), Mark Knudsen (Ghost); *Third Story:* Jaimi Paige (Olivia), Justin Loyal (Marc), Ryan Deal (George), Zarah Mahler (Stacey). **Credits:** Producer: Nichelle M. Protho, Kim Moses, Ian Sander. *Director:* Claudio Fah, Felix Enriquez Alcala. *Writer:* Ann Shrake.
Comment: One of the earliest web series in the horror genre that benefits from having excellent production values (being overseen by CBS). Although *Ghost Whisperer* star Jennifer Love Hewitt is not a regular here, stories are well presented without her (although, if a fan of the *Ghost Whisperer* series, you can almost picture her helping). Each of the stories is creepy enough to sustain interest and could have made good series episodes with some revisions to include the Melinda Gordon character.
Episodes:
1. An accident claims the life of a young bike courier (Zach).
2. Zach begins his journey to the other side.
3. Zach meets Luke, a spirit who asks him to help him hunt down other souls.
4. Zach encounters temptation when he is seduced by a beautiful ghost (Haley).
5. Zach meets B.J., a skate-boarding ghost who tries to put some "fun in his afterlife."
6. B.J. reveals to Zach how he fell from grace and became a part of the Dark Side.
7. Zach and B.J. seek a way to avoid the vengeance of the Shadow Spirits.
8. Zach and B.J. are unsuccessful and captured by the Shadow Spirits.

9. To save himself, Zach makes a deal with the Shadow Spirits.
10. The Second Story begins with the Tyler family (parents James and Meg and their daughter Daisy) moving into their new home, unaware that it is haunted.
11. Strange occurrences arouse Meg's suspicions that she and her family are not alone.
12. As Mike tries to ease Meg's apprehension, the ghost (Bo) befriends Daisy.
13. Strange occurrences continue, driving Meg to the point of hysteria.
14. Meg and James see that a ghost is in their presence and attaching itself to Daisy.
15. Meg begins to fear for Daisy's safety but discovers that Bo is a powerful spirit.
16. Meg and James devise a plan that will release Daisy from Bo's control over her.
17. Bo has plans of his own—to rid his house of James and Meg.
18. The Third Story Begins. At her tenth year high school reunion, a ghost attaches itself to Olivia without her knowledge.
19. The ghost, now a part of Olivia, tries to intersect with the world of the living.
20. The ghost takes refuge in Olivia's home and strange things begin to happen.
21. Olivia seeks to discover why she has become the target of a ghost.
22. As Olivia's behavior becomes a bit strange, her fiancé, Marc, becomes concerned.
23. Olivia's prenuptial dinner plans enrage the ghost, who wants Olivia for himself.
24. Marc and Olivia attempt to share a romantic evening despite their ghostly onlooker.
25. Marc fails in an attempt to rid the house of the ghost.
26. Olivia and Marc call on their friend Melinda Gordon in an effort to help the ghost see the light and move on.

165 Ghostfacers. webserieschannel.com. 2010 (Fantasy).

A spin off from the CW series *Supernatural* that follows a team of amateur ghost hunters (who consider themselves professionals) as they investigate paranormal occurrences. The program details the team's (Ed, Maggie, Harry, Spruce and Ambyr) efforts to solve the mystery of a theater haunted by ghost.
Cast: A.J. Buckley (Ed Zeddmore), Travis Wester (Harry Spangler), Brittany Ishibashi (Maggie Zeddmore), Mircea Monroe (Ambyr), Austin Basis (Kenny Spruce), Kelly Carlson (Janet Meyers).
Credits: *Producer:* Peter Johnson, Jeff Grosvenor, Eric Kripke, Phil Sgriccia. *Writer:* A.J. Buckley, Patric J. Doody, Chris Valenziano, Travis Wester.
Comment: Played more for laughs than horror, the program is well produced and acted and encom-

passes Kelly Carlson (from the series *Nip/Tuck*) as its guest star (Janet Meyers). With *Supernatural* wearing its welcome thin on the CW, *Ghostfacers* could make a good replacement should the CW realize that *Supernatural* has virtually played itself out. The original series concept was to have the cast investigate a real haunted house; this was dropped in favor of the haunted theater.

Episodes:

1. Meet the Facers (3 min., 55 sec.). The team receives the case of an actress (Janet) who was murdered in front of her dressing room mirror and now haunts the theater in which she died.

2. The Grand Showcase (2 min., 45 sec.). The team secures their facts before beginning their investigation.

3. The Big Break (3 min., 56 sec.). At the Grand Showcase Theater, the team begins their investigation.

4. CSI: Maggie (2 min., 50 sec.). An old film gives the team an idea of just who Janet Meyers was.

5. Dead Time (3 min.). Hoping to catch an image of Janet, the team sets up a series of mirrors throughout the theater.

6. Finishing the Job (2 min., 59 sec.). A ghostly image appears to have been captured on video by the team.

7. The Comeback (2 min., 55 sec.). Now positive that a spirit exists in the theatre, team member Spruce attempts to exorcise it.

8. Cutting Room Floor (2 min., 32 sec.). Things do not go as expected as the enraged ghost of Janet attacks Ambyr.

9. Shattered (2 min., 58 sec.). Additional problems plague the team after they rescue Ambyr.

10. Why We Fight (3 min., 1 sec.). The team attempts one more trick to rid their lives of Janet.

166 Ghouls. webseriestoday.com. 2010 (Horror).

The 1920s and 30s were a great time for movie monsters, especially Frankenstein, Dracula, the Wolfman, the Mummy and the Phantom of the Opera. They flourished as the screen's greatest fright figures but as America's fascination with them grew less, they blended into the background and became unnoticed for decades. But that was then. They have returned to the modern world and, having lived a sheltered existence now face a world that is totally unfamiliar to them. Stories follow their efforts to recapture the glory of their pasts by again becoming the screen's greatest monsters.

Cast: Dan Merket (Frankenstein), Julian Martinez (Dracula), Bryce Wissel (Wolfman), Sweet P. (Mummy), David Hall Page (Phantom of the Opera), Jose Rosete (Jason), Geoffrey Dwyer (Royce McCutchens), Patrick Waller (Michael Myers). **Credits:** *Producer:* Alisa Allen, Sandy Haddad, Shelby Sexton, Mathew Lancaster. *Director:* Benjamin T. Ross. *Writer:* Benjamin T. Ross, Kris Simonian. **Comment:** Light comedy mixes with stupidity as movie monsters from the past take center stage. The idea is nothing new as it has been done on television before with the live action *Monster Squad* and the animated *Drak Pack*. Even *The Munsters* and *The Munsters Today* conceived of such an idea. Here, however, the monsters are anything but convincing and are horribly depicted (Frankenstein, for example, has a green face, a bad toupee and two bolts on his neck; Dracula looks normal; and the Mummy has a bad case of loose bandages). The program begins with no introduction as to how the monsters came to be (in the present) or how they acquire their friend Jason. Had some time been taken to present the monsters as they should look and couple that with a decent story line, *Ghouls* would have made a good series. As it stands now *Ghouls* is ghoulish.

Episodes:

1. Episode 1. The Ghouls have returned and begin to ponder their future, especially how to earn money.

2. Episode 2. As the Ghouls figure out how to get back in the movies, Wolfman seeks a way to invest their earnings.

3. Episode 3. The Ghouls plans are slowly backfiring with their continued failures to accomplish their goals.

4. Episode 4. Jason, the Ghouls friend and agent, meets with a studio head with hopes of securing a deal. In the meantime, Mummy believes that they should use the computer for some social networking.

5. Episode 5. Mummy finds social networking a blast while Dracula and Frankenstein hope to scare up business at the local Vampfest. Jason continues his talks with the studio head (Royce).

6. Episode 6. The series ends with the anxious-to-work Ghouls going over Jason's head and meeting the studio head themselves.

167 GIFTED. webserieschannel.com. 2013 (Science Fiction).

Peyton, Scarlet and Will are teenagers who, during a school trip to a park, are exposed to an eclipse explosion. There are no immediate side effects; but the following day they each discover they have been endowed with amazing powers. But others that were caught in the explosion are not as fortunate and have turned criminal-like. Concealing the fact that they have changed, Peyton, Will and Scarlet use their powers to secretly deal with the problems no one else can seem to handle.

Cast: Tagan Robbins (Peyton Elliott), Lewis Phillips (Will Kaplan), Isi Simona Fink (Scarlet Jones), Sophie Haynes (Bella Knight), Louise Elliott (Louise Elliott), Pete Bennett (Matt). **Credits:** *Producer:* Lewis Phillips. *Writer-Director:* Lewis Phillips,

Tagan Robbins. **Comment:** Despite the fact that some of the episodes are quite long for a web series, the story is worthy enough to hold one's attention. Acting and production values are good.

Episodes:

1. Alignment, Part 1 (14 min., 58 sec.). Introduces the series concept.

2. Alignment, Part 2 (12 min., 14 sec.). The teens discover their powers and try to adjust to what is happening to them.

3. Paranormal Activity, Part 1 (14 min., 28 sec.). The teens use their powers to investigate the aftermath of a séance gone wrong.

4. Paranormal Activity, Part 2 (14 min., 15 sec.). Continues the investigation from the prior episode with the team discovering paranormal activity has been released.

5. Mind Over Matter (27 min., 13 sec.). A new girl in town (Bella) takes a liking to Scarlet and tries to become close to her by breaking up the team.

6. The Copy Cat, Part 1 (32 min., 11 sec.). A side effect emerges in Scarlet. She discovers she can replicate power and now feels the urge to steal as much power as she can.

7. The Copy Cat, Part 2 (20 min., 46 sec.). Will, Peyton and Bella seek a way to save Scarlet whose power consumption has taken complete control of her.

168 *Girl Number 9.* webserieschannel. com. 2009.(Horror).

Seven women have been brutally murdered and the police search for a culprit leads them to arrest a suspect: Vincent Boylan. Boylan, however, is only a suspect and the police have only a limited amount of time to get a confession or they must release him. As lead interrogator Matheson questions Boylan, he learns that he has kidnapped another girl and the police have only 30 minutes to find her before she dies. The situation becomes tense when Matheson learns that his daughter, Holly, is the victim. Stories follow Matheson as he plays a psychological game and a race against time to save his daughter. **Cast:** Gareth David-Lloyd (Det. Matheson), Joe Absolom (Vincent Boylan), Tracy Ann Oberman (Det. Lyndon), Lee Ravitz (Weinberg), Laurie Saunders (Jones), Ryan Spencer Wilson (Dunbar). **Credits:** *Producer:* Peter Coogan, Martin G. Baker. *Director:* James Moran, Dan Turner. *Writer:* James Moran. **Comment:** Although technically not a horror series in the true sense, it is a good psychological thriller that is well produced and acted. The program, produced in England, plays out in real time encompassing only 30 minutes of the viewer's time (real time also being done on the television series *24*).

Episodes:

1. Episode 1 (5 min., 8 sec.). The police have arrested the suspected serial killer (Vincent Boylan)

who claims to have kidnapped another girl—Detective Matheson's daughter.

2. Episode 2 (4 min., 2 sec.). Based on clues given to them by Boylen, Matheson and his team search the suspected area but come up empty handed—a ploy by Boylan to make a strange bargain with Matheson.

3. Episode 3 (4 min., 52 sec.). To convince Matheson that he is not lying Boylan is given a laptop and brings up a video image of the girl (Holly) he has kidnapped.

4. Episode 4 (6 min., 4 sec.). As the web cam image of Holly plays, Matheson learns that the door leading to her release is booby-trapped and only Boylan can open it.

5. Episode 5 (5 min., 1 sec.). As time begins to run out, Matheson attempts to figure a way to outsmart Boylan. Unfortunately, it is Boylan who holds all the cards: he will spare Holly's life if Matheson takes his own life (his bargain from episode 2).

6. Episode 6 (3 min., 18 sec.). Matheson's decision is revealed as is Holly's fate.

169 *Girly Ghost Hunters.* ovguide.com. 2005 (Horror).

Four young women, who call themselves The Girly Ghost Hunters, investigate documented or alleged haunted locations throughout Ontario, Canada. The women travel in a motor home and use modern technology to capture evidence of ghosts or other phenomena. Each episode concludes with a wrap up of the investigation but leaves the viewer to decide if what happened was real or just an elaborate hoax.

Dana Matthews is the group's spiritualist; Corrie Matthews is Dana's sister, a scientist; Jen Kieswetter is the researcher; Nicole Dobie is the "adventurer" (the one that leads the way into a haunted locale). **Cast:** Dana Matthews, Corrie Matthews, Jen Kieswetter, Nicole Dobie (Themselves). **Credits:** *Producer:* Sean Buckley, Jim Kiriakakis. *Director:* Sean Buckley. **Comment:** While the idea is not new, having women as the ghost hunters is different and the women are as attractive as most of the creepy sites they choose to investigate. The decision to leave what was investigated as true or a hoax is also different although this was done on television with the series *Beyond Belief: Fact or Fiction*.

Episodes:

1. The Grand Theater. The Girls probe the supposedly haunted Grand Theater in London, Ontario.

2. Fort George. An investigation into haunted Fort George in Old Fort Niagara, Ontario.

3. Ottawa Jail Hostel. A haunted hotel, formally a jail, is investigated by the team.

4. The Bytown Museum. Strange occurrences at the Ottawa museum are probed by the Girls.

5. The Masil Farmhouse. A farmhouse in Ajax,

Ontario, becomes a concern when the present owners claim it is haunted by its former owner.

6. Drummond Hill Cemetery. The Girls face the uncertain when they investigate the Drummond Hill Cemetery, the site of one of the bloodiest battles during the War of 1812 (The Battle of Lundy's Lane) in Niagara Falls.

7. The Banting House. A haunted bed and breakfast in Toronto receives a visit from the Girls.

8. The Werx. The Girls attempt to discover if strange occurrences at a nightclub in Hamilton (The Werx) are caused by an employee who perished in a fire when it was a spice factory.

9. The Cherry Hill House. Reports of a Native American Indian spirit finds the girls investigating the Cherry Hill House, an Italian restaurant built from wood and stone from an Indian burial ground in Mississauga.

10. Fort Henry. Cannon's firing in the night coupled with sightings of ghost soldiers bring the Girls to the haunted Fort Henry in Kingston.

11. Angel Inn. The Girls investigate reports of the ghost of a British Army captain haunting the elegant Angel Inn in Niagara-on-the-Lake.

12. Cedar Island. The Girls spend a night alone on Kingston's Cedar Island, a camp ground surrounded by water to determine if it is haunted.

13. The Hermitage. The concluding episode that finds the Girls investigating the remains of the Mermiatge Mansion in Ancaster, Ontario, reputed to be the site of murders and satanic rituals.

170 *Giving Up the Ghosts.* www.gutg.tv. 2011 (Horror).

Ghost Stalkers is a company, run by Anton and Ed in their spare time that attempts to uncover evidence of paranormal activity. Anton and Ed, co-owners of a medieval-themed liquor store, are assisted by Regina, the daughter of a rich father, who is addicted to new age spirituality (and wine). Ghost Stalkers however, is anything but successful and it faces expulsion from The Paranormal Society due to its inability to uncover anything supernatural. The program charts the team's efforts to remain in the society by finding concrete evidence that ghosts exist. **Cast:** Jared Moore (Anton), Kristofer James (Ed), Monica Reich (Regina), Tony Riech (Roy). **Credits:** *Producer:* Tony Riech, Nick Hartman. *Director:* Nick Hartman. *Writer:* Tony Riech. **Comment:** While only one investigative story was presented, using ghosts with a sense of humor (like vaporizing the bottle of vodka) is a bit different than other such media ghost hunting series. The acting and production values are good and the ending leaves the possibility open for more episodes to follow.

Episodes:

1. Liquor Fools (4 min., 35 sec.). Regina joins the team as news arrives that they face losing their affiliation with The Paranormal Society.

2. Cooler. We Have a Problem (3 min., 36 sec.). A client (Roy) contacts the team, claiming he has a ghost in his kitchen.

3. All That Glitters (3 min., 47 sec.). Regina helps Anton and Ed devise a way to deal with Roy's call.

4. Tormented by Spirits (5 min., 13 sec.). Anton and Regina begin the investigation at Roy's house.

5. Hostage Negotiations (3 min., 51 sec.). Ed attempts to capture the entity that attacked Roy on his thermal imaging camera.

6. Lights Out (5 min., 3 sec.). The unthinkable happens while the team investigates—something unknown vaporizes a bottle of vodka.

7. TNT (5 min., 54 sec.). Believing that they have captured evidence of a ghost, the team submits it to The Paranormal Society hoping to remain active members.

171 *A Good Knight's Quest.* blip.tv. 2010 (Fantasy).

Dorian and Gabriel are friends who live to play video games. One day Dorian's dream becomes a reality when Adrianna, the beautiful princess in his favorite game, magically comes through his game screen and appears in his living room. Her kingdom is in danger and she needs his help to save it. With Gabriel by his side, Dorian follows Adrianna back to her fantasy kingdom and stories relate Dorian and Gabriel's efforts, incorporating their video game skills as knights, to save Adrianna's kingdom. **Cast:** Craig Frank (Dorian West), Paula Rhodes (Adrianna), Charlie Bodin (Gabriel), Cathy Baron (Raine), Angie Cole (Sandrine), Douglas Sarine (Lord Galen), Brian Smith (Agent 1), Benjamin J. Cain, Jr. (Agent 2), Brett Register (Cooper), Yuri Lowenthal (Marcus), Kristen Ortiz (Karen), Maxwell Glick (Tidler), Brea Grant (Agent Zero). **Credits:** *Producer:* Russ Pitts, Paula Rhodes, Rick Rey. *Director:* Brett Register. *Writer:* Rick Rey. **Comment:** Enjoyable story, good but limited special effects and capable acting (although Dorian can come off as a bit annoying). Modern-day cars seen in the background sort of ruins the illusion of what is happening, but that can be overlooked for the gorgeous female villains in their sexy attire.

Episodes:

1. Episode 1. Princess Adrianna appears in Dorian's living room to request his help in saving her kingdom.

2. Episode 2. Dorian and Gabriel try to comprehend what has just happened and agree to help Adrianna.

3. Episode 3. Adrianna leads the way for Dorian and Gabriel to enter her fantasy world.

4. Episode 4. Dorian, called "The Chosen One," begins a quest to find a magic crystal (which must be destroyed to save the kingdom) in The Land of the Sun.

5. Episode 5. As Dorian, Gabriel and Adrianna

pursue the crystal they encounter warriors, sorcerers and Adrianna's enemies.

6. Episode 6. Guided by a map that they do not fully comprehend, Dorian, Gabriel and Adrianna seek someone to decipher it (as it is the key to finding The Land of the Sun).

7. Episode 7. The trio continues their uncertain journey for the evasive crystal.

8. Episode 8. Hope brims as the trio reaches The Land of the Sun (also called Sunland).

9. Episode 9. Hope now dims as Dorian must battle Adrianna's enemies, Sandrine and Raine who are also seeking the crystal.

10. Episode 10. More trouble plagues the trio as they defeat their foes, but are still unable to ascertain the crystal's whereabouts.

11. Episode 11. Trouble again plagues the trio as they encounter Agent Zero.

12. Episode 12. Agent Zero and Dorian confront each other—with Agent Zero determined to rid her life of The Chosen One.

13. Episode 13. When Agent Zero fails in her quest, Lord Galen dispatches Agent 2 to help her.

14. Episode 14. Dorian feels that he needs to re-generate himself by taking a metaphorical pit stop.

15. Episode 15. To continue his quest Dorian feels he must find The Creator, who can guide him between the worlds of reality and fantasy.

16. Episode 16. Dorian is confronted by a vision (appearing as a female) that tells him he must either join the forces of Light or Darkness before continuing his journey.

17. Episode 17. Dorian sides with the Light as he continues his quest.

18. Episode 18. Lord Galen's agents, Sandrine and Raine, pursue The Chosen One.

19. Episode 18. Dorian, Adrianna and Gabriel continue their journey, unknowingly being pursed by the enemy.

20. Episode 20. An ally (Karen) attempts to help Dorian, Adrianna and Gabriel as they continue their search for magic crystals.

21. Episode 21. With the map as his guide, The Chosen One believes the magic crystals are close by and his quest will soon be ended.

22. Episode 22. Sensing that The Chosen One may accomplish his goal, Lord Galen readies his Dark Army for an attack on Dorian.

23. Episode 23. Dorian senses danger as he, Adrianna and Gabriel come closer to finding the crystals.

24. Episode 22. The Dark Army poses a threat as Dorian comes within striking distance of acquiring the crystals.

25. Episode 23. Dorian's quest, to meet The Creator, is granted.

26. Episode 24. Dorian's game skills are put to the test when the battle for good over evil begins.

172 *Gotham Girls*. youtube.com. 2000–2002 (Fantasy).

Characters from the DC Comics universe are seen in animated form as they uphold the peace, battle crime and deal with their own personal lives most notably, the villains Catwoman, Poison Ivy and Harley Quinn and the superhero Batgirl.

Voice Cast: Adrienne Barbeau (Selina Kyle/Cat-woman/Renee Montoya), Arleen Sorkin (Dr. Helena Quinzel/Harley Quinn), Diane Pershing (Dr. Pamela Lillian Isley/Poison Ivy), Tara Strong (Barbara Gordon/Batgirl/Elizabeth Styles), Stacie Randall (Zatanna Zatara), Jennifer Hale (Det. Selma Reesedale/Dora Smitty/Caroline Greenway), Bob Hastings (Commissioner James Gordon). **Credits:** *Producer:* Alan Bruckner. **Comment:** Currently the official website no longer exists but users will be redirected to the Warner Bros. web site. Aspects associated with the original presentation have also been discontinued (like trailers, screensavers and games). Third season episodes were also restructured from the comedy-like first two seasons to a more dramatic approach (especially with the introduction of the transsexual Det. Selma Reesedale).

Episodes:

1. The Vault. Poison Ivy and Harley Quinn plot to rob a vault containing diamonds.

2. Lap Bat in a Rooftop Chase. Catwoman attempts to steal The Jade Gato, a mystical statuette worth millions of dollars.

3. Trick or Trick. On Halloween Harley Quinn seeks to steal a diamond necklace as a present for her mentor, Poison Ivy.

4. A Little Night Magic. After completing a stage show, Zatanna, the magician, must deal with a number of problems as she returns home (from muggers to a speeding truck).

5. More Than One Way. Poison Ivy, Harley Quinn and Catwoman team to steal a valuable painting.

6. Precious Birthstones. Selina Kyle, in her Catwoman alias, plots to steal the million dollar Jewel of the Empress from a Baroness visiting Gotham City.

7. The Three Babies. To cheer up a depressed Harley, Poison Ivy tells her a fairy tale based on "Goldilocks" called "The Three Babes" with herself, Harley and Catwoman as the main characters.

8. Pave Paradise. Poison Ivy attempts to thwart the Mayor's plans to turn Gotham City's wetlands into a shopping mall.

9. The Gardener's Apprentice. Harley Quinn attempts to remedy a situation—getting rid of clones of herself when she accidentally pricks herself on Poison Ivy's "don't water, touch or look at" mimmitia plant when it begins producing pods that grow into little green Harley's.

10. Lady X. Catwoman, Poison Ivy and Harley Quinn attempt to stop the mysterious Lady X, a criminal who has invaded Gotham City and stealing its treasures.

11. Hold That Tiger. Zatanna enlists the help of

Catwoman to find her white tiger after it is stolen following a stage performance.

12. Miss Un-Congeniality. Catwoman, Poison Ivy and Harley Quinn compete for the coveted crown in the annual "Miss Criminal Mastermind Beauty Pageant."

13. Strategy. Believing that Harley Quinn's naiveté is constantly ruining her capers, Poison Ivy sets out to make her a master criminal.

14. Baby Boom. Poison Ivy and Harley Quinn's plan to steal jewels off a wax figure of Princess Adjani backfires when a special plant pollen prepared by Ivy causes Harley to regress to infancy.

15. Cat-n-Mouse, Cat-n-Mouse. Catwoman attempts to capture the girl who is impersonating her and stealing in her name.

16. Bat'ing Cleanup. Barbara Gordon reflects on an uneventful day she experienced as Batgirl.

17. Catsitter. Rather than steal a big screen television, Harley elects to buy one—and begins by earning money by babysitting Bongo, Catwoman's baby lion.

18. Gotham Noir. A take on the old detective films of the 1940s wherein Harley becomes a private detective and is hired by Catwoman to find her missing cat, Velma.

19. Scout's Dishonor. When Poison Ivy discovers that Harley was a Mandy Scout (Gotham City's version of the Girl Scouts) she decides to teach them the merits of being bad and other disreputable "life skills."

20. I'm Batgirl. Batgirl becomes a victim of one of Poison Ivy's flowers when the pollen reverses her moral outlook and turns her into a thief.

Note: The following third season episodes are a complex arc story wherein the men of Gotham City mysteriously vanish, leaving the women to take over and of the principal efforts of Batgirl to uncover what happened (Mr. Freeze sent all men into an alternate temporal dimension where time stood still until they were brought back) and return the city to normal.

21. Missing in Action. *22.* Gotham in Pink. *23.* Hear Me Roar. *24.* Ms.-ing in Action. *25.* Gotham in Blue. *26.* A Cat in the Hand. *27.* Jailhouse Wreck. *28.* Honor Among Thieves. *29.* No, I'm Batgirl. *30.* Signal Fires. *31.* Cold Hands, Cold Heart.

173 *The Great Dying.* the thegreatdying.com. 2011 (Horror).

An apocalyptic America now exists. The catastrophe, called The Great Dying, has erased almost all traces of society. Surviving humans (here in Seattle), who must evade the increasingly growing zombie population, can only remain in one place for a short

The Great Dying cast, from left to right: Ralf Beck, Fredrik Wagner and Jennifer Lila-Knipe (photograph by Klas Persson, Ödmården Filmproduction).

period of time and must move on before their blood becomes the feast of ghouls. Hope, however, does not seem to be lost. While all of America has been struck, it appears that the East Coast is ghoul free as the dead have not risen. Stories follow a group of survivors as they begin a treacherous journey (on foot) to a promised land that may not be a promised land after all.

Cast: Jennifer Lila-Knipe (Lily), Fredrik Wagner (Sam), Ralf Beck (The Man), Robert Prowse (The Chief), Pontus Olgrim (Billy). **Credits:** *Producer-Director:* Karin Engman, Klas Persson. *Writer:* Klas Persson. **Comment:** Intriguing series with sustained interest to tune into the next episode. Production qualities and acting are good and episodes can sustain themselves but should be watched in sequence.

Episodes:

1. Has Already Occurred (13 min., 20 sec.). Establishes America as a world infested with zombies and introduces a character called The Man who will come to lead a group of survivors to a better place.

2. Is Still Going On (12 min., 5 sec.). The Man discovers that a group of zombie meat eaters is being led by The Chief and scouring Seattle for survivors.

3. And Burning Coals Went Forth At Their Feet (9 min., 56 sec.). The Man teams with another survivor, Sam.

4. Trust (9 min., 4 sec.). As The Man and Sam struggle to evade the Chief, they encounter another survivor, Lily.

5. Episode 5 (12 min., 17 sec.). The Man, Sam and Lily are captured by the Chief and appear to become a feast for his man eaters.

174 *A Guy, a Girl and Their Monster.* youtube.com. 2013 (Fantasy).

The girl is Jenn. The guy is Phil, her husband. The monster is Henry Monster, Jenn's childhood plush toy. As a young girl, Jenn had a best friend, a monster (whom she called Henry Monster) that lived under her bed. As she grew, Monster became less important and gradually disappeared from her life. Jenn is now married and she and her husband, Phil, live in a small apartment. As Jenn recalls her childhood, she decides to readopt Monster. Unfortunately for Phil, he too can see Monster and the three must now share the apartment. Stories follow Jenn and Phil—and their Monster as they struggle to live together.

Cast: Jenn Daugherty (Jenn), Phil Hughes (Phil), Matt Zunich (Henry Monster). **Credits:** *Producer-Writer:* Jenn Daugherty. *Director:* Phillip Hughes. **Comment:** Short and right to the point (although longer episodes would be just as enjoyable). The acting and production values are good as is Henry (a likeable plush doll come to "life").

Episodes:

1. Bacon (1 min., 34 sec.). It is the middle of the night and Henry gets a craving for what he loves most—bacon. With the only dialogue in the episode, Henry saying "bacon," Jenn sets about to make his favorite food.

2. Steve (2 min., 14 sec.). Henry goes berserk when Jenn tells Henry that they are out of bacon; he taunts Phil to buy more by endlessly repeating the name Steve.

3. Hollywood Monster (1 min., 12 sec.). Henry believes he is destined to big in Hollywood—and is when he stands distant from the Hollywood sign (which appears small when the camera focuses on Henry).

4. A Monster's Revenge. Henry seeks a way to get back at Phil when he buys Monster Off, a spray to keep Henry off his back.

5. Henri Le Monstre (1 min., 39 sec.). Henry becomes obsessed with French films and now hopes to star in one (the entire episode features only Henry acting with a French accent).

175 *H+.* hplusdigitalseries.com. 2011 (Science Fiction).

A look at an apocalyptic future where technology has reached heights that have never been seen before. It is a time when a third of the world's population has retired and embraced an alarming new device: H+ (a high tech implant that allows people to be connected to information and each other through their thoughts). Some embrace it; some despise it and stories relate the impact H+ has on those who have changed for the better (?) and of a group of people, trapped in an underground parking garage, who must find a means of escape after an explosion has devastated the world above them.

Cast: Alexis Denisof (Conal Sheehan), Caitriona Balfe (Breanna Sheehan), Hannah Simone (Leena Param), Karrien Marsukhan (Ritu Param), Amir Arison (Y. Gurveer), David Clayton Rogers (Kenneth Lubahn), Francesca Fanti (Simona Rossi), Nikki Crawford (Julie Martin), Sean Gunn (Jason O'Brien), Samuli Vauramo (Topi Kuusela), Hannah Herzsprung (Manta), Lela Loren (Francesca Rossi), Melvin Abston (Lee Martin). **Credits:** *Producer:* Bryan Singer. *Director:* Stewart Hendler. *Writer:* John Cabrera, Cosimo De Tommaso. **Comment:** Like the television series *Lost* the program can become confusing as it jumps back and forth between present, past and future events. While it does not introduce an overabundance of characters, it stretches a particular character's predicament over several nonconsecutive episodes and offers very little in the brief time allotted to each episode. Although there is a running theme, especially with the character of Kenneth and his involvement with H+, it might have played better if the episodes had been edited to focus on a particular character and what happens to that character in sequential episodes then move onto a new chapter and a new character. While the first episode captures your attention, additional episodes can easily drive you away.

Episodes: (Because of the series set up, episode comprehension is non-consistent and, like the series, confusing. The descriptions provided below follow their presentation and may also be confusing as scenes continually jump from the present to the past and future and back again to the present):

1. Driving Under: San Francisco, USA—5 Minutes Before It Happened Prologue (7 min., 26 sec.). Introduces the concept as people in an underground parking garage, especially Lee and his wife Julie, appear to have their lives spared when a great explosion traps them.

2. On Their Level—15 Seconds After It Happened (4 min., 9 sec.). A stranger (Kenneth) offers to lead the people down to Level 6 of the garage, where he insists they will be safe.

3. Prophetess—Helsinki, Finland—7 Years Before It Happened (6 min., 10 sec.). A young man (Topi) and woman (Manta) who found each other online, agree to meet in person at a bar.

4. Airport Security—San Francisco, USA, 1 Minute After It Happened (5 min., 19 sec.). Rising water from the sprinkler system poses a threat to Kenneth and Lee.

5. A Large Family—Mumbai, India, 5 Months Before It Happened (6 min., 49 sec.). A young couple (Breanna and Conal) meet with a doctor (Gurveer) to discuss the prospect of a surrogate pregnancy.

6. Voci Dal Sud—Oria, Italy, 2 Years After It Happened (5 min., 27 sec.). A priest (Matteo) tries to help the people of a small village despite the fact that he lacks the necessary medicine.

7. Implanted—Mumbai, India, 5 Months Before It Happened (3 min., 46 sec.). Leena, the surrogate for Breanna and Conal, is implanted with H+ so her pregnancy can be monitored by Breanna and Conal.

8. Makeshift Engineering—San Francisco, USA, 45 Minutes After It Happened (4 min., 58 sec.). Kenneth seeks a way to save Lee's life after he is injured using circuit boards and spare wiring.

9. The Snow Viper—Helsinki, Finland, 7 Years Before It Happened (5 min., 22 sec.). Topi and Manta are now in a physical relationship; more insight is given to Topi's job as a homicide detective.

10. Out—San Francisco, USA, 50 Minutes Before It Happened (5 min., 18 sec.). Kenneth and the group of survivors make plans to stay where they are while Lee's condition changes.

11. Mana—Helsinki, Finland, 7 Years Before It Happened (6 min., 39 sec.). Topi and Manta share a growing intimacy.

12. Searching Over—San Francisco, USA, 20 Hours After It Happened (5 min., 53 sec.). Kenneth raises suspicions among the group when it appears he knows too much about H+.

13. Questions—Portland, Oregon, 5 Years Before It Happened (5 min.). It is revealed that Breanna, a software developer, met with Kenneth to discuss a private venture.

14. The Gates—San Vito, Italy, 2 Years After It Happened (5 min.). Unknown to Matteo, he is being observed by someone with a keen interest in what he is doing outside the gates of a base.

15. Their Connection—Mumbai, India, 3 Months Before It Happened (3 min., 48 sec.). Leena's implant needs adjusting so she can coordinate her sleep schedule to Breanna's work demands.

16. From Above—San Francisco, USA, 2 Days After It Happened (3 min., 46 sec.). A young boy is reunited with his mother in the parking structure and gives Kenneth some insight as to what is happening in the chaotic world above them.

17. Salmiakki—Helsinki, Finland, 7 Years Before It Happened (4 min., 55 sec.). Looks at Topi and Manta's on-going relationship.

18. Advent—Oria, Italy, 2 Years After It Happened (2 min., 58 sec.). Matteo experiences a dream wherein he meets someone he has never known before.

19. 7500 Kilometers—Mumbai, India, 1 Month Before It Happened (3 min., 54 sec.). Leena and Conal grow closer as Conal reveals his personal life to her via his H+.

20. Partenza—Oria, Italy, 2 Years After It Happened (4 min., 21 sec.). Matteo prepares for a week-long trip.

21. Managing—Dublin, Ireland, 4 Years Before It Happened (3 min., 37 sec.). As H+ technology advances, Breanna and Kenneth part company when Kenneth travels to South America to observe human H+ test subjects.

22. Road Block—Southern Italy, 2 Years After It Happened (3 min., 37 sec.). Matteo and his traveling companion are approached by armed thugs as they continue their road trip.

23. The King—Dublin, Ireland, 3 Weeks Before It Happened (3 min., 16 sec.). Breanna becomes suspicious (not knowing he is involved with Leena) when Kenneth begins spending too much time on his H+.

24. Function—San Francisco, USA, 1 Week After It Happened (4 min., 6 sec.). Kenneth and his group, stranded for one week in the parking structure, finally make an exit.

25. Meta Data—Tierra del Fuego, Chile—4 Years Before It Happened (4 min., 13 sec.). At the lab in South America, Kenneth views how H+ technology is being synthesized into the genetics of the human mind.

26. African Aid—Brazzaville, Republic of Congo, 1 Year After It Happened (3 min., 27 sec.). In Africa Topi encounters a soldier he first believes is an enemy (not the ally he turns out to be). The soldier joins Topi in his search for a village.

27. Il Portavoce—Oria, Italy, 3 Months Before It Happened (5 min., 4 sec.). Matteo (a priest) encounters a woman (Simona) who confesses to visions of the past and the future.

28. Coming Clean—Northern California, USA,

2 Weeks After It Happened (5 min., 6 sec.). Shows that Kenneth escaped the underground parking lot and is preparing for a special mission.

29. After Party—Dublin, Ireland, 3 Years Before It Happened (3 min., 58 sec.). Breanna and Kenneth reunite in Ireland.

30. Lord of the Body—Mumbai, India, 7 Months After It Happened (3 min., 11 sec.). Unknown to Leena, her pregnancy is the subject of an H+ experiment.

31. Original Sync—London, UK, 9 Years Before It Happened (4 min., 56 sec.). It is learned that Dr. Gurveer had been approached for an underground medical experiment using H+ technology.

32. Seeds—Dunbara, Republic of Congo—1 Year After It Happened (6 min., 14 sec.). Topi and the soldier search for a village (Dunbara) that had been destroyed many years ago (from episode 26).

33. On the Exterior—Northern California, USA, 3 Years Before It Happened (4 min., 47 sec.). A fringe political clan (called Neo Luddites), led by Jason, becomes a threat to survivors.

34. Endure—Mumbai, India, 8 Months After It Happened (4 min., 39 sec.). Leena is visited by Dr. Gurveer, who is eager to check her progress, in her village.

35. Query String—Northern California, USA, 3 Years Before It Happened (2 min., 44 sec.). It is revealed that Kenneth had a dream (vision) of a pending catastrophe three years before it happened.

36. How to Hack a Data Center—Southern Alberta, Canada, 8 Months After It Happened (3 min., 31 sec.). Simona, the girl who can see the past and future, teams with Kenneth to set up a network regarding H+.

37. Gross Figure—New York, USA, 8 Months Before It Happened (4 min., 50 sec.). Jason, the future rebel leader, is seen as a test subject of LPW, the biotech firm experimenting with H+ technology.

38. On the Inside—Rome, Italy, 2 Years After It Happened (4 min., 39 sec.). Topi receives a message from Manta that is only meant for him.

39. Long Term Benefits—Dunbara, Republic of Congo, 7 Years Before It Happened (2 min., 56 sec.). Dr. Gurveer is seen negotiating with a tribal chief to use his people as test subjects for H+.

40. Two of Them—Rome, Italy, 2 Years After It Happened (5 min., 2 sec.). Manta, suffering from hallucinations, reaches out to Matteo for help.

41. Pronto—Oria, Italy, 3 Months Before It Happened (4 min., 30 sec.). It is slowly being revealed that Kenneth has a plan for H+ technology but has no idea of the catastrophic fallout.

42. Temporary—Yozgat, Turkey, 1 Year After It Happened (3 min., 48 sec.). Leena gives birth to the baby (Vadish) and connects with Conal for the first time in a year. She also discovers that she was an H+ test subject.

43. Make Things Right—Northern California, USA, 2 Weeks Before It Happened (6 min., 32 sec.).

Jason suffers a breakdown when his mechanical body-brace fails and is now unable to rally his troops.

44. From/To Level 6—Southern Alaska, USA, 1 Year After It Happened (3 min., 34 sec.). Kenneth embarks on a trip with Francesca and Simona to explore the Alaska Delta in a hope for a new beginning.

176 *Hamilton Carver, Zombie P.I.* hamiltoncarver.com. 2010 (Science Fiction).

In a lonely city (Noir City) lives a lonely man— Hamilton Carver, a private detective with few clients and little of anything else. His life changed when he met a beautiful girl called The Lips. Unfortunately, for Hamilton, she was a Mob Princess and not longed for this world. When The Lips is found shot to death, Hamilton and his partner, Harry Callahan, begin an investigation. Days led into weeks and weeks into months with Hamilton's investigation becoming increasingly fruitless. Everything changes, however, when the ghost of The Lips appears to Hamilton to give him the information he needs to bring her killer to justice. However, before Hamilton can accomplish his goal, he is killed by those who killed The Lips. But Hamilton cannot rest. He returns as a zombie to continue in his capacity as a private investigator. The program follows a most unusual detective as he solves crimes as a zombie.

Cast: Ben Cunis (Hamilton Carver), Clint Herring (Lucifer), Ryan Sellers (Harry Callahan), Kelsey Rae Grouge (The Lips), Laura Keena (Stiletto Jean), Lucy Savage (Hilary). **Credits:** *Producer:* Ben Cunis, Pete Markowsky. *Director:* Clint Herring. *Writer:* Ben Cunis, Ken Gagnon, Peter Cunis. **Comment:** If nothing else, an unusual take on the private eye genre that plays well. Although the program focused only on Hamilton's search for The Lips killer, the concept has many more possibilities although that now seems unlikely as several years have passed with new episodes not being produced. The concept and characters were introduced in a short Internet film called *The Choices of Ghosts.*

Episodes:

1. Old Friends. Establishes how Hamilton became a zombie private investigator.

2. Exposited. Hamilton faces the wrath of thugs Stiletto Jean and Punny Jack as he investigates The Lips death.

3. The Devil and the Details. Becoming a zombie is not all that easy when Hamilton discovers that if he does not solve The Lips murder within seven days, his soul will be claimed by Lucifer and he will spend eternity in Hell.

4. To Catch a Ninja. With Hamilton now a full fledged zombie (having made the deal to solve the murder or forfeit his soul), he and Harry investigate a group of ninjas.

5. The Long Arm of the Law. Hamilton and Harry are arrested by the police after a confrontation with the Ninjas involve them in a wild car chase.

6. Continuing Education. Now released from jail, Hamilton and Harry, believing the Ninjas, who were at the scene of The Lips murder, know more than they are saying receive help from Yosake, a Ninja expert, to learn the way of the Ninja.

7. Keystone Nights. After completing their training, Hamilton and Harry again confront the Ninjas, this time capturing one of them.

8. Dating Service. In an attempt to discover who else may have witnessed The Lips murder, Hamilton convinces Stiletto Jean to date Yosake (who also may know more than he is revealing).

9. The Long Pun Goodnight. Learning that mob boss Punny Jack may be the key to solving the case, Hamilton and Jean probe further. Unfortunately for Hamilton, he also receives a visit from Lucifer as his deadline is nearing.

10. Iambic Pentameter. Harry attempts to save Hamilton from Lucifer who has returned to claim his soul.

11. Whodunit. Saved from Hell, Hamilton now seeks Punny Jack, who appears to be the link to The Lips death.

12. Le Fin. Hamilton finally acquires the vital clue to bring The Lips killer to justice.

177 Haywire. haywireseries.com. 2011 (Horror).

The setting is the village of Monroe, New York. It is a Saturday afternoon and all appears to be normal. Then, suddenly, a burst of light coupled with massive electromagnetic pulses causes power outages and disables all electronic devices. People are placed in an Amish-like environment that also affects their minds and scrambles their thought processing abilities. They are now living in a never-ending loop of repeating the same chores they were performing before the burst of light. The series begins two days after the burst of light with people within the affected area trying to cope with what is happening and outside efforts (The Task Force) seeking a way to infiltrate the affected area and resolve the unknown situation (which continually grows worse as repeating the same tasks continuously causes the brain to malfunction and madness sets in).

Cast: Rebecca Nyahay (Nikki Blaylock), Michael Edan (Willie Hebert), Vince Umbrino (Maj. Vince Phelan), Colleen Conroy (Annie Strickland), Donna Polichetti (Madeline Freene), Jennifer Crane Turner (Caroline Weaks), Jessica Buck (Cassie Heyward), John Lenihan (Trick Moran), Larissa Laurel (Gracie Garcia), Sal Polichetti (Howard Greene), Brandon McCluskey (Connor Strickland), Misti Dawn Garritano (Leah Rizzo), Ronald Trapani (Rick Manningham). **Credits:** *Producer:* Scott Klein, Luis Martinez, Arlene So, John Lenihan. *Director:* Scott Klein, E.B. Martinez, John Lenihan. *Writer:* Scott Klein, Luis Martinez, E.B. Martinez, John Lenihan. **Comment:** A pre *Under the Dome* (CBS, 2013) like

series that presents an interesting concept (although a similar concept was also presented as a segment of *The Twilight Zone*) and follows through with enough intrigue to make the viewer want to see what happens next. Acting, camera work, directing and writing are also good.

Episodes:

1. The Gardner (4 min., 41 sec.). Establishes the storyline (through comic book-like panels) as a gardener goes on a rampage.

2. The Beaten Path (6 min., 10 sec.). A woman seeks her missing son while trying to evade a group of local vigilantes.

3. Return to Sender (9 min., 18 sec.). More evidence of madness develops as a postal delivery man becomes Haywire (crazy).

4. The Situation (6 min., 26 sec.). A government official attempts to communicate with a scientist in the affected area.

5. Duct Tape and Demons (9 min., 14 sec.). The government's Task Force begins its assessment of the situation in Monroe.

6. Grace Under Pressure (8 min., 2 sec.). Grace, one of the unaffected people, finds her life threatened by a sudden Haywire rampage.

7. The Usual Suspects (14 min., 17 sec.). The Task Force enters the affected area and begins its investigation into what happened.

8. Rules to Live By (7 min., 1 sec.). Citizens of Monroe, living outside the affected zone, must now cope with friends who are not the people they once knew.

9. The Ties That Bind (7 min.). Two unaffected citizens, Grace and Carol, search for a missing child with a healing touch.

10. Getting Ahead (10 min., 49 sec.). The Task Force, reaching the perimeter, encounters its first evidence of the unusual: a Haywire local hunter.

11. Homecoming (8 min., 36 sec.). A missing girl, Cassie, found by Nikki, is returned to her mother—a woman who is showing signs of Haywire (as continually cleaning is driving her insane—evidenced by the dark circles around her eyes).

12. Convergence (13 min., 2 sec.). As The Task Force continues its probe, they encounter a local (Willie) who has organized his own team (The Searchers) to help others.

13. Inside and Out (9 min., 33 sec.). Willie informs The Task Force of the situation and how people are being driven insane.

14. No Rest (11 min., 13 sec.). Panic ensues as word spreads about what has happened in Monroe.

15. One for the Road (13 min., 30 sec.). The villagers come to terms with what has happened, with some villagers feeling they are more qualified to lead than Willie.

16. It Never Rains (8 min., 2 sec.). Major Phelan of The Task Force lays out a plan as to what his team must do.

17. The Eyes Have It (11 min., 13 sec.). Strange

events begin to unfold as villagers begin to distrust each other; Major Phelan begins an investigation of Airplane Park Base.

18. A Matter of Perspective (10 min., 25 sec.). As Willie's basement bar provides refuge for weary villagers, Major Phelan finds help investigating the abandoned airfield base from villagers Trick and Kip.

19. The Odyssey (17 min., 37 sec.). The Airplane Park Base appears to hold the key to what has happened. The last episode ends with unresolved issues that will possibly be resolved if additional episodes are produced.

178 *Hemlock Grove.* netflix.com. 2013 (Horror).

Brooke Bluebell is a pretty high school cheerleader in the small town of Hemlock Grove, a once thriving Pennsylvania steel town. It is suggested that Brooke is a lesbian and has been having an affair with one of her female teachers. One night on her way to meet the teacher (called "Bansky"), Brooke stops her car at a train crossing, apparently texting Banksy, when a creature (obviously a werewolf) attacks the car. Brooke manages to escape and begins running into the woods, where she takes refuge in a lone standing shed (that happens to be in the middle of nowhere). Her safety is short lived when she is attacked and mauled to death by the creature. Prior to Brooke's death, a 17-year-old Gypsy (Peter Rumancek) and his mother (Lynda) arrived in town. Peter aroused the curiosity of Christina Wendell, a girl who yearns to be a journalist, and begins talking to him. When she sees that his index and middle fingers are the same length, she associates that with being a werewolf and soon after begins spreading rumors that Peter is a werewolf. When Brooke's body is found, suspicion falls on Peter (due to Christina's rumors) and serial-like stories relate the investigation that follows to find the killer.

Cast: Famke Janssen (Olivia Godfrey), Bill Skarsgard (Roman Godfrey), Landon Liboiron (Peter Rumancek), Penelope Mitchell (Letha Godfrey), Freya Tingley (Christina Wendall), Nicole Boivin (Shelley Godfrey), Ted Dykstra (Francis Pullman), Kandyse McClure (Dr. Clementine Chasseur), Joel de la Fuente (Dr. Johann Pryce), Laurie Fortier (Marie Godfrey), Eliana Jones (Alexa Sworn), Aaron Douglas (Tom Sworn), Emilia McCarthy (Alyssa Sworn), Lili Taylor (Lynda Rumancek), Kaniehtiio Horn (Destiny Rumancek), Holly Deveaux (Jenny Fredericks), Lorenza Izzo (Brooke Bluebell). **Credits:** *Producer:* Michael A. Connolly, Brian McGreevy, Deran Sarafian, Mark Vergeiden. *Director:* Deran Sarafian, T.J. Scott, David Semel, David Straiton, Eli Roth. **Comment:** The story line is good but the program is rather slow moving (editing the lengthy, non action scenes would have helped). Character development is long; although necessary, it could have

been done in far less time and not used to stretch episodes. There are several gory scenes involving blood and flesh but considering the horror element is dragged out, it can easily bore non die-hard fans of the genre.

Episodes:

1. Jellyfish in the Sky. After the mangled body of teenage girl is found murdered in the woods, evidence indicates that she was attacked by an animal.

2. The Angel. Due to Christina's accusations, suspicion falls on Peter, a Gypsy newly arrived in town.

3. The Order of the Dragon. Christina's investigation uncovers another victim; Sheriff Sworn requests outside help from a doctor (Johann Pryce) in an effort to determine what kind of animal is responsible.

4. In Poor Taste. Dr. Pryce is unable to make a determination while Peter, having befriended Roman Godfrey (of the family owned Godfrey Institute) at school begin their own investigation to find the killer.

5. Hello, Handsome. Destiny, Peter's cousin, attempts to help him understand with and cope with the accusations brought against him.

6. The Crucible. Peter and Roman continue their investigation.

7. Measure of Disorder. Peter is taken into custody to be questioned by Dr. Pryce.

8. Catabasis. Mysteries surrounding Roman and his family are revealed when he falls into a coma after a drinking binge.

9. What Peter Can Live Without. Peter has ventured into a relationship with Letha, Roman's cousin, against her parent's wishes; Dr. Pryce prepares a plan to capture the killer.

10. What God Wants. As another full moon is about to occur, Roman awakens from his coma to join Peter in a search for the killer.

11. The Price. The moon has risen and Christina has disappeared while Peter and his mother seek escape from vigilantes who believe Peter is the killer.

12. Children of the Night. It is revealed that members of the Godfrey family have been concealing a horrifying secret—they are werewolves but Christina, also a werewolf is the actual killer being sought for Brooke's death.

13. Birth. Although the episode ends in a cliff hanger (setting up a possible second season), there are numerous twists and turns presented as tragedy strikes both the Godfrey and Rumancek families as authorities seek to unravel the truth (and the concluding scene indicates that Christina will return—maybe not as a werewolf, but a vampire).

179 *Heroes of the North.* heroesofthenorth. com. 2009 (Fantasy).

It is the present but it is also the Earth in an alternate universe where Canada is protected by a legion

Heroes of the North **cast in a costume pose (photgraph by Sergio Rico, copyright 2009–2014 Movie Seals Digital, Inc.).**

of super heroes. When a terrorist organization called Medusa threatens Quebec, the Canadian government incorporates the services of The Canadian (Canada's principal super hero) to battle its enemy. Unable to accomplish the feat alone, he recruits his Montreal-based squadron (Fleur-de-Lys, 8 Ball, Nordik, Black Terror, Canadian Shield) and together set out to not only destroy Medusa but others who threaten their homeland.

Heroes: The Canadian, real name: Christopher Adam Newman; a descendant of the original World War II hero, the Canadian Shield. He was raised from his childhood to become a hero and is now the field leader of the Eastern Division of the Canada Organization. 8 Ball, real name Tony Falcon, is an expert pool shark (hence his nickname 8 Ball) who was recruited from prison to join the team. Fleur-de-Lys, real name Natalie De Verscheres, is aged 25 and gorgeous. She takes chances that do not always pay off and put her in danger. Nordik, real name Manon Desches, is 24 years of age and was recruited from the Canadian Arctic. The Canadian Shield, real name Charles Alfred Newman, is the oldest member of the team, having been born in 1917 and Canada's first hero. The Black Terror, real name Robert "Bob"

Benton, has connections to the underworld and is struggling to break his addiction to drugs.

Villains: Dr. Joseph Mengele (Medusa Commander) is a World War II Nazi scientist who found a way to revive the dead. Madame Doom, real name Dominique Ophelle Martin, was a 1990s beauty queen whose face was partially disfigured when acid was thrown in her face by a feminist who disagreed with her beliefs. She now covers the scars with a partial mask. Masquerade, alias Diana Adams, was a socialite who, to find excitement in her dull life, became the vigilante Masquerade. Hornet, real name Hortense Netter, is the Executive Vice President of Medusa Industries and the intelligence officer to the Medusa Commander. Crimson is a gorgeous hired assassin who often works for Medusa.

Cast: Larry Vinette (The Canadian), Edith Labelle (Fleur-de-Lys), Vanessa Blouin (Nordik), Anderson Bradshaw (8 Ball), John Fallon (Black Terror), Constantine Kourtidis (Medusa Commander), Bianca Beauchamp (Crimson), Anne-Marie Losique (Madame Doom), Pia Metni (Masquerade), Yann Brouillette (Alpha Q), Michel Brouillette (Canadian Shield), Marie-Claude Bourbonnais (Hornet). **Credits:** *Producer-Director:* Christian Viel. *Writer-Director:*

Tann Brouillette, Michel Brouillette. **Comment:** Gorgeous heroines coupled with gorgeous villains (targeting the male audience) adds to the enjoyment of a well produced super hero saga. The costumes, especially for the females, are striking and special effects, though limited are well done. The acting is above average (for an Internet series) and the episodes are just long enough so as not to become overburdened with needless talk.

Episodes:

1. The Canadian: Origins (4 min., 9 sec.). Recalls The Canadian's origins and how he was raised from childhood to become a super hero.

2. Fleur-de-Lys: Origins (5 min., 51 sec.). Explores how Fleur-de-Lys, a research scientist, became a super hero after developing a high tech weapon.

3. 8 Ball: Origins (4 min., 7 sec.). Tony Falcon, alias 8 Ball (for his wizardry at the game of pool) is recruited from prison for his skills after he is arrested for seeking justice (killing the thugs who attacked and killed his girlfriend, Bronwyn).

4. Nordik: Origins (5 min., 8 sec.). Nordik, a girl with an inner strength she acquired from a Shaman, is recruited from the Canadian Arctic to Montreal after she risks her life to arrest Russian soldiers trespassing in her territory.

5. Black Terror: Origins (3 min., 49 sec.). Although addicted to drugs and suffering from intense pain when he is without the strongest drugs, the man known as Black Terror is recruited because of his connections with the underworld.

6. Canadian Shield: Origins (5 min., 22 sec.). Canada's first super hero is traced back to the days of World War II when, in Berlin, he and his troops battled a squadron of Nazi soldiers.

7. Kiss of Death (10 min., 45 sec.). The Canadian begins his task of recruiting his team to battle the evil Medusa.

8. Brothers-in-Arms (5 min., 3 sec.). Assigned to stop homegrown terrorists who are blowing up mail boxes, Fleur-de-Lys faces a conflict when she discovers they are her brothers.

9. Secret Lives (4 min., 10 sec.). The Canadian and Fleur-de-Lys attempt to cope with their growing feelings for each other—both in their civilian and super hero identities.

10. Cold Turkey (5 min., 21 sec.). With most of the team formed, Nordik and 8 Ball must now convince the drug-addicted Back Terror to align with them for the greater good.

11. All That Masquerade (8 min., 24 sec.). The evil Madame Doom assigns her top agent, Masquerade, to steal deadly chemicals from a laboratory.

12. Crimson (4 min., 16 sec.). Nordik, aware of Madame Doom's sinister plan to acquire chemicals for Medusa, attempts to stop Masquerade and her accomplice, Crimson, from acquiring the chemicals.

13. Fashion Statement (6 min., 14 sec.). Nordik fails and the chemicals are delivered to Madame Doom.

14. Enter the Zombots (5 min., 54 sec.). The Canadian steps in and battles agents at Madame Doom's lair where he captures a Zombot (resurrected dead World War II soldier) and delivers it to his commander, Alpha Q.

15. Wardrobe Malfunction (7 min., 12 sec.). Madame Doom hires a fashion designer to create new designs for a spring collection fashion show that will serve as the catalyst for a devious plan to disrupt the upcoming Canada Day celebrations.

16. Operation Rock and Roll (8 min., 49 sec.). The Canadian and 8 Ball uncover hints that something sinister is planned for Canada Day and set out to discover more.

17. Past and Present (10 min., 44 sec.). Dr. Joseph Mengele, now known as the Medusa Commander, seeks to accomplish something now that he couldn't during World War II: conquer the world with his Zombots and achieve what Hitler could not.

18. Brave New World (6 min., 35 sec.). A new radical group, the Nouveaux Felquists appears in Quebec at the same time Fleur-de-Lys mysteriously vanishes.

19. Falling Masks (6 min., 51 sec.). In a strange turn of events, Masquerade reveals that Fleur-de-Lys has been kidnapped by Madame Doom and is being held in a warehouse where the Zombots are being readied for attack.

20. Hornet's Nest (6 min., 56 sec.). As The Canadian and Nordik follow up on the lead given to them by Masquerade to save Fleur-de-Lys, a new (and beautiful) threat arises—Hornet. The program ends in an unresolved cliffhanger.

180 Heroic Daze. heroicdaze.com. 2012 (Fantasy).

Nottywood is a city in turmoil. It is corrupt, its citizens live in fear, the law doesn't seem to help and the average citizen has no one to look up to for salvation. All changes when two rather lame-brained step-brothers, Bryan and Matthew decide to do something about it. Having dreamed of becoming superheroes, Bryan dons the guise of The Redd Robbyn and Matthew becomes his sidekick, Mr. Nyce Guy. The villains believe they have nothing to fear but Bryan and Matthew think differently and wage a war against the city's nefarious bad guys—Big Boss and Me-No—as the JustUs League. Episodes chart their rather inept efforts to bring an end to crime in Nottywood.

The Redd Robbyn and Mr. Nice Guy are adopted step brothers (their rich parents, Donny and Marie, adopted one child from every state). Although they have 48 other siblings, they became close due to their interest in comic books. They also asserted themselves as the law enforcers of the family thus alienating them from their other brothers and sisters. Having only each other for companionship, they soon began to fantasize about becoming superheroes.

The Redd Robbyn has styled himself after heroes such as Batman, Superman and Spider-Man while Mr. Nyce Guy has chosen heroes who looked like him (like Green Lantern, Black Panther and Shadow Hawk).

Cast: Bryan Lugo (The Redd Robbyn), Matthew McKinley (Mr. Nyce Guy), Harold Stancle (Me-No Black), Neil Brown, Jr. (Oliver), Joshua D. Lewis (Repo), Derrick White (Big Boss), Marlon Bivens (Bishop). **Credits:** *Producer:* Bryan Lugo, Anthony Soriano, Matthew McKinley. *Director:* Bryan Lugo. *Writer:* Harold Stancle, Matthew McKinley. **Comment:** An African-American themed program that needlessly incorporates foul language and violence. The acting and production values are somewhat amateurish and the costumes rather pale in comparison to other such superhero series. The program tries to be street smart but fails when reality clashes with hero mythology. Adding a sexy female superhero or villain would have helped to keep viewer attention.

Episodes:
1. Rise of Me-No Black (7 min., 8 sec.). Establishes the story as the JustUs League is born.
2. Rise of Me-No Black, Part 2 (7 min., 47 sec.). The team tries to stop Me-No Black from taking over Nottywood.
3. You Repo What You Sow (10 min., 58 sec.). JustUs battles Repo, an international hit man.
4. You Repo What You Sow (The Glow) (10 min., 58 sec.). The concluding episode wherein the brother's brother (Oliver) becomes addicted to Bryan and Matthew's cause.

181 *Heroics 101: The Series.* webseries channel.com. 2012 (Fantasy).

Oren the Mighty and Tal the Intelligent are best friends who are also saviors in a medieval time. Like television heroes Hercules and Xena, who each fought to save people threatened by evil, Oren and Tal have embarked on a similar journey, coming to the aid of people in need of help and risking their lives to save those who cannot fend for themselves. Although this was not Oren's original intent. He claims that he is "a professional hero" and will only save Queens, Kings and royalty. Anna, his friend convinced him otherwise—that "the little guy" needs help too and changed his philosophy to follow her advice.

Cast: Will Bangs (Oren the Mighty), Sean Chen (Tal the Intelligent), Taylor Marxhausen (Anna). **Credits:** *Producer:* Derek Wayne Aiello, Dane Fogdall. *Director:* Derek Wayne Aiello, Jason Aiello. *Writer:* Derek Wayne Aiello. **Comment:** Kids play all the roles and the production suffers for it. While the story idea is good, the acting is bad. The costumes and dialogue are lame and the locations appear to be some wooded area that is near the producer's home. There is no attempt to be serious (and it shows) as everything is played for laughs.

Episodes:
1. To Rescue a Princess (6 min., 7 sec.). Oren and Tal attempt to rescue a Princess that is being held captive by a tree.
2. A Hero's Calling (11 min., 6 sec.). Danger lurks around every bend as Oren and Tal attempt to rescue their friend, Anna, from a Warlord (Koronus) who has kidnapped her.
3. Magic (7 min., 16 sec.). Oren and Tal encounter more than they bargained for when they battle an evil genie, a dishonest merchant and a seemingly cursed wishing stone.
4. Legendary Beginnings (5 min., 13 sec.). Explores how Oren and Tal became heroes.
5. The Lord of Scoundrels (10 min., 48 sec.). Oren and Tal take to the road to capture a thief that has relieved Tal of his possessions.
6. Anna's Journey, Part 1 (9 min., 28 sec.). Having witnessed Oren and Tal's heroics, Anna becomes infused to join them.
7. Anna's Journey, Part 2 (9 min., 58 sec.). When Oren and Tal find themselves in a perilous situation, it becomes Anna's turn to show them that she can be a hero too.

182 *Hollywood Wasteland.* hollywood wasteland.net. 2010 (Science Fiction).

An apocalypse has occurred and much of the world has been turned into a vast wasteland with zombie hordes roaming the planet looking for humans to feed on. Burbank, home to Jeff Collins, has been destroyed by nuclear explosions, but he is so involved helping his friends that he has not had the time to notice what has been happening around him. Unknown to him at first is that he has been proclaimed "The Savior of Humanity" by the people of a futuristic earth. However, to ensure that Jeff does save the world from what will happen in the future (by an evil organization called Illuminati International) Synthia, a gorgeous female android has been sent back in time by two ragged-looking future scientists to protect him as he carries out his pre-ordained destiny (stop Illuminati International). Stories follow Jeff as it slowly sinks in that something has happened in the world around him and, once meeting Synthia, fulfill his mission. Jeff's close circle of friends are Veronica Diaz, a self-centered production assistant for Reali-TV; Chlora Clever, a Midwestern girl hoping to become an actress; Chad Patel, a not-so-successful entrepreneur; and Walter, a basement-dweller who has been preparing for what has happened for years.

Cast: Caley Bisson (Jeff Collins), Kaitlin Clark (Synthia), Paula Rhodes (Chlora Clever), Diana Gouveia (Veronica Diaz), Paul K. Daniel (Chad Patel), Scott Berman (Walter). **Credits:** *Producer:* Paul K. Daniel, Beth Dunham, Kaitlin Clark, Diana Gouveia. *Director:* Matt Newcomb. *Writer:* Matt Newcomb, Caley Bisson, Ellwyn Kauffman. **Com-**

ment: Comical science fiction parody that is well done and leaves the viewer asking for more. Unfortunately only four episodes have been released and they conclude unresolved. While television has presented female robots in the past (*My Living Doll, Mann and Machine* and *Small Wonder*) and most recently with *Terminator: The Sarah Connor Chronicles, Hollywood Wasteland* most spoofs the *Terminator* series as there too a gorgeous female robot (played by Summer Glau) was sent back in time to protect a future savior of mankind.

Episodes:

1. Episode 1 (5 min., 35 sec.). Synthia is sent to the present to find Jeff and protect him as the Savior of Mankind. Her arrival in Jeff's backyard stirs suspicions—as she is nude (although her assets are obstructed by a fence) and has not quite adjusted to her surroundings.

2. Episode 2 (5 min., 37 sec.). After much thought Jeff accepts Synthia for what she but is hesitant to believe her story. He has just realized the world around him no longer exists and wonders where he can get another job.

3. Canticle for Collins (7 min., 2 sec.). As Synthia tries to convince Jeff of the gravity of the situation, Illuminati International has become aware of Synthia's presence and dispenses agents to silence her and Jeff.

4. Attack of the Jones (7 min., 47 sec.). Film actor Roy Jones, believed to have been killed in the explosions, resurfaces as an Illuminati agent with one directive—kill Jeff.

183 Horror Bizarre. webserieschannel. com. 2013 (Horror).

Anthology series of horror tales, produced in Norway that follow the premise of such established series as *The Twilight Zone, The Outer Limits* and *One Step Beyond*. All actors listed with the episodes are known Norwegian performers. **Cast:** Varies for each episode; see listing below. **Credits:** *Producer-Writer-Director:* Raymond Dullam. **Comment:** All episodes are in Norwegian with English subtitles which distracts from the overall effect as one's attention is drawn away from the visual aspects of the story. All of the stories appear to be based on something that was already done (although this could just be a coincidence as it is not an American-made series) and produced on a rather tight budget (just the story and nothing more).

Episodes:

1. The Insane Mr. Emrich (7 min., 40 sec.). A writer finds he has the ability to make what he writes come true. Starring Jon Gjerde, Caroline Andersen and Ronny Bank. A similar story was presented on the "A World of His Own" episode of *The Twilight Zone* wherein a writer (Keenan Wynn) possessed a Dictaphone that granted the desires he described.

2. Lieberman (8 min., 30 sec.). A girl seeks revenge after she is raped. Although done many times in feature films and on television, it appears to be based more on the revenge feature film *I Spit on Your Grave*. Starring: Geir Borresen, Anette Lobach and Caroline Andersen.

3. Infomercial (4 min., 17 sec.). Intriguing tale of the dangers some professionals face, like craftsmen, when they accept "goodies" (for example, cakes) from their customers. Starring Henning Lee Yang and Tor Itai Keilen.

4. Ripperologist (4 min., 13 sec.). A new spin on the infamous Jack the Ripper. Here an expert on the killer, being interviewed by a journalist, plans to hold a séance to conjure up his spirit and uncover his true identity. Starring Geir Borresen and Lars Mjoen.

5. William Wilson (9 min., 40 sec.). Edgar Alan Poe–like story about a man who believes he is haunted by his doppelganger (a person's evil side). Starring Stein Winge and Sossen Krohg.

184 Horror Haiku. seraphfilms.net. 2013 (Horror).

Horror vignettes, based on Haiku poems, that are submitted by fans of the website. The "Horror Hosts" introduce each episode with actors portraying the various characters in the stories. Haiku is a short poem, of Japanese origin that has a meter of 5 syllables, 7 syllables and 5 syllables. **Horror Hosts Cast:** John C. Epperson (Priest), Anne Leighton (Sexy Girl). **Credits:** *Producer:* Cindy Cullom, Nick Somers, Esther Biggs, Gene Blalock, Tanya Gorlow, James Tumminia, Phil Goldberg, James Boring. *Director:* Gene Blalock. *Writer:* Gene Blalock, James Borning, Gary McCoy. **Comment:** Very dark productions (hard to tell what is happening at times) but good, eerie stories. All the stories show potential for longer versions should the producers decide to take that path and expand them.

Episodes:

1. Jack Face Was Here (2 min.). A young woman, hosting a party, receives a package that, when opened, reveals a human arm. Suddenly the killer, Jack Face, invades her home. *Cast:* David Delagarza (Jack Face), Brittany Littleton (Woman), Chelsey Hemstreet, Erin Cecilia Pfeifer, Karla Usagi (Partygoers).

2. The Haunted Video Tape (2 min., 20 sec.). A young woman receives a video tape in the mail and proceeds to play it. A mysterious beam emerges from her television set and draws her into the set—where she becomes trapped. *Cast:* Tanya Gorlow (Girl).

3. Blood Red Bath (1 min., 48 sec.). A man dreams that he is dead. But is he? Up to the viewer to decide. *Cast:* Dax Spanogle (Man in tub).

4. Honey, I'm Home (1 min., 49 sec.). A husband, returning home from work, finds his wife being eaten by a zombie. Is he next? *Cast:* DeMarco Hernandez (Husband), Cindy Cullom (Wife), James Boring (Zombie).

5. The Art of Murder (2 min., 21 sec.). A young

artist finds a new way to create works of art—with human blood. *Cast:* Tonya Kay (Artist), Devin Goodsell (Victim).

6. 'Til Death Do Us Part (2 min., 2 sec.). Strange tale of a ghost that drains the life force from the men she marries. *Cast:* Angela Meyer (Ghost Wife), Nick Somers (Husband).

7. Mommy's Wrong (1 min., 58 sec.). A young girl tells her mother that there is a monster under her bed. Her mothers disbelieves her—until she becomes its victim. *Cast:* Felix Rossell Hemstreet (Little Girl), Tanya Gorlow (Monster under bed).

8. Night Swimming (2 min., 34 sec.). A man decides to go for a swim in his backyard pool—unaware that a fierce creature lurks in the water. *Cast:* Tanya Gorlow (Monster in Pool), Louis Dezseran (Man in pool).

9. Drag Me Screaming (2 min., 49 sec.). A young woman, walking through the woods when her car stalls, encounters a group of zombie children—who attack her and drag her off. *Cast:* Kamila Davies, Makayl Walsh (Zombie children), Ciddy Fonteboa (Woman).

10. Moonlit Walk (2 min., 4 sec.). A walk in the moonlight with her boyfriend is anything but pleasing to the girl when he transforms into a hideous beast. *Cast:* Terri J. Freedman (Girl), Edward Gusts (Boyfriend/Monster).

11. Still at Large (3 min., 1 sec.). The Jack Face killer (from episode 1) returns to terrorize a young woman in her home. *Cast:* David Delagarza (Jack Face), Sarah Karjian (Woman).

12. Foul Fetid Reeking Bones (2 min., 31 sec.). Comical overtones as a little girl unknowingly stalked by a zombie, always manages to escape his grasp. *Cast:* Stu Hammill (Zombie), Chalee Ray (Little Girl), Jessica West (Mother).

13. I Am Not Alone. (2 min., 6 sec.). A man believing he is alone in his home finds he is not when a little girl appears, then reveals her true self as a demon. *Cast:* Alexis G. Zall (Little Girl), Aaron R. Smith (Man).

14. Rituals (2 min., 5 sec.). A young woman's sacrifice at a mysterious cult that worships fire. *Cast:* Tanya Gorlow (High Priestess), Lynn Trickey (Sacrificial Virgin), James Boring, Jessica West, Jola Cora (Pagans).

15. Face of Beauty (2 min., 38 sec.). A prostitute is anything but when she acquires a customer who quickly discovers she is a vampire. *Cast:* Raquel Houghton (Vampire), Abel Horwitz (Lover).

16. Duck Face (2 min., 3 sec.). A beautiful girl constantly admiring herself in the mirror suddenly finds that beauty gone when her lips grow to an enlarged size. *Cast:* Rachel Amanda Bryant (Girl).

17. Message in the Blood (1 min., 54 sec.). Creepy tale of a young girl with the ability to control her family with her blood. *Cast:* Tara Emerson (Mother), Preston Sarnowski (Girl), Steve Spiro (Father), Peyton Ray (Sister).

18. Up All Night (2 min., 31 sec.). A man's insomnia, caused by dreaming of clowns, may not be a dream after all. *Cast:* Ciddy Fonteboa, Tanya Gorlow, Nick Somers (Clowns), Nicholas Jaqua (Victim).

19. The Art of Murder II. A second story about the unique ways a beautiful artist creates her paintings. *Cast:* Tonya Kay (Artist), Kyle Cristian Hatch (Victim).

20. Burn My Eyes (2 min., 57 sec.). Alone and stranded in her car, a woman is drawn to a light she sees coming from the woods. Following the lights she sees an alien—and is swept away. *Cast:* Marissa Licamara (Woman).

21. Curtain Number 3 (3 min., 22 sec.). A woman, a contestant on the game show *Matchmaker* questions three men (hidden behind curtains) then must choose one. Her selection—a crazed killer. *Cast:* Walter Cox (Game Show Host), Paula Schmitt (Suzy Simmons), Jason Rosenwach (Sam Gamble).

22. The Phoenix (2 min.). Single scene of a vampire rising from a pool of blood. *Cast:* Laura Hunter, Geoffrey Allen Harris (Vampires).

23. The Art of Murder III (2 min., 46 sec.). A third way to kill and create art is explored. *Cast:* Tonya Kay, Kylie Cristian Hatch.

24. I Know What You Know (3 min., 9 sec.). A young woman fears that what she sees but no one else does, may be something sinister and after her. *Cast:* C. Thomas Howell, Melissa Hanson.

25. It's Only a Game (3 min., 23 sec.). A séance, being played for fun, is nothing until one of the participants is possessed by a spirit. *Cast:* Mindy Robinson, Beth Delia, Alan Michael Ross.

26. That God Awful Smile (5 min., 15 sec.). A man, being drive insane by his wife, kills her—but is haunted by the smile she left on her face. *Cast:* Nicki Steele, Valentino DelToro.

27. I Know Your Name (2 min., 42 sec.). A voice in the night awakens a woman—who investigates and is abducted by an alien. *Cast:* Julia Reis, Daniel James Malone.

28. Night of the Samhain (2 min., 9 sec.). A young girl, being pursued by witches, finds that she too is a witch. *Cast:* Luna Dwyer, Michelle Morgan.

29. Always Check the Backseat (1 min., 47 sec.). It's not so much checking the backseat of one's car—but what is outside as a young woman learns. *Cast:* Rose Keigh, Dan Bentley.

30. Kuchisalla-Onna (2 min., 51 sec.). At a masquerade party, a man discreetly kills his wife. At the party he becomes attracted to a woman dressed in red—a woman who proceeds to kill him. *Cast:* Grace Feeney, Anderson Edwards.

31. The Night Shift (2 min., 25 sec.). A lone night shift worker finds that what the surveillance cameras sees is not there when he investigates. *Cast:* Cliff Mefford.

32. I Believe in Mary Worth (3 min., 11 sec.). A girl finds that the legend of Bloody Mary (by saying

her name three times in front of a mirror to evoke her spirit) is anything but legend when she appears and kills her. *Cast:* Anita Kate, Risa Ramsey.

33. Life Is Like an Onion (3 min.). A wife believes she killed the intruder who attacked her while preparing dinner—or did she? *Cast:* Kit Sheean, Tyson Prince.

34. Suffer the Little Children—Or Slender Man Fairy (3 min., 38 sec.). Are a young girl's visions of a tall, slender Fairy true or imaginary? Imaginary to her parents—but true to her when she is whisked away. *Cast:* Tyson Prince, Emmett Dwyer, Ana DeBaso.

35. The Art of Murder IV (3 min., 6 sec.). A woman finds a unique way of killing—stringing her victims up as a marionette. *Cast:* Tonya Kay, Apollo Staar.

36. Simple Words (3 min., 29 sec.). The scene appears to be that of a mother giving birth—but what comes out is anything but human. *Cast:* Audrey Hill Thompson, Sarah Schacher.

37. The Evil Inside (2 min., 8 sec.). Are Doppelganger's real? A man, alone in his home, discovers they are. *Cast:* Glen Upton.

38. D.J. Face Collector (4 min., 1 sec.). A young woman discovers that an innocent-looking music box is anything but when she opens it—and it steals her face. *Cast:* Lila Shreeve, Jimmy Walker Pearson, Calvin Kelly.

39. The Attic (2 min., 11 sec.). A man, seeing mysterious lights from the attic of an abandoned house, investigates—only to encounter an evil alien. *Cast:* Alex Wayne Trugman.

40. Together Alone (3 min., 37 sec.). A couple, seemingly happy and in love find more happiness when they are apart. *Cast:* Allison Shaffi, Christopher Shaffi.

41. Death by a Thousand Pups (5 min.). A woman, walking her dog at night, is abducted by a woman who plans to use her as food her countless puppies. *Cast:* Jessica Matthews.

42. The Shower (2 min., 22 sec.). A young woman is menaced by a creature that emerges from her shower. *Cast:* Sam LaRocco, Eviland Ross.

43. 10.31 (5 min., 18 sec.). On Halloween a man appears to be menaced by a home full of eerie Jack-O-Lanterns—but it his wife whom he should fear as she is an evil witch.

185 *Horror Hotel.* horrorhotelwebseries. com. 2013 (Horror).

Anthology program of weird tales that mix the elements of horror, fantasy, mystery (twisted plots) and suspense that occur at an establishment called Horror Hotel.

Cast: Varies for each episode; see listing below. **Credits:** *Producer:* Debbie Hess, Errol Sadler. *Director:* Brandon Thaxton. *Writer:* Al Hess. **Comment:** Nicely woven tales similar to those presented

on *The Twilight Zone* and *Alfred Hitchcock Presents.* Each is well acted and produced and worthy of a network or cable broadcast.

Episodes:

1. Tilt (16 min., 33 sec.). A computer hacker turns the tables on an android and her master when they attempt to kidnap him and sell him to the highest undesirable bidder. *Cast:* Marie Barker, Johnny Harvill, Nathan DeRussy, Tanner Gould.

2. Invader (11 min., 59 sec.). Suspicion falls on a science fiction writer when hotel residents suspect him of concealing evidence of an alien. *Cast:* Susan Moss, Troy Henderson, James Edward Thomas, Jerry Irwin, Darian Johnson.

3. Guillotine (16 min., 17 sec.). A beauty pageant contestant, acquiring a charm cut from the guillotine that ended the life of Marie Antoinette, finds more than she bargained for when it provides beauty—but with a price to pay. *Cast:* Stephanie Stevens, Ann Marie Gideon, James Edward Thomas.

4. Bookworm (10 min., 48 sec.). A psychotic woman's deranged plan to acquire the unpublished work of her favorite author. *Cast:* Ellie Trapkin, Hugh Higgins.

5. Houdini's Hand (18 min., 41 sec.). The consequences that befall two small time thieves when they steal the mummified hand of Houdini, the world's greatest magician. *Cast:* Tony Folden, Montrel Miller, James Edward Thomas, Mike Bend.

6. Telsa's Tooth (18 min., 41 sec.). Horror Hotel houses people of all kinds; here a geek seeks to get even with a gangster who delights in bullying him. *Cast:* Ted Parker, Neil Ransay, Tony Folden, Darian Johnson, Matt Rogers.

186 *Horror Porn Parodies from Hell.* fear net.com. 2012 (Horror).

There are sex parodies of television shows that have been released on video (for example, *Married with Hormones* [*Married with Children*], *The Horneymooners* [*The Honeymooners*], *The Maddams Family* [*The Addams Family*] and *Funky Brewster* [*Punky Brewster*]). There are also numerous movie parodies and *Horror Porn* presents a selection of the "the most faithful, terrible and funniest horror porn parodies out there." While the actual parodies contain sex and nudity, the trailers chosen for the program are and overall look at the project without the sex and nudity.

Cast: Varies for each episode; see listing below. **Comment:** Although only the trailers (or previews) are presented it is interesting to see a small sampling of the parodies that have been done in the horror vein (there are also numerous parodies of other television series and movies in the comedy and drama genres).

Episodes:

1. The Human Sexipede. Take on the cult film about a deranged doctor that stitches people together,

making a human chain for sex (while the actual film was gory, the parody is the sex minus the gore). Cast information not given.

2. Scream XXX. *Scream 4* parody about a masked killer who can't quite get the stalking and killing right. Features Ron Jeremy, an iconic porn star of the 1980s. Starring Lily LaBeau, Zoe Voss, Sarah Shevon, Scarlett Fay, Angelica Lane.

3. Friday the 13th. The camp (Crystal Lake) featured in the original *Friday the 13th* in 1980 has become Crystal Lake Nudist Camp with the teens being stalked by a killer. Starring Sara Sloane, Kagney Lynn Karter, Asa Akira, Brooke Lee Adams.

4. Silence of the Lambs. A serial killer, Hannibal the Cannibal, has human meals as the FBI begins a search to stop his reign of terror. Stars Ben English, Kagney Lynn Karter, Isis Taylor, Mark Wood.

5. The Blair Witch Project A Triple X Thriller. A group of adult film stars are lost in the Maryland woods—with sex reprieving them from the dangers of the unknown that lurks around them. Cast information not given.

6. Day of the Living MILIF. Parody of *Night of the Living Dead* wherein a group of deceased MILIF's (middle-aged housewives) are resurrected as zombies and seek prey for sex. Cast information not given. The program is also a parody of the adult film series of MILIF films.

7. Saw: A Hardcore Parody. Gorgeous adult film star Ginger Lynn appears in a rather difficult to transfer parody (from hardcore horror to sex) about a killer who replaces torture with sex. Starring Lexi Belle, David Lord, Evan Stone, Asa Akira and former adult film star Ron Jeremy.

8. Tru: An XXX Parody. A television spoof of HBO's *True Blood* which delves further into the world of New Orleans vampires through more explicit sexual encounters. Cast information not given.

9. Rocki Whore Picture Show. Reworked lyrics but a faithful visual reproduction of *The Rocky Picture Horror Show* about a transsexual scientist from Transylvania. Cast information not given.

10. The Twilight Zone Porn Parody. Another television series parody about a strange couple who sexually ravish a small town neighborhood. Cast information not given.

187 *The Human Strain.* youtube.com. 2009 (Science Fiction).

An unknown virus has spread across the globe transforming non-resistant humans into vicious zombies. With the zombie population seemingly outnumbering unaffected humans, the struggle for survival has become even more difficult with the decreasing food supply and safe havens quickly disappearing. The program follows a group of humans as they battle for survival in a world that appears to soon become infested with zombies.

Cast: Rhiannon McClintock (Heidi), Megan Mc-Manus (Jerri), Julian Peck (Kade), Andrea Clouser (Christina), Josh Peters (Thomas), Bob Strouse (Colt), Donovan Schwartz (Brian), Jason Hastings (Mikey). **Credits:** *Producer-Writer-Director:* Chris Schwartz. **Comment:** As can be seen by the views listed this was not a popular series. The views also indicate that while the first episode drew a larger number than all the other episodes, it did not hold much attention for most to see what happens next. Those that stuck with the program apparently just chose random episodes to watch with the concluding episode receiving fewer views than the episode that preceded it. The program is not as bad as the views indicate. The production is somewhat amateurish although the actors turn in a relatively good performance. There are plenty of zombies (and vicious too) and the project is described as "The first ever, no-budget, graphic novel style zombie series with a single goal: to get enough views to prove that it is time for a REAL zombie TV series." While it didn't receive considerable views, the goal could have been achieved as a "real" zombie series did premiere on cable—*The Walking Dead*, and it could have been influenced by *The Human Strain*.

Episodes:

1. Jerri and Kade's Contact (10 min.). It has been three days since the transformations have begun and a small group of humans are on the run, seeking to find a place of safety. 542 views.

2. Mikey's Contact (6 min., 10 sec.). Mikey and Jack attempt to guard a safety area, Alpha 6 despite the approaching zombies (called Revenants—humans that have disappeared and come back as something else). 184 views.

3. Heidi's Comet (6 min., 15 sec.). Heidi, an analytical biologist, is introduced. She has been studying the creatures but has been trapped in her lab since the outbreak. 221 views.

4. Thomas' Contact (9 min., 42 sec.). Reveals that Thomas, one of the survivors, was serving a five year prison sentence deep within the mountains when the plague struck—possibly what saved him. 258 views.

5. Road Trip (8 min., 5 sec.). Heidi, having escaped from the lab, and Thomas cross paths and form an unlikely partnership for survival. 127 views.

6. Seeking Shelter (3 min., 23 sec.). Kade and Jerri attempt to traverse a dense forest before sundown—at which time the zombies become most active. 90 views.

7. Welcome Home (2 min., 28 sec.). Mikey finds his way into a seemingly safe neighborhood where he seeks a phone to contact his fellow soldiers at base camp. 82 views.

8. Frolic in the Woods (5 min., 14 sec.). Continues to follow Kade and Jerri's trek through the forest with sundown nearing and their exit seemingly unlikely. 73 views.

9. All in the Family. (5 min., 17 sec.). Thomas attempts to reunite with his family while Kade and

Jerri have to resort to zombie killing to survive. 75 views.

10. Anybody in Here? (4 min., 33 sec.). Mikey, believing he is safe by barricading himself in an abandoned house, finds that barricades are not all they are cracked up to be. 97 views.

11. The Last Farm on the Left (Time unknown; episode taken off line). Jade and Jerri, reaching a farm find that their safety is threatened by a horde of zombies armed with deadly tools. 77 views before deleted.

12. Exodus (2 min., 49 sec.). Unable to find a working phone, Mikey decides to venture onto another town, hoping to find one that has electricity. 61 views.

13. To Grandmother's House We Go (5 min., 34 sec.). Feeling that they need to take a rest, Kade and Jerri set up camp in the middle of nowhere—an apparent safe haven for the time being. 77 views.

14. The High Price of Oil (2 min., 1 sec.). Heidi, running low on gas, seeks to fill up—but finding a gas station on the outskirts of town and away from zombies proves to be a difficult task. 71 views.

15. Empty Thoughts (4 min., 5 sec.). Despite the fact that he is in a zombie-infested location, Thomas plots out his next move—and prepares a selection of clothes—just in case he needs to rush off on a moment's notice. 69 views.

16. Zombie Camp (9 min., 2 sec). Tired and needing to rest, Heidi elects to stop off at an old family vacation stop—only to find that it is overrun with zombies. 76 views.

17. In the Still of the Night (2 min., 49 sec.). As night falls, Kade and Jerri appear to be at ease—despite the fact that they are in a zombie infested area. 81 views.

18. No Town Is Safe (6 min., 7 sec.). Mikey and Brian stumble upon a seemingly deserted town that may be more sinister than it appears as it has electricity but apparently no zombies. 71 views.

19. Under a Full Moon (2 min., 27 sec.). Heidi's efforts to find some cover as night falls fail as she encounters a group of zombies. 53 views.

20. Back to the Beginning (3 min., 24 sec.). While Jerri feels safe in the home they have found, Kade tries to convince her to seek out the nearest non-affected town to replenish their dwindling supplies. 49 views.

21. Breakfast in Bed (1 min., 22 sec.). A close call for Thomas as he awakens to see a zombie standing just a few feet from him. 54 views.

22. Fire Down Below (3 min., 48 sec.). As Jerri and Kade head toward a town they believe to be inhabited, they encounter a deadly gas that destroys everything in its path. 52 views.

23. The Scenic Route (2 min., 17 sec.). With a civilized town in sight Mike and Brian must plan their next move—cross an area crawling with zombies. 70 views.

24. Beyond the Safe Zone (3 min., 32 sec.). Jerri and Kade enter a town where a toxic nerve gas residue has destroyed all signs of life (even zombies). 69 views.

25. Junkyard Dogs (7 min., 24 sec.). Brian and Mikey, being tracked by zombies, attempt to make it across a desolate landscape to safety. 114 views.

26. New Blood (4 min., 46 sec.). The concluding episode wherein Kade and Jerri are able to replenish their supplies despite being stalked by zombies, but their ability to destroy the zombies is less certain as the zombies far out number their rounds of ammunition. Ends in a cliffhanger. 107 views.

188 Hurtling Through Space at an Alarming Rate. htsaaar.com. 2009 (Science Fiction).

Mike and Stuart are roommates of the future whose apartment can travel through time and space. The roommates cannot leave their apartment but other people are able to enter and exit without a problem. Mike and Stuart are actually on a mission—but for whom and what is unknown (as they are in a daze as to what they are doing). The program charts their various mishaps as their apartment lands on various planets and they are left to deal with the alien inhabitants who often find them anything but amusing.

Cast: Michael Davies (Mike), Stuart Paap (Stuart), Stephanie Thorpe (Elizabeth), Taryn O'Neill (Michelle), Jacob D. Smith (Gary), Barry Alan Levine (Kalm, Master of the Universe). **Credits:** *Producer:* Amber J. Lawson, Taryn O'Neill, Stephanie Thorpe. **Comment:** The comedy accented program is as absurd as the episode titles read. With elements of the television series *Doctor Who* and the web series *Vincent Kosmos* (see entry), *Hurtling...* tries to be different by using a traveling apartment, ignoring every law of physics (not to mention science in general) and present something different (and when the apartment chooses to touch down, it does so with an impact so intense that only the land on which it sets down suffers damage). The producers have succeeded on that point and the program itself is good for a few laughs.

Episodes:

1. The Planet of Tons of Dirty Laundry. On their first landing Mike and Stuart face off against a nasty laundry monster on a planet called Tons of Dirty Laundry.

2. The Planet of Extremely Sticky Floors That Make It Impossible to Do Anything. After escaping from the Laundry Monster, Mike and Stuart's apartment takes them to a planet were everything is sticky but they have a solution—their favorite beverage (beer) dissolves stickiness and allows them to function.

3. The Planet of Eventually Exploding Time Bombs and Calamitous Proportions. With the sticky planet behind them, the traveling apartment manages

to find a troublesome planet where Mike and Stuart must contend with constant explosions.

4. The Planet of Fairly Attractive Women with Terrible Fashion Sense. With themselves and their apartment intact, the roommates find themselves landing on a planet where women are beautiful—but their sense of fashion leaves a lot to be desired.

5. The Pizza Man Cometh/The Episode of Mostly Exposition. Mike and Stuart find ordering a pizza is simple then realize that their mission has to do with something that hasn't happened yet but soon will.

6. The Wrath of Kalm. The concluding, unresolved finale wherein Mike and Stuart face their nemesis Kalm with the fate of their friends, Elizabeth and Michelle hanging in the balance.

189 I Am Tim. iamtimhelsing.com. 2010–2012 (Horror).

Timothy Ronald Helsing, called Tim, believed he was just an ordinary guy leading an ordinary life with two ordinary friends, Anna (a charity shop manager) and Poncho (occupation: sidekick). He soon learns, however, that he is anything but ordinary: he is the last in the bloodline of the Van Helsings, a family of vampire hunters. Now, with an inherited mission (from Abraham Van Helsing), Tim, assisted by Anna and Poncho, battle the forces of evil that lurk in the darkness (often at times trying to reform them rather than destroying them). Stories are introduced by Richard Timmons, the creator, in a comical version of Rod Serling's hosting chores on *The Twilight Zone* (Richard also involves himself in the plots to help move things along).

Cast: Jamie Simcox (Tim Helsing), Jennifer Jordan (Anna Elena Mondragon), Tom Cockram (Poncho de la Cruz), Richard Massara (Hannibal King), Richard Timmons (Himself). **Credits:** *Producer:* Richard Timmons, Peter Crump. *Director-Writer:* Jamie McKeller. **Comment:** Comical British produced series that spoofs the old Van Helsing family of vampire hunters. The characters are likable, the plots unbelievable, the production values above many other web series but it suffers at times from difficult to understand British accents.

Episodes:

1. York, England, Planet Earth (6 min., 28 sec.). Tim tries to teach a mischievous goblin about the rules of human behavior.

2. The Total Cycle Path (7 min., 57 sec.). While Tim battles the demon Empusa, Poncho and Richard become involved in a heated discussion about the disadvantages of touch screen devices.

3. Romance Is Deadified (6 min., 49 sec.). As Tim and Anna search the woods for a Grue demon, they meet Hannibal King, "the coolest vampire ever."

4. It Is Pitch Dark (6 min., 44 sec.). Tim and Anna meet the Grue and learn of his bewilderment and how difficult it is being a forest-dwelling serial killer.

5. The Thing About Poncho (4 min., 44 sec.). Tim and Anna try to help Poncho deal with a recent dragon killing that destroyed all their equipment as well as his inability to clear clogged sink drains.

6. Sparkle Free Vampires (6 min., 53 sec.). Tim, Anna and Poncho begin a vampire hunt—with Tim armed with a new weapon, his demon-disposing WTF gun.

7. Don't Fear the Red Shirt (5 min., 32 sec.). Tim battles his first vampire (which he calls a Red Shirt).

8. Fan Service (7 min., 51 sec.). Tim steps out of character to face his fans and discuss Red Shirt (vampire) issues.

9. Sibling Rivalry (8 min., 30 sec.). Tim introduces his fans to the non-monster-hunting side of his family.

10. The Daily Grind (6 min., 48. sec.). Tim reveals his day job to his fans: agent at Your Fault Accident Claims "deep in the heart of York City" along with observations about dogs, Paris Hilton and his sleeping arrangements.

11. A Staple Diet of Violence (7 min., 25 sec.). As Tim deals with office problems, Hannibal decides to visit and unload his troubles on Tim.

12. The Fork in the Road (7 min., 13 sec.). Bruce Dickson, the series cameraman, tries to film an interview with a disgruntled Hannibal King (the regulars also step out of character to help Bruce).

13. What a Wonderful World (9 min., 45 sec.). Poncho must solve a mysterious riddle to escape "a mildly dissected vampire" that has taken him captive.

14. For the Viewers at Home (7 min., 25 min.). Tim intervenes in an effort to save Poncho.

15. 110% Epic (12 min., 5 sec.). Tim loses control as he risks his life to save Anna from almost certain death from a vampire.

16. Out with the Old (5 min., 35 sec.). The cast (out of character) reflect on Tim as he puts his monster hunting aside to enjoy life as he once did (his top priority: playing Nintendo video games).

17. Nothing Like Doctor Who (8 min.). Tim's new life is short lived as he returns to battle a demon.

18. Not So Fresh Meat (8 min., 54 sec.). Tim battles a stylish mummy that is plaguing a local café.

19. Tim vs. the Sheeple, Part 1 (8 min., 23 sec.). A countryside outing turns disastrous when Richard gets abducted.

20. Tim Vs. the Sheeple, Part 2 (9 min., 38 sec.). As Tim, Anna and Poncho seek Richard, who has been kidnapped by weird local villagers, they encounter mysterious sheep (called Sheeple).

21. Back to the Daily Grind (8 min., 29 sec.). After rescuing Richard, Tim returns to his boring job at Your Fault Accident Claims.

22. Night of the Living Bread (7 min., 15 sec.). A man, obsessed with toasting bread, becomes a menace when his yeast creation becomes a threat to the local village.

23. Return of a King (8 min., 8 sec.). While battling a trio of vampires, Tim takes time out to demonstrate his arts and crafts skills.

190 *I Heart Vampires.* fairiesvampires.com. 2009–2010 (Horror).

Corbin and Luci are best friends who host a web site called "I <3 Vampires" (their stylized version for "I Heart [Love] Vampires"). The girls are also amateur vampire hunters (hoping but so far not encountering one) and have based their site on the book *Confessions of a High School Vampire* by Siona McCabre (who, at first unknown to them, is involved in the world of the supernatural). Corbin, the more outgoing and aggressive one, actually relates the blogs while Luci, more laid back, assists her when necessary. Life changes for the girls when Luci receives an anonymous e-mail containing the first six chapters of Sonia's new book about the world of vampires (in her on-going *Confessions* series). Believing the information is the scoop of the year, Corbin posts the chapters on her website only to encounter problems when Sonia discovers what has happened (someone leaked the chapters) and threatens to stop publication of the book. The program follows Corbin and Luci's encounter with real vampires when they seek to find Sonia and set things right by uncovering the person responsible for leaking the information.

Cast: Cherilyn Wilson (Corbin), Erin Way (Luci), Martha Hackett (Siona McCabre), Adam Chambers (Wyatt), Alli Kinzel (Sam), Josh Nuncio (Nick McCabre). **Credits:** *Producer-Director:* Oren Kaplan, Shaun Peterson. *Writer:* Julie Restivo, Kate Feldman. **Comment:** Only a scattering of the 42 episodes produced remain online (and only on YouTube). While some of the available episodes do depict Corbin and Luci's encounters with vampires there are storyline gaps as not every episode is sequential (and thus episode descriptions are not presented). Judging by what is online, the program is well done with good acting by all cast members. The production values are very good and, despite the episode gaps, the available episodes are enjoyable.

191 *I Kissed a Vampire.* youtube.com. 2012 (Horror Musical).

Music and songs built around Dylan Knight, an ordinary teenager who is bitten by a vampire and must now contend with life as one of the undead. Particular focus is on his relationship with Sara, his next-door neighbor and the girl he loves—but how to control his vampire urges and still be with her. Trey is an evil vampire who becomes Dylan's mentor; Luna is Trey's seductive vampire girlfriend.

Cast: Lucas Grabeel (Dylan Knight), Drew Seeley (Trey Sylvania), Adrian Slade (Sara Lane), Amy Paffrath (Luna Dark), Katie Seeley (Lydia Bloodworth), Sally Slade (Sally Sucker), Autumn Grabeel (Penny Plasma), Emily Morris (Desiree Damned), Mike Slade (Dr. Payne). **Credits:** *Producer:* Laurie Nolan. *Director:* Chris Sean Nolan. *Writer:* Laurie Nolan, Chris Sean Nolan. *Music:* Frankie Blue. *Lyrics:* Frankie Blue, Chris Sean Nolan. **Comment:** Surprisingly well done mix of music, songs and horror (somewhat like *Zombie College Musical,* which see). The songs and music are performed well and the overall production is far above many web series. With added material, the web series has been re-edited and released as a ninety-minute feature film.

Episodes:
1. Act 1 (10 min., 43 sec.). Sets up the story as Dylan begins developing his fangs and how he attempts to control his urges not to bite the girl he loves—Sara.
2. Act 2 (7 min., 56 sec.). Trey, displeased that Dylan will not fully encompass his new life, invites Dylan to a vampire party—with a hypnotized Sara as one of the guests.
3. Act 3 (12 min., 34 sec.). Sara's fate lies in the balance—in her mesmerized state, she is willing to be kissed (and bitten) by Dylan—who refuses to do so, but Trey's influence over her has her eager to succumb to Trey's world.

192 *The Immoral Dr. Dicqer.* blip.tv. 2011 (Fantasy).

Seeking a life other than the one he is now leading, a doctor (Dicqer) steals a pirate ship from a crew of blood-thirsty mercenaries, abducts the bride (Sheena) of a powerful sorcerer (The Baron of Hells Island) and sails into a futuristic 1980s-like netherworld suburb called Lowtown (where he begins his practice as "a back alley gynecologist"). As the doctor tries to settle into his new life, he finds it is not as easy as he imagined as the Baron has sent a bounty hunter to track him down and he must now not only avoid the Baron but keep his medical practice going.

Cast: Alex Baker (Dr. Dicqer), Cindy Merrill (Sheena Dicqer), Gregory Blair (The Baron), Cody Rhyse (Aggie), Matt Andrews (Henry Dicqer), Victoria Masina (Janet), Anita Borcia (Betty), Kaylee Brown (Trudy Darling), Erika Elyse (Alice), Babetta Juergens (Nurse Dregg), Deanne Mencher (Eileen) **Credits:** *Producer:* Jan Anderson, Nakai Nelson. *Director:* Lindsey Schmitz. *Writer:* Brad Lusher, Lindsey Schmitz. **Comment:** One of the most unusual of the fantasy web series. Live actors, appearing in bizarre animal masks, perform against comic book style animation and computer imaged backgrounds. With its 1980s dreamscape presentation and noir undertones it is certainly worth checking out—even, if at times, you may be saying to yourself, what the heck is going on here. In summary—it is strangely addictive.

Episodes:
1. Episode 1. The nightmare begins for the doctor when he steals a ship and abducts a Sorcerer's bride.

2. Episode 2. Assassins of the Baron descend on Lowtown seeking the doctor and his stolen bride Sheena.

3. Episode 3. The Baron finds that Sheena has married the doctor but he is boorish and an uncaring husband.

4. Episode 4. The Baron plans his revenge on the doctor and hopes to lure him into a device that will trap him in Hell.

5. Episode 5. The concluding segment wherein a seductress (Aggie) attempts to lure Dr. Dicqer into the Baron's trap.

193 Immortal U. immortaluwebtv.com. 2011 (Science Fiction).

As the planet Earth faces continual climatic changes, the struggle for survival has become increasingly difficult. It is also a time when a powerful organization, the Global Control Faction, has become the supreme ruler. Immortals, people with advanced abilities, are the ruling class while Latents, individuals with a high potential for immortal abilities, are the lower class of society. The Faction seeks to bring all Latents to their side and incorporates fear as their weapon to control them. There are rebels who oppose the Faction and its goal to enslave the world's population. The conflict between the two is depicted as the series relates the events that occur when the elixir to bring Latents to immortals is stolen and a substitute elixir is developed that changes the course of life on the planet. **Cast:** Paula Wilson (Caymin), Donny Boaz (Adam Wash), Matthew Willis (Grayson), Aisha Melhem (Alexi), Andrew Staton (Dutch), Jonathon Itchon (Zachary Bloom), Ian Floodgate (Veros), Corey Wallis (Mark Soley), Clint Hansen (Jacob Weiskoff). **Credits:** *Producer-Writer:* Rhonda Abrons. *Director:* Scott Cummings. **Comment:** Quality science fiction adventure with good acting and production values. A lot happens (several series could have been made) and although everything seems to be happening at once, it is all explained as the stories unfold.

Episodes:

1. Guinea Pigs. Genocide plans by the Global Control Faction are sidetracked when Immortals steal the elixir that grants them paranormal abilities.

2. Kid Stuff. As Faction scientists attempt to develop a substitute elixir, the Earth is subjected to a sudden axis tilt that, at first appears not to pose a danger.

3. Empath Rising. Having developed what they feel is an acceptable substitute elixir, its distribution causes unseen side effects when people exhibit signs of madness. The axis tilt begins causing earthquakes.

4. Fear No Good. The Faction seeks a way to control what has occurred while madness begins to empower emotionally imbalanced citizens.

5. Alien Nations. The axis tilt makes it possible

for aliens, called the Visitors, to land on Earth. As high winds now engulf the series setting, Texas, a music video is misinterpreted by the Visitors who see it as a declaration of war.

6. Emotional Boomerang. As weather conditions become more severe, the Faction cuts back on the fear factor and urge Latents to eliminate fear from their lives in order to survive the approaching disaster.

7. Dark Shadows. An apparent understanding with the aliens brings some solace amid Tsunamis, the sinking of the Canary Islands, and an increasingly alarming rate of suicides. The situation worsens, however, when a huge asteroid blocks the sun and the Earth is propelled into total darkness. Is it the end? The Immortals now know the meaning of fear.

194 In Fear Of. youtube.com. 2012 (Horror).

An exploration of the fears that haunt certain people. **Cast:** Varies for each episode; see listing below. **Credits:** *Producer:* Scott W. Perry. *Director:* Scott W. Perry, Jennifer Kipp, Mike Polizzi. **Comment:** Surprisingly intriguing program not so much for the unusual phobias it tackles but for its style of presentation (which varies by episode). Eliminating unnecessary dialogue, the program relies on visuals to evoke the feelings that a person experiences having a phobia.

Episodes:

1. Monophobia. The fear of being alone is explored through a woman (Debbie Rochon) who fears loneliness and overly attaches herself to people making her appear as unstable.

2. Podophobia. A young couple (Xiomara Cintron, Alejandro Santoni) face a crisis when the wife recalls a tragic childhood event that culminates in her fear of feet.

3. Selenophobia. Tells of a young woman (Louisa Ward) who fears a full moon.

4. Thanatophobia. After a night of partying, a young woman (Suzi Lorraine) with a fear of death wakes up in a cemetery to find herself reflecting on her life choices.

5. Apehephobia. Kelly Rae LeGault as young woman, suffering from a fear of being touched, who has recurring nightmares about being followed and touched by a series of faceless hands.

6. Achluophobia. A woman (Raine Brown) suffering from a fear of the dark, begins to experience her fear when, during a blackout she lights a series of candles and one by one they begin to flicker out.

195 Issues: The Series. issuestheseries.com. 2008 (Fantasy).

Comic Relief is a comic book store where a select group of friends, all with an interest in action-adventure and super hero comic books gather to not only savor the world of comic books but live out their wildest fantasies. But into this fantasy land comes the menace—Jared, a shock jock who is determined to break their sanity (uncover their secrets—do they really have powers and are they really super heroes?). The program details this aspect as Jared taunts the staff to find out.

Jackson DeWitt, an architect, enjoys vintage comic books and rare prints. His heroes are Gene Roddenberry, George Lucas and Leonardo DaVinci and *The Third Man, Taxi Driver* and *Goodfellas* are among his favorite movies. His musical tastes include the classics (from Bach to Beethoven) and is best known for his knowledge of unusual trivia and impeccable taste in comic books. He is also a big comic book spender and deplores such things as empty lots, shock jocks, spies and bad writing.

Madeline, known as "that cheery Goth Girl," is a college freshman, who enjoys bewildering customers with her deep thoughts. Her dress makes her appear as though she celebrates Halloween every day of the year and loves the poetry of Edgar Allan Poe (and Emily Dickinson). *The Wizard of Oz* and *Reservoir Dogs* are two of her favorite movies while her musical interests lie between Red Hot Chili Peppers, Nirvana and Smashmouth. Before her Gothic awakening Madeline was a cheerleader and represents that new breed of female—one who enjoys comic books in the relatively male-dominated world. She hates people who pretend to be something they are not.

Edgar is an ex–Specials Forces operative turned bouncer. He has patterned his life after his heroes George S. Patton and George Washington and is famous for tying Chuck Norris in an arm wrestling competition. He has a secret crush on Madeline and hates loud noises.

Leslie Michaels is the store manager who also teaches surfing and tutors students in history and philosophy. His taste in moves range from *Harvey, North by Northwest* and *Ruby* while his musical tastes run the gambit from The Beatles to John Williams. Cary Grant, Benjamin Franklin and P.T. Barnum are his heroes and he dislikes people with greasy fingers, people who purposely use foreign coins when they pay and comic books that are not in their proper place. He is known for his ability to track down any comic in the hundreds of back issues in the store but is also easily manipulated and bullied.

Roberta "Bobby" Shane is the store manager who is best known for her ability to hold her liquor, sleeping in the store after a hangover and her karaoke skills. She is a fan of any comic book by Frank Miller and her musical tastes run from The Rolling Stones and Jimi Hendrix to ACDC. She dislikes overpriced liquor, covers that are unsuited for the comic book it is meant to sell and people who dispose of their chewing gum on city streets. *Snow White, Shaft* and *The Rocky Picture Horror Show* are among her favorite movies while she claims her heroes are Frank Sinatra, Janis Joplin and Ozzy Osbourne.

Zeke Oros is a college student who works as the store's clerk. He is like a magnet and draws the attention of oddball customers. He likes music that ranges from David Bowie to The Clash and *The Time Machine, The Evil Dead* and *A Clockwork Orange* are his favorite movies. Zeke is the nice guy of the group but hates pushy people and his job of cleaning the bathroom.

Mackenzie "Mack" Riley is a clerk at Comic Relief who is working her way through grad school. She enjoys the adventure comics like *Buffy the Vampire Slayer, Superman* and *Daredevil* but her movie tastes are just the opposite with favorites like *The Three Faces of Eve, One Flew Over the Cuckoo's Nest* and *A Few Good Men*. Mary Shelley (author of *Frankenstein*), Amelia Earhart and Katharine Hepburn are her heroes while her musical tastes range from Janis Joplin and KISS to Aerosmith. She hates DVD bootleggers, girls in comics with excessive cleavage and the flawed judicial system.

Cast: Katie Ritz (Madeline), Louise Flory (Mackenzie), Autumn Weisz (Bobby), Kevin Sebastian (Jackson), Noah Rothman (Zeke), CJ Maldonado (Edgar), Daniel Halden (Leslie), Tom Hanley (Jared). **Comment:** Comedy mixes with fantasy to follow a group of comic book fans taunted by a bully. The acting and production values are standard and worth a look if one is such an enthusiast.

Episodes:

1. Year One, Day One. Introduces Zeke as he begins work at Comic Relief as a means of earning money to pay for school.

2. The Coalition of Superior Individuals. Zeke soon realizes that working for Comic Relief is anything but the relaxing job he thought it would be as he encounters religious fanatics, backroom interrogations and even mysterious riddles that need to be solved.

3. Thirty Minutes of Morning. Zeke meets Leslie, Bobby's partner in running the store and sees first hand that Bobby is addicted to alcohol as Mack has to run operations while she sleeps it off.

4. The Judas Receipt. The store's resident "evil," shock jock Jared Sain and his lady, Jane, introduce Zeke to anything but the idyllic life he thought he was going to have at the store.

5. The Uncivil War. Jared continues to taunt the store's bookies (comic book fans) as he becomes more determined to find out who they really are.

6. In Brightest Night, In Darkest Day. The bookies, tired of being abused by Jared, plan their own little surprise for him.

7. The Non-Lethal Prank. The bookies execute their plan of revenge—but Zeke is not all that eager to get even with the mean-spirited Jared, fearing for his own safety.

196 Jobs of the Damned. fearnet.com. 2010 (Horror).

Reality-like format that focuses on a young woman (Angie) as she learns about the business of making horror films by becoming a part of the various aspects that comprise the making of such a film. **Cast:** Angie Greenup (Herself). *Guests:* Greg Mc-Dougall, Doug Jones, Brian Patrick, Jo Ellen Elam. **Credits:** *Producer:* Rhianne Paz Bergado, Sarah M. Shannon, Peter Block. *Writer-Director:* Rhianne Paz Bergado. **Comment:** Although the Syfy network has presented similar ideas, the web version is still entertaining and informative.

Episodes:

1. Zombie Girl. Angie experiences the time, makeup and patience that are required to be transformed into a movie zombie.

2. Doug Jones. Actor Doug Jones teaches Angie, made to look like a zombie, how to act and move like a zombie.

3. Vampire Hunter. Angie learns how to kill vampires (with a crossbow).

4. Slasher Lessons. Angie learns about movie violence and the art of using machetes, hammers "and other heavy, pointy and rusty objects."

5. Knott's Scary Farm. At the Knott's Scary Farm's Halloween Haunt, Angie becomes one of the creatures inside the Delirium Maze.

6. Stunts. Angie is taught how stunts are performed.

7. Paranormal Investigator. Angie accompanies a group of ghost hunters on their latest assignment.

8. Guts. A behind the scenes look at how various horror film props and make-up is created.

9. Costume. Angie is shown how movie monster costumes are designed.

197 *Journey Quest.* journey-quest.com. 2010–2012 (Fantasy).

It is an age of dark magic, wicked kings, strange creatures, angels and demons. It is also the word of a pretty bard named Wren. Wren attends bard school but has yet to graduate. She has attempted to write an epic tale in words and song but has not been able to find a story that will please her teacher, the Headmistress, and allow her to graduate. Life changes for Wren when she is assigned what she believes can be the epic tale she has been seeking: record the quest of a band of dysfunctional companions who are seeking the Magical Sword of Fighting which, if destroyed, will end the reign of the three evil kings and return the land (called The Wicked Kingdoms) to a peaceful state. Her quest is not as easy as she believes as the band she follows is on the lower scale of the intelligent quota: Perf, a wizard who lacks the ability to do anything right; Nara, an elf who wants to pursue her own destiny (but won't state what it is); Glorion, a delusional knight who enjoys killing (especially Orcs); and Carrow, a priest of Vieris and a healer. Complications ensue when, after finding the sword, the evil kings hire a beautiful bounty hunter

to capture the band and present them before the royal court before they can destroy the sword. The program charts the mishaps that befall the band, Wren and the bounty hunter as each tries to accomplish a goal (Wren feels she is the most fortunate because, despite the danger she faces, she has a "Bard Immunity" card that spares her life; bad luck will befall anyone who elects to kill a bard).

Cast: Emilie Rommel Shimkus (Wren), Christian Doyle (Perf), Anne Kennedy Brady (Nara), Brian Lewis (Carrow), Kevin Pitman (Glorion), Samara Lerman (Bounty Hunter), Jesse Lee Keeter (Rilk), Jeremy Spray (Grellnok), Fran Kranz (Silver Tom), Scott Brown (Strong Like Bull), Bob Sapp (Karn), Bryan Watcher (The Watcher), Luke Amundson (Yart), Nikki Visel (Headmistress), Bill Johns (Wicked King), Cornelia Moore (Wicked Queen), Matt Shimkus (Wicked Prince), Paige Bennett (Death). **Credits:** *Producer:* Ben Dobyns, Matt Vancil, Jeff Deneui, Brad Roberts. *Director:* Ben Dobyns, Matt Vancil. *Writer:* Matt Vancil. **Comment:** The episode listing comprises the first season. Only three of the ten second season episodes are available and, because there is no consistency, they are not listed here. Enjoyable (at least first season) medieval fantasy with good acting, sets and costumes. The three available second season episodes follow Wren and the hapless band as they continue with their quest (including the quest of the bounty hunter—to see that they are brought to the evil King, Queen and Prince).

Episodes:

1. Onward (7 min., 34 sec.). Wren begins her quest to find her epic story while Perf, Nara, Glorion and Carrow begin their quest to find the Magical Sword of Fighting.

2. Sod the Quest (7 min., 26 sec.). The team finds their first clue as to the whereabouts of the sword but must first solve its puzzling riddle.

3. A Rather Violent Turn of Events (7 min., 47 sec.). The puzzle is solved and the team must find a mystical portal that lies across a river.

4. Deadly Ancient Magicks (7 min., 54 sec.). After finding the cave hidden by the magic portal, Perf touches the Magical Sword and becomes its wielder.

5. Not a Zombie (8 min., 11 sec.). Glorion faces a gargoyle while Perf tries to adjust to the abilities contained by the sword.

6. Bard Immunity (6 min., 28 sec.). Wren receives her assignment from the Headmistress to record her epic story.

7. Duplicitous Bastards (6 min., 28 sec.). It is learned that the wielder of the Magical Sword will lead a rebellion against the wicked kings; the band is tracked by the beautiful bounty hunter known as The Assassin.

198 *Justice Woman.* justicewoman.com. 2012 (Fantasy).

Sofia Escala is an Assistant District Attorney who is secretly Justice Woman, a daring, masked crusader who battles the corrupt legal system when she feels swift action is required to bring criminals to justice. She is assisted by her sidekick, Roberta Gallion and together they help avenge the wrongs committed against the powerless and innocent victims of the legal system.

Cast: Vanessa Verduga (Sofia/Justice Woman), Lee J. Kaplan (Roberta Gallion), Luke Guldan (Kevin Mirchinson), Lino Del Core (Rufus Leakin), Mary S. Porter (Ruby Stone), Tom Mahon (Brent Renard), Nina Rochelle (Sofia's mother), Chris Schultz (Judge Bernstein). **Credits:** *Producer-Writer-Director:* Vanessa Verduga. **Comment:** Although played for laughs, the fantasy outing is well done and acted. Vanessa Verduga is delightful as the girl with a secret identity—glasses as Sofia; a mask as Justice Woman.

Episodes:

1. Luck Be a Lady (10 min., 11 sec.). Sofia is introduced as an ADA who longs for cases more important than traffic and DWI and finds her big break when she is assigned to assist star prosecutor Brent Renard on the State vs. Lopez criminal case.

2. A Bit Much (13 min., 13 sec.). Sofia's research into the case leads her to uncovering a discrepancy and danger when she and Roberta investigate an abandoned warehouse.

3. Crossing the Line (8 min., 32 sec.). Realizing that the rich and powerful are actually controlling events in the case, Sofia infiltrates a criminal organization—hoping to destroy it from the inside out.

199 *Kip Perry: Adventures in the Unknown.* youtube.com. 2010 (Fantasy).

Kip Perry is an Australian monster hunter and crypto-zoologist who is anything but successful at what he does. He is what most people would consider a career failure as he never gets what he goes after. While this would discourage anybody, Kip only becomes more enthused to prove to everyone that they are wrong. Assisted by Francis and Kate, Kip ventures into the world of the unknown and stories relate his efforts to stay alive while he investigates strange phenomena.

Cast: Michael Robert Kelly (Kip Perry), James Hess (Francis), Amy Funder (Kate). **Credits:** *Producer-Writer-Director:* Michael Robert Kelly. **Comment:** Worthy spoof of the real-life monster hunters with just the right amount of humor. The program is well cast, written and directed and the stories interesting to watch. The creature special effects are done on the cheap side, but passable here as it is not meant to be taken seriously (especially with the kind of creatures Kip seeks).

Episodes:

1. The Monobaboso (14 min., 41 sec.). Kip risks life to enter a secret U.S. military base to investigate reports of a secret experiment "of simian generic origin."

2. Kip vs. Zombies (13 min., 45 sec.). In an Australian preserve for zombies, Kip and the team investigate reports of zombie attacks on wildlife.

3. Kip vs. the Werewolf (14 min., 51 sec.). Visual footage of a werewolf caught on tape, sends Kip and the team after it—with Kip, as usual, getting the worse (bitten) and capturing nothing to bring back as proof.

4. Kip vs. the Aquapig (12 min., 14 sec.). Kip and the team search the Pacific for evidence of an aquapig, the result of a whale-hippopotamus mating.

5. Kip vs. Survivorman (12 min., 52 sec.). Kip on a lone mission to find what he calls a "Tik Taalik Roscac," a creature mutated from fish and land animals.

6. Kip vs. the Landsquid (12 min., 40 sec.). The team heads to the desert to uncover the Landsquid, a creature with octopus-like tentacles that thrives beneath the desert sands.

200 *L-5.* l5-series.com. 2011 (Science Fiction).

With Earth becoming overcrowded, hope for relief comes in the discovery of a star (Barnard's Star) that appears to be able to support life. An exploration ship, the *Argo* is prepared and launched into space. All is progressing well until the ship returns to earth earlier than scheduled and the crew discovers there appears to be no signs of life on the planet. A greater elapse of time has apparently occurred (it remained constant for them but progressed faster elsewhere). With no idea as to what may have happened and with an inability to raise any radio communications, the crew feels they may be the only survivors until L-5, a cylinder colony orbiting earth is detected—although it too appears lifeless. With no choice but to investigate, Commander Richard Adams and Dr. Rodney Lewis begin their exploration of L-5 to hopefully solve the mystery of what happened.

Cast: Will Finson (Richard Adams), Chad Burns (Rodney Lewis), Tony Gratz (Allen Carmichael), Bryn Packard (Kason), Mario Garcia (Charlie), Miriam Mintz (Samantha Tanner), Peter Navis (Carl O'Connell), Christine Thodos (Hoffberg), Kaelen Strouse (Evan Thomas), Joel Thompson (Voice of Charlie). **Credits:** *Writer-Producer:* Tom Ptasinski. *Director:* Stanley Von Medvey. **Comment:** Well produced sci fi mystery that moves right along without padded dialogue. The actors are convincing in their roles and the directing well scripted. The special effects (a combination of animation and 3D art) are quite obvious as being fake and distracts from the overall story.

Episodes:

1. The Pilot (27 min., 37 sec.). Establishes the series storyline as described above.

201 *L.J.'s Trip.* ljstrip.com. 2013 (Fantasy).

L.J. is the host of an educational television series wherein he relates historical facts to children. But unlike any other such host, L.J. possesses a time machine that allows him to return to a specific area and report first hand on what happened. Accompanied by his robot (and photographer) Cambot, the program charts L.J.'s mishaps in various time periods as a time traveler who can't quite adjust to time travel.

Cast: Joel Stigliano (L.J.). **Credits:** *Producer:* Ben Guenther. *Writer-Director:* Mike Gray, Matt Brunson. **Comment:** Comedy blends with fantasy in a concept that was presented in a more serious side on the television series *You Are There* and *Captain Z-Ro* in the 1950s. The program has possibilities as there is a lot to explore—whether it is by comedy or drama.

Episodes:

1. The Salem Sisters (5 min., 1 sec.). L.J. and Cambot return to 17th century Massachusetts to discover the real truth about the Salem Witch Trials.

2. The Origin of Toolz (5 min., 1 sec.). L.J. and Cambot encounter mishap as they travel back in time to discover what could be considered man's first tool.

3. Magic (5 min., 3 sec.). L.J. and Cambot travel back to the days of Harry Houdini to learn the secrets of magic.

4. To the Future (5 min., 4 sec.). A trip to the future is planned to discover the new science of resurrection.

202 *Lady Wasteland.* ladywasteland.blogspot.com. 2007 (Science Fiction).

A woman, known only as Lady, wanders across a desolate wasteland, the remnants of a war that has ravaged the planet. Life as it was once known no longer exists and survivors must become scavengers to live. But Lady is no ordinary survivor. Several years ago, at the beginning of the apocalypse, seven men murdered her best friend. Bitter and angry at herself for not being able to save her friend, Lady has sworn to hunt them down and kill them. She has begun her trek and stories follow her travels as she seeks to carry out her vow of revenge. Henry and his young daughter Samantha are two lost souls Lady encounters along the way. Although wounded by scavengers seeking to kill Henry and Samantha, Lady recovers and becomes their apparent only hope for survival (as Henry is not the most aggressive of men and Samantha has known nothing else but life in the post apocalyptic world). As they journey they encounter Yuri, a psychopathic killer and hunter who joins with them for reasons that appear to be for his own survival as his murderous ways have made him not only feared as a brutal killer and torturer but a target for those seeking to kill him.

Cast: Brynne Worley (Lady), Harold Phillips (Yuri), Jon Lee (Henry), Kyra Walters (Samantha). **Credits:** *Producer-Director:* Mark Roush. *Writer:* Mark Roush, Greg Demchak. **Comment:** Tightly wound but gritty production that gives one the feeling of experiencing the emptiness of Lady's life. The outdoor scenes are well chosen and the characters, especially Samantha, are well made up to look like they have been through hell trying to survive. The acting is good but it appears the story will remain unresolved as production has not resumed since 2007.

Episodes:

0. The Lady and the Wasteland. A preview episode wherein the Lady takes viewers through the history of the Wasteland.

1. A Piece of Food (3 min., 35 sec.). Establishes the story as Lady begins her quest of revenge.

2. The Rules of the Road (4 min., 32 sec.). Henry and Samantha are introduced as they escape into the woods.

3. Fond Memories (3 min., 18 sec.). The quartet is slowly being formed as Yuri reflects on his past and what he has become.

4. The Sludge (4 min., 15 sec.). Wounded in a confrontation (gunshot wound to the shoulder) Lady finds her life threatened by the Sludge (the scavengers).

5. No Breaks (3 min., 27 sec.). Yuri's expertise as a marksman saves the day as the group battles the scavengers.

6. Walkers and Canns (3 min., 27 sec.). As the group pushes forward, Samantha almost falls prey to the scavengers who "walk asleep" as opposed to those who "walk awake."

7. The First (3 min.). It has been several years since Lady began her quest. In the cliff-hanging concluding episode, she comes across the first of the seven men she is seeking.

203 *The Last Stand.* thelaststandonline.com. 2010 (Science Fiction).

Without warning, an airborne virus called the Campion Virus, begins a rapid spread across the world. Affected people appear normal at first—until the virus mutates, kills its hosts and resurrects them as zombies. There are survivors and stories follow the efforts of one such group as they seek a way out of their city to "a place across the river," a place of safety (St. Teresa's) reported by the media before it went black, but face a threat from zombies who are seeking to feed on "the left-overs."

Cast: Dan Kroon (Shots), Sarah Robertson (Beth), Evan Phillips (Davis), Shawn Mesman (Tenison). **Credits:** *Producer:* Martin Vavra, Rachel Bennett. *Director:* Martin Vavra. **Comment:** Fast-moving tale of survival that is well played and worth checking out. The acting and production values are good.

Episodes:

1. Our Heroes. Following the outbreak, a group of survivors begin their trek to St. Teresa's with little food—and little hope.

2. Dearly Departed. The trek becomes more treacherous with food gone and the zombies becoming even more of a threat.

3. Between Two Tides. The group comes across a small party of survivors but with zombies rapidly approaching and supplies nearly depleted, the trek becomes more of a hurdle than originally thought.

4. Purpose in Chaos. Disappointment becomes the result of the trek when the survivors discover that St. Teresa's has also been infected.

5. A Paved Road. With hope apparently gone, the survivors turn their attention to finding an origin to the virus.

6. Death Road. The survivors battle the Remains (zombies) as they seek to make a stronghold before moving on.

7. Best Intentions, Part 1. A survivor of the attack, a young boy, is rescued by the group while chances for their survival now look bleak.

8. Best Intentions, Part 2. The rescued boy becomes infected while Shots, Beth, Tenison and Davis, the last remaining members of the group, realize that St. Teresa's may be just what they have been looking for—the origin of the virus.

204 Legacy. vimeo.com. 2013 (Fantasy).

In a time when the earth was young Shaman from civilizations around the world feared that a global reset could destroy life on the planet. Unable to predict when or where such a catastrophe would begin, members of the various tribes vowed to save civilization by pre-arranging marriages to produce a male and female capable of surviving "The Great Reset" and further mankind with their wisdom, strength and special abilities. Over the centuries countless such marriages occurred but not all with the intent to help mankind. Greed and self-serving motives also produced bloodlines where evil ruled and vowed to destroy the good. It soon became apparent that another threat had emerged and the program relates a battle of good against evil as the various tribe survivors seek supremacy and control of the destiny of the world when the reset occurs. Emily Chance is such a woman. Although she is unaware of her destiny at first, she later learns through her Protector (Will) that she is a Cypher (woman with amazing abilities of the mind) and in possession of one piece of a mysterious puzzle that, when connected, holds the key to an unknown destiny. Unfortunately for Emily, Rachel Kilgore, an evil descendant of the Shaman, is seeking that puzzle piece (an odd-looking medallion-like object) and will stop at nothing to get it as she believes the connected puzzle will yield her unlimited power. Now, Emily and Will must evade Rachel's assassins as Emily, possibly the last living Cypher, and Will seek to complete the puzzle before Rachel.

Cast: Scarlett James (Emily Chance), Christopher Howell (Will Harper), Mallory Leach (Rachel Kil-gore), Mark DeMaio (The Major), Savannah Packan (Angel O'Neal), Anna Houser, Jason Barnes, Heather Lannan, Stanley Louis, Lauren Staggs. **Credits:** *Producer:* Mark Mosrie. *Writer-Director:* Chris Hollo. **Comment:** Intriguing, well-done fantasy series. Scarlett James as Emily is especially good and convincing in her role. Each episode is an arc and so well constructed that you want to find out what happens next. Production values, acting and story continuity are comparable to any broadcast or cable television series.

Episodes:
1. Legacy Episode 1 (5 min., 54 sec.). A young woman (Emily Chance), suffering from a slight case of amnesia, awakens in a wooded area to find herself next to a dead man.

2. Emily (7 min., 22 sec.). Emily begins a search to find out what happened and why, knowing that she could never kill anyone—or at least she thought.

3. It's Your Legacy (6 min., 6 sec.). As Emily regains her memory, she returns home and encounters a man seeking to kill her and recover the puzzle piece (of which Emily is unaware of even having). Having taken the gun from the man she supposedly killed, Emily kills the intruder when he admits killing her parents and now he intends to kill her.

4. I Know What I Am (9 min., 5 sec.). Emily meets Will and learns that he is her Protector and that he killed the man in the woods to save her life.

5. Here We Go (7 min., 1 sec.). Will informs Emily of her destiny that descendents of the good Shaman are being killed and her life is also in jeopardy. He has been assigned to protect her so she can fulfill an unknown destiny.

6. We Need Answers (7 min., 43 sec.). Emily learns of the puzzle piece she possesses, but her life is in immediate peril as Rachel's assassins close in.

7. Are You Crazy? (6 min., 25 sec.). Emily and Will outsmart Rachel by freeing captives in a trap that was set for them.

8. That's Close Enough (8 min., 53 sec.). Emily learns of her abilities, that she is a Cypher, and may be the only one who can solve the mystery of the puzzle.

9. This Can't Be (8 min., 46 sec.). Emily learns that she is part of that puzzle and she must find and connect the other puzzle pieces (which could take the shape of anything) that could relate to the imminent global catastrophe the Shaman feared.

10. Have We Met Before? (11 min., 51 sec.). The concluding, unresolved finale wherein Emily, safe (for the moment) at stronghold, begins to suspect one of its members (Angel) may be a threat to their safety.

205 The Legend of Neil. cc.com. 2007 (Fantasy).

Spoof of the Nintendo video game *The Legend of Zelda* wherein Neil Grimsley, a beer-guzzling ex-gas station attendant with little respect for anyone or anything, finds his life completely thrown into chaos when, while playing *The Legend of Zelda* he falls asleep and wakes up inside the game and mistaken as the hero of the game, Link. Neil is anything but a hero and he must now fight his way out in order to get back to reality. Old Man is Link's mentor; Fairy is the girl who replenishes Neil's health (through sex) and becomes obsessed with him. Princess Zelda is the imprisoned character from the video game (she appears to Neil in visions; in the video game she is Caucasian; here she is African-American). Ganon, the villain, is the one who captured Zelda and sent her parents into "some vortex." He is assisted by Wizzrobe. Dark Nut is a Dark Knight and Neil's (Link's) invincible enemy.

Cast: Tony Janning (Neil/Link), Angie Hill (Princess Zelda), Mike Rose (Old Man), Eric Acosta (Wizzrobe), Felicia Day (Fairy), Scott Chernoff (Ganon), Jeff Winkler (Dark Nut). **Credits:** *Producer-Director:* Sandeep Parikh. *Writer:* Sandeep Parikh, Tony Janning. **Comment:** The pilot episode launched on YouTube.com in 2007; the series played on atom.com beginning in 2008 and ending in 2010. Enjoyable series even if you are not a fan of the video game. Easily followed but contains foul language and sexual humor. Costumes and special effects range from adequate to good and overall, the viewer feels like he is watching a video version of the game. Felicia Day as the Fairy is especially good (and eye-catching in her brief red attire); her special effect sequences are also above average.

Episodes:

1. The Beginning. Neil, naked after waking up in a forest, is given elf clothing by the Fairy and soon afterwards learns from Old Man that he is Link and must defeat Lord Ganon to save Princess Zelda.

2. First Blood. After being attacked by a rock-throwing monster, Neil kills the Octorok beast and discovers a heart-shaped cookie has appeared. By eating the cookie, his heart meter is refilled and he is now able to shoot lasers from his sword.

3. The Fairy's Obsession. After being defeated in a battle with the Octoroks for killing one of their clan, Neil is healed by the Fairy through sex.

4. The Skeletons in Link's Closet. Neil has reached Level 1 of the game but must now battle skeletons and bats; Lord Ganon and Wizzrobe devise a plan to defeat Neil.

5. Map Questing. As Neil continues his journey he is warned by Old Man that he may encounter the boss of Level 1—a dragon with a unicorn horn.

6. Who's the Boss? Neil encounters the dragon and is knocked unconscious. He awakens (after dreaming of being in bed with Zelda) and finds safety in a room the dragon cannot enter. When the dragon complains that Neil cheated, they compromise and decide to become friends.

7. A Link to the Past. A flashback is used to explore Neil's life before he entered the game; Old Man

informs Neil that he can buy a bigger shield to protect himself at "the store."

8. Death in Store. When Neil finds he lacks the necessary funds to buy the shield, he joins a poker game hoping to win the money. In the meantime, an evil Moblin captures Fairy and places her in a jar.

9. Les Neilerables. A musical episode wherein the captured Fairy sings of her degrading sexual encounters; Ganon and Wizzrobe, astonished that Neil has progressed so far in the game, plot his doom in Level 2.

10. Getting High in Hyrule. Neil finally encounters something he can relate to—a pub where he sees wanted posters of Link. When he is recognized, Neil flees with the help of a good Moblin.

11. The Secret Moblin. Pippi, the Moblin who helped Neil escape, teaches him how to use his abilities and about a magic whistle, contained in Level 5 of the game, that can send him anywhere he wishes.

12. The Fairy Strikes Back. Neil locates the kidnapped Fairy and rescues her by killing her captor.

13. A Date with Destiny. Neil enters Level 3 on his quest seeking the Magic Whistle. However, before that can happen, Neil is captured by Dark Nut and reveals that he does not love Zelda nor would he risk his life for her. Ganon appears and stabs Neil (who then awakens in his apartment at the point he was playing the game. He is also given an option—quit or continue playing the game).

14. Quitters Never Continue. Neil transports himself back to the game—even though his life had improved in New Jersey (he had gotten his job back and seemed to be less of an alcoholic). He reunites with Old Man and a now pregnant Fairy.

15. The Gloffice. Ganon learns of Neil's return to the game while Neil ventures through Level 4 and onto Level 5 where he finds the sought whistle.

16. Fairyhood. As Neil searches for Level 6, he finds Fairy, who is having multiple babies and prevents her from eating them due to her "Maternal Hunger." As he continues, he uses the Magic Whistle only to find himself on a battlefield, where he meets Zelda's brother, Tyrelda.

17. 40 Acres and a Zol. After helping Tyrelda, Neil escapes to continue his quest to rescue Zelda but first stops off to see Fairy—who is leaving to be with her mother.

18. Every Hero Needs a Montage. Neil meets with Old Man who tells him to find the Magical Sword in the Graveyard of Living Nightmares. Upon doing so, Neil meets his Doppelganger—who is dressed as Neil in his gas station uniform.

19. Death Becomes Neil. As the Doppelganger plays tricks with Neil's mind, Neil uses the sword to destroy it. Neil next proceeds to Level 8.

20. Restart of the King. The series finale finds Neil reuniting with Fairy and his last ditch effort to defeat Lord Ganon and rescue Princess Zelda.

206 *Legends of Atoll.* youtube.com. 2011 (Fantasy).

Ardek, Tanrissa, Riald and Hughland are medieval-era adventurers who seek rare treasures but who have also become heroes (although reluctantly) and must now use what (limited) abilities they have to help the defenseless. During one such quest to unearth a treasure, the heroes enter a dungeon, find a mysterious box and open it. While there are riches to he had, they unknowingly release The Endless One, a dark sorcerer who was imprisoned many years before and now, that he is free, seeks revenge on those who imprisoned him. When the heroes realize what they have done, they begin a quest to stop The Endless One. With drawn swords and more cowardness than bravery, they battle everything that sands in their way to save their kingdom of Atoll before The Endless One destroys it.

Cast: Michael T. Coleman (Ardek), Samantha Mason (Tanrissa), Dustin Hess (Hughland), Samwise Aaron (Riald), Commodore Jones (The Endless One), Forest Nui Cobalt (Dahlia), Alicia Castle (Wood Nymph). **Credits:** *Producer-Director:* Mario N. Bonassin. *Writer:* Michael Axelsen. **Comment:** Enjoyable medieval tale with good acting, costumes, special effects and production values. The only problem is a slight sound distortion at times.

Episodes: (all have the title "The Return of the Endless One" before the episode number)

1. Episode 1 (6 min., 35 sec.). Our heroes enter a dungeon seeking treasure unaware of what evil lurks there.

2. Episode 2 (8 min., 1 sec.). The Endless One is released as our heroes, still unaware of what they have done seek a way out of the dungeon.

3. Episode 3 (8 min., 21 sec.). As the heroes find their way out of the dungeon they discover they have magical powers.

4. Episode 4 (9 min., 41 sec.). The battle to save Atoll begins with the heroes battling not only The Endless One, but his beautiful assistant, Dahlia.

207 *Lesbian Space Invaders.* onemoreles bian.com. 2010 (Science Fiction).

It is the year 2069 and on a planet called Femgina, women rule a world that is apparently without men and where technology has advanced to a state where its lesbian citizens can travel through space in crafts powered by estrogen. Zelda, Tawny, Blurfy and Lou Lou are four women who are part of the planet's exploratory space force and in command of their own ship (Zelda is the captain; Lou Lou, the medic; Tawny the maintenance engineer; and Blurfy the navigator). The program charts their only assignment: search the universe for a new source of pelvic devices to satisfy their queen.

Cast: Kathy Betts (Zelda), Tierza Scaccia (Tawny), Jessica Londons (Lou Lou), Cameron Esposito (Blurfy), Marsha Mars (Avery), Nicki Shields (Crazy Cat Lady), Kerry Norton, Rosemary C. McDonnell, Jen Bullock. **Credits:** *Producer-Writer-Director:* Christine Collins. **Comment:** There are no special effects; there is no nudity, no kissing, no foul language and no graphic sexual encounters—but it is produced in black and white! The acting and production values are good with comedy thrown in as the women encounter life on Earth although some will be disappointed in the lack affection between the Lesbian Space Invaders and their encounters with Earth women.

Episodes:

1. Caught Between a Rock and a Hot Spot (6 min., 31 sec.). The quest is begun to satisfy their queen.

2. You Know They Do Aliens, Don't You? (10 min., 2 sec.). As the ship's fuel becomes depleted, the women must land on a forbidden (to them) planet called Earth and find a source of estrogen.

3. And I Thought They Were Crazy on Planet Femgina (9 min., 9 sec.). As the women explore their new surroundings, they encounter a man for the first time, become involved with a group of female Bible worshipers and find shelter with the Crazy Cat Lady (who believes her plush cats are real).

208 *Lesbian Vampires.* lesbianvampires. org. 2010 (Erotic Horror).

A group of beautiful women, who are not only vampires but lesbians, engage in a night of sensuous blood feasting and love making at the Vampire Den.

Cast/Credits: This information is not online. **Comment:** Very risqué program that contains mild amounts of blood (as the girls draw it from each other) coupled with kissing and caressing scenes. The girls are very scantily clad but the cinematography is not as good as compared to other such series (appears a bit washed out like it was a dub from a VHS tape). The cast and credits are not given and the program appears to have been created by re-editing a soft-core feature film.

Episodes: Six episodes, with basically no story description (as the concentration is on the blood/love making scenes) that are labeled as Lesbian Vampires, Part 1, Lesbian Vampires, Part 2, etc.

209 *Level 17.* level17webseries.com. 2013 (Science Fiction).

In a time in the not-too-distant future, an Australian city (Adelaide) is placed under a lockdown by the paramilitary branch of the I.O.B. Corporation when a viral outbreak is detected and confinement within the affected area appears to be the only way to stop its spread. But is it more than just a viral outbreak or something more sinister? The program hints at such and follows several people (Ethan and Danielle in particular) as they struggle to survive in a new regime and uncover the truth as to what exactly happened and what the military in concealing in Level 17 of I.O.B.

Cast: Hjalmar Svenna (Ethan), Melissa Martins (Danielle), Ben Todd (Prof. Anderson), Kerry-Anne James (Deidre), Patrick Clements (Rob), Ali Stokes (Crazy Lady), Amara Young (Alien Noticer). **Credits:** *Producer:* Adam M. Carter. *Writer-Director:* John de Caux. **Comment:** A good story idea that it is badly presented. Instead of establishing the premise right off, it begins with an action scene of the Hazmet agents on the prowl making the viewer feel like he missed the whole beginning. The premise is eventually presented but waiting is not the way to go. The Australian-produced program is well produced with good acting and it appears, if additional episodes are produced, it will be a situation where the after fact is presented before the fact that caused it.

Episodes:

1. Pilot (7 min., 28 sec.). Partially establishes the storyline as Hazmet agents of the I.O.B. Corporation begins its patrol of the city by destroying anyone that might be infected.

210 Life, with Zombies. lifewithzombies. com. 2013 (Horror).

An apocalypse has devastated the earth. Zombies are roaming the streets seeking human brains on which to feed and people are, for the most part, confined to their homes until authorities can figure a way to destroy the increasing zombie population. The program focuses on seven people who now live together as they figure out how to survive the situation that surrounds them.

Cast: Gary Rolin (Barry), Jennifer Losi (Sara), Julia Carpenter (Cathy), Michael Perrick (Lester), Tim Sands (Banks), Perry Daniel (Megan), Robbe Henke (Floyd). **Credits:** *Producer-Writer-Director:* Gary Rolin. **Comment:** Played strictly for laughs with a cliff hanger ending. Worth watching for a few chuckles but do not expect much horror (basically only in the last episode).

Episodes:

1. Episode 1 (4 min., 2 sec.). As Barry and his daughter Sara are pursued by zombies, Barry fiddles with a key trying to open a gate that is their only means of escape.

2. Episode 2 (3 min., 40 sec.). Barry and Sara join with four other survivors including Barry's brother, Lester, who has been bitten by a zombie, but has not turned as he invented a device that prevents his brain from telling his body what has happened.

3. Episode 3 (5 min., 23 sec.). The group makes contact with a military rescue unit. Clint Howard guest stars as the sergeant promising them they will be rescued.

4. Episode 4 (3 min., 35 sec.). Sara balks at her father's complete control over her, causing a rift among the survivors.

5. Episode 5 (6 min., 31 sec.). Floyd, one of the survivors, begins showing signs of a zombie infection. Lester's device begins to fail and he too is reverting to zombie. While the two battle, the four remaining survivors sneak out the door.

211 Lifelike. watchlifelike.com. 2012 (Science Fiction).

It is the year 2321 and Artificial Intelligence has been taken to the point where personal computers are shaped like people. In Anchorage, Alaska, now the capital of North and South America United, the Lifelike Corporation controls both the production of androids and the energy market. One of its creations, SIM, has been progressed to a state beyond all previously produced androids. She has natural human mannerisms, convincing emotional responses and a highly developed neural network. While being tested, SIM wanders out of the Lifelike lab and into the city where she is found by Tense, a young news blogger. Tense and her friends soon realize that SIM is not human but an illegal creation and built for reasons that are unknown. The program follows Tense as she and SIM react with each other and Tense's attempts to keep her secret and uncover the reason for her creation.

Cast: Maria Voylokov (SIM), Michael Sanchez (Run), Emily Wilson (Tense), Stephen Chang (Mono), Jssica Amal Rice (Indigo), Timothy Fannon (Neo), Christina Jun (Sally), Graham Clarke (Doctor), Lauren Swann (Lifelike Spokeswoman), Alejandro Ruiz (News Anchor). **Credits:** *Producer-Writer:* Joel E. Salas, Maria Voylokov. *Director:* Maria Voylokov. **Comment:** Stories about beautiful female androids (or robots) have been done countless times before both in feature films and on television (perhaps best exemplified on the series *My Living Doll* and *Mann and Machine*). Here, however, some intrigue has been thrown into the mix and SIM lives up to her television counterparts as not only being gorgeous, but so human-like that no one would ever suspect her as being a robot.

Episodes: Only a 70-second teaser has been released that reveals that SIM (Simulant 3) is a secret creation of the Lifelike Corporation.

212 The Living. webserieschannel.com. 2010 (Horror).

Following an outbreak of what is called "a freak virus" (for which there is no cure) infected people become zombies within six days. Certain people are apparently immune and for them, a struggle for survival has begun. Episodes follow one such group of survivors through and after the zombie apocalypse as they battle the new world conditions hoping that scientists will discover a cure and save mankind before all traces of human life are destroyed by the virus.

Cast: Johnny Brilliantes (John Laruso), Katherine Park (Katherine McClane), Richard Dreyling (Rich Thornhill), C.J. Thomas (Sam Stephens), Seychelle Gabriel (Anne Stephens), Douglas Despres (Mark Masters), David Toda (Geno Thornhill), Caroline Yee-Seul Tilghman (Nurse Caroline). **Credits:** *Producer:* Frank Hernandez, Dani Yuan. *Writer-Director:* Johnny Brilliantes. **Comment:** Tense struggle for survival that is presented like a movie serial of the 1930s or 40s (cliff-hanging episodes). The acting and production values are good and additional episodes are planned.

Episodes:

1. Miracles Happen (3 min., 4 sec.). Establishes the storyline as a young man, realizing that his wife has become infected, has no choice but to kill her.

2. Alone (5 min., 9 sec.). Fleeing from his home and into the woods, the husband fears that he too may have contracted the virus.

3. Trust Flynn (5 min., 54 sec.). A former soldier, seeking safety, encounters the husband (who introduces himself as Flynn; although is real name is John).

4. Answers (3 min., 44 sec.). Rich and Flynn form an uneasy alliance with Rich suspecting Flynn is hiding something.

5. Monster (8 min., 28 sec.). Rich, hopeful that his father is among the survivors, makes plans to return home.

6. Bait, Part 1 (4 min., 59 sec.). As Rich begins the search to find his father, he encounters a couple (Katherine and Mark) that have been attacked by zombies.

7. Bait, Part 2 (6 min., 26 sec.). Katherine appears to be okay, but time may be running out for Mark, who has been affected.

8. Disconnected (9 min., 10 sec.). Flashback-like episode wherein Rich recalls the events that led to his current predicament.

9. Suffering (6 min., 13 sec.). John's hopes for a cure look promising when he and the group reach a medical facility.

10. Go (7 min., 33 sec.). The medical facility becomes a battleground as the infected begin to attack it.

11. Victory (10 min., 26 sec.). The group has managed to survive the attack, but John has become increasingly ill—and may now pose a threat to the group.

12. Hold On (11 min., 23 sec.). With hope that there is not only treatment but a cure for John, the group continues their trek in a concluding, unresolved cliff hanger.

213 *Living with Frankenstein.* blip.tv. 2012 (Horror).

In the year 1818 Mary Shelley wrote the book *Frankenstein* apparently basing it on an actual creature that was created by Percy Shelley (her now her ex-husband) by bringing the dead back to life. She, the creature (called Frank), Percy and their friend, Lord George Gordon Byron have survived the decades by injecting themselves with Frank's blood. After living in England for nearly 200 years, Mary

Living with Frankenstein **cast, from left to right: Steve Brian, Jennifer Neala Page and Patrick Thompson** (copyright toute suite productions).

believes she needs a change of scenery and moves to Los Angeles, hoping to find the atmosphere she needs to write a second book. But not is all as Mary deemed it would be as she, Frank, Percy and Lord Byron have aroused suspicions, especially with a reporter (Ernestine), who has uncovered their secret and has vowed to expose them. The program follows Mary as she tries to protect her family from becoming a major news story.

Cast: Jennifer Neala Page (Mary Shelley), Matt Kelly (Frank), Tatjana Bluchel (Ernestine), Patrick Thompson (Percy Shelley), Steve Brian (Lord Byron), Laura Waddell (Claire). **Credits:** *Producer-Writer-Director:* Deborah Baxtrom. **Comment:** Horror spoof that places the actual Frankenstein monster in the modern world in a well produced story that, although it ends unresolved, is a new approach to the legend with Mary Shelley herself involved in Frank's plight.

Episodes:

1. The New Romantics (4 min.). Establishes the storyline as Mary rents an apartment in Los Angeles in the year 2012.

2. Temper, Temper (4 min., 17 sec.). Mary laments over the fact that she is living forever but always having to spend her time in hiding to keep Frank secret.

3. Mary Shelley (5 min., 47 sec.). To get her mind off her troubles, Mary sets out to write a second book, hoping to recreate the success of *Frankenstein*.

4. PB Shelley (6 min., 43 sec.). Percy Shelley becomes jealous when he believes Mary is sleeping with Frank.

5. Lord Byron (5 min., 40 sec.). Lord Byron is also upset, feeling that he has lost his fame and that he will soon be exposed by Ernestine.

6. Frank Grows Up (5 min., 6 sec.). The threat of exposure frightens Frank, who runs away from home, threatening Mary's life as she needs his blood to live.

7. Dangerous Decisions (6 min., 30 sec.). Frank becomes a threat to their exposure when he begins talking to Ernestine.

214 *Loved Ones: A Vampire Story.* metacafe.com. 2012 (Horror).

A beautiful woman, dressed in white, rises from her coffin as a vampire covet baring torches approach a woman on a sacrificial table and stand around her. She is stripped (all but her panties) as three topless female vampires approach her. The female vampires begin feeding on her until they are ordered to stop from a nod by the mysterious Mr. Trivio, who himself is followed by three seductive female vampires (all clothed). The sacrificial woman becomes a covet member and the program explores the secret society of vampires that exist in present-day Seattle, Washington.

Cast: Chuck Williams, Lisa Cash, Neil D'Monte, Mike Ricker, Larry Laverty. **Credits:** *Producer-*

Writer-Director: Shawn Cain. **Comment:** Filmed in black and white to not only give it a more eerie feeling but to incorporate scenes of Bela Lugosi (as Mr. Trivio) from the 1931 feature film *Dracula*. The film scenes are well blended and Bela Lugosi, being the icon of vampires, is well chosen for the presence he gives. The program contains nudity and foul language and is difficult to assess any further as its content makes it unsuitable for many websites and those that still host it are not very informative. There are apparently five episodes but only two episodes available—all of episode 1 (7 min. and 17 sec.) and an edited version (15 min. and 7 sec.) that contains elements of episodes 1, 2 and 3. What is available doesn't establish much and leaves the viewer totally unsatisfied. The eerie, well filmed images presented in the first episode are lost as the story progresses (even though further images of Bela Lugosi are inserted). There is no website episode information given and a storyline would not have been possible without the actual episodes. The program does have a warning indicating that it contains nudity and foul language but it is easily accessible simply by clicking on the icon that asks if you are over 18 years of age.

215 *The Lucidity Saga.* thirdproductions. com. 2010 (Science Fiction).

George and Jason are roommates but they are no Oscar Madison and Felix Unger (from *The Odd Couple*). Each has a mysterious connection to the other but they cannot determine its exact origins. Each night they share each others dreams but have no control over them. As the situation worsens (their dream worlds encroaching on their real lives) they decide to lucid dream and not only control what they dream but find the reason why it is happening.

Cast: Sean Oliver (Jason), Danny Torgersen (George), Cassidy Hilgers (Dream Girl), Keenan James (Ricky), Kandyce Hughes (Miss K). **Credits:** *Producer:* Sean Oliver, Danny Torgersen, Simon Navarro, Jason McClellan, Drew Leatham, Keenan James, Christopher Lue Sang. *Writer-Director:* Sean Oliver, Danny Torgersen. **Comment:** Played more for laughs than presenting a solution to lucid dreaming. Overall the series is enjoyable and made even more so when the Dream Girl enters their world and Jason and George must not only contend with their problems but a happy-all-the-time girl who has no idea what happened to her.

Episodes:

1. Decisions (10 min., 12 sec.). Introduces George and Jason as they feel something is wrong and they need to do something about it.

2. Responsibility and Endurance (12 min., 17 sec.). Although they are getting agitated with each other, Jason and George try to look past what is happening and begin the search for a third roommate.

3. Liquor, Money and Premonitions (15 min., 33

sec.). The situation worsens for Jason as he is being driven to a point of hysteria.

4. Lucidity (19 min., 44 sec.). Jason and George find a DVD that explains how to lucid dream to control their dreams.

5. Fu**ing Imbeciles (18 min., 42 sec.). The techniques described on the DVD fail to work as Jason and George find they have only minimal control over their dreams.

6. Clearly Glitched (42 min., 5 sec.). During a return to normal from one of their dreams, Jason and George inadvertently bring a girl from the future back with them—a very pretty girl who also appears to be a bit unstable.

7. Neogenic Nightmare (22 min., 42 sec.). A chest brought from their dream world to their world has dire consequences when they open it and release a demon that thrives on eating humans. Their problem: how to get the demon back in the chest and prevent its rampage.

216 *Lumina*. luminaseries.com. 2011 (Fantasy).

Three known realms exist: Earth (the Light Realm), Corwaith (the Dark Realm) and the Bastion (the mysterious Realm of Jewels). In the late 1800s a young British sailor (Gordon Rhoads) uncovered the existence of the Dark Realm when he met a beautiful woman in a mirror. When she provided information that his employer was plotting to kill him and she found she was able to learn about his word from him, they made a deal to help each other by spying for each other. Gordon then developed the Light Realm Mirrorati and spent twenty years identifying and enlisting people who had the ability to see across the Realms. Working with his Dark Lady mirror companion, he built a guild of mirrors that still exist. Today Laetitia Ricon heads the Light Mirror Mirrorati, a powerful guild that regulates the flow between the Light and Dark Realms. Over time the reach of the Mirrorati, as they are now called, has spread far and wide throughout Hong Kong. Every business and every corner of society that has a reflective surface is within their grasp. They are well funded and well connected and each helps the other by spying. The information they gather demands high compensation and can be used for whatever means the two realms desire.

Lumina Wong is young, beautiful and living in a dream world. While she is dedicated to her job (at a think tank called INIT, owned by Eliza Chan), she works too much, has no time for social activities and dreams of falling in love with "someone spectacular." That dream becomes a reality when she believes she has found that special someone—Ryder Lee, who

Lumina. JuJu Chan and Michael Chan in their roles as Lumina and Ryder (photograph by Bettina Enigl).

can only be seen in mirrors or reflections. Lumina becomes infatuated with Ryder until a mirror spy (Eben Sanchez) appears to tell her that Ryder is from the Dark Realm of his world and that her life could be in danger. The story follows Lumina as she contemplates living in her world or joining Ryder in his unknown (to her) world. (Ryder, a thief on the run from agents of the Queen of Corwaith, was first seen by Lumina in a building's refection after he stole incriminating personal letters from the chambers of the Prince of Corwaith.)

Cast: JuJu Chan (Lumina Wong), Michael Chan (Ryder Lee), Shell Z. Zhu (Eliza Chan), Vince Matthew Chung (Teddy Waits), Jacob Ziacan (Eben Sanchez), Emilie Guillot (Laetitia Ricou), Lawrence Jacob Milman (James Weston), Kate Sullivan (Serena Fong), Jamie Cham (Yuri the Master Thief). **Credits:** *Producer-Writer-Director:* Jennifer Thym. **Comment:** Production qualities and acting that compares to anything Hollywood has produced. The story, shot on location in Hong Kong, is suspenseful with twists and captivating from the first episode. JuJu Chan excels as Lumina (you actually feel for her) and overall it one of the best fantasy web series thus far produced.

Episodes:

1. Single Women (7 min., 17 sec.). Lumina encounters Ryder for the first time and soon becomes infatuated with him.

2. Wake Up Call (5 min., 27 sec.). Unable to get Ryder out of her mind, Lumina skips work to meet him and is caught by her friend Teddy talking into a mirror.

3. Enter the Mirror Spy (5 min., 50 sec.). The Mirror Spy (Eben) warns Lumina of the dangers of associating with people from the Dark Realm of his world.

4. Still of the Night (7 min., 26 sec.). After her meeting with Eben, Lumina realizes that Ryder only exists in reflections.

5. Give the Lady a Hand (7 min., 56 sec.). Ignoring Eben's warning, Lumina continues seeing Ryder.

6. Windows (7 min., 6 sec.). With her infatuation becoming stronger, Lumina returns to Ryder, asking him to redeem himself so they can be together.

7. Tick Tock Little Rabbit (7 min., 7 sec.). James Weston, Lumina's co-worker, becomes concerned about Lumina when he learns about Ryder.

8. Et Tu Yuri (5 min., 31 sec.). Eben again warns Lumina about the danger Ryder is facing; Ryder confronts his mentor, Yuri, the Master Thief.

9. Endgame (9 min., 5 sec.). Concludes the story with Lumina making a decision that could change the course of her life.

217 Lust of the Vampires. lustofthevampires-webseries.com. 1998 (Horror).

As the program begins, a beautiful young woman (Angelique) approaches an equally beautiful woman standing next to a bed. Angelique disrobes then begins kissing what appears to be her lover. As the camera angle changes to focus on Angelique kissing the woman's neck, an unexpected beat of music blasts, Angelique's fangs appear and she drains the girl of her blood. In a voice over narration by Angelique it is learned that Angelique is not only a vampire, but a lesbian who has sworn to destroy the female vampire that killed her girlfriend Amber (seen in flashback sequences) and turned her into a creature of the undead. Angelique believes that a vampire known only as The Countess Dracula is responsible and by drinking her blood she will not only end her curse but avenge Amber's death. The Countess, however, is very powerful and possibly one of the Ancient Vampires that has risen from her grave to control the current vampire world. Although Angelique is beautiful and very seductive, she is careless and really does not have a plan of attack. Her connections in the lesbian community are her biggest asset as the vampire slaves of The Countess prey on gorgeous women that, after being bitten, become minions for The Countess. The program, which contains nudity and very suggestive girl/girl love scenes, follows Angelique as she continues her quest—seducing lesbian vampires and extracting what information she can from them about The Countess (and where she is hiding) before she kills them (by driving a stake through their hearts. Angelique carries a small oblong case with her that contains pointed stakes and a hammer-like object).

Cast: Nicole Galiardo (Angelique), Madison Gorman (Amber), Sabrina Leigh (Countess Dracula). **Comment:** A very early Internet horror series that was no doubt influenced by the WB series *Buffy the Vampire Slayer* that expanded upon the lesbian character of Willow (Alyson Hannigan). Only the three principal performers receive credit. There is virtually no text information available on the series and the exact number of episodes is unknown (only three could be found). The production values are acceptable (it is obvious that it was shot on video tape) and the acting is quite good. The three main performers are beautiful and do appear nude suggesting that the program could be a soft core adult film that had been re-edited into a web series. While Angelique is depicted as a loving vampire (she is soft and gentle with her victims), The Countess is vicious, seducing her victims then violently draining them of their blood—something she needs to do to prove her power to rule (which could also mean Angelique's demise as she is not prepared to encounter such a vampire). Based on what can be seen, the program is very much like the made-for-video film *Muffy the Vampire Slayer*.

Episodes:

1. The Countess (12 min., 47 sec.). A flashback reveals that Angelique and her lover, Amber, were attacked by a mysterious woman as they left a night-

club. Amber is killed but Angelique, although bitten, managed to survive.

2. Angelique (10 min., 26 sec.). Angelique learns that a powerful vampire, known only as The Countess, has risen from her grave and is responsible for killing Amber and turning her into a vampire.

3. The Oath to Destroy (17 min., 6 sec.). Bitter and vengeful, Angelique vows to destroy The Countess and begins her quest by seducing the female vampires who have infiltrated the lesbian community (for victims) for information. Unknown to Angelique, The Countess has become aware of her actions.

218 *Malice: The Web Series.* eaglefilms.com. 2012–2013 (Horror).

Following the death of her grandmother, Jessie Turner, a recovering alcoholic, inherits her stately old mansion in Virginia. Nate, her husband, a Navy SEAL just returning from a tour of duty in Afghanistan, and their teenage daughters, Abbey and Alice, decide to relocate and occupy the home with a hope of beginning a new life. The move is accomplished, but the very first night brings a frightening realization that all is not right with the house: strange and macabre events occur and one by one, family members disappear; first Jesse, then Nate, then Abbey. Alice, untouched, is left to solve the mystery as to what is happening. With the help of a mysterious stranger (Jed Spry), Alice begins her investigation and attempts to rescue her family from forces that are anything but human.

Cast: Brittany Martz (Alice Turner), Mark Hyde (Nate Turner), Leanna Chamish (Jesse Turner), Rebekkah Johnson (Abbey Turner), Matthew James Culbranson (Jed Spry), Philip J. Cook (Narrator), Samuel Garman (Ghost Kid). **Credits:** *Producer:* Omar Attia, Philip J. Cook. *Writer-Director:* Philip J. Cook. **Comment:** Broadcast television quality production. Superb special effects, enough suspense to keep you interested into finding out what happens next; excellent acting, direction and writing. Would have made an excellent television series for any network had the producers chosen that route.

Episodes:

1. Episode 1 (5 min., 13 sec,). The Turner family relocates to their new home in Virginia.

2. Episode 2 (5 min., 24 sec.). Strange occurrences begin to plague the family.

3. Episode 3 (6 min., 20 sec.). Nate tries to keep his family together after a frightening night in the house.

4. Episode 4 (5 min., 19 sec.). Alice discovers her father's military rifle; Jesse mysteriously disappears after a walk near the cemetery (where the house has been built).

5. Episode 5 (5 min., 18 sec.). Alice, reading the book *Alice in Wonderland* will soon come to realize that she will be living a real life version of the book;

Alice encounters the spirit of a young boy called Ghost Kid.

6. Episode 6 (7 min., 45 sec.). Alice becomes increasingly aware that something strange is happening to her as her dreams present her as a savior; Nate mysteriously disappears.

7. Episode 7 (6 min., 25 sec.). During a party, Abbey vanishes, leaving Alice the only family member apparently unaffected by whatever is happening; the police arrive to investigate the disappearances.

8. Episode 8 (6 min., 13 sec.). Alice explains what she believes is happening but is disbelieved.

9. Episode 9 (5 min., 22 sec.). As Alice investigates she realizes that there is something unnatural about the adjacent cemetery.

10. Episode 10 (10 min., 53 sec.). Alice encounters a mysterious stranger (Jed) who knew (and loved) Jesse before she married Nate—and learns that an evil entity has taken refuge in the cemetery.

11. Episode 11 (11 min., 11 sec.). Alice and Jed enter a cave that leads to the lair of the entity—a female demon with plant-like tentacles.

12. Episode 12 (9 min., 23 sec.). Alice and Jed rescue Abbey and Jesse but find it is too late to save Nate. The demon now wants Alice and Alice, armed with her father's military rifle, battles the demon to save her mother and sister.

219 *Malwalkers.* youtube.com. 2012 (Horror).

A zombie infestation seen from another perspective—that of never-before-seen footage of a corporate video that goes horribly wrong when a camera crew begins filming a new branding at Aristotle Video's offices and the actors begin to turn into real zombies.

Cast: Abbey Ebarb (Abbey), Casey Donson (Sam), Jason Shivers (Cameron), Ike Peters (Mark), Chris Bopp (Porter), Dustin Stock (Indy), Rob McBryde (Tex), Vincent Flesouras (Vincent), Mona Parson (Mona). **Credits:** *Producer-Writer-Director:* Rhen Wilson. **Comment:** Played more for laughs than anything else, the program is not one of the better Internet series. The writing and acting are amateurish and the directing is annoying with cameras constantly panning back and forth from character to character as they speak. For zombie fans only.

Episodes:

1. You've Got Zombies (3 min., 25 sec.). On October 5, 2012, Aristotle Inc. brings in a camera crew to film a new branding when an e-mail spreads a zombie virus and turns people into Malwalkers.

2. The Zombie E-Pocalypse (4 min., 49 sec.). The camera crew finds itself not only filming what is happening but battling company employees who are seeking their brains for food.

3. When the Dead Call Tech Answers (3 min., 32 sec.). The camera crew (Abbey, Sam and Cameron) find themselves trapped in a dark room—with zombies at the door and their only hope being the technical personnel who may be able to reverse the e-mail's effects on the office workers.

220 *Marble Hornets.* youtube.com. 2009 (Horror).

In 2006 a film student (Alex) began making a movie called "Marble Hornets," the story of a twenty-something year old man returning to his childhood home to recapture the memories of his youth. His friend, Jay, a film student also, assisted him for a few days that summer and most of the film was shot outdoors. Several months later Alex completely dropped the project, citing "unworkable conditions" as the reason. Alex himself also changed— from an outgoing person to becoming very distant and preferring to be alone. Hoping to find out what has happened Jay tries to approach Alex but gets a cold reception. When asked about all the raw footage he shot regarding "Marble Hornets" and what he plans to do with it, Alex told him simply, "Burn it." Alex then placed all the tapes he had recorded in plastic bags, gave them to Jay and told him to leave, never to let him see the tapes and never bring up the subject of "Marble Hornets" again. Alex later transferred to an out-of-state school and Jay, too freaked out to even look at the tapes, placed them in a closet and eventually forgot about them. When Alex suddenly stopped communicating with Jay, Jay remembered the tapes and decided to see what Alex had captured on them. As Jay views the tapes he notices a mysterious figure in a black suit (called the Operator) appears in the background of nearly every scene. The figure is a Slender Man (a being capable of bending time and space) and Jay figures it may be the key to solving the mystery. With the tapes as his guide, Jay decides to become involved and solve a mystery that also has him being stalked by the mysterious Operator. (The Operator is an assumed name for a Slender Man in the Marble Hornets universe. It is described as a tall, strange figure that dresses in black. It is faceless, bald-headed and uses light and shadow to stalk, terrorize and even kill.)

Cast: Troy Wagner (Jay), Tim Sutton (Tim), Jessica May (Jessica), Bethann Williams (Amy), Mary Kathleen Bishop (Sarah), Joseph DeLage (Alex Kralie), Brian Haight (Brian), Seth McCay (Seth). **Credits:** *Producer:* Troy Wagner, Kirill Baru, Joseph DeLage. *Director:* Troy Wagner. *Writer:* Kirill Baru, Joseph DeLage, Troy Wagner. **Comment:** Intriguing beginning but excessively long (three and one-half hours) with so much padding that interest is quickly lost. The lead is also ineffectual as nothing seems to phase him (he shows no signs of fear) and the annoying shaky camera can only be taken for a short period of time, not hours. The idea is good but the ambitious presentation becomes incoherent (to stretch the time) and sometimes confusing to figure out what is happening (like the writers just assumed you could figure out what is happening without actually putting it in the script; no sense of narrative here). Had the episodes been edited (by at least 90 minutes) to tighten the script; the shaky camera used to a minimum and the lead (Jay) expressing some signs of fear, a well constructed, suspenseful Internet series would have resulted. See also *Tribe Twelve*.

Episodes: A listing in chronological order of the series that presents a logical look at what happens. An event listing (Events 1 through 80) as the series was originally presented is very confusing as scenes jump back and forth and descriptions will not make sense.

1. Entry 5. Jay and Alex's conversations are heard as they scout locations.

2. Entry 12. While filming a scene in a park, the cast and crew see the figure of a tall, slender man (the Operator) in the background.

3. Entry 20. Alex and Jay begin filming some behind-the-scenes footage.

4. Entry 17. The Operator watches from outside Alex's house as Alex prepares a scene.

5. Entry 54. As Alex plans a soundtrack for the film, the Operator enters the house just as the tape runs out.

6. Entry 55. Alex considers an abandoned doctor's office as a filming location.

7. Entry 2. Alex begins a search for his dog, Rocky, who was scared off by a tall figure.

8. Entry 70. While looking for Rocky in the abandoned playground, Alex encounters the Operator.

9. Entry 4. While still in the playground, Alex has a second encounter with the Operator.

10. Entry 13. At a location shooting (an abandoned warehouse) Alex again encounters the Operator.

11. Entry 3. Without explanation, Alex constantly begins to film himself.

12. Entry 7. Alex abruptly cuts the filming short when he sees the Operator in the background during a car scene.

13. Entry 9. As Alex films a scene at a gazebo, he begins exhibiting irritation and paranoia.

14. Entry 8. Alex returns home and begins drawing cryptic messages on his walls.

15. Entry 1. Alex films the Operator standing on the front porch of his home.

16. Entry 6. The film shows the Operator circling past the windows of Alex's home.

17. Entry 10. Frightened, Alex runs out of his house and into the woods.

18. Entry 11. The following night the Operator watches Alex's house as he sleeps.

19. Entry 14. The Operator enters Alex's bedroom. Thirty minutes later Alex awakens with a wound on his forehead.

20. Entry 56. The following day, shooting begins at an abandoned doctor's office where Alex shows signs of strange behavior.

21. Entry 57. Alex attacks a cast member (Tim) for no apparent reason.

22. Entry 51. Filming resumes with a cast member (Brian) encountering the Operator.

23. Entry 22. Alex films his remarks saying that he will burn the tapes and move away.

24. Entry 71. Jay visits Alex and persuades him to give him the tapes.

25. Entry 16. Jay believes he can continue the film after Alex leaves.

26. Entry 18. As Jay returns to his home, he is attacked by someone wearing a mask.

27. Entry 19. Home video surveillance shows the masked intruder breaking into Jay's home and sitting near him as he sleeps.

28. Entry 21. Jay finds a misplaced tape that reveals additional footage of the Operator.

29. Entry 23. The masked man traps Jay in his home as the doors and hallways appear to change their arrangement. Jay is then transported to the abandoned warehouse where he encounters the Operator.

30. Entry 24. Was it a dream? Footage from Jay's home surveillance cameras shows him awaking in the middle of the night and leaving his room for several hours (but Jay has no memory of doing this).

31. Entry 25. Jay uploads a YouTube video wherein he shows footage of his apartment building on fire.

32. Entry 26. Alex finds a package outside his hotel door that contains tape that shows Alex and a cast member (Amy) encountering the Operator.

33. Entry 34. Jay traces the return address on the package to an apparently abandoned house.

34. Entry 35–52. Footage concerning Alex and Jay and their additional encounters with the Operator.

35. Entry 58–67. Jay meets with a cast member (Tim) to discuss finishing Alex's project. Both have unexpected encounters with the Operator and the mysterious Hooded Man.

36. Entry 69. Jay and Tim return to the area where "Marble Hornets" began filming to find some burned tapes of the project.

37. Entry 70–80. Jay manages to salvage one of the tapes that reveal Alex's former home may hold clues about the Operator.

221 *Mari-Kari.* fearnet.com. 2010–2012 (Horror).

Mari is a young girl who attends the Gilles de Rais Elementary School. She is sweet and shy and constantly being ostracized by other kids. Mari had a twin sister, Kari, who looked out for her. Kari, however, recently died (an unexplained death) but has not left Mari. She has returned as a spirit in human

form to be at her sister's side. Shari, the school's prima dona and other students fear her; Larry, the dead kid who "lives" in the shed in the back of the sisters' home, understands her and Mari is just glad to have her sister back. Animated stories follow Mari as she tries to live a normal life with Kari plotting revenge on anyone who taunts Mari especially Shari and the Cool Girls, who hate her cheery demeanor and naturally adorable fashion.

Voice Cast: Shannen Doherty (Mari and Kari), Steve Blum (Larry), Georgette Perna (Shari). **Credits:** *Producer-Director:* Jody Schaeffer, Austin Redding, Jim Burns. *Writer:* Keith Fay. **Comment:** Well done animated series that is as much for kids as it is for adults. Mari is a cute blonde with an enchanting smile and wide blue eyes; Kari is seen in a ghostly bluish image and stories, which are presented like a serial, are amusing and well done.

Episodes:

1. She's Back. Kari returns from the dead to be with her sister Mari.

2. Kill Them with Kindness. Kari decides to teach Shari and the Cool Girls some lessons in basic manners after they insult Mari.

3. Hey Dead Girl. Kari is displeased to see that someone else is sitting in her seat at school.

4. Unsatisfactory Diva. As the school's big event, the Sadie Hawkins Dance nears, Kari attempts to find Mari a date.

5. Hang This. Kari discovers that finding Mari a date is a bit more difficult than she imagined.

6. Big Man for Mari. Kari sees that a boy (Mason) shows interest in taking Mari to the dance.

7. A Fate for the Dance. Kari finds that she too has the attentions of a boy—Larry.

8. The Super Fantastic Mari-Kari Season Finale Sadie Hawkins Day Dance Mega Bloodbath Finale. As the school dance approaches, the Cool Girls plot to humiliate Mari—unaware that Kari has her own little surprise for them.

9. Mari-Kari Special Report. A newspaper headline reads "Creepy Local Girl's Gruesome Death Delights Community." A flashback is then used to look into that "gruesome death" of the beloved twin of Mari. It is revealed that Kari was an evil child—disliked by her teacher, her schoolmates and some unknown person who decided to do away with Kari (she is seen tied to a telephone pole and bloody; how she died is not mentioned).

222 *Medium Rare—Viewer Discretion Is Not Advised.* blip.tv. 2010 (Horror).

Harry Costas is a director of Hollywood B-movies whose reputation in the industry apparently rests on the legend of his wife, Helga, a film icon. When an upstart young producer (Mitch) threatens to expose Helga's unsavory background, Harry devises a most unusual way to silence him—by baking his brain in a microwave oven (an idea he hatched after seeing his wife drying her French poodle, Fifi in one after giving her a bath). It didn't work for the dog and it didn't work for Harry as Mitch emerges from the ordeal as a deranged killer with weird superpowers. The program follows Mitch as he becomes deranged and Harry as he seeks a way to stop him from going on a killing spree.

Cast: Burt Young (Harry Costas), Brad Dourif (Mitch Malone), Lainie Kazan (Helga), Brenda Bakke (Rosie), Al Ruscio (Det. Hill), Timothy Leary (Dr. Kyle), Alex Winter (Timmy), Sy Richardson (Marv), Frances Bay (Gertrude), Larry Storch (Willie) **Credits:** *Producer-Writer-Director:* Paul Madden. **Comment:** The story plays as crazy as it sounds. It is a comedy-horror mix and features singer Laine Kazan and television actors Burt Young and Larry Storch. It has its truly unbelievable moments (like the baking of Mitch's head) and, despite all the silliness, plays like an episode of a typical silly television sitcom.

Episodes:

1. Episode 1. Harry finds his career threatened when a young producer (Mitch) threatens to ruin his wife's (Helga) image.

2. Episode 2. Harry tries to bribe Mitch to back off as Helga, bathing her French poodle (Fifi) in the kitchen sink, decides to dry her off by placing her in the microwave oven.

3. Episode 3. Helga's loss of Fifi gives Harry the idea of baking Mitch's brain in the microwave to make him forget.

4. Episode 4. In a comic scene, Harry bakes Mitch's head, but the end result is not what he expected.

5. Episode 5. Mitch overcomes his ordeal—but with a deranged mind and a super machismo.

6. Episode 6. When all thought was lost for Fifi, the now flattened dog (called Alfie) becomes a concern to Helga as she tries to figure a way to bring her back (the dog has also developed super powers and has taken a disliking to Harry).

7. Episode 7. As a deranged Mitch goes on a killing spree, Helga takes the dog to Dr. Kyle in the hope that he can help her.

8. Episode 8. Mitch plans revenge against Harry for what he did to him.

9. Episode 9. As Dr. Kyle continues his experiments on Alfie, Harry hires a hit man to stop Mitch once and for all.

223 *The Mercury Men.* mercurymen.com. 2012 (Science Fiction).

It is Pittsburgh in the year 1975 (where the first 9 episodes are set on the same night; the concluding episode is set in an unspecified time in 1976). Although in reality scientific advances never accomplished what is presented here, drones are highly advanced and an intricate part of society. In one government office building a drone named Edward Borman is performing his hum-drum duties when he discovers that his building has been overtaken by aliens from the planet Mercury (who are made of pure light). Jack Yaeger, an aerospace engineer with a mysterious organization called The League (that secretly battles alien invaders) is at the building at the time. Teaming with Edward, they discover that the aliens (the Mercury Men) have installed a doomsday device called the Gravity Engine (which they have attached to the building's steel framework to act like a magnet and draw the Moon into the Earth). The story follows Edward and Jack as they attempt to stop the aliens before they destroy the world.

Cast: Mark Tierno (Edward Borman), Cut Wooton (Jack Yaeger), Amy Staggs (Grace), James Fitzgerald (Dr. Tomorrow), Nathan Hollanbaugh (The Battery), Aaron Kleiber (Janitor), Kevin Vinay (Patrick Glen), Nick Keeley (League General), Devin Reilly (Mercury Engineer). **Credits:** *Producer:* Christopher Preksta, Kari Lightholder. *Writer-Director:* Christopher Preksta. **Comment:** Filmed in black and white to capture the 1950s style of science fiction motion pictures of that era. Done effectively with good special effects.

Episodes:

1. Invasion (6 min., 59 sec.). Establishes the premise as the Mercury Men invade the building.

2. Skyscraper Saboteurs (7 min., 19 sec.). As the Mercury Men conceal themselves within the massive skyscraper, Edward and Jack begin a desperate search to find them.

3. Contacting the League (7 min., 19 sec.). Seeing that he and Edward are the only apparent survivors, and totally outnumbered, Jack seeks a way to contact the League for help.

4. Engineer Attack (7 min., 28 sec.). Edward, separated from Jack, encounters a Mercury Man engineer.

5. The Battery (5 min., 58 sec.). Edward, defeating the engineer and finding Jack, uncovers the plot to destroy the earth.

6. The Men of Tomorrow (8 min., 33 sec.). Jack, unable to escape the pursuing Mercury Men, is captured while Edward narrowly manages to escape.

7. Enemies of Earth (8 min., 5 sec.). Edward, making contact with the League, informs them of the situation.

8. The Gravity Engine (7 min., 48 sec.). In a daring move, Edward frees Jack from his captors and together they set out to disable the Gravity Machine.

9. Magnetic Tower Assault (9 min., 36 sec.). Jack, disguised as a Mercury engineer, attempts to destroy the Gravity Machine while Edward attempts to stop pursuing Mercury Men.

10. The First World (7 min., 36 sec.). Jack, using alien technology, attempts one last effort to save Earth by disabling the launch facility on the planet Mercury.

224 Milgram and the Fast Walkers. fast walkerseries.com. 2013 (Science Fiction).

Explores the concept that aliens and UFOs have become a part of life on earth. Dr. Daniel Milgram is a world-renowned expert on the subject but has never encountered a first contact. He has investigated numerous reported incidents and has written an award winning book on the subject. Sally Lemm is a corporate litigator who is about to change Milgram's life forever. Having experienced an unexplained UFO incident two years ago but not knowing what it meant, Sally has lived a normal life. Until recently, however, she has been experiencing anxiety and strange dreams about medical facilities in space. Unable to handle the situation alone, Sally confronts a psychiatrist (Dr. Milgram) and together they begin a quest to uncover the reason behind her nightmares. Stories follow their probe of the unknown—a situation that plunges them deeply into the dark world of UFOs and the realization there have been alien intrusions on earth.

Cast: Richard Cutting (Dr. Daniel Milgram), Walker Hays (Sally Lemm), Kate Revelle (Evelyn Milgram), Stephen Jules Rubin (Dr. Peter Steck), Johnny Alonso (Dean Savage), Alexa Davidson (Young Sally), John C. Bailey (Dr. Fred Robinette), Twila Ilgenfritz (Mrs. Lemm), Devon Brookshire (Susie Kramer), Brian McDonald (Reiss), Laura J. Scott (Pam), Danielle Davy (Lisa Hill). **Comment:** Intriguing detective turned UFO hunter concept that is told in the style of a daily television soap opera. Well acted with good production values.

Episodes:

1. Prologue (3 min., 33 sec.). An introduction to the series and what to expect.

2. Episode 2 (7 min., 30 sec.). Looks back on Sally's life two years earlier when, late at night barking dogs and a commotion in the back of her home led her to her encounter the unknown (aliens).

3. Episode 3 (9 min., 29 sec.). Gives insight into Dr. Milgram, his wife, Evelyn and his receiving an award for his outstanding work on UFOs.

4. Episode 4 (7 min., 19 sec.). Dr. Milgram's work is explored.

5. Episode 5 (7 min., 46 sec.). As Sally reunites with her old college roommate (Mimi) and her boyfriend (David), Sally's world starts crashing down around her.

6. Episode 6 (8 min., 28 sec.). Seeing that Sally needs help, David approaches Dr. Milgram at a book signing and urges him to see Sally.

7. Episode 7 (9 min., 34 sec.). Just as Sally begins to experience flashbacks that she is struggling to suppress she receives a phone call from David urging her to see Dr. Milgram.

8. Episode 8 (11 min., 24 sec.). Sally reluctantly agrees to see Dr. Milgram but their first meeting gets off to a rocky start until Sally tells him about the UFO incident.

9. Episode 9 (10 min., 27 sec.). The series concludes with Sally, uneasy with Dr. Milgram, hiring an investigator (Dean Savage) to dig into Milgram's background; and Bix, Sally's boss, becoming uneasy over her strange behavior as she is handling the firm's most important case to date.

225 Mind's Eye. mindseyeseries.com. 2010–2011 (Fantasy).

Dream Weavers are beings with the ability to alter reality through their thoughts. For untold ages there has been a secretly fought war between the evil Daemon and the righteous Seraphim. And for untold centuries there has been prophesized that a special human can bring the war to an end. A search by both factions has never uncovered that special human—until now. It is revealed to be Illia Fairchild, a twelve-and-a-half year old boy who is a bit nerdy but always fantasizing about mystical lands inhabited by beautiful princesses, pirates, wizards and brave knights. Illia has been protected by the Dream Weavers but his life could soon change as both warring factions now seek him. The Dream Weavers have not forsaken Illia; they have taken on the persona of innocent children (with magical abilities) and must now protect and guide Illia until he is ready to assume his destiny.

The Dream Weavers: Mark, born as an English peasant in the 1100s, is the brightest and most optimistic of the Dream Weavers (he rose above his status to become a traveler and adventurer). As a Knight Templar in his late twenties, he nearly died in a conflict between Daemon and Seraphim and was granted his Dream Weaving abilities when he risked his life to save an innocent bystander. He has the ability to become a mighty knight and is the leader of the team guarding Illia. Patrick was an inventor of the early 1700s. When one of his inventions backfired and killed many people, the guilt and shame he felt sent him to find solace in Japan. He studied the ancient meditations of the Samurai and received his Dream Weaving status when he repented. He has vowed to see that Illia does not cause the same death and destruction that he caused.

Darius is the oldest of the Dream Weavers (received his status in Ancient Egypt when he survived a ritual meant for another). He has the ability to become a powerful wizard. Elyssa, born in the early 1500s, became a Dream Weaver when her fiancé, a Spanish admiral, abandoned her and set her adrift at sea to face certain death. She has the power to battle evil as a swashbuckling pirate. Nadia, a former Dream Weaver who was killed by the evil Dolgrath for refusing to reveal the name of Illia, now functions as a mysterious figure in Illia's dreams to guide him through the dream world and keep him from falling into shadow realms. Koji, the youngest of the Dream Weavers, was an extreme sports enthusiast who became a guardian after suffering a skateboarding accident. He is only now discovering his various powers and incorporates the skills of a Ninja to battle evil.

The Villains: The Dolgrath is a powerful demon of ancient origins. His one goal appears to be to gain control over the fate of humanity and create a new world in which he is the absolute rule. Maya is the Dolgrath's dedicated servant who uses her Shadows Hand Minions to hunt the Dream Weavers on behalf of the Dolgrath.

Cast: Nicholas MacMillan (Illia Fairchild), Kyle Harrison Breitkopf (Brendan), Jodre Datu (Young Koji), Nathan Fryer (Young Darius), Aidan Harris (Young Patrick), Andrew Ellis (Young Mark), Thomas Gofton (Patrick), Laura Nielsen (Maya), Lily O'Coin (Young Elyssa), Michael Hamilton (Darius), McKinlee Philips (Chloe), Johnny Quinn (Dolgrath), Candice Barrett (Nadia), Danika Czubak (Elyssa), Sean Liu (Koji), Claire Moran (Young Nadia). **Credits:** *Producer-Writer-Director:* Thomas Gofton, Thomas Roper-Brown. **Comment:** Intriguing storyline that has all the aspects for a good television series for children. The acting and production values are good (based on what could be viewed) and perhaps the episodes will reappear on the Internet for future generations to enjoy.

Episodes: Unfortunately most of the 23 episodes that were produced have been pulled and only a few remain in various websites. It was not possible to give a continual storyline rundown, as has been done elsewhere, for this particular series.

226 *Mission Backup Earth.* missionbackupearth.com. 2013 (Science Fiction).

It is the year 2213 and the Earth faces its greatest challenge as the Sun depletes its source of hydrogen and it quickly becomes a devastating ball of fire (called the Red Giant). Humanity appears to be doomed as large blasts of cosmic rays begin to spread across the solar system in tsunami-like waves that are destroying everything in its path. The SpaceTec Corporation, the organization responsible for space flight, has deemed that to save mankind, it is necessary to preserve embryos and establish a colony on Sedna, a Trans-Neptunian dwarf planet in the outer regions of the Kuiper Belt. In order to reach Sedna, a deep space transport vessel, the *Telsa,* dubbed *Backup* is launched. Meanwhile, on the planet Triton, which is also being struck with cosmic blasts, exo-biologist Jenna Brennagan and her husband Dr. Gordon Brennagan, believe the planet could also support life beyond the dwarf-like planet inhabitants, the Albino (who have long white hair and have adjusted to the cold and harsh climate; one of its species, Giyome, has befriended Jenna). With Sedna still only a possibility, and with the nearest habitable planet being in the Gliese 581 System, Jenna believes she may be on the threshold of discovering Triton is habitable for human life. Complications ensue when

Jenna is ordered back to Earth. The program charts Jenna's experiences as she rejects her orders intent on proving she is correct.

The story described above is based on the episodes that have been released. Website information is quite different and presents a story wherein the *Telsa,* caught in a cosmic storm, is forced to land on Triton when its fuel supply has been depleted. Jenna and Gordon are apparently eager to leave Triton but J.D. Carpenter, the captain of the *Telsa* refuses to let them or any of the planet inhabitants (here called Homo-Stellians) board the ship as it is not equipped to support human life—only the frozen embryos destined for Sedna. Episodes would apparently relate the conflict that ensues as Jenna battles Carpenter to ensure that she and all inhabitants of the planet board the *Telsa* and escape the approaching disaster.

Cast: Drifa Hansen (Jenna Brennagan), Anthony Straeger (Gordon Brennagan), Caprice Crawford (Captain Horton), Richard Bray (J.D. Carpenter), Mark Windsor (Giyome Nobale), Don McCorkindale (Narrator). **Credits:** *Producer-Writer-Director:* Alexander Pfander. **Comment:** While the special effects are good, there is very little action and the acting a bit stiff (perhaps due to the limits of shooting against green screen technology). The production values are also good and the series is well worth watching.

Episodes:
1. The Prototype (6 min., 24 sec.). As the *Telsa* heads to Sedna, it encounters a radiation storm that could endanger its cargo of human embryos.
2. Shockwave (5 min., 21 sec.). Jenna believes that, despite Triton's cold and ice-like environment, that life exists below the surface and has begun a series of drilling experiments.
3. Episode 3 (5 min., 16 sec.). Jenna receives a message from SpaceTec headquarters to stop her drilling project and return to earth.
4. Episode 4 (4 min., 21 sec.). Having established plant life in a greenhouse-like experiment, Jenna becomes reluctant to obey orders and feels she needs to continue her work as Triton could be the salvation of mankind.
5. Episode 5 (5 min., 1 sec.). Jenna risks her life to save Gordon, who has been injured on the planet's surface during an explosion. Ends in a cliff hanger.

227 *Mr. Creepy Pasta's Story Time.* youtube.com. 2011–2012 (Horror).

Tales of horror read to the viewer as opposed to being seen as an actual play.

Cast/Credits: This information is not online. Comment: All programs are narrated by a gentleman who calls himself "Mr. Creepy Pasta" but does not reveal his true identity. While Mr. Creepy Pasta narrates most episodes by himself, when "guest voices" are used, their billing is just as strange (for example,

"The Creepy Dark," "Lady Mischievous 577" and "Creepy Ms. Pasta"). The program is apparently produced, directed and written by Mr. Creepy Pasta as this is the credit that appears. Overall the program is a bit of a chore to watch as its stories are told in monotone over still images with a musical backgrounds and slight sound effects. If you are a fan of old time radio then "Mr. Creepy" will appeal to you.

Episodes:
1. Candle Cove. 2. Ed Edd 'n Eddy Lost Episode. 3. Slender Man Is Real. 4. Mr. Mix. 5. Followers. 6. Edgar Alan Poe Collection. 7. Bubby the Clown. 8. Tourist Trap. 9. Dream Emulator. 10. They Come. 11. The Voice. 12. Jeff the Killer. 13. Tall, Thin and Faceless (2 Parts). 14. The Thing That Stalks the Fields. 15. Cupcakes. 16. Smile.dog. 16. You're Not Scared, Right. 17. Squidward's Suicide. 18. Emma. 19. Tulpa. 20. Doors. 21. The Gunshow: Tales from a Creep. 22. Ben (The Haunted Majora Mask). 23. The Clifton Bunny Man. 24. How Rorschach Stole Christmas. 25. I Used to Be Fearless. 26. Thumbs. 27. Playing the Part. 28. Under the Bed. 29. The Willow Men. 30. Listening In. 31. Gateway of the Mind. 32. A Memory. 33. Self Preservation.

228 The Mistress of Illusion. youtube.com. 2011 (Fantasy).

Reagan Martin, the daughter of a world famous magician called The Mistress of Illusion, became an orphan at a young age when the smoke her mother used in her tricks seriously affected her and eventually took her life. Reagan enjoyed the time she spent with her mother backstage at her performances and had always been intrigued by the wonder of her mother's performances. But that was then. After her mother's passing, Reagan was sent to live with her grandparents. When her grandfather died and her grandmother was unable to care for her, Reagan was placed in the custody of her aunt, a woman who had no time to care for Reagan. Reagan, now 15 years old, was sent to a boarding school (St. Michael's Catholic School) where she quickly adjusted and acquired a best friend, Janice Brook. One day, on a field trip to the local museum to view an exhibit of the recently uncovered Egyptian mummy, Ava Net, Reagan hears chanting from a jewel-like box that is part of the exhibit. Reagan thinks nothing of it until she and Janice return to their dorm room and Reagan discovers that the jewel box is in her school bag. But how? As she looks at the box, a mysterious light emerges, followed by a bracelet that floats in the air and attaches itself to Reagan's arm—making her a real life version of what her mother could only do by trickery. Reagan, however, is confused and, having befriended Father Bradford, her ancient languages professor, learns from him that she is someone special. The bracelet selects only women it feels can fulfill its purpose—use its pantheon powers to help mankind. Reagan has been

chosen and Janice is to assist her. Once selected, the chosen one cannot remove the bracelet and must embrace her destiny. Any attempt to remove the bracelet will result in the wearer's death. Father Bradford tells Reagan that her powers can cure the sick, stop famine and make the word peaceful again. She is a hero. But Reagan does not see herself as a hero and, as the story concludes, does accept what she has become.

Voice Cast: Hannah May (Reagan Martin), Nicole Zambrano (Janice Brook), Mark Jones (Father Bradford). **Credits:** *Producer-Writer-Director:* Jacob Newbum. **Comment:** A very unusual program. Visuals appear at the beginning to reveal the title and production company then disappear to present an audio rendering of the story. The visuals reappear at the end to credit the cast and production crew. The program itself is very good and you can easily visualize what is happening as the story unfolds. The narration by Reagan is well written and descriptive and actress Hannah May, who provides Reagan's voice is so captivating that she literally makes the whole program (even despite the bits of foul language she uses at times). Presumably it was (is) intended as an animated series, but with only an audio pilot being released one cannot be sure. If it were done as a live action program, it would make a good candidate for network or cable television.

Episodes:
1. The Mistress of Illusion: Pilot (48 min., 31 sec.). Establishes the storyline as described above.

229 Monster High. monsterhigh.com. 2010–2011 (Horror).

Frankie Stein is a girl ghoul who attends Monster High, a school that caters to students who are anything but human. Stories follow Frankie (a female version of Frankenstein) and her friends as they traverse life in high school.

Frankie Stein, the daughter of Frankenstein and his bride, is 15 days old, but suffers from clumsiness as her body parts have a tendency to fall off. Draculaura is the daughter of Count Dracula but does not drink blood. She thrives on vegetables and is 1,599 years old. Clawdeen Wolf, the daughter of the Werewolf, is covered in fur and outgoing and sweet. Lagoona Blue, the daughter of the Creature from the Black Lagoon, is sweet and sensitive and carries her pet piranha, Neptune, in a fishbowl purse. Abbey Bominble is the offspring of the Abominable Snowman of the Himalayas. Cleo De Nile is the daughter of the Mummy and considered the mean girl of the ghouls. Deuce Gorgon, the son of the Gorgon Medusa, is friendly but must wear sunglasses to prevent his turning people into stone. Ghoulia Yelps is a zombie offspring and the smartest girl at Monster High (although she only speaks zombie—moans and groans). Holt Hyde and Jackson Jekyll are the offspring of Dr. Jekyll and Mr. Hyde.

Gill, a child of Aquaman, must wear a bubble of water over his head to survive. The New Guy is the student whose head catches fire when he becomes excited. Ramona is a member of the Ghoul Squad Fearleading Team.

Voice Cast: Kate Higgins (Frankie Stein), Laura Bailey (Lagoona Blue/Headmistress Bloodgood), Ogie Banks (Clawd Wolf), Cameron Clarke (Heath/Mr. Rotter), Erin Fitzgerald (Abbey Bominable/Spectra), Dee Dee Green (Draculaura), Andrew Duncan (Narrator), Julie Maddalena (Rebecca Seam/Venus McFlytrap), Mark Mercado (Gargoyle), Audu Paden (Ghoulia Yelps), Cindy Robinson (Holt Hyde/Jackson Jekyll), Salli Saffioti (Clawdeen Wolf), Evan Smith (Deuce Gorgon/Gil Webber), America Young (Howleen Wolf), Wendee Lee (Nefera De Nile). **Credits:** *Producer:* Ken Faier, Asaph Fipke, Chuck Johnson, Audu Paden. *Director:* Steve Sacks, Mike Fetterly. *Writer:* Mike Montesano, Ted Zizak. **Comment:** One of the longest of the Internet series with new episodes scheduled. The animation is standard and the situations creepy enough for any fan of animated horror series. Presented as a tie in with Mattel Toys, who distribute dolls based on the characters.

Episodes:

1. New Ghoul in School. Finds a new girl ghoul seeking to become a member of the school's Fearleading (cheerleading) team.

2. Jaundice Brothers. The school ghouls try to convince the Jaundice Brothers to perform at the Monster High Homecoming Dance.

3. The Talon Show. At the talon (talent) show, Cleo tries to outperform Clawdeen.

4. Fear Squad. The new girl ghoul makes a spectacular showing at fear leading tryouts, which displeases the Fearleader squad captain, Cleo, who believes she is the best.

5. Substitute Creature. The new substitute creature teacher tries to improve things, but only finds itself failing miserably.

6. Party Planners. As Frankie plans a Sweet 1600 Party for Draculaura, Draculaura is secretly planning a Sweet 16 Days Party for Frankie.

7. Blue Lagoona. Lagoona draws a picture of her sea crush then desperately seeks it when she misplaces it.

8. Copy Canine. Clawdeen, who neglected to study for a test, attempts to copy the answers from Ghoulia's test paper.

9. The Hot Boy. In an attempt to impress the new boy in school, Cleo gives Draculaura a scary makeover.

10. Bad Scare Day. While dressing, Frankie puts her neck bolts (for electricity that gives her life) on backwards, causing havoc for anyone who gets next to her.

11. Photo Finish. The ghouls prepare to look their most ghoulish for yearbook photos.

12. Cyrano De Ghoulia. Ghoulia receives help

from her friends as she tries to impress her latest heartthrob—a zombie named Slo-Mo.

13. Bad Zituation. A zit, from eating too much eyeball candy, causes Frankie to panic as she is now disfigured.

14. Clawditions. Cleo and Clawdeen vie for the top role in a school play.

15. Freedom Fight. Lagoona plots for a way to set the science lab frogs free.

16. Totally Busted. Frankie and Cleo's bickering gets them sent to the principal's office when they accidentally break a bust.

17. Freakout Friday. The ghouls face a double dose of disaster—it's not only Halloween but Friday the 13th.

18. Mad Science Fair. Having failed miserably to make a science project, Cleo attempts to steal Ghoulia's to win.

19. Sock and Awesome. When her friends learn that she has not seen any of the "Twighheart" (Twilight) movies, they plan to see that she does.

20. The Good, the Bat and the Fabulous. Draculaura struggles to encompass the oldest vampire feat—turning into a bat.

21. Rumor Run Wild. To win the school's Scream Queen competition, Cleo begins to spread unsavory rumors about Clawdeen.

22. Fur Will Fly. Clawdeen attempts to win a race against the furry Heath.

23. Horroscope. When her friends learn that Draculaura's horoscope predicts she will meet the ghoul of her dreams, they attempt to make it come true.

24. Idol Threat. Cleo uses the magic of an idol to get the ghouls to do what she wants.

25. Hatch Me If You Can. After their teacher claims that sea monsters are bad parents, Lagoona and Gill attempt to prove he is wrong when they are given an egg to care for as if were a real baby.

26. Date of the Dead. Frankie tries to help Ghoulina when she is stood up for a date.

27. A Scare of a Dare. A sleepover at Clawdeen's house is anything but normal for her ghoul girl friends.

28. Parent-Creature Conference. Parents meet their children's teachers for the first time.

29. Scream Building. Frankie and Cleo try to find new ghouls for the Fearleading team when the girls quit.

30. Why We Fright. The Fearleading tryouts are a bust until Frankie gets her friends to help.

31. Fear-a-Mid Power. With a new team formed, Cleo orders that they fear cheer at every school event.

32. Beast Friends. Clawdeen's sudden crush on Clawd, has Clawdeen becoming jealous that someone else is trying to steal her boyfriend.

33. Varsity Boos. The Fearleading team plans to surprise Cleo by giving their best performance ever at the Big Spirit Rally.

34. Gloomsday. The ghouls try to overcome the fact that they have been denied an invitation to Gloom Beach.

35. Falling Spirits. Disappointment reigns as the ghouls, posting a FrightTube (YouTube) video only gets six hits.

36. Fatal Error. The ghouls find dismay when they are issued tickets to Gloom Beach but find they are not valid.

37. Screech to the Beach. With the error corrected, the ghouls are back in high spirits and embark on their bus trip to Gloom Beach.

38. Witch Trials. Trouble brews when the Fear Squad balks at performing some brutal routines.

39. Don't Cheer the Reaper. Ghoulia's creation of a cheer routine that appears scientifically impossible but guaranteed to win a competition is stolen and given to the rival team.

40. Road to Monster Mashionals. With their routine stolen and the chances for the "Mashionals" (Nationals) looking dim, the team seeks a way to come up with a better routine.

41. Queen of the Scammed. Cleo, fearful that she will be replaced as the Monster High Queen, seeks a way to retain her status.

42. Frightday the 13th. Cleo and her friends plan a Halloween sleepover in the school's spooky halls.

43. HooDoo You. Feeling unlucky in love, Frankie seeks help from *Teen Scream* magazine.

44. Fear Pressure. Clawdeen attempts to salvage her floundering romance with the vampire Clawd by introducing a stake into their life.

45. Fear the Book. Toralei plots to break up Lagoona and Gill's relationship by exposing it in the school's newspaper—The Fear Book.

46. Desperate Hours. Toralei's plans to set up the students finds the ghouls plotting to turn the tables on her.

47. Miss Infearmation. Cleo tries to cope with a Ghostly Gossip report that an epic summer bash has been planned at her house (when it hasn't).

48. Hyde and Shriek. Unable to squelch the rumors, the party is held—with trouble appearing as uninvited guests.

49. Daydream of the Dead. A look at the dream held by Ghoulia: to win a first edition Deadfast comic book at the Nekrocon Convention.

50. Nefera Again. The ghouls prepare for the fall semester at Monster High.

51. Back to Ghoul. Frankie clashes with the new girl at school, Abbey, when they meet but do not appear to hit it off.

52. Abominable Impression. After an altercation with Abbey, Frankie finds herself handcuffed to Abbey as punishment.

53. Frost Friends. Abbey tries to convince Frankie that she is not her enemy and only wants to be her friend.

54. Hyde Your Heart. Now friends, Frankie and Abbey move on with Frankie asking Jackson to take her to the movies on a date.

55. Ghostly Gossip. The ghouls attempt to uncover the identity of the columnist who is spreading rumors about them.

56. Hiss-teria. Cleo and her friends attempt to find out what secrets lay in the school's catacombs.

57. Phantom of the Opry. Operetta seeks to get even with Cleo when she falsely accuses her of stealing Deuse away from her.

58. The Bermuda Love Triangle. Cleo's accusation actually backfires when Deuce asks Operetta out on a date.

59. Here Comes Treble. Despite his date with Operetta, Deuce performs a musical tribute to Cleo.

60. Dueling Personality. Frankie plays matchmaker between two ghouls with differing personalities.

61. Neferamore. The Fearleading Squad faces a crisis when Nefera's overbearing attitude threatens to breakup the team just as they are preparing for the Monster Mashionals.

62. Rising from the Dead. Nefera replaces Frankie and the girls with a team made up of her own girl ghouls.

63. Monster Mashionals, Part 1. Frankie and Cleo reorganize a squad of Fearleaders just in time for the competition.

64. Monster Mashionals, Part 2. Cleo and Frankie face stiff competition when Nefera uses every dirty trick in the book to defeat them.

65. Dodgeskull. Frankie attempts to help the school's zombie Dodgeskull team overcome their fears of facing rival teams.

66. Game of DeNile. A sleepover at Cleo's house has the girl ghouls embarking in a monster version of Truth or Dare.

67. Uncommon Cold. Just as the ghouls are planning a trip to Monte Scarlo, a nasty cold virus breaks out and threatens to ruin their trip.

68. Ghosts with Dirty Faces. Spectra attempts to help Heath prove he was not guilty of a school prank.

69. Hickmayleeun. Cleo attempts to teach Operetta how to act at a concert when she acquires tickets to hear and meet her favorite singer, Hickmayleeun.

70. No Place Like Nome. As Abbey becomes homesick for her snow-bound home, the ghouls try to make Monster High feel more like home to her.

71. Sibling Rivalry. Burdened by the fact that he has two feuding sisters, Clawd devises a plan to end the feud by having them do his chores.

72. The Nine Lives of Toralei. Spectra, the school's newspaper reporter, seeks to uncover Toralei's secret past.

73. Unlife to Live. Follows Ghoulia as her life at Monster High is explored.

74. Abyss Adventure. Frankie and Lagoona venture into the unknown waters of the deep end of the school's swimming pool to retrieve Draculaura's necklace.

75. Unearthed Day. Venus teams with Frankie to get the ghouls into a much needed recycling program.

76. Creepfast Club. The ghouls find themselves being sentenced to detention by their teacher, Mr. Rotter.

77. HooDoo That, VooDoo That You Do. Toralei persuades HooDude to use his power of torture on the ghouls—but they are aware of her plans and plot to turn the tables.

78. I Know What You Did Last Fright. The ghouls try to help Jackson, who wakes up with red paint on his hands, remember what happened last night.

79. Honey, I Shrunk the Ghouls. A visit to Frankenstein's lab turns into an adventure when the ghouls are reduced in size.

80. HooDude Voodoo. HooDude appears to be the only hope the ghouls have of retuning to their normal height—and he must transform them within five minutes or they will remain small forever.

81. Undo the Voodoo. The ghouls are made normal again, but to make HooDude feel he performed a good deed, the ghouls attempt to rewire his brain.

82. Night of a Thousand Dots. Draculaura faces the worst day of her life when an acne breakout may cause her to miss Cleo's big party.

83. Beast Ghoulfriend. When Frankie acquires tickets to a haunt concert, the ghouls seek to find out who she will invite.

84. Aba-Kiss Me Deadly. Robecca becomes the school's savior when a power failure knocks out all technology and her robotic ways save the day.

85. Bean Scare Done That. Still bitter over losing the Fearleading championships, Nefera plots to spoil the Fear Squad's fundraiser.

86. A Perfect Match. The ghouls team to find Abbey a date for the upcoming Dance of the Dead.

87. His-toria. A nostalgic look back at the history of Monster High School and how the student ghouls have changed.

88. The Need for Speed. The ghouls get together to discover who stole Ghoulia's new scooter.

89. The Halls Have Eyes. The ghouls face harsh punishment from Rochelle, the new Safety Monitor, if they disobey the school rules.

90. Mauled. A spectacular sale at the mall has Cleo upset as the zombies have camped out making it impossible for her to be there first.

91. Scare-Born Infection. Frankie tries to figure out a way to stop the spread of a cootie infection at Monster High.

92. Boo Year's Eve. The ghouls plan to celebrate the approaching year (2013) with hopes for a better frightening year.

93. Franken-Styled. The ghouls seek the most outlandish outfits for Freaky-Fab Picture Day.

94. Defending Your Lagoona. Gill tries to protect Lagoona's heritage from his prejudiced parents.

95. Freaky Fridate. It's Friday the 13th and as Ghoulina and Cleo embark on a double date, an ancient curse threatens to spoil Ghoulina's first kiss.

96. The Ghoulest Season. A class project assignment has the ghouls arguing over who should do what.

97. Fright Dance. An upcoming dance has the girl ghouls seeking to outperform the other by performing the most spectacular routine.

98. Scare-Itage. Reveals through Skelita's creepy background that any situation can be overcome if you can find the good in it.

99. Tough As Scales. It takes a girl (Jinafire) to show the male ghouls that a sharp mind can help them overcome any problem.

100. Tree of Unlife. The students rally to prevent their favorite dead tree from being cut down.

101. No Ghouls Allowed. The girls seek to acquire dates despite the fact that their boyfriends have proclaimed a guys night out only.

102. I Scream You Scream. Cleo seeks a way to pass an important test—one that she forgot to study for.

103. Frankie's Joltin' Juice. Frankie, made refreshment chair-ghoul for a dance, concocts a beverage that becomes the life of the event.

104. Tortoise and the Scare. Toralei learns from Ghoulia that it pays to be scary smart rather than freaky fast.

105. Fierce Crush. In her attempts to impress Romulus, Howleen fails to notice that she has a secret admirer.

106. Invasion of the Ghoul Snatchers. Frankie and Draculaura attempt to prove that aliens have invaded Monster High.

107. Flowers for Slo-Mo. Zombie Slo-Mo goes overboard to impress Ghoulina by devouring a brain with a higher IQ.

108. Ready, Wheeling and Able. The ghouls rally together to welcome a new student with a need for speed.

109. Creature of the Year. The school's headless Headmistress, Bloodgood, places Cleo and Frankie in charge of picking the next Monster High Creature of the Year.

110. Party Undead. With Friday the 13th approaching, Heath fears that creatures from his video games will emerge to destroy the Freaktacular Dance.

111. Student Disembodied President. Frankie runs against Slo-Mo for the office of Student Body President.

112. Clawbacks. Cleo and Toralei compete for top positions in the school play.

113. Field of Screams. Toralie and the Werecat sisters plot to win the local corn maze race.

114. Angry Ghouls. The ghouls become obsessed with a new app that has them constantly on their iCoffins.

230 *Monster of the Week.* webserieschannel.com. 2013 (Horror).

A drawback to the early years of television when late night horror hosts presented mostly B-horror films of the 1930s through the 1950s (the best example being the more modern *Elvira's Movie Macabre* with the sexy Cassandra Peterson playing such a host). In a twist here, those movie monsters become real and are unleashed on society—with only the show hosts (Ed and Dave) able to stop their evil rampage. Ed and Dave host "Ed and Dave's House of Horrors."

Cast: Ed Rodriquez (Ed), Dave Ragone (Dave). **Credits:** *Producer-Writer:* Ed Rodriquez, Dave Ragone. *Director:* Ed Rodriquez. **Comment:** Modern take on the movie monsters of the 1930s and 40s. Nicely photographed and acted and well worth checking out if you are a fan of those old black and white horror films.

Episodes: (each story features a creature from filmdom's past with our horror hosts out to return it to the film from which it emerged).

1. The Werewolf. Starring Marie Bianci as Carla Kurkowski.

2. Curse of the Werewolf. Marie Bianci repeats |her role as Carla from episode 1.

3. The Zombie. Starring Ward Benoit as the Creepy Caretaker.

4. Crypt of the Zombie. Starring Ward Benoit (Creepy Caretaker) and Gary Flugge (Zombie).

5. The Vampire. Starring Lelac Skellie as a very sexy and seductive vampire.

6. House of Wax. Wax figures coming to life with Lelac Skellie repeating her role as the vampire and Christina Grabowski as "The Wax Figure."

231 *Moon Creek Cemetery.* markapierce inc.com. 2013 (Horror).

LaSalle, Illinois, appears to be a charming farming community—but it is anything but. During the 1830s, emigrants from Salem, Massachusetts, fled their homes to escape their satanic legacy. They chose to settle in LaSalle but faced a new enemy: the Native American Indians who opposed "the white man" taking their land. Lives were lost in the battle between the settlers and Indians and one powerful family, the Moons (who still worshiped Satan), found a way to resolve the problem: they initiated an attack that massacred the Indian tribe. The victims were mass buried in what became known as the Moon Creek Cemetery. As time past, local legends told of strange happenings and sights occurring at

Moon Creek Cemetery **series poster art (copyright 2009 Mark A. Pierce, Inc., and Lundy Street Productions).**

the cemetery. Where the loud noises and turned over tombstones vengeful Indian spirits rebelling against non–Native Americans also being laid to rest there? No one could say for sure.

It is the present day when Modus Pettet, an L.A.P.D. police detective returns to LaSalle (his home town) to not only look into a series of strange murders that have been occurring in the town, but try and re-connect with his ex-wife, Kat Westrum, a Native American Princess (who was an exotic dancer known as Satan's Angel). Kat, a survivor of satanic abuse, also fears for her daughter, Prima, both of whom are connected to the cemetery's legacy, and who could be affected by what is happening: satanic worshipers are planning to invoke the being of Satan and if they succeed the sacred Indian burial ground will no longer be concentrated and allow for the rebirth of her ancestors. The story follows Modus as he seeks to solve the mystery of Moon Creek Cemetery.

Cast: Mark A. Pierce (Modus Pettet), Dawn Marie Ferrara (Kat Westrum), Amy Lawhorn (Prima Pettet), Maria Olsen (Hatchet Lady), Joe Billingiere (Singing Wolf), Corey Richarson (Crazy Carl), David Arrow (Sgt. Hayne), Brittani Noel (Delores Biers), David M. Edelstein (Dr. Harland). **Credits:** *Producer-Writer-Director:* Mark A. Pierce. **Comment:** Since the actual episode has not been made available, changes could occur from the above storyline and what actually develops. The story is not all that original (Satan worshipers and vengeful Indian spirits have been done countless times before) and further comments are not possible.

Episodes: Although the project is listed as current (as of August 2013) at least one episode has been produced but has been labeled "not approved."

232 *Moonbound 24.* moonbound24.com. 2013 (Science Fiction).

It wasn't thought possible, but in the year 2024 when the meteorite X14-0C entered the earth's atmosphere, it exploded and toxic material spread across the planet. Soon all natural resources were depleted and the earth was titled three point thirteen degrees off its axis. This caused the planet's temperature to rise by eleven degrees Celsius, thus resulting in the length of sun-lit days, land becoming parched and oceans drying up. To survive, humans must now wear reflective clothing in the daytime and are governed by the AluBinum Corporation, which controls all resources and enforces extremely strict conservation and recycling laws (violators are terminated by android agents). But AluBinum is not all that bad. They have engineered the first moon colony and had been sending humans to the moon for years. Unfortunately, due to recent developments, there is only enough fuel for one more trip to the moon and only room for 24 people. As can be expected, AluBinum is saturated with Rocket Ship Applicants and the

program relates the stories of such applicants as they explain why they are vital to the mission and should be chosen (each of whom must make his case within sixty seconds).

Cast: Mona Marshall (Kramer Cosmos), Cuyle Carvin (Kar Kasso), Mercedes Young (Sadie-Cat), Tobias Forrest (Scooter Scagnetti), Laura LaMonaco (Xabvrahe Naex), Christopher Karl Johnson (Dr. Otto von Braum), John Devereaux (Lil' Dipper), Lisa Temples (Sally Sullivan), Rachel Tolliver (Dee Dee), Nancy Keuss (Starla Skye), Krystle McMullan (Spsilona Cosmos), Raquel Bell (Alena 5000), Rebecca Both (Princess Violet Lightening), Steve J. Palmer (Prof. Avil Solemncrest) **Credits:** *Producer-Writer-Director:* Ward Edmondson. **Comment:** With only very short sampling it is not possible to make an accurate appraisal of what potential the program may or ay not have. It looks intriguing—but that is based on only seconds of footage.

Episodes: Only a 36-second trailer has been released which briefly explains the premise.

233 *Mrs. E.* mysteriousmrse.com. 2013 (Science Fiction).

Mrs. E's is a tea shop that is everywhere in time, space and reality. Its owner, who has an unknown past, is known simply as Mrs. E (Elizabeth) but she is a woman (perhaps mystical) who has seen evil beyond imagination. Like Doctor Who (from the series *Doctor Who* and his time-traveling machine, the TARDIS) Mrs. E travels the endless regions of time and space battling the evil that lurks and is about to strike.

Cast: Steffani Benton (Mrs. E), Jenna Clark (Jenna), Alicia Hughes (Stella O'Reilly), Josh Clark (Nevermore), Ray Lowther (Brent Jeremy), Christopher Vandiver (Det. Cooper).

Note: On screen Steffani Benton is credited as Mrs. E. On the official website, both (and only) Rachel Bush and Elsha Suzanne Vandiver are credited as Mrs. E. No explanation is given as to why three women are credited for the same role. **Comment:** Based on the only episode that has been released, the program has all the ingredients to equal a first-rate television series. The eerie antiqued-like sequences (resembles an old silent film from the 1920s that has scratch lines and border issues) immediately captures the viewer's attention. The acting and other production values are good and stories are played within a time frame that gives the sought chill without dragging things out with padded scenes and dialogue. Nine episodes are mentioned as being produced but, as previously stated, only one actually released. Two others have brief teasers ("48 Sleepless Hours" and "A Domestic Dispute") but have not been released.

Episodes:

1. Nevermore (19 min., 42 sec.). A young woman enters the eerie cave-like dwelling of Nevermore, a

teller of tales, seeking information about the mysterious Mrs. E. The episode also served as the pilot for the web series *The Nevermore Tales* (see entry).

234 *The Multinauts*. multinauts.com. 2010 (Science Fiction).

The planet of Protesia thrived under the rule of Tetra. She was wise and kind but when the planet was destroyed in the Wars of Cancellation, she abandoned her bodily form and infused her consciousness into a starship to preserve her kingdom's wisdom. With a single goal to save the other planets of the Multiverse from the evils of the corporate warlord, Oysters Rockafeller, Tetra secures the help of three warriors (the Multinuats): Centari, Xanthor and Gigs. Stories follow the intrepid trio as they, aboard the ship *Tetra* seek to defeat Oysters Rockafeller.

Centari, who wields a magic bow, is familiar with the whims of gods and strange beasts. She had been living in the mythical lands of Olympia and had studied the scrolls of wisdom and warfare. She mastered archery under the guidance of a centaur named Nectarious.

Xanthor, with the strength of a bear and the cunning of hawk, has devoted his life to destroying evil. He wields the Icefire Sword, a weapon handed down from his ancestors.

Gigs is a technical genius who became a wanted criminal when she hacked into the Cartesia Corporation's computer files and halted several projects that posed a threat to life forms in her star system. She now serves as Tetra's engineer.

Oysters Rockafeller is determined to rule the Multiverse through his mechanical and genetic weapons. Following the Wars of Cancellation, he became the Supreme Head of the Nork Korp.

Bananas Foster is Oysters' lethal assistant. She follows his every command and her corporate phone contains a button that can destroy planets.

Coco Vaughn is the lead engineer at Nork Korp Konsumer Products division (which also manufacturer's weapons alongside food products for the military).

Freckles is Oysters' flunky, the "guy" (she's a girl) who does all the dirty work for her boss.

Falco Quasar is the entrepreneur and Universal Class dancer (he transverses the Multiverse in his quest for exciting nightlife).

Indigirka is an evil priest who rules the dark temple of Cherotec (wherein he can deflect attacks through his mirrored hands).

Terracota is a being who feeds on the energy of others (who then become her slaves).

Cast: Christine Adolph (Centari), Jennifer Juniper Stratford (Gigs), Riley Swift (Xanthor), David Mason Chlopecki (Oysters Rockafeller), Michael Hsuing (Falco Quasar), Geneva Jacuzzi (Terracotta), Sarah Low (Freckles), Corydon Ronnau (Indigirka).

Credits: *Producer-Director:* Jennifer Juniper Stratford. *Writer:* Christine Adolph, Jennifer Juniper Stratford, Riley Swft. **Comment:** Begins well with the ship's female narration and good special effects, then quickly digresses with noticeable green screen backgrounds (there is a slight ghostly-like image around the characters) and some pathetic attempts at comedy. The idea is good but the presentation is very amateurish. Had the program been played more dramatically it would have made a world of difference.

Episodes:

1. Flashback. Falco Quasar attempts to convince the Multinauts to relax after a harrowing battle with Oysters Rockafeller's troops by joining him at a wild party in a galaxy hot spot.

2. Mirrorman. On the planet Cherotec, the Multinauts begin a dangerous quest to obtain the lost power crystal that sustains Tetra's life force.

235 *My Future Girlfriend*. blip.tv. 2011 (Science Fiction).

Clark is a young man who works for United Environmental, a company whose policies shape the future. Clark is also a comic book nerd who hopes to one day create his own comic book. Recently he has envisioned and drawn the likeness of a girl he calls "My Future Girlfriend." One day while at the comic book store Comics Mast, Clark meets a girl who bares a striking resemblance to the girl he drew—Lisa. It was as if fate had intended them to meet as Lisa immediately becomes attracted to Clark, approaches him as says, "I'm your future girlfriend." Clark, although a bit shy, asks Lisa out for a date but in doing so, he ditches an important meeting at work to be with her when she accepts. Later that night, after their date, Clark is visited by Kelly—a girl from the future who is actually Clark's future girlfriend. Kelly is from the year 2015 and has been sent back in time to put Clark on the right path in life. Had he not met Lisa, the meeting he ditched would have changed the course of the world and helped solve such matters as global warming. Clark would have been an important figure in the future of the planet—but Lisa changed all that. Lisa too is a girl from the future and part of a scheme by a powerful figure (only referred to by Clark as "The guy looks like actor Michael Ironside") to keep the world of the future as it will evolve without Clark, not what it will become because of Clark. Lisa accomplished her goal by preventing Clark from presenting his solutions; now he and Kelly must undo the damage caused by Lisa and prevent the current future from happening by changing the past (Kelly was destined to meet Clark at a bar; but because Lisa met him first that aspect of history never occurred. Had Kelly and Clark met on that night, he would have made the presentation and the future would have progressed as it should have). (The Man from the Future is explained as scientist who worked for United Environmental but was discharged when Clark's theories were implemented. In the year 2014, the Man developed further thinking strategies and used Lisa to become Clark's ideal mate to make sure he missed the meeting by seeing that he never met Kelly).

Cast: Evan Gaustad (Clark), Cheryl Texiera (Kelly), Brigitte Hagerman (Lisa), Kirsten Scoles (Christina), Patrick Cohen (Alan). **Credits:** *Producer:* Brian Amyot, Patrick Cohen. *Director:* Brian Amyot. *Writer:* Steven Tsapelas **Comment:** Enjoyable blend of science fiction and comedy with good acting (and appealing characters) and production values (with a storyline that moves right along).

Episodes:

1. My Future Girlfriend, Part 1 (7 min., 36 sec.). The Man from the Future (the Michael Ironside look-a-like) sends Lisa (programmed with all knowledge about Clark) back in time to prevent him from attending a meeting that will change the future.

2. My Future Girlfriend, Part 2 (6 min., 37 sec.). Kelly, sent back in time, teams with Clark to reverse time so that Clark attends the meeting he ditched to be with Lisa.

3. My Future Girlfriend, Part 3 (6 min., 44 sec.). Time is reversed and Clark meets the future Kelly as the present day Kelly as fate intended at a bar.

4. My Future Girlfriend, Part 4 (7 min., 10 sec.). Complications set in when Lisa appears and threatens to take Clark away from Kelly.

5. My Future Girlfriend, Part 5 (11 min., 2 sec.).

Kelly and Lisa face off with the fate of the world relying on Kelly's ability to defeat her and set history on the path it was meant to take.

236 *My Ghost Sister and Me.* myghostsisterandme.webs.com. 2010 (Horror).

Rosie Jenkins is a very pretty teenage girl who feels that her life is not complete, that something is missing, something she cannot place but something that continually haunts her. Her parents (Susan and Nick) are divorced and Rosie now lives with her mother in England. One day fate intervenes and Rosie discovers what has been missing from her life: her younger sister, Amy, who has returned from the dead as a ghost, first to be a sister to Rosie then to warn Rosie and protect her from a demon (The Dark One) who is seeking her soul. (Amy was killed in a tragic accident that so traumatized Rosie that she created a mental block to conceal all memories of Amy). As Rosie and Amy become close, Rosie learns that she is a Seer (can communicate with the dead) and that The Dark One seeks to bring her to his side (evil) by stealing her soul. Amy's efforts to protect Rosie from The Dark One form the basis of second season episodes. The first season relates Rosie's efforts to convince her disbelieving mother that Amy has come back as a ghost while the concluding third season explores Rosie's efforts to help people with her newly discovered abilities.

Cast: Heather O'Connell (Rose Jenkins/Amy Jenkins/Kate Evans), Jason O'Connell (Susan Jenkins/Nick Jenkins), Brianna Lynn (Alison Gemmer-

My Ghost Sister and Me **poster art featuring Heather O'Connell as sisters Rosie and Amy (photograph and copyright Jason O'Connell).**

son), Dominic O'Connell (The Dark One), Leon Ward (Justin Jenkins), Jack Elm (Jacob Tyler), Ann O'Connell (Mary Smith), Hannah Wilson (Young Susan), Nicola O'Connell (Julie Burkins). **Credits:** *Producer-Writer-Director:* Jason O'Connell. **Comment:** Heather O'Connell is delightful and convincing in her dual role as Rosie and Amy. Although the program is produced in England, it is not hampered by thick British accents and is easily understandable. The production values are good even though the split screen effect is not used for the sisters (Amy and Rosie do not appear together or side by side in the same scene; the camera instead focuses on the individual character as she speaks. This is understandable as limited budget programs cannot encompass stand-ins and the cost involved in creating the illusion of one actress appearing as two people in one scene). It works here and the program, which has a man playing the role of the mother, is enjoyable and worth watching for the ghostly aspect it presents.

Episodes:

1. The Meeting (2 min.). Amy returns to Rosie as a ghost.

2. A Plan Is Formed (4 min., 16 sec.). Rosie is unable to convince her mother that Amy has come back from the dead.

3. Guilty (7 min., 31 sec.). As Amy tells Rosie about her childhood memories, they devise a plan to convince their mother that Amy is a ghost.

4. Goodbye (7 min., 29 sec.). Amy's possession of Rosie's body (the plan) convinces their mother that Amy is a ghost and allows her to see the light and move on.

5. Ouija Boo, Part 1 (5 min., 20 sec.). Rosie, feeling lonely without Amy, uses a Ouija board to summon her back.

6. Ouija Boo, Part 2 (5 min., 20 sec.). Amy reappears to Rosie but the meeting is tense as Rosie may have also unleashed something evil.

7. Gone But Not Forgotten (9 min., 13 sec.). Amy and Rosie are now reunited, but Rosie becomes plagued by nightmares about a ghostly figure taking her soul.

8. The Seeer (5 min., 54 sec.). Rosie discovers that she is a Seer. Heather O'Connell also plays her cousin Kate, who has been visited by Amy.

9. A Haunting Revelation (6 min., 55 sec.). Through Amy, Rosie learns that The Dark One is seeking her soul.

10. Something Suspicious (6 min., 33 sec.). Nick, Susan's husband, meets Amy for the first time.

11. Paranormal Activity (6 min., 11 sec.). The Dark One appears in the form of Amy to begin his evil plan.

12. Protect Me Not (6 min.). The real Amy tries to protect Rosie with a circle of light.

13. Crossover (7 min., 24 sec.). The Dark One makes one final attempt to take Rosie's soul.

14. Surprise (4 min., 37 sec.). Having defeated The Dark One, Rosie celebrates her 15th birthday.

15. What Was Then (4 min., 37 sec.). A flashback is used to show life as it was before Amy's death.

16. A Visit from the Past. (6 min., 58 sec.). A friend of Susan's arrives seeking help (she is being haunted by a ghost that has unfinished business and can't move on).

17. The Sleepover (6 min., 25 sec.). Amy becomes jealous when Rosie invites a friend for a sleepover.

18. Spirit Away (5 min., 8 sec.). Rosie experiences some paranormal activity at her father's house.

19. Truth (5 min., 40 sec.). Rosie discovers that her father has been keeping secrets about a ghost from his family—that of a brother she never knew she had.

20. The Christmas Episode (5 min., 5 sec.). Although not a part of the series, it is a special episode that has Rosie and Amy celebrating their first holiday together.

237 (My) Immortal: The Web Series. my immortalseries.com. 2013 (Fantasy).

Enoby Darkness Dementia Raven Way is a student at Hogsmeade, a magical high school that teaches future wizards how to embrace their special abilities. Enoby, is not the brightest of girls and while she has trouble pronouncing her own name, she believes she is the number one Goth girl and will stop at nothing to prove it. Students like Harry Potter, Hermione Granger and Ron Weasley have become victims of her misguided efforts and stories follow Enoby as she turns the fantasy world of Harry Potter, including the Hogwarts School, upside down.

Cast: Justine Cargo (Enoby Darkness Dementia Raven Way), Joseph Bradley (Harry Potter), Eli Terlson (Draco Malfoy), Justin Kosi (Ron Weasley), Jennah Foster-Catlack (Hermione Granger), Jen Matotek (Bellatrix Lestrange), Tanya Casole-Gouveia (Narcissus), Richard Chuang (Yaxley), Jeff Stone (Snap), Brian McLellan (Loopin), Dani Alon (Millicent Bulstrode), Amie Everett (Pansy Parkinson), Michael Demski (Viktor Krum), Gabriel Mansour (Vlad). **Comment:** The original source material for this parody of *Harry Potter* has been reviewed as "A masterpiece of wretchedness"; "The worst fanfic (fan fiction) ever written"; and the program as "Faithful to the spelling errors, plot holes, Gothy clothes, hyperbolic characters ... the web series captures the best-worst aspects of its source material and puts them all on display"; "Having read *My Immortal*, I can only cheer these brave souls for trying to translate this masterpiece of literary disaster to live-action. Cheer, and pray for their souls." Although most reviews have been harsh, fans of the Harry Potter stories will find it amusing when taking into account that its source material was not altered to correct all the mistakes. Watching all the episodes (or even sampling one) is all a matter of personal taste. If you like

a heroine who has trouble pronouncing her own name (although she is pretty), dancing (maybe attempting to dance) Goths, satanic faith, a confused Harry Potter and a "classic" in the vein of an actual feature film called *The Incredibly Strange Creatures Who Stopped Living and Became Crazy Mixed-Up Zombies* then *My Immortal* is your cup of tea.

Episodes:

1. Episode 1 (8 min., 19 sec.). Introduces the main characters at the Hogsmeade School.

2. Episode 2 (8 min., 17 sec.). Raven, for short, begins her quest to become the best Goth girl.

3. Episode 3 (10 min., 31 sec.). Preps Snap and Loopin, thinking they are above everyone else, get a dose of reality when they encounter Raven.

4. Episode 4 (10 min., 1 sec.). Raven becomes upset when the upcoming Yule Ball is announced as she can't seem to find anyone willing to escort her.

238 My Roommate the Cylon. myroommatethecylon.com. 2009 (Science Fiction).

Can a beautiful young woman (Jessica) save the world by uncovering the identity of a Cylon robot before it can lead the way for an invasion of the Earth by aliens? Cylons are human-skinned robots created for the ABC and Syfy television series *Battlestar Galactica*. One such Cylon has made its way to Earth and has established himself as a normal human being. But is he Bennett, Peter or Dale, three degenerate friends who are also roommates. Jessica, who is Bennett's live-in girlfriend, can't even be sure, so to un-

cover the Cylon, she devises a series of gruesome, subhuman and outlandish tests that each must endure with the hope of humiliating the Cylon into revealing himself and saving humanity (a letter was sent from Cylon Headquarters to the roommates informing them that one of them is a robot thus creating the situation).

Cast: Dorien Davies (Jessica Yarborough), Alex Enriquez (Bennett Jacobs), Tyson Turrou (Peter Odama), Kenny Stevenson (Dale McKinney). **Credits:** *Producer-Writer-Director:* Robert Gustafson, Alec McNayr. **Comment:** Do not expect a serious story, in fact do not expect a story based on scientific fact. What you can expect, even if you are not a *Galactica* fan is comic sci fi tale of what could happen if android technology actually could create something so real that it is indistinguishable from an actual human.

Episodes:

1. Episode 1. A letter arrives indicating that one of three roommates is a Cylon and must be detected before it is too late to save the Earth.

2. Episode 2. Taking the meaning of the letter in the wrong way, Bennett claims to be the Cylon thinking of the status that goes with it.

3. Episode 3. Jessica discovers that Bennett and his idiot roommates have received a strange letter and, since they can't figure out who the Cylon is, decides to take charge.

4. Episode 4. Bennett believes he is the Cylon (and dons an eye patch to protect his roommates from his laser-eye) while Jessica is not sure as she begins to fear Peter and Dale.

5. Episode 5. Jessica devises a series of tests to uncover the true Cylon.

6. Episode 6. Jessica's tests are a bit frightening and even include drinking battery acid—but still the Cylon can't be determined.

239 Necrofusion. webserieschannel.com. 2012 (Fantasy).

Lilith is a 13-year-old girl who led a happy, normal life until the day a refugee soul reaper named Kuro chose to spare her soul and live within her to avoid capture by others of his kind. Kuro is a member of a society of beings called Soul Reapers that process and recycle human souls. When the Designator assigned Kuro to repossess Lilith's soul, he chose not to, instead choosing her to hide from the Designators for something he apparently did (but not revealed) and now does not want to be caught. Lilith would have died without Kuro and now she lives but must share her body with him (they co-exist and through Kuro, Lilith can see into his world, which moves alongside our world). While Kuro cannot control Lilith's body, she can grant Kuro control if he requires it. Kuro, however, is still not safe. The Designator has discovered what Kuro has done and where he is hiding and now seeks to do what Kuro didn't—reclaim Lilith's soul. The program follows Kuro as he seeks not only to protect himself but Lilith as well from the Designator.

Voice Cast: Felecia Angelle (Lilith), Amit Tishler (Kuro), Victor Miller (The Designator), Brett Donnelly (Todd). **Credits:** *Producer-Director:* Amit Tishler. *Writer:* Amit Tishler, Luke Ellison. **Comment:** While only an animated pilot film has been made it does establish that Lilith and Kuro must work together to survive while also telling a story about a young girl coming of age in a way that no other girl has. The animation is good and the program shows potential for some intriguing stories.

Episodes:

1. Pilot (15 min., 16 sec.). Establishes the storyline as described above.

240 Neibauer. scifiriot.com. 2013 (Science Fiction).

It is the year 2024 and the work of private detectives has changed drastically. Gone are the days of Sam Spade, Philip Marlowe and the Thin Man (Nick Charles). Science and advanced technology have replaced the grueling investigative process by enabling detectives, such as Gene Neibauer to bring-to-life (reboot) recent homicide victims in the form of sophisticated holograms—and learn first hand who the killer is. His only job is to find the clues to prove it. During one such case, Gene reboots a murder victim (Arch Fletch) hoping to find out who killed him. Arch instead is more concerned about the welfare of his mistress and chooses to remain as a hologram so

he can watch out for her. With the philosophy "I Think, Therefore I Am," Gene finds himself with a holographic partner who calls himself FletchBoot. Stories follow Gene, a post-mortem detective and his holographic partner as they solve crimes in a new age of technology.

Cast: Trevor Foley (Neibauer), Justin Leahy (Arch Fletch), Natalie Kim (Vivienne), Jamil Ellis (Bob Tray), Cassandra Fletch (Rebecca Robertson), Matt Gaetano Levin (Borghouts). **Credits:** *Producer-Writer-Director:* Chris Chan Roberson. **Comment:** Although not an overall original idea (the ABC series *Pushing Daisies* used a similar concept) the use of a holographic partner as well as presenting it in black and white gives it a unique perspective (it also captures the flavor of those black and white detective films of the 1940s). The acting and production values are also good.

Episodes:

1. Onverso's Reversal (4 min., 24 sec.). After rebooting a recent murder victim (Ruby "Red" Pyon), Gene faces opposition from The Champions of the Dead, a group that morally opposes holographic necromancy.

2. Fighting Champions (4 min., 12 sec.). Gene's efforts to question Red fail when the Champions prevent him from doing so.

3. Crossed Thresholds (6 min., 18 sec.). While investigating Red's murder in the old fashioned way, Gene teams with his former NYPD partner, Borghouts.

4. Buried Secrets (4 min., 29 sec.). Unknown to Gene, the leader of the Champions has blackmailed Borghouts and to avoid being exposed, must kill Gene.

241 The Nevermore Tales. thenevermore tales.com. 2013 (Horror).

A spin off from *Mrs. E* (see entry) that is set in an eerie cave where Nevermore, a teller of strange tales, reveals stories of the supernatural.

Cast: Josh Clark (Nevermore/Manny), Jeff Simmons (Nick). **Credits:** *Producer:* Josh Clark, Brent Jones. *Writer:* Joel Rook. **Comment:** Although only one episode has been released, *The Nevermore Tales* looks to be a promising series of good supernatural stories. It incorporates the same antiquated look as *Mrs. E* for the introductions (resembles an old silent film from the 1920s that has scratch lines and border issues) but using normal photography for the actual story.

Episodes:

1. Rest in Motion (8 min., 32 sec.). A spin on Edgar Alan Poe's "The Tale Tale Heart" wherein a man (Nick) believes he is being haunted by the spirit of a man (Manny) he just killed and buried in the woods.

242 New Gods. youtube.com. 2013 (Science Fiction).

Star City is an affluent futuristic society on a distant planet that has enjoyed peace within its boundaries for over a century. But now, political machinations coupled with arrogant youths who use nanotechnology to establish themselves as (unworthy) gods, has threatened that peace. New to Star City are a father (Michael Ares) and his teenage daughter (Kaela) and their experiences as they attempt to begin a new life (having moved from the planet Avalon) and become involved in the crises that are developing are the focal point of the program.

Cast: Katie Garfield (Kaela Ares), Jason Casella (Michael Ares), Chelsea Reeves (Lori), Alethea Delmage (Trish). **Credits:** *Producer:* Kelly Rhodes, Vince Barnett. *Writer-Director:* Vince Barnett. **Comment:** Thus far only a pilot film has been released and based on that the acting is good and the special effects, though limited are also good.

Episodes:
1. The Devil's Garden (5 min., 31 sec.). The pilot that establishes the story as Michael and Kaela journey to their new home in Star City.

243 Night Is Day. sillyweefilms.co.uk. 2007 (Science Fiction).

Jason MacKenzie is a man who is determined to change his future. He lives in Glasgow, Scotland, and one day is approached by a mysterious man who offers to help him—by bestowing upon him the power of electricity and the ability to see brief incidents in the future—abilities he is to use to help people he sees that are in danger. The stranger tells Jason that he is special and has been special all his life. He was destined to receive powers—powers he can use to help, but powers that prevent him from touching anyone (as they will be electrocuted). Jason wished for his future to be changed and his wish was granted (although not in a way he expected) and stories follow Jason as he attempts to accept what he has become and help those threatened by evil, always remembering that his touch means death.

Cast: Chris Somerville (Jason MacKenzie), Shian Denovan (Amy Campbell), Mark Harvey (Stevie), Steven McEwan (Di Mullan), Vivien Taylor (Sarah), Tam Toye (Mr. Phillips), Karen Bartke (Newspaper Chief), Alexandra McKenzie (Miss Jones), Eileen Young (Sakura). **Credits:** *Producer-Writer:* Fraser Coull, Kim Ferrie. *Director:* Fraser Coull. **Comment:** Scottish produced, low budget (but nicely done) program with an unusual super hero (although one such character was incorporated into the American television series *The Misfits of Science*). While the program ends unresolved, several years have passed and it is unlikely additional episodes will appear.

Episodes:
1. Genesis. Establishes the story as Jason, saving the life of a girl (Amy) who is attacked in an underpass, reveals what he is and why she cannot touch him.
2. Villains. Jason intervenes in the plight of a woman (Miss Jones) who is seeking the thief (Stevie) who stole property from her boss (Mr. Philips).
3. Trapped. Jason again comes to Amy's assistance when Amy, a writer for her college newspaper, seeks a sensational story that will please her editor.
4. Demons. Amy's rescue causes an unexpected side effect when, after witnessing Jason's use of electricity to save her, she becomes fearful of their relationship.
5. Sides. Amy, still uneasy after Jason saved her, decides they need time apart and moves in with her friend Sarah. Meanwhile, Jason seeks to help a pregnant woman he envisioned as being murdered.
6. Sacrifices. Amy's decision to relocate to London shatters Jason while Mr. Phillips devises a plan to release demons on the city. Sakura, a powerful entity appears to Jason to offer him guidance as the program concludes in a cliff hanger.

244 Night Terrors. dreadcentral.com. 2011 (Horror).

Anthology program of horror yarns based on HBO's *Tales from the Crypt* series (that encompassed somewhat twisted stories of terror). After two episodes, the program was reworked as the web series *In the Dark* (although episodes have not appeared) with Gwendolyn Sweet, a Playboy Mansion House Bunny, as the host.

Cast: *The Keeper:* Katie Groshang, Emily Byrd, Tristan Jackson, Clay Brocker, Jordan Stephens, Adam Sanner; *Dummy:* Olivia Bishop, Andrea Armstrong, Cooper Guy, Leslie Mills, Matt Rosenbaum, Gary Willis. **Credits:** *Producer-Writer-Director:* David Buchert, Chris St. Croix. **Comment:** Because the program contains nudity and foul language (totally not needed in both aspects), it was banned by sharing sites YouTube and vimeo but found a home at Dread Central. The episodes themselves appear to have been withdrawn, although two versions of the two presented episode teasers are still online—one at dreadcentral.com (unedited) and an edited (no nudity or foul language) version on YouTube.com and vimeo.com. The program itself is well acted and the stories tightly written and directed.

Episodes:
1. The Keeper. Strange tale that is set in a fancy strip club where a battle for good against evil begins when a mysterious stranger enters—and all hell breaks loose when the living battle the undead.
2. Dummy. A hospitalized young woman becomes the target of masked psychopath (wielding an axe) who has set his sights on killing her.

245 *Nightmare House.* vimeo.com. 2008 (Horror).

Creepy and unusual tales of people who either confront the unnatural or cause it to happen. **Cast:** Varies for each episode; see listing below. **Credits:** *Producer:* Fewdio (the producing company). *Writer-Director:* Kirk B.R. Woller. **Comment:** The remaining online episodes are each creepy in their own way and well acted, written and directed. There is no reason given as to why six episodes were removed.
Episodes:
  1. Anniversary (6 min., 7 sec.). A very pretty young woman's unique way of celebrating her wedding anniversary—by killing her husband, burying him, digging him up, having sex, then killing him again (presumably a vampire) and burying him until next year. Starring Azure Parsons, Donnie Jeffcoat.
  2. The Collector (5 min., 14 sec.). A young woman, alone in a parking garage, finds herself being stalked by something unnatural. Starring Azure Parsons.
  3. The Easter Bunny Is Eating My Candy (2 min., 6 sec.). A young girl, excited about getting candy on Easter Sunday finds that something evil has beaten her to the punch (a demon wearing a rabbit mask). Starring Abigail Daywalt, Marichelle Daywalt, John Crye.
  4. Creep (2 min., 19 sec.). The fears faced by a young woman as she drives on a dark and desolate road at night. Starring Molly Beth Ferguson, Paul Hungerford.
  5. Cleansed (2 min., 16 sec.). A crime scene cleaner finds that the only way he can cleanse a scene is by finding the murderer. Starring Azure Parsons, Paul Hungerford, Michelle Gardner.
  6. The Tale of Haunted Mike (11 min., 42 sec.). A man who sells "haunted" items that are actually fakes as real encounters one that isn't so when he acquires the prosthetic arm of a child. Starring Thomas Rhoads.
  7. Viral (3 min., 12 sec.). The nightmare that ensues when secretive photos of a cannibalistic criminal, Albert "The Carnivore" Carneghy" are placed online. Starring Brian Carr, Paul Hungerford, Marlene Stang, Jim Stoddard.
  8. Marie (11 min., 37 sec.). A killer's efforts to retain his sanity when the last words of his victim, "Marie," begin to haunt him. Starring John Crye, Abigail Daywalt, Paul Hungerford.
  9. The Feed (9 min., 45 sec.). A man's fascination with a mysterious woman when a technical glitch allows him to see security camera feeds on his television set and she appears to be everywhere. Starring Thomas Rhoads, Mary Thornton, David Combs, Tim Brown.
  10. The Caller (7 min., 42 sec.). Two men, hearing a child's cries for help coming from an abandoned house, find nothing that is normal, when they decide to investigate. Starring Paul Hungerford, Chris Snyder, Abigail Daywalt.
  11. Scare (3 min., 7 sec.). As a man, returning home, enters his driveway, he believes he has hit a man. It is Halloween and two teenagers have pulled a prank—stuffing clothes with paper to make a scarecrow. The prank is anything but when the Scarecrow comes to life. Starring Adam Conn, Bob Telford, Hunter Robinson.
  12. Curse (6 min., 35 sec.). A hit man finds himself with a most unusual assignment: take out a man who talks to God. Starring Kirk Walker, Bradley James.
  Off Line **Episodes:** "Breach," "Conviction," "Door 17," "The Prey," "Smoke" and "Tap."

246 *No Warning.* youtube.com. 2008 (Science Fiction).

In June of 2007 an unexplained, sinister phenomena occurred in Northern Ireland: strange lights appeared in the skies and people suddenly began to disappear. A year later, film footage of missing individuals has been found and released on the Internet (where people are seen chatting over the Internet then just vanishing as their signal fades). At this same time Nexcorp, a telecommunications and software corporation emerges and promises a bright future, although its origins are shrouded in mystery. Is Nexcorp the hope of the future? People believe so until an emissary named Gabriel appears and claims to know the secrets behind Nexcorp but cannot deliver his message directly as dark forces are watching him and, to save mankind, he must outsmart Nexcorp so the truth may be told. Gabriel represents the Nexus, humanity's last hope against the ancient Fraternity of the Eternal Brotherhood (now manifesting itself as Nexcorp after a long period in hiding). The program follows Gabriel as he schemes to deliver the series of cryptic clues (the Nexus Gospel) that will expose Nexcorp and save the world. **Cast:** Michael Smyth (Gabriel). **Credits:** *Producer-Writer-Director:* Bill Taylor. **Comment:** Somewhat confusing and difficult to follow story although the acting and production qualities are good. Produced in Northern Ireland.
Episodes:
  1. Webcams in Northern Ireland (3 min., 47 sec.). Sets up the storyline as giant beams of light streak across the sky and begin to affect people using computers.
  2. Gabriel's First Broadcast (1 min., 10 sec.). Gabriel makes his first appearance after the mysteriously found tapes to state that he is a representative of the Nexus and that the Fraternity of the Eternal Brotherhood has re-emerged after centuries of inactivity.
  3. Gabriel's Second Broadcast (1 min., 11 sec.). Gabriel, talking from a new location, warns that Nexcorp is not what it seems.

4. Prisoner (1 min., 51 sec.). Gabriel's next broadcast states that he has begun preparations to oppose Nexcorp.

5. Propaganda Rising (1 min., 10 sec.). Unable to stop Gabriel's broadcasts, Nexcorp begins an on-the-air campaign extolling their mission to enlighten and bring freedom to the world.

6. Statement Under Duress (2 min., 55 sec.). Gabriel appears to state that the Nexcorp goal is to control by fear and what they are offering is false hope.

7. Not Careful Enough (7 min., 46 sec.). A young reporter (Izzy Montgomery) emerges to cover the story and eventually become involved in the battle between good and evil.

247 *Nuclear Family.* syfy.com. 2012 (Science Fiction).

A sudden, mysterious explosion has caused apocalyptic-like chaos on earth. Society as we know it no longer exists and what areas of the world that have been spared, are now ruled by lawless and ruthless clans. Stories follow one family's struggle for survival in an area where one clan, led by The Man, rules. **Cast:** Corin Nemec (John), Danielle Harris (Zoe), Ray Wise (The Man), Kinsey Packard (Lynn), Sharon Lawrence (Karen), Lee Arenberg (Ben), Pauline Cohn (Pauline), Parker Croft (Grant), Cindy Vela (Karen), Jim Cody Williams (Rebar), Jennifer Blanc (Jen). **Credits:** *Producer:* Jesse Albert, Clay McCall Keeley, Jaime Burke. *Writer-Director:* Kyle Rankin. **Comment:** A rarity for a web series as it has known television performers as its stars (Sharon Lawrence, Ray Wise and Corin Nemec). Acting and production values are good with a serial-like story that makes the viewer want to see what happens next.

Episodes:

1. Chapter 1 (7 min., 57 sec.). Introduces the family that is the heart of the story: John, his wife Lynn and their daughter Pauline. The family also has a son, Grant, but he disappeared when the disaster struck and John and Lynn are seeking a way to find him.

2. Chapter 2 (4 min., 14 sec.). John and Lynn recall events before the mushroom cloud appeared and changed the world.

3. Chapter 3 (4 min., 21 sec.). A stranger approaches John and, after seeing a picture of the family, tells him that he knows Grant's whereabouts. Trusting the stranger, John, Lynn and Pauline follow his lead, but sense danger when affected humans, called Berserkers, can be seen in the distance.

4. Chapter 4 (5 min., 53 sec.). The stranger betrays the family and leads them to a camp run by the leader of the Berserkers, The Man. For entertainment, The Man places John in an arena where he must battle to save his life.

5. Chapter 5 (4 min., 34 sec.). Successfully de-

feating his arena enemy, John and his family meet The Man, who wants Pauline. John's refusal sends him back in the arena and in a second battle against the same foe.

6. Episode 6 (3 min., 40 sec.). The foe turns out to be a lifesaver for John when he, having lost his wife, sacrifices himself to help John and his family escape from The Man.

7. Chapter 7 (2 min., 49 sec.). A look at exactly who The Man is (seen as a self-help writer before the disaster struck).

8. Chapter 8 (4 min., 21). John, taking The Man hostage, learns that Grant is being held in a place called Tent City.

9. Chapter 9 (3 min., 42 sec.). As the family heads toward Tent City, The Man's followers begin pursuing them.

10. Chapter 10 (4 min., 24 sec.). Having diverted the pursuing Berserkers, John, Lynn, Pauline and their captive, The Man, near Tent City, where they hope to find Grant.

248 *Oh, Inverted World.* ohinvertedseries. com. 2010 (Science Fiction).

In a small American town, Mina, a recent college graduate, and her three friends, Art, Finn and Rob (called The Bearded Three) receive a visit from a mysterious woman (Selene) who tells them of a strange prophecy: the moon is going to fall into the earth. The friends dismiss it as being unheard of—until the prediction comes to light and the world is thrown into chaos—with time rifts, zombies and numerous other unnatural occurrences. Stories follow the survivors, in particular Mina and the Bearded Three as they struggle to survive on a devastated planet. **Cast:** Pamela Bell (Mina), Krystal Bua (Selene), Christian Nilsson (Art), Terence Krey (Finn), Alex Longo (Rob), Rob Hinderliter (Sol), Samantha Cajade (Jenni), Tim Kelly (Art of the Future). **Credits:** *Producer:* Terence Krey, Daniel Fox, Jacob Cohen. *Director:* Terence Krey, Daniel Fox, Jacob Cohen. *Writer:* Terence Krey. **Comment:** A little bit of everything in an enjoyable little package with good acting and production values.

Episodes:

1. Neighborhood (9 min., 23 sec.). At a bar Mina and the Bearded Three meet the mysterious Selene.

2. The Perfect Space (8 min., 16 sec.). Shrugging off Selene's prediction, Mina and the Bearded Three head for the Mare Tranquillitatis Palace for some relaxation.

3. There's a Low Moon Caught in Your Tangles (6 min., 26 sec.). Selene follows Mina to the Mare to tell her that it is no coincidence that she befriended the Bearded Three as they have a destiny to fulfill.

4. Head Full of Doubt (9 min., 57 sec.). Mina

struggles to comprehend what Selene has told her while at the same time deal with her own personal problems.

5. Will You Make a Grave? (9 min., 14 sec.). As the prophecy begins to come true, zombies begin rising from their graves.

6. I Will Be Home Then (8 min., 12 sec.). Mina learns that the Bearded Three have a connection with the moon.

7. Time Won't Let Me Go (9 min., 15 sec.). A time rift opens a doorway where Art's future self is propelled into this world.

8. Every Time You Close Your Eyes (7 min., 20 sec.). With zombies on the rise and the earth in turmoil, tension erupts between the Bearded Three.

9. Nine Crimes (7 min., 32 sec.). Hoping to resolve their differences, the Bearded Three spend time away from each other, but their personal problems still confront them.

10. Intervention (11 min., 7 sec.). As the situation worsens, it is learned through Selene that the Bearded Three, who had the power to stop the moon from falling out of the sky, did nothing to prevent it from happening.

249 Osiris. osiristheseries.com. 2011–2012 (Science Fiction).

Osiris is a most unusual man. He is over 300 years old and can never die. He can be killed but he returns to life in exactly 37 minutes each time—and each time the process causes excruciating pain. Is his ability a gift? A power? Or is he a freak of Nature? Whatever the reason, his many deaths and rebirths have made him uncaring for others. He is a womanizer and treats everyone like dirt because he fears any long term relationships or friendships. One person, however, knows his secret—his great, great granddaughter Paula, who is also the only person who can keep him in check. Osiris works as a private detective and stories follow his case investigations and efforts to hopefully find out how and why he possesses eternal life. It is revealed that at one point in his life Osiris (who takes his name from the ancient Roman god) worked as a scientist with a man named Wexler—a man who, in the presented story line, wants to capture "his old friend" and dissect him to find out why he is who he is.

Cast: Brad James (Osiris), Nicky Buggs (Paula Castleberry), Stephen Caudill (Gregory Barnes), Aaron Simmons (Vaughn), Rico Ball (Oscar Michaels), Anthony Zhang (Daniel Kim), Erica Page (Nicky), Kermit Rolison (Wexler). **Credits:** *Producer:* Sy Hudson, Rodney Breedlove, Redd Caliborne, Donnie Leapheart, LaQuanda Plantt. *Writer-Director:* Donnie Leapheart. **Comment:** While not a totally original idea (the 1970 television series *The Immortal* immediately comes to mind), the series is presented well with good acting and production values.

Episodes:

1. My Name is Osiris (8 min., 31 sec.). Establishes a case wherein Osiris teams with the FBI to solve a case involving a serial killer that may also be linked to a brilliant but deranged scientist who is seeking to perfect a device to drain energy from one person to another.

2. Even I'm Impressed (8 min., 26 sec). Shows how Osiris, killed in the prior episode during the investigation, returns to life.

3. I'm Not Some Superhero (7 min., 46 sec.). A witness to one of the serial killings (a housekeeper) becomes the killer's next victim.

4. You Think She Likes Older Guys? (9 min., 22 sec.). After finding the body of the housekeeper stuffed in a car trunk, Orsiris vows to find her killer.

5. I Am Not a God (12 min., 46 sec.). Osiris finds himself alone during an investigation when his tracking devise fails.

6. I Don't Need a Warrant (9 min., 2 sec.). As Osiris continues his probe into the killings he learns that Wexler has sent agents out to abduct him.

7. Everyone I've Ever Known Is Dead (6 min., 57 sec.). With Paula by his side, Osiris laments on how his life has changed over the years.

8. You Are Safe Now (7 min., 31 sec.). Unknown to Osiris, Wexler's men have him and Paula in their sights.

9. You're Still Stuck No Matter What (10 min., 35 sec.). Osiris and Paula are captured and brought to Wexler.

10. Transference (14 min., 2 sec.). Wexler begins the transference experiment with Osiris as the subject. It looks as if Wexler has succeeded until Osiris begins to absorb all the energy in the room—including that of Paula. As Wexler's men explode from the experience, Osiris is gaining power—but can he save Paula? The program ends in a cliffhanger.

250 Out of Time. outoftimeseries.info. 2012–2013 (Science Fiction).

Chris Allman is a man who is able to return to the past (by jumping). The Sosumi Company has perfected a chip that, when implanted in the brain, enables him to return to the past. The actual effects of time travel have not been researched and Dr. Marianna Sheppard believes that the effects of jumping through time could eventually kill Chris. Chris's jumps are monitored by Dr. Osborn and his assistant, Samantha, and life changes for Chris when his girlfriend, Sara is murdered and he begins returning to the past to stop Sara's death from occurring. Each trip brings Chris one step closer to Marianna's theory—but it also brings Chris one step closer to achieving his goal. Stories follow Chris as he attempts to alter events in the past to save the life of Sara in the present.

Cast: Steve Kasan (Chris Allman), Katie MacTavish (Samantha Park), Robert Nolan (Dr. Harold

Osborn), James Dalzell (Philip Anders), David Dalzell (Hugo), Shailene Garnett (Alice Winters), Dulcie Felix (Dr. Marianna Sheppard), Catalina Yue (Angie Liu), Julia MacPherson (Sara), April Miranda (Kari Chang). **Credits:** *Producer:* Rodney V. Smith, Dulce Felix. *Director:* Rodney V. Smith, Shailene Garnett, Mike Donis, Jonathan Robbins. *Writer:* Erin Gould, Steve Kasan, Rodney V. Smith. **Comment:** Interesting, well constructed take on time travel (even though this concept dates back to shows like *Quantum Leap*). The acting is good although comprehending the time travel aspects are presented in a manner that can become confusing at times.

Episodes:

1. The Accidental Time Traveler, Part 1. Establishes the storyline as Chris begins his jumps into the past.

2. The Accidental Time Traveler, Part 2. Although Chris knows he is being monitored by Dr. Osborn and Samantha, he also becomes aware that Sosumi agents (dressed in black) are also appearing where he appears. His jumping has also caused him to blackout.

3. Transmissions from the Future. As Chris's implant begins to malfunction, he needs to return to the past within his 5-minute, 55-second window in time and find Kari, the doctor who can repair it.

4. Stop Loss. Chris, having blacked out from his last jump, is unaware what has happened and finds an ally in Angie, who is willing to help him.

5. Fall of Innocence. Samantha attempts to retrieve Chris by shutting down his implant.

6. Safe. As Chris believes he has the key to changing the past to save Sara, he begins to distrust Angie (as an agent for Sosumi) while Samantha initiates the MK Protocol to bring Chris back to Sosumi.

251 *Overturn*. overturnseries.com. 2011 (Science Fiction).

Christopher Gabriel is a young man with an undiagnosed condition wherein he suffers from continual nightmares. One night Christopher is awakened by a strange man who tells him that his nightmares have been artificially created and that he is special. Like magic, Christopher is transported to an unknown place where a multi-national group of people seem to know everything about him. He is suddenly subjected to a number of experiments that are meant to uncover the mystery that surrounds him. During one such experiment, conducted by Lisha, a Nigerian telepath and hypnotist, it is learned that Christopher was once Gavriil, a citizen of 19th century St. Petersburg, who experienced the same condition. As the experiments continue, Christopher meets Maria, the Russian head of the group and learns that his nightmares are the key to unlocking his special abilities, abilities that are destined to be used in a war of good against evil, the evil being the Servant, representative of a mysterious supernatural phenomenon called the Source, which thrives on submissive arrogance. At first Christopher is unsure of what is happening and what he should do: live in his present reality, regardless of its deceptive appearance, or follow what destiny has intended for him. Choosing the later, Christopher begins his training, developing the powers of his mind, body and spirit through intellectual cognition, hypnosis and the martial arts. The program follows Christopher as he prepares for the greatest challenge of his life: defeating the Servant in an invisible war that involves all of humanity without its awareness.

Cast: John Deryl (Christopher Gabriel), Maria Glazunova (Maria Baturina), Philippa Peter (Lisha), Bill Konstantinidis (William Higgins), Paolo

Overturn. John Deryl and Maria Glazunova in their roles as Christopher and Maria (copyright Deryl & Mellow Productions).

Nicosia (Fabrizio Conti), Alexander Galius (The Chaser), Konstantin Gerasimuk (The Servant). **Credits:** *Producer:* John Deryl, Mary Mellow, Eric Ross Gilliatt. *Writer-Director:* John Deryl. **Comment:** Intriguing concept that is played out in too short a time. The acting is good and the production flows smoothly with a suggestion that Christopher will end his nightmares and face the Servant. A feature film, *Overturn: Awakening of the Warrior*, has been produced based on the series.
Episodes:
1. Overturn, Part 1 (5 min., 17 sec.). Actually the first half of the pilot film that introduces Christopher as he makes a You Tube video describing himself.
2. Overturn, Part 2 (3 min., 5 sec.). Explores Christopher's first days as he comes to realize what he has to become.

252 *Pale Force.* funnyordie.com. 2005–2008 (Fantasy).

Web spin off from a series of animated skits that aired on the NBC television series *Late Night with Conan O'Brien.* Show host Conan O'Brien and his side kick, Jim Gaffigan are a team of super heroes that battle evil with the power of paleness. Jim is the tall, muscular super hero while Conan is the wimpy, scrawny and always needing Jim's help to accomplish something side kick. Although mismatched and possessing the power of paleness, the duo believes they are saviors and episodes depict their comical efforts to battle evil villains.
Voice Cast: Jim Gaffigan (Conan/Jim), Eartha Kitt (Lady Bronze). **Credits:** *Producer:* Jim Gaffigan, Paul Noth. *Director:* Paul Noth. *Writer:* Jim Gaffigan, Patrick Noth, Paul Noth. **Comment:** Well produced and amusing fantasy that pokes fun at a network and the celebrities associated with it.
Episodes:
1. Meet Pale Force, Parts 1 and 2. After foiling a diamond robbery (by shining their chests and blinding the thieves with their whiteness), Conan is captured by the villainous Lady Bronze. The second half of the story finds Jim attempting to save Conan from his captor.
2. Pale Force Begins, Parts 1 and 2. Recalls how Conan joined The League of Pale and became a member of Pale Force (it started when he was bullied as a kid and Jim came to his rescue, teaching him how to use paleness as a weapon).
3. Pale Impostor, Parts 1 and 2. The evil Philip Seymour Hoffman, always having to live in Jim's shadow, seeks revenge by impersonating Jim and doing "dastardly" things in his name.
4. Sidekicks, Parts 1 and 2. Feeling inferior as a side kick after Jim's face is added to Mount Rushmore, Conan seeks help from the Side Kick Support Program in the hope of receiving equal treatment.
5. Miss Massachusetts, Parts 1 and 2. Believe it

or not, Lindsay Lohan, Clay Aiken and Scarlett Johansson were once pale stars who have become famous by gaining a tan. Jim theorizes that it has something to do with the Miss Pale America Beauty Pageant (wherein they were all contestants) and sends Conan in drag as a contestant to find out.
6. Charlie Rose. Jim and Conan are interviewed by Charlie Rose (on his PBS talk show) only to learn that their arch enemy, Lady Bronze, hates only pale people and that they should not pursue her as she does work to help non-pale children.
7. Conan and the King, Parts 1 and 2. While cleaning their hideout, the Shade Cave, Conan discovers the time machine Jim created for future crime fighting. Although told not to touch it, Conan does, is transported back to England in the year 1665 and becomes what he has always wanted—flamboyant and the center of attention.
8. Conan in Love, Parts 1 and 2. Unknown to Conan, the on-line romance he has started with a woman is none other than the evil Lady Bronze.
9. Pale Christmas, Parts 1 and 2. With the holidays arriving and Conan being mocked for his paleness, Conan wishes he were never pale and a parody of the movie *It's a Wonderful Life* begins as Conan sees what the world would be like if he had a tan.
10. Pale Force: The Movie. Parts 1, 2 and 3. A movie starring the pale duo could change Conan's outlook and make him the real hero he always wanted to be.
11. Law and Order: Pale Force, Parts 1, 2 and 3. A *Law and Order*s poof featuring the team of Jim and Conan.
12. The Cliffhanger. As Jim parties in a hot tub, a stray, inflatable beach ball taps Conan on the head and causes severe trauma. Medical tests reveal that he is in a deep coma and, due to his paleness, may never wake up. Doctors also see that the incident caused complete muscle failure and retardation ("We have never seen anyone this weak and this untalented recover"). It appears that the only way Conan can survive is for the real Conan O'Brien to fund additional episodes so that paleness can awaken the animated Conan and bring him back to the wimp he will always be.
13. Carnival Conan, Parts 1, and 3. Jim tries to find a missing Conan when he learns that NBC's president abandoned him at a carnival when it was discovered that Conan has no audience appeal and the network needed to rid themselves of him.

253 *Pandora's Blog.* webserieschannel.com. 2011 (Fantasy).

After viewing a horror movie called *Shadow Fear*, a very pretty 16-year-old high school girl (Pandora) receives the ability to see the unearthly creatures that inhabit the dark. Not knowing how or why such a thing happened, Pandora accepts it but soon realizes that the Shadow Creatures (as she calls them) can also see her and she must become a savior to protect innocent people whose lives are threatened by such creatures. Through Pandora's video blog, stories of her encounters with the Shadow Creatures are presented with Pandora explaining what has happened as opposed to a play in which such encounters are performed.

Cast: Alix Maria Taulbee (Pandora). **Credits:** *Producer:* Richard Hays, Steve Hendrick, John Josephs, John Kemper. *Writer-Director:* Richard Hays. **Comment:** Although Pandora is the only person seen, she is so endearing that she makes the program work. Normally this type of program suffers from becoming overly boring. But that is not the case here. The story is well constructed and just enough is given in each episode to make the viewer want to hear what happens next. It is a clean-cut show (no nudity or foul language) and could make it as a cable program with the use of flashback sequences as Pandora talks about what happened.

Episodes:

1. Pandora's Blog 1 (2 min., 40 sec.). Introduces Pandora as she explains how she went from a normal teenage girl to a girl who could see unearthly creatures.

2. Pandora's Blog 2 (3 min., 40 sec.). Pandora attempts to contact "The Prince of the Paranormal," a man who has the same abilities as her.

3. Pandora's Blog 3 (3 min., 52 sec.). Pandora, approached by a Shadow Creature, is asked to deliver a book on witchcraft to a drug user named Jenwan.

4. Pandora's Blog 4 (4 min., 40 sec.). Pandora delivers the book as ordered, but now the Shadow Creature wants her to help Jenwan cast a spell; the problem: Jenwan has disappeared and Pandora has no idea where to find her.

5. Pandora Blog 5 (3 min., 52 sec.). Pandora explains that if she can't find Jenwan, the Shadow Creature has threatened to cut her tongue out. Nervous, Pandora begins a search to find her.

6. Pandora's Blog 6 (3 min.). Pandora, finding Jenwan, must now help her place a curse on the owner of a club as instructed by the Shadow Creature.

254 *ParaAbnormal.* paraabnormal.tv. 2009 (Horror).

Motel rooms that kill guests? Ghostly images caught on sex tapes? To anyone this would seem just a hoax, but to Ken Livingston, a self-proclaimed supernatural investigator, these are not stories, but real and with his assistants sets out to investigate such reports and uncover the truth. Ken and his team (Wendy, Bunky, Tony) operate from his grandmother's garage and consider themselves ParaAbnormal.

Cast: Ken Livingston, Alexander "Bunky" Hunt, Joe Schmidt. Tony Kryczeskiwica, Wendy Donigan. **Credits:** *Producer:* Demetrea Triantafillides. *Direc-*

tor: Jamie Nash, Eduardo Sanchez. *Writer:* Jamie Nash. **Comment:** While a take off on the numerous ghost hunting programs on cable television, it is an amateurishly produced and acted comical variation that presents stories that would be seen nowhere else.

Episodes:

1. Case 1, Part 1 (3 min., 59 sec.). Reports of a ghost caught on a sex tape brings the team to the home of the occurrence.

2. Case 1, Part 2 (3 min., 51 sec.). The tape is no hoax as there appears to be something unnatural about it.

3. Case 1, Part 3 (3 min., 43 sec.). As the team investigates, they uncover signs that spirits are stalking them.

4. Case 1, Part 4 (3 min., 9 sec.). Wendy encounters a poltergeist while Joe appears to have angered a spirit.

5. Case 1, Part 5 (3 min., 22 sec.). The team uncovers evidence that a ghost was actually caught on the sex tape and must now seek a way to help it move on.

6. Case 1, Part 6 (2 min., 56 sec.). With the angry spirits reluctant to leave, Ken conducts an "Ambush Exorcism" in an attempt to rid the home of its evil spirits.

7. Case 2, Part 1 (3 min., 5 sec.). Barely escaping with their lives from the haunted sex tape caper, the team turns their attention to a motel room that kills its occupants.

8. Case 2, Part 2 (2 min., 54 sec.). At the motel, the team meets its creepy owner, Norm Norman, and learn that the haunted ground-floor room has attempted to kill 32 people.

9. Case 2, Part 3 (3 min., 22 sec.). Wendy has an uneasy feeling about the hotel—not aware that it may be coming from Norm—who, like Norman Bates in Alfred Hitchcock's *Pyscho* had a "thing" for Janet Leigh.

10. Case 2, Part 4 (3 min., 23 sec.). As Norm tries to seduce Wendy, Ken begins his investigation of the haunted room.

11. Case 2, Part 5 (3 min., 4 sec.). As the team uncovers evidence that something is not right, Tony uses his contraption, a sensory depravation device "to see dead people."

12. Case 2, Part 6 (3 min., 32 sec.). With shades of the movie *Psycho* the team uncovers the mystery of the haunted room.

13. Case 3, Part 1 (4 min., 30 sec.). Again after just escaping with their lives, the team braves another case—that of strange occurrences at the Baltimore City Morgue.

14. Case 3, Part 2 (4 min., 12 sec.). The morgue attendant, Phunkfaise, guides the team through the creepy morgue.

15. Case 3, Part 3 (3 min., 38 sec.). Something is not right at the morgue as the team soon discovers.

16. Case 3, Part 4 (2 min., 27 sec.). Tony attempts to discover what paranormal activity haunts the

morgue by activating his "communicate with the dead device."

17. Case 3, Part 5 (3 min., 55 sec.). Something definitely evil is present and Tony continues hoping his "High Tech Ghost Communication" devise will give them the answers.

18. Case 3, Part 6 (4 min., 39 sec.). Seeing that Tony is accomplishing nothing, Bunky believes that rational thinking is the only way to solve the case and rid the building of its spirits.

19. Case 4, Part 1 (7 min., 22 sec.). A Succubus feeding on patrons at a bed and breakfast becomes the team's next case.

20. Case 4, Part 2. At the bed and breakfast the team learns that several guests have not only seen but become the victims of what appears to be an insatiable Succubus.

21. Case 4, Part 3 (4 min., 53 sec.). The team begins its investigation.

22. Case 4, Part 4 (7 min., 57 sec.). The concluding episode wherein the team solves the case but its future is uncertain as the pay is small and the risks too great.

255 *Passenger.* passengershow.com. 2011 (Fantasy).

Michael, a demoted Archangel has been sentenced to duty on earth as God's "Hit Man." He still retains his immortality but to regain his salvation and return to his former status, he must find and terminate shape shifting demons (Passengers) that seek the souls of humans. As Michael carries out his assignments, the program presents an underlying theme as to whether Michael's orders are coming from God or something else wherein he is a tool in a celestial conspiracy of spiritual warfare. **Cast:** Al Galvez (Michael), Cassandra Jean (Sarah/Zoon), Eric Frentzel (Burly), Braxton Davis (Bucky). **Credits:** *Producer-Writer-Director:* Al Galvez. **Comment:** Rather slow-moving story with good acting and production values but no real interest to watch even the first episode, not alone five more. **Episodes:**

1. Episode 1. Establishes the somewhat murky storyline as Michael begins his mission at a seemingly desolate bar.

2. Episode 2. At the bar, Michael meets a seductive girl (Sarah) who immediately becomes drawn to him.

3. Episode 3. The girl, actually the Cherub Zoon, is Michael's superior and presents him with his orders: kill a man called "The Slayer."

4. Episode 4. Michael discovers that the bar owner, Burly, is the slayer—a demonically possessed man and plots to carry out his assignment.

5. Episode 5. The assignment is completed (although not without complications when Burly's associate Bucky must also be dealt with) and Michael returns to his wandering.

6. Episode 6. Michael's next assignment: terminate a rock star (Billy Pain) who, Michael soon discovers may not be the enemy, but angelic ally (the cliff-hanging episode concludes the series).

256 *Pete Winning and the Pirates.* youtube.com. 2013 (Science Fiction).

An Internet continuation of the 2011 short film of the same title. It is the year 2029 and global warming and an ensuing world war has caused massive flooding that not only turned the seas radioactive, but covered most of the world in water. To survive, some land dwellers, like Pete Winning, have turned to ships and become pirates; others have rented and live on radiation-free land—land that is under the reign of a self-proclaimed Queen. The program follows one such pirate, Pete Winning, as he and his crew uncover a legend and begin a search for three supposed maps that hold the key to a new world. **Cast:** Mike Donis (Pete Winning), Saffron Cassaday (Eva), Terry He (Victor), Robert Nolan (Remy), Sandra DaCosta (Jane), Shawn Devlin (Finch), Dani Barker (Carmen), Shane Dovey (Steubing). **Credits:** *Producer-Writer-Director:* Mike Donis. **Comment:** Meant to be styled after the swashbuckling feature films of Errol Flynn but falls quite short of that claim. The main characters do dress as pirates (Eva is especially eye-catching in her pirate attire) and production values are good. **Episodes:**

1. The New Swashbuckling Adventures. Establishes the storyline as pirate crews are formed by surviving humans following the great flood of 2029.

2. The Pursuit of a Pathfinder. Pete and his crew, feeling that being sea dwellers excludes them from paying taxes, find themselves being held hostage by the Queen's tax collectors when they dock on royal territory.

3. An Intriguing Proposition. Pete and his crew begin their quest to find the Queen's maps which hold the key to a new land.

4. A Leaky Endeavor. Pete and his crew, having obtained two of the map pieces, set sail for The East for the elusive third piece—unaware that they are being tailed by a motley group of pirates seeking the same map.

257 *Pieces.* minglemediatv.com. 2012 (Science Fiction).

One morning while showering, a man (Jacob Clarke) slips and hits his head. He awakens in a hospital with the good news being that there is no extensive cranial damage but they have discovered a cancerous tumor. What the doctors do not detect is an after effect that occurs—Jacob's ability to hear a voice that only he can hear. Jacob, however, believes the voice is just a side effect of the medication he is taking until it does not go away and Jacob now believes it may be more than just the medication or his disease, but the voice of God. The voice begins directing Jacob's life (telling him what to do) and, as Jacob obeys, the program charts what happens as he comes to the aid of people in trouble.

Cast: Dylann Bobei (Jacob Clarke), Amber Plante (Claire Jermaine), Jesse Laing (Det. Max Edwards), Trevor Kristjanson (Det. Carter McNeil). **Credits:** *Producer-Director-Writer:* Dylann Bobei. **Comment:** While the program is fast-paced, the acting is a bit amateurish (especially with Claire) and the writing and directing okay. The program does establish a supernatural mystery, but it really doesn't explain or resolve the origins of the voice.

Episodes:

1. The Voice (12 min., 7 sec.). Establishes the storyline with Jacob acquiring the mysterious voice that only he can hear.

2. The Truth (12 min., 30 sec.). When the voice instructs Jacob to help a girl who is being chased by a man (possibly a rapist), Jacob intervenes and saves the girl (Claire) by killing the culprit.

3. Witness/Protection (12 min., 37 sec.). Jacob kidnaps Claire to protect himself (as she is the only witness) while police detectives Edwards and McNeil begin an investigation into the killing.

4. The Visit (11 min., 40 sec.). The detectives search brings them closer to discovering that Jacob is the killer.

5. Request (10 min., 58 sec.). Jacob allows Claire to leave after she promises not to reveal what happened.

6. The Choice (11 min., 40 sec.). The voice instructs Jacob to find Claire and reconnect with her as she is the only person who can clear his name.

7. R.I.P. (14 min., 49 sec.). The voice tells Jacob that Claire's life is in danger and that he must rescue her to save his own life.

258 *Pink Five.* pinkfive.com. 2002–2006 (Science Fiction).

Three-part spoof of the *Star Wars* series of motion pictures that focuses on a Jedi pilot named Stacey (code name Pink Five). The Rebel Alliance's destruction of the Death Star made Luke Skywalker a hero throughout the galaxy. But there were other untrained pilots that risked their lives in that epic battle. Pink Five (a.k.a. Stacey) was one of them. She fought bravely and assisted Yoda; even the evil Darth Vader was amazed by her abilities. It was Yoda who told her, "A Jedi you will be. Save the Galaxy you will." With her Valley Girl accent, her pink squadron wings, pink space ship exhaust, pink necklace and pink belt, Stacey risks her life to battle the evils of the universe.

Cast: Amy Earhart (Stacey/Pink Five), Stephen Stanton (Obi-Wan Kenobi/The Emperor), Vince Sanchez, Chris Hanel (Han Solo), Cherise Bangs, Ara Roselant, Christy Marie (Princess Leia), Mar-

kika Piday (Lyn Me), Brendon Ewers, Chris Hanel (Darth Vader), George Manley (Darth Vader's voice), Eric Moody (C-3PO), Tom Kane (Voice of C-3PO), Shawn Sullivan (Chewbacca), Robert Lee (Imperial Officer). **Credits:** *Producer:* Christopher Reed. *Director:* Trey Stokes. *Writer:* Trey Stokes. Based on characters created by George Lucas. **Comment:** Although only three episodes were produced, each is visually attractive and very well acted. Each also captures the flavor of the original *Star Wars* films and will please any fan (even non-fans) of the saga.

Episodes:

1. Episode 1: Pink Five. Begins the saga with Stacey serving on Tatooine in the court of Jabba the Hutt. Life changes for her when she fails in an effort to save Hans Solo (being outdone by Princess Leia) and abandons the Alliance Rebels to forget her love for Han. She travels to the second Death Star where she aligns herself with the evil Darth Vader (but the uniforms made her look "hippy") and later abandons them.

2. Episode 2: Pink Five Strikes Back. Stacey enlists the help of C-3PO, R2-D2 and the Ewoks in another effort to save Han Solo but abandons it when she hears Han profess his love for Princess Leia. She then encounters the ghost of Yoda and is told that the Rebel Alliance is in danger as a second shield exists around the Death Star reactor and she must return to the Death Star to deactivate it.

3. Episode 3: The Return of Pink Five. Picks up where the prior episode left off with Stacey's further adventures in the Star Wars universe.

259 *Pioneer One.* youtube.com. 2010–2011 (Science Fiction).

Without warning, a spaceship enters the earth's atmosphere, spreads radiation across Montana, veers off and crash lands in Canada. U.S. Homeland Security, suspecting it was an act of terrorism, dispatch agents to the crash site where they discover that the object they are seeking, a spaceship, is of Russian origin and to their amazement, there is a survivor, a young man they call Yuri. As the crash site is put under quarantine and the supposed alien placed under protective custody, the mystery to solve what happens begins. Episodes relate what happens when Yuri is discovered to be the child of two Soviet astronauts sent on a secretive Mars exploration mission during the 1980s and of the standoff that ensues when information leaks out and the Russians demand the return of their citizen and spaceship.

Cast: James Rich (Tom Taylor), Alexandra Blatt (Sofie Larson), Jack Haley (Dr. Zachary Walzer), Aleksandr Evtushenko (Yuri), Einar Gunn (Secretary McClellan). **Credits:** *Producer-Writer:* Josh Bernhard. *Writer:* Josh Bernhard, Bracey Smith. *Director:* Bracey Smith. **Comment:** Although it is a speculative series, suggesting what could happen when a human is born in space and returned to earth, it is well done and intriguing. Some scenes are overly talkative and there is little in the way of special effects but it is thought-provoking enough for die-hard sci fi fans.

Episodes:

1. Earthfall. Establishes the storyline as an object from space becomes the concern of both Canada and the United States.

2. The Man from Mars. An expert on space flights (Dr. Zachary Walzer) is consulted regarding the debris—and passenger found at the crash site.

3. Alone in the Night. The passenger is brought to the Calgary base for questioning but doctors are having a difficult time communicating with him.

4. Triangular Diplomacy. As the media gets wind of the space craft, the State Department tries to keep the situation under control as the language barrier has been broken and the passenger (Yuri) is now capable of communicating.

5. Sea Change. Tom Taylor, the man in charge of Yuri's security (who is in quarantine) confronts a Russian source that claims Yuri is a citizen of his country.

6. War of the World. A media conference reveals the truth about Yuri and what happened during the 1980s.

260 PIT: The Paranormal Investigative Team. freewebs.com. 2010 (Horror).

Big Yellow is a diner on Pico Boulevard in Los Angeles. It was founded by Art Mack and "The" Deuce Moran. By day they serve food, by night they become ghost hunters and investigate paranormal occurrences in and around Southern California. They are assisted by Pam Duberry, a research specialist; Lear Levin, a tech wizard, and investigator Clark Dunwoody.

Cast: Art Mack, Pam Duberry, Lear Levin, Clark Dunwoody (Themselves). **Credits:** Not given. **Comment:** Syfy channel *Ghost Hunters* rip off that offers investigations that are more comical than serious. Enjoyable but not to be taken seriously as the PIT team sets out to debunk supposed unnatural occurrences.

Episodes:

1. Grant Me Asylum/Stapler Me Death. The PIT team investigates reports of ghosts at a mental asylum and a stapler factory.

2. Dead and Breakfast. The team investigates reports of unusual happenings at the Meridian Bed and Breakfast.

3. Ghostus Interruptus. The Meridian (from the prior episode) presents more challenges than expected when evidence appears to support a real ghost.

4. No, Not the Robot. The team continues their investigation of the Meridian B&B.

5. You Know What They Say: Bigfoot. A reported attack by a Bigfoot in the central California forest captures the attention of PIT.

6. Something Approaches ... It Looks Blonde. The team's investigation of the Bigfoot incident continues—with a Bigfoot in sight.

7. Pheromones Gone Wild. The Bigfoot investigation continues with the team seeking a way to capture the Bigfoot, who appears to enjoy taunting the team.

8. Unzipped. The series finale with the PIT team also concluding their Bigfoot investigation.

261 Playing Dead. youtube.com. 2008 (Science Fiction).

Grace is a 32-year-old actress who is down on her luck. She has bills to pay but no job offers. One day, while on her computer, she receives an e-mail chain letter that states if you forward it to 15 people within five minutes, a wish will be granted. Grace wishes for an acting job then forwards the e-mail. Seconds later there is a knock at her door—and it is Death, dressed in black, who has come to grant her wish with a job offer—assisting him in escorting people into eternity. Needing the job and feeling it will be an easy gig, Grace accepts. Stories follow Grace as she begins her job as the assistant to Death (to allow him to take some much-need time off).

Cast: Suzanne Keilly (Grace Bass), Noel Orput (Death), Kristen Roberts (Mona, Grace's friend). **Credits:** *Producer:* Ted Raimi, Kurt Rauf. *Director:* Ted Raimi. *Writer:* Suzanne Keilly. **Comment:** Suzanne Keilly is delightful as Grace in a nice comedy-horror mix that moves right along. The acting is good and the program itself is well produced with an ending that leaves the doorway open for more episodes.

Episodes:

1. Curtains (3 min., 43 sec.). Establishes the story as Grace receives a visit from Death.

2. Dead End Job (3 min., 5 sec.). Death just happened to be in the neighborhood when Grace made her wish. It caught his attention and she is offered the job.

3. Rots the Matter (3 min., 29 sec.). Grace makes her first mistake—telling her best friend what has happened (as telling will cause that person's death).

4. Dead in the Water (5 min., 14 sec.). Grace appears at a children's birthday party to claim the clown entertainer (who will drown in the pool).

5. Death with a Side of Sickles (4 min., 37 sec.). Grace tries to audition for an acting job before she claims the producer.

6. You Oughta Be in Coffins (4 min., 9 sec.). Death becomes upset when Grace tries to get acting lessons from the clown whose life she previously took.

7. The Totally Dead Show (5 min., 59 sec.). Fearing Grace will screw up, Death gives her a tool to bring back to life anyone she accidentally touches.

8. That Girl's a Reaper (5 min., 32 sec.). Pleased with how well Grace is progressing, Death offers to keep her on permanently if she wants the job.

262 Possum Death Spree. youtube.com. 2007 (Horror).

Scientists, attached to the U.S. Research Station 37-5X in Kuntishna, Alaska, uncover evidence that, during the prehistoric age, killer possums roamed the earth and were in part responsible for the demise of the dinosaur. More startling than that is their discovery of frozen possums in a glacier. Unfortunately, their discovery comes on the hottest day of summer and melts the glacier containing the possums. While the possums appear to be harmless, the scientists soon discover they are anything but as they attack anything that moves. The program follows the scientists efforts to destroy a new enemy when the ravenous possums attack—and appear virtually indestructible.

Cast: Gareth Smith, Michael Horowitz. **Credits:** *Producer-Writer-Director:* Gareth Smith, Michael Horowitz. **Comment:** Horror (extreme amounts of violence, blood and gore) mixes with comedy (plush animal possums whose conversations are seen in view-able dialogue) in a very fast moving program that would appeal to a wider audience if the violence and blood were kept to a minimum. As it stands now, it has no parental warning (for violence) and is viewable by anyone, even children. The program itself contains no information regarding the cast.

Episodes:

1. Episode 1. Establishes the story as the possums awake from their deep slumber.

2. Episode 2. After a deadly first attack in which two of their team are killed, the remaining scientists prepare for a second wave of attacks.

3. Episode 3. The final battle as the scientists try to figure out a way to kill their carnivorous predators.

263 Posthuman. whatisameme.com. 2010 (Science Fiction).

Charlie Porter, a detective with the Capital City Police Department, is now a man obsessed with only one thing: bring down the Memes, a powerful and elusive subculture that is believed to be an evolved hybrid of human and machine. The Memes are destroying the city and threatening any future peace and happiness. Charlie's obsession, plus his growing inability to retain his sanity, makes him a department outcast—a man whose actions are disavowed by the police (he is eventually dismissed from the force when it learned Gina, who is considered a terrorist for leading a rebellion against the city, is friends with Charlie). The program follows Charlie as he struggles to gain a sense of reality and pursue his obsession to uncover the mystery of the Memes.

Gina, once a seamstress now leads a rebellion against the powerful that run Capitol City, hoping her actions will bring relief to those of the lower class societies. Dorothy Ascher is a scientist who created the medical nano-robots that revolutionized the medical industry (and most likely created the Memes). She mysteriously vanished shortly after and many believe she was killed; others praise her as a hero and a cult, the Ascherists, believe that she will one day return to save all humanity. Gibson is a man whose loyalties lie with anyone who is willing to pay his price. He once operated as Charlie's informant is resourceful and well connected with the underground of the city.

Cast: Jason Martorino (Charlie Porter), Sara Mitich (Gina), Joanna Haughton (Dorothy Ascher), Will van der Zyl (Gibson), Roger Kell (John Wilson), Amanda Phillips (Ricky Reynolds). **Credits:** *Producer-Writer-Director:* Lyndon Horsfall. **Comment:** The overall plot is nothing new (a loner seeking to uncover a mystery and save something) but its presentation here is a bit intriguing as Charlie seeks to fulfill a mission. Production values and acting are typical of an Internet series.

Episodes:

1. Strain Theory (4 min., 33 sec.). Charlie receives his first case from a mysterious woman who appears to know more about him than she is letting on.

2. Strange Bedfellows (6 min., 43 sec.). Charlie seeks out an old friend for help in his investigation.

3. The Past: Promises Reckoned (6 min., 1 sec.). A flashback to Charlie's days as an officer with SWAT (Special Weapons and Tactics) and his meeting with the girl (Gina) who may become the love of his life.

4. Kiss & Tell (3 min., 37 sec.). Charlie trails a man (Gibson) whose actions have aroused his suspicions.

5. Recidivist (7 min., 5 sec.). Gina feels that her memory is playing tricks on her when she tries to figure out what past events actually happened as opposed to those she remembers as happening.

6. Arrested Developments (7 min., 45 sec.). The concluding episode finds Charlie being captured and about to be interrogated by someone he knows—his former boss.

264 Pretty Undead. youtube.com. 2012 (Horror).

Spring Valley appears to be a normal American town. It is home to four best friends (Alice, Jess, Amber and Taylor), teenagers who attend Spring Valley High School. But all is not normal as the friends know that a series of bizarre killings can be attributed to zombies but no one will believe them. It all began when Taylor and her boyfriend, Jason, returning home after seeing a movie, were attacked by a zombie. Taylor managed to escape, but was disbelieved by police when she reported what killed Jason (authorities believe it was a homicidal maniac on the loose). But Taylor's friends believe her and start a blog to tell their story when they begin their own investigation to find Jason's killer. Stories follow the girls (the "pretty" of the title) as they risk their

lives to stop the killings and prove that zombies are responsible. **Cast:** Thais Vieira, Savannah Reinitzer, Cassidy Alla, Irene Tarshi, Savannah Lee, Mike McGongel, Brooke Lavoia, Colleen King, Sierra Reinitzer. **Credits:** *Producer-Director-Writer:* Seng Varipath. **Comment:** No doubt meant to attract a teenage audience (although the four girlfriends are pretty enough to attract any age group) as stories focus mostly on the girls and how they try to resolve adult problems—without help from adults. The acting is exceptionally good and the writing and direction just as good.
Episodes:
1. Episode 1 (24 min., 23 sec.). Introduces the four friends and establishes the story as Taylor and Jason are attacked by a zombie.
2. Episode 2 (9 min., 59 sec.). While patrolling, the girls come to the rescue of a teenage girl being pursued by a zombie—but Taylor finds herself unable to kill it when she faces it.
3. Episode 3 (7 min., 26 sec.). Although not shown, the girls have apparently disposed of prior zombies with the exception of Taylor. At Alice's insisting, Taylor kills her first zombie.
4. Episode 4 (5 min., 11 sec.). The girls learn that they are now the targets of the zombies.
5. Episode 5 (8 min., 35 sec.). The girls devise a plan to discover where the zombies are coming from and stake out the local graveyard. The wait is not long as they are spotted by zombies who are now closing in on them. The program ends in a cliffhanger.

265 Project Breakwater. webserieschannel. com. 2011 (Science Fiction).

It is June 23, 2010, a seemingly normal day. But at 1:41 p.m. Eastern Standard Time, a magnitude 5.0 earthquake strikes Ontario, Canada. During this same time frame, a section of downtown Toronto was blocked to allow high-ranking government officials to attend a G20 Summit. One week later, at 6:45 p.m., Eastern Standard Time, a massive power outage struck Toronto but lasted only one hour. The events however appear to be random, or are they? Unknown to all but a chosen few, an outer space alien (The Entity) has arrived on Earth.

Several months later the death of prominent journalist (Sandra Templeton) arouses the curiosity of police detective Benoit Michaud whose investigation begins to uncover more than just a normal suicide. He uncovers evidence that she had a stalker, a man who underwent secret military training. Was Sandra getting too close to uncovering something? The program follows Michaud's probe of Sarah's past (discovering she was working on an expose of G20) and his efforts to continue where she left off and expose a conspiracy by shadowy forces that can apparently control events (like the earthquake and the power outages).

Cast: Matthew Devon Hemans (Benoit Michaud), Sarah Cody (Sandra Templeton), Luke Marty (Det. Jansen), Robert Nolan (The Informant), Allan Turner (The Entity), David Staruss (Harlan Maguire). **Credits:** *Producer-Writer-Director:* Brian Clement. **Comment:** Although only two episodes have been released, the program shows promise as being an intriguing science fiction mystery. The writing, acting and directing are fine but with the last episode airing in 2011, future episodes do not look promising.
Episodes:
1. Chapter 1 (11 min., 18 sec.). Detective Michaud begins his investigation following Sandra's suicide.
2. Chapter 2 (8 min., 25 sec.). As Michaud investigates, he notices a similarity between Sandra's death and a case he investigated several weeks before.
The Prologues:
1. Reactivation (2 min., 53 sec.). In Toronto, Canada during the winter of 2009, two agents discuss taking into custody the person they require to begin The Project.
2. Debriefing (2 min., 53 sec.). It is June 27, 2010 and immediately following the G20 conference, several members are debriefed on events that occurred within the secured area.
3. Probe Telemetry (2 min., 8 sec.). It is July 5, 2010 and Dr. Richard Kershaw launches an inter-dimensional robotic probe after activating the quantum interflow drive of the recently captured vessel.
4. Special Report on G20 Fences (1 min., 12 sec.). Sarah Cody portrays reporter Sandra Templeton as a fake news report is released as a tie-in to *Project Breakwater.*
5. Suspicion (5 min., 47 sec.). Detective Benoit Michaud becomes frustrated when a meeting he arranged with a contact with mysterious predictions about a monumental crime fails to appear.

266 Project S.E.R.A. youtube.com. 2013 (Science Fiction).

In 2004 S.E.R.A. (Simpson Eames Regeneration Agenda) was formed to develop a drug for the military to expedite a soldier's recovery and enable him to return to the battlefield. In its first incarnation (2009), labeled SERA-130, the drug was distributed to the military and had a sixty-five percent success rate. Soldiers were redeployed to the front in record time, but for the government that wasn't fast enough. Research continued and a more powerful version resulted, SERA-131, which in 2010, proved to be one hundred percent affective. Without warning, and under mysterious circumstances, S.E.R.A. was shut down and all sources of 131 were ordered destroyed—or so it was thought. A short time later it was discovered that samples of 131 were being sold on the black market. Now, concerned that what could result from the use of 131, the government assigns Gillian Eames, daughter of the project founder, and Lieutenant Riggins on a secretive mission to stop the sale of the highly volatile biological drug before its potential could be used for something more sinister.

Gillian Eames is the daughter of the founder of Project S.E.R.A. After her mother's murder, when Gillian was a child, her father, a decorated General, trained her in hand-to-hand combat and how to handle guns. While she did not enter the military, she secured a job as a mapping specialist for the U.S. government.

Lieutenant Riggins (no first name given) is a decorated former SEAL (with Team 6) and served under Gillian's father, General Dennis Eames. During the Iraq War he lost his left arm in a roadside bombing and was awarded the Silver Star. After his return home, he became a test subject for S.E.R.A. and was able to re-grow his missing arm.

Cast: Julia Voth (Gillian Eames), Derek Theler (Lt. Riggins), Victor Webster (Bryan), Thomas Arana (Corvallis), Dennis Keiffer (Gen. Eames), Jacob Zachar (Adam), John Rubinstein (Gen. Simpson), Dimitri Diatchenko (Zakir). **Credits:** *Producer:* Ben Howeshell, Travis Milloy, Hayden Roush. *Director:* Ben Howeshell. *Writer:* Ben Howeshell, Bill Kirchen, Nathan Miller. **Comment:** Well done, fast-moving story with good acting, writing and directing. The story could have been concluded as all the twists and turns were already revealed.

Episodes:

1. Episode 1 (7 min., 50 sec.). Establishes the story line as Project S.E.R.A. is explained.

2. Episode 2 (9 min., 24 sec.). Gillian and Riggins face off in a violent confrontation from those seeking the formula.

3. Episode 3 (8 min., 56 sec.). An attempt to frame Gillian, by claiming she killed her father, Dr. Dennis Eames, the creator of S.E.R.A., succeeds as Gillian, without an alibi, finds herself on the run.

4. Episode 4 (9 min., 11 sec.). Gillian confronts the man (William Simpson) who worked with her father and learns that her father went beyond the original plans and enhanced the formula to a point where it became too dangerous to continue.

5. Episode 5 (9 min., 18 sec.). Gillian finds her father's notes regarding S.E.R.A. and, with Riggins help, decides to destroy the plant where the formula originated.

6. Episode 6 (9 min., 42 sec.). Gillian and Riggins are captured by the men seeking to secure the formula (to sell it to a foreign power) before they can destroy the plant. In a cliff-hanging conclusion, Gillian and Riggins escape capture—but now they are not sure who they can trust.

267 *Project X.* youtube.com. 2007–2008 (Science Fiction).

In November of 2004 an explosion destroyed the Mt. Diablo power plant. *Project X*, subtitled "The True Story of Power Plant 67," relates a fictional account of what caused the disaster: an unknown creature that thrives on power. Drawn to the plant, the creature breached security and, in its efforts to replenish itself through electricity, trapped a group of workers inside the plant. The workers are safe at first but become the prey when the creature discovers their presence. Serial-like stories follow the workers, in particular night manager David Scott, as they seek to out wit the creature and escape.

Cast: Jamie Hobert (David Scott), Christina Rosenberg (Claire Hamilton), Bart Shattuck (Steve Jackson), Kalimba Bennett (Emily Knight), John Mellies (Cameron Bate), Kevin English (Ian Weaver), Adriano Aragon (Dr. Parks), Kyle Vogt (Agent Harris), Kevin Rock (Agent Flint). **Credits:** *Producer-Director:* Joshua Sikora. *Writer:* Joshua Sikora, Clint Cullum. **Comment:** Even without seeing the program and just reading the episode descriptions, three movies will come to mind: *Alien, The Thing* and *It! The Terror from Beyond Space* all of which dealt with people trapped in a small place by an unknown creature. *Project X* is well acted with good writing and directing and does present a fast-moving program of survival.

Episodes:

1. The Arrival. The program begins following the explosion with government agents finding one lone survivor—David Scott.

2. Running Late. Flashbacks are used to recount the incidents leading up to the disaster with David recalling what happened at Power Plant 67.

3. Insubordinates. Introduces some of the night shift crew—Emily, Cameron, Steve and Ian.

4. Thunderstorm. The first indication that something is wrong begins when the phones malfunction.

5. Overqualified. When Marshall, sent to investigate the problem, fails to return, David and his crew (Steve, Cameron and Stanley) begin a search for him.

6. In the Dark. The crew is attacked in the power distribution room by something they can't identify.

7. Dead End. Although Stanley is injured in the encounter, the team manages to make it to safety.

8. Comic Book Logic. A power systems check reveals a power drainage that David believes was caused by what they encountered.

9. Run Like Hell. A plan is devised to call for outside help—but that means getting past the creature.

10. Following Orders. A flashback reveals that David had confronted his father, a plant supervisor, about discrepancies he noticed at the plant.

11. Shutdown. A plan is devised—shut down the power plant and thus depriving the creature of energy.

12. Repercussions. The shutdown fails putting the crew is imminent danger.

13. Lost Love. With the creature apparently becoming stronger and more aggressive, the crew ways their options.

14. When We Die. Fear is spreading among the crew as they have few options and apparently no chance to acquire outside help.

15. Powerless. With the team becoming increasingly passive, Emily tries to instill the fact that there is hope if they all work together.

16. Face Off. Emily's words appear to help as a second plan is devised to escape.

17. Descent. The plan fails as Steve, attempting to evade the creature and get to the outside, is caught by the creature.

18. Shadow of Death. Steve is rescued, but only clinging to life.

19. Broken. With the creature gaining the upper hand, the team begins to realize that none of them may live to see the morning.

20. Facing the Truth. David must deal with his insecurities, his biggest being his failure to act when he first realized the problem (from episode 10) to better be able to lead the crew.

21. Plan of Action. Overcoming his doubts, David theorizes that if they can trap the creature and blow it up, they can destroy it and save themselves.

22. Requiem. The plan is put into action—but does not go as expected as Claire finds herself trapped alone in the control room.

23. High Voltage. Claire holds the key to the solution—but it means sacrificing her life if she ignites the explosion.

24. Out of the Ashes. Opens where the first episode began with the agents finding David as the lone survivor.

268 Quantum Shock. webserieschannel. com. 2012 (Science Fiction).

Quantum Shock is a process that endows ordinary people with extraordinary abilities (strength, stamina and ability to see into the future). Colt Stahl is one such subject, a Super Soldier of the future (a special ops agent). He is also the only person who has been able to survive the process for any length of time and is also being sought by military officials who want him (as Colt has chosen to live free and is on the run). But Colt is also in a time without time— a side effect of the Quantum Shock procedure. When the side effect becomes full blown, Colt finds himself in a strange dream-like world where he encounters a being that is the culmination of all consciousness. The being is the ocean and Colt a drop. The being desires that Colt accept him (enter his body) so that through him, he can set things right and achieve revenge against those who use Quantum Shock for profit and not caring what results.

Cast: Anselm Meyer (Colt Stahl), Tracey Roath (Rebecca Conway), Ben Gerbrecht (Josh Thomson), Ralph Haenel (Conrad Matheus), Rhonda Hem-

street (Bianca Hawthorne), Rick Lee (James Darren), David Mackenzie-Kong (Garret Tyram). Credits: Producer-Writer: Anselm Meyer. Director: Dave Campbell. Comment: Borrowing ideas from the television series *The Immortal* (1970; a man sought for his unusual blood) and *The Six Million Dollar Man* (1973) evolves *Quantum Shock*, a rather long web series if you watch episodes back-to-back. The story is well constructed and produced and those with the time a patience to sit through such a long production will not be disappointed.

Episodes:

1. Hollow Hope (16 min., 50 sec.). Introduces Colt Stahl as a man whose past is gradually driving him insane as he struggles to cope with his new life and abilities.

2. Empty Justice (19 min., 1 sec.). While Colt uses his abilities to help society, he is also sought for his blood (to create an army of super soldiers) and now knows he is worth more dead than alive.

3. Dark Origin (19 min., 14 sec.). Explores the evolution of Colt Stahl.

4. Bitter End (22 min., 58 sec.). As the Quantum Shock overload continues, Colt finds himself struggling to accept what he has now become.

5. Fall from Grave (21 min., 37 sec.). The concluding episode reveals aspects of Colt's life before he became a Quantum Shock subject and how he must now accept what he has become.

269 Rainbow Falls. rainbowfallstv.com. 2013 (Horror).

Rainbow Falls appears to be a typical American town. But beneath the surface lies a word that outsiders have not seen—a world of strange phenomena and horrific tales. Episodes, which have a *Dark Shadows*–like series air about them, relate incidents in the lives of the people who live and work in Rainbow Falls, a place from which there also appears to be no escape.

Cast: Sarah Thrash (Katie), Grace Patterson (Tori Springfield), Montanya Pierre (Myrtle), Larry Jack Dotson (Sheriff Omar Dally), Roni Hummel (Molly), Kolt Atchley (Calvin), Brandon Pentecost (Aaron), Ashley Zamora (Lisa), Emma Lou Cunningham, Vandi Clark, Scarlette Martin, Bryan Quinn, JuliAnna Briscoe, Caden Large, Sarah Thrash, Mark Edward Howell. Credits: Producer: Danilk Rosales. Director: Ike Duncan. Writer: Wayo Benaviees. Comment: While the *Dark Shadows* aspect is conceivable, it is difficult to be certain from what has been released. The acting is good but the production values a bit questionable as the presented scenes are rather badly lit (just too dark). The story appears to be good and it could develop into a good horror-suspense program if that is what the producers have in mind.

Episodes:

1. The Sitter (14 min., 48 sec.). Establishes the

storyline as Katie joins the Hass household as their babysitter.

Note: Four trailers have also been released:

1. Trailer 1 (26 sec.). Briefly shows Katie becoming a "member" of the Hass family.

2. Teaser for Rainbow Falls (1 min., 7 sec.). Introduces the characters of Tori and Lisa.

3. Trailer 3 (46 sec.). A quick overview of the townspeople.

4. Sneak Peak at Rainbow Falls (2 min., 11 sec.). Introduces the characters of Myrtle and Calvin.

270 RCVR. youtube.com. 2011 (Science Fiction).

Sigma is a government agency that investigates reports of UFO sightings. RCVR (pronounced receiver) is a term for humans selected by extraterrestrials to act as channels for advanced technologies (such as major scientific breakthroughs to nuclear power; they also hold the key to time travel and limitless energy). Sandy Bergson and Luke Weber are Sigma agents who investigate such cases with the intent being to cover up what actually happened. The program follows their investigation of one such case—that involving a young boy's (Tommy) claims that he witnessed a UFO landing.

Cast: Catherine Kresge (Sandy Bergson), Daniel Bonjour (Luke Weber), Lexi DeBenedetto (Charlene), Jacob Hopkins (Bobby), Garrett Ryan (Tommy), Kathleen M. Darcy (Mrs. Crosby). **Credits:** *Producer:* Taylor Clyne, Jennifer Levine. *Director:* David van Eyssen. *Writer:* Brian Horiuchi, David van Eyssen. **Comment:** Well acted and intriguing case investigation program. The writing and production values (special effects) are good and the episodes just the right length so as not to become a chore to watch in succession.

Episodes:

1. Little Green Men (11 min., 45 sec). Establishes the series story line as a report of a UFO incident in rural Arkansas arouses the agency's suspicions.

2. Birdfall (11 min., 7 sec.). In Arkansas, Weber meets with the boy (Tommy) who claims to have witnessed something very unusual.

3. Dry Weather (10 min., 50 sec.). As Weber and Sandy question Tommy, other team members begin their investigation of the crash site.

4. Mission Failure (9 min., 13 sec.). Weber tries to convince Tommy that what he saw was nothing out of the ordinary, but Tommy refuses to listen and is insistent that an alien landed.

5. DCVR (10 min., 14 sec.). In a final attempt to convince Tommy otherwise, Weber and Sandy walk Tommy and his family through the manufactured remains of a horrific plane crash. Tommy refuses to budge on his story of what he saw.

6. The Chosen (9 min., 22 sec.). The concluding episode finds Weber wrapping up the case and about to begin a new one.

271 The Real Zombie Hunters of America. realzombiehunters.com. 2013 (Horror).

"There are real zombies in the world and there are real zombie hunters. These are their stories" claims the opening to a program that profiles Robert Daily, a modern-day zombie hunter as he goes about destroying zombies that are becoming an increasingly dangerous part of society.

Cast: Richard McGonagle (Robert Daily), Jennifer Norkin (Nellie Robinson), Joe Desoto (Interview Zombie), David Schwartz (Det. O'Malley), Joe Desoto (Zombie Woman on Street), Michael J. McDonough (Michael), Nancy McDonough (Nancy). **Credits:** *Producer-Writer-Director:* Michael J. McDonough. **Comment:** Enjoyable take on zombie hunters with a likable lead and well written and directed episodes. The situations are played comically as Robert has the best intentions, but their executions rarely work out as expected.

Episodes:

1. Interview with a Zombie (4 min., 56 sec.). Robert presents what he believes to be a television first—an interview with a real zombie and his interpreter, Nellie Robinson.

2. 4-D Zombies (5 min., 44 sec.). News of a new breed of zombies brings Robert to a small town where he encounters fourth dimensional zombies— zombies who travel between dimensions to strike and eat without being seen.

3. Human Bait (5 min., 20 sec.). Faced with a serious problem Robert theorizes that to catch the 4-D zombies he must set up an elaborate trap.

4. Revenge of the Zombies (5 min., 55 sec.). A married couple volunteer to be the bait to catch the 4-D zombies.

5. Zombies Aloha (5 min., 15 sec.). The trap fails, the couple become zombies and Robert is left to ponder what to do next. The concluding, cliff-hanging episode.

272 Red Scare. redscare.tv. 2013 (Horror).

The small town of Plainview, Connecticut, in 1956 is the setting. During the East-West basketball game at West Plainview High School, an air raid siren sounds, forcing several students and a security guard to take refuge in the school's fallout shelter. Is it an air raid drill or has Russia, then the Red Menace, attacked the U.S.? A waiting game plays out with unexpected consequences—one member of the group is a vampire. But who? Unable to go outside the shelter due to what may be nuclear fallout (had a war occurred) the group must determine who the vampire is as it has already killed the security guard and needs the blood of the others to survive.

Audrey is the senior cheerleader at West Plainview High School. She is not only beautiful but smart and involves herself in many extra curricular activities (she is also the dream girl of many of the male students). Johnny is the school's star basketball player who has dated fellow student Audrey and is seeking to attend college on a basketball scholarship. Judy is the beatnik, a girl who loves jazz and considers herself a self-imposed outcast. Lois, a junior, is the prim and proper, intensely religious girl. She is set in her ways and has profound dislike of communists, heathens or people she simply does not like. Gert is a foreign exchange student (from Romania) who has been raised a Communist but has quickly adapted to the American way of life. Irene is a cheerleader with a fast-girl reputation who manipulates others into doing what she wants. Vivienne personifies the June Cleaver (from *Leave It to Beaver*) housewife look of the 1950s. She is always cheerful and believes cookies and hot cocoa can solve any problem. Dino is the Fonzie-like (from *Happy Days*) greaser who acts tough and likes girls and fast cars. Huey, a freshman, is Irene's brother and the classic nerd who loves comic books and is prepared for a potential Communist attack.

Cast: Brianne Howey (Audrey Stone), Chelsea Alden (Irene Miller), Kevin Joy (Johnny Clemens), Heather Howe (Vivienne Lee), Jordan Stavola (Dino DiGiulio), Ellington Ratliff (Huey Miller), Teresa Decher (Judy Graves), Brittany Ross (Lois Henrickson), Nathaniel Weiss (Gert Bumbescu), Dominic Conti (Officer Hover). **Credits:** *Producer:* Sam Roberts, Tom Keenan, Steven Roberts, Meg Roberts, Dorothy Roberts. *Writer:* Sam Roberts, Tom Keenan. *Director:* Lee Citron. **Comment:** Well acted, produced, written and directed program. Although the production is limited to the one shelter set, everything is so well choreographed that the set becomes secondary and attention is focused totally on discovering who the vampire is and who will exit victorious. Each of the characters also captures the feel of the 1950s, especially Vivienne.

Episodes:

1. The Nuclear Club (8 min., 18 sec.). An air raid warning forces ten strangers to lock themselves in a fallout shelter when they believe Russia may have attacked the U.S.

2. Mark of the Vampire (8 min., 38 sec.). The killing of the security guard brings to light the fact that one of their group is a vampire.

3. Auf Wiederser'n, Sweetheart (8 min., 35 sec.). As fear and tension mounts, each begins accusing the other as being the vampire.

4. Brinksmanship (7 min., 13 sec.). With three victims, the latest being Irene, suspicion begins to fall on Audrey, who appears to get jealous when any of the other girls get close to Johnny, the boy she loves.

5. Kill a Commie for Mommie (6 min., 6 sec.). Suspicion diverts from Audrey to Dino—who was born in Romania and that he is the vampire.

6. Fallout (7 min., 54 sec.). As Audrey becomes the next victim, the remaining survivors attempt to put their distrust of each other aside and come up with a plan to expose the vampire.

7. Vault of Horrors (7 min., 56 sec.). Vivienne,

becoming the next victim, leaves only Judy, Johnny and Dino. Believing that Dino is the vampire, Johnny and Judy overpower him and, for safety, place him in the freezer with the bodies of the victims.

8. Mutually Assured Destruction (6 min., 3 sec.). Thinking they are safe, Judy and Johnny find they are not as Audrey, who faked her death, is the vampire who now seeks to kill Judy so she can have Johnny for herself.

273 *Redwood*. blip.tv. 2012 (Fantasy).

In an attempt to save his sister (Skylar) who is dying of leukemia, a vampire hunter (Sonny) arranges for a transfusion using the blood of a vampire. The blood cures Skylar but an allergic reaction transforms her into a vampire. Legend states that blood from a different vampire line can cure the affliction but if the wrong blood type is chosen, the subject will die. As Skylar slowly begins to adopt the attributes of a vampire, she feels she cannot accept it and the only way out is to end her life. Before she is able to do so, Max, a young vampire with morals (refuses to drink human or animal blood) saves her by offering her his blood. As the vampire affliction slowly begins to reverse itself, Skylar finds herself becoming attracted to Max—a situation that becomes increasingly dangerous as his exposure could also mean his death if Sonny should uncover Skylar's secret. While Sonny may be a vampire hunter, he also appears to be in a relationship with one—Ana, a centuries-old, evil vampire. While she is aging and yearns to live the way she did 100 years ago, she has now abandoned all her ethics and believes the world is hers to enjoy as she pleases. But she is also bored, exhausted and apparently showing signs of madness. Four people—two humans and two vampires—and their efforts to hang onto their lives, their sanity and their sense of identity.

Cast: Alisha Peats (Skylar Jones), Rane Jameson (Max Sandoval), Joey Kloberdanz (Sonny Jones), Jasmine Hester (Ana), Alli Miller (Harper), Jeff Torres (Xander), Laura Soares (Vera), Mark Berry (Dr. Raja). **Credits:** *Producer-Writer:* Alisha Peats. *Director:* Michael Willer. **Comment:** A simplistic yet effective storyline coupled with good acting (especially Alisha Peats as Skylar) and production qualities that make the program better than many of the Hollywood produced vampire-themed stories.

Episodes:

1. As I Lay Dying (11 min., 25 sec.). After suffering an allergic reaction to a vampire blood transfusion, Skylar retreats to a cabin in the Redwood forest and meets the man destined to save her (Max).

2. The Wicked Within (6 min., 48 sec.). Skylar's sudden recovery arouses Sonny's suspicions that a vampire is responsible.

3. Out of This Darkness (10 min., 13 sec.). Sonny begins probing the situation, intent on uncovering the truth behind Skylar's reversal.

4. First Blood (9 min., 2 sec). As Skylar's cure progresses, she finds that to survive, she must drink blood.

5. Past Is Prologue (8 min., 23 sec.). When Sonny discovers that Max is a vampire, Skylar places her life on the line to save him.

6. This Midnight Madness (12 min., 9 sec.). Sonny spares Max's life, realizing that he is Skylar's only chance for survival; Skylar leans the truth about Ana, Sonny's girlfriend.

274 *Residenz.* redharvestpictures.com. 2013 (Science Fiction).

In an unspecified time, an apocalypse has changed the course of life on earth. Survivors have established a new world (Anthill) below ground and an artificial intelligence called Sequence 1 controls all vital systems, including life support, communications and law enforcement. As the program begins the citizens of Anthill face a crisis when a mysterious virus affects Sequence 1 and threatens to destroy the city's life support system. At this point, and with each episode that is scheduled to follow, the viewer becomes part of the story. Numerous alternative scenes have been filmed that determine how the story should continue. The viewer is given a choice of options for the cast to take. Once a selection is made the corresponding video continues the story from that point thus each episode's progress will be different for each viewer. The concept is based on the 1980s series of books called *Choose Your Own Adventure* wherein, at certain points in the story, the reader was offered a choice of actions to take as the story unfolded. *Residenz* is an experiment in interactive Internet television programming and could pave the way for future series to follow the same format.

Cast: Zara Durrani (Connie), Shaun Andrews (Mr. Haik), Benjamin Hanson (Jules), Evans Johnson (Grace), Kristian Messere (Simon), David Milchard (Keaton), Brendan Riggs (Alex), Julia Sarah Stone (Beverly), Victoria Vice (Natalee), Wrem Walker (Jennifer), John Samaha (Travis). **Credits:** *Producer:* Batteo Saradini, Barbara Gregusova, Ricjard Metzker. *Director:* Matteo Saradini. *Writer:* Domenico Cutrupi, Matteo Saradini. **Comment:** Based on what little is available, the program does show promise as a new wave of programming. The production values are above normal but, with numerous alternative scenes to film and coordinating additional scenarios with the established storyline could make for a confusing situation for producers and viewers alike as serial-like stories will have numerous twists and turns based on what the viewer selects.

Episodes: Thus far only two trailers have been released that establishes the storyline and how the series will progress:

1. Trailer 1: Residenz Official Trailer #1 (2 min., 24 sec.).

2. Trailer 2: Thora and Keaton (2 min., 5 sec.).

275 *The Resistance.* theresistanceseries. com. 2010 (Science Fiction).

Aurordeca is a futuristic world that has been devastated by a deadly plague. As the death toll rises, a brilliant chemist (Syrus Primoris) discovers a resistance drug (Noxe)—but it comes at a price. Those who seek the cure must grant Syrus absolute power over them. With Noxe being the only way to survive, virtually all of the remaining population succumbs to Syrus's wishes; those that defy Syrus and his regime have become known as A.R.M. (The Aurordeca Resistance Movement). Lana, a brave and courageous woman leads A.R.M. and stories follow her and her group's efforts to find an alternate cure and free the people from the iron-hand rule of Syrus.

Cast: Katrina Law (Lana), Sunny Jain (Arclite), Adrian Zaw (Syrus Primoris), Adam Gray-Hayward (Vince), Paul Statman (Vero Motalvo), Kendhal Beal (Circe), Rachel Hostetler (Eve), Vincent Guisetti (Horace), Ricardo Vargas (Bran), Danny Arroto (Cian). **Credits:** *Producer:* Eric Ro. *Director:* Adrian Picardi. *Writer:* Matt Ragghianti, Kevin F. Pietila. **Comment:** A well done series that combines a sexy heroine (Lana) with numerous action sequences. The sets and costumes add that final touch for an enjoyable medieval-like story of good attempting to triumph over evil.

Episodes:

1. Welcome to Aurordeca (5 min., 24 sec.). The evil dictator Syrus begins his conquest by offering his citizens their only hope for survival.

2. Drug Store Cowboys (2 min., 59 sec.). Lana and her resistance group begin their battle against Syrus.

3. Lost and Found (5 min., 55 sec.). A drifter (Arclite) joins Lana in her fight against Syrus.

4. Close Call (4 min., 43 sec.). As Lana seeks an alternate cure for the plague, Syrus steps up his battle to destroy all those who oppose him.

5. Lady Killers (4 min., 20 sec.). Syrus sees that Lana, who is willing to do anything to achieve her goal, is more of a threat to his regime than he previously thought.

6. Behind the Curtains (4 min., 21 sec.). Scientists working for Syrus discover a new formula and a possible cure for the plague.

7. Hide and Seek (4 min., 1 sec.). Arclite's desire to see action comes to fruition when Syrus attacks A.R.M.'s camp.

8. Revelations (4 min., 47 sec.). A final battle wages as Syrus and his troops battle Lana and the resistance.

276 *Rhyme Animal.* webserieschannel.com. 2010 (Horror).

Shiva is a rapper who dominates the freestyle hip scene in New York City. He is a rising star and has displaced Heaven, a now fading diva. The situation has ignited a war between the two to claim the top spot, but something unnatural has also entered the picture—a shadowy figure that appears to kill the people who are somehow connected with Heaven and the hip-hop community. As Shiva's reputation grows, his lyrics become disturbing, twisted and cannibalistic and it is learned that his philosophy is based on the religious virtues of destruction and consumption. When he hooks up with Judah (his paranoid DJ), life again begins to change when he scores a deal with Urban Scene Records. Stories relate the rivalry that exists between Shiva and Heaven and hint at the fact that Shiva may be the serial killer sought by the police—even though suspicion falls on Judah.

Cast: Al Thompson (DJ Judah), Craig Grant (Shiva), Bridget Barker (Heaven), E.C. LaRock (Rufus), Dani Marco (Erica), Jackie Reynolds (Rick), Stephen Lova (Daria). **Credits:** *Producer:* Jorge Rivera. *Director:* Phil Roc. *Writer:* Jorge Rivera, Aaron F. Schnore, Billy Fox. **Comment:** Although built around an unlikely premise of rap music, the program is fast paced and able to hold one's interest to see what happens next.

Episodes:
1. The Jump Off (Bum Rush, the Freak Show; 4 min., 45 sec.). The first killing occurs as Heaven's hype man, Jo Jo, is killed by an unknown entity during a stage show featuring Shiva and Heaven.
2. Speak of the Devil (3 min., 55 sec.). Judah begins to believe that a terrifying dream he had about Shiva being something other than he appears may actually be true.
3. Dreams Is Visions (4 min., 37 sec.). Judah is now convinced that Shiva is more than he pretends when Urban Scene Records suddenly expresses interest in signing them.
4. Idolatry of Flesh (4 min., 17 sec.). Judah's fears grow worse as Shiva reveals his philosophy of consumption and destruction during a radio show interview (are his lyrics just part of his act?).
5. A Taste of What's to Come (6 min., 3 sec.). Judah finds himself in a rock and a hard place when Heaven tempts him to join her team.
6. A Real Bad Bitch (4 min., 13 sec.). Heaven soon regrets lashing out at Judah for rejecting her offer when she begins to fear for her life (a mysterious figure begins stalking her).
7. We're All Consumers (3 min., 53 sec.). At a dinner party to celebrate their contract with Urban Scene Records, the bizarre string of murders is discussed—with all fingers pointing to Judah as the culprit. The story concludes unresolved.

277   *Riese: Kingdom Falling.* syfy.com. 2009 (Science Fiction).

Eleysia is futuristic kingdom plagued by dwindling resources. Anxiety and distrust have caused people to regress to a primitive state and rituals and mythology have begun to resurface with the darker side of mankind slowly beginning to reveal itself. Riese, the Crown Princess of Eleysia, is thrust into a new world when her family is slaughtered by the powering cult, the Sect, and she escapes into the wilds. She soon finds herself as a catalyst for a group of heretics called the Resistance and involved in a civil war against the Sect. Stories follow Riese as she risks her life to restore her kingdom to a time before the regression.

The Sect is a group of religious fanatics who worship the Goddess Sonne and believe the end of the world is coming. They have established itself as the official religion of Eleysia and believe the only way to salvation is to eliminate anyone who refuses to follow their leadership. They have chosen Amara, called "The Chosen One" as their Empress, but unknown to her, she is merely their puppet until their opposing force, The Resistance (who seeks to end the reign of the Sect) is destroyed.

Riese is the daughter of Empress Kara and King Ulric of the Kingdom of Eleysia. Fenrir is her wolf, a former royal bodyguard. Empress Amara, the cousin of the late queen, was a baroness who rose to her current position by joining the Sect and murdering members of the Royal Family. Herrick is a senior member in the Sect and the one assigned to capture Riese. Trennan is a Sect member and the liaison between the Sect and Empress Amara. Rand is the leader of the Resistance group opposing the Sect. Aliza is Rand's second-in-command. Garin is the tactical commander of the Resistance. Marlise is the manipulative, sadistic Sect member.

Cast: Christine Chatelain (Riese), Sharon Taylor (Empress Amara), Ben Cotton (Magister Herrick), Patrick Gilmore (Trennan), Ryan Robbins (Rand), Emilie Ullerup (Aliza), Alessandro Juliani (Garin), Allison Mack (Marlise), Amanda Tapping (Narrator). **Credits:** *Producer:* Galen Fletcher, Nicholas Humphries. *Director:* Kaleena Kiff, Nicholas Humphries. *Writer:* Ryan Copple, Kaleena Kiff, Miguel Valdez Lopez, Alyssa Ciccarelli. (Note: Kaleena Kiff is a former child star and appeared as a regular on the television series *Love, Sidney*). **Comment:** Fast moving story with good acting and production values.

Episodes:
1. Hunt (9 min., 44 sec.). In a battle with hunters from the Sect that were sent to capture her, Riese is wounded. She and her wolf, Fenrir escape and seek help in the village of Helmkin.
2. Bind (9 min., 6 sec.). While recovering at the hospital Riese discovers a secret ward that houses newborn babies. Meanwhile, the Empress assigns Herrick to track down Riese.
3. Fragments (9 min., 16 sec.). Riese's investigation uncovers evidence that the infants are to be transported to a new location.
4. Spares (8 min., 25 sec.). As Riese discovers documents that implicate the Sect to the infants, she escapes from the hospital.

5. Dawn (7 min., 27 sec,). Now safely out of the town, Riese begins tracking the infant shipments.

6. Prey (6 min., 22 sec.). In the town of Vidar, where the trail leads, Riese finds that there appear to be no signs of life.

7. Beast (9 min., 16 sec.). Riese uncovers evidence of a movement to raise infants as members of the Sect—some of which have become mutated in failed experiments.

8. Indoctrination (8 min., 25 sec.). The Sect becomes aware of Riese's probe and assigns their mutated creations to kill her.

9. Retribution (8 min., 17 sec.). Riese escapes her pursuers but learns that her brother is still alive and involved in a Sect plot.

10. Reunion (11 min., 18 sec.). Riese finds her life in peril when she is caught off guard by Herrick and his henchmen.

278 RoboGirl. blip.tv. 2011 (Science Fiction)

In the near future, after a devastating third world war, an alien virus, called The Host, invades the Earth. With fifteen percent of the human race now being affected by the alien parasite (wherein each affected person becomes host to a central brain wherein they act and think as one) scientists believe that the only way to stop the spread is to go back in time and prevent it from ever happening. A beautiful female android, called Huntress, is programmed with all known knowledge of the Host and sent back in time to 2008 to destroy the original Host probe and stop the spread before it begins. Huntress is beautiful and skilled as a fighter but her time jump (as it is called) does not go as planned. Her trajectory is off by three weeks and the Host has already begun to infect people (beginning with a scientist who heads Advance Genetics, a company that has the resources for the Host to propagate itself). With the original plan aborted, Huntress begins a mission to find the people infected by the Host and not only destroy them—but the original alien Host.

Cast: Elle Parker (Huntress), Peter Davis (Commander), Kinsey McCartor (Female Alien Host). **Credits:** *Producer-Director:* Ed Glaser. *Writer:* Ken Polliard. **Comment:** The type of program that could easily become a hit on broadcast or cable television. Has everything required—from a beautiful heroine, great production values, above-average acting and stories that are fast-moving and exciting. The special effects are television program quality and Elle Parker as Huntress is an eye catcher in her black shorts and bikini-like top.

Episodes:

1. Huntress (2 min., 48 sec.). Introduces Huntress and her jump back in time to 2008.

2. Ally (2 min., 22 sec.). Huntress discovers her mission is in jeopardy when she finds she arrived three weeks too late.

3. Seduction (2 min., 42 sec.). Huntress seduces the scientist first infected by the Host in an effort to learn its other victims.

4. Call Girl (2 min., 55 sec.). To destroy the second Host victim, a Las Vegas boxer, Huntress poses as a call girl to stop him the only way she can—by killing him.

5. Death Trap (2 min., 40 sec.). After defeating a third Host victim, the alien Host becomes aware that a human is becoming a threat to their plans to take over the Earth and plans to trap her.

6. Chained (2 min., 55 sec.). After picking off Host victims one by one, Huntress is captured by a Host agent and slowly tortured to find out whom she is and what she knows.

7. Darkness (3 min., 1 sec.). Discovering that Huntress is an android, the Alien Host attempts to reprogram her.

8. Sorority Girls (3 min., 49 sec.). When the reprogramming fails, thus allowing Huntress to escape, Huntress tracks the next Host agent to a girls college locker room where she encounters something she not seen before—a stronger opponent that almost gets the better of her.

9. Showdown (2 min., 15 sec.). Huntress tracks down the Alien Female Host and, in a battle to the death believes she has defeated it until it disposes of its human skin and appears as a green metal skeleton.

10. Naked Steel (2 min., 45 sec.). Huntress and the now Alien Host skeleton continue the battle with Huntress apparently destroying it with an energy blast. Huntress closes out the episode: "Its cycle broken, I remain the sole monument to the hell they created. Rest assured, it will never repeat—not while I live."

279 Route 666: America's Scariest Home Haunts. youtube.com. 2013 (Horror).

An investigative-like program that explores the "haunted house" and other "haunted location" tourist attractions.

Host: Danielle Harris. **Credits:** *Producer:* Bruce David Klein. **Comment:** An interesting presentation of Halloween-like tourist attractions across America with a behind-the-scene look at how they were created and why.

Episodes:

1. Camperlino's Frightmare. Actor's perform terrifying scenes from such films as *Halloween*, *The Ring* and *Nightmare on Elm Street*.

2. D.C. Cemetery. A look at a computer-run "haunted" cemetery designed to scare the living daylights out of tourists.

3. Mourning Manor. A trip to the Mourning Cemetery and Manor for a look at the props, blood and gore used to frighten tourists.

4. Hagan Haunted Mansion. A tourist site of the undead based on an ancient mortuary.

5. Reign of Terror. A haunted house designed to evoke all five senses.

6. Dead End Cemetery. A haunted site where all the "comforts" of an autopsy room is designed to attract tourists.

7. Rebel Yell Haunted House. Tourists are "treated" to decapitated heads, blood-soaked rooms and other haunted house "niceties."

8. Franklin Square Horror. What appears as an ordinary site turns frightening for tourists as they encounter madmen—one that even chases them with a chainsaw.

9. Mitchell Cemetery. Fog, ghosts and other eerie effects to attract visitors to a haunted cemetery.

10. Bates Haunt. A haunted house treat that incorporates projecting horror into a house.

11. Davis Graveyard. Light effects coupled with large sculptors that turn an ordinary home into a haunted one.

12. The Final Un-Resting Place. Zombies coupled with theatrical tricks and props treat tourists to the world of the undead.

13. Killer Clowns. An exploration of why clowns can be both fun—and terrifying.

14. Haunt on Williams Street. An elaborately decorated Halloween home featuring a skeleton wedding ceremony and real animal skulls.

15. Haunted Wolf Hollow. Horror with ghosts and comedy with two talking skeletons that deliver a series of jokes.

16. Nightmare on Maple Court. An elaborately decorated home that encompasses live actors portraying movie monsters.

17. Fore Galore. Movie magic is incorporated to give the spectator all the gore he or she wants.

18. Terror Tour. Especially themed rooms of horror to scare anyone by encompassing the art of not knowing what to expect next.

19. Haunt 31. Pop-up figures and a working guillotine (with a headless body that gushes blood when the guillotine blade falls) highlight the tourist attraction.

20. It's Alive! Actors, dressed in the things nightmares are made of, "welcome" guests.

21. Cauldron of Invention. A come-to-life Frankenstein and other cleverly conceived horror props for the discriminating tourist.

22. Graveside Manor. A backyard converted into a cemetery with a house just as creepy to attract tourists.

23. Torture Me. Instruments of pain and torture for the tourist seeking a different kind of horror.

24. Dreadnight Bay. A nautical haunt with zombie sailors, a shipwreck and nasty pirates.

25. Morbid Manor. An exorcist-inspired room coupled with decapitated doll heads that move and the horror film–like "creepy kid."

26. McKamey Manor. Blood and gore themed haunt designed to attract visitors.

27. Lowe Family Party. A haunted party that includes a naval battle, elaborate decorations and entertainment from a skeleton rock group.

28. Dr. Haunt's Chamber of Fear. Actors portray everything from a blood-soaked bride to killer clowns in an effort to scare visitors.

29. Robertson Family Cemetery. An elaborate live action show of ghouls designed to scare one and all.

30. Movie Mayhem. Incorporates fears presented in feature films to scare tourists.

31. Best of Home Haunts. A recap of the best moments from the program.

280 Rover's Hill. youtube.com. 2012 (Science Fiction).

In the small town of Rover's Hill, Texas, four teenagers (Blake, Ira, Leo and Lexi) suddenly develop special abilities: teleportation, telekinesis and clairvoyance. But how and most importantly why? Stories follow the teens as they seek to discover who they really are and why they have such impossible powers.

Cast: Kostas Pagoulatos (Blake Emerson), Larissa Dawn (Ira Miller), Julio Torres (Leo Velesquez), Laiken Thompson (Lexi Davenport), Brian Robinson (Holden), Brooke Livingston, Eric Weiss, Brendon Hernandez, Ronald Clemmons, Sonia Alcala, Suzann Thompson, Cody Daniels, Amber Higgins. **Credits:** *Producer-Writer-Director:* Charley Asonibe, Ruben S. Conner. **Comment:** The teens appear as ordinary kids and not made to look like they are special. There are twists and turns as the story progresses as the teens learn who and what they are. The acting and production values are good but there is an annoying background noise on some episodes that makes crucial parts of dialogue difficult to understand.

Episodes:

1. Who Are You? (8 min., 54 sec.). Seventeen-year-old Blake becomes the first teen to discover that he is different.

2. Not Who You Think (10 min., 35 sec.). Blake soon discovers that there are two other people like him (Leo and Ira).

3. Answers (9 min., 6 sec.). Blake and Leo begin their quest to find out who or what is responsible for the changes in their lives.

4. Witch Hunt (9 min., 51 sec.). Leo, Blake and Ira seek a mysterious girl (Lexi) who may be able to answer their questions about what has happened to them.

5. Recon (11 min., 17 sec.). Ira finds Lexi and as they talk, Ira learns that Lexi's deceased sister, Lizzie, shared the same phenomena.

6. Perspective, Part 1 (4 min., 14 sec.). With her abilities to tele-transport, Lexi attempts to go back in time 25 years when her sister was alive to find the answers each needs to solve the mystery.

7. Perspective, Part 2 (8 min., 19 sec.). Lexi talks

with Leo's father and learns that at the local college (A-W University) experiments on genetic mutation were conducted on the grandparents of Lexi, Ira, Blake and Leo. While they did not acquire any abilities, their grandchildren did (it skipped their parents' generation) and now they must learn to control what they have.

8. The New Formula (5 min., 4 sec.). It is also learned that if one of the select group should black out or fall into unconsciousness, their self-destructive abilities will be activated and they will die within a year.

9. Chances (12 min., 54 sec.). Ira, Lexi and Leo have been told of others from that original group of test subjects, totaling seven in all, but have yet to connect with them.

10. Truth Hides from Lies (4 min., 45 sec.). Leo, Ira and Blake feel uneasy as they try to come to terms with what has happened to them—and what will happen in the future.

11. Dissension (5 min., 50 sec.). Another teen—Holden, who appears to have greater powers, seeks out Ira, Leo, Lexi and Blake.

12. Seven, Part 1 (8 min., 37 sec.). Leo gathers Ira, Lexi and Blake for a meeting to discuss matters in the Dendromes (woods) when they are confronted by Holden.

13. Seven, Part 2 (6 min., 54 sec.). Holden reveals himself as being evil and his powers can activate the self-destruct system. He is the catalyst—and he has come to kill them. Concludes in a cliff hanger.

281 Run Invisible. runinvisible.com. 2012 (Science Fiction).

It is a time when Trackers, also called Chasers, are incorporated by a government organization called Department 71 to bring to justice Runners, people who defy authority (not wanting to be controlled by the government) and need to be stopped. One such Tracker is Peter Hale. Hale is aging and company officials feel that he is getting to old for the job and needs to be retired. Hale believes differently and the presented story follows Hale as he attempts to continue his job by proving he is a capable Tracker.

Cast: Rick Katz (Pete Hale), Cal Barnes (Zenders), Melissa Katz (Roberts), Jack Bornoff (Washington), Kelli Lessie (Tang), Nadia Lanfranconi (Grimes), Kyle Katz (Corchoran), Matt Feige (Shargrove), Ego Nwadim (Dr. Neimans), Jonathan Wesley (Garrett), Michael Rush (Cloud). **Credits:** *Producer-Writer-Director:* Rick Katz, Kyle Katz. **Comment:** Rather badly acted, poorly photographed and amateurishly written and directed. While the story idea is good its presentation suffers greatly.

Episodes:

1. Cloud (3 min., 5 sec.). After Hale fails in an attempt to capture a Runner called Cloud, the company psychologist, Dr. Neimens, believes he is getting to old to continue in his present capacity.

2. The Buffalo Still Roam (3 min., 2 sec.). Hale is assigned to capture the Runner Corchoran but must still report to Dr. Neimens for evaluation.

3. Vertigo (3 min., 7 sec.). After Hale encounters trouble tracking Corchoran in downtown Los Angeles, he is assigned an assistant Chaser, Roberts.

4. Freedom (3 min., 38 sec.). Hale and Roberts now join forces to track Corchoran.

5. Tang's for the Memories. The tracking problem takes a turn for the worse when Corchoran teams with two other runners and their leader—Tang.

6. Garrett's Ultimatum (3 min., 57 sec.). Hale's failure to bring in his assigned target nets a reprimand from Department 71 supervisor Garrett.

7. So You Wanna Be a Chaser (3 min., 38 sec.). Hale is ordered to return to his psychological evaluation while another Tracker captures a Runner, who is brought to Department 71.

8. Birds Fly Home (2 min., 58 sec.). A confrontation at Department 71 allows the captured Runner to escape—but he becomes suspicious when he is not chased.

9. Evaluation (8 min., 28 sec.). While the Runner's suspicions are correct (a ploy by Department 71 to secretly follow him to Tang) Hale's evaluation reveals that he is too old to continue as a Tracker and poses a threat to Department 71 if he is allowed to continue.

282 Sage the Mage. webserieschannel.com. 2013 (Fantasy).

Sage is an adorable eight-year-old girl who lives in Los Angeles. Sage is also a very special girl. She is a magician and, with her magic chicken bone (wand), she can bend the laws of nature and explore mystical realms. Sage is in the third grade and is known as Elementary Sage to her neighbor Simon, a galaxy-hopping Ultra Magician (Level 23) who has established a vacation home on Earth (or to his people, Planet MW6371). Simon is a member of the Arcane Order of the Great Sapphire Atom, an outer space society of magicians and has become sort of a mentor to Sage as he oversees her progression into a first-class magician. Sage, however, is very curious and constantly experiments with the abilities she already has, causing her numerous misadventures as she tries to undo the mischief she creates. Stories follow Sage as she works her way from Young Elementary Class Mage to an Ultra Magician like Simon.

Cast: Grace Goodell (Sage), Georgia Goodell (Rosemary), Milo Goodell (Parsley), Sean O'Donnell (Simon). **Credits:** *Producer-Writer-Director:* Sean O'Donnell. **Comment:** A program worthy of cable's Nickelodeon channel as it has qualities that match any of its programs. Grace Goodell is captivating as Sage and stories do not lack for humor or action. There are numerous, well executed special effects as Sage creates magic and stories are well constructed so as not to become tiresome. Network television producers could take some lessons on how to produce a quality program on a limited budget from *Sage*.

Episodes:

1. Sage Rocks (4 min., 57 sec.). Introduces viewers to the adorable, fun-loving Sage.

2. Parsley's Perplexation (5 min., 52 sec.). Parsley, Sage's brother (both named after cooking herbs) discovers Sage's secret.

3. Let It Snow ... Indeed! (6 min., 54 sec.). Yearning for a change in the weather, Sage attempts to make it snow—causing instead a blizzard.

4. Push Echo (6 min., 45 sec.). Rosemary, Simon's superior, arrives on Earth to check on Sage's progress.

5. Sage on the Evil English Ivy (7 min., 1 sec.). Sage creates an ivy vine nightmare when she experiments with a plant fertilizer.

6. Sage's Most Awesomest Ever Show (9 min., 21 sec.). Sage and Parsley join Simon for a vacation that turns into anything but relaxing.

7. Trick or Donut? (5 min., 9 sec.). Although it is not October, Sage creates havoc by creating a Halloween in March.

8. Out of the Frying Pan (6 min., 13 sec.). *Attack of the 50-Foot Woman* movie take-off with Sage creating chaos when she turns herself in a 50-foot girl and goes about exploring the city. Excellent special effects abound.

9. Into the Fire (6 min., 40 sec.). Actually a continuation of episode eight wherein Parsley and Rosemary experience Sage's developing magic—magic that she seems to have little control over.

283 *Saint Seiya Rebirth.* saintseiyaliveaction.com. 2011 (Fantasy).

Based on the Japanese animated series *Saint Seiya—Knights of the Zodiac* (which in turn is based on the comic *The Manga of Saint Seiya* and its concluding Hades chapter). The magna tells the story of an 18th century Holy War and of the battle between Tenma, one of the 88 Saints that worship the goddess Athena, and Alone, the reincarnation of the god Hades. The series begins with Hades, the Lord of the Underworld, being defeated by the Saints of Athena and the aftermath as survivors battle their own demons and regroup for future confrontations with Hades.

Cast: Carlo Trevisan (Shun), Rita Rusciano (June), Alessandro Bruzzesi (Seiya), Jonny Triviani (Ikki), Damiano Verocchi (Baal), Pierluigi Ferrero (Gigas), Carlo Gavazzi (Hades), Carlotta Gargiulo (Shaina), Alessando Chiovini (Aiolos), Lorenzo Farinalli (Dohko). **Credits:** *Producer:* Dream Factory Studio. *Director:* Carlo Trevisan. **Comment:** Produced by the Saint Seiya Live Action, a non-profit organization dedicated to Saint Seiya and the Knights of the Zodiac on the occasion of its 25th anniversary. The program is produced in Italy and has English subtitles. Its official English website is a combination of

the English and Italian languages with a heavier lean toward Italian. It is a bit of a chore watching the series as having to read the subtitles as the action unfolds can easily frustrate some people. Otherwise, it is well done with good acting and production values.

Episodes:

1. Shun Redemption (14 min., 43 sec.). The battle has taken its toll: Seiya, the leader, is in a coma and the warrior Shun is in a desperate search to find his beloved one, June.

2. Return from Hades (14 min., 23 sec.). As June is found, Seiya breaks free of his coma.

3. The Birth of a New Dragon (11 min., 8 sec.). Shiryu is training future warriors (Kiki and Shunrei) when an enemy (Cancer) makes an unexpected return.

4. Phoenix Destiny (21 min., 31 sec.). Shiryu wins the battle against Cancer and soon afterward discovers that he is going to be a father. At the grave of his beloved Esmeralda, the warrior Phoenix encounters the unexpected (as revealed in Chapter 5).

5. Mystery from Ice (9 min., 4 sec.). Phoenix battles the ghosts from his past, which gives him the strength to fight again.

284 *Sanctuary: The Web Series.* syfy.com. 2007 (Science Fiction).

Internet spin off from the television series *Sanctuary* that follows Dr. Helen Magnus, a 160-year-old British scientist who heads the Sanctuary Network, a mysterious organization that seeks Abnormals, non-human intelligent creatures, to help and learn from them. Her search, however, often leads to encounters with creatures far more dangerous and the web series delves into both such aspects (as can be seen by the episodes below).

Dr. Helen Magnus was born on August 27th, 1850. She is an Abnormal and has longevity and a heightened I.Q. She is the daughter of Gregory Magnus and Patricia Heathering and the mother of Ashley Magnus. She specializes in crypto-zoology and xenobiology and her eternal youth resulted from a vampire blood-based serum. John Druitt is the only man Helen has really ever loved. Helen discovered him to be the notorious Jack the Ripper but kept that secret (which caused her terrible pain); because of her feelings for John, she considered him the only man with whom she would have a child (a union that produced Ashley).

Cast: Amanda Tapping (Dr. Helen Magnus), Robin Dunne (Will Zimmerman), Emilie Ullerup (Ashley Magnus), Peter DeLuise (Ernie Watts), Christopher Heyerdahl (John Druitt). **Credits:** *Director:* Martin Wood. *Writer:* Damian Kindler, Martin Wood. **Comment:** Has all the attributes of the popular television series, including production, story and acting. A perfect companion series.

Episodes:

1. Webisode 1 (17 min., 6 sec.). In her search to find a new protégé, Helen crosses the path of Will Zimmerman, a psychiatric patient with amazing abilities.

2. Webisode 2 (16 min., 28 sec.). As Will becomes drawn into Helen's world, the search begins for a young boy with dangerous powers.

3. Webisode 3 (18 min., 8 sec.). The sought child, a mutant boy, is captured while Helen meets with her old flame (John Druitt) and Helen's daughter (Ashley), a demon hunter, seeks the help of demon hunter Ernie Watts in tracking a monster.

4. Webisode 4 (17 min., 27 sec.). Will must make a decision: return to his old life or join Helen in the world of Sanctuary.

5. Webisode 5 (17 min., 6 sec.). Ashley begins a search for answers to her father's existence; Helen and her team are confronted by deadly creatures as they investigate an ancient crypt.

6. Webisode 6 (16 min., 28 sec.). Helen and her team confront three mysterious women found inside the crypt.

7. Webisode 7 (18 min., 8 sec.). The three mysterious women weave their magic spell over Will while Helen seeks to unravel who or what they are (as they appear in a glowing light).

8. Webisode 8 (11 min., 36 sec.). In an unresolved finale, Ashley appears to have met her match when she encounters an unbeatable foe; and Helen and her team struggle to protect Sanctuary from a deadly attack.

285 *Satacracy 88.* youtube.com. 2006–2007 (Science Fiction).

In a mystical realm called Satacracy, an evil force attacks a community of peace dwellers. A young girl (Angela) becomes the only survivor when she is rescued by a leader of the Satacracy Army (mysterious protectors of the human race). Angela is raised as an avenger and taught to become an expert assassin. Angela, now grown, becomes Satacracy 88 (the 88th member of the Army) and must use her skills to save the earth from its destruction by destroying (assassinating) those humans that pose a threat. Episodes follow Angela as she struggles to live two lives—that of an assassin and that of a woman wanting to be a normal human being. **Cast:** Diahnna Nicole Baxter (Angela/Satacracy 88), Cassie Pappas (Susan/Satacracy 112), Andy Dugan (Satacracy Leader), Marc Cittadino (Calloway), Adrian Zaw (Arial Zim), Loyce Baxter (Lois), Max Ghezzi (Dr. Johnson), Marc Anthony Samuel (Martin). **Credits:** *Producer:* Diahnna Nicole Baxter, Brad Winderbaum, Andy Dugan. *Director:* Brad Winderbaum. *Writer:* Diahnna Nicole Baxter, Brad Winderbaum. **Comment:** Although the program concludes with "To be continued in *The Knights of a Hundred Sorrows*" this has not yet materialized. The program is well acted, written and directed but also a bit confusing at times to figure out what is hap-

pening (especially with the voice of the Satacracy Leader which is very difficult to understand [it takes rewinding several times to hopefully figure out what he is saying]; the closed captioning is of no use as it is very badly presented and makes no sense).

Episodes:

1. The Pill. Angela's life appears to be controlled by a pill that supplies her agility as well as control her bizarre and dangerous powers.

2. The Dagger. Angela has come to realize that she needs to break free of her addiction to the pill as it is causing her to rely on it for her very being.

3. The Mission. Angela and her assistant Susan are assigned a strange mission: acquire the mystical hand of Arial Zim, Angela's former partner.

4. Infiltrate. Angela and Susan attempt to infiltrate a mystical nightclub in an attempt to acquire the hand.

5. Off Line. Angela visits a psychic and learns that her boyfriend, Martin is a clone.

6. The Crime. Angela is arrested and placed in a prison hospital for killing the clone (whom she believed was a threat).

7. The Doctor. A Satacracy agent, posing as a doctor, helps Angela escape from the hospital.

8. The Plastic Bag. Acting alone, Susan begins a quest to find out what happened to Angela.

9. Her Next Mission. Angela is instructed to find a magic amulet that protects her boss, Sandy Carter (who is working against Satacracy) and destroy it.

10. The Past. Angela learns about her past from the Satacracy leader (seen in a flashback when Angela was a child).

11. The Betrayal. The warrior that is to become Angela is awakened and she is now the assassin that she was trained to become.

12. The Battle. The history between Angela and Susan is revealed (both were killers) before joining Satacracy.

13. The Deal. Angela reluctantly accepts her second identity as Satacracy 88.

14. The Hook. Unknown to Angela and Susan, unseen forces are watching their every move.

15. The Map. As Angela and Susan prepare to take down Sandy, a frantic young woman approaches their car, begging for help (running from her abusive boyfriend).

16. The Hitchhiker. Angela and Susan help the young woman (with Susan delivering a punch that knocks out the boyfriend) when Angela notices she has the Satacracy tattoo on her arm.

17. The Tattoo. The hitchhiker leads Angela and Susan to a tattoo parlor operated by a former Satacracy agent who warns Angela that forces are seeking to kill her.

18. The Leaf. Angela becomes 88 and unleashes her fighting abilities when she and Susan are attacked by an assassin.

19. The Cure. Angela is now literally two people—

her human self and her warrior self and learns that the mysterious Yerba plant leaf can provide a cure to make her one person.

20. The Thief. As Angela struggles with her dual personalities, they begin to interfere with her abilities to perform as 88.

21. The Ngombe. It is revealed how Angela grew up—keeping secrets, learning strategy and how to kill while it is also said that Susan is the 112th member of the Satacracy Army.

22. The Savior. Angela learns that her blood is special and that it can save the lives of injured Satacracy warriors.

23. The Dream. Angela's dreams are becoming a reality when her human side and her assassin side battle for supremacy of her mind and body.

24. The Choice. Hoping to help Angela the Satacracy Leader appears to tell her 88 side that he needs her "and the world needs you." "The world does not need another killer," responds Angela. The scene fades to black and reopens with Angela seen working for a security company. Has she abandoned 88? The episode concludes unresolved.

286 Save Me. webserieschannel.com. 2011 (Science Fiction).

A mysterious rock, apparently from an alien civilization, falls from the sky and lands on Earth. Anyone who comes upon the rock will acquire enhanced abilities by embracing the sun's rays and turning it into energy. When it is discovered that a young woman named Rose has acquired the rock, she becomes the target of people not only seeking it for evil, but of the Shadow Voice—the alien being who meant for the rock to help humans evolve into a greater species. The story follows Rose and those she comes in contact with as she attempts to protect the rock and overcome the powerful mind-bending influences of the Shadow Voice, who requires her help to achieve his goal.

Cast: Nancy Villalongo (Rose), Ramon Medina (Shadow Voice), Enoc Perez (Mr. Cortez), Edwin Gonzalez (Angel), Jennifer Matos (Liana), Jean Ibanez (Derman), Luis Gaetan (Carlos). **Credits:** *Producer-Director:* Ramon Medina. **Comment:** Rather lame production with very limited special effects and amateurish acting and production values. The whole production looks as if were just thrown together with no thought given to a smooth-flowing story or even likeable characters.

Episodes:

1. Episode 1 (6 min., 18 sec.). Introduces Rose, the possessor of the rock (she remembers only that she acquired it from another girl [Liana] and nothing else). She is also facing the frightening possibility of being controlled by the Shadow Voice.

2. Episode 2 (6 min., 29 sec.). Rose's struggles to overcome the will of the Shadow Voice become increasingly difficult.

3. Episode 3 (5 min., 58 sec.). For reasons that are not quite clear, Rose posts a video of herself (and her powers) on the Internet.

4. Episode 4 (7 min., 35 sec.). It appears that Rose's will is weakening and that she will become possessed by the Shadow Voice (who overtakes her during a lightning storm).

5. Episode 5 (6 min., 26 sec.). Reveals that the Shadow Voice is an alien and the original possessor of the rock and its purpose—to give mankind a chance to evolve further. It also reveals that he has chosen one human, Angel, to take mankind to greater heights.

287 Scared Stiff. scaredstiff.tv. 2011 (Horror).

Anthology based horror yarns aimed at a general audience (like broadcast television's *Tales from the Darkside* as opposed to cable's more adult and creepy *Tales from the Crypt*).

Cast: Jennifer Blanc, Tara Buck, Dana Daurey, Brianne Davis, Alyssa Lobit, Jen Soska, Sylvia Soska. **Credits:** Producer: Jennifer Blanc, Lorna Paul, Susan Wrenn. **Comment:** Not meant to be anything more than "what if" tales that are, despite its low budget productions, well acted and for the most part, interestingly written stories.

Episodes:

1. A Whisper in the Wind. A young girl receives help in dealing with a problem by a voice she hears coming from the wind. See also Episode 19 below.

2. Curse of the Scarecrow. A corrupt realtor soon learns that forcing a farmer off his land was the wrong thing to do when a scarecrow becomes his worst nightmare.

3. Crunchy. A cereal-loving child finds out that Captain Happy's Crunchy O's cereal contains more than just a free toy surprise.

4. Imaginary. A teenage girl (Jamie) attempts to cover the problems she causes by blaming her friend Samantha—until Samantha realizes an opportunity has arisen for her to turn the tables.

5. Alone. A young woman (Geena) faces a nightmare when she wakes up in an abandoned home and in a neighborhood where she appears to be the only person.

6. 2 Girls, 1 Ghost. Two young women, who are also lovers, find their relationship threatened by the spirit of a woman who haunts the home in which they now live.

7. You Better Watch Out. A Christmas-themed tale about what happens when a young boy sneaks a peak at one of his presents.

8. Predator: The True Horrors of Halloween. A young boy learns what not to do while trick-or-treating: accept a ride from a stranger.

9. Case CF 89. Strange story about a found video tape that reveals what happened to two people who mysteriously vanished.

10. Something in the Water. In an attempt to save his floundering marriage, a man serves his wife water acquired from a mystical source that is guaranteed to change her.

11. Closet Monster. A babysitter attempts to calm her young charge by proving there is no monster in his closet.

12. C Sharp. While hiking along the Appalachian Trail, three hikers are stalked by an unknown presence.

13. The Confessional. Unusual tale of a man, apparently one of the last survivors of a zombie invasion, who seeks to redeem himself by confessing his sins.

14. The Game. A young woman finds, that in order to become engaged to her boyfriend, she must play a strange game with him.

15. Tiny's Halloween 2. A young boy finds that, as treats become scarce, he may have to resort to tricks.

16. Alternative Medicine. When he feels that doctors have let him down, a man stricken with cancer seeks help from a woman who practices black magic.

17. My Last Words. Quirky tale of a man, contemplating suicide, who encounters difficulty writing the note.

18. Nightmares. A seemingly normal young man, burdened by frightening nightmares, seeks help in discovering their cause and what they mean.

19. A Whisper in the Wind 2. A sequel to Episode 1. Here a young woman receives help in dealing with her mentally abusive father by a voice she hears coming from the wind.

20. Welcome Mats. A man attempts to find out why a welcoming mat mysteriously turned up on his front door step.

21. Mother. A boy attempts to contend with his date's over-protective mother, a woman who simply doesn't approve of him.

22. Taking the Bait. A college student (Megan), trying to study for an exam, becomes upset by a noisy neighbor who is distracting her. Unaware that it is bait to lure her, Megan proceeds to confront him.

23. Just My Luck. A man's attempts to end his life do not go as planned when someone offers to help him.

24. Tiny's Halloween. Last year Tiny's Halloween (see episode 15 above) was a bust. This year Tiny has new tricks up his sleeve for those who prefer not to give candy.

25. Stay Away. Mystery-like presentation that follows a young woman's flight from something that is pursuing her.

26. Dance for Me. A dancer, preparing for a show, is seized by a fan who wants nothing but to see her dance—even if it kills her.

27. The Best Day of My Life. A woman reveals the disturbing details of an abusive relationship and how she achieved the best day of her life.

28. 12:00. Explores why, on one day each year at the stroke of midnight, a young woman fears facing that day—made even more frightening this year when she must do it alone.

29. The Break-In. A thief encounters strange happenings when he breaks into a house with a mysterious past.

30. They Soar at Night. Romantic (as can be) tale of a vampire who falls in love with a feeding victim.

31. The Camera. A camera with secretive powers becomes a life savior with a sight-impaired man when an intruder breaks into his home on Halloween.

32. A Victim in the Night. A doctor's efforts to treat a battered man, unaware that he is a killer the police are seeking.

288 *Self Centered*. selfcenteredseries.com. 2011 (Fantasy).

Lydia is a young woman who had it all—fame as a movie actress, wealth, and social status. But as she began to age she lost everything when she turned to drinking and drugs. One night, when she feels life has given up on her, Lydia attempts to end it all by drowning herself in the bathtub. It appears she has succeeded until she awakens in The Clinic, a mysterious purgatory of the future where she is told that she is the only hope of saving the world. People have driven themselves to destruction and they require something to believe in—something to unite them and give them hope. Such an endeavor was attempted with a movie called *For All Our Tomorrows* but, because of a miscast role (the female leading actress) the film failed as no one actually saw it. Lydia learns that she is the actress that is needed to make the film and by doing so it will save the world. She is miraculously returned to her apartment—but did Lydia really live what she saw or was it something her unconscious conjured up as she attempted to kill herself? The program explores Lydia's dilemma as she attempts to get her life back together to make the film.

Cast: Kellie Shirley (Lydia), Simon Tcherniak (The Custodian), Jane Jeffrey (The Manager), Nathan Wright (Christian), Alison Rose (The Doctor). **Credits:** *Producer:* Tamana Bleasdale. *Director:* Kevin Proctor. *Writer:* Steven Keevil. **Comment:** Although the British-produced program ends unresolved, it is well acted, written and directed. While the fate of the world still seems to lie with Lydia, whether or not the film will ever be made remains unknown.

Episodes:

1. Episode 1 (3 min., 54 sec.). The morning after a night of drinking Lydia attempts to commit suicide but instead finds herself in The Clinic.

2. Episode 2 (3 min., 17 sec.). Lydia, informed of what she must do, is returned to her normal life.

3. Episode 3 (3 min., 42 sec.). Lydia begins by

seeking the role of the lead actress in the film *For All Our Tomorrows*.

4. Episode 4 (2 min., 44 sec.). Lydia acquires the leading role—but can she perform as the protagonist the movie requires.

5. Episode 5 (4 min., 33 sec.). Lydia's doubts send her back to drinking—and back to The Clinic.

6. Episode 6 (3 min., 36 sec.). Lydia's condition is discussed and it is determined she needs to move onto the next level. Reluctant at first, she agrees as the screen fades to black.

289 Semi-Dead. semi-dead.com. 2009 (Science Fiction).

A zombie apocalypse has occurred but, unlike other such occurrences (that have been seen) infrastructures are in tact and electricity remains on. In fact, if it were not for roaming zombies, cities would appear normal. Two friends, former soldiers, Chris and Joe, now seek a way to survive the city as they did the war in Afghanistan. Chris is suffering from PTSD and is living his life as if nothing has happened; Joe, on the other hand, has begun his battle against the zombies, doing what it takes to survive. Stories follow the two roommates as they plot to survive the zombie infestation with Joe being the more aggressive and Chris, the passive one (comfortable just the way he is).

Cast: Keith Arthur Bolden (Chris), Andrew McMennamy (Joe), Mike Danner (Sean), Wendy Douglas (Jessica), Mandy Flynn (Christina), Tom Flynn (Proto Joe). **Credits:** *Producer:* James Bond III, Josh Hodgins, Chris Wiltz. *Director:* Tom Flynn, Sean Patrick O'Brien, Will Prescott. *Writer:* Chris Wiltz. **Comment:** Comically portrayed zombie saga that really leaves no interest to see what happens next. It is sort of like an "Odd Couple" paring with zombies being the catalyst that sparks their lives.

Episodes:

1. If You Can't Beat 'Em, Eat 'Em. With their food supply running low, Joe tries to figure a way to get to the outside and find supplies (but all Chris can do is ask for strawberries).

2. If You Can't Eat 'Em, Date 'Em. As Chris seeks a new roommate via the Internet, Joe continues his search for food on the zombie-infested streets.

3. If You Can't Date 'Em, Live with 'Em. Chris gets a response to his ad—but Joe is a bit weary about welcoming another guy (Sean) to share their apartment.

4. If You Can't Live with 'Em, Beat 'Em. Joe must deal with the infected Sean—and possibly help Chris see that he needs to realize what is going on around him.

5. Six Months Ago. A look back at Chris and Joe six months prior to the situation they now face (which isn't much different). Joe is devising a zombie security system while Chris is angered when his cable television goes black.

6. Let's Get It Poppin'. The concluding episode

with Joe and Chris still facing threats to their lives from the zombies—a situation made more complicated when Chris's friend (Proto Joe), a guy with a penchant for violent acts, visits them.

290 The Sentinel Chronicles. youtube.com. 2009 (Science Fiction).

In the not too distant future, with war still plaguing the U.S., scientists develop clones made in the image of humans and able to function as soldiers. Over time the clones were perfected and became known as Bioroids; their engineering, however, was flawed, as they began to think for themselves and united to control their own evolution. A new threat now faced humans: the Bioroids, who believe all lower life forms must be exterminated as they now plan to inherit the universe. The GE (Genetic Engineering) Corp. created the clones with the intent being to replace humans on the battlefield. If a clone was destroyed in battle, their memories would be transmitted back to GE's central cloning facility and be programmed into another copy of the same body. All is progressing well until GE, which controls the cloning technology, begins selling upgrades to the highest bidder, thus igniting the existing war into a nuclear catastrophe. The world becomes a wasteland where only pockets of technology and civilizations dot the landscape and alternative social structures, religious zealots and other such factions battle each other for supremacy. In an attempt to stop GE's unethical dealings, the ISA (Independent States of America), programs two clones as assassins: one to kill Dr. Henderson, the chief cloning scientist, and one to destroy the assassin, thus taking suspicion away from them and making the ISA continue to be seen as the most powerful nation state on Earth. It is the year 2031 when the series begins and the battle for supremacy has begun with a primary focus on two clones (Beth and Leviticus); the God Warrior Jonas; Hannah Dixon, a reporter for V4FW (Voice for a Free World) and Natalie Dickerson, chief of the NA (Northern Alliance) Troops.

Cast: Josie Burgin Lawson, Misty Lane, William Pacer, Lawrence R. Johnson, June Letourneau. **Credits:** *Producer:* Lawrence R. Johnson. *Director:* J. Welin, Heith Bullington. *Writer:* J. Welin, Lawrence R. Johnson. **Comment:** The episodes listed comprise the second season with the first and third seasons now off line thus making an episode descriptive listing impractical (as the events seen in season one carry over into the second season and the second season into the third). Based on what can be seen, it is a poorly constructed program with only adequate acting and production values (the chosen outdoor locations, for example, are not very convincing and the special effects very weak).

Episodes: *1.* A History Lesson. *2.* Origin of Cerino. *3.* Origin of Jonas. *4.* The Commander. *5.* Who Am I?

291 Shadow Bound. shadowboundseries. com. 2013 (Science Fiction).

Veritas is a city living in the faded remains of the 1920s, once called "The Roaring 20s." It is actually the 1930s and Veritas is a mystic city of shadows and hidden terrors that has refused to accept the new decade. Jack Pickman is one of its citizens, a famed horror story writer who has returned to his childhood home following the death of his father. Jack's return however, resembles something he could have written about as his brother has been institutionalized and there are mysterious circumstances relating to both incidents. When Jack meets with two old friends and learns that all is not what it seems in Veritas, they form a team to discover exactly what is happening. Their investigation uncovers an ancient evil—and Jack must now risk his life to save mankind from a terrifying menace that is rising from the shadows.

Cast: Nathan Shelton, Sam Long, Shawn Long, Tim Piland, Mickey Stone, Melissa Young, David Dively, George Cron. **Credits:** *Producer:* David Man, Rick Peterman. *Director:* David Braser, Garrett Tripp, Nathan Shelton, Sam Long. *Writer:* Nathan Shelton. **Comment:** Embracing the actual world of filmmaking as it was during the 1920s, the series is presented in black and white—and as a silent film. Based on the teaser, it is an interesting concept that, even if you have never seen an actual silent film from the era, you will surprised just how good could it can be.

Episodes: Thus far only a short teaser running 73 seconds has been released.

292 She-Hulk. shehulkseries.com. 2013 (Science Fiction).

Jennifer "Jen" Walters is the cousin of Bruce Banner, the doctor whose experiments with gamma rays affected his body chemistry and transformed him into a hulking green creature called The Incredible Hulk. Jennifer, born in Los Angeles, is a lawyer and the daughter of Sheriff Morris Walters. Jennifer's life changes forever when she is shot by agents of a crime lord and near death when Bruce gives her a transfusion of his radioactive blood when no other donors of her blood type could be found. The mutated blood alters her body chemistry and gives her the ability to become the She-Hulk. Although Jennifer has the ability to control her changes (which she can do at will) her initial transformations were savage—until she learned to control them. Now, as a lawyer Jennifer uses her abilities as the She-Hulk to dispense her own brand of justice—always remembering what she is capable of and how to control what she has (unlike Bruce, whose anger triggered his transformations and he had no control over the Hulk). She is also seeking a cure and believes radio activity could be the answer.

Cast: Ulises Vega (Jen), Monseriat Perez (She-Hulk), Paolo Ceja. **Comment:** The storyline information presented above reflects the character history of Jennifer as originally presented in Marvel Comics. Each of the episodes have no specific titles and are listed as (for example) "Season 1, Chapter 2," "Season 2, Chapter 1." The video information consists basically of a one minute preview of the episode as an incentive to purchase the videos.

Episodes: As of March 2014, 22 episodes have been produced but only available for viewing in a buy and download in HD format. Since the program was produced in Spain and not dubbed in English, the decision to watch and buy is strictly up to the individual and thus offering an opinion on the program is not presented here. Information wise, virtually nothing has been released to the Internet.

293 Shifters. webserieschannel.com. 2010 (Science Fiction).

During a school field trip to an old museum, three teenagers (Michael, Sam and Krystal) sneak off to examine the lower levels of the building. While exploring they find a strange artifact (a small, black object) accompanied by a loud noise and a glowing light. The artifact was created by intelligent beings over 50 years ago. When it was found, it was placed in the museum's basement as a safety precaution as no one knew exactly what it was or what powers it beheld. The teens appear to be unaffected at first. The following day brings them to the realization that they have been transported into a parallel universe—one that looks exactly the same as theirs but with a different evolution. With the artifact in their possession and realizing that it can open portals and transport them to various parallel universes, they find they are now lost in alternate universes. Stories relate their experiences in several such worlds and their desperate efforts to learn the secret of the artifact and return to their own time and world.

Cast: Daniel George (Michael Flemming), Tenneille Holden (Krystal Mack), Mansoor Noor (Sam Braden), Josh Ockenden (Evan Ross). **Credits:** *Producer-Writer:* Terrance M. Young. *Director:* Terrance M. Young, Ryan Neil Butler, Mansoor Noor. **Comment:** Well done and exciting with good acting and production values—but could be considered a copy of the television series *Sliders* (and *Voyagers* for its time-traveling aspect) which used the same concept of parallel worlds.

Episodes:

1. Changes (23 min., 10 sec.). Establishes the storyline as the teens find the mysterious artifact.

2. Evolution (21 min., 45 sec.). In a world where prehistoric creatures still exist, the teens are rescued by a beautiful princess and find refuge in her castle in the land of West Haven before moving on.

3. Memories (23 min.). The escape from West Haven lands the teens in a world where they become involved with Evan Ross, the leader of a human rebellion in a time of a post apocalyptic war.

4. East Is West (24 min., 15 sec.). The teens, called Shifters, next appear in a world where the Industrial Revolution never occurred and the colonial pioneer era still exists (and where Krystal and Michael must help Sam, who has been mistaken for the notorious outlaw "Sling Blade Samuel").

5. Echoes of Yesterday (23 min., 15 sec.). The Shifters materialize into what appears to be their home world but soon discover it is anything but home when a catastrophe begins to engulf the planet.

6. The Butterfly Effect (23 min., 50 sec.). Continuing from where the prior episode left off, the teens become involved in a desperate search to find their missing shifting devise (the artifact) and escape the catastrophe—natural disasters that are spreading rapidly across the planet.

294 *The Silent City.* silentcityseries.com. 2012 (Science Fiction).

"I've seen less and less of the others as the years passed.... Maybe they're all gone" are the words spoken by a lone wanderer in a future time when the world has been devastated by an unknown catastrophe. One human, referred to as the Man is followed as he wanders through the abandoned shipping docks, deserted buildings, and crumbling highway overpasses that were once a part of Manhattan.

Cast: Eric Stafford (The Man), Kettie Jean (The Girl). **Credits:** *Producer:* Mathias Schmitt, Rudidius Wu. *Writer-Director:* Rudidius Wu. **Comment:** Actually filmed in the abandoned areas of New York City which gives the project a surreal feel (the first episode was filmed at the Redhook shipping docks and the second at the legendary Staten Island boat graveyard, the Seaview Colony). The program does have an eerie aura about it but does not explain who the Man is or what catastrophe struck—all adding to the mystery of a well done science fiction series.

Episodes:

1. A Fractured World (5 min., 5 sec.). Introduces (but without background information) the Man in a world devastated by some unknown event.

2. The Nameless (4 min., 28 sec.). Cameras follow the Man as he wanders across the eerie remains of an old boat yard.

3. A Bitter Struggle (3 min., 43 sec.). The man attempts to save a young woman who has been kidnapped and tied to a bed.

4. Outlander (5 min., 17 sec.). The man frees the girl from her kidnapper, but the girl now sees him as a protector and attaches herself to him.

5. A Survivor's Greed (5 min., 27 sec.). Danger lurks for the Man and girl as they cross the path of a mysterious group of underground survivors.

295 *Silverwood.* youtube.com. 2012 (Horror).

Silverwood, California, is a small town one does not want to live in, visit or even pass by. It is a town engulfed in a world of the unknown, where each citizen has a dark secret and where things that go bump in the night really exist. Adapting the format most connected to *The Twilight Zone*, *Silverwood* uses the unexpected type of storytelling coupled with the fright aspect of ghosts, monsters and demons.

Cast: Bree Essrig, Bridget Zadina, Drake Bell, Drew Garett, Azure Parsons, Brea Grant, Laura Slade Williams, Jared Krusnitz. **Credits:** *Producer:* Anthony Zucker, Dan Weinstein, Matthew Weinberg, Tony Valenzuela. **Comment:** While *Silverwood* is an anthology program and stories are complete in themselves, there is an underlying thread that ties them all together (the mythology of the town through the character of Alex, played by Bree Essrig) when all episodes are watched. As for what is scary and what isn't depends on each viewer's perception. The acting and production values are good based on what is still available.

Episodes: Unfortunately, *Silverwood*, for the most part, is no longer available. It is difficult to determine exactly how many episodes were produced (various sources put it at 9, 11 and 20). The official website, while still open highlights the episode "Unknown Caller" (with the striking image of two girls kissing) and YouTube, where the available episodes can be seen, lists only the following eight: *1.* Sleepover. *2.* Unknown Caller. *3.* Last Encounter. *4.* The Perfect Night. *5.* The Hunger. *6.* Kidnapped. *7.* Left Behind. *8.* Red Ink.

296 *Silverwood: Final Recordings.* you tube.com. 2012 (Horror).

A continuation of the series *Silverwood* wherein the truth about the California mountain town is revealed (hints of which are revealed through episodes in the parent series. The episodes listed below tell the story).

Cast: Bree Essrig (Alex), Sean-Ryan Black (The Black Box Voice), Bridger Zadina (Liam), Tonya Kay (Dr. Christina Rossi), Marc Raducci (Dr. D.J. Moore). **Credits:** *Producer:* Tony E. Valenzuela, Tony Bryman. *Director:* Tony E. Valenzuela, Stephen Reedy. *Writer:* Steven Reedy **Comment:** There are no recaps and each episode should be watched in order to experience the full effect of the program. The acting and production values are excellent and the story flows smoothly from beginning to end.

Episodes:

1. Alex 4Fun (5 min., 16 sec.). Alex, from the prior series is seen as the host of a fantasy web site and one of the people who will be responsible for the fate of Silverwood (the others are Dr. Christina Rossi, Liam and Dr. Moore). It is also revealed that a massive fire, caused by a lightning strike, is threatening the town.

2. I Can See You (7 min., 32 sec.). News reports continue to warn residents that Silverwood is in the

direct line of the fire. But, as the fire rages, something strange is happening to the town.

3. Hurt (7 min.). Silverwood's security system, the Black Box Recorders, show evidence of a massive magnetic field engulfing the entire community.

4. The Portal Opens (6 min., 55 sec.). As the magnetic field becomes more apparent, town residents are being inflicted with strange behavior.

5. She's Insane (4 min., 40 sec.). It is learned that Dr. Rossi's grandfather founded Silverwood over 100 years ago and soon realized there was a strange alien presence that eventually killed him when it tried but failed to overtake him. Dr. Rossi has uncovered the presence and is seeking a way to have it possess her.

6. The Message (5 min., 48 sec.). As the magnetic field continues its enclosure of Silverwood and residents becoming infected, Dr. Rossi plans an experiment to allow the alien force to possess her.

7. Dark Angel (5 min., 5 sec.). While it appears that the magnetic field is of an alien doing and placed over Silverwood to protect it from the fire, it is having adverse affects on the community and beginning to transform people into disfigured, zombie-like creatures.

8. The End of Silverwood (7 min., 37 sec.). Now concerned with what is happening around her, Dr. Rossi attempts the alien takeover of her body with results that not only destroy her but all hope of saving Silverwood.

297 Sin. webserieschannel.com. 2013 (Fantasy).

Each of the seven deadly sins (Lust, Gluttony, Greed, Wrath, Envy, Pride and Sloth) appear in a dark setting to explain what they are—and how they seek to seduce people to their side.

Cast: Caitlin Becka (Lust), Keith Welborn (Pride), Ashley Murray (Greed), P.J. Barnes (Wrath), Anthony Lawson (Gluttony), Morgan Hoffman (Envy), Charles Johnston (Sloth). **Credits:** *Producer-Director:* Joe Ensley. **Comment:** Strange program that has no action, suspense or horror—just the seven deadly sins addressing the viewer. Well photographed and acted and each episode has a parental warning as some material may be unsuitable for children.

Episodes:

1. Lust (3 min., 43 sec.). A seductive young woman tells how she seduces people to commit her sin of Lust.

2. Gluttony (4 min., 6 sec.). A bearded, heavy-set gentleman approaches the camera to entice people to food and his deadly sin, Gluttony.

3. Greed (3 min., 7 sec.). A distinguished young man appeals to viewers to become obsessed with money and fall into his deadly trap of Greed.

4. Wrath (4 min., 26 sec.). A devilish-like figure with a red glow delights in explaining how to lose all control and seek revenge to become part of his deadly sin, Wrath.

5. Envy (5 min., 8 sec.). A beautiful young woman explains that if she is what you want but can't have and what other people have that you cannot have, then join her in her sin of Envy.

6. Pride (3 min., 36 sec.). A man who extols the benefits of what he has and what he has over others invites viewers to do the same thing and join him in the sin of Pride.

7. Sloth. Episode taken off line.

8. Screw Up TV Presents Sin (16 min., 10 sec.). A dramatization of what happens when a man is faced with three of the deadly sins at once.

298 Singularity. youtube.com. 2013 (Science Fiction).

In an age where computers are becoming increasingly more intelligent, one such server in Brazil has threatened to override its programming. Engineers and programmers are unable to explain what has occurred and call the situation "The Bahlia Incident." Silas Faulkner of the Human Redevelopment Initiative and graduate student Mark Andresen, both antagonistic experts, have been entrusted to find out what has happened and how to prevent it from happening again. As Silas and Mark probe the situation, they are followed by a television documentary crew and stories relate their efforts to stop servers from becoming masters of the computer realm.

Cast: Russell Jordan (Silas Faulkner), Einar Gunn (Andros Palmiotti), Oliver Burns (Mark Andresen), Nathan Faudree (Steve Real), David Lamberton (Allen Forsythe). **Credits:** *Producer-Director:* Brian Neuls, Paul Neuls. *Writer:* Paul Neuls. **Comment:** Good science fiction thriller, although there is a lot more talk than anything else. Probes the idea that, like in the movie *War Games*, a malfunctioning computer could be mankind's worst enemy.

Episodes:

1. Do You Sleep Here, Professor? (5 min., 30 sec.). The Bahlia Incident comes to the attention of Mark and Silas.

2. What If There Was No Two? (4 min., 38 sec.). As they probe the situation, Silas surmises that the incident could be attributed to a computer glitch.

3. One, or the Other, Not Someone to Do Both (4 min., 12 sec.). In Brazil the situation appears to worsen when American factory workers are unable to program their server.

4. There Is Another Way (4 min., 31 sec.). Needing first hand knowledge, Silas assigns Mark the task of heading to Brazil.

5. Then What's the Problem? (2 min., 50 sec.). Silas appears on television to discuss the situation in Brazil with Andros Palmiotti.

6. History Will Determine Which Does Which (4 min., 15 sec.). Feeling that he too needs to see what has happened, Silas accompanies Mark to Brazil.

7. Hello, Silas (3 min., 34 sec.). In Brazil, Silas is

surprised to meet Andros, who has also become interested in witnessing what happened up close.

8. It Will Start Out Like This (6 min., 9 sec.). Silos and Andros meet with American plant manager Allen Forsythe who shows them the malfunctioning server.

9. I Don't Think You'd Be Here If You Didn't Understand (4 min., 41 sec.). Believing that rogue software is responsible for the situation, Silas attempts to install a new server to override the defective one.

10. The Tic-Tac-Toe Scene, from War Games (4 min., 14 sec.). Grant, recalling that in the movie *War Games* the game of Tic-Tac-Toe was used to stop a malfunctioning computer, suggests a similar idea here (as there is no winner in a game of Tic-Tac-Toe when played alone).

11. Uhh ... Dave? (9 min., 54 sec.). Cliff hanger (and unresolved) last episode wherein scientists are faced with an additional problem: if the affected server is not restarted within five minutes, the entire system will shut down—and if the system shuts down?

299 Sinners: Which One Is You? youtube. com. 2013 (Horror).

Italian-produced anthology program that encompasses "The Circle of Hell" philosophy: people are seduced to sin by an evil force, face Hell's punishment then return to earth to serve their new master, the Devil. Each episode focuses on one individual and what happens when he or she gives into temptation. Based on *The Divine Comedy* feature film created David Petrucci.

Cast: *Indolent:* Federico Palmieri (Sinner), Andreea Togan, Marius Bizau (Demons); *Lustful:* Francesca Palmas (Sinner), Alessandro Giuseppe Anselmo, Francesco Randazzo (Demons); *Gluttony:* Veruska (Sinner), Fabrizio Bordignon, Andreea Togan (Demons), Simone Destrero (Priest). **Credits:** *Producer-Director-Writer:* David Petrucci. **Comment:** While not an original concept (similar ideas have been presented on series like *The Twilight Zone* and *Number 13 Demon Street*), it is also presented in Italian with English subtitles for American audiences. The title also makes the entry look grammatically incorrect and performers, while known in Italy, are strangers to American viewers. Stories, however, are intriguing and well done.

Episodes:

1. Indolent (5 min.). A man is seduced to kill then pays the ultimate price: attacked and stung by hornets for all eternity.

2. Lustful (5 min.). A woman, giving into temptation to offer sex for a favor, finds herself being sexually abused for all eternity.

3. Gluttony (5 min.). Unpleasant story about how food, tainted by evil, transforms a woman into a glutton—and how she must endure gluttony forever.

300 Skye of the Damned. skyeofthedamned. com. 2013 (Horror).

Skye MacKenna is a young woman, trained in the martial arts and the art of wielding a sword, who is seeking to avenge the death of her mother by finding her killer (which she believes is a vampire. When Skye was 12 years old her mother was killed in what appeared to be a home invasion. Skye believed that if her mother knew how to defend herself she could have saved herself. She vowed at that point to find her mother's killer.) After acquiring information that the vampire she is seeking has become one of the minions of the Vampire King, the leader of the vampire faction that is battling the FAE (fallen angels) for control of Manhattan, Skye moves to New York (where she hooks up with a college friend [Madison] and her roommate, Joelle, a Goth girl). It is when Skye becomes involved with the Goth scene that clues slowly emerge as to what is happening in Manhattan and that a mysterious man (Finn) may be the key to her finding the vampire she is seeking. The program follows Skye as she uncovers secrets about her own family (why her real parents were targets of the Royal Vampire family) and becomes involved in the deadly, secretive battle between the FAE (Fallen Angel Errant) and the Vampires to control Manhattan.

Amara Raine is a beautiful but vicious vampire (she is referred to as a "bitch" as she adheres to a different set of rules). She has military training and was a drug addict before she was turned; on the bright side, she works at a rehab center. Kyle Lawson, part warlock and part FAE, lives on Manhattan's Upper West Side and has come to New York from Tennessee to study music and hopefully start his own band. Silas Winters is Amara's love interest, an ancient but young-looking vampire. He is elegant, well dressed and works for Cillian Black, the Vampire Prince of Manhattan. Madison Park is Skye's friend (they attended college together). She is part witch, single, works for a temp agency and hopes to become an actress. Joelle Meadows, a Goth clothing store clerk, is petite, tomboyish and moved to Manhattan to get away from her family. Nicolai Jordan is Kyle's roommate, an ex-drug addict (works in design) and is best friends with Jillian and Joelle. DJ Phaedra is an alternative DJ who works at Goth/industrial EBM clubs. She hails from Kansas and reads Tarot cards to earn extra money. Shana Dune, Xavier's personal bartender, has a mysterious past "that will play heavily into the series." Jillian Murphy is a FAE who works for Xavier Keenan, the Vampire King of New York City (she has defied the FAE to do this as they grew up together and feels her place is with him). Hayden Fletcher, a bouncer, is newly arrived in Manhattan. He has a questionable past and becomes roommates with Kyle and Nicolai. Finn Malloy is the mysterious man that appears to be following Skye (and whom Skye believes may have something to do

Skye of the Damned cast, from left to right: Josh Fielden as Kyle, Matt Cullen as Nicolai, Briana Redmount as Joelle, Kelly Driscoll as Amara, Andrew Rogers as Silas, Kara Addington as Madison and Lauren Steinmeyer as Skye (copyright Tamsin Silver, SkyeOfThe Damned.com, VampireFreaks.com).

with her mother's death). Grant Carter and Dorian Steele are detectives with the FAE Police Department in New York City. Brooke Delaney and Ethan Vale are detectives with the Vampiric Police Department. Declan Sinclair is the Deputy Chief of the Vampire and FAE Security Department and next in line to become its chief (he is also the most powerful warlock in the country). Xavier Keenan, the Vampire King, rules with an iron hand, owns many of the clubs and bars in Manhattan and is known for helping the homeless, donating money to soup kitchens and giving jobs to the poor. Cillian Black, the Vampire Prince is next in line to being king as his mother is Xavier's younger sister. Alarica Gage is a Knight of the Royal FAE Household (although she has been associating with the mysterious Finn Malloy as his possible accomplice to kill Skye). Tobias Worthington is the Vampire Prince of Queens, New York (he is nicknamed the Queen of Queens). Garnet Surkov is the Vampire Priestess of Brooklyn. Marcel Montgomery is the Vampire Prince of The Bronx. Portia Jane is the Vampire Princess of Staten Island. Ella is the FAE Queen of the Seelie Court. Danae is the FAE Queen of the Unseelie Court. Alexie Gage is Alarica's brother, a Knight and one of the best fighters of the Unseelie Court.

Cast: Lauren Steinmeyer (Skye MacKenna), Bri-
ana Redmount (Joelle Meadows), Sara Hogrefe (DJ Phaedra), Matt Cullen (Nicolai Jordan), Josh Fielden (Kyle Lawson), Kara Addington (Madison Park), Kelly Driscoll (Amara Raine), Andrew Rogers (Silas Winters), Chris LaCour (Det. Grant Carter), Mark Rosenthal (Finn Malloy), Tyler Jakes (Det. Dorian Steele), Sarah Murdoch (Alarica Gage), Rachel Grundy (Det. Brooke Delaney), Audrey Hayner (Shana Dune), Cedric Jones (Det. Ethan Vale), William Welles (Xavier Keenan), Jet Berelson (Cillian Black), Christa Sparks (Jillian), Vince Phillip (Jackson Reece), Philip de la Cal (Hayden Fletcher), Sarah Mack (Ella), Leanna Renee Hieber (Danae), Erika Santosuosso (Portia Jane), Austin Auh (Tobias Worthington), Aaron Lee Wright (Marcel Montgomery), AnnaMarie Vukmanovich (Garnet Surkov). **Credits:** *Producer:* Jet Berelson (VampireFreaks.com), Tamsin L. Silver, Nyle Cavazos Garcia, Lauren Steinmeyer. *Writer-Director:* Tamsin L. Silver. **Comment:** Lauren Steinmeyer is captivating as Skye and the production values, acting, writing and directing based on the first two episodes are very good. The story flows smoothly and Skye's venturing into the dark realm of the New York Goth scene is something different.

Episodes:

1. Back to the Start. Skye returns to New York

when her father is injured in a car accident and learns the truth about what happened to her mother.

2. Welcome to My City. Skye decides to remain and find the people responsible for her mother's death.

Note: Four additional episodes have been produced but not released as of February 2014: The FAE (episode 3), Jillian (episode 4), Wake (episode 5) and Hayden (episode 6). There is also a promotional episode combined with a fund raiser to help finance the project and four short teaser videos.

301 *Sleeping Awake.* youtube.com. 2013 (Science Fiction).

Los Angeles in a future time provides the setting. It is a time when technology has been raised to newer heights especially with the theory of Lucid Dreaming (where it is believed dreams can be controlled). The process, however, causes certain people to have harmful psychological side effects and the Federal Drug Administration has banned its technology. Although banned, there are those who continue to use it, hoping to develop its potential. Based on the pilot episode the series follows Jesse Logan, an agent with the FBI's Federal Task Force as he investigates unusual crimes that are linked to Lucid Dreaming technology.

Cast: Kelby Cross (Jesse Logan), Alexandra De-Martini (Amelia Logan), Danielle Replogle (Lily Kittridge), Paul Leo Dietz (Joseph Rory). **Credits:** *Producer:* Natalie Henry. *Writer-Director:* Bryan Bailey. **Comment:** Shows potential for some intriguing crimes associated with Lucid Dreaming and how people, affected by the technology, are not even aware of what they are doing (hence the title). The acting and production values are also good.

Episodes:
1. The Pilot: The Ghost of You and I (13 min., 9 sec.). Establishes the storyline wherein Jesse's first case involves his finding a mysterious felon who is killing women who resemble his late wife Amelia.

302 *Solo.* watchsolo.com. 2012 (Science Fiction).

There are rock singers who are brilliant in both their stage careers and in their private lives. Then there is Scott Drizhal, a rock star who is just the opposite; best described by his wife Rebecca as an idiot. With the growing success of reality shows on television producer Jack Spratt believes he has come up with ultimate idea: star Scott in a solo show set on the planet Mars. A ship, the *Artemis* is prepared and launched into space for its three year mission to the Red Planet. After 36 days, the GBC network cancels the program and Scott is now stranded in space; his only companion is PHAL 9000, a smart-alec computer that offers Scott little comfort. To make matters worse, Rebecca, believing Scott will never return,

begins proceedings to have him declared legally dead so she can claim millions of dollars in insurance, and the ship, never meant for such a journey, begins malfunctioning and veers off into Japanese air space where Scott must now fend for himself against the Japanese mafia who want the ship. Stories follow an idiot in space and his desperate efforts to survive the crushing problems that are slowly driving him crazy.

Cast: Jonathan Nail (Scott Drizhal), Jason Burns (PHAL 9000), Michele Boyd (Rebecca Drizhal), Jay Caputo (Jack Spratt), Melissa Dalton (Gerry Simon), Amol Shah (Ratish Gupta), Kimberly Atkinson (Lexi Collins), Tohoru Masamune (Yakuza Bossman), Jade Carter (Tripp Steves), Ron Butler (President of the U.S.). **Credits:** *Producer:* Allison Vanore. *Director:* Jorge Urbina. *Writer:* Jonathan Nail. **Comment:** The program ends in a cliffhanger (additional episodes are planned) and is one of the better science fiction comedies with good acting and production values but limited special effects. Ron Butler as the President bears a strong resemblance to Pres. Barack Obama.

Episodes:
1. We're Canceled. Establishes the premise as Scott's mission is suddenly canceled and he finds himself stuck in space with an intelligent computer (PHAL) as his only companion on a round trip that will take three years to complete. Meanwhile, Jack scrambles to find a way to get Scott back home.

2. That's the Shits. When Rebecca learns of Scott's predicament, she begins proceedings to have Scott declared legally dead; Jack pleads with network executive Tripp Steves to help him get Scott back to Earth.

3. Good Grief. The five stages of depression set in as Scott realizes, that even after calling the President of the United States, he may never return home.

4. Female Persuasion. In a desperate effort to reverse the course of the ship, Scott attempts (but fails) to learn how to pilot the ship.

5. Mole. After entering Japanese air space, the Yakuza (Japanese mafia) plan the takeover of Scott's ship.

6. Turning Japanese. Scott becomes aware of another presence on the ship and encounters the beautiful Space Ninja who has boarded the ship with plans to hack PHAL for the access codes she needs to take over the *Artemis.*

7. Wushu Pork. Scott turns to PHAL for help in defeating the Space Ninja.

8. The Discovery and the Challenger. On Earth the Yakuza have determined a way to take over the ship while on the *Artemis* Scott confronts the Space Ninja.

9. End Game—Is Only the Beginning. The concluding episode finds Scott unable to defeat the Space Ninja and losing control of the ship to her.

303 *Soma.* webserieschannel.com. 2012 (Horror).

While on a shoot in the Amazon, a successful photographer (Emilio) contracts a mysterious infection that he apparently overcomes before he returns to his home in Italy. Soon afterward, however, he notices a strange growth on his neck and that he has become violent and cannot control his actions. The infection soon changes his DNA and transforms him into a vampire-like killer (as he kills victims by drawing blood from their necks). The program follows Emilio as he attempts to control what he has become with the police in hot pursuit of the killer he has become. Produced in Italy and presented in Italian with English subtitles.

Cast: Emilio Vacca, Luigi Di Fiore, Samantha Piccinetti, Roberta Stellato, Carlo De Ruggieri, Nereo Savastano, Gianfranco Russo, Giorgio Sorrentino, Cristiana Dell'Anna, Sasa Pelliccia, Sara Laura Raimondi, Alessandra Asuni, Maria Luna Papa, Leonardo Vecchietti. **Credits:** *Producer:* Davide Devenuto. *Director:* Davide Devenuto, Francesco Sardelli. *Writer:* Fabio Paladini. **Comment:** Although reading the subtitles can be distracting, the program is well done and the concept interesting. The acting is good and additional episodes are planned.

Episodes:
1. Episode 1 (14 min., 1 sec.). Establishes the story line as Emilio becomes infected.
2. Episode 2 (13 min., 40 sec.). Emilio is caught by the police and imprisoned after a killing.
3. Episode 3 (14 min., 52 sec.). Emilio, possessed of incredible strength, kills a guard and escapes from prison.
4. Episode 4 (19 min., 50 sec.). Emilio, able to elude the police, seeks a way to control what has happened to him. Ends in a cliffhanger.

304 Soul Fire Rising. soulfirerising.com. 2009 (Fantasy).

A battle for good (Wingers) and evil (Demons) for human souls and the supremacy of Earth. The focus is on Lilith, a beautiful, rebellious demon (a Succubus) who acquires souls by using Earth's vices. Life changes for Lilith when Gabriel, a Winger, summons her to perform one deed: Find Eve, a Winger who chose to become mortal and return her to him. In return Lilith will receive one million souls—the value of Eve's soul. The story presents the conflict that arises when Lilith begins her mission and faces a dilemma—side with Eva or Gabriel—a decision that could change the world forever. Lilith is seen as three distinct characters: Human, demon and her new human form (when Gabriel summons her).

Cast: Jodi Lyn O'Keefe (Lilith, Reborn), Aimee-Lynn Chadwick (Lilith, Human), Kasey Poteet (Lilith, Demon), Kelly Stables (Eve), Mitchell Fink (Gabriel), Marlene Forte (Nina), Melissa Paolo (Julia), Jackie Geary (Serpica), Jordan Rider (Adrian). **Credits:** *Producer-Director:* Dale Fabrugar, John P. Aguirre. *Writer:* Kurt Patino. **Comment:** The three

actress portraying Lilith are outstanding in an exceptional good vs. evil program. While the concept has been done countless times before, it is well reconstructed with having the main character morph into three separate entities: human, evil and reborn. It appears, now that sufficient time has passed, there will be no concluding episodes but for the time being, *Soul Fire Rising* is one of the better Internet series of its kind.

Episodes:
1. I Give You My Soul. Introduces the demon Lilith as she seeks the soul of a young man.
2. The Messenger. Lilith is approached by Gabriel for a special mission.
3. The Temptation. Lilith and her soul-stealing rivals, Serpica and Syrus, seek the same soul—Adrian.
4. Claims. The battle for Adrian's soul begins with Lilith defeating her rivals.
5. The Deal. With Lilith revealing her human side and saving Adrian, Gabriel offers her a second chance at redemption by finding Eve before her soul is taken.
6. The Transformation. Jodi Lyn O'Keefe becomes Lilith as she transforms from Winger to Human when she accepts Gabriel's offer.
7. The Trio. Lilith, now reborn, must turn to the forces of darkness (the Trio) for help in finding the elusive Eve.
8. Raum Cometh. Unresolved cliffhanger as Lilith, finding Eve, must battle Lord Raum, the evil Demon seeking Eve's soul.

305 Space Guys in Space. spaceguysinspace. com. 2013 (Science Fiction).

A narrator tells us "In the beginning there was nothing which exploded and there was the Earth, which eventually exploded. Humanity tried to escape the explosions by sending a colony of its best and brightest off into space but that exploded too." What was left were two idiots (Stew and Carl), a malfunctioning space pod (*Portaterian*) and a gorgeous female hologram named GUSS that is the life support of the pod—and the only hope Stew and Carl have of surviving. Episodes follow the last remaining members of the human race as they drift in space (the pod has no engines) struggling to survive and hopefully find another planet with an atmosphere capable of supporting human life.

Cast: Jason Marsden (Carl), Dave Levine (Stew), Nicole Pacent (GUSS). **Credits:** *Producer:* Tony Wallace, John Frank Rosenblum, Jason Marsden. *Director:* Daniel Capuzzi, *Writer:* Tony Wallace. **Comment:** Nicole Pacent steals the show as GUSS in a comical science fiction parody of what could happen to the last survivors of a planet. The acting is good, GUSS is sexy, the special effects well executed and the overall production worth watching.

Episodes:
1. The Podd Couple (5 min., 30 sec.). GUSS in-

forms us that she is stuck on the pod with two morons when the Earth exploded.

2. Two Guys, One Pod (5 min., 12 sec.). Carl, being the brighter of the two, tries to figure out how to repair the pod's engines (contradicting what had been previously established—the pod has no engines).

3. Confessional, FlurmJam 4.9 (2 min., 11 sec.). Influenced by *Star Trek* Carl begins a journal he calls his "Captain's Logs."

4. Tension (4 min., 58 sec.). Carl and Stew are trying to adjust to GUSS, who can't seem to adjust to them.

5. Random Log: FlurmJam 16.5 (2 min., 40 sec.). Although she is a highly intelligent, GUSS appears to be attracted to Stew.

6. Hole (5 min., 8 sec.). Carl and Stew find the tight quarters becoming an annoyance as they have to constantly be together.

7. Hunger Pains (5 min., 19 sec.). Carl begins to fear for the worst when their food supply becomes dangerously low.

8. In Dependence (4 min., 22 sec.). A worm hole inside the pod solves the food problem (as it can produce things like pizza and beer).

9. Girl Gab, FlurmJam 10–3 (1 min., 47 sec.). GUSS gets times to shine—by relating her thoughts on "lady stuff."

10. Regrets (4 min., 29 sec.). Carl and GUSS try to work out their differences.

11. Confessional, FlurmJam 12.7 (1 min., 36 sec.). Carl reports that he cannot find any privacy.

12. Albinards (5 min., 52 sec.). Alien's drop by—and soon wish they hadn't when they encounter Stew and Carl.

13. Poddy Time, FlurmJam 8.6 (1 min., 31 sec.). Carl's Captain's Log records the fact that Stew hogs the bathroom.

14. Confessional, FlurmJam 18.2 (2 min., 12 sec.). His Captain's Log continues to relay the fact that he (Carl) cannot find any private time.

15. Amazons (5 min., 52 sec.). Stew and Carl (and GUSS) encounter gorgeous Space Amazons—with the guys thinking of only one thing. But what will happen if an earthling mates with a Space Amazon?

16. Girl Gab, FlurmJam 22.9 (2 min., 7 sec.). A rather delicate episode wherein GUSS shares her "wisdom" about "that time of month" with Stew and Carl.

17. FlurmJam 60.3 (1 min., 51 sec.). Stew recalls memories from his past life on Earth.

18. Ninja (5 min., 7 sec.). Stew surprises Carl and GUSS when he reveals he is a Ninja.

19. Confessional, FlurmJam 44.6 (1 min 28 sec.). Carl reflects on his moronic pod mate.

20. Confessional, FlurmJam 50.1 (1 min., 24 sec.). Having lived with two idiots for a while, GUSS believes she has figured out a way to handle Stew and Carl.

21. Hole Theory (4 min., 34 sec.). How a worm hole exists in a space pod is unknown, but Stew's continual fascination with it has Carl worried.

22. Gee (6 min., 2 sec.). After drifting aimlessly for months, the pod is visited by an alien called The All Powerful Gee.

23. Madness (4 min., 48 sec.). Being cooped up with Carl and encountering aliens has Stew believing he has contracted Space Madness.

24. Box (6 min., 2 sec.). Stew believes he has found a way to reverse what has happened to Earth by traveling back in time and preventing the explosions from occurring.

25. Hygiene (3 min., 3 sec.). Another delicate episode as GUSS too finds personal time for herself a problem—especially with the always leering Stew.

26. Change (6 min., 50 sec.). The concluding episode wherein Stew, Carl and GUSS find they are apparently going to be trapped in space forever.

306 *Space Hospital.* spacehospital.tv. 2007–2011 (Science Fiction).

Space Hospital is a mobile medical facility in deep space that is owned by the Overlords, pan-dimensional beings who run the Centrality sector of outer space. The staff is a bit off-the-wall and stories relate their antics as they attend patients and struggle to keep their facility afloat amid threats of it being closed due to its increasing financial problems.

Cast: Adriana Roze (Nurse Ratknee), Anne Ford Galiana (Nurse Barbara), Rich Hutchman (Administrator Snead), Tim Sullens (Dr. Goode), Robert Poe (Prince Plodd), Mary Buckley (Lindsay Long), Brett A. Snodgrass (Dr. Larry), Jodi Dybala (Nurse), Andy Hungerford (Dr. Drake), Heather Horton (Maggie Morningstar), Vanessa Vaughn (Sister Hilly), Frank Conniff (Pres. Magnavision), Tifanie McQueen (Nurse Ripner). **Credits:** *Producer:* Susan Stoebner. *Director:* Robert Poe, John Baumgartner. *Writer:* Robert Poe, Sigurd Ueland. **Comment:** Sort of a more outlandish version of the television series *Scrubs* that is set in outer space complete with a wacky staff and patients that require the expertise of doctors and nurses that, for the most part, do not have that expertise.

Episodes:

1. Log 1: Happiest Surgeon in Space. Introduces Dr. Goode, a self-medicating physician who is about to marry the lovely Nurse Barbara; and Snead, the Chief Hospital Administrator who tries to impress his zombie nurse (Maggie Morningstar) by performing surgery.

2. Log 2: I'm Pregnant. The Chief Nurse (Ratknee) discovers she is pregnant but can't figure out who the father is.

3. Log 3: Day of the X. As the crew sings carols in celebration of an ancient holiday, a solar flare causes the ship to rattle and sends Nurse Ratknee into labor.

Space Hospital cast in a costume pose (copyright 2013 Robert Poe).

4. Log 4: I, Manbot. Just as intergalactic tennis star Lindsay Austin arrives at Space Hospital to have her bionics upgraded, Nurse Ratknee gives birth to a robot baby—a robot that grows within days into a child-like man and falls in love with Lindsay—much to Ratknee's displeasure.

5. Log 5: Save the Robots. Now that her baby has grown, Nurse Ratknee begins a crusade to raise awareness of the widespread unemployment rate among robots on Earth.

6. Log 6: Father and Clones. Snead, lonely and over-worked, decides to grow a clone as both an assistant as well as a son.

7. Log 7: Boobification. Somewhat sexist episode wherein the hospital, under pressure to increase its revenues or close, comes up with a procedure for women to increase their breasts—to as many as 200.

8. Log 8: Reading, Writing and Reactionary. When an archeological dig uncovers evidence of rebellions having occurred on Earth in its past, Snead orders a ban on reading to suppress what he fears may cause unrest at the hospital.

9. Log 9: Half Dozen of the Other. An emergency operation on an Omacron brings out the feelings both Nurse Ratknee and Nurse Barbara have for the alien.

10. Log 10: New Organ. A line of replacement organs is introduced at Space Hospital—"Just because you weren't born with it, does mean you can't have it."

11. Log 11: Work Better with Svedka Vodka. After Dr. Goode endorses a vodka product to help the struggling hospital overcome its financial woes, he finds that being drunk makes him a better doctor.

12. Log 12: Omagone. Totally dissatisfied with Space Hospital's performance record, the Overlords dispatch Prince Neville Plodd to either whip it in shape or destroy it.

307 *Space Hospital: The Animated Series.* spacehospital.tv. 2012 (Science Fiction).

Animated version of the live action *Space Hospital* series (see prior title) about the antics of the staff and patients of the orbiting space hospital in an unspecified futuristic time. **Voice Cast:** Anne Ford Galiana, Robert Poe, Adriana Roze, Brett Snodgrass, Sigurd Ueland, Vanessa Vaughn. **Credits:** *Producer-Writer-Director:* Sigurd Ueland, Robert Poe. **Comment:** While not as outrageous as the live action series, the stories are well animated and written and an enjoyable companion series to *Space Hospital*.

Episodes:

1. Alien Baby Birth (1 min., 10 sec.). An alien baby is born of a surrogate human man and presented to an alien couple.

2. Lindsay Lohan Kill (1 min., 59 sec.). Celebrity guest surgeon, Lindsay Lohan, performs an operation on a patient.

3. Dale vs. Roach (1 min., 26 sec.). A Dalek-like robot (from the series *Doctor Who*) seeks to "ex-ter-min-ate" a giant roach in the hospital.

4. Darth Vader vs. Space Hospital (1 min., 15 sec.). *Star Wars* Darth Vader encounters difficulty attempting to explain his presence at the hospital when Nurse Barbara continually ignores him while taking phone calls.

5. Baba Fett in Love (50 sec.). Staffer Baba falls in love with the admissions nurse (Barbara) although she has no idea and couldn't care less.

6. Rise of the Storm-Tumors (51 sec.). A Storm Trooper is diagnosed with a brain tumor but apparently kept in the dark about their inability to help him.

7. Brangalin Gone Wild (2 min., 7 sec.). An attempt to meld together the Brangalin space orphan family together as one entity goes horribly wrong when a hideous monster results.

8. Storm Trooper vs. Nurse Barbara (53 sec.). Nurse Barbara is not so discreet in front of the Storm Trooper with the brain tumor when he was supposed to be kept in the dark but hears there is no hope for him when Barbara blabs it to a friend.

9. Alien Family vs. DCFS (1 min., 28 sec.). The alien family from episode 1 faces a loss of their infant when the DCFS (Department of Child Family Services) threatens to take it away from them when it was discovered the couple smoked marijuana.

10. Darth Vader Disney Make Over (1 min., 26 sec.). Darth Vader (from episode 4) gets a sissy make over when he finally gets a chance to tell Barbara the purpose for his visit (to become more attractive).

11. The Fart of Life (1 min., 26 sec.). To save the life of a terminally ill patient, the Vulcan-like (from *Star Trek*) mind-meld is attempted.

12. Justin Bieber vs. Space Hospital (2 min., 57 sec.). Justin, seen as a baby-eating pop star, performs a song at Space Hospital.

308 *Spellfury.* spellfury.com. 2008–2012 (Fantasy).

Medieval-set saga of Druinia, an elf who wields a magic sword she found, as she helps the innocent while evading Kruskull, an evil sorcerer whom she believes murdered her father and now seeks to regain his lost sword for the power it will afford her.

Cast: Julie O'Halloran (Druinia), Penu Chalykoff (Kruskull), Ian Quick (Xorn), Debra Ereaut (Velura), Travis Gordon (Bip), Matt Ficner (Tarek). **Credits:** *Producer:* Jason Devlin. *Writer-Director:* Travis Gordon. **Comment:** Good acting and production values that make for a pleasant medieval tale.

Episodes:

1. Hit the Ground Running. Druinia and her human friend, Tarek, confront a forest demon.

2. Play Misty for Me. As Druinia battles the demon, she finds the magic sword that allows her to defeat it.

3. Sword Demon-Stra-tion. With the demon destroyed, Druinia also discovers that Tarek has been killed.

4. You Drive Me Batty. Distraught over Tarek's death, Druinia begins wandering in a forest when she attacked by a horde of huge bats.

5. Thrak Off. Kruskull, the evil sorcerer, and his henchman, Grokonion Thrak are introduced in a story that finds the thief Xorn stealing the magic sword from Druinia.

6. Fights, Plights and Insights. Believing that Kruskul is out to kill him

Space Hospital: The Animated Series. **Animated renditions of the live-action cast (copyright Brett Snodgrass and Robert Poe).**

Bar scene from an episode of *Spellfury* (copyright 2014 Travis Gordon).

for failing to get the sword, Thrak forsakes Kruskull while Druinia continues to pursue Xorn for her sword.

7. Don't Cross Me. As Druinia confronts Xorn, she finds herself helpless without her magic sword.

8. A Hairy Situation. Now having to work without Thrak, Kruskull dispatches two demons to kill Druinia and get the sword from Xorn.

9. Druinia Unleashed. Druinia manages to get her sword back and uses it to fend off Kruskull's demons.

10. To Errol Is Human. The demons get the best of Druinia, who is knocked unconscious but is saved by a cleric named Errol.

11. I Get Grok'd Down, But I Get Up. During a fight against Kruskull's demons, Druinia is injured— but healed by Errol.

12. Out of the Frying Pan. As Druinia and Errol defeat the enemy, they encounter more trouble when they encounter the Fire and Ice Demon.

13. Mum's the Word. Druinia and Errol, unable to defeat the demon, seek a place to hide.

14. Very Ice to Meet You. Unable to evade the demon, Druinia and Errol face it one last time.

15. The Legendary Magic Sword. With the help of the sword, Druinia defeats the demon.

16. Spiders, Faeries and Dragons, Oh My! In the conclusion, Kruskull enlists the aid of a witch to free a dragon that he believes will be his salvation when it kills Druinia and he acquires the sword.

309 Spider-Woman: Agent of S.W.O.R.D.
marvel.com. 2009 (Science Fiction).

The Scientific World Observation and Response Department (S.W.O.R.D.) is an organization that responds to alien threats, especially those of a race called the Skrull. Prior to their current round-up by S.W.O.R.D., the Skrull secretly invaded Earth with a diabolical plan to use their shape-shifting abilities to overtake the bodies of America's greatest super heroes and use their abilities for their own means. One super hero, Spider-Woman (alias Jessica Drew) was one such victim whose life was ruined before her shape shifter, the Queen of the Skrull could be caught. Jessica, angered by what happened, leaves The Avengers (America's super hero fighting team) and, at the urging of Abigail Brand, the director of S.W.O.R.D., joins her organization to get her life back and bring an end to the Skrull invasion. Stories follow Jessica as she begins her quest to capture the Skrull imposters who are still posing a threat. Also hindering Jessica's efforts is HYDRA, a diabolical organization headed by the evil Lady Hydra. Jessica is an Avenger with super strength, endurance, reflexes and capable of producing bioelectric venom blasts (as a result of her transformation when her father used an experimental spider venom to save her life after she was bitten by a poisonous spider).

Cast: Nicolette Reed (Jessica Drew/Lady Hydra), Stephanie K. Thomas (Abigail Brand), Andy MacKenzie (Det. Chong). **Credits:** *Director:* Joe Quesada. *Writer:* Brian Bendis, Sal Buscema, Archie Goodwin, Jim Mooney. **Comment:** In 1949 a series called *The Telecomics* used panel drawings to tell stories. *Spider-Woman* incorporates that same concept but in a much more sophisticated manner. Although the presentation will seem a bit odd at first, it will soon become an intriguing series to watch. There is limited action animation and the story is told mostly through the narration of Jessica over expertly executed panel drawings of what happens. It is like watching a comic book come to life and it does capture the viewer's attention. Smartly produced program.

Episodes:

1. Episode 1. Bitter at the injustice that was done to her by the invading Skrull (who ruined her life), Jessica joins S.W.O.R.D. Her first assignment: kill a Skrull hiding on the island of Madripoor.

2. Episode 2. During her quest, Jessica encounters a new threat, HYDRA, but is captured by its leader (Lady Hydra) and imprisoned before she can do anything.

3. Episode 3. As Jessica seeks a way to escape from the compound, she encounters a Skrull imposter that she is eventually forced to terminate.

4. Episode 4. Jessica, with the blood of a Skrull on her hands, escapes from Lady Hydra but encounters a group of mercenaries (the Thunderbolts) who are attempting to kidnap her for their boss, Norman Osborn, the head of a black ops team.

5. Episode 5. Jessica escapes the threat of the Thunderbolts but faces her greatest challenge when she finds the Skrull she has been seeking.

310 Spine Chillers. spinechillerswebseries. com. 2013 (Horror).

Anthology program that combines elements of *The Twilight Zone, The Outer Limits* and *Tales from the Crypt* to present stories that also combine elements of horror, fantasy and light comedy. **Cast:** Bruce Campbell, Christopher Dinnan, Carol Ilku, Josh Becker, Paul Harris, Robbie Gordonier, Rob Rose, Jessika Alura. **Credits:** *Producer:* Christopher Dinnan. *Writer-Director:* Christopher Dinnan, Josh Becker, Paul Harris. **Comment:** The series tagline, "Submitted for your approval," immediately establishes the fact that a *Twilight Zone*–like program has been produced (as those words were spoken by "Zone" host Rod Serling). Like its predecessors, *Spine Chillers* is imaginative and a bit creepy and presents new takes on stories that have been done before.

Episodes:

1. Frontier Style (15 min., 26 sec.). A man (Timmy), addicted to gambling, suddenly finds his life changing (for the better?) when he becomes enthralled with a mysterious girl that captures his attention—and appears to be a serial killer.

2. Sorry I Couldn't Make It (14 min., 46 sec.). After an argument with his girlfriend, a man (Chad) looks up a former love and believes he has found the girl of his dreams—until he learns that she committed suicide five years ago. But then who (or what) was the girl he met?

3. Roadkill (15 min., 56 sec.). A worker for Crit-

ter Catchers, (Robbie), sent into the woods to investigate reports of broken steel traps, encounters the deadly creature (Sawtooth), a creature now out to kill him.

311 Spirits. wogglebox.com. 2012–2013 (Horror).

Kaelyn Farrow is a teenage girl whose life is anything but normal. While she is loved by her family, has lots of friends and attends Empire High School, she is also being haunted by the spirit of her younger sister, Abigail, who died ten years ago (seemingly by a demon created by a Dr. Edison) in a mental institution. The haunting, however, is not to menace Kaelyn, but warn her that "Hell is coming for you Kaelyn Farrow and I'm its passenger" and that she needs Kaelyn's help in finding a secret door that will bring them together and enable them to join forces and prevent a great catastrophe from happening (apparently a doctor named Samuel Edison created a process to extend life by separating the spirit from the body and transferring it into another body. But the process is not always successful and spirits are damaged. Damaged spirits can reanimate their bodies and become a deadly menace. Such was the case with Fred, a failed experiment that Kaelyn was forced to kill. Fred, now called Dead Fred, is angry at Kaelyn as she was there when he died and she is now connected to the experiment. He has gone on a killing spree and Kaelyn must stop him). The program follows Kaelyn as she tries to accept what is happening to her and help Abigail achieve her goal so she can see the light and move on. As the story progresses, Kaelyn involves her friend Alyssa, first only to document what is happening (prove that she is being haunted) but help her put an end to killings caused by Dr. Edison's experiments (Kaelyn and Alyssa grew up together and have a connection to the supernatural as they encountered demons when they were children).

Cast: Lia Marie Johnson (Kaelyn Farrow), Brittanie Brant (Alyssa Walker), Hannah Swain (Abigail), Brad M. Bucklin (Dr. Samuel Edison), Alexis G. Zall (Ayla Walker), Jon Amirkhan (Dead Fred), Chloe Ewing (Young Kaelyn), Avery Rose (Young Alyssa). **Credits:** *Producer:* Kristian Gabriel, Toi Juan Shannon, Brad M. Bucklin. *Writer-Director:* Kristian Gabriel. **Comment:** Although the story remains unresolved, it is a good supernatural thriller. Lia Marie Johnson is especially appealing (and convincing) as Kaelyn while Hannah Swain and the special effects provided present the kind of creepy little girl that could give one nightmares. The producers have achieved a series worthy of broadcast or cable television. The series is also known as *Woggle Box Spirits.*

Episodes:

1. Nightmares (13 min., 41 sec.). Kaelyn assists the help of her friend Alyssa to document the strange

events that are occurring after a spirit appears to her.

2. School Daze (15 min., 37 sec.). The spirit reveals itself to be Abigail and that she has returned to acquire Kaelyn's help in saving the world.

3. The Secret Door (15 min., 45 sec.). Alyssa reflects on what she and Kaelyn have encountered, stating that what happens in her city (Empire) is not always what they seem.

4. The End of All (30 min., 44 sec.), Kaelyn and Alyssa recall their experiences as children and their first encounters with the supernatural, which gives them the courage to confront what is happening—but is something more sinister waiting? (The concluding episode).

312 *Splatter.* Neflix.com. 2009 (Horror).

Feeling that he has been betrayed by those close to him, legendary rock star Johnny Splatter commits suicide in a devious plan to come back as a zombie and kill those who ruined his life by taking away everything he achieved. At the reading his will, a former band mate (Mortis, who stole his song), his manager (Spencer Pope), his therapist (Dr. Bellows) and a groupie (Fiona Crown) gather to drool over the riches they will receive. It's what they didn't expect and the program relates Johnny's efforts to eliminate them one-by-one and achieve his revenge. **Cast:** Corey Feldman (Johnny Splatter), Erin Way (Fiona Crown), Mark Alan (Mortis), Tony Todd (Spencer Pope), Tara Leigh (Krule), Stuart Pankin (Dr. Bellows). **Credits:** *Producer:* Roger Corman, Julie Corman, Elizabeth Stanley. *Director:* Joe Dante. *Writer:* Richard Christian Matheson. **Comment:** Considering the talent involved (from a well-know cult producer [Roger Corman] to a notable television writer [Richard Christian Matheson] and several known television actors [Corey Feldman, Stuart Pankin] a rather disappointing project resulted. Corey's makeup as a zombie is good and Erin Fay (the groupie) steals the show (with her performance actually the best part of the program). Roger Corman's name alone will draw fans to the show despite the clichéd writing and needless references to then current pop culture events (even Stuart Pankin's character is named after Dr. Alfred Bellows from the 1960s television series *I Dream of Jeannie*).

Episodes: All 10 episodes have been taken off line although it can be viewed as an edited 29-minute short on various websites.

313 *Spook House Dave.* spookhousedave. com. 2009 (Horror).

Dave is a 12-year-old boy who attends Mount Savage Middle School in the town of Mount Savage, Pennsylvania. He is an average student, likes video games and is starting to show an interest in girls. He is also an unusual kid. He is called Spook House

Dave because he lives in a haunted castle on top of Mount Savage and is cared for by a group of lovable unearthly creatures (a crazy mummy, a cranky vampire, a mischievous witch and a romantic werewolf). Legend has it that as a baby Dave was left on the doorstep of the castle with a note attached saying "Please Take Care of Dave." The creepy family took him in and now Dave must actually live in two different worlds—one with a family of monsters and one in the world of ordinary humans. The program follows Dave's experiences as he contends with the antics of his adopted family.

Morlock is a 700-year-old grumpy vampire that sleeps all day and complains all night about the local villagers. He "earned his fangs" in Medieval Europe and is now the owner of the haunted castle in which Dave lives. His age has slowed him down a bit (his back may go out when he transforms into a bat—but he can still drain the blood out of a young woman at a moment's notice).

Bobo is the Frankenstein-like monster created by a mad scientist in the 1800s from a mix of body parts and steam engine coils. He is literally a grown baby and very strong and kept locked in the castle's dungeon (to keep him from stomping through the village and destroying it).

Umberto, a werewolf, is the seventh son of a seventh son and was born in Argentina. Although he is a werewolf, he is treated by the others as the family's pet dog (until the full moon rises and transforms him—not only into a wolf, but sometimes, he dons a dress and calls himself Margarita).

Old Pharris is a 3,000-year-old mummy from the Pyramids of Giza in Egypt. Although he has no brain and his skull has been stuffed with sawdust, he enjoys life although he occasionally loses a limb if he is too active (his bandages need to be tightened now and then to keep all his parts together). He also has a mummified pet cat named Edgar.

Ghost is a castle resident who comes and goes as he pleases. Who or what he was is unknown (and no one seems to care) and his job appears to be giving the castle its haunted reputation.

Hagatha is a 296-year-old ugly witch (wart on nose and all) who rides a broom, cackles and delights in casting spells on unsuspecting villagers. Her potions for youth (goblin heads and roaches) keep her young at heart and she hopes that Dave will become a warlock and someday marry a witch.

Forry is Dave's pet monster, an unknown creature with large grin and razor-sharp teeth (whom Dave found living under Hagatha's cauldron).

Voices/Puppeteers: Lucky Yates, Jason von Hinesmeyer, Scott Warren. **Credits:** *Producer:* Melissa Honabach, Michael Koziol. *Director:* Deb A. Davis. *Writer:* Lucky Yates. **Comment:** Enjoyable horror-comedy mix that is well produced with characters that will appeal to both children and adults.

Episodes: While episodes are still online, it is difficult to determine just how many. The official website claims eight episodes but it also has pages for 31 Halloween accented mini-episodes and several episode extras. Only four of the eight episodes are available ("Mascot," "School Dance," "Backpack" and "Soup Night"); all the mini-Halloween episodes are available as are the episode extras for episode four ("Soup Night"). Like the actual series episodes, the holiday-themed and extras episodes involve the characters in a brief predicament.

The episode *Mascot* finds Dave wanting to change his innocent boy persona into that of a beastly Mount Savage Goat. Dave searches the catacombs of the castle seeking his missing backpack in the premiere episode, *Backpack*. In *Soup Night*, the family prepares for the scariest evening of the year—the night Hagatha makes her homemade soup. Dave seeks to find a date for the upcoming school dance in *School Dance*.

The extras are *Pharris' Story* (wherein the mummy relates how the game of hide-and-go-seek was invented 3000 years ago) and *DNN Nudists* The Dave News Network reports a startling fact: "Naked nakedness in Mount Savage."

Stage Fright series poster art (copyright American Wasteland Entertainment, LLC).

314 Stage Fright. americanwastelandent.com. 2012 (Horror).

A newlywed couple (Laney and Emmett) seeking to begin their own business, purchase the old Vanguard Theater, unaware that its sinister past will affect them in the present. **Cast:** Brittney Greer (Laney Summers), Zac Rantz (Emmett Summers), Mickey Stone (Magnus Blackwood), Chris Greig (Craig), Elaine Jenkins (Crazy Old Lady), Stephen Nations (Creepy Cashier), Jennifer Eiffert (Creepy Crawler), Haley Bertrand (Burn Victim), Kevin Keppy (Glomo, the Happy Jester), Marci Manna (Mrs. Johnson), Angel Gonzales (Ghost Kid), Jason Knight (Two Faced Piano Player). **Credits:** *Producer-Director:* Jason Brasier. *Writer:* Jason Brasier, Brittney Greer. **Comment:** Well done chiller that holds viewer interest, making it a well-worth watching.

Episodes:

1. Chapter 1 (11 min., 44 sec). Emmett is thrilled by the purchase of an old theater but Laney has an uneasy feeling over their new venture as people tell them that the theater is evil.

2. Chapter 2 (7 min., 52 sec.). Laney's uneasiness begins to manifest itself as her fears are being realized by strange occurrences.

3. Chapter 3 (10 min., 29 sec.). Laney finds a mysterious box that could hold secrets regarding the theater.

4. Chapter 4 (6 min., 5 sec.). Laney, left at home alone when Emmett rushes off to the theater, uncovers disturbing information about the theater (the previous owner killed himself [slit his throat] in front of a packed house).

5. Chapter 5 (8 min., 21 sec.). Laney rushes to the theater where she encounters several deranged actors who believe that to save their beloved theater they need a blood sacrifice in front of a packed house. Their choice is Laney. In a surprise ending, the

sacrifice is fulfilled with Emmett unable to save her.

315 *Standard Action.* standardaction.zom bieorpheus.com. 2010–2013 (Fantasy).

A medieval-set program that follows four would-be barbarians (Edda, Martin, Wendy and Fernando) as they set out on a self-proclaimed quest to rid the world of evil—despite the fact that evil keeps coming back to haunt them.

Cast: Joanna Gaskell (Edda), Edwin Perez (Fernando), Tara Pratt (Wendy), Daniel S. Johnston (Martin), Nicole Riglietti (Kev), Edward Foy (Torval), Mike Klemak (Dragan), Ilze Burger (Astrid), Stuart McLean (Steve the Wraith), Rebecca Husain (Ikosa), Lawrence Tse (Marcus). **Credits:** *Producer-Writer:* Joanna Gaskell, Rob Hunt. *Director:* Rob Hunt. **Comment:** Whether or not female barbarians had pointy ears (like Edda) doesn't really matter as a humorous take on medieval barbarians is well presented with somewhat convincing costumes and well executed outdoor sequences.

Episodes:

1. The Barbarian (10 min., 1 sec.). Introduces Edda, a female barbarian who believes that only violence can resolve a situation (and the more the better).

2. The Druid (10 min., 29 sec.). Edda forms an adventuring party with Wendy, Martin and Fernando.

3. The Bard and the Sorcerer (9 min., 6 sec.).

Wendy and Martin, separated from Edda and Fernando, must fend for themselves until they reconnect with their better halves.

4. The Tavern (13 min., 13 sec.). The team reunites at a tavern called The Lonely Dragon.

5. Adventure Hook (10 min., 15 sec.). The team returns to the woods to begin their adventuring quests.

6. Questing (10 min., 16 sec.). Before continuing, the team believes that, for them to become a team, they must face a right of passage (here deciding upon low-level questing).

7. Standard Action: Episode 7 (12 min., 32 sec.). An unrelated (to the prior episodes) recap of what has happened thus far.

8. Don't Split the Party (12 min., 18 sec.). After completing their questing feats, the team continues their journey—this time having to battle a group of Halflings.

9. Hail to the King, Baby (15 min., 36 sec.). Fernando, a bard, takes center stage, when he and the team attempt to track down a band of cannibals that stole their gear.

10. Hero Worship (12 min., 11 sec.). The team attempts to come with a plan to rescue a cleric (Torval) from a group of hobgoblins.

11. The Breaking of Friendship (12 min., 15 sec.). The "brilliant" plan devised by the team begins to fall apart when the hobgoblins close in.

12. Of Keys and Cages (14 min., 23 sec.). As their plans backfire, the team is captured and imprisoned by the hobgoblins; Wendy has second doubts about

Standard Action **cast, from left to right: Tara Pratt, Daniel S. Johnston, Joanna Gaskell and Edwin Perez (copyright Critical Success Productions, Inc.).**

why she is doing what she is doing and is separated from the team.

13. Will and Fortitude (14 min., 52 sec.). Edda, Fernando and Martin free themselves, but unite in an effort to find Wendy.

14. Hell Hath No Fury (10 min., 46 sec.). Wendy proves to be more of a fighter than she thought and realizes what she is doing is for the better good (the season finale).

15. The Board Is Set (7 min., 48 sec.). Season two begins as the team, as bumbling as ever, "hit the road" to "save the world from evil."

16. Watching the Watchers (9 min., 2 sec.). Edda and the team decide to return home after their long journey (from season 1) and, as can be expected, must battle several villains before they even start.

17. Reckless (10 min., 58 sec.). As the intrepid team enters a forest they must contend with a band of evil Kobolds.

18. Inconceivable (10 min., 28 sec.). As Edda battles a masked man in the swamps, Fernando faces his biggest fear—a vicious hobgoblin.

19. Mine Is an Evil Laugh (8 min., 14 sec.). After capturing a villain (Orlando), the team learns through interrogation that they are destined for greater things.

20. Don't Panic (7 min., 38 sec.). Wendy finds an artifact and wonders what it could mean to her and the team.

21. Countless Doorways (8 min., 14 sec.). Edda encounters a rock monster while an explosion transports Martin and Fernando to the present.

22. Watching the Watcher (8 min., 2 sec.). With Edda and Wendy in their own time and Martin and Fernando in the future each duo must now navigate new circumstances. However, when Wendy encounters the Mysterious Woman in White and asks for help, the woman partially grants her request and returns Fernando to them. Martin remains stranded in the future and the series ends in a cliffhanger.

316 Star Trek Equinox. hiddenfrontier. com. 2013 (Science Fiction).

A *Star Trek* franchise program that charts the voyages of the Starfleet space ship U.S.S. *Equinox* under the leadership of Captain Rudy Ransom.

Cast: Robert Thomas Hawke (Capt. Rudolph "Rudy" Ransom), Michael Dempsey (Cmdr. Charlie Rea), Jeff Harth (Lt. Cmdr. Ruko Sullivan), James Butterfield (Lt. Cmdr. Mike McCullough), Lee James Sands (Lt. Cmdr. Tom Fitzgerald), Michael Liebmann (Dr. John Pass), Thomas Barnes (Lt. Maxwell Burke), Eleiece Krawiec (Counselor Bridget Olsen), Christine Burton (Ensign Marla Gilmore), Mat Weller (Crewman Lessing), Jennifer Cole (Voice of Equinox computer). **Credits:** *Producer:* Carmen T. Burton, Charlie A. Rea, Rob Caves. **Comment:** The lengthy episode manages to tell the whole story of the *Equinox* in *Star Trek* like fashion

with good acting, writing, directing and special effects.

Episodes:

1. Shakedown (58 min., 16 sec.). Three Starfleet Academy cadets must come to the rescue when the senior staff of the *Equinox* are injured during a battle with the Cardassian force and save their ship.

317 Star Trek Odyssey. hiddenfrontier. com. 2007–2011 (Science Fiction).

Star Trek spin off about the U.S.S. *Odyssey*, a Federation star ship that has been equipped with slipstream technology (that enables it to traverse millions of light years in a matter of weeks) as it begins a mission to investigate reports of raiders operating in the Andromeda Galaxy.

Cast: Brandon McConnell (Lt. Cmdr. Ro Nevin), Michelle Laurent (Cmdr. T'Lorra), Julia Morizawa (Lt. Maya Stadi), Matthew Montgomery (Dr. Owen Vaughan), Tim Foutch (Ensign Josh Gillen), Sharon Savene (Seram), John Whiting (Gen. Morrigu), Adam Browne (Caecus), Sam Basca (Lt. Alex Wozniak), Jennifer Cole (Grand Majan), David O'Neill (Vito), Heather Ashleigh (Ensign Kristen Laws), Beau Williams (Dagad). **Credits:** *Producer:* Rob Caves, Jennifer Cole, Simon Fraser, David O'Neill, Adam Browne, Sharon Savene. *Director:* Simon Fraser, J.D. Tepnapa, Adam Browne, David O'Neill, Dave Mason, Sharon Savene, Carmen T. Burton, Janice Willcocks. *Writer:* Rob Caves, E. Robert Dunn, Kevyn Eiselt, Simon Fraser, Brian S. Matthews, Gene Roddenberry, Eric Weaver. **Comment:** Enough outer space intrigue and action to please any science fiction fan. The acting and production qualities are excellent.

Episodes:

1. Iliad. Establishes the storyline as the *Odyssey* journeys to an uninhabited section of Romulan space to investigate an invasion by mysterious ships in the Andromeda Galaxy.

2. The Wine Dark Sea. After surviving a battle with the Archiens, the *Odyssey*'s future is at risk when its antimatter storage units become depleted through an emergency pod dump.

3. The Lotus Eaters. Regaining control of the ship, the *Odyssey* continues with its mission: prevent the Archiens from committing genocide.

4. On the Knees of the Gods. One year has passed and the *Odyssey* is still trapped in Andromeda—and still being pursued by the Archien warships. Ro determines that the only way to survive is to negotiate with the Great Ones of the Archien High Command before it's too late.

5. The Immortal Loom. With an apparent truce between the *Odyssey* and the Archien, the *Odyssey* begins its long journey back home, but weary if the truce is a trap to destroy them.

6. For All Time. As Ro Nevin meets with the Great Ones, Searm prepares the *Odyssey* for battle with the Archiens.

7. A Light in the Dark. A flashback is used to re-call events in Ro's past as the fate of two galaxies hangs in the balance.

8. Tossed Upon the Shore. The crew of the U.S.S. *Helena* joins the *Odyssey* in the battle against the Archiens and helps the *Odyssey* return to its home base in the Milky Way.

318 *Star Trek: Federation One.* hidden frontier.com. 2003 (Science Fiction).

A *Star Trek* spin off that focuses on the Presidents of the United Federation of Planets and their en-tourage aboard the Federation's diplomatic flagship, *Federation One.*

Cast: Wayne Webb (Matt McCabe), Heather Ashleigh (Mara Onshul), Risha Denney (Commodore Shelby), Joni Bovill (Praetor Yeshva), Andrew Foster, (Deesus), Karl Puder (Korg), Kurt Wilson (Cmdr. Beckett), Wendy L. Smith (Marion), Consuela Sanchez (Alice), Gregg Knapp (Kramer). **Credits:** *Producer:* Rob Caves. *Director:* Jennifer Cole, David O'Neill. *Writer:* Brian S. Matthews. **Comment:** An unusual twist in the *Star Trek* franchise. While the episodes presented below are filmed, seasons two and three are presented only in an audio format (reminiscent of old time radio). Like other series in the *Star Trek* universe, the program is well done and is not only for Trekkies.

Episodes:

1. Institutions. Matt McCabe, the head of Presidential Security, must uncover the source of an information leak that threatens the office of the Presidency.

2. Unity. Matt institutes Operation Beta Shield after the death of a Federation member.

3. Intel. Matt is joined by Mara Onshul, the Science Intern, as he investigates the murder.

4. Family. Family members complicate matters on the ship as tensions run high among the dignitaries.

5. Obligations. Matt's investigation uncovers a conspiracy concerning the diplomat's death.

319 *Star Trek: Hidden Frontier.* hidden frontier.com. 2002–2007 (Science Fiction).

Star Trek spin off (set between the eras of the television series *Star Trek: Deep Space 9* and *Star Trek: Voyager*) that focuses on the crew of the U.S.S. *Excelsior*, based on Deep Space 12 in the Briar Patch, as it explores deep space.

Cast: David Dial (Admr. Ian Quincy Knapp), Risha Denney (Capt. Elizabeth Shelby), Larry LaVerne (Capt. Tolian Naros), John Whiting (Lt. Cmdr. Dr. Henglaar), Kelly Jamison, Joanne Bsch (Cmdr. Robin Lefler), Wayne Webb (Lt. Matt McCabe), Barbara Clifford (Lt. Cmdr. Myra Elbrey), Arthur Bosserman, Bobby Rice (Lt. Ro Nevin), J.T. Tepnapa (Lt. Cmdr. Corey Aster), Adam Browne (Lt. Jorian Zen/Dao). **Credits:** *Producer:* Rob Caves. **Com-**

ment: The program is based on a fan-created 2000 web series called *Voyages of the U.S.S. Anegles* (which see for information). *Hidden Frontier* is also a fan based production and is not as sophisticated as other *Star Trek* web series. The acing and writing are fine but the presentation is a bit awkward and, because green screen technology was used (presenting the virtual backgrounds) some scenes are flawed with a green-like glow around the characters. Before one can download season one episodes, a polite message will appear from producer Rob Caves: "We'd like to invite you to sample 'Hidden Frontier' by viewing one of our more recent episodes before starting from the beginning. We understand the desire to 'watch from the start', but as with anything, Season 1 was a learning experience for us. We believe that if you enjoy one of our recent season 6 or 7 episodes, you'll enjoy the episodes from the start. All we ask is a chance to put our best foot forward. Thanks."

Episodes:

1. Enemy Unknown, Part 1. The *Excelsior* is as-signed to protect the planet of Ba'ku, which is located in the mysterious Briar Patch.

2. Enemy Unknown, Part 2. The *Excelsior* cautiously approaches the Briar Patch unsure of what they will encounter.

3. Enemy Unknown, Part 3. Concludes the arc story with Capt. Knapp successfully completing their assignment.

4. Two Hours. The crew of the U.S.S. *Independence* is ordered to investigate an anomaly detected by a deep space probe.

5. Perihelion. The *Excelsior* embarks on a mission to investigate the mysterious disappearance of the Nova-class U.S.S. *Perihelion.*

6. Echoes. An enemy, the Grey, reappear and pose a threat to Starfleet.

7. Refugees. Captain Knapp and his crew attempt to stop the Grey from attacking Deep Space 12.

8. Yesterday's Excelsior. A flashback of sorts that shows what could have happened if the *Excelsior*, under the command of Captain Sulu, had been affected by a temporal anomaly, and the Federation had come under the control of the evil Borg Empire.

9. Old Wound. Elizabeth finds herself in a difficult position when she must prosecute Knapp, who has been accused of killing a Federation Ambassador while seeking to learn more about the Grey.

10. Great Starship Robbery. Orion Syndicate pirates kidnap Knapp's security chief, Luko, as a ploy to get the *Excelsior* to help them siphon off an explosive warp engine by-product from a derelict Starfleet ship.

11. Encke. Knapp is ordered to investigate the circumstances surrounding the destruction of the Encke, a terraforming vessel.

12. To the Stars. Focuses on Artim Ibanya, a visitor on *Excelsior* as he contemplates whether to remain with Starfleet Medical or accept the position of scientist in Danula II.

13. Fire in the Heart. *The Excelsior*, damaged in a Grey attack, seeks to escape a pursuing Grey fleet to affect repairs and fight back.

14. Coward's Death. Problems arise in the *Excelsior* when a conduit ruptures and kills an Andorian crew member.

15. Worst Fears, Part 1. Knapp is removed from the *Excelsior* when Starfleet questions his handing of the prior Grey attack (from episode 13).

16. Worst Fears, Part 2. Cleared, Knapp is reinstated as Captain but immediately faces a crisis when Deep Space 12 is surrounded by Grey battleships.

17. Worst Fears, Part 3. Concludes the arc story with Deep Space 12 being spared destruction.

18. Heroes. Trouble brews for the crew of the U.S.S. *Independence* when it is drawn to the Briar Patch through ancient archaeological artifacts.

19. In Memory Of. Corey Aster recalls a mission wherein he encountered a Borg Collective.

20. Modus Operandi. A retired Commander (Naros) boards the *Excelsior* to aid Knapp with a mission involving the Cardassians.

21. Santa Q. The crew prepares to celebrate Christmas at the same time worry is being expressed over the Briar Patch.

22. Ashes. Knapp must solve a dispute between two feuding colonists following the death of a Federation colonist.

23. Voyage of the Defiant. Luko and Lefler attempt to return an old Starfleet ship to service.

24. Hell's Gate, Part 1. Knapp and his crew investigate a deadly incident that occurred at a Grey Research facility.

25. Hell's Gate, Part 2. Concludes the story with Knapp resolving the situation.

26. Piracy of the Noble. Elizabeth charts a course for the *Excelsior* to track down a rogue Starfleet officer who now leads a group of space pirates.

27. Addictions. An investigation is begun to uncover who is responsible for the deaths of hundreds of Bajoran refugees in the Briar Patch.

28. Crossroads. The Federation attempts to help the Cardassian protect a ship from a possible Tholian attack.

29. Entanglement, Part 1. As the *Excelsior* investigates signals emanating on Ba'ku, the *Independence* prepares for a mission to explore the currents that allow access to the Briar Patch.

30. Entanglement, Part 2. The *Independence* has entered the subspace of the Briar Patch while the *Excelsior* has a run in with a Breen vessel.

31. Imminent Danger. It is learned that the Tholians have made inroads in the Brian Patch and pose more of a threat than previously thought.

32. Darkest Night. Danger lurks for the Federation when it encounters an enemy force while considering using Centris III as a listening post.

33. Security Counsel. Matt McCabe, the Security Chief, becomes the key player when the *Excelsior* at-tempts to help a Federation colony deal with supposed terrorist activities.

34. Epitaph. Secrets regarding the Grey are revealed.

35. The Battle Is Joined. A routine surveillance mission turns to a deadly confrontation when the *Antietam* oversteps its bounds.

36. Counter Measures. As Knapp deals with his rebellious daughter, the Tholians begin a series of events that will change the galaxy forever.

37. Dancing in the Dark. The *Excelsior* begins preparations for a Ba'ku scientific expedition.

38. Homeport. The Federation begins preparations for what could be a battle against the Grey.

39. Beachhead. The Tholians begin their plan by testing a new weapon against the Federation's Starfleet.

40. Vigil. Elizabeth assists a Romulan ship as it attempts to navigate the dangerous Brian Patch.

41. Her Battle Lanterns Lit. Knapp takes charge of the fleet (commanding from *Excelsior*) while Siroc, the Tholian enemy, plots to disrupt the Federation attack forces.

42. Heavy Loses. Defeated by Siroc and the Tholian Assembly, the *Excelsior* retreats, hoping to make it back to Deep Space 12 for repairs.

43. Bound. As the *Excelsior* journeys, the Allied fleet makes preparations to counter the Assembly's next attack.

44. Past Sins. Deep Space 12 has survived and the *Excelsior* has returned to her home base to recuperate.

45. Hearts and Minds. With no let up between battles, the Breen and Tholains again target not only the Federation's Starfleet but civilian ships as well.

46. Widening Gyre. The *Independence* is lost in battle while the Klingon and Romulans threaten to withdraw their support from the Federation against Siroc if Starfleet remains in charge.

47. Things Fall Apart. Siroc's plans to conquer progress while the Federation's Allies are collapsing, leaving Siroc the prime player.

48. The Center Cannot Hold. Elizabeth manages to sway the Klingon and Romulans to remain as Allies but Siroc may have the upper hand as he is ready to strike.

49. Its Hour Come Round at Last. The series finale with the Grey attacking Deep Space 12, *The Helena* in pursuit of Siroc and the *Excelsior* rejoining the fleet to protect the station's civilians.

50. Orphans of War. A special wherein Starfleet searches for one of its ships, the *Odyssey* after a battle with the evil Archien Empire.

51. Operation Beta Shield. Starfleet prepares for another battle from the mysterious Archien Empire, rulers of the Andromeda Galaxy.

320 Star Trek: Phase II. startrekphase2.com. 2004 (Science Fiction).

Created by fans of the Star Trek franchise by James Cawley and Jack Marshall in April of 2003. On January 16, 2004 they released the first of eight episodes (approximately one per year) that details the voyages of the starship *Enterprise* during the fourth year of its five year mission "to explore strange new worlds, seek out new lives and situations and boldly go where no man has gone before." Originally titled *Star Trek: New Voyages* and proposed as a network series continuation of the first *Star Trek* series (NBC, 1966–1969).

Cast: James Cawley, Brian Gross (Capt. James T. Kirk), John M. Kelley (Dr. Leonard McCoy), Charles Root (Montgomery Scott), Brandon Stacy, Ben Tolpin, Jeffrey Quinn (Mr. Spock), Kim Stinger (Lt. Uhura), Jonathan Zungre (Chekov), John Lim, J.T. Tepnapa (Sulu), Meghan King Johnson, Kelly Heffernan (Rand), Jeff Mailhotte (Sentell), Ron Boyd (DeSalle), Jay Storey (Kyle), Patrick Bell (Xon), Ron M. Gates (Ross), Paul Sieber (Ahrens), Bobby Rice (Peter Kirk), John Carrigan (Kargh), Shannon Quinlan (Nurse Chapel), Kurt Carley (Captain Pike). **Note:** Several former *Star Trek* regulars made guest appearances: Walter Koenig (Pavel Chekov), George Takei (Hikaru Sulu), Grace Lee Whitney (Janice Rand), Denise Crosby (Dr. Jenna Yar). Eugene Roddenberry, Jr., son of Star Trek creator Gene Roddenberry, served as the consulting producer for the first episode, "In Harm's Way." **Credits:** *Producer:* James Cawley, Jack Marshall, Pearl Marshall, James Lowe, Jeff Quinn, John Muenchrath, Max Rem. *Director:* Jack Marshall, Marc Scott Zicree, Jon Povill. *Writer:* D.C. Fontana, Marc Scott Zicree, Michael Reaves, David Gerrold, Dave Galanter, Shirley S. Maiweski, Patty Wright, Rick Chambers. **Comment:** The main characters are a bit younger-looking versions of the original 1966 *Star Trek* series regulars. The acting, writing, directing and production values are good and the program remains true to the original concepts presented when the *Enterprise* was first launched on NBC in 1966.

Episodes:

1. Center Seat. Introduces the former Ensign Sulu, now a Commander after completing command training as he returns to the *Enterprise*.

2. No Win Scenario. Captain Kirk faces his Klingon enemy, Kargh in a mock version of the "no win scenario" game.

3. Going Boldly. The *Enterprise* embarks on a mission to reverse time to stop "The Doomsday Wars" from ever occurring.

4. In Harm's Way. Kirk and his crew attempt to destroy the "Doomsday Machine" and prevent a devastating series of events that will change the future.

5. To Serve All My Days. With the *Enterprise* being threatened by a warring Klingon ship, Kirk finds himself at a loss when his chief weapons officer, Lt. Chekov, is stricken with an aging disease for which Dr. McCoy can not cure.

6. World Enough and Time. When a Romulan weapons test does not go as planned, the *Enterprise* is swept into an inter-dimension warp with time running out for Kirk to escape and return to his own dimension or be trapped forever.

7. Blood and Fire, Part 1. After escaping from the inter-dimension, the *Enterprise* is damaged when it is fired upon by a Klingon ship. As the crippled *Enterprise* drifts, a nearby star threatens to consume it—and the Klingon ship if they come within the star's gravity pull.

8. Blood and Fire, Part 2. Concludes the above story with the *Enterprise* narrowly escaping destruction but, even though not fully restored, must respond to a distress call from a research vessel in trouble.

9. Enemy Starfleet. The *Enterprise* finds itself under attack by Alersa, the commander of the long-lost Federation ship, the U.S.S. *Eagle*.

10. The Child. A mysterious alien entity affects a female crew member, impregnating her and allowing the birth of a child with remarkable—but dangerous abilities.

11. Enemy of Starfleet. The series conclusion that finds the *Enterprise* assigned to explore a new sector of space—only to find themselves immediately involved in a war between two alien factions.

321 *Star Trek: The Helena Chronicles.* hiddenfrontier.com. 2008 (Science Fiction).

Star Trek spin off about Theresa Faisal, captain of the Starfleet space ship U.S.S. *Helena* as it begins a journey to explore the newly found frontiers previously concealed by the deadly and mysterious Briar Patch.

Cast: Sharon Savene (Capt. Theresa Faisal), Adam Browne (Cmdr. Jorian Dao), PK Eiselt (Lt. Cmdr. Arvin Rockney), Gina DeVettori (Lt. Dais), Ben Euphrates (Lt. Mordan Ness), Beau Williams (Lt. Artim Bandya), JT Tepnapa (Lt. Cmdr. Corey Aster), Joanne Busch (Cmdr. Robin Lefler), David W. Dial (Adm. Ian Knapp). **Comment:** Not only for Star Trek fans, but for anyone interested in a well produced, exciting sci fi adventure.

Episodes:

1. Pilot. Establishes the storyline as the *Helena* begins its mission.

2. Under Pressure. As the *Helena* journeys through space, it learns that the Orions have gained control of a deadly Thelaron device and must now stop them from selling it to an enemy alien nation.

3. Letter of the Law. The *Helena* encounters the stranded *Odyssey* (from *Star Trek Odyssey*) and, against Starfleet orders, attempts a rescue mission.

4. The Minstrel Boy. Defying orders forces *The Helena* to destroy an Orion ship, causing concern among Starfleet officials who fear retaliation.

5. Red Sky at Morn. Starfleet assigns the U.S.S. *Phoenix* to find the *Helena*, which is now considered a rogue ship.

6. Leased Thunder. While the pursuit continues, Theresa uncovers evidence that the *Helena* may be the ploy in a Starfleet conspiracy.

322 *Starship Regulars.* Icebox.com. 1999 (Science Fiction).

An animated spoof of movie and television science fiction offerings that details the antics of Tycho, Wilson and Dave, soldiers stationed aboard the 24th century Federation starship *Integrity*, as they explore space, seeking less exploration and more women and alcohol.

Voice Cast: Diedrich Bader (Wilson), Billy Ragsdale (Tycho), Amy Pietz (Mara), Michael Dorn (Capt. Bellagen), Karl Wiedergott (Jackson/Blinka), Megan Price (Lees). **Credits:** *Producer:* Joanne Lee, Patricia Parker. *Writer:* Rob Lazebnik. *Animation Director:* Wes Archer. **Comment:** Not for children but for adults; a silly animated space spoof dealing primarily with a crew that lusts booze and women (although not necessarily in that order).

Episodes:

1. War. As a battle rages, the crew decides to engage in a drinking game to determine who is best at holding their liquor.

2. Hostage. The enemy takes not only the captain hostage but a rare bottle of alcohol (Cordomite).

3. Raid. With the loss of their rare bottle of Cordomite upper most on their minds, the crew plots to retrieve it by using an old transporter to beam it up (the captain is second on the list).

4. Enemy Engaged. The crew risks their lives to rescue a gorgeous but stranded Gerex woman.

5. Conquest. With the Gerex woman aboard, Tycho contemplates whether or not to seduce her—as intercourse with her means his death.

6. Galien Nation. Although straight, Tycho becomes the attraction of a male alien ambassador.

7. The Ultimate Weapon. The captain, faced with a decision as to whether or not introduce a virus into the evil Koraeg empire finds himself having a much more difficult time of it when the crew gets him drunk.

8. Obsession. Wilson becomes frustrated when a concert by is favorite singer, Dido on Rantor 6, may be cancelled due to a pending war in the Ashtar Nebula.

9. Virgin Territory. Temptation looms when Tycho is trusted to guard a beautiful alien princess.

10. Untouched. Wilson's dream of power becomes a reality when he is believed to be a god to the people of the planet Kaligian.

323 *Stephen King's "N."* stephenking.com/n. 2008 (Horror).

Animated adaptation of the Stephen King novel. A patient, referred to as only "N" by his psychiatrist, Dr. John Bonsaint, has related his beliefs about a circle of stones in a field on the outskirts of a nearby town (Ackerman's Field) conceal the portal to an alternate reality where a terrifying creature called Cthun lives. The creature is seeking to break free of his world and enter ours. John disbelieves him and diagnoses "N" as suffering form obsessive-compulsive disorder. "N" however, believes what he said is real and, unable to handle the situation, commits suicide. Shortly after, John begins to suffer the same symptoms as "N." Was "N" right? The story follows John as he tries to figure out exactly what the stones mean all the time slowly being driven insane by what he may discover.

Voice Cast: Jeff Perry (N), Ben Shenkman (John Bonsaint), Karen Ziemba (Sheila), Holter Graham (Charlie). **Credits:** *Illustrator:* Alex Maleev, Jose Villarubia. *Writer:* Stephen King. *Adaptation:* Marc Guggenheim. **Comment:** All 25 episodes have been taken off line ("This Video No Longer Exists" will appear); an opinion or even episode titles are not possible.

324 *Still: The Web Series.* chroniclefactory.com. 2013 (Science Fiction).

It appears as a day like any other day in the small picturesque Washington town of Sloughtown until strange noises are heard coming from the sky. At first it also appears that the sounds were nothing to be concerned about until people begin to become disoriented and, in some cases, zombie like with the ability to emit sound waves from their mouths and kill. The program follows the after affects the mysterious sounds have on the people—those that become affected and those that remain normal but now face danger from friends and even family members.

Cast: Joseph R. Porter (Hank), Angela Andrews (Cassy), Gregory Marks (Dr. Evans), Simone Leorin (Luca), Tabitha Bastien (Emily), Kael Wagner (Mark), Chloe Holbrook (Nina), Tim Forehand (Gabriel), Michael Chamberlain (Nelson), Thomas Murphy, David Ledingham, Michelle Stah, Nathan Christopher Hasse, Meredith Binder. **Credits:** *Producer-Writer-Director:* Jonathan Holbrook. **Comment:** Suspenseful, chilling program that has excellent production qualities and acting (broadcast worthy). The eighth episode is current as of March 2014 and establishes that more of the town's citizens have become infected and that they may become a threat to other areas of the country unless they are stopped. Cassy's fate is revealed (rescued by Hank) but concludes with a vengeful Levi determined to...? (additional episodes are being produced). Nominated for several awards, *Still: The Web Series* has also run as Official Selection at several Web Series Festivals.

Episodes:

1. Pilot (8 min., 9 sec.). The people of Sloughtown are suddenly bombarded by strange sounds emanating from the sky.

Still: The Web Series cast, from left to right: Joseph R. Porter, Angela Andrews, Gregory Marks, Simone Leorin, Tabitha Bastien, Kael Wagner, Chloe Holbrook, Tim Forehand and Michael Chamberlain (copyright Jonathan Holbrook).

2. Levi (9 min., 57 sec.). Continues to explore how the sounds affect certain people.

3. Neighbors (9 min., 52 sec.). As night falls for the first time since the sounds, some people are becoming disoriented while others are showing signs of madness.

4. Slingshot (5 min., 33 sec.). It is the day following the sounds in the sky and the effects of the sounds are becoming more apparent—some people are acquiring the ability to emit dangerous sound waves from their mouths.

5. Companions (14 min., 43 sec.). Those that have acquired the sound-emitting ability are now becoming zombie-like and apparently out to bring the unaffected to their side.

6. Family (12 min., 22 sec.). How the sounds have affected families is seen as a young woman returns home to find she is the only member that has not become zombie-like.

7. Peers (11 min., 2 sec.). Business is not what it seems when a factory foreman (Hank) finds that most of his employees have called in sick and those that remain are acting a bit strange.

8. Yearning (12 min., 40 sec.). Hank's situation goes from bad to worse when an infected employee (Levi), armed with a military-style rifle, begins a shooting spree as he seeks a specific target (Cassy), apparently not to kill her, but bring her over to his side.

325 *Suck and Moan*. suckandmoan.com. 2010 (Horror).

In a time, perhaps the not-too-distant future, a crisis has befallen the vampire population. A viral outbreak has ravished the planet and zombies have begun to appear, depleting the vampires' supply of human blood. Now vampires are forced to battle the brain-eating zombies for what is left of the human race and stories follow a group of vampires as they plot to survive in their battle against a new enemy.

Cast: Eric Hailey (Henry), Carmen Elena Mitchell (Myra), Courtney Geigle (Banyan), Alex Wood (Luke), Lauren Baldwin (Annie), Jared Young (Douglas), Joel Bryant (Mac), Amanda Rowse (Ashley), Kyle Eliason (Harold), Chris Mollica (Ed). **Credits:** *Producer:* Danny Ohman. *Writer-Director:* Brendon Fong. **Comment:** A clever mix and struggle to see what species will win with good acting, production values and zombie makeup.

Episodes:

1. Pilot. It is the end of the word and vampires Luke and Myra must now contend with a changing world as zombies become the ruling class.

2. Luke and Myra. Realizing that their food supply is diminishing, Luke and Myra begin discussions on how to sustain themselves.

3. Vampire Support Group. Luke and Myra attend a vampire support group to determine the best means of survival.

4. Transformations and Tooth Decay. The zombie population is growing and vampires have begun staking out what humans can be found before they become zombie meals.

Suck and Moan. **Posed scene for a vampire meal (photograph and copyright 2010, Brendon Fong).**

5. Bloodlust. The vampires realize that they must defeat the zombies in order to survive and begin a plan of attack.

6. The Death of Immortality. A member of the vampire group (Henry) becomes a victim of starva-

tion when his fangs fall out and he contemplates facing death for the first time.

7. Shelf Life. A vampire (Ed) theorizes that if they destroy a zombie's flesh they can also eliminate the zombie.

8. Breaking and Entering. Vampire rules of entering a home without permission are put to the test when vampires Annie, Mac and Ed attempt to acquire guns from a home without asking permission first.

9. The Count. Banyan, Luke and Henry visit their leader, the Count, in an effort to learn if vampires and zombies ever before co-existed.

10. Let's Call It a Night. The concluding, cliff hanging episode that finds the vampires contemplating whether to hibernate in their coffins or continue the battle come sundown.

326 *Super Knocked-Up.* superknockedup. com. 2012–2014 (Fantasy).

Jessica James, alias Darkstar, is the nation's prime super villain; nothing stands in her way of achieving her ill-gotten means. Michael Masters, alias Captain Amazing, is America's number one super hero—and Darkstar's mortal enemy—at least when she is wrecking havoc and he is out to stop her. But Captain Amazing is also a super womanizer and Darkstar is a gorgeous woman. One day the unthinkable happens—a one night-stand results in Jessica becoming pregnant and mortal enemies become a couple to raise a baby (Matthew). Michael has continued his battle against injustice while Jessica has become torn over a decision to become good or remain evil. Becoming parents was not on either one's agenda and, as Michael and Jessica try to figure out a way to remain together for the sake of the baby, episodes follow what happens as each returns to their prior good (and so far) evil lives.

Jessica James, age 28, and alias Darkstar, was born in Virtue City. Although she is an independent super villain, she often takes orders from the evil Dr. Destruction. Her powers include strength, martial arts skills and energy blasts (which are discharged from her hands).

Michael Masters, alias Captain Amazing, is 30 years old and affiliated with the Guardians of Justice (a super hero organization). He was born in Virtue City and encompasses powers that include super strength, invulnerability and the ability to fly.

Dr. Destruction is 50 years of age and affiliated with the Sinister Society. He was born in Westhaven as Nathaniel Cross and is possessed of enhanced senses. He is extremely intelligent, skilled in technology and a master strategist.

Carol Masters, alias "Mom" (Michael's mother) is 50 years of age and was born in Starlight City. She is a doctor and affiliated with the Guardians of Justice. She appears younger than she really is and has the power of healing.

Cheery Villain, alias Katie Campbell, is 20 years old and, despite her cheery attitude, is a member of the Sinister Society (although, like Darkstar, she is also an Independent). She was born in Logan, Pennsylvania, and considers herself "a sidekick wannabe." If being a geek were a power, Cheery could be considered a "super geek" as she is super smart and an expert computer hacker.

Shadow Girl, age 25, was born in Japan as Kasumi Kisaragi. She is a super villain and a member of the Sinister Society. She has the ability to turn into a shadow, travel along shadows and create shadow ten-

Super Knocked-Up. **The cast in costume (copyright Jeff Burns).**

drils from her fingers. She is skilled in the martial arts and is an expert swordswoman (uses the Shadow Sword).

Cast: Natalie Bain, Jourdan Gibson (Jessica James/Darkstar), Mark Pezzula (Michael Masters/Captain Amazing), Yvonne Perry (Carol Masters), David Bunce (Dr. Destruction), Daniela Malave (Darcy Danger, the reporter), Catherine Mancuso (Katie Campbell/Cheery Villain). **Credits:** *Writer-Director:* Jeff Burns. *Producer:* Jeff Burns, Jourdan Gibson, Christopher Schiller, Hans Olav Bakken, Mike Feurstein. **Comment:** Something different—in the saga of super heroes. While played comically, having mortal enemies trying to work together for the greater good (their child) is something that hasn't been done before and it took the Internet to bring it to audiences. The acting is good and production values comparable to a television sitcom. The action sequences with Jessica doing battle—and holding her baby at the same time—are very well done.

Episodes:

1. One Night Stand (5 min., 36 sec.). After a one night stand Jessica becomes pregnant and must now not only curtail her life of evil, but plan on becoming a mother (seen as a flashback).

2. Mom (5 min., 57 sec.). With Michael adjusting to the fact that he is to become a father, he attempts to break the news to his mother (Carol).

3. Sinister Society (4 min., 55 sec.). As Jessica's life takes a new turn she must decide whether or not to continue helping Dr. Destruction with his sinister plan to eliminate the world's super heroes.

4. Dr. Destruction (5 min., 34 sec.). Dr. Destruction is not pleased to learn that Jessica is to become a mother; Doris is also not happy to hear that her grandchild could follow in his mother's footsteps.

5. I'm Taking the Bedroom (7 min., 31 sec.). Trouble threatens to end the relationship when Jessica catches Michael in bed with another woman.

6. Welcome to the Family (6 min., 47 sec.). When an unknown assassin fails to kill Jessica (by blowing up her apartment) Jessica moves in with Michael and he too must now share her concerns about becoming a parent. Michael's mother, an OB/GYN, becomes Jessica's physician.

7. Super-Preggers (10 min., 1 sec.). Jessica and Michael learn that, because they are super beings, their baby's life is in peril and Jessica must take extra precautions to protect it.

8. Super-Baby (10 min., 13 sec.). Time advances quickly as Jessica gives birth (in a hilarious delivery room scene). Complications set in when Jessica finds she cannot follow Dr. Destruction's orders and instead must become a stay-at-home mother. It is also revealed that Matthew has powers (thus far the ability to make things disappear).

9. Super-Family (8 min., 6 sec.). After a visit from her super hero friends, Jessica realizes she cannot become a normal mother while Michael resumes his

life. With the baby (Matthew) by her side, Jessica returns to the life she once led.

10. Super-Battle (7 min., 30 sec.). On orders from Dr. Destruction, Jessica steals an ancient artifact—with her baby by her side. Problems ensue when Michael appears and Jessica must keep him from discovering Matthew is involved.

327 Super Life. rhinocrate.com. 2012 (Fantasy).

Mike Mightoffski is a super hero, known as Captain Might, who suddenly finds himself out of work when he loses his position with the Pegasus Justice Squad, a super hero organization run by Percy Axworthy. With no money and with no other choice, Mike is forced to move back home with his parents and sister Lana. Rather than feel sorry for himself, Mike continues his battle against injustice—in the same bumbling manner that got him fired in the first place.

Cast: Michael Wayne Smith (Mike Mightoffski), Kris Moreau (Percy Axworthy), Bailey Libby (Lana Mightoffski), Michael Jameson (Mike's father), Jenny Gutzbezah (Mike's mother), Kate Paulsen (Amy Athers). **Credits:** *Producer:* Christian Hegg. *Director:* Troy Minkowsky. *Writer:* Christian Hegg, Troy Minkowsky. **Comment:** Comedy blends with fantasy to present aspects of a super hero who can help others but is helpless when it comes to himself.

Episodes: Only a 50-second pilot has thus far been produced.

328 Super Scary Horror Theater. youtube.com. 2011 (Horror).

A sexy host (Ms. Dementia) showcases "classic" horror movies from the past coupled with audience chat (via Skype) and comments regarding the films being streamed.

Cast: Kat Steel (Ms. Dementia). **Credits:** *Producer:* Elaine Ewing, Travis Rink. **Comment:** Like the television series *Elvira's Movie Macabre*, *Horror Theater* encompasses the same sexy-style hosting making the less-than-spectacular featured films more enjoyable then they would be without Ms. Dementia. The actual movies that are presented were not made for the Internet and reflect horror films produced for theaters. The following films have been shown: *House on Haunted Hill*, *The Devil Bat*, *The Brain That Wouldn't Die* and *The Tingler*.

329 Super Girl. youtube.com. 2011 (Fantasy).

Adaptation of the *Super Girl* legend about Kara, a survivor of the planet Krypton (the home of Superman) after it was destroyed in an explosion caused by it being drawn into its sun. Kara, a teenager, has established herself on the planet Earth and is now attending college and appears to be just an ordinary co-ed; however, when evil strikes, Kara dons a blue costume and becomes Supergirl, a hero to those who are unable to protect themselves. The program was to follow Kara as she struggles to lead two lives—college student and the mysterious Supergirl. Kara lives with her roommate Barbara, who is secretly Batgirl; however, although they share a room neither knows of the other's secret identity (even when they team to battle evil, their dual identities are not revealed).

Cast: Tiffany Giardina (Kara/Super Girl), Kaight Zoia (Barbara/Batgirl), David Klein, Ryan McIntyre, Eric Rhodes, Jarda Beeber, Kyle Rutchland. **Credits:** *Producer-Writer-Director:* Tom Madigan. **Comment:** Only a pilot has been produced (and well at that). Tiffany Giardina is perfect as Super Girl and the special effects, though very minimal, are good. The program has no character introduction and just assumes the viewer knows who Kara is. Not so as Kara's history is not as legendary or common knowledge as Clark Kent/Superman. While Kara is dazzling as Super Girl, there is no explanation as to how she came to Earth, where she lives, how she got the costume, or what college she attends. Adding to the mystery is Barbara. While her identity (to the viewer) is unknown at first, at the program's conclusion, her Batgirl costume is seen under her bed. But is she Barbara Gordon (one of the Batgirl aliases?) or someone else? Her costume is lighter in color than prior Batgirl incarnations and not as sexy, leading to the conclusion that had more episodes been produced, the mysteries surrounding Kara and Barbara would have been explained. Despite the continuity problems, the episode is enjoyable.

Episodes:

1. Super Girl—The Pilot (8 min., 41 sec.). Kara comes to the aid of a girl being threatened by male students—a trap set to destroy her with Kryptonite acquired by a vengeful geology student to stop her from "wrecking their fun" (mischief). The green-glowing Kryptonite is affecting Super Girl and weakening her—until the mysterious Batgirl appears to rescue her.

330 *The Supernatural Adventure.* web serieschannel.com. 2011 (Horror).

Ghost Hunters–like project wherein Shawn Li, founder and lead investigator of the Supernatural Team and the Supernatural Crew, travels around the world to investigate reports of supernatural occurrences. He is accompanied by Steve Wong, his assistant and tech guy.

Cast: Shawn Li (Shawn), Steve Wong (Steve). **Credits:** *Producer-Director:* Steve Wong. **Comment:** Interesting program that runs longer, without commercials, than the programs it copies. While intriguing, it needs editing to tighten scenes and increase the suspense; otherwise it becomes rather tedious to watch and enjoy.

Episodes:

1. Pulau Ubin: The German Girl Shrine (45 min., 40 sec.). On the offshore island of Pulau Ubin in Singapore, the team investigates reports of paranormal activity at the Shrine of the German Girl, a tourist attraction that attracts people from all over the world to pay respects and give offerings.

2. Singapore Haunted Places, Labrador Park (47 min., 15 sec.). In Labrador Park, the team investigates World War II bunkers—and captures what appears to be a full body apparition on video.

3. Malaysia Haunted Places: Puchong House (33 min., 57 sec.). The team investigates reports of paranormal activity at the Puchong House in Malaysia.

4. Singapore Haunted Places: Istana Woodneuk (51 min., 59 sec.). The team investigates rumors of ghosts at Istana Woodneuk, reputed to be the most haunted site in Singapore.

5. Singapore Haunted Places: Suicide Tower (45 min., 8 sec.). At the Suicide Tower in Pasir Ris Park, the team investigates reports of seeing the spirits of suicide victims.

331 *Sweethearts of the Galaxy.* www.sweet heartsofthegalaxy.com. 2013 (Fantasy).

Katelyn and Lily, young women who work for a catering company, are best friends (since they were ten years old) and now share an apartment together. To earn extra money they have acquired second jobs as "cosplayers" (costume players) wherein they appear dressed as comic book characters at comic book conventions. Katelyn, a fan of super heroes (having always wanted to be one since she was a young girl) dresses as Trinity Infinity, a gorgeous Galactic Ranger with the Intergalactic Office of the Law. She wears a sexy purple and silver costume and has been battling evil for over 500 years. Lily appears as her sidekick, Element 47 (because "I make this [her figure in her costume] look damn good"). At one such convention, while attempting to perform a stunt for a television interview, Katelyn stumbles, falls and hits her head on the floor. Having read the latest issue (Number 48) of *Trinity Infinity* before leaving for the convention, Katelyn can only recall the comic book's characters and believes she is Trinity Infinity and Lily is Element 47, together known as "The Sweethearts of the Galaxy." As her alter ego becomes more real to her, Katelyn (as Trinity) begins to wonder why she has lost her powers (like the ability to fly) but realizes that she has a mission: to find the velocity vortex (the plot of that comic book).

Concerned over Katelyn's mental well being, Lily believes that by indulging Katelyn's fantasy (by devising comic book scenarios for her to solve) it will bring her back to reality when she finds she cannot conquer them (her enemies). The situation becomes complex when Paul, their friend, is seen by Katelyn as Trinity's enemy, Necrocide and Morgan, Paul's ex-girlfriend (who has become jealous over the fact that he is showing interest in Katelyn) is seen by Katelyn as Trinity's mortal foe, Wretched, the evil woman who can expose Katelyn as Trinity Infinity and reveal her true identity to the world. The program follows Katelyn as she attempts to deal with Morgan/Wretched and keep her dual identity a secret, but also risking her life when her fantasies become real to her and she sets out to capture actual villains as Trinity Infinity.

Cast: Kit Quinn (Katelyn/Trinity Infinity), Lola Binkerd (Lily/Element 47), Tallest Silver (Silvia/Dark Element 47) Megan Alyse (Morgan/Wretched), David Dickerson (Paul). **Credits:** *Producer-Director:* Dexter Adriano. *Writer:* Michael Premsrirat.

Sweethearts of the Galaxy. **Kit Quinn (left) and Lola Binkerd as Trinity Infinity and Element 47 (photograph copyright 2012 Michael Premsrirat, copyright 2013 Dexter Adriano and Michael Premsrirat).**

Comment: Although Katelyn's superhero is only alive in her mind, she believes she can defeat evil and stories are well constructed around that element. Kit Quinn is charming as Katelyn and Trinity and the series is an enjoyable spoof of superheroes.

Episodes:

1. Wish Granted (10 min., 24 sec.). Establishes the storyline as Trinity Infinity makes an appearance at a comic book convention.

2. Capturing Necrocide (10 min., 35 sec.). Concerned for Katelyn's well being, Lily pretends to be her companion, Element 47 while Paul, who has a crush on Katelyn, becomes involved in the game by pretending to be the evil villain Necrocide.

3. Becoming a Super Villain (7 min., 43 sec.). After Katelyn believes Morgan, Paul's ex, is her enemy, Wretched, Morgan decides to play along. But for Trinity Infinity, Wretched is real as her pretend energy blasts actually effect Trinity.

4. Faking Normal (10 min., 35 sec.). As Lily sees that Katelyn is slipping further into her fantasy world, she attempts to snap her out of it by making her see the real world and that she must report to work or lose her job.

5. Stopping Real Crime (6 min., 52 sec.). Katelyn's strange behavior at work causes her dismissal but to Katelyn it is only the beginning of something better. After witnessing a mugging, Katelyn becomes involved in a real crime when Trinity Infinity, possessed of no powers, comes to the rescue of the young woman who was robbed.

6. Hanging Out in Bars with Guys (9 min., 1 sec.). Having assisted Katelyn, Lily, dressed as Element 47, wanders into a bar where she begins lamenting about the situation she has gotten herself into and how Katelyn is now putting her life in danger.

7. Behold: The Committee of Evil Doers (6 min., 20 sec.). An imposter Element 47, dispatched by Morgan, captures Trinity Infinity and brings her to a meeting of villains to make Katelyn see that she is living in a fantasy world.

8. Some Romantic Notion (7 min., 57 sec.). Trinity, believing that Wretched is out to kill her finds that she has no protection from the fake energy blasts Morgan emits from her hands and that she appears to be doomed.

9. Reality Bomb (7 min., 39 sec.). In one final effort to make Katelyn see the truth, Morgan shows her a cell phone video of her falling at the comic book convention. Reality sets in and a depressed Katelyn leaves, followed by Lily. Lily tracks Katelyn to a building roof top where Katelyn feels life is no longer worth living. In a surprise ending, Katelyn, unable to be saved by Lily, jumps off—but is not killed. She soars back—as a real life Trinity Infinity.

332 SYNC. youtube.com. 2012 (Science Fiction).

In the year 2025, the world's first computerized man, Charlie Cooper, is created. A result of fringe science and the government coded program SYNC, Charlie, a human government agent, was "digitized" to change his intellect and personality to meet a specific need: highly intelligent and cunning covert operative. To keep Charlie "going," numerous clones have been made. If Charlie should suffer a fatal injury, his entire being is simply transferred into "a new body shell" thus making him appear immortal. Stories follow Charlie as he not only performs missions, but struggles to balance what is left of his humanity with his apparent immortality.

Cast: Tanner Thomason (Charlie Cooper), Cooper Harris (Eleanor Delaney), Carlos Ciurlizza (Carlos Ruiz), Kelly Walker (Zoe LaPierre), Dead Lee (Juan). **Credits:** *Producer:* Sarah Penna, Steve Raymond, Mike Rotman. *Director:* Sam Gorski, Niko Pueringer. *Writer:* Ira Parker. **Comment:** Well acted, fast-moving (although a bit confusing at times) story that has hints of the television series *The Six Million Dollar Man* and the web series *RoboGirl* (see entry). The special effects, though minimal are well done and the program lengths are just right so as not to become tedious to watch.

Episodes:

1. Episode 1 (9 min., 31 sec.). Introduces Charlie Cooper, as the first human to be transformed in a carefully supervised restricted system (and his control via SYNC Headquarters).

2. Episode 2 (9 min., 31 sec.). Explores Charlie's personal life as he must now adjust to new circumstances.

3. Episode 3 (8 min., 28 sec.). Charlie's deal with SYNC now makes him immortal—but he must literally sell his soul for that immortality (endlessly perform missions).

4. Episode 4 (10 min., 43 sec.). A situation begins to brew in China when an extraordinary computer virus is detected.

5. Episode 5 (7 min., 10 sec.). SYNC discovers that if the virus continues to spread, it will affect servers around the world and humans will no longer be the dominant intelligent life form on Earth.

6. Episode 6 (6 min., 50 sec.). When it is discovered that a sixteen year old girl (Yoshi) could be responsible for the virus program, Charlie is ordered to find her.

7. Episode 7 (8 min., 40 sec.). In China, Charlie finds Yoshi—but also encounters problems when persons unknown are seeking to kill her.

8. Episode 8 (8 min., 38 sec.). Convincing Yoshi that he has come to help her, the duo seeks a way to escape the pursuing assassins.

9. Episode 9 (7 min., 46 sec.). A confrontation with the assassins proves successful when Charlie, with his enhanced strength, defeats them and he is able to get Yoshi to SYNC Headquarters in the U.S.

10. Episode 10 (7 min., 25 sec.). The virus has caused numerous problems with the SYNC system and Charlie, learning that he is in danger of being shut down, must face what could happen to him.

11. Episode 11 (13 min., 21 sec.). Charlie breaks ties with his girlfriend and begins a quest to find the source of the SYNC program.

12. Episode 12 (11 min., 20 sec.). In a seemingly deserted desert town Charlie finds what he has been looking for—the SYNC source—a system of alien technology and the alien that constructed it. But what will become of Charlie if the technology is destroyed? The program ends in a cliff hanger.

333 *Tales from the Lab.* dagburgos.com. 2013 (Fantasy).

Anthology program of stories dealing with the supernatural—from ghosts and celestial beings to premonitions of the future.

Cast: Meghan Burns, Brian Luna, Dean Noble, Walter Plinge, Tanya Klein, Simon Burgos, John Jameson Mahers, Jeff Karr. **Credits:** *Producer-Writer-Director:* D.A.G. Burgos. **Comment:** The first three episodes are well done and present the real feel for what the project should be. The remaining episodes are poorly acted and not in the proper aspect ratio (images are stretched to fill the screen, indicating that these sequences were produced before HD and look as if they are dubs from a video tape). The production values on these episodes are poor and have no horror or fright aspect about them. Appears they were pickups from something else and just used to stretch the length of *Tales from the Lab.*

Episodes:

1. View from My Window (5 mi., 7 sec.). A man's torment as he sees a woman dressed in red from his window, then a murder—but is it real or a delusion.

2. The Gauntlet (2 min., 47 sec.). A woman, awakened each evening by a nightmare, fears that it may be a premonition of the future—her own murder.

3. Till Death Due Us Part (9 min., 47 sec.). A man, about to be married, finds his nuptials questioned when the spirit of his first wife appears to him.

4. Madam Tape 3 (2 min., 58 sec.). A suspect in the murder of a young woman claims he is innocent, the actual killer being his doppelganger.

5. The Quest for the Key of Chi (7 min., 59 sec.). An ancient demon, released when a mortal finds the mystical Key of Chi, sets out to claim our world.

6. Tribunal: The Trial (9 min., 2 sec.). Celestial beings, engaged in a religious war, must judge which planet to save.

7. Tribunal: The Deliberation (8 min., 53 sec.). Two alien enemies, face each other in a battle for supremacy in the war.

8. Tribunal: The Verdict (9 min., 25 sec.). The Tribunal must now decide the fate of the planets.

334 *Teen Wolf: Search for a Cure.* mtv.com. 2012 (Horror).

A companion web series for the MTV cable series *Teen Wolf* that explores the search begun by Scott, a teenager who was bitten by a werewolf, and his friend Stiles as they seek the cure for Scott's affliction.

Cast: Tyler Posey (Scott McCall), Dylan O'Brien (Stiles), John Posey (Dr. Conrad Fenris). **Credits:** *Producer-Writer-Director:* Jeff Davis. **Comment:** Well produced companion series that provides sort of a back story for the Scott character but his continual search for a cure.

Episodes:

1. Episode 1 (2 min., 38 sec.). Scott and Stiles learn of a werewolf expert who may be able to help.

2. Episode 2 (2 min., 32 sec.). Scott and Stiles begin their search.

3. Episode 3 (2 min., 39 sec.). After finding the lycanthropy expert (Dr. Fenris) Scott and Stiles find him reluctant to help.

4. Episode 4 (3 min., 9 sec.). Refusing to take no for an answer, Scott and Stiles break into the doctor's house seeking answers.

5. Episode 5 (3 min., 5 sec.). Caught, Scott and Stiles are held at gunpoint by the doctor.

6. Episode 6 (4 min., 28 sec.). Dr. Fenris lays down his gun and agrees to answer their questions regarding werewolves and a possible cure. But what they learn is not the cure they will accept (only by cutting a werewolf in half can the disease be stopped).

335 *Teenage Vampire Killers from Hell.* teenagevampirekillersfromhell.com. 2013 (Horror).

Father Boyd is a Catholic priest. Frank is a street thug befriended by Father Boyd. In an unusual move, the Archdiocese assigns Father Boyd a most unusual task: destroy the teenage vampires that are terrorizing the community. With Frank as his assistant, a team of vampire hunters is formed and stories follow the unlikely pair as they set out to rid their community of the vampire plague. **Cast:** Andy Rocco (Father Boyd), Matt DeCoster (Frank), Michael Delaney (Father Sidney). **Credits:** *Producer:* John Robert Wilson, Lisa Herring, Teresa Tai-yi-Lee. *Director:* Russell Costanzo. *Writer:* Andy Rocco. **Comment:** A rather different approach to vampire killing with an "Odd Couple"–like team that has enough dark moments to make one at least check it out. The acting is okay but its production values common (acceptable) for a low budget production.

Episodes:

1. Into the Woods at Sunset. Father Boyd and Frank begin their quest by destroying a group of teens that were just turning after having been bitten.

2. Hotel of the Damned, Part 1. Father Boyd and Frank stake out a hotel that they believe is a breeding ground for female vampires.

3. Hotel of the Damned, Part 2. Having captured a vampire, Father Boyd and Frank face the unpleasant task of disembodying it.

4. The Problem with Apartment 4C. Father Boyd questions his ability to continue in his capacity when he kills an innocent teen he mistakes for a vampire.

336 *Terminator Salvation: The Machinima Series.* youtube.com. 2009 (Science Fiction).

Animated prequel to the feature film *Termination Salvation* that strays from the traditional John Connor character and his efforts to destroy Skynet, the futuristic organization that has sent terminator robots after him to prevent him from changing the future, to focus on Blair Williams, a soldier in the human resistance against Skynet's machines before she met John and Marcus Wright. It is the year 2016 and stories follow human survivors of the war against Skynet's machines as they prepare troops and underground communications to defeat Skynet. **Voice Cast:** Moon Bloodgood (Blair Williams), Cam Clarke (Laz Howard), Jim Meskimen (Command). **Credits:** *Producer:* James Middleton. *Director:* Tor Helmstein, Kelly Ward, Ian Kirby. *Writer:* Andy Shapiro. **Comment:** Rather poorly animated program (looks like the video game from which it was adapted) but a good story and voice characterizations compensate for the program's crudeness.

Episodes:

1. Episode 1. It is two years before the events of the feature film and Blair begins establishing a resistance group in Los Angeles.

2. Episode 2. Blair and her partner, Laz Howard, face deadly T-600 Terminator Robots as they seek the safety of their command headquarters.

3. Episode 3. As Blair and Laz battle the robots, Command instructs Blair to retreat and, if necessary, leave Laz behind.

4. Episode 4. Blair defies orders and risks her life to save Laz. As they escape from the robots, they take refuge in an abandoned office building.

5. Episode 5. Blair and Laz find little safety as they are soon attacked by the Terminator robots.

6. Episode 6. The concluding episode wherein Laz saves Blair from a robot and Blair discovering that the war is not lost, that there is a savior and the war against Skynet can be won (which leads to her role in the feature film).

337 *Tether.* youtube.com. 2013 (Science Fiction).

In a future time humanity is plunged into a viral pandemic when tethers (strange cables) drop from the sky and fall onto the Earth. Exactly what they are and where they come from is unknown. They are suspected of being alien but their significance is also unknown. The phenomenon splits society into those who survived through immunity and those who survived through power and influence. As time passed and the quarantined zones became livable again, the true survivors were left to build a devastated planet. The program explores what happens in a post-apocalyptic world when all must work as one to rebuild their world. **Comment:** Although only a pilot film has thus far been produced, the program does show promise with amazing special effects, good performances and grand cinematography (especially if watched in the HD option on YouTube). Unfortunately, for such a well done production, the cast is not identified (or even given) and credits are also absent from the production.

Episodes: Only a 12-minute and 42-second pilot film has been produced that introduces the proposed series concept.

338 *They Live Among Us.* theyliveamongus.com. 2011–2013 (Horror).

Los Angeles, called the City of Angels, for at one time being one of the least corrupt cities in the U.S., is also the present-day home of fallen angels, demons and star-crossed lovers that have been reincarnated and must now live new lives among humans. Stories, played against a supernatural backdrop to explore the darkest parts of the human condition, follow several characters: Lillith, a gorgeous Succubus who preys on the lonely seeking romance; Caim, a fallen angel who, to gain redemption, must encounter then lose his true love over countless lifetimes; Ted, a lonely man who encounters a beautiful spirit near the Hollywood sign; and Father Buer, the Catholic priest seeking redemption from his dark past.

Cast: Nina Rausch (Lillith), Ivet Corvea (Serafina), Geoffrey M. Reeves (Caim), Rolf Saxon (Father Buer), Marcia French (Beliala), Allen Marsh (Lucian), Kendra Munger (Peg), Terence J. Rotolo (Rocco), Don Shirey (Sam), David Standford (Ted), Jessica Nicole Webb (Beth), John Thomas Gilbert (Craig), Brittani Ebert (Jane), Don Shirey (Sam), Justin Baker (Jimmy) **Credits:** *Producer:* Anne Lower, Steve Harshfield, John Maguire, Russell Southam. *Director-Writer:* Anne Lower. **Comment:** Not a horror series in the normal vein as there is more talking than anything else. The writing, special effects and acting are good but the program encompasses the annoying shaky camera method of filming that is simply a turn off for many people (you don't need to see the camera bouncing up and down and from side to side as people talk or action unfolds). With the exception of Lillith, there is no real character development and no interest to see what happens next (unless one becomes a Lillith fan).

Episodes:

1. Pull My Strings (12 min., 55 sec.). At the Paradise Bar a man (Craig) becomes intrigued with a mysterious girl (Lillith)—a girl who has been reincarnated as a Succubus and finds Craig a most tempting subject to fulfill her sexual needs (by draining his life force).

2. Fall from Grace (15 min., 26 sec.). Star-crossed lovers Serafina and Rocco rediscover each other—but not as they were before. Serafina has been reincarnated as a prostitute and Rocco as a drug addict.

3. All Her Angels (15 min., 34 sec.). Continues from where episode two left off with Lillith feeding on Craig and Rocco, discovering that another man (Caim) has set his sights on Lillith, bursts into a drug-infused rage intent on killing Lillith.

4. Night's Candles (10 min., 34 sec.). Ted, a park ranger, saves the life of a young woman who is about to jump off the Hollywood sign only to discover that she is the ghost of a doomed actress named Peg Entwistle. Serafina contemplates returning to Rocco.

339 *The 3rd Floor.* webserieschannel.com. 2010 (Horror).

Comical horror extension based on the NBC series *The Office* that encompasses several of its cast regulars. Erin and Kelly, two of the employees of the Dunder-Mifflin Paper Company are eager to expand their horizons by breaking into show business. Their dreams become a reality when they write a horror story script and convince their friend Ryan to produce it. The story, titled "The 3rd Floor," begins when a woman approaches Erin and asks to buy some paper. When Erin finds she has no money, she refuses to give her the paper. Angered, the woman (dressed like a Gypsy) places a curse on her—to become all the serial killers who ever existed. Erin shrugs it off, but slowly she begins to change. She develops the right arm of Lizzie Borden, the left arm of Jeffrey Donner, the heart of Jack the Ripper and the legs of all the serial killers who escaped the law. Now, wielding an axe, Erin begins her rampage, killing all the third floor employees—or at least attempting to do so. Also known as *The Office: The 3rd Floor.*

Cast: Ellie Kemper (Erin Hannon), Mindy Kaling (Kelly Kapoor), B.J. Novak (Ryan Howard), Kate Flannery (Meredith Palmer), Brian Baumgartner (Kevin Malone). **Credits:** *Producer-Director:* Mindy Kahling. *Writer:* Kelly Hannon. **Comment:** Played strictly for laughs and actually funny, especially the last episode. Ellie Kemper (Erin) is a standout and just her performance as the crazed serial killer is worth the price of admission.

Episodes:

1. Moving On (2 min., 47 sec.). Erin and Kelly seek a way to get their horror film produced.

2. Lights, Camera, Action! (2 min., 9 sec.). Ryan makes preparations to begin production on Erin and Kelly's movie.

3. The Final Product (3 min., 3 sec.). The movie is filmed (and explained in the above storyline).

340 *13 Witches.* youtube.com. 2012–2013 (Horror).

During the 17th century, thirteen women, sisters in a Coven were accused of being witches and in a strange twist on normal stories, they were burned alive at the stake by those they loved (as opposed to the traditional "angry villagers"). One sister (Nemesis), escaped the death sentence and swore an oath of revenge on those who destroyed her family. It is the present day when the series begins. Nemesis, although centuries old, is young and beautiful, but full of hatred, and has made a deal with the Devil: her

13 Witches cast members, left to right: Andrea Stefancikova, Victoria Vice, Adiam Asrat, Sabine Mondestin, Laura Watson, Ashley Young (copyright Sabine Mondestin, MyDestiny Production, and Steve Lareau).

soul for her sisters' reincarnation. The thirteen sisters, now reunited, begin a quest to destroy those of today whose ancestors took their lives centuries ago.

Cast: Sabine Mondestin (Nemesis), Marie E. West (Athena), Victoria Vice (Andromeda), Lila Popa (Pandora), Wanda Ayala (Eurybia), Lauren Watson (Themis), Lea Kovach (Venus), Paula Elle (Lilith), Natasha Davidson (Isis), Valerie Pauwels (Persephone), Ferrone Gavriel (Salome), Dominique Brownes (Danica), Jennifer Koening (Abeona), Sara Akeera (Hera), Nicole Rockman (Diana), Andrea Stefancikova (Diana 2), Julia Lawton (Sheila), Clayton Chitty (Christian), Matthew Mandzij (Steve), Edwin Rodriquez (Anubis), Lionel Maye (Ben), Randy Rafuse (Mark), Ashley Young (Tina), Anelora Popa (Selena), Steve Lareau (Asmodeus), Edward Rodriquez (Anibus). **Credits:** *Producer-Writer-Director:* Sabine Mondestin. **Comment:** The billing is right on—"Sexy," as it does encompass a bevy of beautiful girls. The story line and production values are good and for something different when it comes to programs (or movies) about witches, *13 Witches* does offer an enjoyable alternative.

Episodes:

1. And the Journey Begins (10 min., 53 sec.). A long prolog begins the series that explains how women, accused of being witches, were tortured and burned at the stake. The scene dissolves into a modern apartment occupied by a woman named Diana. Unexpectedly, she is visited by Nemesis and her witch sisters. The viewer learns that through a spell cast by Nemesis that Diana's ancestors were among the loved ones who destroyed her sisters.

2. You Are Sentenced to Burn (5 min., 28 sec.). The flashback from the prior episode continues as Diana is made to see how Nemesis's, sister, Abeona, was burned at the stake.

3. I Gave My Soul to the Devil (11 min., 9 sec.). Shows Nemesis escaping the witch burnings and making a deal with the Devil to one day avenge their deaths.

4. A Mistress Will Get You Killed (9 min., 20 sec.). Diana, under Nemesis's spell, becomes a pawn in Nemesis plan to destroy Steve, whose ancestors helped destroy the witch sisters.

5. The Goddess Inside (7 min., 59 sec.). Diana, assisted by her sisters Lilith, Pandora, Envo and Andromeda continue to reveal secrets about Diana's former life (in the 17th century) hoping to make her join their cause.

6. The Awakening. (6 min., 20 sec.). Nemesis conducts a mystical ceremony that not only gives special powers to Diana, but makes her one of the witch sisters.

7. Bloody Fest (5 min., 30 sec.). The newly transformed Diana becomes a threat to the people close

to her—people, like herself, whose ancestors destroyed the witch sisters.

8. A Slave's Wish (5 min., 7 sec). Anubis, the Devil's (Asmodeus) slave, is granted a wish by Asmodeus to help Nemesis achieve revenge (but also to spy on Nemesis and report back to Asmodeus who wants her soul before she achieves her goal).

9. Deadly Threesome (5 min., 32 sec.). Andromeda, assisted by Diana, plots to kill Ken, the man whose ancestors killed her.

10. Never Betray a Mistress (8 min., 41 sec.). Hera, reincarnated by Nemesis, and believing she is a goddess, begins her quest for revenge.

11. Twisted Sisters (4 min., 41 sec.). Nemesis, distraught that her relationship with Athena has taken a turn for the worse, seeks a way to befriend her.

12. Obscure Conspiracy (6 min., 12 sec.). Athena discovers an evil conspiracy behind Nemesis' attempts to befriend her.

13. A Clumsy First Time (5 min., 18 sec.). Athena begins to develop powers that outweigh those of Nemesis.

14. Who's the Bitch Now? (5 min.). Themis, reborn as a powerful goddess, seeks revenge on the man (Mark) who abused her for years.

15. The Tale of Nemesis (5 min., 54 sec.). Diana, Pandora, Themis and Venus discover that their leader, Nemesis, had a hidden human desire (in a flashback it is shown that Nemesis yearned for a husband [Christian] and a family).

16. A Love-Hate Relationship (8 min., 2 sec.). The present-day Christian, whose ancestors initiated the 17th century witch burnings, meets his fate when he is confronted by Nemesis.

17. Quest for Power (9 min., 50. sec.). It is learned that for Nemesis to gain more power to rule both the world and underworld, she must not only kill more humans, but Satan (Asmodeus) as well.

18. The Game of Evil (7 min., 10 sec.). It is the 17th century and Eurybia plots to change the future and become queen of the world by pitting Nemesis and her sisters against those who will eventually kill them—but making sure her witch sisters will not triumph. The episode concludes in a cliff hanger with the fate of the witches unknown.

341 30 Days of Night: Blood Trails. ov guide.com. 2007 (Horror).

A prequel to the feature films *30 Days of Night* and *30 Days of Night: Dark Days*. It is two days before the events in the first film begin and introduces George Fowler, a drug addict who earns money by secretly conveying information to Judith, a vampire hunter. George is hoping to use the money he earns to leave New Orleans and begin a new life with his girlfriend (Jenny). The program charts the nightmare George faces when Jenny is bitten by a vampire (and he is forced to behead her) and how his involvement with a sect of vampires transforms him from

addict to vampire hunter. See also *30 Days of Night: Dust to Dust.*

Cast: Andrew Laurichas (George Fowler), Dani Owen (Jenny), Marilyn Johnson (Judith), Trip Hope (Eddie), Brittney Kara (Kate), Jeremy Shranko (Luis), Shawn G. Smith (Cal), T.J. Zale (Pat), Geoff Stirling (Chad). **Credits:** *Producer:* Jim Burns. *Director:* Victor Garcia. *Writer:* Steve Niles, Ben Katai.
Comment: While not as suspenseful or gory as the films on which it is based, it has its moments and the story flows smoothly across all seven episodes. The acting is good and production values above the standard.

Episodes:
1. Blood Trails, Part 1 (5 min.). Introduces George Fowler, the drug addict who supplies information to Judith, a female Vampire Hunter.

2. Blood Trails, Part 2 (3 min.). George finds a new calling—Vampire Hunter when his girlfriend (Jenny) is bitten by a vampire.

3. Blood Trails, Part 3 (4 min.). A series of attacks brings George to the realization that he must do something to stop them.

4. Blood Trails, Part 4 (4 min.). As Jenny succumbs to the bite and begins transforming into a vampire, George seeks a way to protect her and hopefully find a cure for her.

5. Blood Trails, Part 5 (5 min.). George and Jenny continue their search for a safe haven amid the chaos that surrounds them.

6. Blood Trails, Part 6 (4 min.). As Jenny becomes progressively worse and without an apparent cure, George contemplates a most heart-felt decision.

7. Blood Trails, Part 7 (4 min.). Knowing that if Jenny fully transforms she will become a killer, George does what he has to—save her by beheading her (the act that leads to *30 Days of Night: Dust to Dust*) wherein George is arrested and imprisoned for killing Jenny.

342 30 Days of Night: Dust to Dust. vimeo.com. 2008 (Horror).

Internet continuation of the 2007 feature vampire film *30 Days of Night* that begins one month after the movie ended to focus on Sara Maguire, a young prison nurse who was attacked by a vampire and is now becoming one of the undead and of her police detective brother's (Nick) efforts to find and help her.

Sara's plight begins when she reports to work and is bitten by a vampire while transporting a prisoner (George Fowler), a vampire hunter convicted of a beheading, to a maximum security location. Nick, informed of the prison break, begins the search for George and Sara (who has also disappeared). Sara has begun nursing her throat wound but soon realizes that something is happening to her (as her fang teeth are already manifesting themselves). As Nick tracks George, Sara finds her first victim—Tracy and feeds off of her. The program continues in this vein with Nick and George hoping to find Sara before she progresses into a full vampire and can only be stopped by beheading.

Cast: Mimi Michaels (Sara Maguire), Andrew Laurich (George Fowler), Shawnee Smith (Det. Gina Harcourt), Christopher Stapleton (Det. Nick Maguire), Rainie Davis (Tracy), Andrew Laurich (George Fowler). **Comment:** Although based on a feature film, the Internet version bears little resemblance to it. There are few chills, the production values are fair and the vampires are far less frightening than their feature film counterparts. For fans of girl/girl scenes, the program's highlight is Sara "putting the bite" on Tracy (but it is also rather disappointing as it lasts only a few seconds). Making the scene more erotic and investing some time on production values could have made for a much more pleasing program.

Episodes:

1. Dust to Dust, Part 1. Explains the storyline as Sara becomes a vampire when vampires descend on the New Orleans County Penitentiary to assassinate George, the Vampire Hunter.

2. Dust to Dust, Part 2. Nick, called in on the case, finds George, who escaped the assassination attempt.

3. Dust to Dust, Part 3. As Nick learns from George what has happened to Sara, Sara begins to realize she is transforming into a vampire.

4. Dust to Dust, Part 4. Nick must confront the truth that Sara is becoming a creature of the undead and must feed on human blood.

5. Dust to Dust, Part 5. George must face the truth and destroy Sara to save her.

343 31. 31theseries.com. 2011 (Horror).

Thirty-one episodes, each running 31 seconds and broadcast for thirty-one consecutive days (premiering March 31, 2011 at 3:31 p.m.) that encompass the cliff hanger style of the movie serials of the 1930s and 40s. A young woman wakes up alone in an area of total darkness. She has no memory of who she is or how she came to be where she is. Has she been kidnapped? Why is she being held a prisoner? The program relates her torment as she seeks to learn what happened to her.

Cast: Becky Briggs (The Girl), Ben Bryant, Rob Kiely. **Credits:** *Producer:* Dawn S. Smith, Tammy Good. *Writer-Director:* L.C. Cruell. **Comment:** Intriguing program that holds interest and plays better now then it did when originally broadcast as all the episodes can be watched back-to-back. For the very short program that it is, it is well produced and, while it does imitate the movie serials of the past, it does not contain the death-defying episode cliff hanger, the recap in the next episode or the resolution (how the hero escaped) from the prior chapter in the next chapter.

Episodes: All the episodes have the title "Transmission" followed by a number. They have been re-edited and can be seen in a series of packages as opposed to 31 individual programs. *1.* 31: Transmission 1–7. *2.* 31: Transmission 8–14. *3.* 31: Transmission 15–21. *4.* 31: Transmission 22–28. *5.* 31: Transmission 29–31B.

344 *Thor and Loki: Blood Brothers.* marvel.com. 2011 (Fantasy).

Animated rendering of the legend of Thor and Loki, the younger and older sons of the Norse God, Odin. It is a time when Loki has taken over the rule of Asgard from his father and who with Thor, has been placed in chains. Stories follow the conflict that exists between the brothers, with Thor attempting to escape and return rule of Asgard to his father.

Voice Cast: Daniel Thorn (Thor), David Blair (Loki), Deborah Jane McKinley (Frigga), Elizabeth Diennet (Sif), Joe Teiger (Odin), James Hampshire (Baldar). **Credits:** *Producer:* Ruwan Jayatilleke. *Director:* Mark Cowart, Joel Gibbs. *Writer:* Robert Rodi. **Comment:** Striking animation that is done as a comic book come to life (characters are basically stationary and placed in detailed backgrounds). The male characters, especially Loki, are very harsh looking (weathered faces) while the women are quite sexy. The dialogue is like listening to a Shakespeare play with Loki lamenting over what he has done and what he still has to do (keep all parties who backed him in the take-over happy). The static presentation coupled with a morality tale could work both ways—an attraction or a deterrent. Only two-minute previews of each 16–20 minute episode are available for free viewing; full viewing requires purchasing the episode (beginning at $1.99).

Episodes:

1. Episode 1. Loki has claimed rule of Asgard and imprisoned Thor, the powerful son of Odin and the rightful heir to the throne.

2. Episode 2. Loki begins his rule while Thor contemplates the fate Loki has arranged for him: death.

3. Episode 3. Loki's misguided rule threatens to topple Asgard as Odin and Thor seek a way to stop him.

4. Episode 4. Thor, escaping his bounds, faces Loki in the ultimate battle for control of Asgard. The concluding episode ends unresolved.

345 *Throwing Stones.* youtube.com. 2011–2012 (Horror).

There is a theory called "The Broken Window" that claims if a building window is broken and it is not fixed, the structure decays and crime moves in. If that window had been fixed, the crime would not have happened. Believing that several of his students at Blair High School (Paige, Dontrelle, Staci, Tad, Asher, Rachel, Chrissy) are broken windows (troublesome and need "fixing") Richard Beckett, the assistant principal, secures them in a classroom for Saturday detention and tests his theory by asking the students to identify the broken windows. Sounds simple enough. But Beckett is deranged and believes the only way to fix the school's broken windows (students) is to kill them. Episodes relate the students' efforts to survive Beckett's insane plans to eliminate them one by one.

Cast: Cherami Leigh (Robyn Goode), Lynn Andrews III (Dontrelle Williams), Kayla Carlyle (Staci Lambert), Chad Cox (Richard Beckett), W. Tom Hamlett (Tad Wadlow), Spencer Harlan (Asher Van Deen), Lindsay Seidel (Rachel Black), Rebekah Kennedy (Chrissy Holden), Jon Christie (Jackson Cole), Brina Palencia (Finley Jaymes), Rachel Verret (Paige Dennis), Bryan Massey (Officer Glover). **Credits:** *Producer:* Jason A. Wheeler, Bart D. Van Bemmel, Ron Gonzalez. **Comment:** Well produced and acted, including tense moments but the story can be a bit confusing at times as you try to figure out what is going on. Knowing what the Broken Window Theory is before watching is essential as it is the key to the whole series (other than the fact that Beckett is insane).

Episodes:

1. Don't Forget About Me. Begins with a girl (Robyn) running through the school halls as if she were being chased by someone.

2. Can You Hear Me Now? A flashback to before Robyn's plight with Beckett addressing his class.

3. The Broken Windows Theory. Becket explains to the class the meaning of the theory.

4. Sticks and Stones. Beckett leaves the students alone to ponder the theory and figure out why they are the broken windows.

5. Pawn Stars. As the situation becomes tense, the students feel it is best if they find Beckett and end the class. Beckett however, has no intentions of doing so.

6. Death Beds. The situation worsens when the students discover they are locked in the building and cannot escape.

7. Ashes to Asher. The students attempt to make it to the gym, where they feel it is their best chance establish a stronghold.

8. Hallway to Hell. The students exit the classroom—but are pursued by Beckett who is now planning to kill each one of them. The first season ends.

9. Welcome Back. The second season premiere episode that recaps the prior episodes with Beckett in pursuit of the students.

10. Full Court Press. Robyn is captured by Beckett and must now fight for her life.

11. Two's Company. Beckett continues to torment Robyn.

12. The Scarlet Letter. Two of the students, Chrissy and Tad, having escaped Beckett's pursuit, plot a way to outwit him.

13. The Shepherd and the Lamb. Robyn manages to escape, leaving Beckett extremely bitter as he believes she is a slut and needs to be eradicated.

14. The Armor for God. Tad and Chrissy's efforts to escape fail when Tad is captured and demands to know where Robyn is hiding.

15. Breaking Good. Robyn begins running for her life (as seen in the first episode) and takes refuge in the science lab.

16. Sincerely Yours. Robyn, trapped in the science lab by Beckett, finds a bottle of acid and throws it in Beckett's face, blinding him. But did it stop him? Ends without resolution.

346 *Tights and Fights: Ashes.* tightsandfights.com. 2010–2012 (Fantasy).

Superheroes (Fantabulous Gal, Leopard Woman, Major Faultline, Captain Euchre and The Plumber) seen in a different light: as seemingly ordinary people (although they dress in leotards) who battle evil (namely Evil Trojan Borscht) but are personally troubled and experience problems of everyday life (in the series setting, Toronto, Canada).

Fantabulous Gal, as she calls herself, was born in a small town in Canada and is the younger of two sisters. The sisters were raised by a single mother whose inability to make ends meet forced the family to constantly uproot themselves and seek greener pastures. Although Fantabulous Gal had hoped for a job as a Hooters waitress when she reached 18, her mother thought it would be best if she moved in with relatives in Toronto. The big city found Fantabulous Gal as part of the urban life and it became the key to her future: become a super hero (as Toronto "is lousy with 'em ... but villains too"). She soon discovers that Ronin Force, formed by Captain Euchre, is the most prestigious super hero organization, but becoming a super hero, with no training and only her abundant enthusiasm as "her power," it would be best to become a sidekick. This became a problem when she discovered that most side kick positions go to children who graduate from Professor McRoninson's School for Gifted and Profitable Youngsters. Unable to enroll in the school, Fantabulous Gal volunteered her services as side kick and came to the attention of Dyna Gal, who hired her as both a side kick and personal assistant. She first fought along Dyna Gal in the Snailen Invasion Crisis. When the pressure of work caused Dyna Gal to have a breakdown and be institutionalized, Fantabulous Gal lost her job. With no recourse, Fantabulous Gal reinvented herself, striking out on her own as a gorgeous super heroine with a can-do attitude, enthusiasm, business acumen—and the crime-fighting equipment once used by Dyna Gal.

Leopard Woman was born in Leopardia, the Cat Kingdom in the center of the planet (where the earth is hollow and various animal species have survived for centuries). She became a Queen at an early age and has ruled, in her true form as a feline, for many

***Tights and Fights: Ashes*. The cast in their costume roles (copyright 2010 GopherX).**

years until an earthquake virtually destroyed her kingdom and took the fifth of her mother's nine lives. It was at this time that Bill Faultline, a Ronin Force super hero known as Major Faultline, "fell" into Leopardia and Leopard Woman became infatuated with him, but in her cat form, could only become his pet. Fate intervened when Leopard Woman found and unearthed magic amulet that gave her the power to assume the human form of a woman. To be with Bill, she relinquished her Cat Throne and journeyed to the surface to find Bill, only to discover, at first that humans kept cats as pets. She eventually found romance with Bill and married him. Leopard Woman became a charter member of Ronin Force but their marriage has suffered over time with their super hero activities threatening to breakup their relationship.

Evil Trojan Borscht, Ronin Force Dossier Number 164735 is a man of mystery, even to himself. He first came to prominence by posting videos and it soon became apparent that he was under some sort of mind control (but its source could not be determined). He considers himself to be a genius hacker although his grasp on technology is quite limited. He taunts superheroes and average citizens with videos and blogs from his hidden lair in Toronto.

Major Faultline was born in Toronto (the suburb of Thornhill) and is the scion of a wealthy and affluent family. As William "Bill" Lyon Mackenzie King

Faultline, he began his career to becoming a super hero at the age of 13 when he joined the Canadian Army Cadets. While he will claim it was his enthusiasm that advanced him to the rank of major, it was actually the fact that no one else wanted the position (it can also be told that Bill "bribed" his drill sergeant with the flan desserts he made in his home economics class to recommend him for the position). Life soon changed for Bill when budget restrictions forced the Canadian Space Agency to recruit cadets for an interplanetary mission. The mission turned deadly when, on the planet Seti Alpha 9, Bill and his cadet soldiers were captured by the giant, cube-faced Asparagusians and subjected to genetic experimentation. One by one the cadets succumbed to horrific deaths and it was thought that Bill had also been terminated. But fate deemed otherwise and Bill survived the genetic experiments. He has no memory of what happened, but when he was returned to Earth he discovered he was endowed with strange electronic parts embedded in his chest and right hand and has the ability to create earthquakes (discovered when he tripped getting out of bed, his hand hit the floor and the earth engulfed his parents' home). Bill, now feeling that his last name has significance, also found that he could fight evil with the power of earthquakes (it was when he tried to stop runaway pigs from an over-turned truck that he created a rip in the earth that caused him to fall through to the center of it and into Leopard Woman's world and eventually marry her). Major Faultline also has the ability to time travel (acquired when he had a brush with a nuclear missile).

The Plumber, alias Robert Strovesco, is the son of Oscar and Lucinda Strovesco. Oscar, better known as The Electrician, is a man with the power to control electrons ("with the proper, certified equipment, of course"). Despite the fact that Robert was dropped three times on the floor by the doctor delivering him, he appeared to grow into a normal person. At a young age, Oscar felt it was time for Robert to follow in a family tradition and began mentoring him as a super hero. But it seemed fruitless as Robert failed at every test his father gave him; it was a wonder that Robert even lived to continue. But when Robert turned 15 his world changed. He returned home from school to find a note from his father saying that he and his team, the Mega Powers League, had been called to duty to fight in the Obfuscated Wars. It was first reported that Oscar and his squad were killed; it later surfaced that Oscar had actually run off with a fellow super hero, a famous pin-up girl known as The Showgirl Woman. The news depressed Robert but he knew he had to continue without him. After graduating from high school Robert attempted to become a plumber and joined his Uncle Sal's business, Strovesco Plumbing. But Robert could never really master the art and was assigned to the tackle the dirtiest unclogging jobs. As time passed, Robert met his future wife (Tanya) and they became the parents of Justin. It was also at this time that Robert decided to become the super hero his father wanted him to be and took up the alias The Plumber ("Snaking the Drains of Justice"). Robert is also known as The Damp Defender, The U-Bend in the Pipe of Life and the Ronin Force's least wanted member. He has donned a mask but has no super abilities; he is experimenting (for example combining water with electricity) but not having much luck.

Captain Euchre was once an ordinary man (an expert at the card game Euchre) who, after refusing to fix the 1997 World Series of Euchre, was a mob target and left for dead. But fate intervened. Wounded and alone, he stumbled into the gutter when a stray ray of pure energy shot out of the sky and struck the deck of Euchre cards he was carrying (which absorbed its energy); the super-charged cards now enable him to battle injustice. With a vow to bring all criminals to justice, Captain Euchre created the Ronin Force, which unites Toronto's superheroes as a super-powered crime fighting force (similar to The Justice League of America). **Cast:** Chelsea Larkin (Leopard Woman), Jeremy Knight (Major Faultline), Melanie Hunter (Fantabulous Gal), Scott Watkins (The Plumber), Scott Albert (Captain Euchre/Evil Trojan Borsht). **Credits:** *Producer:* Courtney Wolfson, Scott Albert, Christopher Guest. *Writer:* Scott Albert, Christopher Guest, Neil James, Kristin McGregor, Conor O'Hegarty,

Melanie Hunter, Scott Watkins, Chelsea Larkin. *Director:* Christopher Guest. **Comment:** Exceptional video quality; well acted, written and directed (the lightly comedy-accented episodes feature the characters addressing the camera to talk about what happened. While it would seem unlikely that such a premise would work with so many episodes, it does). Having watched all the episodes back-to-back, the Fantabulous Gal episodes (identifiable by a thumbnail picture of the yellow-haired, blue attired super heroine) are the most enjoyable.

Episodes:

1. Phoenix or the Cuckoo? Introduces Evil Trojan Borscht, who awakens after a long sleep.

2. Always During an Evil Ultimatum. Evil Trojan Borscht makes plans to do what he does best—spread evil.

3. While the Rat's Away. Leopard Woman finds it a bit difficult becoming close to hubby Major Faultline when he returns home after spending time in jail.

4. The Best Laid Flans of Mice and Men. Major Faultline decides to retire and do nothing at all.

5. Jobless. Fantabulous Gal's life is turned upside down when she returns from vacation and finds she no longer has a job (as her employer, Dyna Gal, has been sent to a mental institution).

6. My Chair, My Frenemy. Evil Trojan Borscht enters into an uneasy truce with his superior.

7. Counseling. Leopard Woman and Major Faultline enter therapy to resolve their problems.

8. Blocked at Every Turn. The Plumber, separated from his wife and son, tries to reconnect with his son (Justin).

9. Trickle to a Torrent. A glimpse into the Plumber's past as he attempts to win over Justin.

10. Acting Director. With Major Faultline declaring his retirement, Leopard Woman is made Permanent Acting Director of the Ronin Force.

11. Snail Mail. With no other choice, Fantabulous Gal moves into her former employer's apartment.

12. Going My Way. Focuses on Evil Trojan Borscht as he plans his next insidious move.

13. Barry. Evil Trojan Borsht acquires a new evil friend—Barry.

14. Major Faultline Wants Back In. Major Faultline believes he may have made a mistake by retiring and seeks a way back into Ronin Force.

15. The Obligatory Groveling Episode. Attempting to reconnect with his weird family, the Plumber tries to find his Uncle Sal.

16. The Plumber's Call. With his life in a state of shambles, the Plumber tries to find the only person who can help him—Captain Euchre.

17. Shopping for Super Clothes. Fantabulous Gal feels she needs a new look and goes shopping for a superhero costume.

18. Hello, My Name is Fantabulous Gal! Now that Fantabulous Gal looks fantastic in her new

costume, she struggles over a tag line to fit her new persona—like "Fantabulous Gal, Your Savior, Your Pal!"

19. This Ain't No Texas Hold 'Em. Evil Trojan Borscht appears a bit dazed as something seems to be controlling his mind and directing his evil actions.

20. A History of PFO Letters. With her new look, but a stack of rejected letters from Ronin Force, Fantabulous Gal feels she is now ready for acceptance into the super hero union.

21. Trojy's Recruiting Drive. When Evil Trojan Borscht sees that Ronin Force has used Captain Euchre's image for a recruiting drive, he devises his own methods for a recruiting drive of evil.

22. Those Other Plumbers. The Plumber feels he is a superhero and applies for admission in Ronin Force (the title refers to video game plumbers the Mario Brothers).

23. Power Pointed. Much to her surprise, Fantabulous Gal is approved for acceptance in Ronin Force—if her Power Point presentation meets the standards.

24. Crème of the Crap. Leopard Woman begins her duties by evaluating applicants from the recruitment drive.

25. Ask a Silly Question ... Get 17051 Junk Mails. While Ronin Force appears to have been successful with recruiting, Evil Trojan Borscht has gotten nothing but negative responses.

26. Turned Down. Despite her new look and enthusiasm, Fantabulous Gal is rejected by Ronin Force. Depressed, she takes to drinking and begins bad-mouthing Ronin Force.

27. Plumb Out of Luck. The Plumber is accepted into Ronin Force—and he even disbelieves it, but he has a letter to prove it.

28. Welcome to 1994, Chump. Leopard Woman may not have been the right choice for the job as she shows a lack of empathy and it is causing concern among the society's leaders.

29. Shaken Up. As Fantabulous Gal recovers from a hangover, Toronto is hit with an earthquake.

30. The Great Quake of '10. Ronin Force, as well as the common folk, attempt to readjust their lives following the earthquake.

31. Hint: Ticking Bomb? Not Good. Evil Trojan Borscht attempts to capitalize on the earthquake by claiming that he caused it.

32. One Sweet Heist. A heist pulled by Evil Trojan Borscht reveals that he stole an abundance of candy necklaces.

33. Shook Me All Night. Leopard Woman is not pleased to learn that Major Faultline caused the earthquake.

34. Thank You for Calling, Part 1. Angry that she has been rejected by Ronin Force, Fantabulous Gal decides she is not going to take no for an answer.

35. Thank You for Calling, Part 2. Fantabulous Gal decides to plead her cause for acceptance to join Leopard Woman.

36. The Yard Patrol. Although he had a letter indicating that he was accepted into Ronin Force, The Plumber discovers it was a mistake and decides to become his own super hero.

37. Wet and Dirty. In his first attempt to become a super hero, The Plumber experiments with water (and fails).

38. A Wrench in the Works. If water didn't work, what about electricity? The Plumber learns that it too doesn't provide super powers.

39. Bean Bag Chairs Weigh Heavy on the Soul of Injustice. For reasons that he cannot explain, Evil Trojan Borscht steals a bean bag chair.

40. Counseling Redux, Part 1. Leopard Woman and Major Faultline, still experiencing marital issues, return to Internet instant message counseling.

41. Counseling Redux, Part 2. Despite all the instant messaging, it appears the couple is still far apart on healing their strained relationship.

42. Puzzle, Puzzle, Toil and Trouble. Major Faultline tries to decipher a cryptic message left by Captain Euchre before he disappeared.

43. Name Change? Again rejected by Ronin Force, Fantabulous Gal believes the way to admission may lie in changing her secret identity to something else.

44. A Drip for Hire. Still without any powers or a job, The Plumber resorts to infomercials for results.

45. A (Very) Simple Plan. In an effort to find the missing Captain Euchre, Leopard Woman thinks using interns may be the answer.

46. Captain Euchre Is in Trouble! Fantabulous Gal swings into action to find Captain Euchre as a means to gaining membership in Ronin Force.

47. A Plumber for Hire: Hired. The infomercial results in a job offer for The Plumber—at a suspicious underground euchre club.

48. Party All the Time. With the rescue mission a failure, Fantabulous Gal figures the way to admission is by throwing a fantabulous party.

49. Watch Your Butter. Continues to focus on Evil Trojan Borscht as he does not appear to be himself, but being controlled by something or someone.

50. Rule Number One of Euchre Club. The Plumber, taking the euchre club job, may be the key to uncovering the whereabouts of Captain Euchre.

51. The Plumber Is Flushed. In an attempt to once again connect with his son, The Plumber bribes his wife to let him see him.

52. Wasn't That a Party? Fantabulous Gal is once again depressed when the party turned out to be a bust.

53. Stretching the Bounds of Good Taste. Fantabulous Gal ponders her next scheme, but feels she has given it her best shot already.

54. Can't Go Home Again. The Plumber meets with his son, but it just isn't the same as things have changed between them.

55. Making Up. In an effort to save their faltering

marriage, Major Faultline asks Leopard Woman out on a date.

56. Crazy Ultimatum Time. Wanting to get even with Captain Euchre for what he has done to him, Evil Trojan Borscht threatens to unleash his prize evil pupil Barry on Toronto if the city does not turn the captain over to him. The only problem: no one knows where the captain is.

57. Have You Seen This Cat? Major Faultline, stood up for his date with Leopard Woman (who has been kidnapped), returns home—and waits, and waits and waits.

58. A New Hope. An unexpected letter from Ronin Force arrives at The Plumber's home asking him to join.

59. Fantabulous Gal to the Rescue. Not discouraged, Fantabulous Gal hopes, that by capturing Evil Trojan Borscht, and finding Leopard Woman and Captain Euchre, Ronin Force will see that she is worthy of acceptance.

60. Barry's Big Day. With Toronto unable to produce Captain Euchre, Evil Trojan Borscht plans to unleash Barry (equipped with a nuclear missile) on the city.

61. Space Time Talk. Although a bit intoxicated, Major Faultline swings back into action, determined to save the city from nuclear bomb Barry.

62. The Importance of Being Thwarted. Wondering why his evil plans never amount to anything, Evil Trojan Borscht decides to review his constant failures.

63. Fantabulous Gal Shafted. Fantabulous Gal finds Leopard Woman and reunites her with hubby Major Faultline, but finds she is not getting recognition.

64. Credit Where It's Not Due. Leopard Woman recounts her lone and daring escape from her kidnapper, not once mentioning that it was Fantabulous Gal who rescued her.

65. Job Snaked Out from Under Me. The Plumber is delighted. He is accepted into Ronin Force—but ousted just as fast.

66. In Search of a New Barry. With his diabolical nuclear plan a failure, Evil Trojan Borscht seeks a new Barry.

67. Honey, I'm Home. Leopard Woman returns to Major Faultline.

68. Fantabulicious Sex Must Wait. The Plumber laments that what he had hoped for—sex with Fantabulous Girl was nothing more than a fantasy.

69. Sticking It to the Mail Man. As Evil Trojan Borscht complains that his mailman delivers him all the wrong mail, he begins slipping in and out of various delusions, not knowing who he really is.

70. The Plumber Is a Multi-Tool. The Plumber finally devises a super weapon that will not kill him—a Leatherman copy Multi-Tool.

71. Time Travel 101. Major Faultline explains his recent adventures in time traveling.

72. Desperate Encounters Profile: Plumbing Go

D673. Still desperate to find a girl, The Plumber hits the Internet with new dating techniques (Desperate Encounters).

73. Looking for Love in All the Wrong Toilets. The Plumber is delighted to find that his Desperate Encounters inbox is loaded with hits.

74. Worst Rickroll Ever. Evil Trojan Borscht's efforts to bad-mouth Ronin Force backfires (again).

75. The Yoke's on You. With undesirables being hired by Lungfish, Leopard Woman's assistant, Leopard Woman seeks a way to discreetly dismiss them.

76. Trojy Gets Fired. Evil Trojan Borscht's plan to become a French superhero fails miserably.

77. The At-Odds Couple. Ninjas invade Fantabulous Gal's home.

78. Learning Japanese. Fantabulous Gal attempts to deal with her Ninja intruders and learns why they attacked her (to steal a file she compiled—"Weaknesses of Superheroes").

79. Go Fly a Kite. A report from Major Faultline on the past and future of Toronto based on his time travels.

80. Monkeying Around with the Plumber. The Plumber hits on a new way to achieve superhero status—by teaming with a monkey (Mr. Tibbles).

81. A Few Cars Short. Fantabulous Gal takes up the cause of finding the again missing Captain Euchre.

82. Lessons in Love from Elmer Fudd. Love finds Evil Trojan Borscht.

83. Monsieur Popular. The super villain, Le Gros Chapeau, seeking status information, infiltrates Ontario's superhero squads.

84. Alexander Graham Bull. Once again hoping to repair their relationship, Leopard Woman and Major Faultline return to therapy.

85. Robbin' the Hood. Figuring that she can stop a crime by committing a crime, Fantabulous Gal and her Ninjas steal a suitcase full of money from the Mafia (which she says she will hand over to authorities at a later date).

86. We-ell I'm Movin' on Up. Fantabulous Gal uses the money (which she is only borrowing) to move out of Dyna Gal's apartment and into her own digs.

87A. You Killed the Monkey. The Plumber mourns the loss of his monkey, Mr. Tibbles, whose fate was determined by an on-line vote.

87B. You Didn't Kill the Monkey. It is revealed that in an alternate universe, on-line voters opted not to kill off Mr. Tibbles.

88. Caffeine Conundrum. Leopard Woman's efforts to brew a cup of coffee are not so simple when she gets a new coffee maker.

89. AAA Plan. A reformed Fantabulous Gal has bold new ideas—establish her own superhero/custodial business.

90. The Plumber Cleans Up. The Plumber becomes the first to join Fantabulous Gal's new business—AAA Cleaners.

91. Cat Kingdom Come. Leopard Woman faces a difficult decision—remain with Ronin Force or return to her former kingdom.

92. Plumbed Out. The Plumber finds he is not as young as he used to be when he tries to party hard like Fantabulous Gal's Ninjas.

93. Plumber on the Run. Someone has impersonated The Plumber and committed a crime—and now the real Plumber is on the run, fearing the police will be looking for him.

94. For Whom the Pants Tent. Le Gros Chapeau explains how car trouble prevented him from getting to a club to meet with Fantabulous Gal and Evil Trojan Borscht.

95. Kiss and Tell. As Fantabulous Gal continues to recruit agents for her business, she becomes infatuated with men with foreign accents.

96. The Plumber's Going Alone. The Plumber, still on the run from the law, believes he has found the perfect hideout.

97. Kick You Out Before I Go-Go. Seeking to bring some integrity back into Ronin Force, Leopard Woman begins dismissing those she considers non productive (with a song).

98. Confessions of a Super Villain. Le Gros Chapeau decides to hold a press conference for an important announcement—but technical difficulties prevent it from being heard.

99. The Transmigration of Evil Trojan Borscht. After dealing with a number of mental issues, Evil Trojan Borscht realizes that he is actually Le Gros Chapeau.

100. Visiting Hours. Fantabulous Gal, infatuated with the French-speaking Le Gros Chapeau, is unaware that he is her enemy, Evil Trojan Borscht.

101. Special Delivery. Fantabulous Gal receives an unexpected "romantic" gift for her new heartthrob—a supply of canned foods.

102. We Love You, Simon Le Bon, Jr. An old Betamax video tape (the competition for VHS tape technology) reveals Leopard Woman's life a teenager.

103. Council This! Major Faultline attempts to explain his collection of future pornography when it is discovered by Leopard Woman.

104. The Secret Plumber's Other Ball. The Plumber returns to his old room in his mother's house.

105. Trojy Finds Religion ... His. The mentally unstable Evil Trojan Borscht now declares himself as a god.

106. It Figures. Fantabulous Gal plots new ways to expand her business.

107. Kitty Bidding. In an attempt to raise money for Ronin Force, Leopard Woman devises a Bachelorette Auction—where nothing goes as planned.

108. The Plumber, the Player. The Plumber reveals that at the Bachelorette Auction he won a date with Leopard Woman by raising the $50 bid to $1700. Now he needs to find a way to acquire the money.

109. Boom and Greetings. With his new proclamation as a god, Evil Trojan Borscht declares a holy war.

110. The Audit. Trouble brews for Fantabulous Gal when she receives a letter stating that AAA Cleaners is being audited.

111. Dating Licks. A date between The Plumber and Leopard Woman is revealed when Leopard Woman tells all.

112. No Poon for Plumber. The Plumber tells his side of the date—which cost him a small fortune and left him broke.

113. Prison Letters to the Leader. Evil Trojan Borscht's new religion has its drawbacks when he receives mail from disgruntled worshipers.

114. So Sue Me. Fantabulous Gal faces another challenge for AAA Cleaners—Ronin Force's claim that she infringed on their patented trademark.

115. Signal to Noise. Evil Trojan Borscht is now struggling to come to terms with his multiple personalities.

116. Doing the Can Con. Fantabulous Gal forgot to pay the tax due to the city from her business and faces a loss of her Can Con accreditation.

117. Adieu and a Warning. In a surprise move, Leopard Woman decides to return to her kingdom.

118. Don't Cry for Me, Mississauga! Le Gros Chapeau plots revenge after Leopard Woman reveals his nefarious ways.

119. Blogs of Future Passed. In the future Major Faultline, now Admiral of the starship *Jefferson* sends a message warning the world to destroy the evil Suckers (robots) as the future of the world depends on it.

120. Dyna Worry, Be Happy. After months apart, Fantabulous Gal visits Dyna Gal.

121. Electrifying Reunion. The Plumber is reunited with his father, The Electrician.

122. Electronically Grounded. The Plumber finds that he has not lived up to the expectations his father had for him.

123. Ninjas, I'm Home. Captain Euchre, found by Fantabulous Gal, is invited to her home and her Ninja houseguests.

124. Swing Time. The Electrician becomes a problem for The Plumber when he tries bonding with every man and woman in town.

125. Urine for a Heck of a Future. A time trip by Major Faultline turns hectic when a group of monkeys hop on board.

126. That Is Why the Plumber Fails. To make him more of a man, The Electrician attempts to use electric shock therapy on The Plumber.

127. What the Deck. With Captain Euchre more of a problem than she thought, Fantabulous Gal seeks a way to control him.

128. Shoulda, Coulda, Woulda's. Leopard Woman returns to her kingdom, which has fallen into a state of ruins.

129. Fantabulicious Visit. The Plumber recalls the visit he received from Fantabulous Gal.

130. Digging Up the Past. Major Faultline discovers, that without Scotch, he is an ineffectual time traveler.

131. The Gathering Storm. Le Gros Chapeau returns with a machine capable of tunneling through any surface.

132. Straight Up. Fantabulous Gal figures that the best way to save Major Faultline is to stop him from drinking. But that is not as easy as it sounds as he is useless without his bottle of Scotch.

133. Getting Ducks in a Row. Leopard Woman, now back home, faces a threat from her enemy, Sucker.

134. The Ninja Blues. Fantabulous Gal misses her Ninjas, who appear to have left her to wreck havoc elsewhere.

135. The Evil Villain's Guide to Self Love. Le Gros Chapeau's love for Leopard Woman continues to grow as a battle rages in the Leopard Kingdom.

136. Going Undercover. An assignment finds The Plumber going undercover at the mysterious Euchre Club.

137. AAA What's Going On? Fantabulous Gal attempts to reorganize her company without the Ninjas.

138. Here, Kitty Kitty! As Major Faultline returns from one of his time trips, he discovers that Leopard Woman has returned to her kingdom.

139. Le Blog of Le Dead. Just when it seemed to be the end for Le Gros Chapeau, he is reactivated as a cyborg.

140. Sucker's Been Euchred. The Plumber discovers that a computer program is behind and controlling the evil Sucker robots.

141. Down and Out ... of Business. Just when things looked bright, Fantabulous Gal finds that her cleaning/superhero company is just not working.

142. In Too Ted D-eep. The Plumber's alter-ego, Ted D. Rock Spin is beginning to overtake his real personality.

143. Liquor in the Front, Euchre in the Back. Down in the dumps, Fantabulous Gal finds that a bottle of Scotch is now her best companion.

144. The Boning Sessions. The Plumber's alter-ego has transformed himself into a 1930s-like two-bit gangster.

145. Do Cyborg's Dream of Half-Electric Sheep? Le Gros Chapeau struggles to adjust to the fact that he is now a cyborg.

146. Winning Is Half the Battle. Major Faultline reports that Sucker has defeated Leopard Woman's kingdom—but she is safe, but assumed missing in action.

147. The Weird Part. During a blackout Evil Trojan Borscht was captured by the Sucker robots, killed, taken apart and reassembled as a cyborg. He is now on the run from the Sucker robot army after escaping.

148. Into the Woods. Cyborg Evil Trojan Borscht, still on the run, believes that a nearby farm could offer him the safety he requires.

149. Back on Top. Following the battle against Sucker, Leopard Woman believes it is time for her to return to hubby Major Faultline.

150. The Rubber Glove Procedure. Evil Trojan Borscht appears to be adjusting to life on a farm, despite the fact that he is not only evil, but also a cyborg.

151. Plumber's Up for Air. Hoping to help each other overcome trying times, Fantabulous Gal, The Plumber and Captain Euchre have decided to become roommates.

152. This Is Why We Can't Have Nice Things. Evil Trojan Borscht realizes that his evil needs to be exploited—and working on a farm is not the answer.

153. All Day Sucker. Now back in the surface world, Leopard Woman relays a message that humans and animals must be prepared as Sucker is their enemy.

154. Or a Mustard and Cheese Sandwich Perhaps. Evil Trojan Borscht, finding safety in a cave in the woods, recalls how nice it was being human.

155. Battle Fatigue. A battle is looming between good and evil—and the media believes it is not significant enough to warrant coverage.

156. The Plumber's First Real Battle. Since the media failed to provide coverage, The Plumber relates his experiences in the Battle of Dundas Square.

157. The Alyssa Milano Maneuver. Having managed to escape the robots after a battle, Evil Trojan Borscht is safely back in his lair.

158. After the Rumble. The battle-weary Fantabulous Gal, addicted to Scotch, is too impaired to notice that she suffered injuries in the insignificant (to the media) war.

159. Stupid Cult. As Evil Trojan Borscht tries to reattach his severed camera hand, he realizes that in his battle with the robots, he was fighting on the wrong side and helping to destroy his own cult members.

160. Therapeutic Breakthrough. Now back together, Leopard Woman and Major Faultline decide to return to therapy to save their troubled marriage.

161. The Package. Fantabulous Gal receives an unexpected package in the mail—a candy necklace and assumes that someone is sweet on her. She is unaware that the necklace has hypnotic powers and will control her if she wears it.

162. Mail Order Plumber. The Plumber, captured by Sucker, becomes a victim of their brainwashing plans.

163. The Little Death. Fed up with Major Faultline, Leopard Woman believes killing him may just be the answer.

164. Le Evil Monologue. Le Gros Chapeau faces the camera to express his feelings about what has happened to him since he met Leopard Woman.

165. Sucker Says. Surviving the death attempt, Major Faultline realizes that Leopard Woman had been hypnotized by Sucker to kill him.

166. Brainwashed and Waterlogged. Sucker's

plan to brainwash The Plumber into disrupting the city's water system appears to be working.

167. Match Game. Sucker's influence now has both Fantabulous Gal and Captain Euchre under their control.

168. That Guy Again. Major Faultline snaps Leopard Woman out of her hypnotic trance—and now has more hope that their marriage can be saved.

169. Captain Euchre Does a Three Way ... Fight! Fantabulous Gal, Captain Euchre and The Plumber battle to overcome Sucker's influence over them.

170. I Did What to Who Now? The battle proves most successful to Fantabulous Gal who, despite causing damage to structures, appears to have overcome her addition to alcohol.

171. Stupidity Saves the Day. The battle makes The Plumber realize that he is a failure, not a superhero (although his failures sometimes save the day).

172. They Always Escape. Ronin Force's efforts to capture Evil Trojan Borscht appear to be even less effective now that he is a cyborg.

173. Funny Story. The Plumber and Major Faultline recall some of their experiences together.

174. On the Bright Side of Life. As Fantabulous Gal relates her feelings about living with Captain Euchre, she also reveals that she has re-established her cleaning business but on a smaller scale.

175. Second Time's a Charm. Leopard Woman and Major Faultline agree to give their marriage a second try and get back to the business of battling evil.

176. The Plumber Hangs Up His Wrench—for a Wrench. Realizing that he was never meant to be a superhero, The Plumber decides to go back to his plumbing business.

177. New—Finally Some Respect. Overcoming Sucker's influence over her, Fantabulous Gal is rewarded for not sabotaging Ronin Force.

178. Euchre Rising. Having apparently been cured of his addiction to Scotch, Major Faultline, now also broke and homeless, is forced to move in with another superhero.

179. See Ya Later Sucker. As Ronin Force reorganizes itself, Major Faultline feels that he is no longer needed and leaves the organization.

180. Reformation Party. Fantabulous Gal embarks on a new mission—reform Ronin Force.

181. ETB: The Next Generation. Evil Trojan Borscht decides to encompass his cyborg abilities to wreck even more havoc on the city.

182. Unclogging Ronin Force. Unable to become the plumber he was meant to be, The Plumber decides to once again attempt to become a Ronin Force superhero.

183. New—Future Fodder. Leopard Woman reflects on past experiences as she signs off and ends the series by stating that she is pregnant—"and if it's a girl, she better not be prettier than me."

347 Time Keeper. timekeepershow.com. 2011 (Science Fiction).

Mitch Manners is a man with a power he does not understand or even know how he acquired. He can travel through time through thought but the experience leaves him unable to remember those experiences. His purpose appears to be returning to the past to change an incident that could change the future if it is not altered (or set on the right path). When the planet Jupiter suddenly vanishes from space and asteroids (normally held back by Jupiter) threaten Earth, Mitch jumps back in time to find an answer and hopefully stop what will happen in the future (the only arc storyline presented).

Cast: Matt Lunsford (Mitch Manners), Chris Jackson (Dave), Joanna Sycz (Susan), Brandii Banks (Jan), Jessica Alexander (Jill), Miranda Rivers (Emily). **Credits:** *Producer:* Daryn Murphy, Jessica Alexander, Matt Wightman, Wes Pratt. *Director:* Daryn Murphy, Matt Wightman, Wes Pratt. *Writer:* Daryn Murphy. **Comment:** The time traveling sequences are well done and, although a bit talkative at times, the story is compelling enough to draw the viewer back to see what happens. Acting, writing and directing are on the level of a regular television series.

Episodes:

1. Inane Stuff (8 min., 3 sec.). The planets are in alignment but Mitch has a vision of his returning to the past to kill a young woman—someone who may be something other than she appears.

2. Purpose (6 min., 42 sec.). Mitch is sent back in time to the day before Jupiter disappeared and begins his search to find the girl.

3. Initiation (8 min., 18 sec.). Without warning Mitch begins to have recollections of past time travels.

4. Incoming (9 min., 42 sec.). Television news reports the alarming disappearance of the planet Jupiter and of the disasters that will affect the planet Earth.

5. Feedback (7 min., 13 sec.). Back in the present, Mitch feels that he needs help and visits a psychic—who, surprisingly, knows about Mitch's abilities.

6. Do-Over (10 min., 44 sec.). The psychic tells Mitch that clues to what he is seeking lie in something that he has seen before. As Mitch retraces his steps, trying to recall what that might have been (the young woman), he believes he will have a second chance (a do-over) to relive prior events but will now be armed with new evidence to save the world.

348 Time Traveling Lesbian. fuunyordie. com and afterellen.com. 2009 (Science Fiction).

Rebecca Drysdale is a young woman working as a clerk in the video store Reel Life. She is a lesbian and part of an improvisational comedy group. One day, while stocking DVD's she finds one marked "Recommended by Carl." At home, Rebecca plays the DVD and learns that in the year 2319 science has accomplished something that was thought impossible—time travel. But with the good comes the bad. As agents called The Leak seize upon the abilities of time travel to alter history to suit their own sinister purposes, Carl, as he identifies himself, needs someone to champion their cause—a lesbian who will return to the past to fix any events that have been altered by The Leak. Although reluctant at first, Rebecca agrees to become Carl's Time Traveling Lesbian to not only seduce historic beauties, but reverse historical events that have been altered and keep the natural order of time and space.

Cast: Rebecca Drysdale (Herself), Drae Campbell, Hanna Cheek. **Credits:** *Producer:* Bryan Carmel. *Director:* Brendan Colthurst. *Writer:* Rebecca Drysdale. **Comment:** Rebecca is cute; the stories are sexy and play well; there are gorgeous girls for Rebecca to encounter; and there are numerous possibilities for storylines (it is even a good candidate as a television series for the Here! and Logo cable channels). Although there is no nudity there are plenty of girl/girl kissing scenes and its one major fault is the continual (and needless) use of foul language. Episodes are humorous, fun to watch and will leave some viewers wanting more.

Episodes:

1. Studio Fifty ... Whore? (3 min., 55 sec.). Although the episode opens with "Last time on *Time Traveling Lesbian*," there was actually no last time. It establishes the storyline as Rebecca finds the DVD and is faced with a decision—whether or not to become the unseen Carl's agent.

2. Sappho's Sacrifice (4 min., 5 sec.). Rebecca is equipped with a wrist communicator (to contact Carl and vice versa) when she agrees to become his agent.

3. When in Rome. (3 min., 58 sec.). Rebecca journeys back to Ancient Rome to stop an imposter of Apollo from preventing the Fall of the Roman Empire.

4. Hats. (3 min., 41 sec.). The Leaks become aware of Rebecca and feel she is a threat to their goals.

5. Dangers of Improv (4 min., 55 sec.). Rebecca returns to the past to become an unknown again in the present (as she has to remain anonymous) when the Leaks change the present to make her a world-famous improv performer.

6. Summer of Love (3 min., 58 sec.). Rebecca's time traveling experiences have allowed her to encounter and make love to many beautiful girls (although only kissing is seen). Carl's worst fears come to light when Rebecca falls for a girl in the 1960s and wants to remain with her. She learns that if she chooses to remain in a time period not of her own, history will be changed (as here, where if she remains, The Leaks plan to set the women's movement back 10 years will succeed).

7. 12 Monkeys (2 min., 43 sec.). As Rebecca prepares to be whisked back to the Old West days of Kate Winslett, she is sidetracked when she feels something is not right.

8. To Be Cunt-inued ... Get It? Never Mind (2 min., 22 sec). Rebecca's feelings grow stronger when Carl assigns her to return to the days of Genghis Khan but Rebecca discovers something else. She spies two of The Leaks conversing with a computer and hearing Carl's voice. Have her travels been for the greater good or has Carl planned something else for her? A cliff hanger ending with a degrading title.

349 *Transformers: Cyber Missions.* youtube.com. 2010 (Science Fiction).

A computer animated project in the Hasbro toy franchise *Transformers* that is a supplement to the live action film series that takes place between *Transformers: Revenge of the Fallen* and *Transformers: Ark of the Moon*. Like the films, it continues to depict the Autobots (robots capable of transforming themselves into vehicle-like weapons) battle against the evil Decepticons. Optimus Prime is the leader of the Autobots (which include Bumblebee, Ironhide, Ratchet and Sideswipe), while Megatron leads the Decepticons (Starscream, Soundwave, Bludgeon, Lockdown, Mindwipe, Barricae and Frenzy).

Voice Cast: Eric Edwards (Optimus Prime), Tom Anderson (Bumblebee), Tony Gialluca (Megatron/Smolder/Chopster/Barricade/Bludgeon/Frenzy/Ironhide), Bronco D. Jackson (Bludgeon/Frenzy/Ironhide/Lockdown/Mindwipe/Ratchet/Sideswipe/Soundwave/Starscream). **Credits:** *Producer:* Aaron Archer, Erin Hillman, Michael Verrecchia. *Writer:* Scott Beatty. **Comment:** The animation matches the style of the movie and television versions but it is really directed at fans of the franchise as having prior knowledge of what the characters are helps greatly to understand what is going on.

Episodes:

1. Cyber Missions 1. At NEST Command Headquarters, the history of the Autobot Deception War is reviewed by Optimus Prime.

2. Cyber Missions 2. During a mission, Bumblebee manages to trap Soundwave in an electromagnetic bubble. Meanwhile Bludgeon is being tracked by Ironhide.

3. Cyber Missions 3. With Ratchet on guard at NEST Headquarters, he is unaware of approaching danger from the enemy.

4. Cyber Missions 4. Optimus Prime and Sideswipe confront Meagatron at an abandoned factory.

5. Cyber Missions 5. Ironhide seeks help after a mission fails and he finds himself lost in a jungle.

6. Cyber Missions 6. While being pursued by Sideswipe, Barricade and Frenzy attempt to escape capture by using a hologram to fool Sideswipe.

7. Cyber Missions 7. After being injured in a bat-

tle, Sideswipe encounters difficulty trying to repair Ratchet.

8. Cyber Missions 8. Optimus Prime issues a directive warning the Autobots to always be on guard and alert as the enemy could strike at any moment.

9. Cyber Missions 9. The Autobots are called in to battle a fire in Scramble City.

10. Cyber Missions 10. Jack faces a dangerous enemy (Mindwipe) who seeks what Jack knows about NEST's plans.

11. Cyber Missions 11. Ironhide finds himself in a dangerous situation when he is caught speeding on Interstate 95—but the police he believes are human are anything but.

12. Cyber Missions 12. Megatron and Starscream plot an attack while Bumblebee attempts to track their movements and intercept them.

13. Cyber Missions 13. Optimus Prime arranges a meeting with the Decepticons in the final effort to avoid a war.

350 *Transitions.* transitionstheseries.com. 2010 (Fantasy).

Kingdom City appears to be like any other city with one major exception: it is also a city of the supernatural. It is here where Ed Loomis has been attacked by a vampire but not killed. He has the virus and is slowly being transformed into a creature of the night. Stories follow Ed as he attempts to accept and adjust to life as a vampire. **Cast:** William Ellwood (Ed Loomis), Tudor Dixon (Claire), Liza Zaczek (Amber), Todd Spratt (Joseph), Patricia Gray (Megan), Adam Slager (Kevin). **Credits:** *Producer-Director:* Chad Ream. *Writer:* Jeremiah Coe, Chad Ream. **Comment:** While the subject of vampirism is explored, it is not an action-packed vampire saga. It does have its moments and the production is well executed. **Episodes:**

1. Pilot (9 min., 6 sec.). Ed begins the early stages of his transition.

2. Introductions (7 min., 10 sec.). Zachariah, a member of clan of Joseph Klein, introduces Ed to his new lifestyle.

3. Acceptance (11 min., 10 sec.). Ed encounters difficulties adjusting until he speaks with Claire, a vampire who also faced uncertainty about her transition.

4. Day Tenders (10 min.). As Ed adjusts, he begins to wonder if there are other clans in the city and seeks to uncover the mystery surrounding a woman named Amber.

5. A Taste Of (9 min., 20 sec.). Claire offers Ed his first taste for blood.

6. The First (7 min., 45 sec.). At a Halloween party, Claire seeks a "meal" for Ed.

7. Delete (13 min., 30 sec.). Ed's first taste of human blood revitalizes him and makes him more favorable toward his new life.

8. Anxious (11 min., 30 sec.). Ed begins to adjust to his new life and confronts Zachariah about his feelings.

9. Define (8 min., 35 sec.). Zachariah explains to Ed what it truly means to be a vampire in today's world.

10. Watching (8 min.). Claire learns from Zachariah about Ed's succumbing to his life as a vampire.

351 *Transolar Galactica.* transolargalactica.com. 2011 (Science Fiction).

Star Trek spoof about the crew of the S.S. *Transolar*, a UGCA star ship that is captained by an incompetent (Remington) and staffed by a crew who are just as ignorant about space travel as they begin a voyage into deep space. **Cast:** Isaac Joslin (Capt. Elliott "Remington" Trigger), Adam C. Boyd (Petty Officer McCall), Clancy Bundy (Reginald Murdock), Adam Harum (Samson), Jade Warpenburg (Charles Yasaki), Crystal Pointek (Nurse). **Credits:** *Producer:* Adam C. Boyd, Clancy Bundy, Adam Harum. *Writer-Director:* Adam Harum. **Comment:** Knowing that kids would be attracted to such a premise, the producers chose to overlook that and present foul language (should have a parental warning, but doesn't). There have been several *Star Trek* spoofs, many funnier and done better than what is presented here. Luckily, there are only three short episodes, so the comedy is swift and not dragged out. **Episodes:**

1. Second Star (5 min., 6 sec.). The crew of the S.S. *Transolar* begin a voyage into outer space.

2. Beam Them Aboard (3 min., 32 sec.). McCall, the Chief Petty Office, tries to figure out a way to save a scouting party when they become lost on Canyon World VI.

3. The Will to Live (4 min., 58 sec.). The crew has to put their heads together and figure out a way to save Samson, the Communications Officer, when he is injured.

352 *Trenches.* trenchesonline.com. 2010 (Science Fiction).

Futuristic drama about two warring enemies (Lt. Andrews, a Rossdale Evacuation Specialist, and Racine, a Kuzaan Army Captain), stranded on a primitive planet, who must learn to work together to survive the dangers of an unknown world. **Cast:** Aaron Mathias (Lt. Andrews), Mercy Mallick (Capt. Racine), Lev Gorn (Cpl. Traina), Scott Nankivel (Pvt. Janeski), Daz Crawford (Sgt, Verro), Hong Chau (Specialist Wing). **Credits:** *Producer-Director:* Shane Felux. *Writer:* Dawn Cowings, Sarah Yaworsky. **Comment:** Enjoyable tale of survival with twits and turns to keep the viewer interested enough to see what happens next. **Episodes:**

1. Behind Enemy Lines (5 min., 46 sec.). Establishes the story as Andrews becomes stranded on a hostile planet.

2. Fubar (5 min., 46 sec.). Andrews encounters a group of Rossdale survivors who are seeking safety following a battle with the Kuzaan Army.

3. Field Promotion (4 min., 54 sec.). Andrews takes charge of the band of survivors but meets with hostility as some blame him for the predicament they now face.

4. Dead Reckoning (3 min., 54 sec.). As the survivors move forward, Andrews finds himself faced with unrest among the group. He is now weary of who can and who can't be trusted.

5. Shallow Grave (4 min., 22 sec.). The survivors find temporary shelter at what appears to be an abandoned Kuzzan base.

6. Whisky Tango Foxtrot (2 min., 59 sec.). Unrest with the group forces Andrews to exert his authority and insure everyone that they will reach safety.

7. The Suck (4 min., 14 sec.). Andrews discovers that their temporary sanctuary is only that and they must move on as the enemy abandoned it for a reason—it is a trap.

8. Snafu (4 min., 23 sec.). When Racine, the Kuzaan Captain, fails in an effort to become the group leader, he realizes that he and Andrews must put their differences aside for the greater good.

9. Defecation Hits the Oscillation (5 min., 27 sec.). As the group nears a tunnel that could lead to their safety, Andrews and Racine must now work together to figure out the right path amid the numerous twists and turns that confront them.

10. Charlie Foxtrot (6 min., 52 sec.). Concludes the program as Andrews must gamble as what move he must now make to save everyone and get off the planet.

353 Tribe 12. youtube.com. 2013 (Fantasy).

A Shadow Man is a being, usually tall and slender, bald and dressed in black, that can bend time and space. Milo Asher is college film student who began work on a project called "The Twelve Tribes of Israel." Shortly after filming Milo discontinued the project and was later found dead in his room. His cousin, Noah Maxwell, who had been posting news about his cousin's (Milo) project on YouTube, retrieves the tapes Milo had been shooting with a hope of turning the page from a project page to a dedication page. While viewing the tapes, Noah notices something strange in the scenes—a Shadow Man, a figure that haunted Milo and that now is apparently haunting him as he has been hearing unexplained strange noises in and around his house. Believing that his life may also be in danger Noah begins recording himself, especially when he sleeps, in the hope of catching whatever is causing the strange sounds and what could have possibly killed Milo.

Episodes follow Noah as he views Milo's tapes to discover why he is being stalked, what really happened to Milo and most importantly—how to escape the Shadow Man.

Cast: Adam Rosner (Noah Maxwell). **Credits:** *Producer-Director-Writer:* Adam Rosner. **Comment:** There are no screen credits for cast or production crew. An excessive use of the annoying shaky camera method of filming. The production values and acting are amateurish. The story can (and does) become confusing and interest is quickly lost (as can be seen by the views listed). The views also show that the program was not watched with any consistency as there are thousands of view differences between most of the episodes. While *Tribe Twelve* is based on *Marble Hornets* (see entry) it is a much more confusing presentation.

Episodes: It is not possible to present a consecutive storyline that makes sense based on the episodes that are still available online. The available episode titles are listed with the views each received, showing how interest was gained and lost.

1. Introduction: In Memory of Milo (223,209 views). *2.* Submission 1 (136,315 views). *3.* Submission 2 (99,131 views). *4.* The Live Stream Incident (80,531 views). *5.* November 11th (98,718 views). *6.* Several Months of Hell (51,274 views). *7.* Interception (103,211 views). *8.* The Manifest (40,461 views). *9.* The Order (81,674 views). *10.* Obituary (28,676 views). *11.* The Device (54,366 views). *12.* Milo's Tape (20,206 views). *13.* Our Meet-Up (34,082 views). *14.* Deus Ex Machina (62,095 views). *15.* Happy Birthday (91,966 views). *16.* Come Closer (119,413 views). *17.* Northern Trip (74,897 views). *18.* Summer Update (49,486 views). *19.* Submission 4 (80,096 views). *20.* Submission 3 (90,337 views). *21.* The Live Stream (80,531 views). *22.* Northern Trip Footage (74,897 views). *23.* Summer Update (49,486 views). *24.* Slenderdansen (79,332 views). *25.* Halloween Hotel (64,166 views). *26.* The Envelope (55,012 views). *27.* The Unbox (70,463 views). *28.* Let's React (6,705 views). *29.* Interruption (184,340 views). *30.* Urban Legends (72,464 views). *31.* Extraordinary Circumstances (29,860 views). *32.* The Token Letter (67,419 views). *33.* Secret Parent Interview (51,823 views). *34.* A Phone Call with John Fletcher (51,927 views). *35.* Complication (8,209 views).

354 The True Heroines. youtube.com. 2011 (Fantasy).

During World War I a secret experiment called Project Paradise Hill began with the intent to breed humans with special abilities (H.S.A.'s). Its purpose was to limit the number of Allies lost during the war and was privately funded by The Corporation, which established Utopian towns across America and allied territories with the intent of enticing returning soldiers into settling down—and unknowingly breed

H.S.A.'s. In 1941, with America's entrance into World War II, the government purchased the ability to produce H.S.A.'s from The Corporation. The government, however, misused the ability and enslaved H.S.A's, forcing them to work as slaves or soldiers on the front lines in Europe. Though many H.S.A's were lost, several escaped and managed to live lives as regular humans worldwide. The government, however, displeased with that fact, hired agents to find and eliminate fugitive H.S.A.'s. Stories, set in New Paradise Hill in the 1960s, follows a group of female H.S.A.'s (Pearl, Margie and Dottie) as they attempt to uncover the secret of their abilities and who or what they actually are.

Pearl Andrews is an ex-war nurse who lives in New Paradise Hill. She dresses as and is typical of housewives of the 1960s. She is rather uptight and constantly willing to help others with her power of invisibility. She is also seeking to learn the truth about herself and what happened to others of her kind.

Margie Hepburn is married (her husband is an executive at Milk King Corporation). She is a very tidy person and possesses the power of super speed. She has come to New Paradise Hill to avenge her kind and suspects that Milk King is now behind what happened.

Dottie Rodriquez is the product of growing up in a tough Cuban neighborhood and, although she too possesses super strength, she has also acquired street smarts from her school of hard knocks. Dottie also shares Margie's concerns that something evil lurks behind the doors of Milk King.

Ethel Worthington is a mother-dominated woman who succumbed to a campaign of finding serenity in New Paradise Hill. She works as the Milk King switchboard operator and considers herself a misfit and knows more than what she lets on about Milk King. Her mother, Doris, and Ethel moved to New Paradise Hill after the war and while Ethel believes she doesn't need a man to be happy, Doris believes just the opposite and is seeking to find not only herself a mate—but one for Ethel too.

Gordon Fitzgerald, a former soldier, is now a deliveryman for Milk King (he is also heir to the Milk King fortune and has been trained as a military assassin). Earl Finch is a former Milk Man for Milk King whose work as a scientist during the war may hold the key to the questions The True Heroines seek. Bobby Fitzgerald, the town's mayor, has lived in New Paradise Hill his entire life; it was his father who initiated Project Paradise Hill. Hugo Rodriquez is married to Dottie (they meet when she worked as a dancer at a USO during the war) and is now a salesman at Milk King. Calvin Hepburn is Margie's husband, a corporate leader at Milk King. Percy Andrews is Pearl's husband, a mechanical engineer at Milk King.

Cast: Fiona Vroom (Pearl Andrews), Jovanna Guguet (Margie Hepburn), Paula Giroday (Dottie Rodriquez), Ali Liebert (Ethel Worthington), Fina Chiarelli (Doris Worthington), Joel Sturrock (Gordon Fitzgerald), Denis Simpson (Earl Finch), Peter Benson (Bobby Fitzgerald), Zak Santiago (Hugo Rodriquez), Brendan Penny (Calvin Hepburn), Neil Grayston (Percy Andrews). **Credits:** *Producer-Writer:* Nicholas Carella, Paula Giroday, Jovanna Guguet, Fiona Vroom. *Director:* Michelle Ouellet. **Comment:** Comedy mixes with fantasy to tell a tale of three women yearning to uncover their roots. The acting, writing and direction are very good. The women dress as though they were 1950s television sitcom housewives (although 1961 is specifically mentioned in one episode) and do give the feeling of how women dressed and acted in that era. The sets appear to be too modern for its setting and the flashback sequences, wherein the leads are seen in their roles as USO (United Servicemen's Organization) volunteers is just too unrealistic. During World War II USO's were set up to entertain soldiers—but here the women are seen in sexy black lingerie-like attire (and in provocative dances) that just not would have occurred at the time. While this does make the series more appealing (and a good deal of time is devoted to it), it distracts from the storyline when the women are seen again as supposedly ordinary housewives. Overall though, it is an entertaining and well produced series to watch.

Episodes:

1 and 2. The Pilot, Parts 1 and 2 (7 min., 12 sec.). Introduces the three main girls (Pearl, Margie and Dottie) and their rising suspicions that the local Milk King Corporation is hiding something behind its making and delivering of milk.

3. For All We Know (11 min., 23 sec.). The girls come one step closer to uncovering the truth about the Milk King Corporation.

4. Count Your Blessings (9 min., 13 sec.). A flashback episode to World War II wherein the girls are seen in sexy attire as well as performing provocative dances.

5. What'll I Do (10 min., 5 sec.). The flashback continues with additional entertainment by Margie, Pearl and Dottie.

6. Come on a My House (12 min., 25 sec.). Back in the 1960s, Doris readies Ethel for a date while the girls attend a lavish party and, using it as a cover, seek more information about Milk King.

355 *The Twisted Mind of Ray Hinkley.* www.webserieschannel.com. 2010 (Horror).

Psychological-based program that delves into the mind of a serial killer. Ray Hinkley appears to be just an ordinary man. He is an engineer and could be your best friend, your neighbor, or even a relative. But he has an uncontrollable passion for killing and within the past year, he has killed five people. As Ray addresses the viewer, a first person account is presented regarding Ray's personal life and how he was transformed into what he has become.

Cast: Rafael Goldstein (Ray Hinkley), Meryl Helman (Norma Jean Hinkley), Oto Brezina (Herbert Hinkley), Umi Vaid (Jaime), Tommy Cooley (Victim 1), Dan Hagen (Victim 2), Robert Enriquez (Domenic). **Credits:** *Producer-Writer:* Chris Sheng. *Director:* Chris Sheng, Ravi Vora. **Comment:** Although only one episode has been released, it can be stated that the idea of a serial killer it is not original (having been done countless times in feature films and on television)—even the one presented here, with the killer addressing the viewer. Series like *Profiler* and *Criminal Minds* have used the same concept and done in a much more suspenseful way than is presented via Ray Hinkley.

Episodes:

1. Season 1 Episode 1 (7 min., 51 sec.). Explores how Ray meets his victims then plots their demise.

356 Twisted Showcase. britishwebseries.com. 2012 (Horror).

Anthology program of horror stories where the unexpected happens (although traces of *The Twilight Zone* and other such television anthology series can be seen). **Credits:** *Producer:* Rhys Jones, Robin Bell, Leigh A. Jones. *Director:* Leigh A. Jones. *Writer:* Ricard Holland, Robin Bell. **Comment:** British produced program that, due to accents, becomes difficult to understand at times. The acting is good but the stories, with the exception of "Something at the Top of the Stairs," (which is suspenseful) are not chilling and are more talk than anything else.

Episodes:

1. Peter and Paul (11 min., 9 sec.). A man (Peter) finds the spirit of his late brother (Paul) returning to him—by possessing his right hand. Starring Gareth David Lloyd, Beth Mascarenhas.

2. Eyeball (2 min., 54 sec.). After a transplant to receive a new eye, a man finds that from his left eye, he sees life through the donor. Starring Rhys James, Derek Evans.

3. Fear of Living (9 min., 41 sec.). A man becomes fearful of leaving his home after receiving a series of death threats. Starring Ian Marksman, Ziad El Hady.

4. Bob Dracula (6 min., 54 sec.). A vampire (David Welsh Price) seeks to adjust to life and live among humans.

5. Something at the Top of the Stairs (4 min., 43 sec.). A young woman (Abigail Law Briggs) alone in her home fears something is upstairs when she hears disturbing sounds.

6. Clone Alone (7 min., 28 sec.). A black and white episode about a clone that must come to terms that other clones exist in his image. A cast is not given.

7. Man vs. Porn (5 min., 42 sec.). A young man, addicted to Internet pornography, seeks the help of a psychiatrist when his attraction to a young female star begins to overtake his life. A cast is not credited.

357 Tyranny. weathermanfilms.com. 2011 (Science Fiction).

It is the year 2012 and Daniel McCarthy, a 30-year-old respected artist, musician and filmmaker, has been struggling to solve a mystery that began on November 22, 1999—when he volunteered for a grad student's neurological experiment and the course of his life would be changed forever. The experiment appeared to be harmless—to record his brainwave patterns as he performed various tasks. At the conclusion of the experiment Daniel found that eight days had elapsed and that he had no memory of what happened during that time. All he can remember is envisioning a future time wherein an unknown people and corporations that do not yet exist, are using technology that has not yet been developed to manipulate the governments and people of the world. Daniel believed that what he saw was not a dream but a vision into the future. But his memory of the future is cloudy and to help him recall more of what he saw, Daniel begins conducting sensory deprivation experiments on himself. The experiments bring to life bits and pieces of the puzzle convincing Daniel that what happened during those eight days were not a dream but an actual vision of the future. The program charts Daniel's self-imposed mission to stop what he saw from happening by finding the people who will affect the future of the world.

Alexandra Hubbard, called Alex, is Daniel's friend, an agent with the Behavioral Sciences Division of the FBI. They met at Berkeley, dated, but ended up as friends. Isabelle Lorenz, Daniel's wife for less than a year, left San Francisco for a marketing job in New York during the summer of 2001. Pavel Novak, a wealthy adventurer, is one of the people Daniel encountered in Sweden during his quest to uncover his puzzle. Ariel Huckster is a woman who became interested in Daniel's quest when she found one of his journals while traveling through San Francisco in 2010. Demas Hunter, a member of the London Underground, teamed with Daniel in the fall of 2008. Myra Ripley, a friend of Daniel's, works in London as a fashion designer. Mina Harud is the international super model Daniel befriended in Paris (she is married to the wealthy banker, Omar Harud and helped Daniel with finances during his quest).

Cast: John Beck Hofmann (Daniel McCarthy), Kieren van den Blink (Isabelle Lorenz), Bitsie Tulloch (Alexandra Hubbard), Olga Kurylenko (Mina Harud), Mikael Forsberg (Pavel Novak), Sarah Coleman (Ariel Huckster), Aric Green (Ethan Chambers), Mimi Ferrer (Myra Ripley), Enrico Piazza (Dr. Jacob Malik), Sasga Townsend (Demas Hunter), Nathan Marlow (Agent Holden), Steve Collins (Edson Cross). **Credits:** *Producer:* John Beck Hofmann, Kieren van den Blink, Sandra L. Rostirolla, Mimi Ferrer, Sarah Coleman. *Director:* John Beck Hofmann. *Writer:* John Beck Hofmann, Sarah Coleman, Mimi Ferrer, Mikael Forsberg, Sasha Townsend,

Kieren van den Blink, Olga Kurylenko. **Comment:** Interesting concept that is well acted and produced. Despite the fact that the flashbacks are interspersed within current events in Daniel's life, the program does hold one's interest as Daniel slowly uncovers the puzzle pieces—although they are never fully connected for the viewer.

Episodes:

1. Beginning of the End (6 min., 44 sec.). During his latest experiment Daniel's subconscious brings to light memories of his late wife and a new piece to add to his puzzle. He also uncovers information that a secret underground exists and may be the key to helping him.

2. Evaluation (4 min., 5 sec.). As Daniel's actions arouse the concern of persons unknown, he is captured and interrogated by a mysterious man (Dr. Malik) seeking to uncover what he knows about the future.

3. That Day in November (4 min., 1 sec.). A flashback to 1999 when Daniel agreed to become a test subject for grad student Edson Cross at Berkeley.

4. Crossing Wires (4 min., 31 sec.). A continuation from the prior episode that shows how Edson's neurological experiment affects Daniel.

5. Wake Up Calls (4 min., 22 sec.). Was what Daniel experienced during the experiments a nightmare, a dream or a vision of the future? Unsure, he begins a quest to find out.

6. Missing the X (5 min., 24 sec.). Daniel's obsession has changed him to the point where he virtually isolated himself, bringing his girlfriend, Alex, into the picture when she becomes concerned.

7. Enter Isabelle (7 min., 28 sec.). After completing the experiment and discovering eight days had elapsed, Daniel checks himself into a hospital—only to be discouraged by a diagnosis of needed rest and prescription drugs (Isabelle is introduced as Daniel's wife at the time; they divorced in 2001).

8. Note to Self (5 min., 15 sec.). Despite doctor's orders to rest, Daniel proceeds with a scheduled art show—only to later find himself in the midst of an emotional breakdown.

9. Man from Atlantis (4 min., 13 sec.). At the suggestion of a friend (Kurt) who has become aware of Daniel's obsession, Daniel visits a bookshop owner who enlightens him about how a conspiracy may play a part in what he is seeking.

10. Déjà Vu (6 min., 25 sec.). Isabelle becomes concerned as Daniel begins devoting all his time to developing the sensory deprivation tank in his loft.

11. Aversion (5 min., 41 sec.). Daniel's actions have aroused the suspicions of the FBI, who bring him in for questioning.

12. Losing It (4 min., 24 sec.). As Daniel's obsession begins to get the better of him, he records a video journal wherein he explains what has happened and how paranoia has been affecting him.

13. Y2K (7 min., 3 sec.). As the clock ticks down to the year 2000 Daniel finds himself confronted by possible hallucinations and Isabelle's growing doubts about their marriage.

14. Out of Ideas (6 min., 49 sec.). Daniel's self conducting experiments are starting to appear as a failure until a mysterious doctor (Ethan Chambers) enters his life. Ethan, suffering from cerebral palsy, is a specialist in the field of neuroscience and can possibly help Daniel. Ends unresolved.

358 *The Undead Diaries.* youtube.com. 2010 (Horror).

On a business trip to New Orleans a young man (Alistaire) is bitten by a vampire. It doesn't seem to phase him at first until he returns home and tells his girlfriend (Danielle). Thinking what happened is cool she asks that Alistaire bite her. Suddenly, the couple become vampires—but has no clue how to deal with what has happened to them. Basing their knowledge on what they've seen in movies and read in books, Danielle and Alistaire must now learn to live a new life. The program relates their "growing pains" as they must now not only give up coffee, and not faint at the sight of blood but find victims, dispose of bodies and accept everything else associated with vampire legends.

Cast: Angelique Mechel (Danielle), Steven Adam Ellison (Alistaire). **Comment:** Episodes (including information relating to them) have been withdrawn from the Internet thus an analysis of the actual horror-comedy mix program is not possible.

359 *Undead Seriously.* undeadseriously. com. 2010 (Horror).

It appeared like any other day until a zombie virus called Munlos "was accidentally" released on the Longwood college campus. While students were turned into zombies something unexpected happened—they found that "death is not all it is cracked up to be" and that it is not much different from life—only they are undead. The program relates events in the lives of the undead that act and live as they previously did before the virus struck.

The people of Longwood University ("affectionately" called Zombie U.): Maria Delaney, a fourth year graduate student studying Immune Pathology who has come to Longwood to help her former mentor, Dr. Bennett, find a cure for the Munlos virus (she has not been infected and wears a HazMat suit in the lab). Jeff Best is a junior and studying industrial engineering; Ian DeCaro is a junior music education major and has his own jazz combo, the Ragdoll Cats. Paul Fortynbras, a sophomore and majoring in biology, works at Lawfen and Rextab, Inc. Kamoa Funkunome, also known as "Ka-mo'a Money, is a ladies' man and philosophy major who can think of nothing else but romanticizing women. Harmony Hastings is an art major and lover of all things in the universe. Alice Springs McKenna, a freshman, is taking a liberal arts course (undecided about her future but considering majoring in either psychology or English). She was born in Chicago and likes "mysterious and dangerous guys." Dr. Todd Bennett is the research scientist seeking the cure for the virus and is responsible for saving the undead as they are now only "technically undead." Bree Michaels is a sophomore and theater major from Key West, Florida. She moved to the town of Longwood to attend its university for its renowned drama department (her biggest qualm is that she lost her tan when she became a zombie). Natalya Romano, a freshman from Washington, D.C., is a Poli-Sci major with a minor in film. She works for the school's literary magazine and hopes to make a documentary film on the effects of the Munlos virus. Jessica Walters is a junior majoring in psychology (although she hates schoolwork and rather party, drink and chill with friends). Cedric Sullivan, a freshman, is majoring in computer science, bio-engineering and gender studies. After graduating he plans to attend graduate school and do research on the Munlos virus.

Cast: Cat Alter (Jessica Walters), Walls Trimble (Harmony Hastings), Farhan Arshad (Dr. Todd Brooks), Caitlin Schneuderhan (Natalya Romano), F. Michael Chua (Cedric Sullivan), Peter J. Hengel III (Paul Fortynbras), Makoa Kawabata (Kaoma Fukunome), Rachel Kenney (Alice Springs McKenna), Ben Gojer (Jeff Best), Bree Michaels (Herself), Andrea Griffo (Maria Delaney), Damian Engelhart (Ian DeCaro). **Credits:** *Producer:* Danielle Calvert, Paul Foryt, Kara Redding. *Director:* Makoa Kawabata. *Writer:* Makoa Kawabata, Peter J. Hengel III, C.J. McFate. **Comment:** A comical horror series that appears to have little horror (the zombie aspect) and more comedy (their attempting to live normal lives as the undead). Based on only the first episode, the acting and production values are good.

Episodes: Twenty-four episodes were produced but only the first episode, which establishes the storyline, remains online.

1. The Pandemic Begins. *2.* Firs-B-Gone. *3.* Whatman? *4.* Triple Dog Dare. *5.* We Just Met a Girl Named Maria. *6.* I Hate You, Maria Delaney. *7.* Mr. Smith Goes to Longwood. *8.* Geek Fest. *9.* Whatman? II. *10.* Stood Up. *11.* Waste of Tape. *12.* Brian, Part 1. *13.* Brian, Part 2. *14.* Mating, Part 1. *15.* Mating, Part 2. *16.* Pheromones. *17.* The Switch. *18.* Whatman? III. *19.* Risky Business. *20.* Mission Accomplished. *21.* Serial Killer. *22.* Shot Down. *23.* Dead Seriously, Part 1. *24.* Dead Seriously, Part 2.

360 *The Underwater Realm.* theunderwaterrealm.cgink.co.uk. 2012 (Fantasy).

Although the oceans cover two-thirds of the world, little is still known about them. Many images are associated with them—from monsters to gods, from calm seas to fierce storms, they are still danger-

ous and unpredictable. The Ancient Greeks feared Poseidon (the God of the Seas) and the Romans, the Titan Oceanus (Neptune) who ruled a great river that circled the world. There also myths of sunken cities (such as Atlantis), islands and mermaids. But what other mysteries are still unknown to modern-day science? The program explores the what if aspect—what if, for example, Poseidon intervened and saved the people of Atlantis and allowed them to live beneath the surface? Mermaids have been seen by sailors on long ocean voyages—but are they real or just hallucinations? (Such a girl is suggested through the character of Aryl, who appears in the episodes that are presented.) Five different time periods (2012, 1942, 1588, 1208 and 149 BC) are explored as to what can and could have happened beneath the surface of the sea.

Cast: *Episode 1, 2012:* Lauren Ashcroft (Rebekah), Dan Richardson (Daniel), Diane Townsend (Old Aryl); *Episode 2, 1942:* Andy Torbet (Walter), Jananne Redman (Young Aryl); *Episode 3, 1588:* Jamie Matthews (Teyo), Frederick Roll (Ignacio), Jessica Blake (Llantus), Gareth Lawrence (Chief Nestor), Beccy MacEnri (Woren); *Episode 4, 1208:* Harriet Moran (Lady Conant), Jon Campling (Lord Conant), Nigel Barber (Acinos), Duran Fulton Brown (Roland), Alex Corbet Burcher (Terath); *Episode 5, 149 B.C.:* Amanda Piery (Iystyn), Gordon Alexander (Quintus), Patt Bauristhene (Cretus). **Credits:** *Producer:* Mike Altmann, Chris Anderson, Erik Beeson, Alison Chapman, George Chiesa, Alan Mandel. *Director:* David M. Reynolds. *Writer:* Rosie Claverton, Jonathan Dupont, David M. Reynolds. **Comment:** Fascinating web series. Even if there is no interest in history or the oceans themselves, the execution is remarkable on what can be produced on a string budget and the technology that was created to accomplish it. The underwater sequences (from the Mediterranean to the North-Cornish Coast) are striking and clear and the actors, well trained in diving (and holding their breath) are excellent. The behind-the-scenes video that is also available on the official website is as compelling as the episodes themselves and shows how sets were created to combine with the actual underwater footage. As the site's press release states "The project is being shot on the Red EPIC camera system, the same cameras that were used by Peter Jackson to shoot *The Hobbit*—despite the complete budget being less than what that project spent on coffee." There are endless possibilities for story telling—and the production qualities are such that they could easily become a network or cable television series.

Episodes:
1. 2012: Present Day Hawaii. Explores the modern day ocean floor—and its dangers as a young couple begins a dive in the Mediterranean and encounter the mysterious caverns and caves that inhabit the ocean bottom.
2. 1942: Shooting the Spitfire. World War II British

Spitfires comes under attack by German Messerch-mitts with a Spitfire being hit and plunging into the sea. A chilling reenactment of the plane, filling with water and the desperate attempts of the pilot to escape.

3. 1588: Building the Galleon. A young man, aboard the Spanish Galleon, is working to keep the cannons loaded when an explosion destroys the ship and hurls him and the crew into the water. Trapped in mid ocean with no hope of rescue, the program explores the watery grave that awaits the crew below.

4. 1208: Underwater Illusions. Eerie tale of a beautiful medieval girl who elects to kill herself by diving off a cliff into the cold waters below rather than face life with a cruel Lord who has claimed her as his wife.

5. 149 BC: Underwater Workflow. At the height of the Roman Empire, another civilization, one that still remains a mystery, is documented—the building of the undersea kingdom of Atlantis.

361 *The Unearthly.* theunearthlyseries.com. 2013 (Horror).

Adapted from the Horror Mythos created by H.P. Lovecraft (a pulp science fiction writer of the 1920s and 30s who developed a theory that human beings are the subjects of powerful beings [extraterrestrial] who understand and obey natural laws which, to limited human understanding, may appear magical). A young man (Chuck Ward), driven mad after inheriting an ancient tome called "The Necronomicon," attempts to understand it (the book tells of ways to reconstruct dead tissue). Although institutionalized, Chuck escapes, and with the book in hand attempts to use its powers to help cultists revive Yog-Sothoth, a god-like extraterrestrial that could mean untold death and destruction if he should succeed. **Cast:** Brian K. Nelson (Randy Carter), Bryce Stanton (Chuck Ward), Christina Longman (Jessica Bell), Corinne Jackson (Jill Carter), Oscar Bramblett (Nick Wolfe), Michael Cirrone (Tyler Bradley), William Howell (Edward Huntington), Mark Mook (Simon Orne), Xander J. Lyons (Victor Anton), Neghan Truckey (Emily Curwen), Josh Nelson (Steve Warren). **Credits:** *Producer:* David Alan Bennett, Mark Fukae. *Writer-Director:* Mark Fukae. **Comment:** With only one episode made available, it clearly shows that the project has potential but it also shows that it is limited in the number of additional episodes that can be produced (that is, how far can the producers stretch the concept before it becomes too repetitive or ridiculous).

Episodes:

1. Missing (19 min., 7 sec.). Establishes the storyline as Randy and his friends begin a search for their friend Chuck, who has mysteriously disappeared while doing research on his family's ancestry.

362 *Universal Dead.* universaldead.com. 2010 (Science Fiction).

Without warning a mysterious disease breaks out that turns affected people into zombie-like, mindless murderers. One doctor, Henry Vataber, appears to hold the key to what is happening and its possible cure. Henry has deduced that an alien parasite is the cause, not a disease. Once infected with the parasite, the victim becomes zombie like with all nutrients (food) being absorbed by the parasite. His once beautiful wife, Angela, has become one such victim and she now cannot be killed (if, for example, she is shot, energy from the parasite will prevent her from dying). Angela now has the physical attributes of a decaying zombie and needs to sustain herself on human flesh. The program charts what happens when Henry attempts to explain his theory to a doctor from the Center from Disease Control (David MacAvoy) and Angela becomes more deadly than just a demonstration. **Cast:** Gary Graham (Dr. David MacAvoy), Doug Jones (Dr. Henry Vataber), Valerie Perez (Angela Vataber), D.B. Sweeney (Capt. John Trent), Michael Broderick (Lt. Melvin Hauk), Craig R. Sawyer (Chief Petty Officer Maxwell). **Credits:** *Producer:* Kirk Harris, Kelly Parks. *Director:* Vernon E. Mortensen. *Writer:* Kelly Parks. **Comment:** Although only three episodes were produced, they are very well done. It is a bit talkative but so well constructed that each episode holds your interest and does so even more when Angela is introduced. Well worth watching even though there is no outcome.

Episodes:

1. The Presentation, Part 1. Dr. MacAvoy is transported to Henry's secret lab by his Navy SEAL bodyguard, Captain Trent.

2. The Presentation, Part 2. Henry begins discussing his theory regarding an alien parasite as being responsible for the outbreak and not a disease.

3. The Presentation, Part 3. Henry presents positive proof that a parasite is responsible when he presents Angela—but all does not go as planned when Angela seeks only to feed the parasite that lives within her (ends in an unresolved cliff hanger).

363 *Unsung Heroes.* dpeacockfilmsonline. wix.com. 2012 (Fantasy).

The Alliance of Really Really Evil is a legion of bad guys (and gals) who have formed their own union to destroy all that is good. While superheroes, like those associated with the Justice League of America (Batman, Wonder Woman, Robin and Superman) have far more important things to do than deal with the evil Alliance, five less-than-efficient heroes have taken up the cause and risk their lives to keep the word safe from the Alliance. The program follows these unknown, fumbling, less-than-spectacular heroes as use what limited abilities they have to

Universal Dead cast and crew production still (photograph by Luz Mcmullen, 2009).

prove to the world that they are the unsung heroes of the world.

Phoenix Black, "a good-looking and ridiculously talented karaoke champ," is the leader of the Unsung Heroes and blends dancing and martial arts to deal with the enemy. Captain Armstrong, a retired member of the Heroes of Tomorrow, is determined to continue his fight (bad back and all) and uses his super strength as his weapon. Heather Royale, "a glamorous drag queen," encompasses the essence of Xenia (the Warrior Princess), Wonder Woman and Beyonce (the singer) and, with her yellow bustier (that exaggerates her breasts), she is blessed with super speed—but is also a bit vain as she loves to admire herself in mirrors. Annie Gloom, rightly named for her "power" of depression, which she uses to depress the enemy. She is considered a gothic beauty and joined the Unsung Heroes out of boredom. Revenant Lad, "a short Indian Fan-boy," uses his power of teleportation to help the team battle evil.

Cast: Devin Peacock (Phoenix Black), Justine S. Harrison (Annie Gloom), Frankie Lapace (Heather Royale), Nick Searles (Captain Armstrong), Jatin Saraf (Revenant Lad). **Credits:** *Producer:* Devin Peacock. *Director:* Sussan Cordero. **Comment:** While less-than-effectual superheroes have been done numerous times before (but mostly in animated form on television) it appears that, based on the teaser, a promising series is in the works.

Episodes: Only a 55-second teaser has thus far been released.

364 *Valemont.* mtv.com. 2009 (Fantasy).

Valemont University is an exclusive Massachusetts college that caters to wealthy students. It has an impressive alumni, an excellent faculty and a dark and dangerous secret: it houses a nest of vampires. The viewer becomes a part of life a Valemont when a murder victim (Eric Greene) is found on campus. The police investigation of the crime uncovers no culprit, but Eric has an estranged sister, Maggie Gracen. When Maggie is informed but learns that there have been no arrests, she steals a cell phone from Eric's personal effects and enrolls as a student at Valemont under the alias Sophie Fields. With the videos and text messages on Eric's phone as clues, Sophie begins a dangerous quest to uncover her brother's killer.

Cast: Kristen Hager (Maggie Gracen), Eric Balfour (Eric Greene), Georgina Reilly (Melissa), Jessica Parker Kennedy (Beatrice), Nikki Blonsky (Poppy), Kyle Mac (Leonardo). **Credits:** *Producer-Director:* Stefan Scaini. *Writer:* Christian Taylor. **Comment:** Well done program with good acting, writing and directing. Only five episodes are viewable as the series has been released on DVD and the remaining 30 episodes taken off line.

Episodes:

1. Family Reunion. Maggie Gracen is informed of her brother's death and recovers his cell phone.

2. Back to School. Maggie assumes the identity of Sophie and enrolls at Valemont University where she acquires a roommate (Poppy) and learns her brother was a member of Panthera House, a mysterious fraternity.

3. The Rules. Sophie defies the rules and breaks into Panthera House seeking information about her brother. When she is caught, she is stripped, placed in a mouse costume and the words "Cat Food" written on her stomach.

4. They Call Him the Archangel. While in the ladies' room removing the words on her stomach, Sophie envisions blood coming from her ribs and the word "Desmodus" written on the mirror. Coming to her senses, she sees Gabriel, who claims to have known her brother.

5. Everything Leads to Desmodus. Sophie seeks to uncover the meaning of Desmodus as it may be the clue she needs to uncover the mystery of her brother's death.

Note: The following episodes have been taken off line: *6.* Sebastian's Rose. *7.* Capital Punishment. *8.* The Laundry Room. *9.* It's in Our Blood. *10.* Take-Out Date. *11.* Breaking and Entering. *12.* Things Are Different at Valemont. *13.* They're Vampires, All of Them. *14.* The Sanitarium. *15.* Are You Sick? *16.* Secrets, Secrets, Secrets. *17.* The Hemoglobins. *18.* Self Defense. *19.* Panthera Promise Pin. *20.* Let Him Go. *21.* Hi, Sis. *22.* Human Nature. *23.* The Story Continues. *24.* What You Really Are. *25.* You Are Desmodus. *26.* Human Relations 101. *27.* The Serpentes Mixer. *28.* The Last Hope. *29.* Butterfly or Beast. *30.* The Vampire Piper. *31.* Takes One to Make One. *32.* The Hunger. *33.* Whose Side Are You On? *34.* Seeing in the Dark. *35.* Just the Beginning.

365 *Vamped Out.* kevinpollak.tv. 2010 (Horror).

Alowisus "Al" Hewson is an actual vampire struggling to make ends meet as an actor in Hollywood. Although he is born to play the part of a vampire, he is continually rejected for actors who look more like vampires. Elliot Finke is a filmmaker who has hit on an idea to produce a documentary about a real vampire. With camera in hand, Elliot begins filming Hewson's daily activities—from his role auditions to his life with his girlfriend (who works at a blood bank) and his meetings with his manager Billy Goldborg. Stories with comical overtones, relate life as faced by a real vampire in a world where he can function as normal people, but whose abilities appear to be his biggest drawback. **Cast:** Kevin Pollak (Elliot Finke), Jason Antoon (Alowisus Hewson), Seana Kofoed (Marie), Samm Levine (Billy Goldborg), Jason McIntyre (Kenneth), Kat Steel (Ginny Lee). **Credits:** *Producer:* Jason An-

toon, Amber J. Lawson, Kevin Pollak. *Director:* Kevin Pollak, *Writer:* Jason Antoon, Kevin Pollak. **Comment:** The writing appears to be quite dull and the story has little humor. The production values and acting are okay but there is nothing of real interest to draw the viewer back for a second look. The traditional vampire legends are all dropped (like not being able to live in daylight or being seen in a mirror—here reflecting his ability to be photographed). The title may draw attention to check it out, but other than that, there is no interest to see what happens next. **Episodes:** The episodes have been taken off line although one episode is available on YouTube.

366 *The Vampire Diaries: A Darker Truth.* ovguide.com. 2009 (Horror).

Companion web program to the CW network series *The Vampire Diaries* that follows the character of Jason Harris as he begins to investigate the death of his sister Joanne in the creepy town of Mystic Falls, Virginia. Jason's video investigation is chronicled as he attempts to acquire evidence to prove that Stefan Salvatore, Joanne's former neighbor in Manhattan, is not only responsible, but a vampire. **Cast:** Matt Peello (Jason Harris), Ian Somerhalder (Damon Salvatore), Paul Wesley (Stefan Salvatore), Molly O'Neill (Mystic Grill Hostess), Kat Slatery (Dead Hiker). **Credits:** *Director:* Christopher Hanada. *Writer:* Sean Reycraft. **Comment:** Well-produced, tense companion to the television series.

Episodes:

1. Episode 1. Jason arrives in Mystic Falls and learns from the Mystic Grill Hostess that the person he is seeking lives at the Salvatore Boarding house.

2. Episode 2. At the boarding house, Jason begins to gather evidence that Stefan is a vampire while at the same time plotting to find his coffin and kill him.

3. Episode 3. Jason encounters Stefan—but the traditional vampire legends about sun light, garlic, holy water and the crucifix does not affect him.

4. Episode 4. With the myths about stopping vampires now not a possibility, Jason theorizes that destroying a vampire's nest (coffin) by fire is the only way to stop Stefan and avenge his sister's death.

367 *Vampire Killers.* youtube.com. 2009 (Horror).

Nicole, Johnny, Katrina, Travis and Orville are college students interested in mythology, especially that which relates to vampires. They live in Los Angeles and find their lives changing forever when their professor solicits them to become vampire hunters when a sect of gorgeous female vampires, led by the beautiful and deadly Vampire Queen, Charlotte Ross, encrust themselves into society. Stories, set at night in the city, follow the students as they seek to destroy Charlotte and her alluring sect members.

Cast: Ania Spiering (Charlotte Ross), Kit Paquin (Nicole), Tim Fields (Johnny), Nick Heany (Orville), Ginger Pullman (Katrina), Marco Mannone (Travis), Katelyn Gault (Amy), Julia Fadiriva (Alekssandra). *The "Vampire Gurlz:"* Sasha Liu, Anna Warn, Theresa Flowers, Amanda Burrill, Katya Lampka. **Credits:** *Producer:* Doug Hutchison, Tim Baldini. *Director:* Tim Baldini. *Writer:* Doug Hutchison. **Comment:** The program begins like a porn flick with alluring girls in their lingerie, a brief girl/girl kissing scene and Charlotte approaching a kidnapped girl she seduces than plans to kill. The girls are very sexy and the pace is rapid but it is also ladled with gutter language, especially in reference to female body parts. The suggestiveness, coupled with the language, has placed *Vampire Killers* in delicate situation as most sharing websites have banned it (it can be viewed, for the most part on YouTube, although all of episode 1 is blocked as are scenes from other episodes). While the girls are attired in black, the typical color associated with vampires, their living quarters are rather unsavory and add even more ambiance to the story (beauty amid squalor). While not recommended for children (and YouTube has taken steps to see to that) it is a well written, directed and acted short web series.

Episodes:

1. Charlotte (2 min., 31 sec.). Charlotte and her sexy vampires have captured a girl (Amy) and Charlotte now plans to feast on her blood.

2. The Feeding (1 min., 57 sec.). The team tries to piece together the clues wherein several girls were reported missing then later found drained of blood.

3. Kat Trap (2 min., 11 sec.). The team sets a trap to bring Charlotte into the open.

4. Your World Is Coming to an End (2 min., 43 sec.). The elusive Charlotte proves to be no match for the team (as she has no heart and can't be killed) when Katrina is attacked and bitten.

5. The Turning. (1 min., 15 sec.). As Katrina lies near death, Johnny stalls in his attempt to kill her before she turns.

6. The Pledge (1 min., 50 sec.). Katrina turns—but is shot by Nicole before she attacks the team. The four remaining hunters vow to destroy Charlotte and her sect.

368 *Vampire Mob.* vampiremob.com. 2013 (Horror).

Don Grigioni is a hitman for the Mafia. He is married to Annie and he appears to have a happy marriage. But Don feels his life is in a rut and believes that becoming a vampire will change all that. Despite the objections of his parish priest, who warns him not to become one of the undead, Don ignores him and through his connections with the mob, allows a female vampire to bite him. Annie is not all that happy—and even more so when Don "becomes hungry" and bites her, turning her into a vampire. The situation goes from bad to worse when Annie convinces her mother, Virginia, to come over to their side and Don finds that after Annie bites her, he must now share his home with his mother-in-law. As Don adjusts to his new life he finds that becoming a vampire was a mistake. He is not more efficient at his job, he can never really be alone with Annie and he must constantly find a source for blood. Don's observations on how tedious life has become since the change are the focal point of the program.

Cast: John Colella (Don Grigioni), Reamy Hall (Annie Grigioni), Marcia Wallace (Virginia Jones), Rae Allen (Carlina Grigioni), Kirsten Vangsness (Laura Anderson), Chris Mulkey (Marty Five), Elizabeth Beckwith (Harry Hickey), Jim Roof (Rob Anderson), Andy Lauer (Smyles), Peter Spruyt (Aldo), Stacy McQueen (Wendy Battella), Chad Wood (Rudy Morelli), Kenny Lombino (Tony Battella), Joe Tabb (Vincenzo Golini), Vincent Guastaferro (Father Eddie), Cris D'Anunnzio (Cadillac Frank). **Credits:** *Producer-Writer-Director:* Joe Wilson. **Comment:** Light humor mixes with light drama in a program tagged as horror with the horror aspect being that the main characters are vampires. The acting and production values are good but there is an abundant use of foul language and none of the blood and gore associated with vampire legends. There are five additional episodes (15 through 19) that, at present, are not available online but included in the DVD release of the program.

Episodes:

1. We Are All Family to a Few People (6 min., 40 sec.). Introduces Don and Annie (both already turned) with Don regretting his choice to become a vampire.

2. You Can't Choose Your Family (6 min., 35 sec.). Annie's sister (Laura) expresses her feelings of remorse that she turned their mother into a vampire.

3. Castle on the Left (4 min., 59 sec.). Don's search for blood leads him to the Castle—which is a castle in the middle of a residential neighborhood.

4. Through the Tunnel (6 min., 17 sec.). In a mysterious underground tunnel Don meets with a Mafia head who offers him a special kind of hit—to blow up a client.

5. Full Nest Syndrome (4 min., 36 sec.). Don's life becomes more complicated when his mother-in-law (Virginia) decides to move in with him.

6. An Uneasy Alignment (5 min., 19 sec.). Annie hopes to convince Don to invest in her new business, Smoke 'n' Tan, a combination smoking parlor and tanning salon.

7. Another to Do (6 min., 29 sec.). Don reveals that jobs are becoming scarce since his change and that his "grocery list" (hit list) is not like it use to be.

8. Hitman's Best Friend (7 min., 33 sec.). Don finds help in obtaining blood from a friend's wife—a nurse in a hospital blood bank.

9. Back to Rectifying the Situation (6 min., 48 sec.). Annie is not too pleased with the taste of the newly acquired blood and demands that Don find a different supply.

10. There's a Ying and There's a Yang (5 min., 28 sec.). Don finally gets an assignment—find a guy with a gunshot wound and finish the job.

11. Full Nest Syndrome Plus One (8 min., 10 sec.). Don's mother (Carlina) and Annie's mother (Virginia) meet to discuss the vampire situation.

12. Dinner for Six (9 min., 15 sec.). Don contends with a dinner wherein members of both families have gathered.

13. Massages and Smiles (7 min., 21 sec.). A meeting with Don and his Mafia bosses is showcased.

14. Same as the Old Boss (7 min., 13 sec.). Don finds his life in danger when the wife of a man he shot orders a hit on him.

369 Vampire Zombie Werewolf. vampire zombiewerewolf.com. 2010–2011 (Horror).

Tad and Bunny appear to be an ordinary (but to some an eccentric) couple. They have no children and live in a moderately furnished home in California. They also have a secret: they are not only vampires but werewolves and zombies (while visiting England, Tad was attacked by a werewolf and infected; he then turned Bunny). Being who they are and who they know (vampires, werewolves and zombies) Tad and Bunny hit on an idea to produce a web series using real monsters, not actors in disguise. To begin the project they contact a web series producer (no name given) who has had experience making horror web series and offer him $50,000 to produce a series. The producer meets with Tad and Bunny and, although not too enthusiastic at first (until Tad and Bunny reveal their true nature), the producer agrees to their terms. The program relates the making of a horror web series using "real" monsters.

Cast: Steven Lekowicz (Tad), Tanya Ihnen (Bunny), Robb Padgett (Producer), Jeremy Sonney (Balthazane), Stephen Simon (Howie), Jeff Carlton (Zombie), Jon Monastero (Werewolf), Jimmy Bopp (Count Von Boppula), Kathy Harmening (Vampinda), Corrie Meyers (Corriolanus), Laura Neufeld (Laurila), Andrea Westby Toaso (Andphelice), Joell Posey (Joellette), Lauren Bopp (Laurenthia), Stephen William Moore (Siddel). **Credits:** *Producer:* Tanya Ihnen, Steven Lekowicz, Robb Padgett. *Writer-Director:* Robb Padgett. **Comment:** Nice mix of comedy and horror with good makeup (depicting the strange transformations of Tad and Bunny). The acting is also good and the program's only real fault is the over-abundant use of foul language in the flashback origin sequence in episode 2 (there was really no need for it).

Episodes:

1. Vampire Zombie Werewolf. Tad and Bunny invite the Producer to their suburban home to discuss a horror web series.

2. An American Zombie in London. A flashback recalls how Tad became what he is.

3. Vampwardly Mobile. The Producer agrees to make the series.

4. Please Feed the Vampires. To celebrate, Tad and Bunny invite some of their vampire friends to a party.

5. Of Webseries and Werewolves. Tad also invites a werewolf but his decision to use real silverware could cause a problem (as silver can kill a werewolf). Clips from the Producer's prior series are seen (*Sand Witches* [*Baywatch* with witches] and *Zombie Coroner*).

6. Wolvers of Endearment. Shows how a microwave oven can transform Tad and Bunny into werewolves.

7. The Great Vampsby. Tad and Bunny's vampire friends are introduced.

8. There Wolves. A full moon causes unexpected problems among the monster guests.

370 Les Vampires. twilightwomen.com. 2011 (Erotic Horror).

Beautiful lesbian vampires are featured in two erotic, bordering on soft-core pornography tales: "Karen's Story" and "Monique's Story." In the first story, a young woman (Karen) is enticed to enter a den of female vampires by Ann and Robin but becomes infatuated with Robin, the gorgeous vampire she meets at the den. The second story begins in a packed bar where a young woman (Monique) is enticed to join several female vampires in a blood orgy. **Comment:** Unfortunately casts and credits are not listed. The programs are very sexy and contain nudity, caressing, kissing and considerable amounts of blood. Both stories play as a seduction with the girls being as sexy as possible without breaking the fine line between soft core and hardcore pornography. Due to the nature of the programs (which appear to have been edited from feature films into a web series) the official website is available to persons 18 years or older ("The content within this site was designed for the connoisseur of erotica") while on its sharing website, Dailymotion.com, the episodes are available to anyone without restriction.

Episodes:

1. Karen's Story. 21 episodes comprise the story but there are no titles except Karen's Story, Part 1; Karen's Story, Part 2, etc.

2. Monique's Story. Comprised of 21 episodes and follows the same titling situation (Monique's Story, Part 1; Monique's Story, Part 2, etc.).

371 Vampirism Bites. vampirismbites.com. 2010–2013 (Horror).

Belle is a beautiful young woman obsessed with

vampire legends. She has immersed herself in all its folklore, watched all related movies and read every book on the subject. One day she discovered that vampires are real and accepted a date with one. Her dream also became real when he bite her and transformed her into a creature of the undead. Unfortunately for Belle, what she had read about vampires is nothing like actually being one. Her first shock came when she apparently lost her BFF ("Best Friend Forevah") Kristy when she turned and must now be on the look out for vampire hunters (although one named Simon Polidori found her crying in a cemetery after she turned and felt she was so pathetic that he refused to kill her). She must also now associate with a group of vampires she believes are "colossal jerks." Belle's transformation also brings to light that she is descended from The Dracula, the original female Countess and that she and The Dracula are also targets of a mythical man-beast known only as The First Hunter who has set his goal to exterminate all vampires. Belle calls The Vampire "Mom" and has been declared "Czarina of the Vampires" by her "Mom." Although she is a vampire, Belle still has feelings for Kristy and seeks to protect her from those who would love to take a bite out of her. Stories follow Belle as she struggles to encompass her new life, while always regretting that she made the wrong decision.

Yekaterina Svyatoi was born in Kiev Rus (before it became Russia) at a time when it was overrun by "The Golden Horde" in the post–Genghis Khan Empire of the Mongols. When she discovered a way to turn the tide of battle, she gave up her mortal life to become The First Vampire. As time passed she declared herself The Dracula. As the new ruler, Yekaterina knew she had to protect her vampires and decreed in misinformation that vampires perished in sunlight, turned into bats and could hide in plain sight if they filed their fangs. To further conceal her secret, she convinced the world to see that The Dracula was a Romanian man in a tuxedo who "wants blood." Although she thought she was brilliant, The Dracula made one mistake. She tried to turn her son, Evgeni into a vampire but it failed as her blood would make him immune to her dominance. She had him executed and declared him "Alucard" (Dracula spelled backwards as an insult).

Kristy Taussig and Belle have known each other since grade school and have vowed to forever remain friends. Their breakup occurred when Belle's initiation into the vampire world required her to kill Kristy's boyfriend (something she has since regretted doing)—with Kristy present. It was when a vampire plan to get Belle and Kristy to kill each other failed that Kristy brought Belle back into her life.

Erica Burgos was born in Toledo, Spain at a time when it was under the rule of Alfonso VIII. Erica, working as an artist at a time when the Moors attacked, organized a group to fight the invading enemy. The Dracula, one of the Defenders, saw her

as a kindred spirit and turned her, making her the Fourth Vampire to exist (she became the administrator of The Dracula's empire). Erica also possesses a thirst for killing and destroys the vampire hunters from the Polidori family for her mistress.

Vincent Franji, also known as "The Crusader," was a warrior during the Crusades. His prowess in battle brought him to the attention of The Dracula who turned him into a vampire (by this time The Dracula had perfected the art of turning humans into vampires to gain dominance over them). When Vincent pledged his loyalty to The Dracula, he became known as The Second Vampire to ever exist.

Cast: Natalie Baxter, Katie Laban (Belle), Lindsey Black (Kristy Taussig), Jacquie Floyd (The Dracula), Jess Dunsmore (Simon Polidori), Ryan Falcheck (Vincent), Adiva Wayne (Erica), Miranda Tully (Syd), Jason Cole (The Litigator), James Fernandez, Richard Raphael (The First Hunter), Michael Meike (Kelvin the Lionhearted), Mary Lynne Gibbs (Jaq the Tripper). **Credits:** *Producer-Writer-Director:* James Fernandez. **Comment:** Slight humor mixes with vampire history as a very pretty girl copes with her new immortality. Although vampire history has been altered for humor, the program is still very enjoyable.

Episodes:

1. Hail to the Teeth (6 min., 32 sec.). Having been bitten, Belle now struggles to accept what she has become—but her fangs haven't formed yet and she is constantly hungry, making her realize she made a mistake.

2. Flaw and Order (4 min., 40 sec.). Simon must answer to the Litigator, the Attorney General of the Hunting Party (the Vampire Hunter's union) for not killing Belle when he had the chance to do so.

3. Warning Plotz (3 min., 48 sec.). Kristy, who remains Belle's roommate, becomes Belle's protector as Belle struggles to become a vampire and avoid the hunters who are seeking her.

4. The Dinner Belle (5 min., 40 sec.). Belle, accompanied by Kristy, begins to feed her hunger by attacking humans—something she still can't adjust to.

5. The First Hunter (4 min., 23 sec.). The Vampire Hunters face competition when an ancient being, the Holy Engine of Destruction, returns to do the job they can't: kill Belle and her clan.

6. Fight Schlub (5 min., 48 sec.). Belle and Kristy are taught the art of protecting themselves from hunters by a vampire couple.

7. Belle of the Brawl (6 min., 20 sec.). Belle and Kristy are pitted against each other in a match by The First Vampire to test their abilities.

8. Parting Plotz (5 min., 31 sec.). The Litigator makes it known that The First Vampire and her clan are about to be abolished by his hunters (or so he thinks).

9. Chagrin and Bare It (5 min., 56 sec.). A confrontation with hunters leaves Belle wounded (taking

a rock to the head) but learns that she has moved up the ladder of vampire status.

10. A Kick in the Math (5 min., 51 sec.). With the backing of the Directors of the Vampire Sciences Division, Simon and the Litigator come up with a mathematics formula to determine when the original male Dracula (The Dark Lord) will rise from his slumber so they can attack him.

11. Here Comes the Doom (5 min., 49 sec.). Belle's efforts to blend into society suddenly fails when her filed fangs re-emerge as sharp; Vincent and his assistant, Erica, await the arrival of The Dark Lord.

12. Yakkity Smack (5 min., 1 sec.). The Hunting Party's master spy, Stakeout, assists the Litigator in their effort to kill The Dark Lord (who has risen and whose powers are slowly returning).

13. Fangs for Everything (6 min., 30 sec.). Belle becomes a full vampire when she is finally able to embrace and communicate with The Dracula. Their fate, however, is still in peril as the Hunting Party closes in.

372 The Vamps Next Door. youtube.com. 2013 (Horror).

They may look like a normal family, but the Tepes are anything but; they are vampires just struggling to live a normal life in modern day suburbia. Beverly is the mother, an emergency room nurse whose job not only provides her with a paycheck, but meals (blood). Walter, her husband, is an IRS auditor who can use his power of hypnotism to make taxpayers "pay up." Kate and Jimmy are their children; Emma is their "batty old grandmother" and the family pet (Shadows) is a vampire cat. Stories follow a *Munsters* (CBS, 1964)–like family just trying to be themselves in a world that doesn't exactly see eye-to-eye with them.

Cast: Rachel Bailit (Beverly Tepes), Robert Smokey Miles (Walter Tepes), Daniela Hummel, Polina Frantsena (Kate Tepes), Matt King (Jimmy Tepes), Annette Pascal (Grandma Emma), Olivia Dunkley (Denise), Rae Latt (Nancy Finster), Dexter Elkin (Hal Finster), Antoinette Abbamonte (Dewey), Holly Beavon (Pamela), Jay Denton (Mike), Lynn Manning (Brian), Gabriel Cordell (Miguel). **Credits:** *Producer:* Laura Feig (Van Scotter), Phil Ramuno. *Writer:* Laura Feig (Van Scotter). *Director:* Phil Ramuno. **Comment:** A nice twist on vampire tales that is played more for laughs than horror. A similar idea was presented on television in the pilot film *Mr. and Mrs. Dracula* and like the pilot, the web series plays well. The program encompasses handicapped performers, something rare in an Internet series. Here Dewey, Walter's co-worker at the IRS, is

The Vamps Next Door. Left to right: Jay Denton, Daniela Hummel, Robert Smokey Miles, Annette Pascal, Rachel Bailit and Matt King (copyright Laura Feig [VanScotter]).

deaf and unable to be hypnotized by Walter's voice; Brian is blind (turned into a vampire by Emma) and serves as the family butler; and Miguel is the family's wheelchair-bound neighbor.

Episodes:

1. Meet the Tepes Family. Begins with the family purchasing a new home and the problems a vampire family are about to face.

2. IRS Party. A typical day in the life of the family: Beverly meets her new neighbor, Nancy; Walter finds working in an office a bore; Kate discovers she must be careful whom she bites as it has consequences; and Jimmy faces his first day at a new school.

3. MMM What's for Dinner. Beverly finds a meal to her liking when a patient fails to survive an operation.

4. Shadows Runs Away. When their vampire cat objects to the way he is being treated he decides to run away.

5. All Tied Up. Kate finds that she is unable to tell her human boyfriend (Mike) that she is a vampire and wants him only for his blood.

6. Eating Dogs for Dinner. The next door neighbor's dog has disappeared and Hal, the neighbor, comes looking for him at the Tepes home. Meanwhile Grandma Emma has developed a crush on President Obama.

7. Season Finale. With unusual happenings occurring at the hospital, school and at their home, suspicion could point to the Tepes family and expose their true being.

8. My Nurse Is a Vampire. Opens a new season with Kate becoming a blood-drawing nurse at the hospital; Beverly lamenting that a lack of fresh corpses has left her hungry; and Jack seeking to conceal his decapitated squirrel heads from his home school teacher.

9. Harvey Gets Hypnotized. In an attempt to communicate with his deaf co-worker (Brian), Walter believes hypnotism may do the trick; Kate tries to convince her boyfriend to become a blood donor.

10. Grandma Got Fang. Beverly hosts a Neighborhood Watch meeting; Kate siphons too much blood from her boyfriend; Jimmy manages to frighten his teacher.

11. Neighborhood Watch. Beverly so impresses the neighbors that she is made Watch Captain; Kate faces problems when her boyfriend begins acting strangely and she could be exposed as a vampire.

373 *Venus Rises*. venusrises.com. 2009 (Science Fiction).

In an unspecified futuristic time the Earth is ravished by a series of cataclysmic events that destroys all world governments. Advanced technology has allowed survivors to escape to the colonized planets of Mars and Venus with Venus becoming home to the working class while Mars becomes the seat of power. Civil unrest soon becomes a problem with the colonists of Venus seeking treatment equal to Mars. Stories follow the developments that occur as witnessed by Sam Reegan and Nathan Griggs, member of the Mars Defense Directorate.

Cast: Damien Amores (Sam Reegan), Joseph Negra (Nathan Griggs), Anne Roig (Dr. Kylara Marinn), Julia How (Aeriana Onaar), Rob Ferreri (Demille Onaar). **Credits:** *Producer-Writer-Director:* J.G. Birdsall. **Comment:** Short, right-to-the-point progression of stories that tell, without padding, a well acted, written and directed tale of a possible civil war between two newly colonized planets.

Episodes:

1. Crossroads. Private Sam Reegan and Sergeant Nathan Griggs, stationed aboard the Earth Orbital Fueling Station, are introduced as civil unrest is fueled by Alex Foster, a radical eco-terrorist.

2. Freefall. Sam and Dr. Kylara Marinn become involved with the Venusians resistance when they are rescued from their fuel-depleted ship by a mining hauler (*Ikarus*) with ties to Venus.

3. Resist. The cliff-hanging conclusion wherein a solar flare could ignite a war between Mars and Venus.

374 *Vexika*. vexika.com. 2010 (Science Fiction).

When the Earth was still being formed some 3.14 billion years ago, a meteorite crashed into the planet and fused with a naturally occurring mineral called Chrysocolla in the hills of what is now Arizona. In the mid 1800s, the mysterious metal was found by the gold-seeking Forty-Niners and remained unknown until only recently when scientists discovered it and found that it can facilitate the biological introduction of nanoid technology when prepared with a specific process and given in exact doses.

Victoria Bloom is a young woman who works as a television reporter for Channel 4 in Arizona. She is ambitious and had always dreamed of doing what she is now doing. She is also Vexika, the only successful test subject of experiments with the newly created nanoid technology (which has endowed her with super abilities). Victoria was coerced by a rogue scientist of what is called the D.A.R.P.A. Project to become a test subject. Believing she would acquire the story of the century, she never dreamed that she would never be able to tell it. Victoria's DNA was altered when the nanoids were introduced into her body and she must now feed off the exotic material that was created to produce the nanoids to survive. It appears that the only source is the failed and now deranged rejects whom she must track and kill (thus absorbing their life-giving force). The program follows events in life of Victoria, television reporter, and Victoria as Vexika, as she seeks the rejects (especially FR#0) to not only sustain life, but prevent

Vexika. Miranda Stewart as Vexika and Dan Stewart as the Ninja (copyright Sun Run Media, LLC).

them from causing harm to others. (FR#0, Failed Reject 0, is her ultimate goal. As once she defeats him, she will absorb enough nanoids to last her forever—not the days or weeks she acquires from other rejects. Only her boyfriend [her cameraman], the government, who sometimes incorporate her abilities on covert operations, and the failed rejects know of Vexika's existence. FR#0 also creates clones of himself as an army to kill Vexika before she kills him.)

Cast: Miranda Stewart (Victoria Bloom/Vexika), Dan Stewart (FR#0/Clones). **Credits:** *Producer-Writer-Director:* Dan Stewart. **Comment:** One of the few Internet series to feature an African-American super hero in the character of Vexika. Miranda Stewart is gorgeous—both as Victoria and Vexika and, even though she plays to the camera (making you know she knows she is being filmed) she pulls it off and makes the program enjoyable as a comic book come-to-life. Dan Stewart, her husband, handles all the other roles and with makeup and trick photography, also makes you believe he is more than just FR#0 and his clones.

Episodes:

1. Vexika Part 1, Pilot: Get Her (4 min., 44 sec.). FR#0, the fugitive test subject, begins plotting to kill Vexika by creating deadly (but imbecilic) Ninja clones of himself.

2. Vexika Part 2, Get Her: Dark Angel Meets Everybody Loves Raymond (4 min., 15 sec.). The Ninja clones uncover a piece of the meteorite that created Vexika and FR#0 plans to use it to destroy her once and for all.

3. Vexika Part 3, Get Her: Mortal Kombat Meets Princess Bride (5 min., 47 sec.). The concluding, cliff-hanging story finds the cloned Ninjas closing in on Vexika and determined to end her life by throwing her into the Grand Canyon.

4. Vexika Special: Valentine Day Message (2 min., 17 sec.). Vexika takes time away from her battle with the Ninja clones to wish her fans a happy Valentine's Day.

5. Vexika Holiday Christmas Special (1 min., 16 sec.). Vexika wishes her fans a Merry Christmas and a Happy New Year while the Ninja clones try to stop her.

6. Vexika Prologue (1 min., 16 sec.). A fast-paced introduction to the series.

375 *Vicky Vixen.* fantasywebseries.net. 2010 (Fantasy).

Vicky Vixen is a sexy teenage girl who battles evil. She is also only a comic book character that is idolized by Victoria Fox, a pretty, but nerdy 17-year-old high school girl. Victoria has a high I.Q., is imaginative and she attributes her overactive imagination to her love of reading. But for Victoria, Vicky Vixen is no figment of her imagination. Whenever teenage problems arise at school or in her neighborhood, Victoria summons her comic book alter ego to settle the score—"by kicking ass." But, does Victoria actually become Vicky or is Vicky an actual person conjured up by her imagination? That fine line between fantasy and reality is explored as Victoria tries to put things in perspective.

Victoria lives with her parents (Mary Beth and Mike) and her brother (Albert) and has become a concern to them (her strange behavior around the house has forced them to send her to a therapist). As Victoria struggles to navigate the worlds of reality and fantasy, stories were to follow her experiences on both levels.

Cast: Teresa Decher (Victoria Fox/Vicky Vixen), Mercedes Rose (Mary Beth Fox), Daniel Nelson (Miles Fox), Harold Phillips (Albert Fox), Sally Spaderna (Vicky Vixen Double), Karen Trumbo (Therapist), Christian James (Todd). **Credits:** *Producer:* Randolph Sellars, Sally Spaderna, Sam Garr. *Writer-Director:* Randolph Sellars. **Comment:** When Victoria becomes Vicky, a very sexy teenage heroine is seen; before Victoria feels the need to call on Vicky, strange things happen (like her dolls coming to life or visions of eerie beings). A good premise, good special effects, good acting and production values, but apparently only a pilot has been produced (there are hints of a second episode but it has not aired). It has all the qualities for a television series debut.

Episodes:
1. Vicky Vixen: The Pilot (9 min., 50 sec.). Introduces viewers to Victoria and her alter ego, Vicky Vixen.

376 *Villains.* youtube.com. 2010 (Science Fiction).

Big Guy, as he is called, is a John Doe without any memory of who he is or what he was. He is currently residing in a halfway house for people with addictions ranging from gambling to drugs to alcohol. Although Big Guy appears to be withdrawn, delusional and paranoid he is also not normal. He soon discovers that he has skills he cannot explain (fighting and weaponry abilities) and a mysterious supernatural power to see and control events. The program follows Big Guy (also called BG) as he befriends three house residents (Ana, Jimmy and Phil) to help him find out who he is and how he acquired his abilities.

Cast: Shavar D. Clark (Big Guy), Frank Sjodin (Phil), Lacie Shayne (Ana), Richard Reed (Jimmy), Phil Whitehouse (Smoke), Lartell Mann (Frank). **Credits:** *Producer-Writer-Director:* Lawrence Lee Wallace. **Comment:** Interesting take on a subject that has been done before (amnesia) but the idea can only be stretched so far before the victim must be made aware of who he is. Once established the idea

could be pursued to have BG appear as a superhero-like crusader. Unfortunately, the production is very amateurish with the annoying shaky camera just adding to its misery.

Episodes:
1. Pilot (20 min., 38 sec.). Introduces the concept as BG is brought to the halfway house and befriends Ana, Phil and Jimmy.
2. Lighter (13 min., 18 sec.). Explores BG's life at the house and his struggles to determine if his dreams are nightmares or memories. A look at Ana's past is also presented.
3. Let the MF Burn (14 min., 39 sec.). BG's abilities continue to evolve causing concern that he may become a threat if he does not remember how to control them.
4. Learning Is Fun (18 min., 50 sec.). The concluding, unresolved episode wherein several more clues are presented as BG appears to becoming closer to uncovering the secret of his past.

377 *Vincent Kosmos.* youtube.com. 2009 (Science Fiction).

A spin off from the Australian television series *Damon Dark* (see title; from the episode "The Time Thief"). Vincent Kosmos, born on Meta Andromeda, travels through time and space via his Red Door time machine. He is a futuristic thief who uses an inter-dimensional gateway to travel through time to relieve people of their rare and valuable treasures, but also help people who are threatened by aliens. Also known as *Vincent Kosmos—The Time Thief.* The character of Damon Dark appears in various episodes throughout the web series run.

Cast: Chris Heaven (Vincent Cosmos), Stefania Moretti (Prof. Julia Jones), Robert Trott (Gary Sutton), Silvio Marchetti (Caleb), Adrian Sherlock (Damon Dark), Trea Cotton (Dr. Lansing), Patrick Murphy (Young Vincent Kosmos). **Credits:** *Producer:* Chris Heaven. **Comment:** Poor man's version of *Doctor Who* that blends science fiction with comedy in a rather cheap and not-so-likable version of the British television series. Produced in Italy and in English, but at times hard to understand (there are only captions available in Italian). Vincent's Red Door time machine is a direct rip off of Doctor Who's blue police phone booth–like time machine, the TARDIS; even the theme music is reminiscent of *Doctor Who.* Vincent Kosmos is rather unsavory-looking and it takes a few episodes to adjust to his quirky ways. The production values are just passable and the special effects done as cheaply as possible. For the most part stories are good, but Vincent's constant whining about having to do this or that is more annoying than the comedy it was meant to be. The aliens encountered by Vincent are also created on the cheap side and more comical than the frightening menace they were meant to be. There are a lot of episodes with opening visuals and the theme music changing but not the overall production values (although the last few episodes are more professional-looking than the others). For *Doctor Who* fans, there is a lot to compare and criticize; for sci fi fans, it is something different (especially if you have never seen *Doctor Who*). Having watched all the episodes back-to-back, it can be said that *Vincent Kosmos* grows on you.

Episodes:

1. The Ghost Painting (5 min., 42 sec.). Vincent plots to steal a valuable painting from the Syrius Delta Art Museum.

2. The Prey (4 min., 45 sec.). Vincent becomes the target of a family seeking revenge for what he has taken from them.

3. Clock Killers (8 min., 54 sec.). Damon Dark attempts to stop Vincent from stealing a Leonardo DaVinci sketch from friends of his.

4. Another Time, Another Space (8 min., 45 sec.). Vincent discovers a ship that appears to have been built in a future time.

5. Space Plague, Part 1 (7 min., 49 sec.). Vincent's attempts to steal an artifact brings him in contact with a deadly space plague.

6. Space Plague, Part 2 (6 min., 5 sec.). Vincent becomes affected by the plague (a cyber virus) and seeks its cure before his days of thievery are abruptly ended.

7. The Void (8 min., 35 sec.). Vincent overcomes the plague—but it has a strange side-effect—he can longer steal.

8. The Black Slime (10 min., 25 sec.). While still unable to steal, Vincent battles a deadly black slime creature that is threatening to expand across the galaxy.

9. The Web (9 min., 56 sec.). Damon contacts Vincent, warning him that a trap has been set in Sector Delta Gamma 389 by his enemy, the Collective, to kill him.

10. A Little Help from My Friend, Part 1 (6 min., 33 sec.). Vincent seeks the help of a friend to escape a Hyper Beholders trap.

11. A Little Help from My Friend, Part 2 (7 min., 4 sec.). Concludes the story wherein Vincent's timeline is restored and he reacquires his ability to steal.

12. Rest Rest Perturbed Spirit (6 min., 48 sec.). Encompasses aspects of the *Damon Dark* episodes "Space Prison," Parallel Man" and "Vincent from Mirror Universe" to explore Vincent's experiences in the Tempus Project wherein an evil clone of him was created.

13. Lazarus (5 min., 35 sec.). Finds Damon Dark and Dr. Lansing attempting to save Vincent from evil entities that have possessed him.

14. Older, Part 1 (9 min., 2 sec.). A time warp brings Vincent into the past—where he now co-exists with a younger version of himself.

15. Older, Part 2 (7 min., 38 sec.). Vincent seeks a way to reverse the time warp as an older and younger version of himself cannot co-exist in the same time frame.

16. The Last of Metians (7 min., 38 sec.). Vincent springs into action when he receives a message from his younger self that their home planet is in danger of attack.

17. Going Back to an Old Job (3 min., 52 sec.). A flashback episode of sorts (a bit confusing) wherein Vincent recalls his days before thievery as what appears to be a monastery or church caretaker.

18. The Pixie (8 min., 33 sec.). Vincent returns to the scene of his first theft (from episode 1) to see what treasures still remain.

19. A Deal with the Devil (7 min., 36 sec.). Vincent encounters The Magician, the arch enemy of Damon Dark.

20. Femborg (9 min., 42 sec.). Borrowing an element from the television series *The Bionic Woman* (and its Fembot characters) Vincent encounters an evil Femborg robot.

21. The Other Time Thief (8 min., 48 sec.). Vincent encounters an old friend, a time thief who now appears to be totally insane.

22. Medea, Part 1 (8 min.). Vincent's encounter with an old girlfriend is anything but joyous when she traps him inside a video game.

23. Medea, Part 2 (8 min., 27 sec.). Vincent's efforts to escape from the video game are depicted.

24. Dorian Gray (9 min., 22 sec.). A young woman with knowledge of the future approaches Vincent to tell him that he needs to stop an old (but dangerous) woman with the power to destroy the Earth.

25. Will You Reap What You Sow (5 min., 25 sec.). Vincent attempts to find who was responsible for the destruction in the Meta Andromeda.

26. Brother and Sister (9 min., 6 sec.). The Magician returns, this time intent on killing Vincent.

27. Escape (7 min., 19 sec.). A doctor contacts Vincent for help in escaping from the evil Tempus Security facility.

28. The Toy Master (9 min., 7 sec.). Vincent battles a strange enemy with the ability to create and bring toys to life.

29. Harbingers of Death, Part 1 (8 min., 22 sec.). Vincent begins an investigation of strange alien activity in the solar system.

30. Harbingers of Death, Part 2 (6 min., 47 sec.). Vincent's mission is complicated when his computer malfunctions and contradicts everything he plans to do.

31. Harbingers of Death, Part 3 (5 min., 43 sec.). Vincent discovers that an alien has penetrated the Red Door and must destroy it before it destroys him.

32. Ghost (10 min., 38 sec.). A ghost appears to Vincent to ask his help in finding the man who killed her—The Magician.

33. The Avenger (9 min., 21 sec.). Vincent encounters a strange man—wearing a gas mask and capable of traveling trough time.

34. Women Are Trouble (6 min., 50 sec.). Female guest stars from past episodes are featured as Vincent succumbs to a virus and recalls his encounters with them.

35. The Cannibal (4 min., 41 sec.). Vincent returns to planet Earth to protect it from an evil being bent on destruction—by eating bodies.

36. Mind Over Body (7 min., 59 sec.). A continuation of the prior episode wherein Vincent lends Department 6 a hand in disposing of the Cannibal alien.

37. Home Sweet Home (6 min., 45 sec.). Vincent begins to suffer hallucinations when he wakes up—married and living a normal life.

38. Catch the Fox (7 min., 38 sec.). Vincent faces still another enemy who would like nothing more than to end his life of thievery.

39. The Order (6 min., 17 sec.). Vincent, who sometimes works for Department 6, receives an order to steal a disk from the department's main computer.

40. No More Jokes (5 min., 17 sec.). Vincent appears to be having hallucinations—or is he when he envisions his planet being destroyed.

41. Gethsemane (2 min., 10 sec.). Continuing from the prior episode, Vincent's visions were real and his home planet has been destroyed by aliens.

42. Ace in the Hole (8 min., 42 sec.). Why Vincent was ordered to steal the disk (from episode 39) is revealed—to trade it (the information it contains) for the life of his younger self.

43. Seeds of Madness (5 min., 45 sec.). Vincent's experiences appear to have driven him mad and he now wants to end his life.

44. The Eyes of the Enemy (8 min., 26 sec.). Continues from the prior episode wherein Vincent tries to come to terms with what he actually is—an immortal—and cannot end his life.

45. Different Tastes, Different Races (8 min., 20 sec.). Vincent comes to the aid of an old friend as she tries to battle a strange enemy.

46. Caleb (10 min., 10 sec.). Vincent is at a loss when his computer (PIR) malfunctions at the same time an alien (Caleb) bent on killing, seeks out Vincent.

47. A Hard Day's Night (6 min., 53 sec.). Vincent sets his sights on stealing a rare first-edition book.

48. Legacy of Evil, Part 1 (9 min., 32 sec.). Vincent comes to the aid of a girl in trouble—unaware that she is the daughter of his adversary, the Toy Master.

49. Legacy of Evil, Part 2 (9 min., 34 sec.). Vincent attempts to escape a deadly trap set by the Toy Master's daughter.

50. Tie Me Up Before I Go-Go (7 min., 40 sec.). Vincent is captured by a female bounty hunter (Mira) who was paid to not only abduct him—but kill him.

51. The Beginning of the End, Part 1 (10 min., 9 sec.). Vincent becomes trapped on a space probe (Phobos 23).

52. The Beginning of the End, Part 2 (8 min., 38 sec.). Vincent seeks as way to escape from the space probe before it is pulled into a black hole.

53. Heart of a Thief (11 min., 55 sec.). Department 6 enlists Vincent's help to steal a microchip that contains information on aliens.

54. Mind Reader (8 min., 20 sec.). The theft of the microchip causes Vincent to be captured by an alien and probed to discover what he knows.

55. The Bomb (7 min., 38 sec.). Vincent finds himself trapped by an enemy who has rigged a bomb to kill him.

56. The Jail (10 min., 46 sec.). Explores the strange relationship between Vincent and one of his enemies, Caleb.

57. The Tear of Wishla (11 min., 6 sec.). A special episode wherein Vincent celebrates the Christmas season.

58. Time Loop (8 min., 16 sec.). Vincent becomes trapped in a reliving of events when he is engulfed by a time loop.

59. MechaDroids (18 min., 37 sec.). Vincent comes to the aid of aliens facing a threat from the evil MechaDroids robots.

60. Skin Trade (24 min., 19 sec.). A friend of Vincent's from Department 6 contacts Vincent, asking him to help find the daughter of an employee who has been kidnapped by aliens.

61. Misfortune Quiz Show (10 min., 42 sec.). An unusual episode wherein Vincent plays for his life against an alien on an intergalactic television game show.

62. Vincent and the Beast (9 min., 37 sec.). The Magician's evil daughter blackmails Vincent into stealing an artifact for her; in return, she will return to normal a friend of his (whom she has transformed into a pig-like creature).

63. Till the Last Breath (17 min., 32 sec.). An expanded episode (length wise) for Vincent as he faces enemies (Caleb, The Toy Master's Daughter, Boris Craven, The Last Metian and Socrds) who have joined forces to kill him.

64. Poker Face (14 min., 34 sec.). Vincent faces the wrath of The Magician's daughter when she learns that he still hasn't granted her request (from episode 62).

65. Who Am I? (11 min., 36 sec.). After having self doubts about his existence, a genius contacts Vincent to prove that he exists.

66. Another Thief, Another Friend (14 min., 24 sec.). Vincent finds competition from a female time traveler and thief (Alex) when he attempts to steal a valuable object.

67. The Comeback (8 min., 57 sec.). Mira, the bounty hunter who kidnapped Vincent (from episode 50) returns to finish the job she started.

68. Where is Gary Sutton? (19 min., 8 sec.). Vincent lends a hand to find Gary Sutton, an agent from Department 6, who has mysteriously vanished.

69. The End (16 min., 5 sec.). When his time

machine comes under attack by androids, Vincent discovers that it contains a secret hiding place—that is larger inside than its outward appearance.

70. After the End (7 min., 42 sec.). Continues from the prior episode with Vincent escaping from the androids seeking to kill him.

71. Rakshadar (11 min., 21 sec.). Vincent, exiled on Earth, seeks Damon's help in retrieving his missing Red Door traveling machine.

72. Exiled (6 min., 37 sec.). Until he can retrieve his time machine, Vincent attempts to make the most of his time on Earth (living with his friend Julia Jones).

73. Laugh in the Darkness (7 min., 36 sec.). Still stuck on Earth, Vincent takes a job (that he dislikes) with the Military Advanced Task Force Elite.

74. Menace from Abandoned Base (9 min., 39 sec.). Vincent begins a mission to explore an abandoned base where, unknown to him, an evil alien is hiding.

75. Chronosphere (10 min., 28 sec.). Vincent, stranded on earth, seeks a way to repair his Red Door to answer a call for help from a friend on a distant planet.

76. Lost in Time (7 min., 39 sec.). Vincent finds mishaps through time—from the prehistoric era (with a really pathetic looking dinosaur) to the age of Napoleon when his Red Door malfunctions again.

77. Alterations, Part 1 (8 min., 14 sec.). Vincent faces his old adversary, Caleb, in a showdown that has adverse effects.

78. Alterations, Part 2 (8 min., 43 sec.). Vincent attempts to reverse a timeline that was altered by Caleb.

79. Small Heads, Big Deals. (9 min., 13 sec.). Vincent, recovering his time traveling machine, encounters numerous problems as he attempts to repair it.

80. A Night in the House of Dolls (10 min., 56 sec.). A seemingly innocent home proves to be a trap for Vincent when dolls come to life.

81. Carbon Copy, Part 1 (10 min., 31 sec.). The Black Slime enacts a devious plan to clone Vincent.

82. Carbon Copy, Part 2 (14 min., 11 sec.). Vincent attempts to escape the Black Slime and stop his evil clone from doing their bidding.

83. The Trial (15 min., 46 sec.). Finds Vincent falling into a trap, being captured, jailed and put on trial to answer for all the atrocities he has caused.

84. Pyramid of Fear (11 min., 13 sec.). Vincent attempts to escape from an ancient Egyptian tomb when he becomes trapped.

85. Three's Company (16 min., 46 sec.). Old enemies unite to once and for all dispose of Vincent.

378 *Vitamin Z.* vitaminzseries.com. 2013 (Horror).

In an attempt to produce perfect soldiers, Chinese government scientists created a "super soldier serum" that was intended to modify their genetic makeup.

However, the compound was compromised before the final testing stage and the developed product caused de-mortification on those who ingested it. Government officials considered this an opportunity and distributed it as a liquid supplement called Vitamin Z. An aggressive advertising campaign, endorsements by sports figures and countless bottles of free samples made Vitamin Z "the thing" to have. Within a week more than half the world had sampled Vitamin Z and were, at first amazed by their increased abilities—until the full effect of Vitamin Z emerges, changing its users into zombies. Those who learned quickly that Vitamin Z was causing a virus were the only survivors; but they too are in danger, as those affected by Vitamin Z now possess a zombie virus and their bite can turn an unaffected person into a creature of the undead. Vitamin Z quickly turned into an apocalypse; food has become scarce and a fight for survival is a daily occurrence. However, the long-term effects for survivors is also turning deadly—turning on each other and resorting to animalistic and barbaric behavior. Stories follow a group of survivors caught in the middle— trying not only to evade zombies but those humans who have turned as well.

Cast: E'va Stepniewska (Becka), Douglas Farra (Don), Zach Silver (Jake), Nailya Shakirova (Jenna), Joe Palubinsky (Tom), Corey Taylor (Sarah), Adriane McLean (Emily). **Credits:** *Producer:* Douglas Farra, Silva Artinjian-Farra. *Director:* Douglas Farra. *Writer:* Douglas Farra, Eric Jacobs. **Comment:** No shortage of zombies here (and frightening too). Good story coupled with fine acting, writing and directing that makes this one of the better zombie series to hit the Internet.

Episodes:

1. Take Out (10 min., 47 sec.). As the plague rages on, survivors find that the food source is becoming depleted.

2. Enhancements (11 min., 6 sec). The survivors, that include Don, Sarah, Jake, Jenna and Becka seek a place of safety after their former safe house is compromised by zombies.

3. Raw Meat (10 min., 11 sec.). Jake, still unable to comprehend what has happened, convinces Jenna to share his supply of Vitamin Z.

4. Conflict (9 min., 38 sec.). After securing a new location and finding food, Jake and Jenna continue using Vitamin Z.

5. Withdrawals (13 min., 9 sec.). Becka lashes out against Don, feeling that his decisions are wrong and could cost them their lives. Jake, influenced by Vitamin Z, leaves the safety of the compound.

6. The Savior (14 min., 33 sec.). As Sarah faces a zombie attack, Jake's condition worsens.

7. Escape the Horde (10 min., 14 sec.). Sarah is rescued; Jake's addiction reaches its final stages; the survivors must battle a horde of zombies to escape.

379 Voyage Trekkers. voyagetrekkers.com. 2011–2012 (Science Fiction).

Star Trek spoof about a self-centered space ship captain (Jack Sunstrike), his unfazed first officer (Blake Powell) and the exasperated ship's doctor (Elaine Rena) as they wreck havoc during assignments seeking to further their positions within the Galactic Union.

Jack T. Sunstrike is a captain and commander of Triumph class G.S.V. *Remarkable* star ship. He is the grandson of Admiral Reginald P. Sunstrike, son of Reginald Sunstrike, Jr. (voted "Mr. Handsome Galaxy" three times in a row) and the brother of Captain Reginald Sunstrike III. Although he comes from a stellar family Jack is anything but stellar. He is most famous for being the only survivor of the G.S.V. ship *The Montgomery* when it was attacked by the Vendrexxi in the Orgo Nullix Nebula (Jack was apparently too drunk to realize what was happening and "was merely sleeping it off in an escape pod"). He now commands one of the last of the Triumph-Class G.S.V. space ships. Jack also has a number of disciplinary actions against him: violated Rule Prime Zero by exposing technology to the people of Promidia IV (thus giving them the ability of hyper speed). He is also accused of terrorizing people with a "magic ray gun," forcing a young girl to admit her religion was a fake and launching an orbital strike into the upper atmosphere after proclaiming he was their god. He is also accused of meddling in a hostage situation and disobeying direct orders. Because of his heritage, he is never brought to trial.

Blake Powell is a lieutenant commander under Captain Sunstrike. He never questions orders and does what is commanded of him. During one voyage the *Remarkable* entered a Class IV Cosmic Wormhole that reversed the gender of all crew members aboard the ship. A method to reverse the condition was later found but it did not work on Powell; a sex change operation was formed to return him to the way he was. Jack claims there is nothing significant to report about Powell other than "he has good hygiene and above-average punctuality."

Elaine A. Rena is a lieutenant and the chief medical officer aboard the *Remarkable*. Elaine "is a troubled soul whose only pleasure seems to be contradicting her handsome captain's authority." Jack thinks she acts like a rebellious teenager who voices her opinion but doesn't stand for anything. Elaine graduated top in her class at Space Academy and first served aboard the Galactic Union's flagship G.S.V. *Republic*. On Space Date 2233.190 an "unfortunate teleporter accident" (not stated what) ended her career on the *Republic* and she was reassigned to the less prestigious *Remarkable*. Elaine, like Jack, has been disciplined. On Space Date 2334.027 Elaine disobeyed orders and cured a plague affecting the alien Draudis population. Instead of gratitude, the Draudis seized the *Remarkable* and stranded the crew on the stink planet Bognil XIII. The ship was later found after being abandoned by its hijackers. If that wasn't enough, Elaine was next reprimanded for conduct unbecoming of an officer. Jack has a favorite chair on the "Captain's Transit Pod." When Elaine took the seat and refused to relinquish it Jack filed

Voyage Trekkers. **The cast in costume (copyright Squishy Studios).**

charges that he claimed "steers dangerously close to mutiny." It occurred in Space Date 2234.059.

Cast: Adam Rini (Capt. Jack Sunstrike), Gabrielle Van Buren (Dr. Elaine Rena), Logan Blackwell (Lt. Cmdr. Blake Powell). **Credits:** *Producer:* Nathan Blackwell, Craig Michael Curtis. *Writer-Director:* Nathan Blackwell. **Comment:** Despite the short episodes the program does present laughs along with science fiction. The acting, special effects and production values are also good.

Episodes:

1. Rescue from the Lizard Man (2 min., 59 sec.). With Jack captured by the deadly Draudis lizard men, he realizes that his only hope of survival is from his less-than-enthusiastic crew.

2. Social Network (3 min., 4 sec.). With Elaine's nasty attitude and Blake's non-caring attitude, Jack finds himself faced with a dilemma when he is assigned to an important diplomatic mission and worries how his crew will help or hinder the assignment.

3. Birthday Surprise (2 min., 46 sc.). Jack finds it's no time for a celebration when he and Blake infiltrate an enemy compound.

4. Language Barrier (5 min., 38 sec.). When the *Remarkable* is assigned an alien officer (Lt. Jayda) communicating becomes a problem when Jack realizes a translator is needed for each to understand the other.

5. Oh Great Space Crystal (4 min., 25 sec.). The discovery of a new life form in the shape of a crystal finds Jack, Elaine and Blake seeking a way to make contact.

6. Formal Charges (4 min., 55 sec.). When Elaine disobeys (yet again) another direct order from Jack she finds herself (yet again) in trouble.

7. The Clutches of General Kang (4 min., 29 sec.). Although there is no real team work among Jack, Elaine and Blake, they find they have to put their heads together to escape the clutches of the evil General Kang.

8. Phoning It In (3 min., 9 sec.). Believing he is seeing a new side of Elaine and Blake, Jack assigns them each a specific duty while he entertains an important diplomatic ambassador.

9. Fabulous Technology (2 min., 17 sec.). The meeting doesn't go exactly as Jack wished when he uncovers evidence of a planned assassination against the diplomat.

10. Many Paths to Eden (13 min., 32 sec.). The first season finale, which is interactive, presents a story (Jack and his crew being assigned their most important mission to date) and leaving its outcome up to the viewer (called here "Choose Your Own Path." Available only on YouTube wherein, once the annotations are turned on, a list of outcomes is presented and viewers can scroll down and click the one he or she wants to see).

11. Welcome Aboard (7 min., 49 sec.). The crew attempts to make their ship less the disaster it looks to impress the visiting General Grissom on the second season premiere.

12. Laser Swords at Dawn (5 min., 57 sec.). Jack and his old adversary, General Kang in a laser sword-to-the-death bout.

13. Set Witchcraft to Stun (6 min., 37 sec.). The crew is assigned to an undercover mission that Jack hopes will not become more than the simple assignment it appears to be.

14. Junior Ambassadors of the Galactic Union (2 min., 46 sec.). Elaine becomes the only hope for a group of children celebrating the Junior Ambassadors ceremony when they are attacked.

15. Powell's Last Stand (5 min., 54 sec.). Although he is rather timid and lacks an aggressive side, Blake must somehow find the courage to face an enemy.

16. The Captain's Ball (6 min., 26 sec.). At a formal celebration for Galactic Union Captains, Jack uncovers evidence that all in attendance are in danger.

17. Revenge of the Lizard Men, Part 1 (7 min., 17 sec.). The Lizard Men return to accomplish what they couldn't before: destroy Jack and his crew.

18. Revenge of the Lizard Men, Part 2 (6 min., 13 sec.). Elaine becomes the only hope for her captain when Jack is captured by the Draudis Lizard Men and she must lead a rescue party.

19. Revenge of the Lizard Men, Part 3. With Jack rescued, the crew returns to the ship—hoping to blast off before the Lizard Men capture them.

20. Revenge of the Lizard Men, Part 4. The second season finale finds escape is not possible and Jack and his crew must battle the Lizard Men.

380 *Voyages of the U.S.S.* Angeles. hiddenfrontier.com. 1998–2000 (Science Fiction).

The first Internet spin off from the *Star Trek* franchise that follows the voyages of the Federation's Starfleet Academy space ship, the U.S.S. *Angeles* as it explores the unknown regions of space.

Cast: Janice Willcocks (Capt. Janice Willcocks), Jennifer Cole (Capt. Jennifer Cole), Dave Mason (Lt. Cmdr. Dave Mason), Katie Moss (Counselor Katie Moss), Jason Munoz (Lt. Jason Munoz), Cliff Gardner (Helmsman Cliff Gardner), Chris Esquibel (Cmdr. Chris Esquibel). **Credits:** *Producer:* Rob Caves, Janice Willcocks. *Director:* Jennifer Cole. *Writer:* Rob Caves. **Comment:** Although the picture quality is poor (looks like copy of a VHS tape), the characters sometimes seen in a green glow (due to green screen technology used for the virtual backgrounds) and the special effects really noticeable as fake, the program is a pioneering Internet series and worthy of watching just to see what was done at the time. The series was produced by (and featured members) of the Los Angeles based chapter of the Star Trek Fan Club.

Episodes:

1. Return to Duty. The *Angeles* is recalled to

active duty to investigate a troublesome situation in the deadly Briar Patch.

2. A Little Night Music. The *Angeles* becomes the center of attention as a mysterious space storm threatens not only the ship, but its home base, Deep Space 12 and the planet Ba'ku.

3. Dreamers. The *Angeles* crew becomes involved in an intergalactic power struggle for control of Ba'ku, a healing planet.

4. Q in the Dark. The *Angeles* faces not only their enemies the Borg—but the Q as well.

5. Last of the Iconians. Crew members investigate what appear to be the remains of an ancient colony (Iconian) following a devastating war.

381 *The Walking Dead: Cold Storage.* amctv.com. 2012 (Horror).

Extension web program based on the AMC series *The Walking Dead.* Two men, Chase and Harris, have survived the zombie outbreak of the AMC series and have taken temporary refuge on a rooftop in Atlanta. Hoping to find safety in a nearby storage facility, Chase and Harris leave the rooftop but are soon attacked by the Walkers (zombies) and Harris is killed. Chase, managing to escape, finds safety inside the unit, which is under the command of a former employee named B.J. The story relates what happens when Chase discovers that B.J. is a madman—killing other employees, taking one female hostage (Kelly) as "his sexual slave" and now plans to kill him.

Cast: Josh Stewart (Chase), Daniel Roebuck (B.J.), Chris Nelson (Harris), Cerina Vincent (Kelly). **Credits:** *Producer:* Michael Petok, Chris Pollack, Jared Hoffman. *Director:* Greg Nicitero. *Writer:* John Esposito. **Comment:** Although produced for fans of the AMC series, it is well done and will appeal to non fans as a gripping story of escape and survival.

Episodes:

1. Hide and Seek (4 min., 29 sec.). Chase and Harris feel that, although they are safe on a rooftop, that a nearby storage facility will provide better protection.

2. Keys to the Kingdom (4 min., 57 sec.). The escape is costly as Harris is killed by the Walkers.

3. The Chosen Ones (5 min., 38 sec.). Chase becomes suspicious of B.J., the man who commands the storage unit he and Harris were seeking.

4. Parting Shots (9 min., 4 sec.). When Chase discovers B.J. is a killer and frees the girl he held captive (Kelly) the two plot to outwit B.J. and escape.

382 *The Walking Dead: Torn Apart.* amctv.com. 2012 (Horror).

A prequel of sorts that traces the history of Hannah ("The Bicycle Girl") from the AMC series *The Walking Dead.* In the series pilot episode Hannah became one of "The Walkers" (Zombies) when she was shot by Rick after he discovered she became infected.

The web series begins at the start of the zombie apocalypse when the world is in chaos and how Hannah becomes affected as she struggles to save her family.

Cast: Lilli Birdsell (Hannah), Rick Otto (Andrew), Madison Leisle (Jamie), Griffin Cleveland (Billy), Danielle Burgio (Judy), Josh Stewart (Chase), Daniel Roebuck (B.J.), Rex Linn (Palmer). **Credits:** *Producer:* Jared Hoffman, Chris Pollack. *Director:* Greg Nicotero. *Writer:* John Esposito. **Comment:** Has all the production values of the television series on which it is based and just as compelling. Fans of the AMC series will savor the web version, despite having to endure a thirty-second commercial before each episode begins.

Episodes:

1. A New Day (2 min., 37 sec.). The world has changed and Hannah and others are struggling to adjust.

2. Family Matters (2 min., 20 sec.). Hannah and her children (Jamie and Billy) take refuge at the home of her ex-husband (Andrew).

3. Domestic Violence (3 min., 10 min.). Judy, Hannah's mother-in-law, becomes infected when she attempts to help a young girl, unaware that she is a zombie.

4. Neighborly Advice (4 min.). Andrew seeks help from his neighbor, Palmer, who has the guns he needs to save his family.

5. Step-Mother (2 min., 22 sec.). Hannah comes face to face with Judy, now a zombie, who is seeking her children.

6. Everything Dies (5 min., 7 sec.). After killing Judy, Hannah and her children seek a place of safety but find their lives threatened by an increasingly growing zombie population.

383 *Walking in Circles.* wictheseries.com. 2011 (Fantasy).

When Sithalazalamazar, a fire-breathing dragon kills his father, an adventurer (Krag) swears to avenge his death by killing the dragon. With the help three friends (Garand, Angie and Markus), Krag sets out on a dangerous (if not comedic) quest to slay a dragon. Angie is a free-spirited Druid who detests violence; Markus is a somewhat incompetent wizard; Garand is a bard who seeks to document his adventures but constantly annoys all concerned with his tales; Alex is the mysterious woman in black who exudes an awe of evilness.

Cast: Eric Radic (Krag), Katie Wilson (Angie), Jonah Priour (Garand), Adam Rady (Markus), Ben Burch (Squire Quigley), Diana Restrepo, Kate Cobb, Chloe Slater, Annemarie Pazmino (Alex). **Credits:** *Producer-Writer-Director:* Adam Rady, James Rodehaver. **Comment:** A humorous look at four friends trying to survive in an age where evil flourishes. The outdoor scenes are well chosen for that medieval forest look and the story flows smoothly across the 11 episode run.

Walking in Circles cast, from left to right: Katie Wilson, Adam Rady, Eric Radic, Ben Burch and Diana Restrepo (copyright Never Red It Productions and ElectricHobo Films).

Episodes:

1. Party Up. As they begin their trek to find the dragon, Krag and his associates encounter a party of bandits.

2. Walking. With no one to assist him, Krag faces the bandits alone, later receiving help from Garand and Markus.

3. Old Debt. Krag faces a vengeful demon that is now dead-set on killing him.

4. Dysfunctional Democracy. Krag decides the time has come for his team to become epic heroes. The only problem—who will lead them.

5. The Master of Darkness. With Krag as their leader, the team faces a Hell Spawn when they inadvertently enter its lair.

6. Horace. Krag enters the netherworld to speak with his deceased father.

7. Counter Song. Angie and Garand attempt to rescue Krag and Markus from a trio of deadly sirens.

8. The Old Man and the Lake. Angie and Garand rescue Krag and Markus but now have to deal with a wizard and barbarian seeking to kill them.

9. Coming Out. Feeling that he can no longer hide who he really is Garand reveals his true being—he is an elf.

10. Random Encounter. As the quartet near the dragon's lair, they encounter a cult of bloodthirsty crazies.

11. Let Sleeping Dragon's Lie. Krag faces the dragon; Angie, Markus and Garand are doubtful he or they will survive the battle.

384 *Warehouse 13: Of Monsters and Men.* syfy.com. 2013 (Science Fiction).

Web extension story based on the Syfy channel series *Warehouse 13* (about a facility, located in Dakota, that houses mysterious relics, strange artifacts, supernatural souvenirs and "fanciful" objects collected by the U.S. government over the years). For the web series, three of its employees, Artie, Claudia and Pete become the victims of a cursed comic book when they are drawn into it, become trapped and seek a way to return to their own world.

Cast: Saul Rubinek (Artie Nelson), Allison Scagliotti (Claudia Donovan), Eddie McClintock (Pete Lattimer). **Credits:** *Producer:* Kenny Micka, Edward Rogers. *Director:* Andrew Seklir. *Writer:* John-Paul Nickel, Benjamin Raab. **Comment:** Fans of *Warehouse 13* will enjoy this story extension which has all the intrigue of the series (not to mention its acting and production values).

Episodes:

1. Episode 1 (4 min., 7 sec.). A delivery of classic comic books will soon affect the lives of Artie, Claudia and Pete.

2. Episode 2 (3 min.). A two dimension world traps the trio in a comic book called The City of Ghouls.

3. Episode 3 (1 min., 35 sec.). As the team realizes what has happened, they encounter a threat from ghouls.

4. Episode 4 (2 min., 22 sec.). Claudia is captured by a ghoul and taken to the underground sewers.

5. Chapter 5 (2 min., 17 sec.). Pete tracks the ghoul and successfully rescues Claudia.

6. Chapter 6 (2 min., 49 sec.). Additional troubles confront Pete and Claudia as they face more ghouls.

7. Chapter 7 (3 min., 31 sec.). Artie manages to bridge the two worlds and contacts an associate (Leena).

8. Chapter 8 (2 min., 54 sec.). As Leena struggles to release the team from the comic book, Pete has a confrontation with Mercer, the man seeking to keep him prisoner.

9. Chapter 9 (3 min., 38 sec.). Pete and Claudia flee from Mercer but face danger from the ghouls.

10. Chapter 10 (2 min., 46 sec.). Pete, Claudia and Artie face one last hurdle in an attempt to escape from the comic book, but Mercer plans to see that it doesn't happen.

385 *Watchers: The Virtual Series.* the watcherscouncil.net. 2003–2008 (Horror).

A spin off from the WB/UPN series *Buffy, the Vampire Slayer* that focuses primarily on that series characters Willow Rosenberg (Alyson Hannigan) and Rupert Giles (Anthony Stewart Head). Here Willow was depicted as a powerful witch that helped Buffy Summers (Sarah Michelle Gellar) destroy demons. Rupert was a Watcher, a man from a long-line of such beings that train and protect female slayers like Buffy. When their Sunnydale, California-based Watchers Council is destroyed by the First Evil, Willow (who has discovered that she was destined to become a Watcher) and Giles establish the New Watchers Council in Cleveland, Ohio, home to a second Hellmouth (a portal through which demons can pass from their realm into our world. Sunnydale was home to the first Hellmouth). The program follows the Council members as they continue their battle against powerful demons, most notably The Presidium.

Principal Characters: Willow Rosenberg (High Priestess and head of the Coven Division of Witches); Rupert Giles (Council Advisor); Rowena Allister (Senior Watcher); Faith Lehane (Head of the Slayer Division); Kennedy Calendar (Lead Slayer); Dawn Summers (Watcher and Coven member) Xander Harris (Weapons Master); Robin Wood (Security Chief and Academy teacher); Andrew Wells (Coven High Priest); Jeff Lindquist (Watcher and Coven Member); Skye Talisker (Vampire and Dawn's lover); Grace Hatherley (a Watcher); Buffy Summers (Head of the Watcher Division); Kadin Van Helsing (Rogue Demon Hunter); Becca Giles (Bookstore owner and Giles' wife); Jason Felix (Head of Bureau Nine); Althenea Dimmons (London High Priestess). Lori Carew (Former Slayer and now Felix's assistant); Vi Joston (a Salyer); Tracey Hausser (Council member and college student); Ethan Rayne (Watcher and Magic Expert); Shannon Matthewson (Dawn's Slayer), Marsha (Slayer assigned to Willow). **Cast:** Anthony Stewart Head (Rupert Giles), Alyson Hannigan (Willow Rosenberg), Eliza Dushku (Faith Lehane), Lyari Limon (Kennedy Calender), Felicia Day (Vi Joston), Michelle Williams (Rowena Allister), Michelle Trachtenberg (Dawn Summers), Nicholas Brendan (Xander Harris), Sarah Michelle Gellar (Buffy Summers), Jennifer Connelly (Althenea Dimmons), Carly Schroeder (Marsha), Elijah Wood (Jeff Lindquist), Helen Shaver (Becca Montague-Giles), Christy Carlson Romano (Hope Lehane), Lindsay Felton, Lacey Chabert (Skye Talisker), Michelle Rodriquez (Kadin Van Helsing), Laura Prepon (Lori Carew), Caroline Dhavernas (Grace Hatherley), Gary Oldman (Jason Felix), Rachel Hurd Wood (Lorinda Sheparton), Steffani Brass (Shannon Matthewson), D.B. Woodside (Robin Wood), Tom Lenk (Andrew Wells), Thora Birch (Tracey Hausser), Robert Sachs (Ethan Rayne). **Credits:** *Producer:* CN Winters, Susan Carr, Dragon Writer 17 (as credited). *Writer:* CN Winters, Susan Carr, Kye Cook, Chris Cook, Dragon Writer 17 (as credited), Dan Joslyn. *Director:* CN Winters, Susan Carr. **Comment:** The program began during the seventh season of *Buffy, the Vampire Slayer* and remained loyal to the feel of the original series. The program incorporates regulars from the original series with excellent acting and production values. With the exception of teasers and fan-produced tributes to the series (available on YouTube), all the episodes, as of March 2014, have been taken off line.

Episodes:

1. Something Ventured, Something Gained. Establishes the premise as Willow discovers her true destiny (a Watcher) and she and Giles begin establishing the New Council.

2. Lake Eerie. The Council battles a lake demon that attacks boaters on Lake Erie.

3. Foreign Presence. Introduces Rowena Allister, a Watcher from the Old Guard, a group of Watchers that is determined to dismantle the New Council.

4. Untimely Arrivals. Giles faces additional opposition to establishing the New Council when Old Guard members arrive in Cleveland.

5. Broken Allies. Seeing that she may have misjudged the New Council, Rowena sides with Giles and joins with him. Meanwhile, Willow becomes a Watcher to a new Slayer (Marsha).

6. Samhain. The Council must stop a demon bent on creating a zombie army.

7. Love and War. Dawn, Buffy's sister, is introduced and finds herself becoming attracted to a warlock named Jeff.

8. Another Year Old. Xander, from the original

series, reunites with Willow to celebrate her birthday.

9. Love Hurts. Willow faces a crisis when her powers are temporarily lost after an encounter with The Presidium.

10. Dark Force Rising. Tara, from the original series (Willow's girlfriend), appears to Kennedy (Willow's current love interest) in a dream with information on how to restore Willow's powers. Meanwhile, Giles finds romance with Becca Montague, a shopkeeper.

11. Blue Christmas. Anya, the demon girlfriend of Xander (from the original series), creates havoc by creating a demon Santa Clause. Meanwhile, as Willow and Kennedy's romance flounders, Giles and Becca's blossoms.

12. Modus Operandi. The Council attempts to stop a demonic Jack the Ripper type of killer.

13. Rash Decisions. A new demon, Sister Sin, becomes a threat to the city that the Council must destroy.

14. Family Ties. A fierce winter storm brings some unexpected calamity when family members of the New Council besiege headquarters and are forced to wait out the storm together.

15. About Last Night. Willow reveals to her parents that she is now a Watcher.

16. Restoration. A flash forward episode wherein a descendant of Willow in the year 2130 (a Colonel in the Military Watchers Council) reunites with a reincarnation of Tara (now a Slayer) as they attempt to stop an army of demons created by the New Council itself.

17. Scarecrow. Willow, a lesbian in the original series, finds herself becoming attracted to Rowena as she, Giles and Rowena battle an evil Watcher/Magic abuser.

18. Gangland. Faith, a New Council member, tries to recruit a group of "lost girls" who acquire strength when they band together.

19. Lessons Learned. Mia, one of the "lost girls" becomes attracted to Kennedy as Faith and Giles begin their recruitment.

20. High Art. As Giles celebrates his 50th birthday, a painting he purchases at an auction becomes more than just a painting when he discovers it can reveal one's inner demons.

21. Child's Play. A hex, placed on Willow, Faith and Xander, returns them to a time when they were children.

22. May Day. As the Watchers and Slayers prepare for the celebration of Beltaine, The Presidium casts a spell that forces religious groups to attack the Council.

23. Another Day. Willow and Kennedy attempt to rescue Faith, who has been kidnapped by a demon.

24. Another Apocalypse. The season one finale wherein the Council members each use their powers in an attempt to defeat The Presidium.

25. Everything New Again. Although the Council failed to defeat The Presidium, it has vowed to make his elimination their number one priority. A new demon, the Lover, from the kingdom known as Vor, rises and becomes a serious threat as it has the power to see what the Watchers are planning. The start of Season 2.

26. New Again. Willow begins mentoring her Slayer (Marsha) as demons plot to turn Faith into one of them.

27. Checkmate. Willow and Rowena engage in a game of chess, magically enhanced by the Witch's Coven, whose chess pieces come to life to reveal incidents from the women's past lives.

28. Swap Meet. Becca's attempt at casting spells backfires, causing Council members to switch identities.

29. True Colors. Becca learns that she is pregnant (by Giles) as Willow and Rowena become sexually attracted to each other.

30. Red Herring. The board game "Clue" becomes all too real when, at a costume party, Council members must defeat a killer who is playing the game for real.

31. Dream Warriors. A demon's spell has Council members dreaming they are in an arena battling a demon named Imbethit.

32. Hell Goddess. The Council battles a group of demons called Mizors, who have besieged Cleveland.

33. Time Out. Council member Tyrrell is exposed as manipulating a plan to eliminate the Council heads.

34. Real World. The Presidium's plan to recruit a human agent to kidnap Rowena and Mia backfires when he is killed and Rowena wounded.

35. Blue Moon. In an attempt to cure a woman (Camille) of her vampirism, Troy (a werewolf) and Cassandra (a vampire) cast a spell that cures her but leaves them both werewolves.

36. Bad Blood. Although Camille believes she has left her past behind her, an unknown figure now threatens her—Kadin Van Helsing, heir to the Helsing legacy (vampire hunters) who has vowed to kill her for killing her father (when she was a vampire).

37. In the Dark. Council members Vi and her twin sister Angie, try to help a disfigured, abused young man who is believed to be a monster.

38. Avatar. An encounter with a supernatural beast leaves Kennedy with super abilities—abilities that if used, could destroy demons—but damage the city as well.

39. Fire Eater. Becca and Giles face a Soul Stealer that is seeking Becca's unborn child.

40. Unfinished Business. Kadin teams with Kennedy to battle a seemingly unstoppable demon.

41. Chapel of Love. Having defeated the Soul Stealer, Giles and Becca set their sights on marrying.

42. Get a Life. A demonic incarnation of actress Jeri Ryan becomes the target of the Council when it begins killing fans at a comic book convention.

43. Rack and Ruin. Xander and Vi become closer while Kennedy and Mia face challenges to their relationship when Kennedy realizes she has deep feelings for Kadin.

44. Resistance. Willow, once turned evil on the original series, fears she may be returning to the dark side when continual nightmares appear to be leading her down that path.

45. Internal Affairs. A shape shifter, pretending to be a lover to both Vi and Xander, threatens to drain their life force while Dawn and Rowena seek a monster of their own—a dragon.

46. Wickerman. Faith and her Black Ops Squad attempt to stop The Presidium from masterminding a plot to invade the earth.

47. Ragnarok, Part 1. The second season finale wherein the Council enter the Vor to battle Lover and The Presidium. Meanwhile Becca gives birth to a girl (Elizabeth) and Buffy becomes head of the Council.

48. Ragnarok, Part 2. Continues the story with the battle against The Presidium.

49. War Zone. Now that he is a father, Giles elects to retire and places Rowena in the position of head of the Council. At this same time, the Council must battle a demonic sand worm that is threatening to wipe out U.S. troops in the Iraq desert. Start of the 3rd Season.

50. Maternal Instincts. The Council seeks to stop a horde of demons that are seeking a human surrogate mother.

51. Both Sides Now. Rowena's first mission as the Council leader finds her attempting to clear Xander, Willow and Vi of charges that their negligence caused the death of several women and the fall of the Vancouver Watchers Council.

52. Just the Facts. A reporter (Robert Devlin) attempts to piece together the incidents that lead to the women's death and the fall of the council. His research uncovers startling evidence regarding the Watchers and their work.

53. Trial by Fury. A spell is put on Devlin to prevent him from revealing what he uncovered to the outside world. Meanwhile, Kadin must come to terms for killing a group of werewolves who had dedicated themselves to living peacefully with humans.

54. Luna. Rowena and Willow contemplate their relationship as the Council battles a series of strange occurrences during a full moon.

55. In the Balance. Rowena and Willow rekindle their stormy relationship as Kennedy and Kadin forge a new bond.

56. Loves Labors Lost. Rowena, Willow, Faith and Robin seek a way to bring an end to an ages-old feud between two families while Willow must also help uncover the source of ghostly occurrences at Giles' new home.

57. No Mercy. Rowena must decide if the mysterious Gregor Kalderash (Kennedy's uncle) is a candidate for the Council after he predicts an agonizing future for Willow and Faith. Meanwhile, Skye (a vampire) begins to raise suspicions about her mysterious activities.

58. Birthright. Assisted by Kennedy, Kadin seeks the other half of a medallion left to her by her father to claim her birthright as a member of the Helsing family. Meanwhile, Dawn becomes concerned over Skye's mysterious behavior.

59. Rule of Three. Vi attempts to come to terms with killing Gregor to save Willow and Faith; Dawn is rejected by slayer Shannon as her Watcher after Shannon befriends a deranged creature.

60. Roses Are Red. The Council must contend with the ghost of young girl (Rose) who has begun haunting the Cleveland Council. Skye turns renegade (killing a slayer) while Kennedy and Faith's relationship is apparently ending as Faith leaves the Council.

61. The Night in Question. Faith finds herself mysteriously transported to an alternate universe where she never achieved the status of a senior slayer with the Cleveland Council but that of a rogue slayer.

62. A Road Trip to Remember. A search is begun to find the rogue vampire, Skye. Dawn, shattered by Skye's death when she is found and destroyed, must come to terms that she has lost Skye and Buffy must realize that Dawn is no longer her kid sister, but a woman.

63. 59:23. The Council members ban together to defuse a mystical bomb that is set to detonate in less than one hour.

64. Skin Deep. Willow and Rowena must come to terms on the inherent differences in their relationship while Kennedy, reunited with Faith, must also choose to strengthen or abandon their relationship; and Xander and Vi appear to have progressed to a state where a relationship is now possible.

65. Strange Bedfellows. The Council must decide if Kadin is worthy of becoming a member (as she acts first and obeys orders later). Meanwhile, Dawn seeks a way to restore Skye's soul and bring her love back to her; Kennedy is assigned the task of testing Kadin in the field—by helping her destroy a nest of vampires, lead by Harmony and Luna, dangerous vampires unleashed by the Hellmouth.

66. Very Bad Ideas. Dawn discovers a way to bring her lover back—by seeking the Witch's Coven's help in restoring Skye's soul.

67. Rules of Engagement. As a nest of demons appear, Rowena assigns Buffy to take her place while Dawn, acquiring the spell she needs, begins preparations to bring Skye back to her.

68. Foucault's Pendulum. The Council learns (from a time traveler) that in 300 years Watchers and Slayers are doomed and that to protect that future, action must be taken now. As head of the Council, Buffy summons Council leaders from around the world to change the future.

69. The Secret Life of D.J. Trace. Council mem-

ber Tracy's college radio program provides the backdrop for a look at a week in the life of the Council as it deals with free lance vampire slayers and as Tracy deals with her own problems—from her encounter with a strange little boy to her work at school.

70. Ouroboros. Giles and Willow investigate the unearthing of a mysterious temple (Ouroboros) found on a construction site.

71. Shomer. Visions of what could happen if the Council were not created are brought to light when an angel appears to the Council to deliver a message: "For behold, I bring you things of great ... Doom."

72. Megiddo. The third season finale finds the Council faced with possible devastation as Hellmouth's from across the world start to open and dispense creatures that could destroy mankind. It appears that a temple in the lost City of Atlantis holds the key to destroying the enemy.

73. Better Days. The Council's battle against the demons from the prior episode makes them known to the world but also reveals to the public that demons really exist. Another organization, called Bureau Nine (led by Jason Felix) is revealed to also abolish demons—but for a substantial fee. Start of the 4th Season.

74. Unspoken. Rowena and Kennedy seek an ancient text that contains magic spells capable of banishing evil.

75. A Little Faith. Hope, Faith's younger sister becomes possessed by a demon seeking to use her to destroy Council members.

76. Based on a True Story. A screenplay, written by Council member Andrew, becomes a movie that is anything but the truth.

77. Withdrawal. Rowena experiments on Skye, hoping to cure her of her vampirism.

78. Hide 'n' Seek. Rowena, Faith, and Vi attempt to escape from a demon (Hell) after they are taken hostage and find themselves trapped in an amusement park fun house.

79. Collateral Damage. Kennedy seeks to help Kadin when she faces the wrath of a werewolf seeking to kill her for killing his werewolf family.

80. Revelation 9:6. Faith must contend with an anti-slayer—whose touch can take away the powers of a Slayer.

81. From the Bottom Up. Incidents in the lives of lesser known Council members are explored.

82. Trinity. A look at the problems facing Council members Dawn, Skye and Shannon.

83. Auld Lang Syne. Stories of the past are related by Giles, Rowena, Faith and Andrew on New Year's Eve.

84. Meiyo. A look at Bureau Nine and its leader, Jason Felix.

85. You Never Know. The Council must stop a pair of bungling demons before they can affect a plan to destroy the world.

86. Drawn Together. Willow and Andrew seek a way to escape a cursed comic book based on Faith's life when they are drawn into it.

87. Hidden. Kadin, Rowena, Faith, Buffy, Willow, Xander and Kennedy must overcome a curse that seizes their abilities to fight demons.

88. Lockdown. Amira, the Muslim Council member, seeks a way to end a fundamentalist Islamic takeover of the Council.

89. Alluvion. The Council clashes with Bureau Nine in an effort to acquire an ancient artifact.

90. Sacrifice. The demon Hell returns seeking to kill Council members with Kennedy determined to stop her. A confrontation forces Kennedy to kill Kadin in order to save Willow from her clutches.

91. Serena. Kadin, able to resurrect herself, returns to the Council—and to her lover, Serena.

92. Tokyo Knights. A lead to Hell's whereabouts brings Kennedy to Tokyo where she finally achieves her goal by killing Hell.

93. Bloodlines. Faith, feeling that she is becoming a less-effectual Slayer, finds her faith restored when she begins mentoring younger Slayers for the Council.

94. The Price. Kennedy's doubts about herself and what she has done to protect the innocent are brought to light when she is propelled into an alternate world without the protection of the Council.

95. Childe Roland. As Willow and Rowena plan to marry, the Council faces a crisis when Jason (of Bureau Nine) begins preparations to rid the world of magic to make it a better place.

96. The Dark Tower. The fourth season finale wherein the Council, helpless without magic, must find a way to stop Jason and the doorway he will open to let demons control the world.

Note: Episodes 97 through 123, which represent the series fifth and last season, have been taken off line. Flashbacks, coupled with flash forwards are incorporated to explore the past and future history of the New Council and its battle against a vicious demon called the Loathestone.

Fifth Season Episode Titles: *97.* Past, Present, Future. *98.* Home Sweet Home. *99.* Games. *100.* Time and Again. *101.* Orientation. *102.* Divination. *103.* Lorinda's Kiss. *104.* Triangle. *105.* Inside the Watcher's Council. *106.* The Unknown. *107.* Savage. *108.* Cone of Power. *109.* Webs We Weave. *110.* Reboot. *111.* Before I Wake. *112.* Turnabout. *113.* Tainted. *114.* Contingency. *115.* Unlikely Heroes. *116.* Underworld. *117.* Breaking Point. *118.* Last Tango in Cleveland. *119.* Asha. *120.* Unto the End. *121.* Generations. *122.* Generations II. *123.* Generations III.

386 *The Weepers.* tktproductions.com. 2013 (Science Fiction).

Unknown to humans there is a race of people called Weepers, assassins who are committed to eliminating the undesirable elements of society. Weepers are under the command of the Tempus Senatorum and the Tempus Prefect determines who needs termination. Stories follow Weepers as they seek and execute their assigned targets.

Cast: Daniel Moresburg (Rob Simms), Joshua Bingham (J.D.), Courtney Allbu (Det. Nicole Brightly), Mara Leite (Mara Jacobs), Gary Winchester (Selkirk Weeper), Karent Wetterhahn (Chief Giardino), Stephen Latshaw (Anon Nown). **Credits:** *Producer-Director:* Thomas Tierney. *Writer:* Matthew Melton, Thomas Tierney **Comment:** The series plays like the backwards episode of *Seinfeld* (where the end is seen first and flashbacks are used to show you what led to the ending). Presumably more episodes are planned and it will continue in that backwards manner showing additional events that leads to a conclusion.

Episodes:

1. The End (11 min., 40 sec.). The story ends. The serial killer (J.D.) who became known as the DIE Killer (as he would leave the word DIE with his victims) is trailed by Detective Rob Simms but meets his fate at the hands of a Weeper.

2. The Beginning (8 min., 24 sec.). The story begins. A serial killer (J.D.) encounters a Weeper Trainer (Anon) while a detective (Rob Simms) investigates one of his latest crimes.

387 *Which Die Is That Again?* whichdie. com. 2012 (Fantasy).

A young man named Brian, whose only joy in life is imagining himself as a brave knight in days of yore, works as a down-trodden employee of Burger Castle. His quest for something bigger happens when he falls asleep and he becomes that brave knight. The story follows Brian when he becomes a knight and attempts to rescue a maiden, tied to a tree, and defeat the evil villain, Doug, who put her there.

Cast: Nathaniel Grauwelman (Brian), Victoria Baker (Maiden), Justin Frechette (Doug). **Credits:** *Producer-Writer-Director:* Nathaniel Grauwelman. **Comment:** The program opens with the shakiest of shaky camera scenes ever seen then progress into something that could have been better if a little care was taken. As it stands now, awful would be a compliment. Not only is it badly photographed but the dialogue is mostly improvised and the acting below par (for example, the Maiden could express some fear as she is being menaced, and the villain, reminiscent of silent film villains needs to take lessons from Snidley Whiplash [from television's *Dudley Do-Right* series] who had a fondness for kidnapping a woman and tying her to railroad tracks). Brian, as the Knight, wearing modern-day eye glasses, also does not help with authenticity.

Episodes:

1. Episode 1: The Pilot. Establishes the series story line as explained above.

388 *Wingman.* webserieschannel.com. 2013 (Fantasy).

Wingman is a superhero with a number of problems, the most embarrassing being that he still lives with his mother, an over-bearing woman who is also his worst enemy (as she thinks he is lazy and being a superhero is not a job). But Wingman has chosen to become a superhero and with his sidekick, Peregrine Falcon, initiates a battle to save the world from its most diabolical enemies—from Cheetah Girl to The Inquisitor. Wingman's obsession began when he was a child and his mother would read him stories about superheroes. While he does wear a costume, he insists that it be called a uniform, not a costume.

Cast: Casey Nash (Wingman), Bryan Siebers (Falcon), Barb Trzcinski (Wingman's mother), Nicolette Sims, Rachel Kirk, Jordan Wagner. **Credits:** *Producer-Writer-Director:* James R. Lawrence. **Comment:** Enjoyable spoof of superheroes with a likable cast and good production values.

Episodes:

1. Secret Identity Crisis (10 min., 31 sec.). Introduces the characters and sets up the storyline.

2. Paws of Fury (9 min., 3 sec.). Wingman's arch enemy, Cheetah Girl, plots to trap him into proposing—and win over his mother.

3. Enter the Man Cave (11 min., 22 sec.). Mary Day, Wingman's girlfriend is not too pleased to learn that Cheetah Girl has her sights set on him.

4. Alliance of Justice (9 min., 49 sec.). Wingman and Flacon seek help battling evil by sponsoring an Alliance of Justice League.

5. Counsel of Terror (12 min., 25 sec.). Although Wingman is engaged to Mary Day, Cheetah Girl continues her pursuit—this time bringing a minister with her.

6. Operation Blackbird (9 min., 39 sec.). After infiltrating the Evil Convention for Super Criminals, Wingman and Falcon discover a new villain has come into their lives—Leopard Woman.

7. Flawless(ish) Victory (11 min., 39 sec.). At a convention where the Inquisitor is the guest of honor, Wingman and Falcon encounter the evil Hypnotist.

8. The Candlelight Vigil (10 min., 44 sec.). Trouble looms for Wingman when Cheetah Girl tricks him into proposing to her at a candle party and he must now keep Mary Day from finding out.

9. The Inquisitor Strikes Back (9 min., 29 sec.). In an attempt to deal with Wingman, The Inquisitor and Bee Boy kidnap Wingman's mother.

10. Threshold of Fear (9 min., 14 min). In an effort to end their engagement, Wingman hopes to have her put away by tricking her into stealing a famous diamond on their wedding day.

389 *Withered World: An End of the World Web Series.* witheredworld.tv. 2013 (Fantasy).

Anthology program of stories about what could take place on the last day of the Earth's existence as seen through a group of diverse people.

Cast: Alicia Cabrera, Ari Bavel, Tosin Morohunfola, McKenna Abercrombie, Curtis Smith, Joe Backer, Kevin Bingham, Jessi Burkette, Paul Burns, Sherry Cain, Brian Cain, Angie Cherry, Michelle Davidson, Deborah Ellison, Rick Ellison, Somyia Finley, Caitlin Gentry, Eric Johansen, Michael Joiner, Doug Marshall, Ariel O'Bannon, Lauren O'Bannon, Wilson Vance, Bill White. **Credits:** *Producer:* Bryce Young, Tucker Keatley, David Brain, Justin Gardner, Rob Turner. *Director:* Chris Bylsma, Jon Davis, Justin Gardner, Bruce Young, Tucker Keatley, Anthony Ladesich, Katie Mooney, Patrick Rea, Brian Reece, Kendal Sinn, Bruce Young. **Comment:** Although gloomy in thought, a well presented collection of what could happen stories.

Episodes:

1. The Field. An elderly man reflects on the life he shared with his wife.

2. A Man's Table. In light of the end of the world, a loving father and husband vows to protect his family at any cost.

3. If Night Comes. A filmmaker begins documenting how people are spending their last day on Earth.

4. New Life. The torment felt by a couple whose baby is due on the last day of the world.

5. The Icarus 1. A young boy with imagination attempts to build a rocket ship before the end occurs.

6. Vows. A young couple makes one last vow to each other.

7. Vindicate. A man seeks to kill the man who destroyed his family before time runs out.

8. Ollie's Oms. A couple celebrates the occasion at a wild "End of the World" party.

9. Champion. A young mother attempts to console her daughter as the end nears.

10. Pop Tarts. A lonely widower invites a stranger to join him in one last breakfast.

11. Last Show. A theater group performs their final show.

12. Return to Sender. A young man seeks to build the courage to face the inevitable.

13. Waiting in Line. Old friends visit for the last time.

390 *Wizard Hunters.* youtube.com. 2012 (Fantasy).

Centuries ago a Vampire warrior of the highest rank and an Arabian Priestess fell in love. The Priestess became pregnant and was now carrying what was to be the first half human-half vampire child. However, when their love was discovered it was condemned by both the human and vampire factions, forcing the couple to flee for their lives. Eventually the couple found refuge in a small settlement and

Wizard Hunters. **A scene from the series (*Wizard Hunters* is a trademark and copyright by Uphill Pictures. Licensed by Uphill Pictures, LLC. Copyright 2014 Uphill Productions. All rights reserved).**

pretended to be humans. At this time, however, there also existed Wizards, both the good and bad, and each side became engaged in a battle for supremacy. Killing was not a concern to them and they abolished anything that stood in their way. The couple found themselves caught in the middle with tragic results—the Wizards killed the Priestess and her child, forcing the Vampire to swear an oath of revenge—to kill all Wizards. Prophecy reveals that a reincarnation of that child with the abilities of a sorceress and possessed of amazing powers will one day surface. That child will be the only hope the world has to save it from a vampire army. Over time vampires have been transforming humans into an undead army and require that child for the power it possesses.

It is the present day when a 12-year-old girl (Crystal) and her adoptive mother (Jessica) are in a parking garage when they are confronted by what appear to be demons. The demons want the child but encounter the unexpected when Jessica uses energy blasts from her hands to protect Crystal. Jessica, however, is not powerful enough to defeat her enemies and is killed; Crystal, confronted by a demon, is saved when the medallion she is wearing (a gift from her birth mother), emits a ray that destroys the demon and saves her. The medallion is also a signal to another realm that brings Zillah, a demon fighter to Crystal's aide. Zillah rescues Crystal and brings her to Orion, an ancient Wizard that tells her she is the reincarnation of that ancient vampire-sorceress child and that Jessica, though lost in the battle, was sent to protect her until it was her time to take her position in the battle between Wizards and Vampires. Crystal also learns that the medallion knew who and what Crystal was and it became activated when the first threat appeared (Crystal's birth mother is not mentioned but it has to be assumed she was either a good Wizard or a Sorceress). Stories follow Crystal as she prepares to take her part in a world few know exist and use her amazing (but still developing) abilities to help defeat the Vampire who has sworn revenge many centuries ago.

Cast: Scarlett Lynn (Crystal), Bob Barr (Orion), Michele Bauer (Zillah), Karita Fleming (Jessica), Gerardo Candelario (Petrus), Alexis George (Lena), Nathan O. Miller (Vampire Captain), Brendan Guy Murphy (Hades) **Credits:** *Producer:* Antonio Villagomez, Cori Di Simone. **Comment:** From the beginning of the attack in the parking garage to the Wizard's recounting the couple's history, your attention is grabbed and kept from episode to episode. The acting, writing, directing and special effects are superior and, although the program ends unresolved, it is well worth watching as it could have easily been turned into a broadcast or cable television series. The Syfy network should take a look.

Episodes:

1. Episode 1 (5 min., 21 sec.). Introduces Crystal as a mischievous schoolgirl whose life changes when

she and her adoptive mother are confronted by demons.

2. Episode 2 (3 min., 24 sec.). Crystal's capture by a demon is thwarted by Zillah, an emissary of the Wizard master.

3. Episode 3 (4 min., 1 sec.). With Zilla's help, Crystal is whisked away to the safety of the Wizard's lair.

4. Episode 4 (5 min., 36 min.). Crystal discovers that she is the last puzzle piece—a powerful sorceress in a puzzle that, if acquired by the vampire army, will mean the destruction of the world.

5. Episode 5 (6 min., 2 sec.). The history of the vampire couple is recounted as Crystal attempts to understand her place in the war.

391 *Woke Up Dead.* crackle.com. 2009 (Horror).

Drex Greene is a young man with a lot to live for—or at least he thought until he catches his on-and-off girlfriend (Diana) making out with a drug dealer at a party; making matters worse, Drex accepts a pill of unknown substance from him. At home, while taking a bath, the pill's effects put Drex to sleep. Although he is found by his roommate Matt after being underwater for 15 minutes, it appears that he is still alive—but as a zombie. The program relates events in Drex's life as he finds romance—first with a pretty nurse (Cassie) then with an equally pretty zombie (Aurora). But romance is not his biggest problem. He soon learns that he is part of something bigger—something that can be attributed to his mother (Marilyn). It appears that when Marilyn was younger, she was in a cult called the Sleepers, wherein members were "trying to awaken their genetic potential." Marilyn knows what is happening to Drex and he is part of that experiment. However, unknown to both Marilyn and Drex, persons unknown are keeping tabs on Drex as he is apparently the key to "The Awakening Underground" and what he possesses others want (unfortunately the program ends unresolved).

Cast: Jon Heder (Drex Greene), Krysten Ritter (Cassie), Josh Gad (Matt), Daniel Roebuck (Shadow Man), Jean Smart (Marilyn Greene), Ella English (Diana Phillips), Wayne Knight (Andrew Batten), Taryn Southern (Debbie), Meital Dohan (Aurora). **Credits:** *Producer:* Brent V. Friedman, Stan Rogow, Jeff Sagansky. *Director:* Tim O'Donnell. **Comment:** Light comedy-horror mix that portrays zombies in a different (less gross) light and even incorporates a zombie romance. Acting and production values are above the normal Internet series (very well done) and features some well-known television names like Wayne Knight and Jean Smart.

Episodes:

1. Up and at 'Em. Establishes what happens when Drex wakes up after being underwater for 15 minutes.

2. The Walking Dead. After wandering out of the apartment, getting hit by a bus, and awakening after being declared dead, Drex meets a pretty nurse named Cassie; Matt makes plans to film Drex's transformation and post it online.

3. Dead TV. Cassie believes a symptom called Hypostatsis-Hematosis could be responsible for Drex's condition, but they can only be sure if they can find the drug dealer from the party.

4. The Working Dead. Drex returns to work where he receives a strange memo asking him if "he woke up dead."

5. Work It All Out. Unknown to Drex, an unknown figure is watching his every move. At home, Matt tests Drex to see if he is a zombie by feeding him calf brains.

6. The Searching Dead. As Cassie, Drex and Matt seek the drug dealer, Cassie believes the drug may have affected Drex's central nervous system.

7. Lost and Found. As Cassie runs some tests on Drex at work, Drex receives another strange memo.

8. Dead Man Typing. Cassie discovers that Drex's system is slowly decaying, but he is not outwardly being affected. Drex, now knowing he is a zombie, finds that he has special skills.

9. Someone Wicked This Way Comes. Trouble brews at work when a co-worker (Andy) witnesses Drex's sudden abilities and calls for him to have a drug test.

10. Pill of the Dead. Hope looms for Drex when Cassie finds the drug dealer they were seeking and is given the mysterious blue pill.

11. Feeling Groovy. Drex's embellishment of his new undead life is not as carefree as he thinks when he trips, falls off a three story building—and winds up dead at the hospital—and again wakes up "alive."

12. IM of the Dead. Drex receives another memo from the IM (Instant Messenger) while Andy, Drex's co-worker, objects to Drex placing pictures of Cassie in the office.

13. Hide and Seek. Drex devises a scheme to make the IM reveal herself.

14. Date Night. The IM, who calls herself Pittsburgh 666, arranges to meet Drex; Cassie and Matt accompany him, feeling it may be a trap.

15. Warehouse of the Living Dead. At the assigned meeting spot, the trio encounters Aurora, a beautiful female zombie—to whom Drex immediately becomes attracted.

16. Single Dead Female. Drex becmes infatuated with Aurora, unaware that she has been assigned to spy on him.

17. My Gun Is Dead. Cassie and Matt begin a search for Drex when he leaves the safety of their company to find Aurora.

18. Back to School. After finding Aurora, Drex questions her about her memos (and learning that she only sought to meet him).

19. Kiss of the Dead. Drex learns that, now that he is a zombie, that he possesses more abilities than he thought.

20. The Not Bank Job. Becoming concerned over Drex's relationship with Aurora, Cassie and Matt use a variety of cameras to keep tabs on them.

21. Night of the Dead Shark. It is revealed that Aurora is the key to discovering the secret of "The Awakening Underworld" and her undead life is now on the line if she can't bring Drex over to her side (people seeking the secrets of genetic awakening).

22. Mother's Day. Drex receives a surprise visit form his mother—who sheds some light on what is happening to him but the program concludes in a cliff hanger with no further information revealed.

392 *Wolfpack of Reseda.* webserieschannel. com. 2012 (Horror).

Ben March is a man living in his own dreary world. He works in a boring job (auto insurance salesman), has little interest in anything (except fellow employee Sophie) and dreads listening to the motivation speeches given by the head of his company (Vance). He also lives with Rudy, an Animal Control Officer and sees his future as bleak. Ben lives in an area of California where the legend of werewolves also thrives. In the 19th century a clan of Gypsies from Eastern Europe settled in an enclave of Reseda. When a Spanish missionary fell in love with a girl, the daughter of the head of the clan, her father, who disapproved, used black magic and cursed him with "the spirit of the wolf." Shortly after, the missionary was attacked by a pack of wolves and, although he survived, he was bitten by one that had been infected. As he too became infected and realized that he was developing strange traits, he took his own life—but his infected blood that drenched the earth has been cursed—anyone in the present that may stumble upon that ground will themselves suffer the same fate as the missionary. Poor Ben. While out one night, Ben crosses the forbidden land, is attacked by a mysterious creature and bitten. Soon effects of the bite become apparent as Ben begins to experience changes—but are they of a werewolf? Episodes hint at that as Ben encompasses his new abilities to enjoy life.

Cast: Tate Ellington (Ben March), Deanna Russo (Sophie), Brian Smith (Vance), Alex Berg (Rudy), Justin Giddings (Stu), Brandon Johnson (Norris), Marc Evan (Rod). **Credits:** *Producer:* Fox Digital Entertainment. **Comment:** With Fox Digital Entertainment behind it, "Wolfpack" is a well produced series that presents elements of horror and comedy (sort of combining elements of the 1940s feature film *The Wolfman* with television's *The Office*). Although the actors are relative unknowns, they handle their parts well and, being it has been done by Fox, it has potential to be broadcast on television.

Episodes:

1. First Bite (14 min., 3 sec.). Ben is attacked by a creature and begins to experience subtle changes.

2. An American Werewolf in Car Insurance (9 min., 14 sec.). Although not typical werewolf powers, Ben finds that he has become more aggressive in selling cars.

3. Hungry Like a Wolf (11 min., 43 sec.). Ben closes a deal with the head of Taco Truck and realizes the car lot is his new lair.

4. Leader of the Pack (7 min., 18 sec.). Ben forms his own "wolf pack" with co-workers Stu and Norris (who, after learning about Ben, want to be like him).

5. Date Night (8 min., 34 sec.). Actual signs of becoming a werewolf manifest themselves when Ben sees Vance with Sophie, the girl he loves, and he flexes his alpha dominance.

6. First Blood (9 min., 21 sec.). As the full moon begins to rise, Ben tries to prevent changes from occurring.

7. Full Moon Party (8 min., 10 sec). As Ben makes the transformation, it is learned that several killings have occurred. Was it Ben?

8. Debbie from HR (11 min., 2 sec.). Ben seeks answers to what has happened to him.

393 *Wormtooth Nation.* theskyisfree.com. 2008 (Fantasy).

In an underground complex there apparently exist the last remaining human beings. It is a complex from which there appears to be no escape and how people came to be there or why they are there are questions to which there appear to be no answers. It is a dark world ruled an Overlord (Baron O'Brien), whose knowledge of the city is such that he should remain in power. It also appears that as long as the Baron rules, the city will produce power, food and water for its residents to survive. There are those who believe another world lies beyond what they are now experiencing. But escaping to find that world seems to be an impossible task as memory loss continually plagues those who try. The story follows one such group of people as they seek a way out to a world they believe exists beyond their own.

Baron O'Brien, ruler of The City, knows its secrets, as he helped shape the city from the beginning. His knowledge of the machines necessary to keep The City functional has citizens bowing to his leadership. Lady Tania is the Baron's mistress, the High Lady of The City. Her voice is heard on every radio in The City, day after day and hour after hour as her voice is their comforter. Serias is a worker (in the furnace room) who heads a revolt (The Worker's Union) against the Baron and his harsh rule. Hella is a furnace worker (repairs boilers) who, like many others, has no recollection of the past, where she came from or of a ruler before the Baron. Dimitri, a city watcher, laments in the fact that he once held an official position (sort of like a security chief) but now has been regulated to a position that that has been forgotten. Bottom is a city entertainer and often performs on stage with Lady Tania. Sam has

faint recollections of being somewhere else and is the one citizen who is determined to find out where that someplace else was.

Cast: Elizabeth Hughes (Lady Tania), Benjamin Estey (Baron O'Brien), David J. Murphy (Bottom), Steve Pappin (Serias), Brendan Thomas (Rufus), Helena-Grace Treadwell (Hella), Steve White (Demitri), Ted Walker (Robin), Matt Ticciati (Sam). **Credits:** *Producer:* Geoff Boothby, Cullen Thomas. *Director:* Geoff Boothby. *Writer:* Geoff Boothby, Cullen Thomas. **Comment:** People trapped in various situations (like buildings) is nothing new. Here, however, the culprit is the loss of memory which prevents them for escaping and they must continually seek a way out. The story plays a little bit like the ABC series *Lost* in that scenes jump back and forth from characters' lives before their becoming trapped in the situation they now face. It is compelling and done well enough to make you want to see what happens next.

Episodes:

1. Episode 1. An introduction to the underground city and some of its residents.

2. Episode 2. Hella is introduced in a separate story that explores the city and what is apparently its heartbeat—the furnaces.

3. Bottom's Dream. As Bottom and Lady Tania rehearse for a show, citizens attempting an escape are captured by the Baron's agents.

4. Tania's Love. A look back at the relationship between The Baron and Lady Tania.

5. Good Fellow. A group of people, led by Sam, reach the surface and see the night sky for the first time—but each cannot remember if they have ever seen it before (as what they are seeing will soon disappear from their memories).

6. The Theory of Serias. Fed up with the conditions (and small pay) he and his fellow workers have to endure, Serias theorizes that the only way to escape is to revolt.

7. Watcher. Serias and his fellow workers begin plotting their take over of The City.

8. Lovers, Fools and Madmen. As Lady Tania and Bottom's show is being performed, a rebellion is building behind the scenes.

9. The Sky Is Infinite. Sam, who is beginning to have recollections of an outside world, leads a group of people on the path to be what he believes is the way to the surface and freedom.

394 *Xombie: Dead on Arrival.* xombified. com. 2003 (Horror).

In a future time when most of the world has been destroyed by an unstated catastrophe, zombies are the ruling class while the few humans that remain are clinging to life and struggling to survive by any means they can. Zombies have evolved to a state where they are aware of what they are but are torn between their cravings and a sense of moral sensibility.

Dirge is one such Zombie, a creature impervious to death but armed with reason and now cursed to a life of endless wandering. The animated program follows Dirge as he wanders, seeking to adjust to what he has become and survive in a world where zombies roam across the wastelands of the future. **Cast:** Geoff Edwards (Dirge), Michelle Fairney (Zoe). **Credits:** *Producer:* Cindi Rice, John Frank Rosenblum. *Writer-Director:* James Farr. **Comment:** Simplistic animation (almost still like) is combined with a good story idea that, unfortunately, has not gone beyond a first episode. It is different and appealing and worth watching.
Episodes:
1. The Dead Sea (4 min., 43 sec.). A young girl (Zoe), a human survivor of the catastrophe, finds her life being threatened by a group of unethical zombies and about to be killed when Dirge comes to her rescue and whisks her off to safety. Accompanied by his undead dog, Cerberus, Dirge now has a mission: reunite Zoe with her family.

395 *The Young Adventures of Damon Dark.* youtube.com. 2009–2010 (Science Fiction).

A spin off from *Damon Dark* (see entry) that relates incidents in his life before he became the world renowned UFO investigator and demon hunter. It all started when Damon was a teenager and he and his friend, Jason, planned a camping trip. Damon arrived at the site first and after setting up a tent, became aware of a glowing light coming from beyond the trees. Believing it was Jason, Damon ventured forth only to discover that he had witnessed the landing of an alien space craft. The craft's landing, however, was no mistake as its inhabitant had chosen Damon to become a hero—to save the people of Earth from the truly evil aliens before they can affect life on the planet. He is given the knowledge and the power but if he refuses to accept it annihilation will result. Damon accepts what he has been told and the program charts his early adventures as he investigates strange phenomena. **Cast:** Jack Knoll (Damon Dark), Rachael Hunt (Lucy Reynolds), James Wilson (Josh Dean), Adrian Sherlock (Elder Damon). **Credits:** *Producer-Director:* Jack Knoll. *Writer:* Adrian Sherlock. **Comment:** Interesting presentation that uses the theatrical serial like format to tell most of its stories. Well produced and acted and spooky and intriguing enough to even warrant a second viewing. The special effects are excellent with the exception of Damon's conversations with the alien which are extremely difficult to understand (if at all). Unfortunately, the close captioning is very poorly done and only makes matters worse.
Episodes:
1. The Origins of Damon Dark, Part 1 (6 min., 54 sec.). Relates the history of the character as explained in the storyline above.

2. The Origins of Damon Dark, Part 2 (6 min.). Damon's history continues.
3. The Origins of Damon Dark, Part 3 (8 min., 15 sec.). Concludes the story of Damon's history.
4. A Look into the Future (10 min., 21 sec). Damon receives a visit for an old friend who possesses the power to see the future.
5. Child of the Dead, Part 1 (7 min., 11 sec.). Josh, Damon's friend, becomes possessed by spirits that are intent on entering the real world through him.
6. Child of the Dead, Part 2 (6 min., 3 sec.). Josh attempts to help Jason, who has now been overtaken by the spirits.
7. Child of the Dead, Part 3 (6 min., 7 sec.). The concluding episode wherein Damon confronts the spirits in an effort to exorcise them.
8. A Forbidden Friendship, Part 1 (6 min., 25 sec.). A girl (Emma) approaches Damon, asking his help in investigating a UFO incident.
9. A Forbidden Friendship, Part 2 (6 min., 38 sec.). As Damon and Emma get to know each other, they come closer to uncovering the mystery when Damon picks up a strong, alien signal.
10. A Forbidden Friendship, Part 3 (6 min., 27 sec.). Damon finds that Emma is anything but a friend when she reveals her true alien self.
11. A War in the Sky (9 min., 56 sec.). Damon intervenes when two alien species land on Earth—the Lallucood, who want to use the Earth's moon to mine rock; and the Bulha, who require the moon for research.
12. Dawn of the Shadowmen, Part 1 (5 min., 30 sec.). Damon faces a new challenge when supernatural forces (shadows) invade his house.
13. Dawn of the Shadowmen, Part 2 (11 min., 54 sec.). Damon attempts to uncover the source of his haunting in the concluding episode.
14. The Dream Monster, Part 1 (10 min., 24 sec.). Lucy, Damon's friend, begins to have strange dreams that are compelling her to do something against her will.
15. The Dream Monster, Part 2 (7 min., 43 sec.). Lucy, unable to resist the will of the Dream Monster, is ordered to kill Damon.
16. The Dream Monster, Part 3 (6 min., 33 sec.). In an attempt to help Lucy, Damon also becomes infected by the Dream Monster (Aloxian) and must find a way to defeat its control over their minds.
17. The Young Adventures of Damon Dark Christmas Special—Snow from Space (33 min., 21 sec.). Damon investigates the strange phenomenon of snow falling in Australia in December—when it is their summer.
18. Genesis of the Collective (33 min., 21 sec.). The series finale that leads into the life of Damon Dark as the famous UFO investigator and demon hunter of the series *Damon Dark*. It is here that Damon sees a vision of his future self and learns that the alien enemy, the Collective, cannot be defeated

without help. At the age of 18 he will contacted by an Australian government agency called Department 6 and share his information about UFOs. He and Jason will then become a team and continue their battle.

396 Zenya: A Fairy Tale. fantasywebseries.net. 2011 (Fantasy).

A young woman has been confined to the Bellevue Mental Institution due to her belief that she is an elf. The patient, Zenya, appears as a normal-looking young woman but all efforts to convince her otherwise have failed. When a newly assigned male nurse (Alvin) learns of Zenya he takes an interest in her and the story follows his efforts to help her, despite objections from Sally, the head nurse (who believes Zenya is delusional) and Dr. Knight, the hospital administrator, who objects to Alvin's interference. **Cast:** Kelsey Carroll (Zenya), Chistine Taylor (Sally Kaplan), Austin Mace (Alvin Edwards), Alan Fritz (Dr. Knight). **Credits:** *Producer:* Amy Brophy, Charles E. Fowler. *Writer-Director:* Charles E. Fowler. **Comment:** Although billed as a fantasy series, the only such aspect is Zenya's belief that she is an elf. Otherwise, the story is interesting and Kelsey Carroll as Zenya is well cast and convincing in her role.

Episodes:

1. Not a Fairy at All. Alvin becomes attracted to Zenya, a young woman who believes she is an elf.

2. Recognize Your Delusion. Dr. Knight questions Zenya about her identity while Alvin, who has fallen for Zenya, researches her patient history.

3. No One Else Will Help Me. Alvin believes he may be able to help Zenya but Dr. Knight refuses to let him try non-approved procedures.

4. Not Exactly. Dr. Knight fears that Alvin is becoming too closely involved with Zenya and the relationship could be harmful to both of them.

5. We're Going Now. Alvin, infuriated over Dr. Knight's attitude, decides to take matters in his own hands (as he believes a better environment will help Zenya realize she is human).

6. Danger to Herself and Others. Zenya escapes from the hospital—with Alvin seeking to find her (to give her a better home) before someone else does (Dr. Knight).

397 Zerks Log. zerkslog.com. 2009 (Science Fiction).

In a futuristic era, Zerks Ganymedewski, captain of the space ship *Venturi 552* disappeared without a trace. Three time fragments later a mysterious black box, Zerks logs were discovered floating in space. The logs were brought to the League of Outstanding Planets for review and possible resolve as to what happened to Zerks and his ship. Episodes relate what the logs contain as reported by the captain himself in recorded diaries.

Cast: Ben Alpi (Captain Zerks), Rob King (Cilanjoe), Beth Smith (Computer Voice), Sarah Babb (Lt. Suva/Ensign Fil Voice), Dave Condon (Abel Farnspet). **Credits:** *Producer:* Steve Lettieri, Rob King, Chris Conway. *Director:* Steve Lettieri. *Writer:* Patricia Pino, Jason Brow. **Comment:** Nicely produced mix of science fiction with light comedy. The Zerks costume and make-up are very well presented (he has a slight resemblance to the character of "Baby" on the television series *Dinosaurs*) and well worth watching whether you are a sci fi fan or not.

Episodes:

0. Zerks Log Intro (1 min., 2 sec.). Abel Farnspet of the League begins reviewing Zerks logs.

1. Zerks Log Episode 1 (1 min., 5 sec.). Records reveal that Zerks has been assigned to become the captain of the *Venturi 553*.

2. Zerks Log Episode 2: Frustration (3 min., 12 sec.). Records reveal that Zerks is becoming frustrated when he learns the duties a captain must perform.

3. Zerks Log Episode 3: Morale (2 min., 31 sec.). Records reveal that Zerks believes that by addressing his crew over the PA system that he can maintain his composure and run a tight ship.

4. Zerks Log Episode 4: Second-in-Command (2 min., 45 sec.). Records reveal that Zerks and his second-in-command, Commander Goorel, have different opinions on how the ship should be run.

5. Zerks Log Episode 5: Love Letter (3 min., 28 sec.). Records reveal that Zerks has been receiving anonymous love letters from someone aboard the ship.

6. Zerks Log Episode 6: Self Doubt (2 min., 58 sec.). Records reveal that Zerks believes he has humbled himself into taking a position that is beneath him when he is destined for something better, as he is of a noble birthright.

7. Zerks Log Episode 7: Hangover (4 min., 23 sec.). Records reveal that at a party for an ambassador, Zerks became intoxicated.

8. Zerks Log Episode 8: Misunderstandings (3 min., 24 sec.). Records indicate that Zerks and his first officer had an argument over Commander Goorel's unusual cranial accessories.

9. Zerks Log Episode 9: A Little Detour (3 min., 37 sec.). Records indicate that, for no apparent reason, Zerks defied orders to take the *Venturi 553* on an exploratory trip.

10. Zerks Log Episode 10: Cleaning the Air (2 min., 21 sec.). Records reveal that Zerks and Commander Goorel have become friends again after Zerks had insulted him (from episode 8).

11. Zerks Log Episode 11: Emergency (52 sec.). Records reveal that Zerks panicked when his ship encountered a troublesome situation.

12. Zerks Log Episode 12: Emergency Aftermath (3 min., 36 sec.). Records indicate that Zerks has reflected on his reactions to the emergency and has vowed to remain calm in the future.

13. Zerks Log Episode 13: Running Together (3 min., 8 sec.). Records indicate that Zerks is becoming increasingly unhappy with the slow pace of repairs being made to the ship.

14. Zerks Log Episode 14: Ensign Fil (3 min., 6 sec.). Records indicate that Zerks approved a test of the ship's weapon system as conducted by second officer Ensign Fil.

15. Zerks Log Episode 15: Inspection (2 min., 47 sec.). Records indicate that Zerks welcomed his girlfriend as she performed an inspection for LOOP Command.

16. Zerks Log Episode 16: Probation (3 min., 7 sec.). Records show that, following the inspection, Zerks had been put on probation due to poor performance.

17. Zerks Log Episode 17: Anticipation of Grand Assignment (3 min., 31 sec.). Records reveal that a reinstated Zerks is excited by a new assignment.

18. Zerks Log Episode 18: Final Recording (3 min., 31 sec.). Records indicate that after beginning his new assignment, recorders were apparently disabled and Log 18 appears to be the last known log of Captain Zerks.

398 Zhon: The Alien Interviews. whois zhon.com. 2012 (Science Fiction).

A man, claiming to be an alien who has just landed on Earth, surrenders to the U.S. Secret Service, but will only talk to Amanda Bella, a television talk show host. Zhon does appear to have amazing powers and he appears to know a lot more than he is revealing. When Amanda agrees to interview the alien, who calls himself Zhon, stories present his version of Earth's history—presumably as witnessed by him. **Cast:** Robert Linden (Zhon), Alida Gunn (Amanda Bella), Michele Holland (Mindy Anne), Eric Schumacher (Agent David Killjoy), Gary McGaha (Agent Gary Grey), Jeffrey Scotland (Chief Robert Killjoy), Tyrel Good (Agent Meyers). **Credits:** *Producer:* Eric Schumacher, Robert Linden. *Director:* Alan Williams, Tyrel Good. *Writer:* Marty Ketola. **Comment:** Intriguing idea that places the alien front and center to tell his story (sort of like a take on the feature film *The Day the Earth Stood Still*). The mystery surrounding Zhon is carefully played out and increases the viewer's interest although there are more episodes than many television series enjoy. The production qualities and acting are good and the characters are good and hated as intended. **Episodes:**

1. Who Is Zhonny? (17 min., 51 sec.). Zhon arrives on Earth and begins his quest for a television interview with Amanda Bella.

2. Everybody's Kung Fu Fighting (13 min.). As the interview continues, Zhon discusses the real origins of Kung Fu.

3. Food Glorious Food (12 min., 30 min.). Zhon begins a discussion about food and makes claim that he created some of the world's most famous dishes.

4. Rehythm (13 min., 3 sec.). Zhon discusses the world from which he came.

5. When I Was an Alien (9 min.). As Zhon continues his background story, he tells of his life in China and Rome.

6. Is It Hot in Here? (9 min., 34 sec.).With government agents present and Zhon continuing his story, agent David Killjoy attempts to interrogate Zhon and get to the truth.

7. A Tangled Web We Weave (9 min.). An attempt is made by Amanda and her assistant Mindy to steal the interview tapes and sell them on the open market.

8. Rome If You Want To (12 min., 8 sec.). Zhon's age becomes more apparent when he discusses his experiences in Ancient Rome.

9. Game On (9 min., 26 sec.). Zhon becomes apprehensive as the intimidating Agent Meyers pressures him to reveal who he really is (not believing he is an alien).

10. The Jig Is Up (9 min., 29 sec.). Having secured the interview tapes, Amanda has second thoughts about leaking the information as she may also ruin her reputation as trusted television host.

11. Ex-Zhonerated (9 min., 27 sec.). Despite the fact that a television promo featuring Zhon has aired, Amanda and Mindy still try to conceal Zhon's existence from a curious public.

12. Punk Drunk Love (10 min., 39 sec.). Zhon's story that he was the creative force behind American dance crazes raises doubt among his listeners.

13. Shake, Rattle and Rome (15 min., 37 sec.). Zhon concludes his story about his connection to Ancient Rome and why he chose Amanda for the interview.

14. The Day After Yesterday (15 min., 33 sec.). David is taken off the case and a new interrogator, the vicious Meyers is assigned the job of extracting the truth from Zhon.

15. Up the Ante (10 min., 39 sec.). While Amanda and Mindy seek to get David back as the interrogator, David begins his investigation of a strange devise found by the NSD.

16. Love (12 min., 50 sec.). As David discovers the object is connected to Zhon, Zhon's feelings toward Amanda continue to grow.

17. Together Like Apple Pie and Pickle Relish (7 min., 45 sec.). Amanda and Zhon share a kiss.

18. Orange Juice and Space Ships (10 min., 6 sec.). Amanda learns that Zhon must soon return to his world; it is also discovered that Chief Killroy had prior knowledge of Zhon.

19. The Past Is Prologue (12 min., 36 sec.). Zhon reveals that what has been speculated about Area 51 in New Mexico (concealing alien spaceship remains) is not speculation—but the truth. Killroy's encounter with Zhon is revealed when Zhon saved his life during the Vietnam War.

20. The End of Television (a.k.a., Ad Astra Per Aspera; 15 min., 32 sec.). Amanda has been given the story of a lifetime but as Zhon departs, has she also lost her lover?

399 The Zombie Apocalypse. rfcentertainment.com. 2013 (Horror).

The unthinkable has happened: world powers have resorted to chemical warfare and the earth is now suffering the consequences: the oxygen supply is depleted and what is termed a zombie apocalypse has occurred; the dead have risen to feed on the living. A group of adults, led by Vince, join forces and the series follows their efforts to find a way to survive. **Cast:** Geovanni Molina (Vince Lorado), Joseph Velez (Tony Vasquez), Max Gonzalez (Santiago Marzino), Dawn Andrews (Jessy Lansburg), Chance Molina (Steve Lorado). **Credits:** *Producer-Writer-Director:* Geovanni Molina. **Comment:** Initially only a 66-second trailer had been released, making it difficult to make a real assessment of the series. However, after the release of a first episode, it is clear to see that while there is potential for a gripping story, the production values lack, especially since it encompasses an over abundant use of the shaky camera method of filming (and coupled with non-centered scenes, it just distracts the viewer). It is also a bit unclear as to exactly what has happened. Vince is a CIA agent whose mission is to stop North Korea from unleashing a chemical attack on the U.S. (according to press material). However, in the episode, the attack has already occurred and Vince has found his son (but not his wife). The provided episode description states that "Vince is trying to save his family and stay on his mission" (but what mission would that be since he already failed?).

Episodes:
1. Escape from the City (9 min., 41 sec.). Establishes the story line as a CIA agent (Vince) and his son (Steve) seek to escape from the city and find the rest of their family.

400 Zombie College. icebox.com. 2000 (Horror).

Arkford University is not a typical American college. Its students are mainly zombies although humans are also accepted as students. It is here that a young man (Scott) has enrolled (after giving up a scholarship to M.I.T.) to be with his girlfriend, Zelda. Scott can see no one else but Zelda despite the fact that they continually fight then break up then get back together again. During one such breakup Scott befriends Zeke, the zombie who tries to kill him, but instead becomes his friend and fraternity mate (with another zombie named Julius). Stories follow Scott's activities as he attempts to cope with college life and with Zelda, who eventually becomes a zombie and may want Scott for his brain rather than lover. **Voice Cast:** David Herman (Scott), Pamela Segall (Zelda), John DiMaggio (Zeke), Billy West (Julius/Graham). **Credits:** *Producer:* Eric Kaplan, Mary Alice Drumm, Patricia Parker. *Writer:* Eric Kaplan. *Animation Director:* John Rice. **Comment:** Although 12 episodes were produced, only the first episode remains online. It is a horror-comedy animated mix that follows the animation style of programs like *The Simpsons* (as the series was originally pitched to Fox).

Episodes:
1. The First Day of Zombie College. Establishes the story line as Scott follows Zelda to Arkford University.

401 Zombie College Musical. youtube.com. 2010–2011 (Horror).

Peter Wells is a college student who, though stricken with swine flu, leaves the protection of his quarantine when he becomes obsessed with a strange craving he can't place. Unknown to him, the flu is turning him into a zombie and the craving is human brains. Peter has one desire, and with the help of his best friend, Joey Crisp, seeks to win the heart of the beautiful Ella Carmichael, an intellectual girl who is not easily won—all of which is told in music and song as Peter soon realizes that not only is he becoming a zombie, but others on campus as well. **Cast:** Lachlan McKinney (Peter Wells), Loghan Bazan (Ella Carmichael), Brian Hamburger (Dr. Villain), Gillian Hassert (Nurse Morrow), Sean Pack (Joey Crisp), Hannah Roberts (Katie Holloway). **Credits:** *Producer:* Alex Rothera, Stefan Dezil. *Director:* Benjamin Welmond. *Writer:* Yulin Kuang, David Grabows. **Comment:** With influences of the web series *Dr. Horrible's Sing-a-Long Blog* and the television series *Glee* students at Carnegie Mellon University (in Pittsburgh, Pa.) created a new twist on the zombie—a musical as it depicts one student's transformation into a creature of the undead. Although student made, it is well done and an amusing zombie horror-comedy and music mix (with characters just bursting into song during dialogue).

Episodes:
1. The Pilot. Peter Wells has been infected with a zombie virus but is not fully aware of what is happening to him.
2. Episode 2. Peter begins his quest to win the heart of Ella Carmichael.

402 Zombie Roadkill. webserieschannel.com. 2010 (Horror).

While driving on an unfamiliar road in a national park, a group of college students run over and kill a squirrel. Unknown to the passengers, the road on which they are traveling is no ordinary road. It is a road where such animals as that squirrel are reanimated as zombies and out to kill the humans who ended their lives. Soon after, when their car crashes, Simon, the only one who is not injured, must now find help to save his brother (Greg) and their friends Amber and Trish. As Simon prowls the woods he encounters a park ranger (Chet) who tells him about the murderous animal zombies and together they set out to survive long enough to help Simon's stranded passengers.

Cast: Thomas Hayden Church (Chet Masterson), David Dorfman (Simon), Michael Blaiklock (Greg), Cherilyn Wilson (Amber), Toni Wayne (Trish). **Credits:** *Producer:* Jim Burns, Sarah J. Donahue, Sam Raimi, Robert Tapert, Aaron Lam. *Director:* Dave Green. *Writer:* Henry Gayden. **Comment:** An amusing, original idea that plays well and is enjoyable to watch. Television producers Sam Raimi and Robert Tapert are familiar with what works and they achieved it here. Thomas Hayden Church, who appeared in several television series, is also good as the park ranger.

Episodes:

1. An Eye for and Eye (6 min., 53 sec.). The terror begins when a road trip claims the life of a squirrel.

2. Smell of Death (3 min., 59 sec.). A smell of fear enters the air when, after the crash, hungry animals go on the prowl.

3. Road Block (5 min., 35 sec.). Simon begins his search for help—and encounters victims of the zombie animals.

4. Fur Kills (5 min., 25 sec.). Simon's friends fend for themselves when they are attacked by blood thirsty creatures.

5. Hot Night in Hell (3 min., 58 sec.). The battle continues.

6. Dead End (5 min., 17 sec.). Simon faces a final confrontation with the zombie squirrel in an effort to save everyone.

403 *Zombie Whisperer.* funnyordie.com. 2012 (Horror).

An apocalypse has changed the world forever. Zombies are now a part of society and, although some pose a threat to the human survivors, most have become as decent as their condition will allow. Tony Mallone is a speech therapist (an expert on undead relations) who has developed PETZ (People for the Esthetical Treatment of Zombies) and realizes there is a whole new market of people, although undead, who need help. He establishes himself as a Zombie Whisperer and the program follows his efforts to train zombies (and humans) how to deal with each other.

Cast: Matt Fowler (Tony Mallone), Lacy Wetmore (Tammy), Kyle Duncan Graham (Bob), Judith McConnell (Jacki), Justin Rupple (Announcer), Matthew Ray Collins (Cujo). **Credits:** *Producer-Writer-Director:* Matt Fowler. **Comment:** A comical

different take on the numerous zombie series although the idea can only be stretched so far, thus far dealing with only humans who possess zombies as pets. The program itself makes an over abundant use of the annoying shaky camera coupled with unflattering extreme close-ups of the cast.

Episodes:

1. Tammy and Bob (9 min., 26 sec.). Tony attempts to help an eccentric but pretty cat lady deal with her pet zombie (Bob).

2. Jacki and Cujo (9 min., 43 sec.). Tony tackles a situation wherein he must teach a woman (Jacki) how to tame her daughter's pet zombie Cujo.

404 *Zombie with a Shotgun.* vimeo.com. 2012 (Horror).

Aaron is a young man who contracts a zombie virus and must come to the realization that he will eventually become one of the living dead. It is a time after a zombie apocalypse has devastated the world and a great many people have become infected. Rachel, his girlfriend, has not been affected and shares his torment but also realizes that the man she loves is slowly slipping away from her. While Aaron, armed with a shotgun, contemplates his next moves, he and Rachel have become fugitives as they must avoid others who have contracted the disease and succumbed to its final results while seeking answers to what has happened and why. As they take refuge in an abandoned building Aaron's thoughts are heard in a voice over (then Rachel's as Aaron begins to change). Aaron is still able to think clearly and uses his shotgun to protect Rachel from approaching zombies. But as he succumbs to the virus, will Rachel still be safe or will she have to use the shotgun on him?

Cast: Braeden Baake (Aaron), Lynnea Molone (Rachel), Sammy Mena, Jonathan Rios (Zombies). **Credits:** *Producer-Writer-Director:* Hilton Ariel Ruiz. **Comment:** While the program is more of a character study than action oriented, it is still a compelling look at a man struggling to come to terms with what the future holds for him. The production values are good (as are the eerie beats of music) and worth watching.

Episodes:

1. Episode 1 (4 min., 47 sec.). Establishes the storyline and introduces the main characters.

2. Episode 2 (5 min., 31 sec.). Impressive makeup as a zombie is seen but more talk than anything else with the main characters as they prepare for what lies ahead.

3. Episode 3 (3 min., 41 sec.). As Aaron's condition slowly worsens, Rachel fears she must accept the fact that her boyfriend will soon become one of the undead.

4. Episode 4 (3 min., 55 sec.). With zombies approaching and Aaron and Rachel being threatened, Aaron, still able to think clearly, begins protecting

her—but will he turn the shotgun on himself to save Rachel from himself?

405 *Zomblogalypse*. zomblogalypse.com. 2008–2011 (Horror).

Hannah, Tony and Miles are friends, living in York (a town in England) that have survived a zombie apocalypse and devised a way to take advantage of it—present a blog. Episodes relate their various mishaps as they attempt to present their blog—and survive the horde of zombies who are taking over the city.

Cast: Tony Hipwell (Tony), Hannah Bungard (Hannah), Miles Watts (Miles), Charlotte Gee (Charlotte). **Credits:** *Producer:* Dominic Brunt, Hannah Bungard, Tony Hipwell, Miles Watts, Dominic Brunt. *Writer-Director:* Miles Watts, Tony Hipwell, Hannah Bungard. **Comment:** Interesting take on the numerous zombie-themed television shows and feature films that have appeared over the years. Using the documentary style presentation is different and worth checking out.

Episodes:

1. Shopping (7 min., 26 sec.). Tony, Hannah and Miles, realizing what has happened, now seek to find a way to acquire food—without getting killed while trying.

2. Boredom (8 min., 11 sec.). The trio takes refuge in their flat, hoping they will be safe from the prowling zombies.

3. Rivalry (8 min., 52 sec.). Hannah, Tony and Miles meet with some rival bloggers.

4. Relationships (8 min., 15 sec.). To relieve the boredom, the trio decides to experiment with relationships.

5. Kiwi (9 min., 30 sec.). The trio receives a visit from a man from another country who has survived a treacherous journey only to meet his fate in York.

6. Cinepocalypse (9 min., 41 sec.). The trio battles zombies to see some of the films they made at the local theater.

7. Ground Z-Ro (8 min., 38 sec.). A flashback that takes viewers back to the first day of the zombie apocalypse but also showcases their pre-zombie blog antics.

8. Homeless (9 min., 21 sec). The unthinkable happens: Hannah is bitten by a zombie and succumbs to the zombie plague.

9. Walkabout (10 min., 30 sec.). With their interest turned toward Hannah, Tony and Miles accidentally lock themselves out of their flat and take refuge on a deserted farm—with zombies not far behind.

10. Natural Selection (8 min., 57 sec.). With Hannah apparently gone from their lives, Miles and Tony contemplate acquiring a new roommate.

11. Ambition (10 min., 15 sec.). Tony and Miles attend a seminar about positive thinking in a time of crisis.

12. Siege (10 min., 14 sec.). Tony and Miles fail to find a new roommate (although they befriend a girl named Charlotte) and settle on a life eating condiments to stay alive.

13. Way of the Ninja (10 min., 33 sec.). Charlotte becomes "one of the gang" and joins with Tony and Miles as they seek to avoid zombie encounters.

14. Splat to the Future. (10 min., 3 sec.). Tony and Miles apparently have no luck when it comes to girls. Charlotte is bitten and Miles and Tony embark on a quest to find a cure for her.

15. Full Metal Hatchet (10 min., 44 sec.). Tony and Miles search through an underground facility hoping to find a cure for Charlotte.

16. Attack of the Moans (9 min., 43 sec.). Hannah re-emerges (as a Ninja) and steals the cure Tony and Miles found for Charlotte, leaving Charlotte on the brink of death.

17. There Will Be

Zomblyogalypse cast, from left to right: Tony Hipwell, Miles Watts and Hannah Bungard (photograph by Ben Bentley [www.benbentleyphoto.co.uk/], copyright 2014 Coffee Films).

Guts (14 min., 6 sec.). With Hannah cured, the trio makes the deserted farm their new home.

18. Zombies in the Mist (14 min., 5 sec.). The trio resumes their zombie blog amid an unsettling rise in the zombie population.

19. Connectivity (6 min., 9 sec.). Hannah, Tony and Miles are back— to the start of season 1.

20. Business as Usual (5 min., 39 sec.). Shows Hannah, Miles and Tony settling into house-sharing during the zombie apocalypse.

21. Hangin' in the Garage (3 min., 1 sec.). As the trio begins to feel safe in their new surroundings, they decide to build a defense mechanism against possible zombie intruders.

22. Cooking and Sports in the Apocalypse (3 min., 1 sec.). The trio begins to feel confident as they continue their blog.

23. The Zombie Postman Cometh (4 min., 41 sec.). Hannah, Tony and Miles engage in a game of poker to determine who does what household chores.

24. The End ... or Is It? (3 min., 1 sec.). As Tony, Hannah and Miles blog, approaching zombies could end their efforts forever.

INDEX